Gourmet Cooking
With
Health in Mind

BY: Sushil K. Hennessy, MSW

Dedication

This book is dedicated to Jim and Carla Dearing and their children. I want to thank their son and our family friend Tony Dearing, from the bottom of our hearts who helped millions of families with his bi-weekly column about the effect of dementia, and how to take care to preserve brain health.

This book is also dedicated to Richard's and my parents. His mother Margaret Quinn and father Lawrence Hennessy, who taught him all about the food. Richard is still my partner in the kitchen. My mother Bhagvati Devi Singh and father Babu Ram Katiyar, had passion to teach us from the early childhood. My father read to us, the famous cookbook: Pakchandrika, and gave us line by line instruction in cooking, on a regular basis.   He was working as a financial accountant (CPA), in a government run Agriculture College, came across the healthy food all his life, and taught us all about it almost on a daily basis.

This book is based on opinions. Consult your doctor and get professional insight. We have made all efforts to make this book accurate and informing. Each body is different, each case is different, what is good for one person may not be right for the other. So, everything may not suit or apply to everyone. Get expert medical and professional advice whenever needed regarding your health matters. This book is not a cure in any way or in any fashion. Neither are any of the products named in the book, nor the recipes, the spices, herbs, suggestions, organizations, authors, publishers. Any outside help, etc. directly or indirectly involved with the book does not accept any legal responsibility for any form of injury or damage, or loss. This book is not the substitute for any treatment by a qualified doctor or other duly licensed health provider whose services and direction you may need.

Spicy meat and vegetables, partially cooked food, and any unfamiliar food or recipes should be avoided by people with allergies, the elderly, infants, pregnant women, sick and weak individuals, and by those who have an impaired or a critical immune system. And are not used to eating this type of food.

Front cover page, L to R: Quinoa squares, luscious jumbo chocolate layer cake, fudge brownies, cream puffs, black sesame seeds squares, mini cannolies, and white chocolate fudge bar.

Bottom: My husband Richard, is holding Light and Dark Chocolate Cake on his 87th birthday.

Back cover page: Photo of the memorial dedicated to Tom, Richard's younger brother. Also listed are the testimonials.

All photographs are taken by the author.

Introduction

I grew up in a family where I thought I had a doctor, a nutritionist, a teacher and a father. My father was all that to us. He worked for a long time in an agriculture college, where he came across various studies and researches about nutritious food, herbs, grains, fruits and vegetables.

He would buy healthy food and help us cook good meals. When he retired he started buying books on health and nutrition. He also became interested in Ayurvedic and Homeopathic medicines. Started giving out free medicines to people who needed them.

Now, looking back to my life when I was growing up, I realize that I was very fortunate to have my mother and father who taught us all about healthy cooking.

My father once said to me, "If people like to eat good food, they can also learn to cook good food. It just takes some practice. First, cook simple things, then try the complicated ones, and keep on practicing until you get perfect."

I believe that practice not only makes you perfect, but can make you an expert. When I came to America, I knew only about Indian cooking, but by tasting, eating and trying different food, I not only developed a taste for good food, but learned a lot about good food and cooking. This is what made me write this book today.

I want to share a personal story with you. I came to America in the 1970s, as a student, to attend a business college for an accounting diploma in Newark, New Jersey.

In the beginning I stayed with our family friend. In a few months, I found a full time clerk-typist job and started attending school at night. I later moved to the YWCA on Broad Street in Newark, as it was close to my school, and I had all the freedom to stay late and do my homework quietly.

I was trying to make the ends meet on my salary. After paying my tuition, weekly rent at the YWCA and bus fare for travelling from and to the work in north Newark, I had almost no money left for anything else. I was fortunate enough to get free lunch at the work, at the Youth Consultation Service, just because my boss did not let us girls go out for lunch in a bad area.

When I got back to my room, I was always starving and always thinking, "If I was in India, my mother would have prepared a nice meal and would have been waiting for me to get back from school and serve me a tasty food. But here I am all alone and have to take care of myself somehow." So I would stock up on cheap food in my room, such as cold cereal, English muffins, ketchup and dry-milk powder. After returning back from my job, I would stop by my room and eat one or two English Muffins with ketchup, drink a lot of water and head to the school to start classes from 6 to 9 p.m., three nights a week.

When I finished school, I would walk back to the YWCA at night, eat some dry cereal and start doing my homework. In accounting school, we used to get big packages to solve problems. Sometimes I would finish the work by 11 p.m., sometimes midnight and sometimes I had to stay up until 3 or 4 a.m. All night long I would take turns eating cereal and English muffins.

Every night I was thinking that my mother is preparing my favorite food - onion, zucchini, cauliflower and potato fritters. I can smell them all over in the house. When we had a cold, she would make us onion fritters that helped us fall to sleep and also helped with the cold.

This imagination kept me going for almost a year and half. Eating the dry cereal or raw English muffins didn't damp my appetite at all. I knew that if I worked hard and got good grades, I would get a better job, could have my own place, my own kitchen, and I would cook a lot of good food and invite lots of my friends. I just had to do it.

Within a year, I met my husband at the same job. On holidays my big boss Mr. Julian Stone, started inviting me to his house for holidays with his family so that I will not be left alone in my room at the YWCA. He also promoted me to assistant accountant. On the other hand my immediate boss Richard Hennessy, was impressed with my work and cooking at work, and started inviting me to his place. I used to do a lot of Indian cooking at his place, and he loved all good food. Shortly after that we got married and the rest is history.

To this day, I help others in need, always cooking a lot of food to give out to others. For me, food is Life, and life is everything. I cook almost three hot meals a day, just like my mother used to do for us. On holidays, I cook extra sweets and give them out to my neighbors all around our complex. I like to see people happy, and when I cook something new, something delicious, I can see it in their eyes, and the word goes around in the complex like the wind. My chocolate brownies are so easy to make but are a big hit for parties. My husband loves a corned beef and cabbage dinner. My nephew Ed Wolfe in Las Vegas will start eating my cheese cake even for breakfast. My deceased brother, R.N. Singh, loved my meat samosas, and would stop by to pick them up hot right out of the wok. I am so glad that my mother and father taught me how to cook and take care of others, and that makes everyone happy. To me cooking is an art, a science and a passion.

I want to follow my father's footsteps. He will leave the house in the morning around 7 a.m, walk about 4-5 miles to his office, work eight or nine hours, and then go out on appointments to help the people in need. He will help them get admission, scholarships, jobs, help as a middleman to get the girls married etc., and at home he will give out free Homeopathic medicines. Almost every night he came home around 9 or 10 p.m. while my mother is waiting and heating the dinner over and over again. He always put others first, and dedicated his whole life helping others. I too want to help the poor, feed the hungry, save the unborn, and help others as much as I can.

The Recipe for Good Cooking:

Start with interest in cooking,

add a teaspoonful of Passion,

a dash of Patience,

a pinch of Humor,

a cup of Fun,

whisk all

&

Garnish with Love

Contents

1

Abbreviations & General Tips

Throughout this book following measurements are used:

1 Teaspoon = 1Tsp.

Tablespoon = Tbsp.

3 Teaspoons = 1 Tablespoon

4 Tablespoons = ¼ Cup

1 Cup = 1C (16 Tablespoons)

Ounces = Oz.

2 Cups = 1 Pint (16 Fluid Ounces)

2 Pints = 1 Quart (32 Fluid Ounces)

Quart = Qt.

2 Quarts = ½ Gallon (64 Fluid Ounces)

4 Quarts = 1 Gallon (128 Fluid Ounces)

Introduction to Buying Food and Cooking

We want to cook healthy and a palate-pleasing meal. While we are buying ingredients to cook, just pay attention how to buy a right and a good, nutritious food that tastes as good as it is healthy.

Breakfast: While buying breakfast, take care of your health. Buy orange juice, eggs, quinoa, oatmeal, farina, Wheatena (toasted wheat cereal), cold cereal, or make pancakes. Whatever your choice is, buy fresh or dry berries: fresh blueberries, strawberries, banana and dry cherries to go with breakfast, especially with cereal and pancakes. Berries are loaded with antioxidants. Start the day with fruits. Have 6 to 7 servings of fruits and vegetables each day.

Lunch: Buy colorful fruits and vegetables. Cook and serve colorful to be more appetizing and more nutritious. Lunch should include salad and yogurt, light protein, low fats, soups etc. My father, who was interested in homeopathic and Ayurvedic medicines, will not allow us to eat yogurt and food loaded with the acidic sauces like tomato sauce at night. According to him, these foods give you inflammation and joint pain. So we ate yogurt during the day only. Also, try to have fermented food and vinegar pickles at lunch. Buy low-sodium fermented food or wash out the salt with water (like in pickles etc.). Fermented food is good for the intestinal tract.

Dinner: Buy greens like kale, spinach, Swiss chard, broccoli rabe, etc. and cook them within a day or two. Buy other fresh vegetables that can last at least a week like zucchini, mushrooms, eggplant, broccoli, cauliflower, brussels sprouts and potatoes, and cook them with fresh red onion, garlic, parsley, etc. Buy frozen peas, soy beans, brussels sprouts and beans etc. Try not to buy too many vegetables that need to be cooked right away. Frozen vegetables like peas, soy beans and lima beans are good to have for weeks. Fresh chicken, turkey, steaks, seafood are good to buy, but buy less-processed food and vegetables. If you are buying canned food, look for low-sodium beans and tomatoes, etc. Fish, tuna and smoked oysters in the can are also good.

Dessert: Cut down on prepared sugary desserts and load up on fresh fruits whenever possible. Dark chocolate is another option. Nut butter and nuts are filling as well as very nourishing. Homemade desserts are better.

Scientists have discovered that the pigment-related nutrients such as colorful fruit and vegetables promote a good health. So cook and make a colorful plate.

General Tips: Before you start cooking with this Book

- Before cooking, follow the recipe, gather all the items, count the number of items that are needed and then start. When having company, make or prepare ahead whenever possible and just put the recipes together that very day. My parents advised us to never time the preparation of food – such as you have to make lunch within 30 minutes. You should be flexible and work according to your skills and convenience. Maybe the others can time their preparation, but you should have option according to your schedule. Take it easy, do what you can, ask for help. And make sure you have eaten and your stomach is not empty, otherwise you will not able to concentrate and will rush to judgement. Use the recipes for company that you have tried before. Never try a new recipe for company.
- Also, know how to fix burnt, overcooked food, etc. If you burn the food, take if off the stove immediately. Leave the pot or the pan covered for a minute or two. Then take out the good food and discard the burnt one. Add chicken broth, tomato sauce, chutney, cooked potato, cream or spices to change the flavor and texture. If most of the food is burned out, then toss the whole thing away and start all over again. Always have some canned food in the house to replace burnt or spoiled food.
- Never use the soap on food. Some people wash celery and lemon (for zesting) with soap, but the soap goes into the food. So just wash a few times, and rub dry with a kitchen towel.
- Keep raw meat and vegetables separate. Wash the cutting board after each use. Try to use a glass cutting board for raw meat and sandy vegetables like greens and herbs, and wash out the board with a little warm soapy water.
- Any utensil or tools that are used in handling meat should be washed right away after using. The cross-contamination can give you salmonella poisoning.
- I line all my baking pans, trays first with parchment paper, then grease them with softened butter. And if need to, I sprinkle a little flour, move around to coat the pan well and then tap out the excess flour. This way baked goods do not stick to the pan.
- Try to bake in the center of the oven. Move the shelf in the center before heating the oven. If you have to bake more than two items, then use the bottom third shelf and rotate the food from top to bottom and from bottom to top halfway during the baking.
- For baking desserts, buy powdered sugar (confectioner's sugar) in a bag rather than in the box so it won't be lumpy. Always sift powdered sugar before using. Because once the powder sugar is mixed in frosting, the lumps will not come out (you can cover them with some decorations).
- If you are going to sauté, shallow -fry and cook in a dry pan, use a heavy bottom skillet or cast iron pan, heat the pan first on low heat, and just before cooking grease the bottom with 3-4 drops of oil or butter, rub the bottom with a paper towel to grease it evenly and then proceed with your recipe. This process protects the pan from burning in the bottom, and also greases the pan well. I do this for the wok and for stainless steel pots and pans. Even if I am going to deep-fry in oil, I still follow this procedure of greasing the bottom and it protects them from burning.

- Try to marinate your meat. The liquid marinade goes inside the meat and the dry rub stays outside, but when you cook some of the rubs soaks in to the meat through steam. Before grilling and barbecuing, add some dark beer to the marinate to reduce the chances of getting cancer from the charred meat. Also, try to cook on a temperature that is under 300 degrees according to the experts. It will cut down on cancer-causing substances and thus will not change the DNA.
- For healthy cooking, use lean meats and a lot of vegetables. I even make my mashed potatoes with either frozen peas, spinach, parsnips, sweet potatoes, celery roots or the grated carrots, and serve some fresh fruit or vegetables and herbs on the side like avocado, kiwi, green chickpeas (whenever I can find them in the Indian markets) radishes, green onion, red onions, garlic leaves, parsley or cilantro, spinach or beets greens, tomatoes and even chopped celery stalks.
- As you must have heard or read in various books, be very careful with handling and consuming raw seafood. Pregnant women, kids and elderly are very vulnerable to food-related diseases. Avoid buying seafood raised in an industrial area. When going to a fish-monger, if the sore smells fishy, avoid buying seafood there, leave the store and go to a fresh seafood store. Fresh seafood should not smell fishy. Freezing the fish solid also kills bacteria.
- When cooking mixed vegetables, start cooking with the heavier or the denser one first, wait a while, and then add the softer ones after. Cook carrots first, then add celery or zucchini after.
- To make your own dry herbs, buy fresh herbs, such as cilantro, parsley, mint, dill and methi (Fenugreek) in bulk, take off the leaves and spread them out over paper towels placed in a large tray, in a single layer. Put the tray over the refrigerator, and they will dry within 4-5 days to use. Grind the leave in a coffee grinder, or just rub them over cooked food, or use the dry herbs as a garnish for the look and the taste.
- You can also use the microwave oven to dry some herbs like mint until they are dried and crisp. And rub over the food or mix with the chili powder or chaat masala and add to yogurt or boiled potatoes to make them tasty.
- To keep the greens fresh and green-looking, boil about 1-1/2-inch deep water in a large sauté pan, dip the green leaves of spinach, broccoli rabe, methi or the broccoli florets, let them boil for 2-3 minutes, rinse out the water, wash under running cold tap water, pat dry a little with a kitchen towel and refrigerate in a bowl covered for 30 minutes. When ready to serve, just sauté the vegetables for 1-2 minutes in hot oil, sprinkle with granulated garlic, salt and pepper and serve warm. You can do the same with the parsley and cilantro, and then freeze them in the ice cube trays, and take out whenever you need them.
- To cook vegetables tasty and healthy, such as soy beans, spinach, cauliflower, broccoli, eggplant, zucchini, etc. (the soft ones). Slice or cut vegetables in small pieces, drizzle with some salt, pepper and oil, toss a little and bake on high heat, about 400 degrees in the oven, for about 15-20 minutes or until they are soft. Turn off the oven and let the vegetables stay there for another 10 minutes they will be ready to serve.
- To reheat snacks, mostly the fried foods like fritters and bread, wrap them in the paper towel, place on the rotating plate of the microwave and heat 1 minute at a time for 2-3 minutes or until they are warm. To keep the fritters crispy, heat them in microwave only for 1 minute (such as samosa or stuffed breads) then heat them in the regular oven or in the toaster oven for additional 2-3 minutes or until heated through. I do the same with pizza slices – just wipe the slices on the edges (no dripping of cheese or sauce) and heat them in the microwave first, then in the toaster oven, curved up or in the regular oven in a baking tray lined with foil.
- After eating do not brush your teeth right away or exert your body by doing exercise etc.

Food & Health

"The ground work of all

Happiness is health."

Leigh Hunt

According to my father, "Before you cook, you have to know what to buy – "The Right Stuff. Food is not only for the taste, it is for the health, it is the life and your future." My father would travel miles and miles to get or eat the unique, tasty and healthy food, and he would describe it or sometime would take us there. Then we all me, my sister and mother, would try to cook the same recipe. Most of the time we would get it right away, and if we did not get exactly the way it should be, he would take us there again. My family was very famous for good and healthy food. Cooking is an ART, and this ART not only helped me, but helped my whole family, friends, neighbors, and also my best friend and my husband – Richard, who loves all my cooking: what I had learnt in India and what I have learnt here in America.

My father was not only our father he was also a doctor to us. According to him: "Health is something you have to nourish, you cannot buy it no matter how much money you have."

He was a chief financial Account Officer (like a CPA) in a government's Agriculture College. When he retired he became a Homeopathic doctor and started giving free medicine to the poor and needy. He had a great collection of health related books. I remember once someone had borrowed some books and returned them, one of them was on garlic, another one on lemon and the third one on turmeric. Since then I got interested in reading about health books.

My father, mother and older brother all had joined Yoga. They used to get up very early in the morning, left the house by 4:30 a.m. and walked to Yoga school about 3-4 miles each way. When my father visited us in the USA, back in 1989, the first thing he did was: drink water that was kept the night before in a copper glass, went to the bathroom, drink more room temperature water, and started doing Yoga for at least an hour. We were told to do yoga, deep breathing and meditation on a regular basis to see the results. Yoga has unlimited benefits. It should be done at least 30 minutes once or twice a day. You can do almost anything. Just make up your mind, do it on a regular basis and stick to it.

When it came to food he always asked us to make the fresh bread daily with a mixed flour of: 2 parts whole wheat flour, and one part each chickpea and barley flour. Our split beans (Dal) were made daily with spinach or other greens. With daily meal we had fresh cilantro, onion, garlic, & amla chutney and/or buttermilk Raita (yogurt salad). We didn't drink tea or coffee on regular basis. But we did drink a large glass of warm milk after dinner every night. My father was never sick and never went to any doctor. Even when we all were growing up, we didn't have to go to any doctor; my father used homemade remedies, ate fresh fruits, vegetables, all sorts of beans and whole grains.

You have to take care of your life, no one else will do it for you. Remember, you have one life, one chance so make it great and make it healthy.

Alzheimer's Disease

This chapter is in memory of Mrs. Carla Dearing, who lost her life with Dementia. Jim and Carla Dearing are the proud parents of Tony Dearing, our family friend, who had done a great job educating families about this disease.

Dementia is the medical term for a decline in mental ability that disrupts the normal working process of the brain.

Alzheimer's is a progressive and degenerative disease that attacks the brain and is the most common form of dementia. It results in impaired memory, difficulty learning and remembering new information; including personality changes, speech problems, and disorientation. It increases with age. According to experts the disease can last somewhere from 4 to 20 years.

Do you know that India has a very low rate of Alzheimer's Disease? Alzheimer's Disease has no effective treatment. Researchers have been working for a long time to find a cure, and have spent billions of dollars. So far, they haven't found any promising cure. It seems that education, diet, and exercise are playing an important role. The Amyloid protein that builds up in the patients' brains (the plaque) is the leading cause of Dementia. In Dec., 2016 Congress passed a law and president Obama signed it, called the 21st Century Cures Act. This included assigning $3billions over a 10 yrs. period for research and cure.

As my family used to say, one of the root cause of all illness is food – how it goes in and out of your body. You need plant-based protein. It is light, digestible, good for all ages, and is healthy. Add to your diet beans, legumes, nuts, seeds, greens, herbs, curry powder and turmeric etc. Eat fresh cucumber with skin on and an apple daily. Don't overeat and try to stay regular. Use Turmeric powder in cooking at least 3 to 4 times a day, about 1/3Teaspoon for two servings. It is good for the brain, stomach and overall health. You also need cow's whole milk (Vitamin B-12). It should be heated with or without water and should be consumed warm so that the milk fat flows through the body and gets absorbed with the food; good for all ages. Any kind of exercise is good for the body, Aerobic exercises are good for brain and Yoga together with meditation and breathing exercises is good for body. You should sit down on the floor at least 5 to 10 minutes with your legs crossed and arms resting on your knees, so that your diaphragm opens up. Take deep breaths, inhale slowly and exhale slowly with the same rhythm. Regular bowel movement is the key to stay disease free and live longer. You will stay active, will have more energy, and the body will get stronger and stronger. Among other things chickpeas, sesame seeds, cow's whole milk, fresh pears, mangoes and papayas are the best to keep you regular.

As you get older, if you see any signs of memory slowing down, take the memory test, eye scan and get professional help. If you have a family history of Alzheimer's or inherited the genes, consult your doctors. If both parents have the genes, take the brain scan before the age of forty.

Keep yourself occupied with new, innovative, and brain healthy activities to keep the memory going strong and preserve brain health with diet and exercise.

Make friends, make phone calls, move around try not to sit for too long, go out for a walk in the fresh air, read newspapers and magazines, listen to music, learn dancing, go to movies, social gatherings, parties etc. Seek out help from support groups (check out the local libraries and churches) and enjoy life to the fullest. Make your New Year's resolution to be happy and make others happy, which has a trickle-down effect.

Alzheimer's Disease and the Indian Diet

The main reason for the low cases of Alzheimer's in India is the Indian diet and exercise. My father, who worked for a long time in a government run Agriculture college and worked his whole life in the Govt. Agriculture Dept., came across various findings and researches, followed those recommendations and kept us informed and practiced a healthy life style. He was also an expert in Homeopathic and Ayurvedic medicines.

We were told not to use aluminum pots and pans. Aluminum melts in the food. In 1989 Britain's medical journal, Lancet reported the result of a study by the British Government: "the risk of Alzheimer's disease has risen by 50% in areas of Great Britain where drinking water contained elevated levels of aluminum." According to experts aluminum is found in food additives, douches, antacids, buffered aspirin, antidiarrheal preparations, shampoos, and in aluminum cookware. So be careful and read the labels.

People wonder what kind of diet Indians follow. Well, here is the diet we grew up with, and even in America I try to follow it, or find substitutions. You just have to make up your mind, get motivated, have discipline, a routine, and a desire to eat healthy, and beat almost any kind of disease. Just try to cook one or two items first until you get used to it. Almost all the food can be cooked ahead; heat and serve.

1. Soak 5 Almonds, and 5 large dark Raisins called Munakka in cold water overnight. Go to bed early, and at the same time if possible, and do not eat anything at least 2 hrs. before going to bed. Take about 2 cups of water in a copper pot (if possible) to drink in the night, and save some to drink in the morning.

2. Get up early in the morning (about 4 or 5a.m), and drink some water (cold or warm). Then go through your daily routine, or drink more water or juice. Then go to the bathroom, go out to walk or take a shower etc.

3. Before Breakfast: First thing you should eat is soaked and peeled almonds and large raisins. Eat slowly chewing well, and drink a little water with it.

4. **Breakfast:**

Oatmeal with Barley: (Serves:2)

Ingredients: 1/4Cup Pearl barley; 1-1/2cup oatmeal (5 minutes); milk; 1/4cup each walnuts or pistachios, and dry cranberries.

Bring 3 cups of water to a boil in a medium pot, add barley, stir, and cook simmering for 10 minutes. Add oatmeal and simmer for five minutes. Turn off the heat, cover, and let rest for 5 minutes. Serve with milk, nuts, and cranberries and/or honey.

Oatmeal with Quinoa: (Serves:2)

Ingredients: 1/4Cup whole grain organic premium quinoa (Keen-wah); 1cup 5-Minute oatmeal; milk, nuts, and dry cranberries to serve.

Follow the same procedure as above, bring water to a boil, add quinoa and simmer for 5 minutes. Add oatmeal and cook 5 minutes, let it rest covered for 5 minutes. Serve with milk, nuts, cranberries etc.

Tips: Drinking juices on an empty stomach can give inflammation to some people. So, drink room temperature or warm water early in the morning. Also, if you have time use Steel-cut oatmeal. It takes longer to cook but it is good for you. It has endosperm, germ and bran that gives you fiber and more nutrients.

Cashews and Berries Smoothie: For four servings.

Ingredients: In a dry pan for about 8 minutes, on medium heat roast: ½ cup quick cooking oatmeal lightly toasted, ¼ cup sunflower seeds, ¼ cup pumpkin seeds, slivered almonds,1/4cup flax Seeds or powder at the end of roasting; 1cup cashews; 4 fresh boiled and chopped eggs; about 3 cups orange Juice; 1cup blueberries; 1/4cup dry cranberries.

In a blender first grind roasted ingredients, then add cashews and puree, add eggs and orange juice and puree, add blueberries and cranberries and pulse 3-4 times. Pour in glasses and serve immediately, or refrigerate for up to two days covered, or cover with double plastic wrap and tie air tight with rubber bands and freeze for later. Defrost wrapped overnight, heat in microwave oven and serve.

Tips: Cashews are good for memory. Almonds are heart healthy and blueberries have a high level of antioxidants, known as flavonoids that boost the brain pathways and cognitive health. Also, berries in general are good for the heart.

Boiled Eggs: (S:2)

Ingredients: 4 large eggs, 1/4 tsp. celery salt; ½ tsp. turmeric powder; 2 tsp. olive oil or clarified butter (Ghee); 2 grain or whole wheat toasts; 2cups fresh blueberries or strawberries.

Bring eggs to a boil covered with water, boil for 5 minutes. Turn off the heat. Let them rest in hot water 2-3 minutes, crack and submerge in cold water. Peel the eggs, cut in half, sprinkle with celery salt, turmeric powder, olive oil or clarified butter. Serve warm with berries and toasts.

Tips: Eggs are good for the brain and body growth. Yolks are good for the vision.

Dal Cheela (Beans Pancakes): (Serves:2)

Ingredients: Soak 2cups of split, peeled, moong dal (Mung beans) for 3 hrs. or overnight in water and grind in the food processor/blender with a little water; 1/2cup diced onion; 2 tbsp. each: diced garlic cloves, ginger, cilantro soft stems; fresh serrano or jalapeno pepper seeded and diced to taste; 1 tsp. turmeric powder; ½ tsp. celery seeds; 1/2cup semolina; salt to taste; mustard or canola oil to cook.

Heat a cast iron pan on medium high-heat, dip a wand of paper towel in the oil and grease the pan. Mix all ingredients together and drop one ladle into the hot pan, spread it out from the back of the ladle, cover and cook on medium heat about 2 minutes on each side until light brown and serve with Cilantro Chutney.

Tips: Just like turmeric, celery seeds are very beneficial for the body. They take out aches and pains from the body, and are loaded with minerals like zinc, magnesium, potassium etc. Try to use them daily in making pancakes, breads, okra, cabbage etc.

Breakfast is the most important meal of the day: Don't skip breakfast. If you do not have time to make breakfast, then just grab a fruit such as banana, apple, guava. Also, nuts, seeds, bran muffin and yogurt. You can also eat whole-wheat or oat-bran cereal or a bowl of mixed-grain muesli (found in India and U.S.) topped with fresh fruits, berries, and yogurt. A study came out that skipping breakfast can lead to high blood pressure, high cholesterol, diabetes, heart disease and much more.

Dosa (Rice and Bean Pancakes): For 2-4 servings. You can buy the Dosa Mixture at the Indian Grocery Store and make it instantly. In South India they use these pancakes for Breakfast, Lunch and Dinner, either plain or stuffed with vegetables.

Ingredients: Make your own batter, ferment for 12hrs.: 1cup of peeled urad beans (Gota) soaked in water for 3 hrs. and grinded with little water in the food processor/blender. Then add 1/2cup rice flour; 1/2cup yogurt; ½ tsp. salt; ¼ tsp. each: turmeric powder, fenugreek seed powder (op) mix all with a little water to a thick pouring consistency (thicker than the pancake batter), and let it rise in the room temperature for 12 to 24 hrs.; oil to cook.

Heat a cast iron pan on medium-high heat. When hot, dip a folded paper towel in the oil and grease the pan. Drop one ladleful of batter in the pan in a circle, spread it out with the back of the ladle, spread out about 6-inches diameter. Cover and cook on medium heat for about 2 minutes; take pan off the heat; scrape off the pancake with a metal spatula. Cook the other side 1 minute and serve with coconut chutney. Once it is cooked you can stuff it with any cooked vegetable. Place about 1cup of cooked warm vegetable lengthwise in the center, and fold both ends over the vegetable cook for 1 minute and serve.

Quinoa and Semolina Halwa (Quinoa & Sooji dry Pudding): For 2-4 servings. This is considered the Brain Food.

Ingredients: ½ cup whole grain organic premium quinoa or sorghum (or coarse grinded Kuttu); 1Cup semolina (or Sooji or Cream of Wheat); 4 tbsp. butter or ghee; 1/3cup packed brown sugar (or Jaggery); ½ tsp. turmeric powder; 1/2cup nuts; 1/2 cup dark raisins or dry cranberries.

Heat a large heavy bottom pan on medium heat and brown quinoa for 5 minutes until light brown. Add the butter and semolina and brown on medium to medium-high heat stirring back and forth for 8 minutes, making sure it is not burning. Lower the heat, add sugar, nuts, cranberries, stir well, take the pan off the heat and cover half way, then stir in 3 cups of cold water and turmeric powder, raisins/cranberries, nuts and sugar. Put the pan back on medium-high heat. Keep on stirring for 5 minutes, then reduce the heat to medium and stir until all the water is gone and the texture is a thick paste, about 8-10 minutes. Serve warm with milk, tea or coffee.

Tip: Eggs have a substance called Choline. It plays an important part in maintaining the bodily functions. It plays an important role in liver function and reproductive health, transport of fat; it aids in cell membrane, muscle control and memory storage; it helps the brain with Dementia and Alzheimer's and works with folate in a baby's brain development during pregnancy. It is found in eggs, firm tofu, peanut butter, pistachios, beef liver, pink salmon and chicken breast etc.

5. **Lunch:** Serve soups and other dishes, follow the recipes in the book.

Sprouted Chickpea Salad: For two servings

Ingredients: 2 Cups *sprouted chickpeas (see Yoga Meal) or 1can, 14oz. can chickpeas washed, drained, and heated lightly in a pan; use ½ of medium sized Lettuce torn in bite size pieces; 2small kirby cucumber cored, sliced in half lengthwise, then thin sliced across with the skin on; 1 small carrot grated; 2 to 4 plum tomatoes chopped into 1-inch cubes; 1small raw beet peeled and grated and kept separate; 1/2cup green onion sliced; 1 tsp. lemon/lime zest; 1/4cup lemon /lime juice and 1/4cup mustard oil or E.V. olive oil; 1cup cheese cubes.

Mix all salad items together except the beets and place in two serving plates, top with grated beet, sprinkle with lemon/lime juice, then oil and serve.

Chutney (The fresh Herb Paste): (M:1-1/2cup)

Ingredients: Chutney is almost like Pesto. 1 tbsp. roasted (browned in dry pan on medium heat for about 6 minutes) caraway seeds; 1 cup packed cilantro leaves and soft stems chopped; 1/2cup fresh mint leaves; 4 large garlic cloves (1tbsp.) chopped; 1/2cup chopped fresh onion; 1-2 serrano or half seeded and chopped jalapeno peppers   1/3cup lemon/lime juice; 1/2cup walnuts, 1/4cup grated coconut (op); salt to taste.

In a Blender or Food Processor first grind the caraway seeds, then add the cilantro, mint, garlic, onion, serrano/jalapeno peppers, a little salt, nuts, and 2-3 tbsp. water puree all together. Add lemon/lime juice, and coconut (if using) and puree again to mix well. Take out in a non-reactive bowl. Serve within two days.

Herb Salad: (S:2)

Ingredients: We make this salad when we don't make any chutney. 1/2cup each fresh chopped: onion, baby spinach, cilantro, mint, tomato; ½ tsp. each: garlic cloves, rosemary, oregano and ginger; 1-2 serrano or jalapeno peppers seeded and chopped; 1 avocado; 2-3 tbsp. lemon Juice; 2-3 tbsp. olive oil or mustard oil; salt and pepper to taste.

In a medium non-reactive bowl combine all herbs, cover and refrigerate. Just before serving pit and peel avocado cut in cubes, add lemon juice, sprinkle oil and a little salt and pepper and serve.
Tips: Avocado has plant based fat, folate, fiber, magnesium, and lutein etc. We use lemon, lime and their zest on salad. We do not use vinegar because it takes out natural nutrients from the cucumber and herbs etc. Also lemon juice helps digest the iron. If possible try to eat raw vegetables such as cucumber, carrots, celery, string beans and beets etc.

Also, herbs help you live longer and disease free. In some parts of middle-east people serve a plate full of fresh herbs with the meal everyday.

Fresh Grinded Spice Mixture to cook vegetables etc.: (M:2cups, for 6-8 servings)

Ingredients: 1 tbsp. broken bay leaves (all veins taken out); 1/4cup each: caraway seeds and coriander seeds, black peppercorns; 2 Large onions chopped; 1/2cup each chopped garlic cloves and fresh ginger; 1 tbsp. cardamom seeds; 2 tsp. turmeric powder; 1 tsp. fenugreek seed powder; 1 tsp. or to taste cayenne Pepper; ½ tsp. cinnamon powder; 1/4cup ghee (clarified Butter) or mustard or vegetable oil; ½ tsp. salt.

In a blender or a food processor first grind the bay leaves, caraway, coriander and cardamom seeds, peppercorns without any water. Add onion, garlic, ginger, and about ¼ (very little) water and grind all into a thick paste.

Heat a heavy bottom pot on low heat. Add ghee or oil add turmeric, fenugreek powder, cinnamon powder and ½ tsp. salt, and cook on low heat for 2 minutes until it is bubbly. Now add all the grinded spices, mix well, increase heat to medium-high and stir well for 2 minutes until it is simmering. Cover with the lid and simmer for 8-10 minutes on medium heat. Now these fresh spices are ready. Add rest of the ingredients or take out in a bowl and use in portions for different cooking.

Tips: The main Indian spice which is used all day long is Turmeric. It has no flavor just yellow color use enough to give some color to food. Use from ½ tsp. to ¾ tsp. for two servings. You will see benefits of Turmeric only in prolonged use. So, use it daily and faithfully to see the benefits. Someone has written that, "Turmeric's health benefits are through the roof." One of the substances found in turmeric is called, "curcumin," a strong antioxidant. It can stop the cancer, and can stop amyloid plaque development in the brain. It regulates triglyceride and insulin levels, protects cardiovascular health, and helps eyes, teeth and gums. It can kill flu virus, germs, gum disease and stomach bacteria. I think this is one of the main reason India has a low rate of Alzheimer's.

Cucumber Raita (Yogurt Salad): For four servings.

Ingredients: 1 to 1-1/2 Pound yogurt; 2cups (about 3 medium) cored and grated kirby cucumbers; salt and pepper to taste; Hot Garnish (Baghar): 1 tbsp. ghee or vegetable oil, 1 tsp. caraway seeds, 1 tbsp. chopped fine garlic cloves.

In a non-reactive bowl whisk together yogurt and cucumber, add salt and pepper to taste. Heat a small pot or pan on medium heat. Add the ghee/oil and brown the caraway seeds for 1 minute light brown, add chopped garlic and cook golden brown for about 5-6 minutes. Stir in the mixture into the yogurt mixture. Keep covered. Serve with almost any dish.

Tip: Yogurt is a probiotic food. It contains good bacteria they promote gut and gastrointestinal (GI) health, may reduce some health risks, aid cardiovascular health and help your immune system.

Khedari (Rice and Beans): For four servings.

Ingredients: 2 tbsp. ghee or vegetable oil; ½ recipe of the fresh grinded spice mixture (from above); 1cup split and with skin on, moong dal (Mung Beans); 1cup long grain or basmati rice; 1cup chopped green cabbage or cauliflower or broccoli cut into 1-1/2-inch pieces; 1/4cup tomato sauce (op); ½ tsp. turmeric powder; salt and pepper to taste.

Heat a large heavy bottom wide pot or a saute pan on medium heat. Add ghee/oil. When hot add the mung beans and rice and brown them for 5 minutes. Add the fresh grinded spices and stir for 5 minutes. Add 3 cups of water, about 1-inch higher than the rice mixture. Top with cabbage, cauliflower or broccoli, turmeric, salt and pepper to taste. Bring to a boil on high heat, lower the heat and cook on medium heat for 20 minutes or until rice and beans are soft. Add the tomato sauce, stir well, cover and cook until the beans and rice mixture are heated through and all the liquid is almost gone. Serve with Cucumber Raita (Yogurt Salad), and Chutney.

6. **Dinner:**

Serve mixed grain bread with Dal (beans made with greens) or 2 different vegetables made with fresh grinded spices (Make vegetables: brown spices in oil for 8 minutes, add small pieces of the vegetables such as zucchini, string beans, asparagus, and cauliflower, brown 5 minutes, sprinkle

2Tbsp. water, cover and cook until soft, add salt to taste and serve), Chutney, or vinegar pickles etc.

Dal (Beans made with greens): For Four Servings.

Ingredients: 1cup whole American lentils (Green) with skin on (If using Indian Lentils, soak them overnight in the water and cook in pressure cooker);1 tbsp., about 4 large garlic cloves chopped;1medium onion sliced; 3cups baby spinach;1 red bell pepper cored, seeded and cut into strips; 1cup, 8oz, tomato sauce; 1 tsp. turmeric powder; 1 tsp. curry powder; salt and pepper to taste. To serve 4 tbsp. ghee or butter.

Heat 4 cups water in a large, heavy bottom pot bring to a boil and make layers: sprinkle the lentils, garlic, onion, spinach, bell pepper, turmeric, curry powder, salt and pepper to taste. Increase the heat to medium-high and bring to a boil, lower the heat, cover and cook on constant simmer for 20 minutes, do not stir. Add tomato sauce, cover and cook on medium heat for 5 minutes until dal is heated through. Serve garnished with butter/ghee and grain bread, chutney, pickles etc. We cook various beans, mostly with spinach and other dark greens such as beats, collard green etc. everyday.

Tips: Spinach and other leafy greens cooked with tomatoes and beans are very good for the eyes and brain. Spinach, kale (has copper), chard, collard green, beets and other dark leafy greens contain vitamin K, iron and magnesium etc. Magnesium increases serotonin level which helps depression and anxiety.

- There are several types of lentils: green lentils (large and greenish brown), lentilles du pub (dark olive green almost black), red and yellow lentils (split and peeled), black lentils (black and small). Indian lentils are small and dark brown, have rich, complex flavor. You have to soak them for a few hours and cook for at least an hour. We mostly use green lentils, which cooks in 15-20 minutes. Cook them whole with skin on to get all the nutrition: protein, iron and fibers.

Brussels sprouts and Cabbage: For four to six servings.

Ingredients: ½ of medium cabbage shredded and ½ pound brussels sprouts core and cut into half of quarter lengthwise; ½ tsp. each turmeric, granulated garlic and onion powder; salt and pepper to taste; 2 tbsp.olive oil or mustard oil.

Move the oven shelf in the middle and preheat oven at 450 degrees. Line a large baking tray with aluminum foil and leave little extra foil on both sides. Grease the foil, spread out the cabbage, wash the brussels sprouts and spread out in single layer over the cabbage. Now sprinkle turmeric, garlic, onion, salt, pepper then oil. Bake at 450 degree preheated oven for about 15 minutes or until almost soft. Turn off the oven, cover the vegetable with foil from both sides and leave in hot oven for up to 15 minutes; serve hot as a side dish.

Tip: Cabbage and Brussels sprouts have Sulfur. According to experts Sulfur disinfects the blood, kills bacteria and protects the protoplasm of cells. It has the ability to protect against the harmful effects of radiation and pollution, slows down the aging process and extends life span. It is found in hemoglobin and body tissues and needed for synthesis of collagen to prevent dryness and maintain elastin in the tissues. These cruciferous vegetables keep cancer away and are good for the brain. My father used to give out free Homeopathic medicine, Sulfur-30 tiny balls to people who had colon polyps (check with your doctor first).

Mixed Greens with Chickpeas: For six servings.

Ingredients: 3-4 tbsp. olive oil or mustard oil; 1medium red bell pepper cored, seeded and cut into strips; 3cups canned chickpeas washed and drained well; ½ pound each: collard greens, kale, swiss chard, spinach with all hard stems taken out, washed then thin sliced across; 1large onion thin sliced, 1/4cup each chopped: fresh garlic cloves and ginger; 1 tbsp. curry powder; 2Tsp. turmeric powder; celery salt and pepper to taste; 1/4cup lemon juice.

Heat a large cast iron pan on medium-high heat. When hot add oil and chickpeas. Shake the pan to coat them with the oil and let them cook on medium heat for 10-15 minutes covered until they are lightly browned underneath. Sprinkle ½ tsp. turmeric powder, shake the pan and turn off the heat. Reheat just before serving.

Heat a stainless steel (non-reactive) pan on medium heat, add 2 tbsp. oil and onion, brown for 8 minutes. Add garlic, ginger, red bell pepper, curry powder, rest of turmeric powder, kale, collard green, swiss chard, spinach. Do not stir, sprinkle 2tbsp. of water, cover and cook on medium heat for 10-15 minutes or until soft. Open the cover, stir well, then add salt and pepper to taste and sprinkle with lemon juice. Serve topped with warm chickpeas on the side or make sandwiches. We make double, and serve the next day.

The Grain Bread: For Four Servings.

Ingredients: 2cups chapati/bread Flour (White Whole Wheat Flour called Atta) plus extra for dusting; 1/2cup chickpea and 1/2cup barley flour (or 1cup chickpea flour alone); 1 tbsp. celery seeds; 1 tsp. each garlic and onion powder (or 1 tbsp. each fresh); ¼ cup thin sliced cilantro stems (op); mustard or vegetable oil to cook.

In a large bowl add all the ingredients except the oil and whisk in 1-1/4 to 1-1/2cup water slowly, as needed to make a firm dough, them make a ball of the dough. Knead the dough, sprinkling about 1 tbsp. of water at a time for 5 minutes until it is pliable, then set aside for ½ hour covered.

Heat a cast iron pan on medium heat. Divide the dough into 8 portions. Take one portion at a time, dusting with flour, make a patty first then roll out each bread into very thin and large (about 8-inch) rounds. Prepare ahead, and cover with a kitchen towel. When the pan is very hot, slap the rolled bread into the pan, and cook on medium to medium-high heat as needed to keep the temperature about 350 degrees, for ½ minute. Keep on turning the bread over and over, until it is all puffed up and cooked has some brown specks, then drop about 1/2tsp. oil on each side, spread the oil out with the back of the large spoon, when it has light brown specks all over take it out and serve hot with Dal, Chutney, pickles etc.

Tips: Do you know that Indians eat fresh made bread "Chapati" (like thin Pita bread) everyday. It soaks up the fat (cholesterol) gives energy, and fills you up.

Also, we serve meals with water (not soda, coffee or juices) but drink very little water with the meals. We drink liquid all day long. According to experts a normal healthy person loses over 2 quarts of water a day in perspiring, urinating, breathing and in other body wastes. So drink enough water and other liquids for your body to function properly. Check with your doctor first in cases like physical activities, urinary incontinence etc.

Yoga Meal:

Yoga meal is simple and mostly natural. The only thing we cook is the grain bread. We serve bean sprouts, yogurt raita made with fresh cucumber, chutney, and some fruits. Yogurt is served for breakfast and lunch only.

My father kept one tradition going almost everyday, a serving of mixed bean sprouts with raw mustard or vegetable oil (you can also use olive oil). Soak the whole beans overnight, wash them and wrap in a thick damped cotton cloth, place in a bowl, cover with the lid, and leave in room temperature overnight or until they sprout (in 2-3 days). You have to wash beans and the cloth daily and rewrap in the cloth. Mung and lentils take 2 days, other larger beans and chickpeas take 4-5 days. Bean sprouts have Sulfur, very important for the body.

Fermented Vegetables (M:2 Jars) These can be served daily with any meal for health.

Ingredients: 2 medium carrots peeled and cut into ½-inch diameter sticks; 2 bulbs of garlic clove peeled and pierced with a wooden toothpick; about 2 cups fresh okra or string beans; 2 cups white vinegar; 1 tbsp. turmeric powder; 1/4cup mustard seeds; 2 tsp salt; 2 clean, 16oz. pickling jars with airtight lids.

Fill each jar with half of the garlic cloves; place okra in 1 jar and carrot sticks in the other. In a pitcher whisk together 2 cups of warm water, vinegar, turmeric, mustard seeds and salt. Pour over vegetables filling up to ½-inch of the rim. Place the jars for two days in the sun, or leave them on the counter, away from the draft. They are ready to serve. After opening keep them in the refrigerator. Serve these fermented veggies, like pickles, daily with meals. They will last up to a month in the refrigerator.

Hot Chocolate or Hot Milk: For two servings.

Ingredients: 2 Cups whole milk; 1-2 tsp. brown sugar; 1/3 tsp. unsweetened cocoa powder or 1 oz. chopped dark chocolate.

In a medium pot bring ½ cup of water to a boil, add milk, sugar, cocoa powder; stir well to dissolve the cocoa powder. Bring almost to a boil. Serve hot.

To drink the hot milk omit cocoa powder and follow the recipe above.

Tips: Cocoa powder is mood boosting, has protein and good for the digestive health. Dark chocolate helps mood and reduces the blood pressure. But stay away from sweet side, use unsweetened cocoa powder and limited amount of dark chocolate.

7. Afternoon Drinks: The British had a tradition of drinking Tea. My father would allow us to drink occasionally milk tea or coffee. We mostly had a Mango drink, a Yogurt drink, sweet or salty with mint (Lassi). Or in hot weather we made Thandai, a drink made with melon seeds grinded into milk with fennel seeds etc. Or we all sat down and ate seasonal fruits, such as Water Chestnuts, Mangoes, Melons, Papaya etc.

8. After dinner, about 2 hrs. later, in a Thali (metal Platter), my mother would bring warm whole cow's milk in a large glass with a little sugar for each one of us. It tasted almost like a milkshake. Just bring 2 cups of milk to a boil and stir in 1Tbsp. of grated dark chocolate or 1/4Tsp. Natural, unsweetened, Cocoa Powder.

9. Whenever possible, after the meal, chew some fine Fennel Seeds to digest the food, and freshen the breath.

10. We also went on a Fast, once a week. At that time we ate fermented and sprouted Mung beans with some chickpeas, with a sprinkle of lemon juice and mustard oil. We ate cooked or steamed vegetables without any salt or spices. If we had any fruits, nuts available we used them as well.

Follow more healthy and vegetarian dishes through out this book.

There are 5 main aspects of this diet:

(A) Eat a lot of fresh herbs (Chutney). They are very nutritious, tasty, and full of vitamins. Whenever possible eat fresh fruits, especially berries every day.
(B) Use Turmeric Powder in cooking at least 3-4 times a day in savory dishes. Turmeric is good for the brain and stomach. Use fresh grinded spices to cook vegetables, beans and rice etc. Helps avoid cold, cancer and diseases.

(C)Use Dal (the Whole and Split Beans) with turmeric, spinach, curry powder and tomato sauce etc: it provides protein, vitamins, and fills you up. According to my father some findings show that beans cooked with spinach and tomatoes cure eyes and brain diseases. Turmeric has no flavor, so use it in all savory cooking. This is an antioxidant, it has a substance called "Curcumin," that can ward off stomach cancer and help alleviate Alzheimer's. I want to reach out to all those who have a family history of Alzheimer's and suggest to incorporate Turmeric in their diets. According to the experts the plaque that causes memory loss (Dementia) builds up in the patients' brain almost 10 years prior to symptoms.

(D)Use mixed Grain Bread (Paratha, Chapati etc). Chickpeas are a must: grains soak up the impurities, give strength, protein and minerals.

(E) Use Yogurt during the day. Make sure you stir in hot oil with spices into the yogurt to stop the fermentation. Fermentation can give inflammation. You can use Greek yogurt. Also the last item consumed should be Whole Cow's Milk. Milk is very important for overall health. It is satisfying and filling, so you don't have to look for more food, helps you sleep, helps bowel movement, brain development, and is good for all age groups. Use Whole Cow's Milk. Bring the Cow's Whole Milk to a boil, with or without Brown sugar, Unsweetened Cocoa Powder (makes the intestines strong and is good for overall health), Dark Chocolate, or a little brown sugar (or Jaggery-unrefined sugar). Pour into glasses and drink hot or warm. The heated milk is lighter, easy to digest, and the unsaturated milk fat gets absorbed into the cells easily, good for all ages. You can also use Whole Milk in warm food as it is such as: Oatmeal, Mashed Potatoes, and Pudding etc.

According to experts some people lose their ability to produce gastric acid and pepsin. This enzyme helps separate vitamin B12 from food. Because of losing gastric acid and pepsin it results in absorbing less vitamin B12. Therefore, these people may have more stomach bacteria that are not killed by gastric acid and pepsin. These bacteria also use up vitamin B12. The long-term deficiency of vitamin B12 can cause nerve damage. Dementia is also a result of vitamin B12 deficiency. Use of Turmeric on a regular basis can take care of stomach bacteria and other stomach illnesses.

Do not drink tea and coffee on a regular basis. Tea can dry up the tissues. Coffee has caffeine that interferes with the blood flow to the brain and disrupts sleep. Eat yogurt and drink whole milk (vitamin B12) daily. Cow's Whole Milk is good for all ages, good for the eyes and brain.

Take CoQ-10 or Fish Oil daily for brain health. According to the experts, CoQ-10 (Coenzyme Q-10) helps the Immune System, fights Heart Disease, High Blood Pressure, Allergies, and Respiratory problems. It makes the brain healthy, especially related to Alzheimer's disease and Schizophrenia; it can reduce Cancer and the mortality rate. We also take a multiple vitamin daily. Check with your doctor first.

Avoid chemicals such as nail polish, hair color and dry-clean clothes etc. These chemicals have a bad effect on the brain.

Beans (Plant protein): Are the backbone of the Indian diet. Also, green chickpeas eaten raw right from the pod are the best (find in Indian grocery stores). There are several types of beans. Lentils and Mung cook fast, Toordal, and Split Chickpeas take longer, So, you can cook them in the pressure cooker. Frozen Soybeans and Peas are very healthy too. If using whole beans, wash and soak them overnight in a large bowl with a lot of cold water. Once they are soaked wash them with fresh water just before cooking. Do not use the soaking water in cooking, it will give you gas. Do not use any salt it will make the skin rubbery. I just add 2-3 Bay leaves, about 1-inch Ginger, and 1Tsp. of Turmeric for 1Pound of beans. Cover them with 2-inch higher with cold water, bring them to a boil on high heat, then lower the heat and cook covered on a constant simmer until soft (about an hour). Add spices and tomato sauce etc. later. In India we use split beans, they cook fast, do not give gas, are easy to digest, are full of nutrients, and go well with other food. Indian vegetable Thali (platter) consist of: Dal (bean stew), one or two Vegetables, Bread and Rice, Raita (Yogurt Salad), and Chutney. This is a complete lunch meal. Use green Chutney with all the meals, it is fresh made with fresh herbs and spices. That can provide enough vitamins and mineral for the day. Beans are filling, loaded with nutrients such as Iron, Protein, Fiber, Folate, Magnesium, Potassium, Zinc, and if you cook with greens and tomato sauce, the combination help you digest the minerals.

Tip: Use soy beans (we use frozen shelled edamame, soymilk, cheese, egg replacers, patties, burgers and beverage powder) and stop drinking caffeine, you will cure Acid Reflux. Acid-reflux is the root cause of many illnesses.

Fresh grinded spices: Do you know that the Curry Powder contains therapeutic power? By combining with fresh Herbs and Spices it has a double dose of healing power. All ingredients are available at Indian grocery stores:

Use nuts: Cashews are good for Memory. Almonds are good protein and take care of over all health; Walnuts, Pistachios take care of the bad cholesterol and Brazilian nuts have selenium. Cranberries contain Proanthocyanidins (PACs) flavonoids that can help improve the blood cholesterol levels and lower the blood pressure. Use raw nuts about 20 a day. Brazilian nuts take roasted one a day only.

Bread: Bread made with Chickpea flour keeps you regular, purifies the blood, and should be eaten every day. Other mixed whole grain flour breads such as wheat, barley, water chestnut flour, corn, and almond flour give nutrition to the body. Paratha, is made in a cast iron skillet, puffed both sides by turning over and over, when it is almost ready to eat, sprinkle 3-4 drops of oil, which helps digest the grains well. Watermelon, Papaya, Green Mango,Turnip and Cauliflower pickles made with Balsamic Vinegar were available with the meals.

Tip: Whole grain consists all parts of the grain: Germ is the inner part of the grain that sprouts, has antioxidants, vitamins B & E, and trace mineral. Endosperm is the inner part surrounding the germ that has mostly protein, carbohydrates and some vitamins. Bran, the outer layer of the grain has antioxidants, trace mineral, B vitamins and fiber. Husk is the outer layer protecting the grain.

Yogurt : Is probiotic, used mostly as a Raita (Yogurt Salad) at lunch time. Kirby Cucumber is the best, the skin is soft and has a lot of vitamins. In India it is known to help Heart Disease. My father said that Yogurt should be eaten during the day; in the night it gives inflammation. Also, it should be heated through hot oil, caraway seeds and fine chopped garlic (baghar) to stop the fermentation.

Clarified butter (Ghee): has no fat, but should be used in moderation. Serve hot Dals (beans) with about 1Tsp. Ghee on the top, and also use Ghee to spread over the hot breads (Roti/Chapati). We used Mustard Oil in cooking. My father would buy Mustard Seeds, then got oil made out of them. The fresh Mustard Oil is so sharp that you can feel in your eyes and nose right away. It is antibacterial, keeps Stomach Viruses, Cancer and Skin Diseases away. We used it for massages as well.

As my mother used to say: do not time your cooking, do it slow, and do it right. Lots of preparations can be done ahead. I always have chutney in my refrigerator. I make it twice a week, I make bread three times a week . The prepared bread dough can stay in a plastic bag airtight for at least a week. The fresh grinded spices I make twice a week. Dal or split beans with greens I make three times a week. Just heat the next day and serve. The only item I make fresh everyday are the vegetables. You can also order from an Indian Restaurant: Vegetable Thali with Dal (Vegetable Platter with Bean Stew), or Dosa (fermented Rice and Bean Wrap, cut in half and eat with hands) with Sambar (Bean Soup), and green Chutney (Herb Chutney) or Bara (Bean Fritters) with Chutney and/or Raita (yogurt Salad).

Even though American food is different, now we also eat lean steak, turkey, chicken, or fish once a week. You just need a system to cook the right food and stay healthy. See Index for all sorts of Indian food.

Other Activities:

In India, we did half an hour Yoga together with deep breathing exercises and meditation, walked once or twice a day (before breakfast and after dinner) or whenever possible for a good night sleep and fresh air for the lungs. Do at least 30 minutes of exercise every day. But if you have a serious illness or a chronic disease then use another 30 minutes of exercises. We grew up walking to schools, and my father walked at least 5 miles each way to his office. Exercise is just as important as is the food.

Once or twice a week we went to Temple. In 2013 I visited India, and one day I went to Temple with my nephew and his wife. For about 2 hrs. people were happy, chanting, ringing the bells, playing various instruments, kept on singing one song after another, swaying the body with their eyes closed and enjoying the ceremony. I felt that I have cured my body and I am re- born into a new body. When I came home I said to my sister, if anyone is lonely, sick, heartbroken, they should attend these worships every day, they will get cured right away. My sister said," these worships are done twice a day and the temple is filled with people, early in the morning and in the evening. People socialize, give donations, do their heart-felt prayers, then just come home eat, relax, they all forget about their problems, and have a good night sleep. This is not only a physical but a mental cure."

Summary:

1. **The Indian diet is plant-based protein**: beans, such as chickpeas, peas, soy beans, lentils, urad, toordal, quinoa, black eye peas, mung, kidney and soybeans etc. The bread is made with whole wheat, barley and chickpeas flours and seeds etc. Beans are made mostly juicy with greens and tomatoes daily, and fresh mixed grain bread is served with them. Fresh grinded herbal chutney is used everyday. The vegetables are made with fresh grinded spices, curry powder and turmeric. Turmeric is used 3 to 4 times a day in cooking, about ¼ for two servings. Desserts are made mostly with milk, home-made cheese, nuts, seeds, squash, carrots, fruits etc. Yogurt is eaten during the day, and the whole warm milk with or without water and a little brown sugar is served after dinner. Fruits, nuts, yogurt drinks, milk tea, milk coffee are served during the day. Early morning (before sunrise) and late evening after dinner are the walking times. Yoga together with the deep-breathing exercises and meditation is a must. Socializing at the temple or other gathering places is beneficial. Eat healthy, exercise daily, be courteous to others and maintain a happy life style, do not drink and do not smoke. This is the key for a disease free life.

2. **Oil treatment for the Brain**: Wash your hair only once a week (but no more than twice) with cold or warm water, do not use hot water. Let the hair dry out naturally. Then in a small bowl take about 3Tbsp. of Mustard or Vegetable oil and leave in the sun for 15 minutes. Dip your 2 fingers in the oil, bend down your head, and drop 2-3 drops of oil in your right ear. Rub the oily fingers starting on the ear, then starting from behind the ear going to adam's apples rub the oil. Now using your thumb brush down the same area. Do the same for the left ear. This will strengthen your ear, nose and throat, eyes together with the brain. Now drop 2Tbsp. of oil right over your head and start hitting the head gently with the palm of your right hand for 1 minute, then with left palm for 1 minute. Take 1Tsp. oil and rub in your palms then put your right hand's fingers under the roots of your hair and rub the scalp starting from forehead going to the back of the head for two minutes. Do the same with the left hand. This strengthens your brain and eyes muscles. Leave the oil in your hair for 10 to 12 hrs. Never use both hands at the same time on your head. Use only one hand at a time so you do not squeeze the brain.

3. **Sleeping for the brain**: An adult should have at least 7-1/2 to 8 hrs. of sleep. Sleep helps healing and repair of blood vessels, promotes immunity, supports healthy growth, helps blood glucose level relaxes your brain and gives energy. During the day after lunch take about 15-20 minutes rest: first lay down on your right side for 5 minutes, then on the left side for 7 minutes, then on your back for 8-10 minutes. Do not go to sleep. If needed more rest, repeat this one or two more times and then get up. You can take 2-3 breaks during the day but never go to sleep after eating. In the evening, right after the dinner go out for the walk. Then drink warm whole milk. There should be at least a 2 hrs. gap after dinner before you go to sleep. Have a lighter meal in the evening. If you get hungry eat a banana or peanut butter and honey on a toast with some warm milk in the night. While sleeping change the sleeping positions often. Sleeping on one side will accumulate the blood on one side of the brain, so distribute it all around by changing the positions. Also, while sleeping on your back never put your arms on your chest; it creates more heart problems.

4. **Exercise and the brain**: According to some experts, "Exercise works on brain tissues. It improves the connections between nerve cells, creates new synapses, new neurons and blood vessels and improves cell energy efficiently."

   Another very important factor for brain development is "Mother's Milk. Mother's milk to the newborn is very important. This is the foundation of brain development. The new mothers either should stay home for a few months or arrange for milk to feed their babies. This is still done in India. It is not any shame but it is a duty of new mothers to help babies grow properly physically and mentally.

   Yoga, together with deep breathing exercises and meditation, is a complete body exercise. Yoga is good for overall health. Deep breathing is good for the heart and lungs – takes out carbon dioxide and brings in oxygen in the body. Meditation brings peace of mind and helps you sleep better. My father went to yoga school and told us that yoga should be done faithfully on a regular basis to see the benefits. Yoga, deep breathing and meditation practicing all these three regularly, you will grow new healthy genes inside the body to fight diseases; you will have more energy; your mind will grow healthy cells and will stop cell decay and not only you will have better sleep, your brain will be disease free that will help you in old age.

5. Make sure you maintain a proper weight, a healthy diet, quit smoking, get vaccinated as recommended by your physician, protect yourself from the sun. With the help of your doctor go for a regular age-related screening such as colonoscopy, memography, bone density, and cancer etc. Also, take extra precautions and check out family and heredity related disease such as Dementia, Alzheimer's Disease, High Blood Pressure, and Diabetes etc.

   Tip: A study came out that overweight is linked to 13 different types of cancers. Overweight defined by the National Institute of Health is an excess amount of body weight that may come from muscles, bone, fat and water. While obesity refers to an excess amount of body fat. So eat right and maintain a healthy weight.

About 8 hrs. of night sleep is very important for adults. Sleep is just as important as food and air for the body. Sleep deprivation can lead to Alzheimer's, diabetes, high blood pressure, cancer and other chronic diseases, as well as cognitive decline, memory and learning problems. In her book

"The Sleep Revolution," Harmony Books, N.Y., 2016, (page 107), Arianna Huffington gives the findings:

"Scientists are also starting to unravel the connection between sleep and memory. A recent study from the University of California, Berkeley, found that there is a circular relationship between poor sleep and poor memory, based on the protein beta-amyloid, believed to be the cause of Alzheimer's. "The more beta-amyloid you have in certain parts of your brain, the less deep sleep you get and, consequently, the worse your memory," said lead author, neuroscientist Matthew Walker. "Additionally, the less deep sleep you have, the less effective you are at clearing out this bad protein. It's a vicious Cycle."

A study came out that "aerobic exercises are good for the brain. They grow new brain cells that detour when the arteries are blocked."

Some experts say, " Ballroom Dancing is good for the brain. It shows significant changes in the brain and makes you smart. But it should be done at least 3 to 4 times a week."

According to a study, "the superagers are aging at a different level. The cortex - the outer layer of the brain is much thicker. Researchers don't know whether the reason is generic or environmental."

I think it is both. My grandmother was a very strong woman. We used to buy our own wheat to get the flour made. One day after washing and drying the wheat in the sun on the 2nd floor, she filled a tin to take the wheat down. I went over and tried to take it down, I couldn't even move the tin. My grandmother said, "you girls can't do anything." And she picked up the tin against her stomach, moved it on the side, carried it down to at least 15 stairs and left it near the door for my father to take it to the flour mill. She always worked outside in the garden, drank warm raw milk with honey (the milk that was just milked), and ate all the raw vegetables and greens right in the garden before bringing them in the house. She also mentioned a few times that her mother was a strong woman as well.

A study was done in Italy, "suggesting that drinking about three cups of coffee can save your life. It can help prevent prostate cancer, heart disease, liver cancer, parkinson's, and about 20% of alzheimer's. People in Italy drink cappuccino in the morning with milk and espresso in the evening without milk." Coffee is an anti-oxidant, so it is beneficial and protects the body from diseases.

A study came out that suggests, "Walking helps Dementia patients. It calms down the brain and helps short and long-term memories".

Electronic devices: a study came out that, "Excessive free radicals triggered by low-frequency microwave exposure from wireless technologies have been linked to cardiac arrhythmias, anxiety, depression, autism, Alzheimer's, infertility and more." So, keep the electronic devices and EMF's away from your body and turn them off whenever is possible.

A new study shows that "a simple, non-invasive eye scan can predict disease years ahead of symptoms. They have found a similar buildup of certain abnormal protein on the retina just like the brain." So, take care of and check out your eyes if you have a family history of Alzheimer's or are getting signs of memory loss.

Also, take a brain scan. According to experts SPECT, scan predicts over 90% of Alzheimer's disease. Brain SPECT also identifies various types of Dementia.

Learn more about brain and how it is affected by Alzheimer's (see illustrations with pictures). Go to www. Alz.org., Inside the Brain: An Interactive Tour. You will see: Three Pounds, three parts of brain; supply lines; The cortex; Left brain/right brain; The neuron forest; Cell signaling; Signal coding; Alzheimer's changes the whole brain; More brain changes: healthy brain and Alzheimer's brain; Under the microscope; More about plaques; More about tangles;

Progression through the brain; Earliest Alzheimer's stages; Mild to moderate Alzheimer's; Severe Alzheimer's disease.

You Have to Take Care of Your Brain

According to Indian Homeopathic and Ayurvedic medicines and modern scientific evidence you have to take good care of your brain.

Stay positive and avoid negatives, so that the body does not have any stress. According to experts reducing stress improves brain function and protects the brain's reserve. Happiness can increase the levels of feel good hormones such as dopamine, serotonin, and adrenaline. Positive emotions such as happiness, love and excitement protect the brain's neural framework. Do yoga, and meditation; take a daily walk and do fasting once a week; listen to music and do memory exercises for a healthy brain. Do not gain excess weight; stay healthy and physically fit to keep your brain young and healthy. Have a companion (even a dog), make lots of friends and stay socially active. Avoid stress, control your emotions and have positive thinking. Stress increases hormones like cortisol that can impair the cognitive function of the brain, including shrinking of the brain. This can lead to Alzheimer's and other brain abnormalities. Try to maintain a healthy diet. A good night's sleep is just as important as food and air for the body. Lack of REM sleep (Rapid Eye Movement sleep makes experience more permanent and focused in the brain.) can increase risk of dementia and Alzheimer's. Take breaks and short rests during the day so the blood flows to the brain. Do brain exercises where you have to think. Meet challenges such as painting, doing puzzles, making a quilt, learning to cook new foods, learning new skills and languages. Travel to your favorite places so your brain will be happy and occupied. Explore and enjoy to the fullest keeping your brain occupied. Don't give up; stay active, healthy and happy. There is no end to learning and challenging your brain; you learn from the crib to the grave.

Dr. Alois Alzheimer, who recognized the Alzheimer's Disease, and is named after it, was a German physician. In 1906 he gave his first lecture stating that, "he has seen an unusual disease of the Cerebral Cortex." Since then several researches have been done, drugs have been invented, and thousands of doctors and scientists have been working on it. So far there is no promising cure. Some experts say that one in nine of the older generation has this disease. President Ronald Reagan had it. It is a disease where body and mind both are affected. The brain is covered with amyloid protein (plaque) that can no longer process the information.

Education, diet and exercise are playing an important role. So follow a healthy life style. Have a discipline, a routine, and a strong will to stay healthy, find a companion, a friend, a partner to share.

Tony Dearing, Director of the NJ Advance Media, at The Star Ledger, is writing about Dementia & Alzheimer's for over a year. Tony's column appears bi-weekly in the Star Ledger's Health section on Thursdays. He interviewed Dr. Howard Fillit, a geriatrician and neuroscientist, founding executive director of the Alzheimer's Drug Discovery Foundation. Dr Fillit says:

"We have known about inflammation in the brain of people with Alzheimer's disease for 35 years, but it's never been addressed as a therapeutic target until recently. Inflammation is a hallmark of aging. Chronic inflammation can affect the brain in negative ways…

Prevention, public health, healthy lifestyles, managing morbid conditions, can delay the onset of Alzheimer's to beyond the time of death. That's the goal. We want to die with our minds, and not in a state of dementia. And I think that can be done."

Alzheimer's Disease and the Caregiver

I admire people very much who faithfully take care of their spouses, elderly parents, and family members, and friends. It is very hard to care for someone who is ill. It takes a toll on everyone involved. But try to get help and get everyone involved. Find out all the resources available and at the same time take care of yourself. Get out of the house, meet your friends, refresh your mind, and get some new energy.

A caregiver should also seek counseling, how to best take care and successfully fulfill their rolls. Long-term care at home is given for the people with chronic condition such as Alzheimer's disease, stroke, and Parkinson's etc. If you can afford a professional or admit the patient in the hospital or a nursing home for long-term care, it will take a lot of the burden off the caregiver and family members. Also, the care will be given 24/7 on a professional basis. Find out all the resources available in your community and on state level. Check out: www.Alz.org or call: 1-800-272-3900.

Martin J Schreiber gave his first hand experience on how to take care of your loved ones in his book:

"My Two Elaines, Learning, Coping, and Surviving as an Alzheimer's Caregiver. By Martin J. Schreiber with Cathy Breitenbucher, Book Publishers Network, 2017."

I read the review and liked the book very much. Next day I went to the local library, then to Barnes & Noble, I couldn't find it so I ordered six copies on Amazon.com. Within 10 days I had mailed the book, together with the summary of the Indian Diet, to four families who had Dementia and/or Alzheimer's. I also gave one to the local library. Mr. Schreiber's experience, and the will to share it and help others is very courageous. He is telling his experience, realizing that he could have done better. On pages 94 and 102 he writes:

What I wish I'd known

"Alzheimer's is a disease of inactivity of both mind and body. As it progresses, the person with the disease becomes slower and less capable. You can try familiar activities, but you need to accept when the brain can no longer process the information...

What I wish I'd known

When your partner gets an Alzheimer's diagnosis, it's important to get started on a bucket list of things you want to experience together. Prioritizing helps you feel comfortable later on when you are alone and must do things without your spouse."

I think people should read the book and learn from his experience. As pastor Rick Warren writes in his book, The Purpose Driven Life, "While it is wise to learn from experience, it is wiser to learn from the experiences of others."

Hot Lines to Get Immediate Help

For emergencies call 911. For a healthier life style, check out the government and other agencies web sites and telephone numbers to get help:

Academy of Nutrition and Dietetics: www.eatright.org/resources/food/planning-and-prep/cooking-tips-and-trends
American Cancer Society: Tel. # 1-800-227-2345, or visit: www.cancer.org.
.Alzheimer, New Jersey: Tel. # 1-888-280-6055, alznj.org.
.Alzheimer's Foundation for National Memory Screening Program: www.alzfdn.org
.Alzheimer's Disease: 24/7 Hot line: 1-800-272-3900 or www.alz.org
Centers for Disease Control and Prevention: www.cdc.gov
.Child Help Line: 1-800-4-A-child, www.childhelp.org.
Food & Nutrition Magazine: www.foodandnutrition.org
USDA, Food Safety: www.FoodSafety.gov.
.Hunger Free America: 1-866-3-Hungry
National Cancer Institute: www.cancer.gov
.Poison Control Help line: 1-800-222-1222.
National Sleep Foundation: www.sleepfoundation.org.

Super Foods

Super foods not only contain super nutrients but they are necessary for the health. According to experts following nutrients are found in these super foods:

Fresh Herbs: A plate of mixed fresh herbs such as Rosemary, Watercress, Fennel, Oregano, Basil, Thyme, Dill, Parsley, Mint, scallion, Garlic leaves, Ginger should be served daily. These herbs not only give you vitamins and minerals but help you live longer and disease free. You can also make chutney with the fresh herbs.

Almonds, Cashews, Walnuts, Pistachios, Pumpkin seeds, Brazilian nuts and Sesame Seeds: Nuts in general are good for you. They have omega-3 fatty acid that helps the brain and heart. They also have vitamin E. A National Institutes of Health study suggested, "smokers who snacked on nuts reduced their risk of lung cancer, possibly because nuts curb oxidative stress associated with smoking." Almonds should be soaked overnight (with their skin on), rub to peel, and then eaten raw with hot milk, coffee or tea. They go directly into the blood stream and help the brain. They also take inflammation away. They have protein, riboflavin, calcium, iron and zinc etc. Nuts should be eaten raw and can be served as a snack or with a drink. Cashews help memory and have vitamins, protein, iron and zinc. Walnuts are high in antioxidants and omega-3 fatty acids. They have folate, potassium, magnesium, iron, vitamin B, protein, and zinc. Pistachios have potassium, calcium, magnesium, iron and protein. They also have copper that helps the lungs and make red blood cells. Brazilian nuts have selenium. Pumpkin seeds have magnesium, protein and zinc. Zinc helps prostate health. Sesame seeds are loaded with protein and minerals.

Avocado: Avocado has healthy fat called monounsaturated fat (plant based). It also has folate, fiber, magnesium, vitamin E – good for the skin, lutein – good for the eyes and brain. Buy unbruised and a little firm, Haas avocado, leave in the room temperature for a couple of days and it will get soft.

Omega-3 fatty acids & DHA: For a healthy brain you must have Omega-3 fatty acid and DHA. Use deep water fish like wild salmon, herring, mackerel, sardines, anchovies, tuna, halibut, halibut, shrimp, lobster etc. Omega-9 fatty acids, or oleic acid in oil are healthy. Omega-9 fatty acids include olive oil, canola oil, soybean oil, raw nuts, etc. Omga-3 fatty acid reduces inflammation in joints and arteries, helps lower the blood pressure and reduces the risk of cardiovascular disease, lowers cholesterol and triglyceride levels, helps eczema etc. Monounsaturated fat is also found in pecans, flax seeds, peanuts etc. Polyunsaturated fats are two types – omega 3 fatty acids found in fish, fish oil and omega 6 fatty acids found in vegetable oils such as canola, corn, olive, soybeans and sunflower. You should include both in your diet. The two main fish oils are Eicosapentaenoic acid (EPA) and Docosahexaenoic acid (DHA). DHA is important for the brain and retina. DHA also influences the thinking part of the brain and how you feel. EPA and DHA also protect from heart attacks. Researchers have shown that dietary omega-3 fatty acids are very important for normal function and brain development. Japanese researchers found that a deficiency of these fatty acids can lead to impaired ability to learn and memory information. So, it is very helpful to Dementia and Alzheimer's patients.

Beans: Beans are plant based light protein, have fiber, and antioxidants. They are loaded with nutrients, easy to digest, keep you regular, lower the cholesterol, help insulin production, and protect against cancer. Chickpeas, Lentils, Urad, peas, Toordal, Soybeans, and Mung, all with their skin on; are very good for you. They have zinc that is needed by the body on a daily basis.

Berries: Berries are good for the brain and heart. They eradicate cancer, make new blood in the body, and should be eaten on a daily basis. Blueberry pancakes or muffins are not only tasty but are very healthy.

Cow's Whole Milk: The milk fat from the cow's whole milk is good for the skin, hair, brain and in general for the whole body. It has vitamin B-12 that's good for the brain. My father never allowed us to drink Buffalo's milk, according to him, it doesn't make you smart and is very heavy. Make sure you bring the milk to a boil and use hot or warm. You can also add some water in heating the milk, if you prefer to drink a lighter version. It is good for all ages. By heating the milk the fat gets thinner, and is easy to digest and easy to absorbed by the body. It is satisfying and filling, so you will not keep on eating. When we were growing up, my mother kept a cow for the milk, and as soon as she would milk the cow my grandmother got her favorite glass filled with the warm milk and drank with honey. We tasted it a few times, it tasted just like heavy cream, but we didn't like raw milk because it had cow's smell. Some studies link prostate cancer to dairy products. So check with your doctor first.

Probiotics: Probiotics found in yogurt culture. It is very important for keeping you hydrated, helps in sweating and keeps your gut healthy. Try to eat yogurt during the day. We were told it may give inflammation if you are using during the dinner or after the dinner. Because you go to sleep and there is not enough time to move around and digest it well.

Eggs: Eggs are the brain, body, hair and eye food. They have a substance called 'choline' that is needed for nerve transmission, it minimizes excess fat in liver and aids in hormone production, plays a big role in brain function and preserving the memory, promotes energy, and enhances immunity. Yolk is very beneficial for the vision. Among other nutrients eggs also have vitamin A, B12, D & E, zinc, iron, amino acids, protein, also contain substance called lecithin, that protects against cardiovascular disease.

Kiwifruit: Kiwi fruit is loaded with nutrients. According to some experts it helps vascular health, lowers LDL (bad cholesterol), reduces blood pressure, it not only helps DNA but also helps damaged cells to repair themselves, and fights cancer. More juicy they are more nutrients they have, so let them ripe on the counter until they are soft. Cut them just before serving. It loses nutrients when exposed to air.

Turmeric and Curry Powder: Turmeric the wonder spice is the cure for the entire body. The curcumin in the turmeric is an antioxidant, and keeps the diseases away, erases inflammation, and helps digest the food. It should be cooked with the food. Use almost the same amount as if you would use for salt. Curry powder also has a therapeutic effect on the body. Use it daily in savory dishes.

Garlic: You can use garlic cloves and leaves both. It is a natural antibiotic. It lowers blood pressure, prevents inflammation in reducing the risk for coronary heart disease, protects from infection, helps reduce arthritis, cancer, colds, flu, heart, liver disease, ulcers etc. Peel, cut, slice or chop just before using. Roasted garlic takes care of bad congestion. Chopped raw garlic together with olive oil and lemon juice can be used on salad.

Celery seeds: help digest food, take inflammation away, clean out the liver and kidney, take toxins out of the body, help in arthritis and fever, and lower the blood pressure. When the seeds are roasted and chewed with water they help digest the protein. They have calcium, zinc, iron and other minerals. They are good for bone health, arthritis and liver problems and take away swelling of the joints. They work both as a sedative and as an antioxidant. Use celery seeds with all bread products, cabbage, broccoli, cauliflower, okra and even eggs.

Alfalfa: This is good for those who need mineral supplement. It comes in a liquid form. It has calcium, potassium, magnesium and all sorts of vitamins. It helps arthritis, ulcers, eczema, asthma, high blood pressure, stops hair loss, and cancer etc. My father used to describe it as a richest mineral food.

Fenugreek: In south India they use these seeds and powder all day long in every type of savory cooking. They help the sinus reduce mucus, help lungs and reduce inflammation, reduce fever, lower cholesterol, are good for the eyes and intestines.

Flax Seeds: They have protein, reduce inflammation, help control high blood pressure, improve heart health, colon, bones, teeth, skin and nails. Use in powder form in cereals or seed form in baking bread etc.

Fennel Seeds: They are good for the breadth, help the intestinal track digest food. Just chew about 1Teaspoonful raw after the meal.

Quinoa: Quinoa cooks in 5 minutes. It has 8 to 9 Amino Acids that are essential for the body. It is complete plant based protein, and can be used in salad, in place of rice, and carbohydrates. You can bake with it, make cake, muffins, bread, and pudding etc.

Beets: Beets are known for brain health and memory. Raw beet juice lowers the blood pressure within an hour of drinking the juice; so drink in moderation. Beets should be eaten almost every day. Peel, grate or slice thin and top it on the salad, bake them in the oven covered with skin on for about 1:15 minutes at 350 degrees, depending on the size. You can take the juice out and use in baking. Use 6 to 8 servings of vegetables and fruits a day.

Cucumber: Just like eating an apple a day, Kirby cucumbers with skin on are good for the heart, brain, complexion, and prevent heat stroke. They have vitamins B. C, folic acid, calcium, magnesium, phosphorus, potassium, iron and zinc. Buy un-waxed, small, and either Kirby or Mini Hot-house cucumbers.

Spinach: Spinach has iron, calcium, vitamin A, C, K, magnesium and folate. To digest it better try to use it with tomato or lemon. Spinach helps vision, protects against eye disease, helps protect brain, and protects against prostate, breast and colon cancers. We use in Dal (beans) on daily basis. If possible try to use some kind of greens on daily basis.

Watercress: and Spinach: Watercress has more nutrients than Kale. According to experts watercress is loaded with calcium, vitamin c, vitamin A, K, and has antioxidant and protective phytochemicals. Watercress does not need to be cooked, should be eaten raw. Just garnish the cooked food with it. I slice it thin and top my dishes with it all day long.

The Art of Eating

Not only is cooking an art, but eating is also an Art. Back in India, when we were growing up, my father always said to us:

1. Make a routine to eat on time. Go to the bathroom and wash your mouth and hands before you sit down to eat. Do the same after eating, to keep your stomach light.
2. Start with the light items such as soup or salad. Don't gobble down the food. Take your time and enjoy it.
3. Chew each bite well (each bite about 18-20 times). If you cannot do that, then take a smaller bite. Don't let your stomach do the work for your teeth.
4. Keep the some water near you while you are eating, but don't drink it unless you really need it. Too much water will flood the stomach, and it will be hard for the stomach to digest the food and get the proper nutrition. With too much water the food will just pass through the body without digesting.
5. Talk very little during the meal so that you can enjoy the food and chew it right. Do not watch TV during the meal, you may end up eating more.
6. Eat colorful and healthy fruits and vegetables.
7. Eat Yogurt during the day, so it will not give any inflammation or joint pain. Drink Milk after super, hot or warm, but drink it by itself.
8. Use whole grain food, brown rice, quinoa etc. that is unrefined.
9. When making fresh bread, make with mixed flours. Use some Chick pea flour to stay regular.
10. Make your plate with small portions. Do not waste any food, or do not overeat. The less you eat the longer you live. Moderation is the key.   As an Indian proverb goes: Kum Khana, gum Khana", Eat less and tolerate more. If you are taking lunch to the office do not use plastic wrap or plastic container. Keep your lunch in a glass or stainless steel container/bowl. Carry your water in a glass or stainless steel canteen/bottle, do not use plastic. Plastic melts in hot sun and heat.

Cooking, Eating and Living Healthy

1. The key to healthy living is to use more plant- based food; lean meat, eggs, fish, whole grain, nuts, olive oils etc. Cut down on refined grains, flour, rice, and sugar etc. Cut down on sugary drinks; use lemon or fresh berries mashed into the water or drink buttermilk with dry or fresh mint and roasted cumin power. Use heated whole milk (with or without adding water) for tea, coffee, and hot chocolate, or just by itself. Use fresh or dry herbs for salt substitute; use more beans and vegetables, including greens and fruits on regular basis. Fresh herb sauce or chutney and turmeric powder should be a must for healing the body of aches and pains and keeping inflammation away. Leave the skin on whenever possible: like potatoes, zucchini and other squash etc.

2. Bake with apple sauce or flavored seltzer water, instead of oil and butter. Whenever possible use heated cow's whole milk; add some water to it if necessary. Whole milk is filling, it is good for the eyes, hair, and brain; or just use milk of your choice. Use oatmeal and brown sugar for crumbs in baking. Oatmeal has soluble fiber, beta glucan, that takes out cholesterol from the body. Also, whole grain fills you up quickly with less calories.

3. Use more beans for fibers and protein rather than meat.

4. Cut down on saturated fats. Use monounsaturated fat (plant based) like canola oil, soybean oil and olive oils. Use polyunsaturated fats found in vegetable oils, nuts and tofu, salmon, albacore

tuna etc. Researchers suggests to use omega-3 fatty acids that help reduce inflammation, heart disease etc.

5. Eat rainbow color fruits and vegetables for a healthy heart.

6. Use smaller portions. For example aim for 3-4 ounces of meat, the size of your palm. Buy more poultry and fish, and less red meat. Use lean cuts of meat that have less fat: like loin and 80-85% lean ground meat.

7. Eating right and exercise are very important for a healthier life. Experts recommend 30 minutes of exercise daily. If you have any chronic disease, such as high blood pressure, diabetes etc., add another 30 minutes extra to your daily routine.

8. Watch your alcohol intake. A glass of red wine or beer occasionally is alright, but consuming on a regular basis can be harmful.

9. Make it a daily routine to cook and eat right. If you have a busy schedule, use the pressure cooker or slow cooker; or cook one day in advance in order to eat right. Shopping and cooking go hand-in-hand, so shop right so that you can cook and eat right. Get your spouse or a partner involved and encourage each other to do the right thing.

Make a Colorful Plate

A rainbow color in the plate is not only is a palette pleasing but full of nutrients. Experts say you should have 7 colors in the plate. The scientists have found that the colorful fruits and vegetables cover a wide variety of vitamins, mineral and nutrients, such as blueberries, nuts, carrots, celery, onion, tomato, dairy, beans etc.

Green fruits and vegetables: have antioxidant, good for the eyes and for warding off cancer. You can find them in Asparagus, broccoli, Brussels sprouts, avocado, kiwifruit, zucchini, artichokes etc.

Yellow and Orange: have antioxidant, vitamin C, and help vision, some cancers, heart etc. They are found in carrot, yellow pepper, yellow beets, papaya, peach, mango etc.

Red: helps eyes, heart, and immune system. They are found in red grapes, strawberries, watermelon, beets, red peppers, tomatoes, red potatoes etc.
Purple and blue: Also are antioxidant, keep you young, help urinary tract and memory. They are found in purple cabbage, eggplant, purple potatoes, blueberries, plum, figs, raisin etc.

Tan brown: These fruits and vegetables reduce certain types of cancer and help the heart. They are found in turnip, onions, garlic, mushrooms, dates, banana etc.

Dr. Joseph Parent with Nancy Parent and Ken Zeiger, have written the book, "The Best Diet Book Ever, The Zen of Losing Weight. On page 102 and 103 they say:

Rule of Thumb (Eating)

"Your stomach's ordinary capacity is about one quart. If you eat more than that, the capacity will expand to accommodate the greater volume (up to three or four times as much). If you get used to pushing the limit, you'll need to eat that much more before feeling you're no longer hungry. You'll get in the habit of eating too much, and gain weight. To lose weight, you need to do the opposite. Stick to smaller portions and you won't overload your stomach.

Here are a few fun rules to help you choose the right portion sizes for:
Veggies – be a two-fisted salad eater
Fruits – one fistful is fine
Protein – as big as your open palm
Carbs – cup them in one hand
Chocolate – no larger than your thumb
Dessert – wave goodbye with your empty hand!

Try This:
Using measuring cups or spoons, portion out foods you commonly eat and put them on a plate. Now you can see what each amount looks like. Practice until you can recognize your ideal portion sizes without using the measuring tools."

Daily Recommended Amount and Type of Food

Earlier we were told to follow the Food Pyramid, but that got too complicated for most of us. So now we are told to follow Pie. Take a dinner plate and divide into four sections: about 30% grain, 20% protein, vegetable 30% and 20 fruits. You also have dairy, the size of a cup on the side (outside the plate). My Plate is to build a healthy Meal. Go to: www.ChooseMyPlate.gov. This is a government run site to remind you of healthy eating habits. So, it is clear that we all must have a balanced meal. Any cooked food should be eaten as soon as possible or within three days of cooking. Frozen food should be consumed within two months or sooner. If you can afford it, buy organic, such as milk, berries, apricots, bell peppers, etc. where you can consume the outer peel without cooking.

Meat: It is good to eat meat in 4 to 1 proportion of white meat (chicken, turkey etc.) to red meat (beef, lamb etc.). Processed meat like cold cuts, franks etc. have more sodium and preservatives so there are more chances of getting cancer and other diseases. Use lien cold cuts within 3 to 5 days, the meat starts breaking down fast. Deep water fish like Salmon is beneficial. It has omega-3 fatty acid that is good for body and has less mercury.

Grilled and smoked meat: Grilling is a lot of fun but cooking with wood, wood chips and adding extra flavor of smoke to the food is not good for the health. The best way to cook meat is precook meat indoors by simmering, sautéing and roasting etc. and just heat the meat on the grill with added sauces etc. Smoked meat and vegetable add carcinogens and harmful substances that can deteriorate our health slowly. If you really like the smoked food then use the liquid smoke to flavor the B.B.Q. sauces etc. Use only the top of the liquid smoke without shaking the bottle and discard the bottom residue. The acid in lemon juice and vinegar will kill some of the bad effect of the smoke.

Vegetables: When buying salad greens, check the expiration date and the freshness of the green. Fresh vegetables get spoiled fast, especially in the package, use as soon as possible. The cruciferous vegetables like broccoli, cabbage, cauliflower are known to clean out the body and fight cancer cells. Turmeric used alone or with curry powder in cooking can be great for the health. Turmeric is an antioxidant and gives a pretty color to the cooked food.

Fruits: Always buy fruits a little firm and unblemished. Check the stem. It should be green not dry and brown. Fruits not only have lot of nutrients but they have fibers and help reduce the inflammation in the body. Like the saying is: An Apple a day keeps the doctor away. Pears are very high in fiber.

Spices: Spices give flavor and keep cancer away. In India, we make a mixture of spices like Curry powder or Garam Masala. You can use roasted and grinded Caraway seeds, Turmeric, Garlic powder and Black pepper, equal amount and use on food. Celery salt takes inflammation away from the body. Celery is loaded with vitamins and minerals.

Vitamins, Minerals and Nutrients

According to experts, Vitamins are substances that help and regulate the body conditions. Minerals are enzymes that can trigger an enzymatic reaction, and they are also part of the cells found in the hard part of the body like bones. They both regulate the body process that provides you with energy, keep you away from infection, and let your body function properly. Each body is different, and each of us are brought up in a different environment, climate, setting, and foods etc. So before you follow any diet or take a supplement consult with your doctor. The four main vitamins are A,B,C & D.

In short, vitamin A is good for the eyes, is an antioxidant that prevents aging. You can find it in animal sources like fish, eggs, milk, liver, oil and plants based in dark green leafy vegetables like spinach, kale, mango, oranges, apricot, papaya, carrots etc.

Vitamin B helps cure cognitive decline. It makes red blood cells working together with folate and helps the body digest the fatty acids and amino acids. It is found in salmon, yogurt, milk, eggs, chicken etc. Folate is also found in beans, wheat germ, avocado, peanuts etc. Avoid processed and refined food.

Vitamin C is helps bones, produces connective tissues, & collagen. It helps the body absorb iron, protects from infection and heals the wounds. It is found in citrus juices, papaya, guava, red bell pepper, strawberries etc.

Vitamin D does many things and is the secret of overall health. Vitamin D3 is very important. Older adults and people who do not get enough sun exposure can consume extra vitamin from supplements. Vitamin D is found in salmon with bones, all types of milk, orange juice etc. About 10-15 minutes of sun exposure can provide enough daily recommended allowance.

Vitamin E is a fat soluble and an antioxidant. It helps prevent the bad cholesterol (LDL) and helps the heart. It is found in oils, vegetables, in fortified breakfast cereals, hazelnut, almonds etc. Vitamin K makes the blood protein for bones, blood and kidneys, it also makes the protein for blood to clot (coagulate). It is found in dark green leafy vegetables like kale and spinach.

Omega-3 Fatty Acids, found in fish, avocado etc. is good for the brain and heart. Experts recommend to use deep water fish two to three times a week.

Minerals help regulate many body processes. They are stored in the body in different ways. Some of the minerals go through the bloodstream and are carried to the blood cells. Excess goes out through the body in urine. Some minerals are attached to the protein which eventually becomes part of the body. Consuming too much minerals for too long can be harmful. Both major and trace minerals are important for the body. The major ones needed more are calcium, magnesium, phosphorus, electrolytes, potassium, chloride, and sodium. The trace minerals are chromium, copper, fluoride, iodine, iron, manganese, molybdenum, selenium, and zinc.

All fats are not created equal – some are good for you and some are bad. They promote bad cholesterol (LDL) like the saturated fat. Polyunsaturated and monounsaturated Omega3 s and Omega6s are beneficial. Omega 3 fatty acids are high in polyunsaturated. They help arteries from clotting and hardening. They are found in salmon, albacore tuna, mackerel, flaxseed, canola and soy. The Omega 6s fatty acid are also polyunsaturated. They help lower the LDL and help the heart. They are found in soybean, safflower and vegetable oils. Trans fatty acids are the result of the partially hydrogenation of fats. The man made trans fat acts almost like saturated fat. The Hydrogenated fats are when the unsaturated (good fat) are processed and made like saturated fat (bad fat), when Hydrogen is added in the process to make them firmer. Like stick of margarine, cookies and cracker.

Tip: Some experts say, "If you eat enough fruits, vegetables, vegetable proteins you do not need supplements."

Also, if you eat one fruit a day like an apple and a cup of berries you reduce 40% the chance of getting stroke and cardiovascular diseases."

Learning from family and the knowledge of Homeopathy , Ayurvedic medicines, natural cures, beans, grains, fruits and vegetables helped us all our life. Now watching TV, reading Newspaper and books, and listening to the health experts, I have learned a lot. Following are the advices from the experts:

Brain Food

Brain is an amazing organ which is made of millions of nerve cells that are called neurons. Brain requires constant flow of the oxygen from the bloodstream. Take a multivitamin and fish oil daily if possible (check with your doctor. Also, see the Alzheimer's disease under Food and Health chapter.

My father's daily routine was to soak 5 whole Almonds with 5 large Purple Grapes (Munakka) overnight in cold water. Peel the almonds and either chew them slowly with the water or rub the almonds on the grinding stone, make the thick paste and eat first thing in the morning.

1. Leafy green vegetables, salmon, eggs, blueberries, nuts all are good for the brain. One egg a day will keep your brain healthy and help in body growth. Yolks are good for the eyes; they improve vision.

2. Beets: Use Red Beets, and do not trim them. Leave some stems and the tail on before baking. Bake them in a heavy bottom baking tray, drizzled with a little oil. Cover the pan airtight with aluminum foil, and bake them 1 hour to 1:30 minutes until they are soft (depending on the size). Beets keep the blood flow to the brain and make memory stronger. Baked beets are the best; they keep all the nutrients. Be careful drinking raw beet juice; it can lower the blood pressure within a few hours of drinking the juice.
3. Cashews are a little high in calories; they boost the memory. Lightly toasted cashews are lighter and more nutritious. Do not salt them.
4. Avocado has vitamin K, Folate and vitamin E. It protects the hardening of the Arteries. Eat fully ripened and raw avocado; sprinkle with lemon juice and a little salt and pepper.

Vitamin E, found in the nuts, especially the pumpkin seeds, are believed to help the memory a lot.

Omega-3 fatty acid, like in Salmon, Herring and Tuna helps protect the brain cells.

Folic acid, found in orange juice and watermelon etc. helps keep the memory part of the brain sharp.

Vitamin B-12, found in dairy products and hard cheeses etc. are very helpful to the brain.

CoQ-10: Supplement helps the brain and overall health. Consult your doctor before taking any supplement.

According to ancient Indian philosophy: Yoga is a full body exercise. It should be done on a regular basis to see results. You will have new cells growing, it will stop cell decay in the brain, will give you energy, and will keep you disease free.

Food that Help Reduce High Blood Pressure

High Blood Pressure is also known as "the silent killer." There are no symptoms. It can be attributed to race, heredity, and life style. But you can control it by a healthy diet, physical activity, lessen the intake of salt by substituting with herbs, maintain a healthy weight, quit smoking and limit alcohol intake. Visit your physician regularly to keep it under control. Thus you can avoid having a stroke, heart and kidney failure.

Celery seeds, celery, beets, spinach, natural unsweetened cocoa powder, mung beans, white beans (Great Northern etc.), pumpkin seeds and pulp, pomegranate all help lower high blood pressure. One cup of raw beet juice will bring down your pressure within an hour, but use in moderation. Slow and long-term use of beets is beneficial.

Make hot chocolate with natural cocoa powder and whole milk (or add some water). It lowers the blood pressure, helps the body, makes the intestines strong, allows a good night sleep etc.

Follow a healthy diet. Daily walking for one hour after dinner, and about 15 minutes after each meal will reduce blood pressure drastically. This is what I have done

Exercises for a Healthy Body

I have three rules for doing exercises: warm up, do variety of exercises and stretch at the end. Stretching should be done right way. Stretch only parts of the body at a time in rotating and gliding fashion. Consult with your personal trainer. I start with slow bike to warm up, then do each machine or exercise only for 5 minutes (I go back to same machine later on if I need to), each day I change the order of doing exercises, and at the end I make sure I do stretch exercises. This way I do not exert the body or get in any injury. Use caution when starting a new exercise routine. Before you get involved in any kind of exercise regime, check with your doctor first, make sure you are doing the right one for your body type. Each person is different and each body needs different type of care. There are so many exercises you can do for a healthy body and a healthy mind. Some of my favorites are as follows:

Avoid Negatives and concentrate on Positives: This is my mother's advice. She always believed that positive thinking is very important for a healthy brain and overall health. My father also gave us advice to take positive steps for a healthier life: read inspirational books, do mood- lifting things that make you happy, make others happy that in return will make you happy, listen to soothing music etc. This will not only make you positive and strong but will give you power and tools to face challenges and keep your brain healthy. You have to nourish your brain with positive thoughts.

Move around, do not sit for too long: Research has proven over and over that the more you sit the more you are prone to diseases such as high blood pressure, diabetes, heart attack, stroke, dementia, depression, week legs, and cancer etc. If you get up and move around every half hour to an hour or go out for a walk in fresh air, you will have a good night sleep, be more active, be more energetic, have less stress. You also will have a sharp mind, your body will function better, and will have a longer lifespan. Some experts suggest to use a pedometer and take 10,000 steps a day. Dr. Sanjay Gupta has a walking meeting with his associates. Growing up in India we walked and move around almost all day long: going to school, work, market, temple etc. Experts suggest to move around every half an hour; even doing exercise will not compensate for sitting too long.

Aerobic Exercises: A study came out that aerobic exercises are good for the brain. They grow new brain cells that detour when the arteries are blocked. At the Gym we do virtual exercises: jumping of rope, rowing, playing tennis, throwing frizbee, and marching knee-high hitting the knee with the palm of the opposite hand. All these exercises have a good effect on the brain.

Breathing Exercises: Breathing exercises are good for lung, heart, nose, mouth and throat. They carry the oxygen into the blood stream, and supply oxygen to the brain.

Dancing and Music: According to a study, "Ballroom Dancing is good for the brain. Dancing should be done at least 4 hours a week." We grew up with dancing at special occasions. I think any type of dancing is good for the brain and even for the whole body. My father used to say," Teachers have young hearts, and Dancers have young bodies and minds." In India, I had joined the classical dance "Bharatnatayam" and here I have joined Zumba. After I finish Zumba I feel like my brain is exercised and the blood starts flowing. This is something I really enjoy very much, I forget my problems for a while; also it uses up my energy, I am satisfied, and get a good night sleep. You can also join vocal music group and sing with the people. Anything that your heart enjoys your brain will enjoy too.

Gardening: Working out in the fresh air, using your hands, legs, brain, and enjoying the fresh herbs and vegetables. They all are very good for a healthy body. I do not have much space, but I do grow flowers and plant herbs in large pots. I have a supply of Rosemary, Basil, Oregano, Thyme, and Mint all year round. I Grind and fill in the bottle for later.

About 5 yrs. ago, I read an article that there is region in Japan where the Japanese people live long. They eat a light and a healthy breakfast, also eat Kimchi (fermented food), and Vinegar pickles with lunch. There was a story of a man who was over 100 yrs. old. He got up in the morning, ate a light breakfast of Guava and an Egg, then worked in his Orchard for two hours every morning. He weeded the Orchard, came home, ate lunch, took a nap, then again went out to work for a short period of time. If you can bend down, and work for 2 straight hrs. it is remarkable.

Knitting, Sowing, Rowing, Tennis, and Swimming: Rowing, Tennis, and swimming are full body exercises. Check with your doctor first, and them get in a routine of doing some kind of exercise that you love. When we were growing up, we all used to do a lot of knitting. My mother used to make long sleeve sweaters for us for the winter. Early in the morning, on our day off, we sisters used to grind the Wheat and used to make our own Oatmeal. None of us ever went to a doctor. They make hands, fingers, heart, and mind strong. My father told us once; keep on knitting and you will not get any pain in your fingers.

Practice for a Good Night Sleep. A good night sleep is just as important as the food for the body. You should have at least 8 hours of good night sleep. Go to bed the same time, and try to get up the same time. If you are having problems getting a good night sleep: eat a light meal in the evening. Do not eat at least an hour before going to sleep, eat a lot of fruits and vegetables during the day to fill yourself up, go out for a daily walk. This will also make a regular bowel movement. Good night sleep is the basis for a disease-free life. If you are still having a problem sleeping, go see a doctor.

Stretching: Stretching not only perks you up and relaxes the body, but helps your lungs, brain, and the gallbladder. Stretching before and after the exercise is very important.

Walking: Walking is a good exercise for the whole body; make sure you have comfortable shoes. Walking also gives you fresh air in the lung and in the brain. Early morning walking in the fresh air has a lot of benefits. Also, walking after the night meal helps you sleep better. Some Researchers say that walking 15 minutes a day can add up to 3 more years to your life. Some doctors say that everyone should walk at least 30 minutes each day. If you have some serious illness such as: Diabetes, High Blood Pressure etc. then you should walk another 30 minutes per day. You do not have to walk all together, as long as you walk several times a day, a total of one hour, it will count.

Yoga exercises: There are various types of yoga. Start with gentle classes such as Pranayam, Restorative, and Hatha yoga. Once you get used to yoga it can be done 3 – 4 times a day. My father used to tell us that best time to do yoga is the morning time, after your morning routines, when your stomach is empty. Yoga is a total body and mind, exercise and discipline when it is done with breathing exercises and meditation.

Do or learn something new: A new hobby or a new challenging activity can keep you occupied for hours. Even painting, swimming, joining a local club, finding a trainer to teach you exercise etc. will improve your mood and can make a big change. Do something you can do easily and are interested in. If possible find a partner that will motivate you to stay on a daily routine.

Fasting: In order to give a rest to the body and make it chemical free fasting is very important. It is a safe method of detoxifying the body. In our family we went on fast once a week in the name of the God, and used that day praying and meditating, visited temple etc. We ate boiled and baked food such as fruits, vegetables, milk and yogurt. We were not permitted to use spices, flour, oil, salt, eggs etc. Some families use fresh made bread, halwa etc. at the end of the day. According to Hindu philosophy, "you live longer and disease free when you fast, pray, and meditate."

Other Requirements: Besides exercise you should maintain a proper weight, a healthy diet, quit smoking, get vaccinated as recommended by your physician, protect yourself from the sun. With the help of your doctor go for a regular age-related screening such as colonoscopy, memography, bone density, and cancer etc. Also, take extra precautions and check out family and heredity related diseases such as Dementia, Alzheimer's disease, High Blood Pressure, and Diabetes etc.

Breathing Exercises

Deep breathing exercises reduce stress, the root cause of most illnesses. They help the brain relax and relieves nerve tension, the brain becomes calm, the pressure goes down, and the body functions well. In 2013, when I visited India, I saw my sister was still practicing the 3 main breathing exercises on a daily basis.

1. Wear loose and comfortable clothes. Sit down on the carpet with legs crossed, keep spine firm and straight. Take deep breaths through chest and abdomen to open up your diaphragm. Inhale on the count of 5 seconds and exhale on the count of 5 seconds through the nose. Try to breathe through the lower stomach. Do it at least once a day and build up more later on. You can also do this breathing standing up.

2. While sitting down, close your left nostril and inhale from your right nostril, then close both nostrils. Hold the air in your lungs for a count of 10 or 15 (whatever is comfortable for you; do not hold air too long) and then slowly exhale from the left nostril (the other side) with the same speed. Breathe deep after exhaling.

   Repeat this slowly and comfortably 4 to 5 times, at one nostril after the other. This exercise also makes the lung and the wind pipe strong.

3. This is a brain- relaxing and feel good exercise. It is done before going to bed at night: Keep your hands about 10-inches away from your face at mouth level. Make an upside down U with both hands, and wrap right hand's fingers over the left hand. Keeping the left index finger near your thumbs, both palms facing each other, and the heel of the palms touching each other. Place your both thumbs over and touching left index finger. Now make a little crack between the two thumbs. Slowly at a count of 5 seconds inhale from the nose, and at

the count of 5 seconds slowly exhale through the mouth, blowing the air in the crack of your thumb. You should be able to inhale and exhale about 10-12 times in a minute. Do about 2 to 5 minutes until you are relaxed.

Deep Breathing Tips:

At the end of breathing exercises, inhale through the nose for the count of 5 , hold your breadth for the count of 6, and then exhale through the mouth for the count of 7, then keep on puffing out air a little longer to get all the bad air out of your lungs so that you can breathe in more oxygen . When you are doing deep exhales, curve up your body, squeeze out your lower stomach, and get air out of your lungs. Repeat this process 4 to 6 times. Then deep inhale the oxygen. About 3 yrs. ago, I had attended some classes on yoga in our local library. When the teacher was exhaling, he would curl up his body and get all the bad air out of his lungs. We were surprised how long he could exhale before breathing in the fresh air again. Deep breathing exercises can be done 3 to 4 times a day, with or without yoga.

Every morning (between 4 to 6 a.m.) and every evening (between 6 to 8 p.m.) go out for a walk in the fresh air or work in the garden to get fresh air in your lungs. This is the time in the early morning my father, mother, and older brother went to attend the yoga school. Your brain needs fresh air and oxygen.

Meditation

Meditation, an ancient Indian practice, is a big part of the Hindu Religion. Gautam Budha, meditated for days under a Pipal tree to find enlightenment (Nirvana). Most of the Hindu religious ceremonies consist of some form of meditation. If it is possible, practice meditation in the morning to get the full benefits, and it will keep your mind fresh and healthy for the day. It's a natural cure for a healthy body and a healthy mind. Try to do Yoga everyday and if possible twice a day, for at least 15 minutes each time. In 1989 my parents visited us to see their first grandson. At that time my father refreshed us again with Yoga and Meditation. According to him:

 "Meditation is a must for a healthy body and a healthy mind, do it for 10-15 minutes daily.

Wear comfortable clothes. Sit down in a quiet, comfortable, and a peaceful place on a carpet. Sit in an Asana position: cross your legs, with toes under the other knees, and back straight. Put your hands at the end of the knees, hand open but index fingers folded and touching the thumbs.

Close your eyes, relax, relax, breathe easily, and be comfortable, start breathing deeply with your stomach. Either chant a Mantra, a famous song, or even do your religious prayers, whatever pleases you. Devote yourself to peace of mind and find your inner self. Concentrate on your mantra, think of someone is pulling out all your stress out of your body. You are nice and relax, happy, healthy, and enjoying the life, nothing will bother you, you are on the top of the world, you control your life, your destiny, and the future.

Now you are getting energy in your body. It's pouring into your head, moving all over, arms, body, heart, legs, and flowing all over the body. You are cured of all diseases, and you will seek peace and happiness in whatever you do or whatever you see around you. So, help me God to live a healthy life. From now on I will lead a happy, healthy, a peaceful life, and the happiness will follow me all over, and I will be happy for ever.

It is believed that in the old days in India, by practicing deep meditation and concentrating on the body, mind, soul, and inner energy, some of the gurus levitated in the air while practicing yoga.

Now a new yoga being practiced that is A minute meditation or Six breath meditation, Keep your eyes open and focus on your peace of mind. Breathe into your nose deeply and let it out slowly from your mouth. Do this for one minute at a time, several times a day.

35

Takeaway Points (Breathing)

We were brought up with yoga, breathing exercises, and meditation. I saw my father, mother, and older brother getting up very early in the morning and leaving the house by 4:00a.m., walk each way for about 4 miles, doing yoga, and returning back in about 4 hrs. Then during the day they would teach us yoga on a daily basis. Yoga is part of our life; it is good for overall health. Deep breathing is good for the heart and lungs, takes out carbon dioxide, and brings in oxygen in the body. Meditation brings peace of mind and helps sleep better.

In her book "Breathe," Dr. Belisa Vranich, St. Martin's Griffin, N.Y., 2016, teaches people to breathe that is very effective. She shows why everything starts with breathing, and how to improve your breathing for mental and physical health, energy, and maximum performance. Following are the Takeaway Points, from her book, pages 176-178:

1. "Having an imbalance of oxygen and carbon dioxide can create serious problems related to inflammation and acidity, but without delving into the chemistry, simply know that you need to pay attention to both.
2. The harder you work out your inhale and exhale, the less you'll tire when you're practicing or competing.
3. Stress in the body raises cortisol in the muscles, and therefore places strain on the back through excess diaphragm tension. What this means is that negative emotions (e.g., sadness, anger) hurt your back.
4. Better inhales and exhales are part of the solution; addressing stress levels (and even deeper, subconscious emotional pain) is a big part of the cure.
5. Vertical Breathing means you're overusing neck and shoulder muscles (at the front and back of your body), which then throws the balance of muscles off all the way down your body. And it really does throw your balance off. Your natural center of gravity is right below your belly button. So you aren't imagining the feeling of being more balanced when you breathe low; it's real. As your center of gravity gets lower, you become both physically and emotionally more balanced.
6. On the inhale, you should be thinking two things: Lower-body Breath and expand. On the exhale, think: Lower-body Breath and squeeze/contract. Remind yourself: "Inhale...expand. Exhale...squeeze."
7. Between each breath, a certain amount of carbon dioxide stays in your lungs, just settling there and getting stale (more if you are a really lazy exhale). The result is that these organs can't expand to their full capacity with fresh air on your next inhalation. In other words, your starting inhalations have to be less than optimal when you haven't exhaled well. Often, the result is that you speed up the rate of your breathing in an effort to compensate, which ripples out as an imbalance of pretty much everything in your body and nervous system.
8. Lower-body Breathing is anatomically congruous; Vertical Breathing is not – you're going against the way your body and organs were built. A Lower-body Breath that expands on the inhale is a healthy breath. Turn your awareness inward: You'll find it "feels good." You're not imagining it...
9. The belly breath really is just the beginner breath that helps break down the habit of keeping the middle of your body braced. It gets you physically used to the idea that there is movement from your armpits to your pelvis when you breathe...
10. The next stage in maximizing your inhalations is to consider the flexibility of your thoracic cavity. If you sit at a desk at work or spend several hours a day in a car, then your thoracic cavity is probably pretty darn rigid – the size of your lungs doesn't matter. Making the intercostals

muscles (between your ribs, and in your sides and back) more flexible means they'll expand more, allowing you to take a bigger breath.

11. At the top of your breath (and remember you aren't really filling up – you are filling out), relax your shoulders again and let the air feel as if it's settling into your body. Then soften your pelvis (meaning relax your glutes and thighs) and notice the feeling of being more grounded. This should only take two to three seconds.

12. At this point, you should be able to imagine in your mind's eye how your pelvic diaphragm is the "bottom" of a container. Your belly and upper abs are the middle of the container, and your thoracic diaphragm is at the top. Some people envision a poster tube, others a long water balloon."

The DASH Diet

DASH means: Dietary Approaches to Stop Hypertension. This combines fruits and vegetables, low-fat or non-fat dairy, and whole grains to provide people with a high-fiber, low-fat diet that has been proven to lower blood pressure. The key is to use less sodium. The DASH Diet recommends that instead of salt, use flavor mixes like Italian seasoning, lemon-pepper mix or Chinese 5 spice, and Indian Curry Powder made with Turmeric.

.

Mediterranean Diet

According to researchers the Mediterranean Diet is very good for health, but be careful of adding extra calories:

- Vegetables and fruits should be eaten several times per day either raw or cooked including some leafy vegetables. Potatoes don't count.
- Legumes, nuts, and Whole grains should be eaten daily.
- Olive oil is the main cooking and use extra-virgin olive oil for salad.
- Fish should eaten more than once per week.
- Saturated fat comes from butter, red meat and eggs are rarely eaten.
- Cured meats and refined sugar and flours should not be used often.
- Wine and alcohol should be used only in moderation .

Per experts: you don't have to follow every one of these principles, and you don't have to follow them perfectly. What is important is to use them often and make a daily routine of it. Some people say that Mediterranean diet is for rich people and others say it is a high calorie diet. So, choose what you can afford and the same time make a healthy choice.

Turmeric – the Wonder Medicine

One of the reason contributing to the low rate of Alzheimer's Disease in India is the use of Turmeric. We use it daily. As I had mentioned before, we never went to a doctor all our life. My father followed the traditions, read the books and led us to a healthy life style. He treated Turmeric as a wonder medicine as follows.

Only prolonged use of Turmeric will give full benefits, so it should be used on a daily basis.
How much to use: We use about 1/4Tsp. per serving in cooking.
How to use: You can use with the spices, or use in the oil in the beginning, or just sprinkle over the food, halfway through the cooking.
What form to use: Use in the yellow powder form.
Where to find it: Most of the supermarkets sell it, or buy at the Indian Groceries.
On what food: You can use on all savory dishes, and some sweet dishes, such as: pudding, halwa, syrups, and in milk products etc. Turmeric has no flavor, it has the yellow color.

1. Turmeric is anti-inflammatory; it takes away aches and pains from the body. We used turmeric in all our vegetables, beans, some breads, and even in some desserts.
2. It takes the itchiness away: If your skin is dry and itchy, or you have rash, take a Turmeric bath or just take 1Tsp. of Coconut Butter, add 1/4Tsp. of Turmeric, clean out the skin first with soap and water, dry it well and then apply the lotion. Rub for a while until all the lotion is soaked up in the skin.
3. It can be used for Gargle: If you have a sore throat, heat about 1C of water, add 1/4Tsp. each of Salt and Turmeric and gargle 3-4 times a day, especially before going to the bed.
4. It can heal the Stomach: If you have aches and pains in the stomach or swelling, heat a cup of Milk, add 1/4Tsp. of Turmeric and 1Tsp. of Jaggery (Cane sugar), stir and drink the warm milk. But drink only once a day for only three days. You can also take it with the warm water.
5. To clean the Face: Make a paste of: 1/4C Chickpea Flour, 1/4C Coconut Milk, 1/2Tsp. Turmeric, and 1Tbsp. Coconut Oil. Mix together and spread all over on the face, let it dry out for 5 minutes then rub it out. If needed add a little more oil and the milk, and take it off the face. Then wash the face with water. It will take out all the dry skin and the black heads.
6. The biggest advantage is that it kills germs: flu virus, stomach cancer, the gut, the gums and works like a natural antibiotics. It should be used on daily basis to see the results.

Food Eaten in a Combination

Balsamic and red wine vinegar both help cut down on fat and sugar, so use these on cooked vegetables, salad and pasta dishes with oil. Also, vinegar helps digest carbohydrates in the body.

Chickpeas and soybeans have iron and should be eaten with lemon, oranges, red bell pepper – the vitamin C, it helps absorb the iron better.

Cooked grains should be served with lemon and oil, or just oil. Also chickpeas require a lot of oil to digest. Grains have tendency to stick so serve sprinkled with oil.

Cook beans such as lentils, mung, peas, soy beans, lima beans with greens and tomato sauce. They help digest the beans and give extra nutrients.

Use broccoli, that has calcium with eggs that are loaded with vitamin D, Calcium helps absorb vitamin D better.

Warm milk should be served with nuts such as Almonds and Cashews. It is healthy for the brain.

Food and Care for the Skin

Chickpea flour combined with milk, turmeric and coconut oil is very good for the skin. We make a face mask and rub all over on the face and neck, leave it on for 4-5 minutes, then just rub it out and wash with warm water. Turmeric is an antioxidant, chickpea gives Iron and rubbing on the face cleans out all dry skin. Coconut oil is also an antioxidant.

Olive oil is believed to be very good for the skin. It has omega-3 that is good for the skin and hair. Ancient Greeks used this for beauty treatment.

Sesame seeds give a glow to the skin, and purify the blood. Just toast them, crush a little and sprinkle on salad and food or add to the chutney.

Turmeric is not only an antioxidant but help clear the skin. Use it every day in the food, just you will use salt and pepper.

Protect your skin from sun, UV can damage your hair, skin and give you skin cancer. So wear loose, white, comfortable, cotton clothes and cover your body from head to toe. Sun rays can penetrate the first layer of skin. According to some experts, wear a good sunscreen with SPF 50. You can also buy a sunblock with active mineral ingredients such as titanium dioxide, zinc oxide or iron oxide. Also, use a good body lotion, to nourish your skin, right after you come out of shower. We use coconut lotion.

Food You Should Buy Organic

According to experts you should try to buy following organic food:

Root Vegetables: Potatoes

Regular potatoes that are grown above ground are sprayed with pesticides, and the soil they're grown in is treated with fungicide. By buying organic varieties, you avoid both these threats. In case you can't find organic potatoes, try sweet potatoes; they are usually grown with less pesticides overall. Organic potatoes cost about $1.49 per pound at grocery stores.

Produce: Peppers and Celery

Both veggies react to pesticides in the same way: like a sponge, absorbing the chemicals through the skin. Because of this you won't be able to reduce chemical ingestion by washing or peeling them. Always choose the organic variety. Organic peppers and celery cost between $3.99 and $6.99 per pound at grocery stores.

Leafy Greens: Lettuce, Spinach and Collard Greens

Usually these plants are doused in pesticides to ward off insects. Organic growers use methods like non-toxic repellents to keep these vegetables free of pests. Organic greens cost between $2.99 and $5.98 per pound. Use them in soups and salads.

Dairy Products: Yogurt, Butter, Cheese and Ice-Cream

It's important to go organic with these kitchen staples because we eat so much of them. The grass-fed cow's milk is the best. Non-organic dairy products may come from cows fed a diet of genetically modified corn, soy, and antibiotics. Organic dairy products can be found at grocery stores and Whole Food Stores.

Herbs That Heal

The famous Indian writer and my father's favorite author; H.K. Bakhru, who has written several books, and articles appearing regularly in newspapers and magazines in India, gives some of the following herbs that heal in his book: "Herbs That Heal", pages 9 through 16, Publisher: Orient Paperbacks, a Division of Vision Books Pvt., ltd, New Delhi, Bombay, 1995.

Index of Diseases and Ailments

Anemia: Ash Gourd, Celery, Chicory, Dill (Sowa), Fenugreek, Hog Weed, Onion, Wormwood.

Arthritis/Rheumatism: Alfalfa, Castor Seeds, Celery, Garlic, Indian Aloe, Indian Gooseberry (Amla),Nutmeg, Pepper, Rosemary, Saffron, Sage.

Asthma/Bronchitis: Aniseed, Asafoetida, Celery, Chicory, Clove, Garlic, Ginger, Hog Weed, Holy Basil (Tulsi), Indian Gooseberry (Amla), Linseed, Marjoram, Rhubarb, Turmeric.

Burns, Scalds & Boils: Cumin Seeds, Curry Leaves, Dill (Sowa), Marigold, Parsley,urmeric.

Cataract: Aniseed, Fenugreek, Garlic, Indian Sorrel, Parsley.

Cholera: Clove, Fenugreek, Lemon Grass, Onion, Poppy Seeds.

Chronic Peritonitis/Colic/Abdominal Pains: Cassia, Coriander, Cumin Seeds, Dill (Sowa), Ginger, Marjoram, Saffron.

Common Cold: Cassia, Cinnamon, Cumin Seeds, Ginger, Holy Basil (Tulsi), Nutmeg, Onion.

Constipation: Betel Leaves (Pan), Cassia, Chicory, Cinnamon, Fennel, Indian Aloe, Linseed, Liquorice, Rhubarb, Tamarind;

Corns: Marigold, Liquorice.

Cough/Sore Throat: Betel Leaves (pan), Cardamom, Clove, Fennel, Fenugreek, Garlic, Ginger, Indian Aloe, Linseed, Pepper, Sage, Turmeric.

Depression: Cardamom.

Diabetes: Curry Leaves, Fenugreek, Indian Gooseberry (Amla).

Diarrhoea & Dysentery: Bishop's Weed (Ajwain or Celery Seeds), Chicory, Cumin Seeds, Curry Leaves, Dill (Sowa), Fenugreek.

Diptheria: Garlic.

Eczema: Linseed.

Falling Hair & Dandruff: Alfalfa, Curry Leaves, Fenugreek, Rosemary, Sage.

Fever/Dengue Fever: Cassia, Coriander, Fenugreek, Lemon Grass, Saffron.

Glaucoma: Indian Gooseberry (Amla).

Gout: Castor Seeds.

Headaches & Migraine: Clove, Ginger, Henna (Mehndi).

Heart Disorders: Alfalfa, Garlic, Indian Gooseberry (Amla), Onion.

Herpes: Linseed.

High Blood Pressure: Alfalfa, Garlic, Parsley.

Hysteria: Asafoetida, Saffron, Turmeric.

Indigestion/Dyspepsia/Flatulence/Acidity: Fennel, Aniseed, Caraway Seeds, Cardamom, Celery, Cinnamon, Clove, Coriander, Cumin Seeds, Fenugreek, Ginger, Lemon Grass, Saffron, Turmeric.

Insomnia: Aniseed, Celery, Cumin Seeds, Nutmeg, Poppy Seeds.

Intestinal Worms: Bamboo, Indian Aloe, Turmeric.

Jaundice: Chicory, Indian Aloe, Parsley.

Kidney Stones: Celery, Holy Basil (Tulsi).

Liver Problems & Cirrhosis of Liver: Chicory, Dandelion, Garlic, Indian Aloe.

Low Back Pain/Lumbago: Betel Leaves (Pan), Garlic, Indian Aloe, Saffron.

Measles: Cinnamon, Turmeric.

Menstrual Problems: Asafoetida, Bamboo, Chicory, Dill (Sowa), Ginger Lemon Grass.

Muscular Cramps: Clove, Ginger, Liquorice, Pepper.
Nausea: Cassia, Curry Leaves.
Pimples/Acne: Cinnamon, Coriander, Fenugreek, Sandalwood (Chandon).
Ringworm/Dhobi's Itch: Cassia, Coriander, Holy Basil (Tulsi), Lemon Grass, Turmeric.
Sciatica: Indian Aloe, Nutmeg.
Scurvy: Lemon, Wood Apple.
Sprain: Marjoram, Turmeric.
Syphillis: Poppy Seeds.
Toothache/Teeth Disorders: Asafoetida, Clove, Marjoram, Onion, Pepper.
Tuberculosis: Celery, Ginger, Linseed, Onion.
Ulcer: Bambo, Fenugreek, Marigold.
Whooping Cough: Garlic.

Food and Dental Health

Your mouth not only helps you to eat but it also plays a big role in your health. Researchers have found that taking care of your teeth is also avoiding the diseases early on. Some researchers even linked gum disease to heart disease. Do few basics: do not snack too often, and brush right after snacking. This will stop plaque from building. Sip plain water or lemon water after drinking or eating sweet food. Some of the food that help your teeth are as follows:

Celery Seeds: Chewing a few raw of toasted celery seeds will cure all your mouth problems.

Cloves: Hold a piece of clove on the tooth that is aching and slowly suck the juice; it will take the pain away.

Fennel Seeds: They are not only good for your digestive system but they also help toothache and gum diseases. Brush your teeth then chew a teaspoonful of fennel seeds slowly.

Pineapple: Easting a small piece of raw or cooked pineapple strengthens your teeth. Just remember that pineapple has a lot of acid, so when you cut and peel it, sprinkle with some salt, let it stand a few minutes and wash out the salt. You can cook it covered in a pan, with or without a little sugar on low heat for 15-20 minutes. This way it will be lighter and will be easier on the stomach.

Strawberries: Eat fresh strawberries to keep your teeth white. Berries in general are good for the heart, and they are an antioxidant as well. So have some on regular basis.

Turmeric: Add about 1/2Tsp. of turmeric in warm water and gargle with it to help soar throat and running nose. If you have swelling in your gums, brush your teeth and then use a thick paste of mustard oil and turmeric (1Tsp. turmeric mixed with 1/2Tsp. of oil) and rub it on the swelling.

Note: To take care of your teeth on a regular basis:
- Brush your teeth three times a day – after getting up in the morning, after lunch and before going to bed. If you have problem with your teeth brush after each big meal.
- After eating the last meal, floss your teeth in the night and then brush your teeth.
- Visit a dentist on regular basis to avoid dental problems.

- Change your tooth brush after getting a cold. Try to change your tooth brush after using it for 3 to 4 months.
- Consult a dentist for dental problems, gums, cavities etc. right away.

Food for the Healthy Hair

These are common practices that we all grew up with in our family. To have healthy hair you have to feed your body with the right food. Vitamin B 12 found in dairy products. Zinc and Iron are very important for the hair. Zinc is found in Oat bran, dairy products, eggs, soybeans, navy beans, and red meat etc. Iron is found in spinach; legumes such as soya, lima, kidney beans & chickpeas; red meat; egg yolks; tuna; and shrimp etc. Use some lemon to digest the iron.

Over the weekends wash your hair, let it dry naturally, and then use Almond Oil in the roots of your hair with your fingers, and gently rub the oil into the roots. Almond oil makes hair grow and thicken.

You should soak about 5 Almonds with skin on overnight in water. In the morning peel them and eat them with breakfast. Soak and eat 5 dark Raisins. They are good for the heart. If you prefer, just drink about 1/2cup of Almond Milk everyday. It is good for the brain, hair, eyes and the skin.

Eat Oatmeal for breakfast (see breakfast) at least 3-4 times a week.

In India, we ate Amla Chutney (see Chutney section) everyday. You can find Amla in Indian Grocery Stores, in powder form or frozen green berries. Make chutney or just sprinkle about 1/4Tsp. per serving on the cooked food. Also use spinach, lentils and soya beans in your diet. Food with iron helps hair, but to digest the iron use some lemon or tomato sauce with it. A few drops of Alfalfa extract taken with the water is known to stop the falling hair, consult your doctor first.

Eat one Apple a day, and some berries: they are good for the heart and hair.

Use Henna powder, mixed with dark brewed Tea or natural dark cocoa powder, to color your hair; the natural color is better than the chemicals that you find in the market. Henna powder can be found in Indian Grocery Stores.

Tip: For healthy hair you need sun, air, nutrition (oil in the roots), and plain shampoo. Wash your hair once a week but no more than twice, let it dry then put some Almond Oil in the roots. Almond oil makes hair thick and healthy. I take care of my hair over the weekend.

Laughter is the Best Medicine

When I was in 8th grade, every Friday afternoon we had a function in our school. We all gathered in a big hall. First, we would have some dance, singing and poetry program, then at the end we will have a laughing program. One of a chosen girl from each class went on stage and told us some jokes and we all laughed so much that we had tears in our eyes. Even later when we will tell those jokes to our family and friends we will make everyone laughed all the time.

Laughing is a full body exercise just like walking. You can laugh with or without any reason. Just start with some breathing exercises, forget your personal problems, sit in a comfortable position, have a positive attitude and laugh with full flow. Make a habit of doing this exercise everyday with your family and friends, maintaining the eye contact with each other.

Good Night Sleep is just as Important as the Food for the Body

To have a good 8 hrs. sleep you should eat light, light protein and complex carbohydrates, and at least 2hrs. before going to bed. Drink warm milk that helps you sleep better. Make sure you wear loose clothes (no bra or underwear), have a properly ventilated room (not too hot or cold), keep the room quiet, use dark shades, make a routine of going to bed and getting up at the same time. You have to develop good habits that your body gets used to. According to experts make some meaningful goals in your life and focus on them. A study in "Sleep Science and Practice links life purpose with better sleep." Sleep deprivation can lead to chronic diseases. Adults need about 8 hrs. sleep to clear their mind and give rest and recharge their brain.

According to some experts, adults (65 and over) should have at least 8hrs. sleep, teenagers (14-17yrs.) should have 8 to 10 hrs., and newborns (0 to 3months) about 14 to 17 hrs.

Inner Peace and Satisfaction for a Disease-free Life

You need both inner and outer health for a disease-free body. When I was leaving India (I was 22 yrs. old), my mother and father were advising and preparing me to live on my own. Just a couple of days before leaving my father said:

"You know we cannot be with you all the time. You have to stand on your own two feet. You are the creator of your own future. Before you make any decision get advice from others, think over and over, and then do whatever is right for you. You were raised in a Hindu family with Hindu values. Apply all that we taught you all your life. Eat healthy, live healthy, respect other, enjoy a stress-free life, and faith in god, he will direct you all the way. Do not let yourself, your family and your values go down. Then you will not have anything left, and you will not succeed in life. Depend on God, be courteous to yourself and to others. Peace of mind is just as important as food and air for the body." Those words are still ringing in my ears. Sometimes, it seems that my parents are there and advising me every step of the way.

My family taught us, "Give people more than they expect, do it cheerfully and faithfully, and you will make friends." Also, "Learn from the experience of others. Because you can not make all the mistakes by yourself." In his book, "Happiness The Mindful Way," Dr. Ken A. Verni, Psy.D. gives life saving advices.

Health Messages from: Doctors, Friends & Health-care Professionals

This message is from a brother, who is in his seventies. He teaches Tennis, Swimming and Math. He goes to Gym at least 5 times a week and works out 4 hrs. each time. He plays tennis, does aerobics, uses the machines, then swims for almost an hour.

"My Philosophy is:

One eats every day, one works out every day.

Eat 3 times a day, workout 3 times a day.

200 calories in one hour each time one eats".

Anil and Veena

This is the message from the personal trainers, the father and son.

"The individual benefits of physical fitness go far beyond simple aesthetics. Regular cardiovascular exercise can help improve heart health, which may prevent heart disease in individuals with higher genetic risk factors. When people age it can become increasingly challenging to move around resulting in long periods of inactivity Resistance training can help prevent muscle atrophy and increase the quality of life for elderly individuals. It can also delay the loss of bone mass postponing the onset of osteoporosis and other conditions that weaken the bones. Exercise can also help the hormone glucose absorb insulin, which helps in treating type 2 diabetes. Finally, it can be an excellent way to reduce stress. These are just a few of the numerous health benefits that make exercise a no brainer in improving a person's quality of life.

Sources:

American Heart Association Recommendations for Physical Activity in Adults. (n.d.). Retrieved May 28, 2016, from

http://www.heart.org/HEARTORG/HealthyLiving/PhysicalActivity/FitnessBasics/American-Heart-Association-Recommendations-for-Physical-Activity-in-Adults_UCM_307976_Article.jsp#.V0mnNI-cG3A

What I need to know about Physical Activity and Diabetes. (n.d.). Retrieved May 28, 2016, from

http://www.niddk.nih.gov/health-information/health-topics/Diabetes/physical-activity-diabetes/Pages/physical-activity-diabetes.aspx

https://www.nof.org/patients/fracturesfall-prevention/exercisesafe-movement/osteoporosis-exercise-for-strong-bones/ ".

Michael Cohen and Offer Cohen

Xceed Fitness

Alzheimer's is one of the diseases that has no treatment. Researchers are working on this for a long time, and have spent billions of dollars. So far they haven't found any promising cure. The Amyloid protein that builds up in the patients' brains is the leading cause of Dementia.

This message is from my friend Tony Dearing, Director at The Star Ledger News Paper. Tony was writing a series of articles in the Ledger, on Dementia. I read all of them, and when I came across this one, I wanted to publish it in my book. I said to him, "since you are so dedicated helping others, I would love to publish your article in my book."   He said, "I am passionate about the topic," and gave me permission:

Six Steps to Brain-healthy Life

Be fit, be rested: Exercise regularly and get plenty of sleep.

Reverse your girth: Shed those extra pounds, keep your cholesterol and blood pressure under control, and eat a healthy diet that includes antioxidants and omega-3 fatty acids.

Attend to what ails you: Visit your doctor regularly, get preventative care and seek treatment for any medical concerns that arise.

Imbibe responsibly: If you drink alcohol, drink in moderation, and don't smoke.

Nurture your mind: Keep your brain engaged by seeking new experiences, learning new skills and staying socially active.

Yen for zen: Calm your mind, manage your stress, maintain a positive outlook and seek spirituality.

Tony Dearing

Local Content Director, NJ Advance Media, The Star Ledger

This message is from my doctor. He is practicing the medicine for over fifty years.

"Heart Disease is a major cause of death in the United States. Genes play a role but cannot be changed. However, a good lifestyle can help minimize the risks of heart disease. For example: no smoking, exercise daily; 30 minutes a day on the treadmill or elliptical trainer, walking outside, weight reduction. Avoiding sugar and carbs can minimize risk. In terms of diet: fruits, vegetables, nuts, and grains will help. Fish is important for Omega – 3, especially salmon. For breakfast I eat O's heritage cereal, steel oats, fiber one, flaxseed, brewers yeast, sunflower and pumpkin seeds, blueberries, hemp hearts, walnuts, turmeric, cinnamon, stevia, chia seeds, and almond or coconut milk. The breakfast takes time to prepare, but try it.

Don't ignore symptoms of heart disease; such as fatigue, arm, jaw and chest pain, upper back pain, shortness of breath, or pain in the pit of the stomach. Be aware of your numbers. Control your blood pressure. Know your blood sugar and A1C, cholesterol, LDL, HDL and triglycerides. EKG and stress tests are helpful. Be heart healthy."

Gilbert Mandel, MD

Denville Associates of Internal Medicine, P.A.

This message is from my friend and doctors Mr. & Mrs. Mehta:

"Charaka, born 300BC one of the founders of Ayurveda an ancient Indian medical practice, wrote that all suffering that afflicts the mind or the body has ignorance for its cause, and all happiness has its basis in clear scientific knowledge.

Ayurveda explains the science of living and discusses the techniques for extending the life span without losing physical, mental or intellectual health. It is based on the principle of eating and living as one ought. According to Ayurveda, one needs to regulate one's dietary habits, external activities, and thinking process in order to stay healthy.

Ancient texts say that in order to have a healthy body, one must learn to consume and eliminate properly. One must breathe correctly and have self-control. One must also consider the influence of climate on the body. Preventive medicine is the best, easiest and most rewarding approach.

It is important to note that we are not only bodies in isolation. We breathe and think as well. We are made up of complex emotions, appetites and desires. Our physical body is affected by our mind and emotions. Just as one needs to have a basic knowledge of one's body, one also need to be aware of one's feelings and thoughts. If one is able to keep clear thoughts and a calm and tranquil mind, one can have healthy body."

Reference: A Practical Guide to Holistic Health by Swami Rama. Published by Institute of Yoga Science and Philosophy of the U.S.A.

Dr. Jyotsna Mehta

Dr. Sudhir Mehta

This message is from my niece and nephew. They are working in New York. I have over eight doctors in the family, both in India and in America.

"The ACC/AHA (American Heart Association/American College of Cardiology) Guideline on Lifestyle Management to Reduce Cardiovascular Risk, in general, advises adults to engage in aerobic physical activity to reduce LDL-C and non-HDL-C (bad cholesterols): 3-4 sessions per week, lasting on average 40 minutes per session, and involving moderate to vigorous-intensity physical activity, for beneficial effects on their blood pressure and lipid profiles.

The ACC/AHA Guideline on Lifestyle Management to Reduce Cardiovascular Risk advises to consume a dietary pattern that emphasizes intake of vegetables, fruits, and whole grains, includes low-fat dairy products, poultry, fish legumes, non-tropical vegetable, oils, and nuts, and limit intake of sweets, sugar-sweetened beverages, and red meats."

Saurav Luthra MD

Vasvi Singh, MD

My Father's Philosophy

The food you cook you smell with your nose, approve with your eyes, eat with your mouth, but it has to pass the Test of Health and Nutrition; make sure it is worthy to eat. So, each time you buy it, cook it, and eat it, Cook with Health in Mind.

My Philosophy

Each time you cook food think of health. Make it healthy and make it tasty. Doctors are here to correct your mistakes and guide you to the right path. Before going to a party or attending a holiday dinner, do not go hungry, eat something at home first, and then leave the house. At the parties, fill up your plates with salad, veggies, and fruits. Cut down on heavy and fattening food by eating in moderation. Remember, you are a creator of your health.

Herbs, Spices, Fruits, Vegetables, Liqueur etc.

Most cooking is based on spices. They are used in both savory and sweet dishes. Indian cooking mostly has different types and forms of spices for different dishes. Some dishes have the main spice: curry powder. Some have fresh- ground herbs and spices, some have dry-roasted spices. Some dishes have a bean mixture and some have citrus mixture. According to my father, "Each dish should taste different, and look different, and that will prove how good of a cook you are."

Storing Spices: Buy spices in a small quantity grind the mixture only for a week or two. Roasted, ground spices should be used the same day or kept airtight for a day or two. Fresh- ground spices should also be kept airtight for a day or two. Dry and ground spices should be kept in an airtight jar, away from heat and light, and use them within 3 months. Use a clean and dry spoon when you take spices from the jar. The whole spices should also be kept in an airtight jar, and most of them can last up to a year. Never sprinkle the spices directly over the cooking pot while it is cooking on the stove or the oven. The spices will get the steam from the cooking and will lump together and will spoil very fast.

The Brine (for a 12-Pound Roasting Turkey)

The purpose of brining is to soak meat in a salted and herbal water before roasting or cooking, such as poultry, steak and pork etc. So that the flavor goes in the meat, and the salty moisture makes the meat tender.

½ cup of table salt or ¾ cup kosher salt; 2 tbsp. each: crushed black peppercorns and coriander seeds, 2 large bay leaves, 1tbsp. each: dried rosemary or oregano, granulated garlic, juice and zest of 1 lemon. Bring all to a boil in 2 cups of water, cool and add to the cold water, just enough to cover the bird.

Brine chicken, turkey and large meat overnight, game hens, and steaks etc. for 2 to 4 hours in the refrigerator or in the cold garage or basement. Bring to a room temperature or about 1 hour before roasting, pat dry, rub with butter or oil and roast, sear or bake.

Chat Masala - Snack Spices (Makes about ½ Cup)

4 tbsp. each: caraway seeds and coriander seeds, 1 tbsp. each: lemon-pepper mix, and cardamom powder, 1 tsp. each: salt, cayenne pepper, and mustard powder, ½ tsp. bay leaf broken and ground into powder

Roast the caraway and coriander seeds in a skillet on low heat until light brown for about 5 minutes, add the broken bay leaves, and stir for 2 minutes, take out, cool and grind them well. Add rest of the spices, stir well. Transfer to a plate. When cooled completely, store in an airtight jar. Use within 6 months on cooked dishes, roasted meat and Indian curries, etc.

Traditional Curry Powder (Makes about ½ Cup)

2 tbsp. caraway seeds, 4 tbsp. coriander seeds, 1 tbsp. fenugreek seeds, 1 about 2-inches long cinnamon stick, 1 tbsp. mustard seeds, 8 whole cloves, 1 tbsp. black cardamom seeds, 2 medium, dry, broken bay leaves, 2 tbsp. turmeric powder, 1 tsp. cayenne powder (hot red pepper).

In a coffee grinder or spice mill, grind all whole spices, sift through a medium sieve, and add the turmeric powder. Store in an airtight jar.

Fancy Curry Powder (Makes about 1-1/4 Cups)

2 tbsp. caraway seeds, 2 tbsp. cumin seeds, 5 tbsp. coriander seeds, 1 tbsp. fennel seeds, 1 tbsp. black mustard seeds, 8 whole cloves, 2 tbsp. black cardamom seeds, 1 tbsp. ginger powder, 1 tbsp. fenugreek seed powder, 2 tbsp. turmeric powder, 1 tbsp. cayenne powder (hot red pepper), 1 tbsp. granulated garlic.

Grind all whole spices, sift through a medium sieve, and add the powdered spices. Store in an airtight jar, and use them within 3 months to keep the freshness and flavors.

The Curry Paste (Makes about 1-1/4 Cups)

¼ c peeled and chopped garlic cloves or 1tbsp. granulated garlic, ½ c peeled and chopped fresh onions or 2tbsp. onion powder, ¼ c peeled and chopped fresh ginger, 1 tbsp. fresh ground black cardamom seeds, 1 tbsp. fennel seeds, ½ cup madras curry powder, 1 tsp. fenugreek seed powder, ½ c canola oil, ¼ c white wine vinegar.

In a food processor grind onion, garlic, ginger, fennel and cardamom seeds using 1-2 tablespoon water if necessary. Add curry and fenugreek powder and puree all together.

Heat a medium sauté pan on medium heat. When hot add the oil and ground spices, stir a little, just to heat, cover for 6-8 minutes. Open the lid and stir for another 5 minutes or until the spices are cooked and they release the oil. Add the vinegar, stir well for 5 minutes. Take off the heat, cool and store in an airtight jar for up a month. Use a dry and clean spoon each time you take out the paste.

Garam Masala (Makes about 1/3 Cup)

The garam masala is used to flavor the food. It does not take place of curry powder, which is the main spice base, but it is used to give extra flavor to the dishes.

1 tbsp. coriander seeds, 1 tbsp. black cumin seeds, 1 tbsp. caraway seeds, ½ or one whole star anise (depending on the size), 2 tsp. fenugreek seeds (or 2tsp. powder), 8 whole cloves, 1 tbsp. black cardamom seeds, ½ tsp. cayenne pepper (op), 1 tbsp. black peppercorns, 1 tsp. crumbled bay leaves, 1/2-inch broken cinnamon stick (or ½ tsp. powder).

Grind all spices in a spice mill or in a coffee grinder and store in an airtight glass jar for up to 6 months, away from the heat and light. Use a dry spoon each time to take out the powder.

Nut Spice Mixture (Makes about ½ Cup)

Ingredients: 2 tbsp. each: coriander, cumin, and fennel, and sesame seeds; ¼ cup shelled and chopped walnuts; 1 tbsp. each: dried mint leaves, black peppercorns; ½ tsp. sea salt.

Heat a dry skillet and roast the seeds on low heat, shaking the pan or stirring with a metal spatula until light brown, about 6-8 minutes and take them out in a bowl. Now roast the walnut on low heat for 5-6 minutes, light brown and take them out. Roast the sesame seeds covered with a lid, so that they do not pop out, by shaking the skillet, for about 4-5 minutes, until they start popping, and take them out. In a spice grinder or a coffee grinder, grind all ingredients together with salt, in batches, and store in an airtight bottle for up to a month. Use on roasted and boiled meat, vegetables, bread and rice.

Sambar Spice Mixture (Makes about ¾ Cup)

This spice mixture is used in sambar (like bean stew), in South India. It is their main protein source for the vegetarian people.

1 tbsp. each: methi seeds, urad dal, chana dal, and black peppercorns, 3 tbsp. coriander seeds, 1 tbsp. caraway seeds, 1Tsp. Fenugreek seeds, 8 to 10 dry red hot chilies or to taste, broken in half, and seeds and stems out, 1 tbsp. cardamom seeds.

In a dry cast iron pan on medium heat, dry roast urad and chana dal for 2 minutes, move them aside and add coriander, methi and caraway seeds, then chilies and cardamom seeds. Shake pan and roast them for 5 minutes or until they are fragrant. Cool and grind them in the coffee grinder into a fine powder. Store in an airtight glass jar for up to 3 months.

I also use fresh spices in the sambar (the famous dal from South India or bean soup with vegetables) for 4 servings, grind together: 1-inch fresh ginger, 1/2cup soft cilantro stems and leaves, 1-2 serrano peppers and 3 tbsp. lemon juice with a very little water. When the sambar is done, add this mixture in last 10 minutes before the end of the cooking and serve.

Punch Phoran (Makes about 4 Tablespoons)

Just like Chinese five-spice powder, Punch Phoran is made with five different spices in India. It is mostly used in East Indian cooking, i.e. from the Bengal region.

1 tbsp. mustard seeds (black or yellow seeds), 1 tbsp. cumin seeds, 1 tbsp. fenugreek seeds, 1 tsp. fennel seeds, 1 tsp. nigella seeds.

Grind all together in a spice grinder or in a coffee grinder. Store in a glass jar, airtight, away from heat and light for up to 3 months. Use a clean and dry spoon each time you take out of the jar.

Lemon Herb Mix (Makes about ½ Cup)

This mixture goes very well with seafood and steaks. I use this mixture in cooking the fish all the time. But you can use it in chutneys, over cooked and buttered bread (roti) and naan and on roasted meat and vegetables, etc.

Ingredients: ½ c lemon pepper mix; 2 tbsp. ground dry thyme; 1 tbsp. each ground dry rosemary and oregano; ¼ tsp. each, cumin powder, granulated garlic, salt and black pepper; 1 tbsp. canola oil.

Combine all ingredients in a blender and store in an airtight glass jar in the refrigerator for up 3 months.

Roasted Herbs with Garlic (Makes about ½ Cup)

These are fresh herbs, roasted with fresh garlic for garnish, or use them as spices.

In an aluminum pie plate place all chopped: 1/2 c chopped garlic cloves, 2 tbsp. rosemary, 1 tbsp. marjoram, ½ c cilantro soft stems and leaves, 1 tbsp. sage, 2 tbsp. oregano, 2 tbsp. butter, ¼ tsp. salt and fresh ground black pepper. Cover airtight with foil, and bake 350 degrees for about 15 minutes. Take out of the oven, but keep them covered for another 10 minutes. Use warm or cold.

Seafood Seasoning Mix (Makes about ½ Cup)

This is very versatile. I use this on seafood before and after cooking, on toasts, on roast meats, even on rice pilaf and vegetables.

Ingredients: 4 tbsp. lemon-pepper mix; 1 tbsp. dry thyme; 2 tbsp. granulated garlic; 1 tbsp. white pepper; 1 tsp. sea salt; 1 tbsp. paprika.

Mix all together and store in an airtight glass bottle for up to six months.

All Purpose Fresh ground Spices (Makes about 2 Cups sautéed,15 Servings)

These are fresh spices ground with very little water, sautéed in oil and used in any vegetable or meat dishes. In North India, we grind them fresh every day and use all day long to prepare tasty vegetables.

½ c whole coriander seeds, 2 tbsp. caraway seeds, 4 large (about 1 tbsp.) bay leaves, veins removed and broken, 2 tbsp. black cardamom seeds, 1 tsp. salt; 4-5 hot dried chiles or to taste, 3 c chopped fresh onions, ½ c chopped fresh ginger, ½ c chopped fresh garlic cloves, 2 tsps. turmeric powder, 2 tsps. fenugreek seeds powder (op).

Grind first 6 items in a blender or a food processor to a fine powder. Add ginger, garlic and ½ C water and grind well. Add onion and another ½ C to ¾ C water and puree all well. Place in a bowl and stir in turmeric and fenugreek seed powder.

Heat about ½ C of canola oil, add spice puree and sauté on high heat for 5 minutes. Reduce heat to simmer and simmer covered for 30 minutes. You can freeze the mixture or keep in refrigerator for 4-5 days covered.

Tandoori Masala (Makes about ¾ Cup)

Tandoori is referred to the Tandoori Oven. This is a clay oven where in India, they bake the nan bread, roast chicken and make kebabs, etc.

Ingredients: 2 tbsp. each fresh roasted in separate batches all the ingredients, until light brown (in a dry skillet, low heat, 6-8 minutes), and then ground together: coriander seeds, caraway seeds, and fennel seeds; 1tbsp. each: dry mango powder (amchoor), cardamom seeds powder, fenugreek seed powder, cayenne pepper, dry ginger powder, mustard powder, turmeric powder, and de-veined, broken and ground into powder 1-2 bay leaves.

Mix all ingredients together with 2 tsp. fine salt. Store in an airtight bottle for up to 4-5 months.

Anchovy Butter (Makes about 8 Tablespoons)

This butter is so versatile that you can use it on almost anything eggs, fish, grilled, broiled, roasted and seared meat, even on some vegetables.

Ingredients: 1 Stick unsalted butter softened; 5-6 anchovy fillets mashed fine; 1 tbsp. fine chopped mint leaves or thyme leaves; 2 tbsp. minced shallot; 1 tsp. grated fresh garlic cloves; 1 tbsp. cilantro or flat leaf parsley; 1 tbsp. lemon juice; fresh ground black pepper to taste.

In a small bowl mashed all together with a fork into a thick paste. Place the butter on a piece of plastic wrap, shape back into a butter stick, wrap all around and chill in the refrigerator for an hour. When it is hard, serve sliced over food.

Apple Butter (M:about 2 pints)

Ingredients: 3 pounds tart (Granny Smith) apples, peeled, quartered and cored; 2cups apple cider; 3 cups sugar; 1tbsp. butter. Use a plastic spatula in working with the butter.

Place apples and cider in a non-reactive or stainless steel pot and bring to a boil on high heat. Lower the heat and simmer on low for about 30 minutes until apples are soft. Puree the apples in the food processor. Add sugar and mix well.

Preheat oven at 300 degree. Grease a 14X8-inch baking glass/stainless steel dish with butter, pour the apple puree, even out the top and bake for about 2 hrs. until it is thickened to hold its shape. Pour into a clean jar, cool and refrigerate for up to 2 weeks.

Gremolata (M:about 1cup)

This is actually a garnish you can use it on soups, steaks, roast meat etc. In a nonreactive bowl combine chopped: ½ cup parsley; 1Tbsp.each mint, thyme, tarragon leaves; 1Tbsp. each lemon and lime zests; little salt and pepper; 4Tbsp. lightly roasted and chopped pumpkin seeds; 1Tbsp. E.V. olive oil. If preferred, add some lemon juice at the time of serving.

Hoisin Type Marinade and Sauce(Makes about ½ Cup plus 2 Tbsp.)

This sauce is very tasty, and goes with almost any meat. For beef, pork and lamb you can also use as a marinade.

Ingredients: 1 tbsp. each cumin or caraway seeds and fennel seeds; 1 tsp. canola oil; fresh ground herbs:1/2 c chop packed soft cilantro stems and leaves, 1 tbsp. fresh mint leaves, 2 tbsp. lemon juice, and 1 tbsp. peeled chopped fresh ginger; 1-2 serrano green peppers all ground in the food processor fine with 1-2 tbsp. water; ½ c concentrated frozen orange juice thawed; 2 tbsp. molasses; 2 tbsp. low sodium soy sauce; 1 tbsp. tamarind concentrate; ¾ tsp. cardamom seeds ground fine; 2 pinches of ground star anise (op); ½ tsp. granulated garlic; ¼ tsp. each salt and fresh ground black pepper or to taste.

Heat a large heavy bottom non-reactive sauté pan over medium heat and toast the cumin seeds for 5 seconds, push them aside, and add the fennel seeds and roast them until light brown (about 5 minutes). Take them out, cool and crush them coarsely. Set them aside.

Using the same pan heat the oil and add the fresh pureed herbs and cook them on medium heat until all the liquid is almost gone. Add the orange concentrate, molasses, soy sauce, and tamarind concentrate, salt and pepper. Bring them to a boil, add cardamom, garlic, and star anise powders. Simmer the sauce over low heat for about10 minutes. Take off the heat. Add the roasted and ground caraway, and fennel seeds. Stir well.

When cooled fill the sauce in a clean, dry, air tight, glass bottle. Refrigerate up to one month. Pour the sauce when serving, do not use a spoon. The sauce may get spoiled, and do not pour over a hot cooking food , the steam may get into the bottle and spoil the sauce.

All Purpose Rub (Makes about ¾ Cup)

Ingredients: ¼ c coarsely ground black peppercorns; ¼ c smoked or plain paprika; ¼ c granulated garlic; 2 tbsp. granulated onion; ¼ c fresh ground fennel seed.

Mix all and store in an airtight bottle up to 6 months. Add coarse sea salt as needed. I use dark beer on dark meats such as beef and lamb so there is no need for the salt.

Tip: Dark beer cuts down the chemical reaction of grilling and cooking of the meat.

Seafood Rub

Sprinkle 1 tsp. of granulated garlic and 1 tsp. of cayenne or fresh ground black pepper to taste, then drizzle 2 tbsp. of lemon juice for each 2 pounds of seafood and let it sit in room temperature for 15 minutes before cooking.

Tip: Before rubbing the spices, wash and pat dry the meat with the paper towels. The rub sticks better and any germs sticking to the meat also get washed out.

All Purpose Marinade

Ingredients: 2 tbsp. crushed cumin or caraway seeds,; 2 tbsp. crushed mustard seeds; 2 tbsp. crushed coriander seeds; 4 tbsp. crushed black peppercorns; 1 tsp. crushed allspice berries; 2 broken medium bay leaves; 2-inch peel and crushed fresh ginger; 2 tbsp. peel and crushed fresh garlic cloves; 1 tsp. sea salt; 1 tbsp. grated lemon zest; 2 tbsp. lemon juice; about 4 c of water.

Bring all ingredients to a boil and simmer for 5 minutes. Pour in a bowl and cool completely. Place 4 to 5 pounds of meat in a large bowl or zip-lock plastic bag, pour in the marinate, refrigerate overnight. Bring meat to the room temperature before cooking.

Basic Vinaigrette (Makes about 1 Cup)

Ingredients: 1 tbsp. dijon type mustard; 1 tbsp. garlic cloves or onion grated or minced; 1 to 2 pinches of salt and fresh ground black pepper; 3 tbsp. cider vinegar; 6 tbsp. extra-virgin olive oil; 1 tbsp. fresh or ½ tsp. dry oregano (op).

Just before serving salad, whisk all vinaigrette ingredients together and pour over the salad and serve. If you prefer, you can whisk in 1-2 anchovy fillets in oil; whisk and pour.

Commercial Spice Blends

If you are in a hurry and/or like to have different flavors on hand, buy some spice blends that are available in the market. There are several different lines of blends, my favorites ones are as follows:

Adobo Seasoning with Pepper (Adobo con Pimienta): When I was working in the bank, I had a friend Maria, she had once given me a bottle of adobo poultry seasoning, I tried it and liked it, and since then I started using all different types of this spice blend.

Creole Seasoning: Emeril Laggasi, the famous chef, has his own line of spices, also there are several other brands of Creole spices. If you have ever visited Louisiana, you will fall in love with this cooking and Creole spices just like we did.

Curry Powder: You can use on vegetables as well as making juicy meat or seafood dishes. Make your own or buy the madras curry powder if you like a little hot.

Dash: If you have high blood pressure or want to cut down on salt, try some Dash seasoning to reduce the hypertension. Lemon pepper seasoning blends, for fish and seafood, and classic Italiano for vegetables, sauces and meat add a good flavor.

Garam Masala: This is a spice blend of hot spices (hot in reaction) that is used in Indian cooking. It is roasted and then ground, then used at the end of the cooking to spice the vegetables and meat dishes. I also use this in making rice dishes.

Grill Mates – Steakhouse Onion Burger with Garlic seasoning: (By McCormick): This mix in the bottle goes with almost anything. You can use as a rub or as a seasoning in the cooking.

Also, **Mesquite Marinade and Brown Sugar Bourbon Marinade**, come in packages, used as rubs and seasoning. I use 2/3rd as a marinade and 1/3rd as garnish, at the end, on meat together with some lemon juice and/or melted hot butter.

Montreal Steak: Good for steaks, burgers, ground beef like keema and samosa, and grilling etc. Goes very well over standing prime ribs.

Old Bay: Seafood and old bay go together very well. You can also sprinkle some as a garnish on the cooked dishes.

Pickling Spices: You can add this mixture as whole spices not only to pickles but to marinade, in the beginning in oil for rice and vegetables, on sword fish, corn beef and pastrami, shrimp boil and clam bakes. A ground blend you can use in place of curry powder.

Poultry Seasoning: This herbal and spice blend is good for chicken, turkey, eggs, potatoes, etc.

Ranch Salad Dressing and Seasoning Mix (By Hidden Valley): for dressing, seasoning and for garnishes.

If you are really crazy about making dressing: puree some buttermilk and blue cheese together in the blender, add some roasted, onion, tomatoes, garlic, capers and pour over roasted root vegetables or fresh salad.

Smoked Paprika: This not only gives the color but also the flavor of smoke in dishes. You can also use this as garnish on prepared dishes.

Roasted Garlic & Herb: If you are a garlic-lover, you will love this mixture. I use this regularly on one thing or the other.

Sambhar Masala: In South India, for split beans cooked with vegetables called Sambhar, this spice blend gives the complete taste. You can also use this on any bean dish, if you like a spicy taste.

Pani-Puri Masala: This spice mixture is to make tasty water for spicy snacks. These snacks are little semolina and wheat balls about 2-inch in diameter. You poke them on the top, make a hole, fill the hole with the cooked chickpeas and potatoes then fill with the tasty water and put in your mouth and eat. This spice mixture is versatile. It goes very well on seafood, kebabs, samosa and any sautéed vegetable.

Original Taco Seasoning Mix: You can use this blend on almost anything. I use this with the samosa meat filling, together with some madras curry powder.

Tandoor Masala: Indian cooking done on open fire (Tandoor Oven) is mostly for the Tandoori chicken, but can be used on meat and vegetables as well. I also use this in garnishing the dishes.

Tuscan Rosemary & Sun-dried Tomato: For baking the whole chicken, steak and making sauces, it works very well.

Dredging Flour Mix for the Fried Food (Makes about 1 ½ Cups)

Ingredients: 1/3 to ½ c Cajun spice mix or jerk seasoning mix; 1 tsp. sugar; ½ c each, medium yellow corn meal and all-purpose flour; 2 tbsp. corn starch; ½ tsp. each salt and fresh ground black pepper or to taste; 1 tbsp. lemon-pepper seasoning mix: 1 tsp. cayenne pepper (op), 1/2Tsp. Baking Powder (op).

Mix all ingredients together in a jar, and refrigerate up to 6 months in the refrigerator.

Spices to use separate

Curry powders, garam masala and roasted and ground spice mixtures are general spices you can use in combinations. There are other spices that should be kept separate: various herbs, lemon-pepper mix, whole nutmeg, grilling spice mix, pickle spices, turmeric powder, caraway powder, fenugreek powder, fennel powder etc. these are often used separate.

Herbs and Spices not only help you in various health related conditions, they are natural remedies and can make food tasty. They are loaded with antioxidants. They prevent food from spoiling. I remember back in India, when we had a solar eclipse we were told to put a piece of Kus (a type of tall grass) in the cooked food until the eclipse passed. You can use herbs in the food, take a herbal bath, make tea and even rub them over the skin.

Herbs and Their Usage

Try to grow the basic herbs in the pot or in a sunny area. Once you grow them, you will fall in love with them, and will start using them on a regular basis, just like I do. Flat Leaf Parsley or Cilantro can be used almost with any savory dish. You can also use 2-3 herbs together, as well making soup, stews, stock, bread, and herbal butter etc. Use Onion, Garlic, Scallions, Shallots, Chives in all savory dishes.

Beef: Use Bay leaves, Marjoram, Oregano, Parsley, Rosemary, Tarragon, and Thyme in rubs, stews, roasts, gravy, and steaks etc.

Eggs: Use herbs and tomatoes with eggs. Use Parsley, Chives, Cilantro, Thyme, and Oregano in scrambled and boiled eggs and in omelets etc. The more herbs you use in eggs the more nutritious they get and the less cholesterol there is.

Ham and Pork: Use Dill Weed, Marjoram, Oregano, Parsley, Rosemary in roasts, rubs, ham omelets, spareribs, and stuffing etc.

Lamb: Use Basil, Dill Weed, Marjoram, Oregano, Rosemary (goes well with Garlic) etc,

Poultry: Use Bay leaves (grinded, mostly in Indian curries), Basil, Dill, Marjoram, Oregano, Rosemary, Savory, Tarragon, and Thyme in salad, curries, roast, rubs, grilling etc. I make about 1/2cup of Coconut Chutney, add about 2Tbsp. fresh chopped Tarragon, and rub it all over the Chicken before roasting, it tastes very good. You can also do the same with the Mint and Cilantro, add Coconut Chutney and rub on Roast.

Seafood: Use Basil, Dill Weed, Marjoram, Oregano, Parsley, Savory, Tarragon, and Thyme in rubs, in crumb, baked, broiled, grilled and poached, fish chowders and in creams etc.

Veal: Use Bail, Dill Weed, Marjoram Oregano, Parsley, and Tarragon in braising, breaded cutlets, roasts, scallopini, stews and in tomato sauce.

Bread, Rice, and Vegetables: Use according to your own taste. Mint goes well with potato and yogurt. Bread takes a lot of herbs such as Parsley, Fenugreek leaves, Scallions etc. A variety of herbs go with different kinds of vegetables. There is more use in juicy vegetables like curries and stews. Chutney takes a lot of herbs, depending what kind of chutney you are preparing.

Herbs, Spices, Fruits, and Vegetables: **Does and Don'ts:**

1. Do not use any herb in any way unless you are 100% sure. Pregnant women should check with their doctors for their use of dry or fresh herbs. Also, use the herbs in moderation, and watch out for any allergic reaction, and side effects.

2. Some herb plants can be used completely and some are used only in part. Such as: Cilantro's roots, leaves and fruits all are useful. But in the case of Tomatoes, only Tomatoes are healthy, the leaves are poisonous.

3. In order to make herbal tea follow the direction on the package. If you are using your own fresh or dry herbs, place the herbs in a strainer, and pour boiling water over them. If you are using loose herbs, in a tea pot, pour boiling water over them, cover the pot, and let the leaves steep for 5-10 minutes; then pour the tea and enjoy. You can also use a few drop of lemon with the herbs. Green Tea is good for Memory, prevents Dementia, fight bad Cholesterol, but use in moderation (about 1 cup a day). Green tea leaves collect the pollution from the air, so too much of it can be harmful. Use fresh herbs in moderation, and for a limited time only.

4. Taking a bath with the herbs for certain health conditions (such as aches & pains etc.) just make a few cups of herbal tea and add to your bath water. You can also fill a cotton sock with herbs, tie them with a cord, and let the hot water run over them. Then soak in the herbal water as prescribed by the doctor.

5. Bay leaves help digest the food so use one or two (depending on the size) in the beginning when you are browning the spices in the oil. This way they will give a good aroma and you will avoid the drowsiness effect if they are not completely cooked. Once they are browned, take out the tough veins and grind them with the spices (onion, garlic & ginger) , and they become tasty and exotic spices.

6. You can use fresh green herbs or dry herbs in food on daily basis such as Cilantro, Parsley, Sage, Chives, Thyme, Rosemary, Oregano, Mint and Ginger roots.

7. To dry the fresh herbs do not wash just pat them dry with paper towels. Then either take the leaves off the stems or just spread them out with the stems on, in several trays, in a single layer; place the trays over the refrigerator and let them dry for at least one week, and then take the leaves off, grind in the coffee grinder. Store them in an airtight bottle. Or store whole leaves, and just before using them rub between your palms and add to the food.

8. Avocado has monounsaturated fat, plant based that is good for the body. It has vitamin K, B5, B6, C, Potassium and Folate. Potassium is almost twice as much in ratio to Banana.

9. Tea: The best way to drink tea is to place the loose tea leaves in a small strainer, place the strainer over a warm cup, and pour the hot water over them. You can also use tea bags in the hot water and take them out when the tea is extracted.

   Per my father: do not grind tea leaves and do not use them whole. Tea leaves have led, they are harmful, so just dip the tea leaves in the water and throw them out.

10. There are certain spices that work better with others. Cardamom is good to use with Cloves and Ginger. Cardamom is cold in reaction, and cloves and ginger are hot in reaction. Cardamom and Fenugreek are very flavorful and give good aroma in the food. But make sure it is browned in the oil on low heat until it is foaming, before adding the other ingredients.

11. Buy Kirby cucumbers, un-bruised, medium or small and use them with skin on. Most of the nutrients are in the skin. The silky part and soft pulp around the soft seeds helps Diabetes, High Blood Pressure, and Relieves joint pain. My mother had heart problems, an Ayurvedic doctor prescribed her to drink the cucumber juice 2-3 times a day, and eat all the left over pulp as well.

12. To grow herbs find a sunny and dry location and plant them as seedlings in garden soil. Seedlings do better growing from seeds. If you want to grow Garlic, plant the Garlic Cloves in soft soil. Fertilize plants with vegetable fertilizer, keep them moist, and by the end of the season you will have garlic bulbs. Take out a few bulbs but leave the middle one to grow again. Let the bulbs dry out in the garage for a couple of weeks to mature, then use them in the cooking. Garlic will come back from the same roots year after year.

13. Purple Carrots: If you can find Purple Carrots they are magic. Besides their antioxidant capability they have vitamin A, and protect against Cell decay.

14. Don't ever plant mint in the ground; it will spread and will take over your garden. Use the leaves for cooking and just plant the brown stems in the pot, fertilize them and within a month you will have mint leaves coming.

15. At the end of the season bring in the Rosemary and Thyme plants indoor. The Sage and Oregano can thrive in the ground over the winter. Parsley, and Cilantro, and basil have to be planted every year.

16. Do not use the leaves of Rhubarb, Peanuts and Potatoes; they are toxic. Do not to use green potatoes. Either peel them deeply and take out all the green coating or just throw the potato away. Do not eat the raw Peanuts. They are harmful for the brain. Either boil them in their shells or roast them in the oven first. Once they are cooked, discard the red skin over the peanuts.

17. Tulsi, is a holy plant in India. It is used in worship, and sometimes 2-3 torn leaves are added to the water or Yogurt (Panchamrit). Avoid drinking Tulsi Tea. According to my father it has led, and can be toxic.

18. My father came across a British study, and told us to use heated cow's whole milk with the Tea all the time, it helps skin, eyes and brain. He also told us, if you drink two cups of Tea a day then drink 1 to 2 cups of water also. Water washes away the toxic substances from the body, and helps you sleep better. I do the same for drinking coffee.

Various Herbs and Spices

There are certain herbs and spices they are good for the health and some have side effects, if not used in moderation:

Amchur: Amchur is the Mango Powder, made from the dried green mangoes. It is very sour, brown color, and is used in place of lemon. Use it sparingly, as it can be overpowering.

Amla: This is Indian Gooseberry, a small, light green fruit with a pit, found in Indian Store, as frozen, pickled, candied or in powder form. It is rich in vitamin C, has vitamin B & E, iron and calcium. It is good for hair, nails, and eyes, helps in allergies, asthma, colds, tuberculosis, cancer, diabetes, hair loss, liver and lung disease, prevents wrinkles. It has iron so use it with lemon. The best use is in Amla Chutney which we had everyday with our lunch. It is also the main ingredient in famous Chyawanprash (an Ayurvedic paste).

Allspice: These are the unripe and dried berries of the tree, famous from Jamaica. It an antioxidant, and antiseptic, has Vitamin B, C, calcium zinc, magnesium, and iron. It helps with diarrhea, high blood sugar, arthritis, sore teeth and gums. It has a combined flavor of Cloves, Nutmeg, Cumin and Cinnamon. It is used both in sweet and savory dishes. The main ingredient of Jamaican Jerk spices is Allspice.

Anardana: These are dried whole or powdered seeds of Pomegranate. They have a therapeutic effect on the body. They also give a tart flavor in the food. This is an ancient Indian medicine, and are still used in cooking.

Annatto Seeds: These triangular, brown color seeds are peppery. They give a very pretty yellow color to food. They are used first in oil in cooking, to color the food or soak in the boiling water for a few minutes before grinding.

Anise: Mostly the seeds are used. They have protein, essential oils, help in asthma, diarrhea, hiccups, menstrual cramps and whooping cough. The seeds are used in soups, sauces, rice, breads, cookies and cakes. Just like Fennel seeds, when chewed raw, they help the digestive tract and freshen the breath.

Star Anise is part of the Chinese Five Spice Powder. The roasted Star Anise also used as garnish in soup and are used in liquid in boiling and roasting pork.

Asafoetida: This is actually a spice extract in a paste form or clumps. Traditionally, this was used mostly by the people who did not eat garlic and onion (mostly the Jains). Buy in a dry mounds, not the powder form. It is used in warm oil, in the beginning of the cooking. As soon as it starts foaming add rest of the spices or ingredients. Don't let it burn. It is supposed to keep inflammation away, help digest the food, and gives a good taste to the food.

Basil: The leaves of the plant either fresh or dried are used in cooking and the flowers and leaves are used in herbal bath. Basil is an antioxidant, anti-inflammatory, antiseptic, has Vitamin C, beta-carotene and essential oils. It helps asthma, colds, constipation, headache. They go well with the Italian cooking. The Tomato and Cheese dishes give extra flavor.

Bay Leaf: It is used both as herb and spice. It helps digest the food, is antifungal, helps arthritis, flu, memory loss, it repels bugs and fleas. We used raw dry Bay Leaves to store flour, rice and beans to keep the moths away. You can use them on woolen, silk clothing and books to keep them from bugs and moths. They are mostly used whole in cooking and discarded after the cooking. In Indian cooking they are browned in oil or ghee and then grinded together with the other herbs and spices. I prefer to take out the tough veins and grind them first and fill them in an airtight jar. When needed just brown them in hot oil and then add the rest of the spices (see Palak Paneer - Spinach with Cheese). Use them cautiously, a little powder goes a long way. They can be overpowering, and too much can make you drowsy.

Capers: These green berries are the flower buds of a wild shrub – Capparis Spinosa, grown in the warm climate. You can buy them whole dry or in vinegar, or brine. When I buy them in the salty brine, I take out the brine and add some good white wine, this way they are not too salty. You can use in garnish, in cooking, stuffing etc. they give a good flavor.

Caraway: These are the seeds used in cooking and pickling etc. They are aromatic, antiseptic, have protein, calcium, magnesium, iron, fatty acid and essential oils. They help digest food, and solve hiccups, memory loss, gastrointestinal conditions, crohn's disease, respiratory congestion, it also makes breathing easier in high altitude and can be used as a breath freshener. We used crushed leaves together with turmeric as a poultice to heal wounds. Dry roast the seeds in a cast iron pan, cool, and grind them, store in an airtight bottle. The powder can be used on cooked vegetable, yogurt, mint and lemon drink (called Jaljeera), and on snacks (called chat). It is aromatic and gives a good flavor.

Cardamom Pods: There are two type of Cardamoms: small greens, and large black ones. They both are used in cooking, the small green are much more flavorful. The large black ones are used whole, in making the famous Garam Masala. They have a cool reaction, give an exotic flavor in the food, and when used in the meat gravy they add a unique flavor. They are used both in sweet and savory dishes. You can chew them raw in the pod, or take the seeds out of the pod, crush, and use in cooking. When used in cooking make sure they are heated through, to give full flavor.

Cayenne Pepper: These are dried hot chilies that are grinded into the powder. I use a small amount to rub the meat or sprinkle on the seafood, that gives a very good flavor to the meat. You can also use in sauces, or sprinkle on cooked dishes, that will give you some heat.

Celery Seeds: Both seeds and stalks are edible. The tiny little brown seeds are magical. They clean out the liver, kidney, take toxins out of the body, help in arthritis, bronchitis and fever and lower the blood pressure. Celery seeds smoke helps relieve the pain in jaws, helps reduce inflammation. When seeds are roasted and chewed with water they help digest the protein. They have calcium, zinc, iron and other minerals. They are good for bone health and also take away swelling of the joint. The seeds go well with making any kind of bread, pancakes and coleslaw. Roasted celery seeds can be sprinkled over cooked food.

Chilies and Peppers: There are several types of chilies and peppers world wide. We use mostly fresh Serrano and Jalapeno, dry Cayenne, fresh ground Black or White Peppercorns, Sweet Paprika, or smoked Paprika. The white, red, or black Peppercorns come from the same plant, they are just matured at different stages.

Chyawanprash: This is a combination of various herbs, spices and berries made into a sweet and mild spicy paste. It is a several thousand year old Ayurvedic medicine that takes care of overall health, mostly for adults and old people. It is made with amla, herbs, ginger, honey, black pepper, clarified butter, Malabar nut, Indian bamboo's internal secretion, various roots, grape fruit & Myrobalan rinds, asparagus, winter cherry, water lily flower, bay leaves, green Cardamom, Cinnamon, and Indian chestnut flower etc. My father's aunt, who lived with us, used the Chyawanprash with fresh warm milk all winter long. We had our own cow, and when my mother milked the cow, within a second or two my grandmother filled the fresh, foamy, warm milk and drank it right away. She was the longest living woman in our family. Also, a couple of years ago, when Dr. Deepak Chopra (who has written several books on health, and has his own health Ashram for yoga and health) attended the Dr. Oz show, he spoke very highly about the Chyawanprash. He handed out a 2 Pound jar to each and every member of the audience on that day. (You can find it at the: Vedic Store or Indian Grocery Stores.)

Cinnamon: Comes from the bark of the cassia tree. It is an antioxidant and antifungal; it has iron, essential oils and zinc. It helps the digestive tract, eyes, skin, headache, it can ward off cold and sore throat, staph infection and can help digest dairy products. It goes well both with sweet and savory ingredients. It is cultivated in tropics mostly in Sri Lanka and south China. Use in moderation; using over 1-1/2 gram can lead to convulsion and hallucination. It is hot in reaction so avoid using during pregnancy, hot flashes and extreme dry conditions. It is good for diabetics, and helps increase the memory.

Cloves: Cloves are used worldwide. They are aromatic, and hot in reaction. So use them in combination with the cardamom seeds. Cloves are used in meat – mostly in ham and lamb, Indian spice mixture the Garam Masala etc. When kept over a swollen gum or tooth they take the pain away from an infected tooth. Gargling with cloves boiled water helps the gums.

Coriander or Cilantro: Coriander is the seed and Cilantro are the leaves of the same plant. They both are used for centuries in cuisines like: Indian, Thai, Asian, Arabic and Latin America etc. You can use the fresh leaves as herbs, or use the soft fine sliced stems in the juicy vegetable and gravies, or use coriander seed powder in curries. The green leaves and soft stems give a pretty green color when used in the Chutney. The best aroma comes from whole roasted coriander seeds, which you can grind and sprinkle on cooked dishes as a garnish. To freeze the fresh coriander leaves and very soft stems, just cut the bunch of leaves and soft stems off the thick and hard stems and roots. Wash the leaves in a few changs of cold water. Leave the leaves to drain in a large platter tilted for about ½ hours. Then pat dry with paper towels, and again spread out on the kitchen cotton towel for a few hours or overnight. Then wrap in paper towels and freeze in the container or chop fine, wrap in small portions in plastic wrap and freeze in the small plastic bags in an airtight container. When needed just take out one or two portions and sprinkle on the food before serving.

Coriander seed tea helps in allergy, diabetes, fever, migraines, sore throat, high cholesterol etc. The green leaves are loaded with calcium and can be use as a garnish on cooked dishes, or juiced and applied on itchiness and swelling.

Cumin: Cumin seeds whole or crushed are used in pickling spices, spice mixture, in rice dishes, and in lot of savory dishes.

Curry Pata or Curry Leaves: These shiny green leaves are very aromatic. They are used in hot oil until light brown, and then used in savory dishes as a garnish or with the spices. Available at Indian Grocery stores.

Dill or Dill Seeds: You can use the leaves as a herb or seeds in the cooking and pickles etc. Dill seeds are tiny brown seeds that are very fragrant.

Fennel Seeds: They are light green color tiny seeds almost like Caraway seeds. The small ones are used raw for chewing and the large ones are crushed and used in cooking. It helps digest the food and gives energy to the body, it stabilizes the blood sugar. It also helps in upset stomach. In India, it is a tradition to chew a few fennel seeds after the meal to aid the body in digesting the food.

Fenugreek: You can use whole seeds or grinded in to powder. Just brown them on low heat in the oil first then add rest of the ingredients. You can use the green leaves in the bread, just like spinach, or use with a vegetable as a herb with potatoes. The seeds are a little bitter, but after browning them in the oil they get a little milder. Fenugreek is used in Indian, Chinese, and Egyptian medicine. It stabilizes the blood sugar, produces the good cholesterol (HDL), helps stop coughing, bronchitis, constipation, menstrual cramps, and tuberculosis. Indian grocery stores have green plants, that come in a bunch, just like spinach. Use soft stems and leaves. After washing well in a few changes of water. The leaves are a little bitter and taste best in bread.

Garam Masala: This is mixture of at least 9 spices. They are used mostly in Indian cooking. This combination of the spices is made of hot, cold, digestive, therapeutic, and tasty spices. So when used in cooking, in hot oil, on low heat, or toasted and grinded powder at the end of the cooking it gives a unique flavor. Use it mostly in winter, it has a hot reaction.

Garlic: Garlic come in cloves and formed in a bulb. You can use raw or cooked in food. When raw garlic is exposed to the air and heat it starts loosing its nutrients. It is good for the heart, helps fight infectious disease, high cholesterol, tuberculosis, asthma etc. In Indian cooking fresh garlic, fresh onion and fresh ginger are grinded together to make aromatic spices. Over use of garlic can irritate the stomach and kidney and even can be allergic. Garlic leaves are edible and can be used in garnishes.

Ginger: The roots are edible as fresh ginger or grinded in powder form. The young ginger roots are very soft but the older ones are tougher and can be used in gravy. It strengthen the tissues in the heart, helps food digestion, reduces inflammation. Ginger tea helps colds and flu. Ginger also helps in treating food poisoning, migraines, pain. It prevents blood clots and helps asthma. Ginger marmalade is very common in some European countries. People with high blood pressure should consume it very cautiously. Too much ginger can be allergic and can result in tumors if used excessively.

Jaggery: This is an unrefined juice of the Sugarcane made into Indian Sugar. It is healthier than the regular refined sugar. It comes in a mound or a mold form. Just cut in pieces with the chef knife and use in cooking, baking etc.

Juniper Berries: These are dark brown berries of a shrub. They are good to use crushed in marinade for all sorts of meat dishes, jelly, roasts, and vegetables.

Kalonji: These are the black seeds of the Onion. They are very flavorful. We use them in hot oil in the beginning of the cooking, to give the flavor to the savory dishes. They are also very tasty in the bread, pickles, and spice mixtures.

Lavender: Lavender has a mood lifting aroma. Lavender oil is rubbed to the body, and the blossom is kept around the house to give the aroma. Lavender is also used in French herbs.

Lemongrass: It is the long and hard grass like plant that has a sour taste. The bottom white or the yellow soft part is crushed or grinded and used in the Asian cooking.

Marjoram: Used in meat and poultry, grilled food, potatoes etc. The fresh leaves are tasty in herb mixture as a garnish over steaks and meats.

Mint: Mint is a refreshing herb. It is used at the end of cooking in making chutney, sauce and jelly. After you buy a bunch of the mint, use whatever needed and then take the leaves off the stems, place on a paper -towel -lined baking tray and place on the top of refrigerator. Within 4-5 days the leaves will be dry. Store the leaves in a large glass bottle. Whenever you are making a smoothie, a drink using yogurt, or making potato salad, just rub a few dry leaves over the food. You not only have a pretty garnish but a wonderful flavor. Use mint and a yogurt drink with a little salt and pepper, some water (Namkeen Lassie) and make mint chutney all summer long to keep cool and fresh on hot summer days.

Mushrooms: The dried Mushroom Caps of Shiitake and other dried mushrooms are very flavorful, available in Asian markets or in some supermarkets. The fresh and grinded mushrooms can be added to the meat stuffing for Samosa, in meatloaf, tasty stocks and gravies. Fresh sliced and browned mushrooms go well with eggs, gravy and as garnish over the cooked food.

Mustard seeds: In America mostly Yellow Mustard seeds are used. In India we use yellow and the black mustard seeds. The black mustard seeds are usually used in hot oil for garnishes, in rice, curries, and even in sweet dishes. The yellow mustard powder and seeds are used in savory dishes to give a sour flavor.

Nutmeg: It is a small brown ball type of fruit (about 1-inch in diameter), and the outside is used as a Mace and inside is as a Nutmeg. It has a sweet aroma, and a nutty flavor, but used sparingly. It goes well with the creamy vegetables, sauces, drinks, meat, seafood, and as a garnish on sweet dishes.

Onion: The much of cooking is based on certain herbs and spices and onion is one of them. You can't do without it. Onion comes in all different form, green onion (scallion), shallots, chives, leeks, sweet, yellow, white, purple etc. Onions have vitamin C, E, fiber, potassium, selenium, polyphenols, fructans -insulin, sulfur compounds, lowers cholesterol etc. It goes well with garlic and keeps away flu, cold. When cutting onion wear glasses, hold a piece of bread in the mouth to avoid tearing. To keep the nutrient in the food, cut onion and let it sit 8-10 minutes before using, use raw onion in the salad, mix with vinaigrette or lemon juice and herbs or cook on low heat to help develop the nutrients. Onion slowly sautéed in purified butter with a little garlic powder, salt and fresh ground black pepper and baked slowly in the balsamic vinegar taste superb.

Oregano: Oregano leaves are used both fresh and dry. They go well with garlic and tomato dishes. They are antioxidant, and anti-inflammatory, has vitamin C and K, iron, magnesium and calcium. It helps digest the food, flu, asthma, fever, headache, measles, mumps, tonsillitis, high cholesterol etc. You can use as a herb, as a oil that is antiseptic, growing in the garden keeps the aunts and bugs away, it is believed when you carry it next to your body it helps protect you from sudden sicknesses.

Peppers: There are several varieties of fresh and dried, red, green, orange, and dried brown peppers. The main heat source in the peppers are seeds and the fiery veins. If you take both of them out the shell itself will not be so hot. The cayenne pepper is the dried grounded hot pepper and when it is cored and crushed in small pieces it is called Red Pepper flakes. The Paprika is the sweeter version which you can also get in the smoked form. Hot pepper used in some cough syrups. The peppercorns, green, red or black are the same peppers, they are just the different stages of maturity. It is believed that black pepper (made from grinding the black peppercorns) is much more healthier than red pepper.

Poppy Seeds: They are white and black and come from the Opium plan. The white ones we grind in the spice mixture to make curries. The black ones are used in garnishes, and in bread, bagels, and buns etc.

Rosemary: Rosemary leaves are used, they are on a sturdy stem so you can use the stems for kebab. It goes very well with chicken, potatoes, tomatoes, rubs, grilling, preserves, and herb stuffing. Rosemary is anti-inflammatory, antioxidant and antiseptic, has Vitamin C, iron, calcium, magnesium, zinc, potassium and essential oils. It helps digestion circulation, fights infection, helps memory, asthma, gallstones, headache, vertigo, migraine eczema and bruises, repels insects, inside the book keeps moths away. You can use in gargle to help gums, soar throat. When used in shampoo it can prevent hair loss, graying of the hair. When used as a wash it can help the eyes get the redness out and relax, and the wash can also help prevent wrinkles.

Although it is beneficial but be careful using in large quantities or too often and too much, it can cause convulsion, heart attack in some, and even death.

Rose Petals: In India, and in some Asian and Mid-eastern countries, we use Red Roses, dried or fresh in garnishes and in cooking. The base where the petals are attached is cool in reaction, and is used in making drinks for the summer. It is also supposed to help your memory.

Safflower: Mostly the flower, petal and the seeds are used. It is used in India in Ayurvedic medicine, Chinese, Greek, and Arabic medicines. It helps in fever, high cholesterol, measles, tumors, the oil helps in tissue regeneration, bruises and inflammation. The seeds also give color to the bread like saffron. The safflower oil has a mild flavor, loaded with polyunsaturated fat, and is considered the good oil for cooking.

Saffron: This is the most expensive spice of the world. It is the stigma of the crocus flower. The only part used is the flower stigma which needs about sixty to seventy thousand stigmas to make one pound of saffron. To buy the pure form use stigma not the powder form. It gives yellow color, and a distinctive sweet and a nutty flavor to the food. Used in Indian, Latin and Mid- eastern cuisines. To use it in the cooking soak it in the warm water or milk or stir in the hot cooking liquid. You can also wrap in single layer of aluminum foil and lightly heat it over the stove and then add to the food to be cooked. Keep it air-tight in a glass bottle away from the light and heat and after opening the bottle keep it in the refrigerator, as it can lose its flavor and color.

My father preferred Turmeric to Saffron. Because the long use of saffron can cause headache, coughs, and even kidney damage.

Sage: Mostly the leaves are used (above ground). It is an antioxidant, antifungal, antiseptic, has Vitamin B, C, calcium, magnesium, iron, essential oils, helps digestion, in infection, helps brain, blood clots, fever, colds, perspiration, insect bites. When used is herbal bath it helps skin conditions, when used as a gargle helps laryngitis, throat and gums, when used as a hair rinse it helps treating dandruff and can darken the hair, as a steam to face it cleans out the spots and glows the skin.

Do not use when nursing the baby, it can dry up the mother's milk. When using therapeutically use in small quantities and for a shorter period of time, and people with kidney disease and high blood pressure can have an adverse effect.

Sandlewood: This edible and a naturally perfumed Sandalwood has a cool reaction. In India, it is sold as a dry, smooth and shiny piece of the wood. It is rubbed in the water over a stone, and the light brown, milky, and perfumed water is used in making the summer drinks. It is supposed to relieve the rash, and heat break outs.

Sesame Seeds: They are white, off white, and black. My father loved the black sesame seeds sweets (see the Desserts). They are the more nutritious ones. In middle-east some places they are considered sacred. They are used all around the world. Use in moderation, they can give you loose stomach.

Star Anise: This is star shape, dried spice, about 1 to 2-inch in diameter. It is mostly used in Chinese and Asian cooking. It is one of the main ingredient of the Chinese Five Spice blend. We use in making broth, in pork etc.

Tamarind: Tamarind is a sour fruit similar to the Lima Bean shape. It is very tart in flavor. In Indian and in Asian cooking, even in making the Worcestershire sauce it is the important ingredient. The best form to use it in thick Paste form. This way you do not have to go boiling the dried Tamarind, cooking and extracting the juice, and then straining it, and filling in the bottle for future use.

Thyme: The fresh herb, that has tiny leave and very thin stems gives a lot of flavor to dishes especially to seafood. It is antibiotic and antifungal. The dry herb is just as good to use in combination with other herbs like parsley and cilantro. Good for cold and Flu and for itchy skin, it loosen the mucus and strengthen the immune system. Inhaling the flower aroma helps mind and body stay young. A tea made with thyme leaves and then cooled to room temperature can be used on hair to take the dandruff off. Also thyme bath can help arthritis and sore muscles.

Tulsi: Also known as a holy basil. This is a holy plant found in homes in Hindu families, in India. It has a therapeutic value of curing fever, flue, skin conditions, headache, and stomach. It is mostly used in religious ceremonies in Hindu families. Thousands of years ago in practicing Yoga the gurus drank Tulsi tea, it is hot in reaction, gave them strength and stamina and the desire to work hard with minimum consumption of food. It is a tradition to keep the plant around the house to keep the disease, mosquito, and bad spirit away.

My father was very fond of reading the herbal books, books on health, books on Ayurvedic and Homeopathic medicine and once he came across that Tulsi has Mercury, and the extreme and longer use over a period of time, can be fatal, he stopped consuming the leaves or any other part of the plant. We were told to take a tiny leaf part (1/4-of an inch of the leaf) only in religious yogurt drink (called Punchamrit) as a offering to god.

Turmeric Powder: Turmeric powder is yellow that gives good color in the food, and is made from the root of the plant which looks almost like ginger roots. Turmeric is antioxidant, anti-inflammatory and antifungal. It takes away aches, pains and helps stomach with virus like symptoms. When we were growing up, my mother gave us warm Turmeric milk (One glass, 8oz, of warm milk, mixed with a little sugar and about 1/4Teaspoon of turmeric powder) to ease aches and pain in the stomach. But use this remedy only a limited time, once a day for about 3-4 days. It helps prevent blood clots from forming, takes the inflammation away, helps arthritis, colds, eczema, flu, uterine tumors and high-cholesterol. It heals the open wounds (make a thick paste with turmeric and water in a large spoon, just heat it over the stove, cool, and apply on open sores and wounds). In India, it is used in religious ceremonies for purification, as a dry powder or diluted in water or yogurt.

Vanilla Beans: The most common extract used in baking is the Vanilla extract. The beans are dark brown color, just split them in half lengthwise, scrape out the seeds and add to the cooking. Vanilla has a rich, little sweet, and a caramel like buttery flavor.

Wasabi: Wasabi is a pungent root vegetable, mostly used in powder form or fresh in sauces and relishes etc. The powder mixed with a little water, made into a paste, served with the seafood.

Various Fruits and Vegetables

Back in India, when I was growing up, we lived on fresh fruits, vegetables and Beans. My mother went to market mostly in the evening, when the farmers are going back home, and got a lot of bargain, paid only a fraction of the price. We ate seasonal fruits that were abundant in the season. To this date I try to do the same. I know back in 2010, my niece was here on my birthday, she had bought some Doughnuts for me, and hid them under the pile of vegetables in the refrigerator, I had 11 fresh vegetables and greens on the shelf, and I didn't even know about the Doughnuts.

According to the experts in various fields, including my father who worked in the government's Agriculture Dept. for most of his life, following are the seasons and specialties of various fruits and vegetables. If the fruits (mostly the berries) and vegetables are grown in a greenhouse they are available all year round.

Fruits

Berries: Blueberries, and Huckleberries are summer fruits. I remember that around July 4th , each year I get a 6 pints basket of Blueberries for almost half of the price in the supermarket. Strawberries come around spring and summer. Blackberries and Raspberries are available in spring, summer and autumn. Cranberries are available around Thanksgiving time.

Citrus Fruits: Grapefruits are available end of summer and winter. Lemons, and Oranges are available mostly in spring and winter. Limes come around summer.

Melons: The most popular melons like Cantaloupe, Honeydew and Watermelon are available in summer.

Stone Fruits: Most of the fruits with hard pits, like Apricot, Nectarines, Peaches and Plums are available summer fruits. Cherries you start getting from spring to summer.

The Fruits Grown on Trees, Bushes and Vines: Apple, Pears, Pomegranates, and Persimmons start coming from the end of the summer into winter. Grapes are available starting from spring up to the start of the winter. Rhubarb available mostly in spring and summer.

Vegetables

Beans, Peas, and Corn: Green Beans, Long Beans and Wax Beans are available in summer. Corn is a summer crop. Peas are mostly available in spring and summer.

Crucifers: Brussels Sprouts, Broccoli, Broccoli Rabe and Green Cabbage are available in autumn and winter. Cauliflower is available from summer to winter. Red Cabbage comes mostly in winter.

Greens: Arugula is available in spring, summer and autumn. Lettuce, Spinach mostly in spring and autumn. Kale from summer to winter.

Root Vegetables: Asparagus in spring and summer. Beets, Celery, Carrots, and Radishes start from spring and are available until winter. Potatoes are mostly spring and summer vegetables. Fennel, Rutabagas and Turnips are available from autumn to winter.

Onion, Garlic and Leek: Onions are mostly summer vegetables. Garlic and Leek are available in spring into summer.

Other Vegetables: Mushrooms are mostly spring and autumn products, but are available during the summer as well. Cucumber, Chile, Eggplants, Peppers, and Tomatoes are mostly available in summer. Avocados are available starting from spring till start of the winter.

Vegetable Storing and Refrigeration

Basics: Never wash any vegetables, until you are ready to cook. The perishables such as herbs and greens, take them out from the original packing, wrap in the paper towels, and store in a clean plastic bag and leave the end open. Try to use with 2-3 days. If herbs are wet, pat dry first then wrap in the paper towels.

 If you are freezing any of the vegetables or herbs, blanch them first, to retain their color, pat dry and freeze them in an airtight container for about 2 months. Longer they may lose their color and flavor.

Artichokes: Artichokes turn brown very fast. So rub the lemon on the cut surface, take out a few outer tough leaves, cut in half, and pull out all the fuzzy center with the potato peeler. If they are large then wrap each artichoke in the paper towel and place in the vegetable box. You can also slice off the dry end of the stem, wash the end with cold water, pat dry, rub the end with the lemon, and place in an airtight container and store in the high humidity drawer of the refrigerator. To freeze, trim the 1/3 top off, rub the cut surface with the lemon, boil in lemon water (use the used up lemon pieces), drain upside down, then freeze in an airtight container.

Asparagus: Take off the rubber bands, just wrap with the paper towel and store in the vegetable drawer for 3-4 days. To freeze, blanch them in the lemon water for 3 minutes, pat dry and freeze in an airtight containe. Before cooking remove the bottom tough part, by bending near the bottom edge, and let them break off the tough part automatically.

Avocado: Buy the Hass avocado. Buy the hard one and leave in the room temperature for 3-4 days until it ripens. If you need to use right away only then buy the soft one. Store them on the counter, but once they are soft, store them in the refrigerator open, and use within 2-3 days, otherwise they will start turning brown inside. Cut avocado just before serving, so that they do not turn brown. To cut the avocado, cut the outer green skin lengthwise, twist the two parts, then take out the pit with the edge of the knife, and then scoop out the pulp, or just peel off the skin. Use about 1Tbsp. lemon juice per avocado immediately over the pulp before serving.

Beets: Beets can be stored for up a month in the refrigerator box. Just make sure they are nice and dry without any stems and leaves. Also, leave the tail on, otherwise they will bleed. To use the leaves, wash each leaf separate, under running cold water, stem side down, slice thin across and use them right away, after washing.

Broccoli, Brussels Sprouts, and Cauliflower: Just store in the refrigerator without opening the original wrapping, and use with 4 to 7 days. Take out the wilted leaves, wash, cut and cook. The stem of the Broccoli and cauliflower, can be peeled, sliced, and used in the salad or in cooking.

Carrots and Celery: Always refrigerate in its original packing. Depending on the freshness, they can be stored for almost a month. Once you open the package, push in a large paper towel under the roots to prevent them from getting spoiled.

Chinese or Indian Bittermelon: This green and bitter skin squash shape melon can be thin sliced and used raw in salad, and cooked in soup or as a vegetable. Store open in the vegetable box for up to 4-5 days. If it is partially cut and used then wrap the cut end in paper towel, and then in plastic wrap and refrigerate.

Fresh Corn: Place one paper towel on the top of the corn, and one in the bottom of the corn, close the plastic bag airtight and store on the refrigerator shelf in the center for up to 4 to 5 days. Make sure the corns with the husk are not wet. If there is any moisture pat dry, and pull out the wilted silk on the top and then store in the bag. If the corn is husked then store overnight, covered with a lid and use the next day.

Cucumber: Always buy the fresh ones, without any bruises, take out from the plastic bag, and just throw them over a paper towel, and store them in the vegetable box. Depending on the freshness, use them within 3 days.

Eggplant: You do not need to refrigerate. Store them lose in a cool place. But if you are not going to use right away, refrigerate 1 to 2 days in the vegetable box, drape with a large paper towel. When cooking cut and sprinkle lightly with the salt on the cut surface, so that it won't turn brown.

Garlic, Onions, and Potatoes: Keep them in the room temperature, in a plastic or bamboo basket, in a cool and dark place. Peeled garlic and onion should be refrigerated and use them within 2-3 days. Some experts believe in not refrigerating them at all, they say they are unhealthy refrigerated. Also, do not use any potato shoots, leaves, and any part of the potatoes that are green, just discard them.

Ginger: We always use the whole ginger without peeling it. Keep the ginger in the refrigerator in a paper towel up a month. When I find ginger on sale I but it extra, and leave open in the box over a paper towel, and keep on using as I need it, in this process some of the ginger will dry out, if left for too long, so I put the dry ginger in a container, wash before using, and throw in a piece or two in the soup, stock, or in a juicy vegetable or meat dishes. It comes handy, when you need it. Ginger is hot in reaction, so use it sparingly in the summer.

Green Beans and Peas: Keep them refrigerated and use with 3-4 days.

Greens, such as Beets, Cabbage, Chard, Collard, Kale, and Spinach: If they are wet then pat dry them with the paper towels, and then store in the refrigerator for 3-4 days. The best way is to take them out of the original package and wrap them in paper towels and store in the vegetable box, and use them soon, also, do not buy too much. You can always cook them and freeze them in a airtight container.

Herbs: If it is Basil, do not refrigerate. Just trim the bottom and place in a half-full glass of water for up a 4-5 days, change the water on daily basis, and snip off the spoiled leaves.

Other herbs should be refrigerated for upto a week, depending on the condition of the freshness. Keep them in a cloth bag or wrapped in a paper towel. If you want to freeze them, grind them first with the oil, and then freeze them in ice cube tray, cover them with the plastic, or in a container, and top with little more oil.

Lettuce: When using the leaves take out the outer leaves, wash first and then use them. Some people just slice the Iceberg lettuce, in that case, wipe out the cut end with the damp paper towel, cover the cut part with a dry paper towel, then put in a clean plastic bag and store in the refrigerator, and use within 3-4 days.

Mushrooms: Refrigerate them right away, and use them within a week. If you have opened the package, and used only a few, then immediately, push in a paper towel in the empty space, and then cover the whole box with the plastic wrap, airtight.

Parsnips: Refrigerate them for up to 2-3 weeks, if needed change the packaging and use a clean, dry plastic bag, the root end should be covered with the paper towel, so that it will not spoil.

Radishes: If you buy them with t he leaves on then trim off the leave and use them first. The root part can be stored in the paper towel lined plastic bag up to 2 -3 weeks.

Squash: If it is a summer squash then store in the refrigerator up to 4-5 days, lose, open in the vegetable box. If it is a winter squash should be stored outside in a cool place for up to 3 weeks, in a basket or in a perforated cloth bag.

Sweet Potatoes: Store them in the room temperature up to a week. Once the skin start drying then use them right away.

Tomatoes: Always store them in room temperature, away from apples, in its original perforated box, or open in a basket. If it is a large tomato, and you are using only a part of it, then wrap in the plastic and refrigerate, and use it within a day of two.

Turnips: If they are small white turnips store them in the refrigerator. If they are the large one and covered with the wax, then keep them in the room temperature in a basket for up to 2-3 weeks.

No matter how much caution you use in storing the vegetables, the key is buy only what you are going to use within a short period of time, and use them as soon as possible. If I buy in bulk, then I usually cook them ahead, cool, and freeze them right away in containers, for different servings.

Wine, Cognac, Cordials, Liqueur and Hard Liquor etc.

Every time I see a miniature bottle in the liquor store I want to buy and taste it if I already hadn't tasted it before. I think you are a real baker if you bake your chocolate and cheese cake with the white and dark chocolate liqueur. Your taste buds will tell you when the chocolate cake and cheese cakes are above and beyond. There are several other brands and flavors out there but I mostly use following to give a little extra flavor to my cooking: I don't drink liquor but I cook with them.

Amaretto Disaronno: 375ML. 28% Alc. By Vol.; **Amaretto di Loreto:** 56 Proof, 50ML (1.7FL.OZ.), or **Amaretto di Galliano:** 56 Proof, 1/16 Pint. All these almond liqueurs can be used in cookies and cakes as well as in milk and water base drinks, and shakes, etc.

Anisette: 60 Proof, 200ML/68 FL.OZ. You can use with soups made with fennel, chowder, over scallops, oysters etc. You can mix with some water and ice and it will refresh you right away.

Apfel: 1 Bottle 750ML, 21% Alc./Vol. This is Apple Brandy. I use this for apple desserts and sauces etc.

Arrow Honeydew Melon: 200ML. 50 Proof. This green liquor goes well with broken fresh mint leaves over pistachio ice cream cake. I make this cake for St. Patrick Day. You can also drink with ice and soda.

Blackberry Flavored Brandy: 200ML or a Pint. You can use in blueberry sauce for pancakes or over the ice cream, cakes, muffins, etc. Fill a glass of ice, add 1 oz. each of blackberry brandy and anisette, and you can sip on a tasty drink.

Brandy: You can use any brand you like. Buy a 200 ML bottle or larger if you use more often. You can drink on ice or make brandy sauce, add in coffee or tea or make a hot toddy. We prefer our "namesake" cognac, Hennessy V.S.O.P.

Champagne: Champagne is very good in punch. Some people in mix orange juice and Champagne to make a breakfast drink. New Year's celebrations start with champagne, or you can use another bubbling wine. We had a boss who loved Dom Perignon, an expensive taste.

White Chocolate Liqueur (by Godiva): 375ML, Alc. 15% by Vol. I make all kinds of cheese cakes using this liqueur, use in eggnog, white chocolate squares etc. If you make icing for carrot cake or for the red velvet cake, don't forget to add some.

Dark Chocolate Liqueur (by Godiva): 15% Alcohol by Vol./375ML. Chocolate cake, chocolate mousse and chocolate sauce will be incomplete without this.

Cream Sherry: These are mostly after-dinner drinks. We also pour over ice cream and custard desserts.

Devonshire: 50ML. 34 Proof. This is a royal cream liqueur from England, has a caramel flavor and can be used in coffee, eggnog, sauces, after-dinner drinks, etc.

43 (Cuarenta Y Tres): 750ML, 31-1/2 Alc./Vol. I buy bigger bottles because it goes fast. This is a product of Spain and is an important ingredient in Spanish coffee. You can use with hot drinks like hot chocolate, coffee and tea, or drizzle over key lime pie, ice cream, or pour in small beer mugs and top with heavy creamfor an instant milkshake. Once you get hooked, you will always enjoy it.

Grand Marnier: 50ML.80 Proof. This orange-flavor liqueur is good for baking cookies and cakes as well as in sauces and glazes. I started buying 750ML, Bottle with 40% alcohol by Vol. that lasts for about 6 months.

Gran Gala: 50ML. 80 Proof. This is imported from Italy. This is my favorite triple-orange liqueur and goes well with orange cakes and pound cakes.

Klrschwasser: 750ML. 90 Proof. 45% Alc./Vol. This is Cherry brandy, an important ingredient in Black Forest cake. You can make chocolate-covered cherries with it. I add to chocolate sauce to serve over ice cream and cakes.

Kahlua: 26.5 G.L. 53 Proof., 1 OZ. This delicious coffee liqueur comes from Mexico, and is an important ingredient in Spanish coffee. You can have with soda or brandy or have with milk.

Monte Alban: 50ML. 80 Proof. This is a famous tequila. Even though it is a miniature bottle, it has Oaxaca with Agave Worm, something to remember. You are supposed to swallow the worm while having the drink. I do not use in cooking but it is a famous drink from Mexico. My Spanish friend Maria told me once, "You are not a man if you don't drink tequila."

Mozart: 50ML. 40 Proof. This is the famous chocolate liqueur from Austria. It is versatile, can be used in coffee, milk, sauces and in chocolate cakes and filling, etc.

Pama: 1 Large Bottle, 750ML, 17% ALC/VOL. This is a Pomegranate liqueur that you can use in Pomegranate molasses, or chocolate sauces to be used with desserts, and with the ice cream and cakes. Just sprinkle around some fresh pomegranate seeds for garnish.

Poole's: 50ML, 34 Proof. This is a product of Ireland and is an old-fashioned fruit liqueur, and has versatile use.

Red or White Wines: For cooking I buy mostly domestic wines. I use whole bottle to make red wine reduction with 1 cup of orange juice and about ¼ cup of light brown sugar, in a large non-reactive pan over medium-high heat, partially covered. I reduce it until it is thick enough and only about 1 C is left. Then you can pour over fruits, cakes, ice creams, steaks, grilled meat, etc. White wine I use with chicken broth in sauces, in gravy and in cooking with Italian sausages, seafood and with some heavy cream, etc.

Royale Chambord Liqueur De France: 50ML. 33 Proof. The round bottle with a crown on the top is very pretty. I use this mostly making fruit sauces.

Rum: Light or dark, you can use both in pound cake, fruit cake or in icing. It is very popular in tropical mixed drinks.

Sabra: Miniature bottle. Sabra liqueur is from Israel. This is an orange liqueur with chocolate flavor. Good for baking, making sauces and for drinking.

Tia Maria: 1 Ounce. 63 Proof. This coffee liqueur comes from Jamaica.

Tom Boy: 1 FL.OZ, 34 Proof. This chocolate liqueur from Italy is good for chocolate cooking and baking.

Truffles: 12-1/2% Alc. By Vol. 25 Proof. This is a dark chocolate liqueur. Good for chocolate-flavored cooking, baking and for using as a liqueur.

Vodka: This is a hard liquor mostly used in making mixed drinks. But you can make vodka sauce for pasta. Also use a small amount in the pie crust in pie crust it will be flaky.

Pantry and Ingredients

Beans

Beans are vegetarian proteins and are cheaper, digestible, nutritious and more versatile than meat. In all cultures around the world, beans are used in one form or the other.

They are used fresh, whole or shelled; dried, whole and split with or without skin; frozen to keep their color and flavor right after they are harvested; and canned green or dried cooked beans. Beans have soluble fiber that is very important for digestion. They give you protein, iron, vitamins and minerals. They give a complete and a flavorful meal, lower cholesterol, blood pressure and are very healthy for diabetics. All beans should be picked over and soaked in water overnight or for several hours, if cooked whole and dry. Usually, one cup dry beans after cooking will yield about two to four cups depending on the type of beans you are using.

Adzuki: These are small, oval-shaped beans in maroon color and have thin white lines. They have a nutty flavor. Soak dry beans overnight covered with water or at least four hours in warm water before cooking. Mostly used in Asian dishes.

Appaloosa: These are large white beans with black spots. They are rich, creamy and very flavorful.

Black Turtle: These are medium-size, oval-shape, matte with small white lines. When cooked, they are sweet and mushroom-like.

Broad or Fava: These are large, light-brown color and oval-shaped beans that are very creamy and nutty in flavor.

Boston, Navy, Haricot: These are small beans, oval-shaped and rounded and plump. They are also creamy when cooked.

Cannellini: These are kidney-shaped, off-white beans, creamy and mild in flavor.

Cranberry: These are cream-color beans with red spots, pretty with or without shells. They are creamy in flavor.

Red and Black Kidney: These kidney-shaped beans come in red and black. They are very flavorful and full-bodied.

Great Northern: These are large white beans and are very creamy.

Flageolet: These are pale-green in color, either small or medium size. They have a rich, nutty flavor and cook fast. They are very popular in France.

Gigante: These are off-white color beans and are huge in size. They are popular in Japan, Greece and Spain.

Pinto: These beans are oval-shaped and have freckles, and are very rich and robust.

Lima: These come both in small and large forms and have a nutty flavor.

Jacob's cattle: These kidney-shaped maroon beans have white spots. They are very rich and robust in flavor.

Black-Eyed Pea: These are medium-size white beans with a thick, long and black lining. They are rich in flavor and cook very fast even without soaking. They are very popular in south, especially on New Year's Day to bring wealth. In India they are very popular too. We used then even as a brunch with chutney and red onion, fresh ginger and lemon.

Chick Pea, Garbanzo Beans, Ceci and Channa: They are medium to small size and come in four colors: cream, green, brown and black. They have a nutty flavor. They are used a lot as beans and ground as flour. They are very popular in northern India.

Dried Pea: They can be small or medium round-shaped, and greenish or pale yellow color. They are very earthy and flavorful.

Lentil: American lentils are greenish and small, round flat-disk like. Indian lentils are tiny, round, plum-light brown to dark-brown in color. When split and the skin is taken out, they are pretty orange, almost like a tangerine color, and cook in a snap.

Mung, Green Grams: These are tiny, long and plump green beans. When peeled they are light yellow color. They are very light and cook very fast. Also used in making bean sprouts. These are used in China and India.

Peanuts, Groundnut: These are peanuts eaten mostly roasted as a nut. But are very popular shelled in cooking in India. Also, creamy and chunky peanut butter is made with these beans, which are loaded with protein.

Pink or Chili Beans: They are sort-of kidney-shaped, plump and round, and pinkish-brown color. They are used mostly in Caribbean cooking.

Soybean: These are small, cream-color, oval and plum-shaped beans, and also come in black. They have a very rich flavor. The green ones also are called Edamame.

Butter, Oils and Ghee (clarified Butter)

Oils have both saturated and unsaturated fat. Saturated fat like from animals is unhealthy, and unsaturated fat is good for the body. Certain oils that have unsaturated fat are good when used raw, like extra virgin olive oil. Shortening also is saturated fat, mostly used in baking and deep frying. In our family we were never allowed to use shortening for any use at all. Store oils in cool and dark places well-sealed in a heavy plastic or porcelain container. For daily use, use a small colored glass bottle to minimize the heat affect. Oils can go bad, and that is unhealthy and can ruin the flavor.

Butter: Salted or unsalted both butter should be kept in a very cold temperature, or frozen, and well wrapped to keep it fresh. Unsalted or sweet butter lasts longer than the salted kind.

Experts advise to smell the butter before buying, it should smell fresh. The butter made in winter is usually white, when the cows graze on hay in an enclosed surrounding. The yellow butter mostly comes from the cows who are fed on grass, roaming freely in the field, mostly in nice weather. The deep-yellow color butter is mostly when it is exposed to the air. You can easily smell rancid butter even through the layers of the paper. Once the butter starts turning rancid, it will spoil the whole package. Butter gives good flavor in baking.

Ghee: Ghee is clarified butter. Where the water from the butter has evaporated and is pure butter. It has high smoke content and lasts longer without refrigeration.

Saturated fat: These are found in animal products like meat, butter, whole milk and in some oils. These fats are artery-clogging and can give you bad cholesterol, heart attack, high blood pressure, obesity and much more.

Some families use shortening for deep-frying for the taste and texture. Any solid fat that does not melt in the room temperature can be harmful for the body. It is a matter of taste, once you start frying in oil, like canola oil, that has a neutral taste, you just get used to it.

Lard: This is mostly port fat, with lot of cholesterol. Avoid using this.

Polyunsaturated fat: These are plant-based and mostly found in vegetable oils. These Omega-3 fatty acids are found in deep-water fish like salmon, and in some seeds, oils and vegetables.

Monounsaturated fat: These are mostly found in olive, natural peanut and canola oils.

Canola oil: This is unsaturated fat, very light and is almost all-purpose. You can use in cooking, salads, and even in your hair. Because of its light weight, texture and neutral quality, I use it in baking a lot. It has a high smoke point.

Coconut oil: Coconut is good to eat raw. Use coconut oil for massage on outside skin. It is used in India to give massage to babies. In Hawaii it is used to protect from sunburn. It is also good for your hair but mostly in summer (gives you dark shiny hair) When you use it in cooking, it becomes mostly saturated fat. So use sparingly in cooking.

Corn oil: This mild and full flavor oil can be used for all sorts of cooking. This is also unsaturated fat. Now with using corn oil for gas (ethanol), there is a big demand for corn oil.

Grapeseed oil: It has mostly unsaturated fat. It has a high burn content, velvety and very close to olive oil. It can be used for all sorts of cooking for its neutral flavor.

Mustard seed oil: This oil is very famous in Northern India, especially if you get your own made at the mill, which we did all the time. When you get fresh oil made, it will be so powerful that if you leave it open is a bowl your eyes will start tearing. It is an antioxidant and can be used for almost anything. The adults use this for Ayurvedic medicine on outside of the body starting from head to toe. We also used it in daily cooking.

Nut oil: Almond, walnut, hazelnut and flax seed all have unsaturated fat to some extent. Flax seed oil, one or two spoonful used daily, can be good for you. Walnuts are better when eaten raw and rough chewed. Almonds we were told to soak in the water overnight, and then peel and eat. Almond oil is good when eaten raw 2-3 times a day with overnight-soaked large dark grapes.

Olive oil: This is a monounsaturated fat (plant based). Store it in a dark glass bottle or a tin, away from heat and light. Extra-virgin olive oil is made from the first cold pressing, is more natural, and is high in antioxidant (dark green). It is good on salad etc. even good for your skin if rubbed raw. Virgin Olive is also made from the first cold pressing. The light variety of Olive Oil is of pale color, more pressed and can be used in cooking. Try not to buy in large quantities. *Once it is opened it can turn rancid if exposed to air for too long. Buy for about 6 to 8 weeks supply. Check out the expiration date and buy oil that is under a year old. Extra-virgin Olive Oil is good for blood pressure, it lowers the bad (LDL) Cholesterol, and has vitamin E.

*Tip: This goes with almost with any oil. Try to buy 6 to 8 weeks supply.

Peanut oil: Peanut oil is loaded with protein and has mostly unsaturated fat. It has high smoke point, so it is good for deep frying. You can also drizzle raw on salad.

Sesame oil: Sesame seeds come in three colors: white, light brown and black. Sesame oil is mostly unsaturated fat both monounsaturated and polyunsaturated fat, therefore it is more beneficial to use raw or toasted seed oil without getting involved in cooking. Also, this oil burns fast, so you have to be very careful in cooking. We made sesame seed candies just by toasting and grinding the seeds and used all winter long. Be careful to use sesame seeds in moderation. Too much or prolong use can give you loose stomach. The light-color sesame seed oil comes from the untoasted seeds that are neutral, mild and light in color. The little darker color oil from toasted seeds has nutty taste and aroma.

Truffle oil: Truffles, white and black, are very expensive subsequently truffle oil is expensive as well. It is used very sparingly, mostly on cooked food and salads.

Vegetable oil: This has both unsaturated and saturated fat to some degrees depending on the type: sunflower, safflower, cottonseed etc. could be anything. This can be used for almost any cooking.

Ghee (Clarified butter)

In India we use butter in purified form. Butter is heated on medium heat in a large wok and when it starts bubbling it slowly burns out all the water and slowly starts turning brown. When brown particles start gathering turn the heat to medium high. The brown particles stay in the bottom but will give a very distinct flavor and aroma and will give antioxidant properties. Now, ghee is left alone in the wok and when it is cooled, strain it into bottles or cans. This process allows the ghee to last longer, in room temperature for almost six months. Ghee is used in cooking vegetables, frying bread (which makes bread very tasty) and on paratha – a pan-cooked bread. But use everything in moderation. Too much fried food is harmful for health.

Bacon Fat: After you fry or cook bacon, the rendered fat may be tasty to some people, but it is very unhealthy. It has cancer-causing burnt particles that can clog the arteries. We hardly use bacon but before cooking the bacon you can blanch it, just like French do. Add the bacon in a large amount of cold water, bring the water to simmer, let it simmer on low for about 10-12 minutes and drain out the water. Wash the bacon under running cold water, drain out the water and pat dry with the paper towels then cook according to your recipe. This process takes out most of the salt, smoky flavor and also some of the fat. A thin-sliced turkey bacon is healthier than other bacons.

Sugar and Sugar Substitutes

White sugar (granulated), light brown sugar, dark brown sugar, and confectioners sugar all are made from various types of refining processes.

White Sugar: Also known as granulated sugar, comes in various crystal sizes. Depending on the size of the crystals, the sugar is dissolved. Larger crystals take longer to dissolve.

Brown Sugar: The light-brown, dark brown sugars are a less-refined process of sugar making. You can make your own brown sugar by adding 4 tablespoons of unsulfured molasses to 1 cup of superfine granulated sugar. Keep brown sugar in the refrigerator to keep it from getting lumpy.

Molasses: This thick and dark color liquid comes from refining sugar at the first state. This is the fine-quality liquid. The third liquid molasses is called blackstrap. It is darker with intense flavor. Some processors use sulfur dioxide to refine sugar. Use unsulfured molasses to avoid the distaste.

Honey: Pure honey is the best natural sugar. Honey can be from light to dark color, depending on the type of flowers used by the honey bees to get the nectar from the flower. Honey is sweeter than sugar. My father, who was an expert of Ayurvedic and Homeopathic medicine, never allowed us to use honey in cooking. We were told to use honey in its natural form to avoid the destruction of the health properties.

Maple Syrup: This is the sap of the sugar maple trees that is collected by making a cut into the trees and attaching pales for a period of time to collect the sap. Then the sap is reduced to make it thick like syrup. This is low-fat sauce to use over food or in cooking.

Corn Syrup: Both light and dark corn syrup comes from corn. The process of making this syrup needs acid or various enzymes to turn the starch granules into syrup.

Beet Sugar: Beets are so sweet that the juice is extracted, refined with chemicals and turned into sugar.

Sugar Free and Sweetner: Nowadays you can find sweetener substitutes for cooking, or mixing with coffee and tea, etc.

Agave Nectar: This is commercially produced syrup found in most of the supermarkets. This is another alternative to the sugar. You can use this in baking as well.

Chocolate and Cocoa Powder

Chocolate not only tastes good, but it is anti-oxidant, good for high blood pressure and an important item for baking. But the key is the moderation.

Among different types of chocolates: semi-sweet, white (is not a real chocolate), dark (good for health), bittersweet, chocolate chips and milk chocolate . Milk chocolate has the most calories. Milk chocolate weighing 4 ounces can contribute up to 588 calories and about 36 grams of fat. White chocolate is not a real chocolate as it does not have any chocolate liquor. But I use white chocolate liqueur in cooking for flavoring, especially making low-fat cheese cake, and around Christmas adding white chocolate liqueur to eggnog is the most amazing taste you can ever have.

There are several brands of chocolate and each and every one of them is a little different in taste. Because each brand uses a different combination of beans, chocolate liquor and cocoa butter. The American chocolates such as Ghirardelli, Hershey, Nestle, Maillard Eagle and Baker's are very common brands. To get a more intense flavor, some of the imported chocolates like Valrhona, Lindt, Tobler and Callebaut are also very good. The pure chocolate contains only chocolate liquor. These are bitter, unsweetened and baking chocolates.

.

Store Chocolate:

No need to store chocolate in the refrigerator. Store it in a dry and cool place with about 60F temperature. I just keep the chocolate packages in an airtight container. Chocolate absorbs moisture and odor so keep it away from dampness.

Cocoa Powder

Cocoa powder is made by removing at least half of its butter. Therefore, cocoa power is good to use for low-fat baking. Some of the cocoas are treated with alkali to neutralize its acidity (Dutch-processed).

Cocoa powder imparts is flavor when it is mixed with warm liquid. I often make my own cocoa melt. In a cup or a small bowl add: ¼ C of cocoa powder, ¼ C of light brown sugar, and 2 Tbsp. Soften butter, stir to mix well. Heat about 1 C of milk, or low-fat milk, or half-and-half or heavy cream to about 115-120 degrees and pour over the mixture, then stir a little to mix all ingredients. Cover with a lid and set aside for 5-8 minutes, stir well and you have an instant melted chocolate ready. Light brown sugar and cocoa powder, together with warm water, works very well.

Various Types of Cooking Flours

Most of baking and cooking is done with all-purpose unbleached and bleached flour, and in India with unbleached white or red (whole wheat) bread flour. For certain recipes, other kind of flours are used. Buy special kind of flours when you are going to use them for a certain recipe as needed. Store flour in a zipper-lock bag and then put the sealed bag either in a plastic container or in a porcelain jar, covered with a tight lid. The smell of the flour invites flour bugs. You can also store large quantities of flour in a large container in a zipper-lock storage bag on the shelf, away from heat. In any case, when working with flour, pour the flour or take it out with a measuring cup carefully, even it out on top with a knife and wipe the bag all around, and then store in a clean and dry container. Do not leave any traces of flour outside the container.

All-purpose flour: This can be bleached or unbleached, but most of the time you use unbleached that has multi-purpose use. This flour usually has a combination of hard and soft wheats and has about 10 to 12% protein per 100 grams of flour, depending on the brand. It is used for almost anything.

Bread flour: This unbleached flour is a little more coarse in texture and used mostly for pizza and bread. It is milled from hard wheat and has more protein, over 12% to 14% per grams of flour depending on the brand. High protein results in strong gluten, and a substantial dough that gives a nice texture and a crispy crust.

Durum Flour: It is a coarse, yellow flour, or it can be a fine flour with coarse particles, and has high protein content, used mostly in pasta.

Whole Wheat flour: This is pure flour without taking out any bran or germ. It contains about 15% protein, vitamin, fiber and has complete nutritional value. As a result it is heavier than other flours. It is mostly used with a combination of other flours. Try to buy in a small quantity and store in the refrigerator after it is opened

In Indian grocery stores, you will find white whole wheat flour. This is mostly ground from the light-color wheat berries. My father preferred to buy our own berries, wash them to take out any dirt, spread them on the white bed sheets in the sun to dry them well, and then send them by the tins to the local flour-grinding mills. I prefer to buy white whole wheat flour at Indian grocery stores. My preference is the Golden Temple brand. It the bread flour that we use in making famous bread called "roti or chapatti." It contains between 13% to 15% protein.

Pastry flour: This contains about 8% to 12% protein, and comes from soft wheat.

Cake flour: This is a finely ground flour that produces delicate and light baked goods. It comes from soft wheats and generally has 6% to 8% average protein. It contains less gluten, therefore it does not need more fat.

Self-Rising flour: This is usually made with all-purpose flour that has salt and baking powder in it. The flour is sifted well so it is easy to use for quick baking. It has usually 8% to 10% protein.

Chick pea flour: Also called besan or graham flour. This is very healthy flour that is made from grinding whole dry white chickpeas. This is loaded with protein and other nutrients. In Indian cooking, after the bread flour, this has more use than any other flour for fritters, pancakes, bread, filling, snacks and crumbs. It is also believed that chickpeas purify the blood and decrease the bad cholesterol in the body.

Urad flour: This flour is made from peeled black or green graham beans and is very sticky when it is mixed with liquid. It is usually used in dosa (stuffed pancakes), fritters and stuffing bread and poories, etc. This flour has a very strong bean taste and is little heavy in texture, so use sparingly.

Corn meal: There are three types: yellow, white and blue cornmeal made from yellow, white and blue dried corn, and ground fine, medium or coarse. Yellow cornmeal is more appealing in recipes as it can be better in texture and flavor. You can store cornmeal in refrigerator for longer shelf life. To make polenta, use coarse corn meal, and to make corn flour, you can simply grind the medium corn meal in a food processor, or buy a finer variety of corn meal.

Cornstarch: Made from the endosperm of the corn kernel into a fine powdery substance. This is used to thicken liquid, gravies and sauces as well as in some baking and puddings. When using corn starch from the box, use a clean and dry spoon, and close it property then store it in a cool place away from the heat.

Mung flour (or Moong flour): This flour is made with green peeled mung beans, the one used for sprouts. It is very versatile, light, tasty and easy to handle. You can also make protein crumbs, use in Halwa, fritters and in breads, etc.

Rye flour: This flour is made by grinding the rye grain into three types: dark, medium and light. Dark flour contains the whole rye berries. This is also used with a combination of all-purpose flour. My father, who was specialized in homeopathic medicine, allowed us to use regular chapatti (bread) flour with the combination of 3 parts whole wheat, 1 part each rye and chick flours. We made small and thin breads and topped hot bread with a little clarified butter. This bread was the best-tasting and healthiest bread you could ever eat with almost anything.

Soy flour: This is made from grinding soy beans. Most of the time it is made with roasted beans, so it is gluten-free and has a nutty flavor. Tofu and fritters are made with this flour in combination with all-purpose flour.

Rice flour: Rice flour is made either with white or brown rice and with small-grain rice that is more starchy. You can use this in dosa (stuffed pancakes), fritters, pudding, stuffing, idle (small steamed rice cakes), crumbs, etc. I sometime use this in desserts as well.

Nut flour: This is made by grinding nuts, mostly almond, walnut, hazelnut and chestnut. Almond flour is used in cookies, walnut and hazelnut and chestnuts in pfeffernusse, and cookies, etc.

Water chestnut flour: This flour is used in India. It is made with ripped water chestnuts when they turn from green to red to maroon. They are peeled, chopped and dried, then ground into flour. This flour is like fruit with a sweet and nutty flavor. It is used to make halwa, and deep-fried breads with the combination of squash or potatoes. This flour is a staple for those Hindu holy days when people go on fast and are allowed to eat only fruits and vegetables.

Measuring Dry Ingredients

Sift flour before using, especially before baking. Set a medium or a medium-fine mesh strainer over a bowl or over a piece of wax paper, stir the flour to loosen it first, then dip a measuring cup into it, or spoon the flour into the cup, level it off with a knife and sift it into the bowl or over wax paper. This method is called scoop-and-sweep or dip-and-sweep.

If you are following a baking recipe, mix flour, baking powder, baking soda and salt first, and then sift the flour after to make sure all dry ingredients are combined well. Keep in mind that too much flour can result in a tough and thick product. So follow the recipes. Liquid is also determined according to the weather.

Wet and humid weather will put more moisture into the atmosphere, therefore it will require a little less liquid.

Thickeners

Thickeners are used to absorb liquid such as that found in pie, sauces and gravies. Some oriental cooking also uses thickener in meat pieces to stir-fry them. Be careful when cooking; overcooking of thickener may break down the thickening quality and eventually may turn into liquid, or some may turn rubbery. They all turn clear after cooking. Cassava is good for glazes as it settles beautifully as it cools.

Cornstarch: This is very common thickener. It is made with corn and blends well with the flavor and the texture of the food.

Tapioca: It is made from the Cassava root. It is the cassava root powder that is turned into tiny drops or beads, and is called cooking or pudding tapioca.

Arrowroot: It is made with the underground stems of the plant. It is not too common as it needs a longer baking.

The Leavening Agents

Baking Powder: Baking powder helps rise cake, pastry and bread etc. Buy the Double Acting Baking Power. It absorbs moisture quickly so keep it air-tight and replace it after 3 to 4 months. Write down the date on the container when you open and use it the first time. Baking powder contains a mixture of dry acid and baking soda with starch or flour. Now-a-days, you find double-acting baking powder (SAS). The double reaction occurs when mixed with the liquid in the dough and again in baking in the hot oven; by releasing the carbon dioxide, it helps to rise the dough.

Baking Soda: It is used in cooking and baking when there is acid in the ingredients to neutralize the acid and to make it rise. Baking soda is also known as bicarbonate of soda. It is an alkali, so it darkens the cocoa and chocolate in the baking. Use it cautiously; overuse can alter the taste and color, even the texture of the finished product.

Yeast: Yeast is used in flour to make dough. It comes in several forms: compressed, dry-granulated and rapid-rise. Fresh compressed yeast comes in a cake form, with light tan color, and should be refrigerated and used up to 4 months. Use equal amounts of sugar to liquidate it. The active dry yeast and rapid-rise yeast both are used the same way. They are granules that bubble when added to lukewarm water and used with a little sugar. If it does not bubble, discard it and buy the active one. The dry yeast, unopened, can be stored in room temperature or can be frozen.

Dairy Products

Milk: Milk contains protein, calcium, vitamins and minerals. It also gives moisture, softness and freshness to recipes. Whole milk contains an average of 3.4% butter fat. In some recipes you can use low-fat milk or skim milk to reduce the fat contents.

Buttermilk: Buttermilk is a low-fat dairy product because the solids and some of the fat are removed. You can also buy buttermilk in a powder form, which is good for some baking and for making dressing.

Canned evaporated skim milk: This canned milk consists of a skim milk where water is reduced in half. It goes through a high temperature of sterilization process, therefore it has a little longer shelf life. I use this milk in place of cream because it is always available in my pantry.

Cheeses: See Cheese section.

Sweetened condensed milk: This milk is thick because by using a vacuum system, half of the water is evaporated, making it thick and tasty. The liquid is homogenized and sterilized to prolong shelf life. Also, the added sugar gives a long life.

In northern part of India, most sweets are made with a reduced milk called khoya or mawa. It resembles cheese, is long-lasting, and makes fantastic sweets with a wonderful flavor like pera (round milk and sugar patties), burfi (milk squares with fruits and nuts) and rubri (milk pudding).

Powdered milk: Most powdered milk is made with low-fat milk to avoid the fat that can contaminate the powder on the shelf. Milk in powder form has a long life. It can be used in recipes as well as for drinking when mixed with water.

I use powdered milk a lot in sweets to absorb the liquid, to give a milky taste and to lower the calories and fat. Milk powder when used in dough not only gives more calcium and nutrients, but it also softens dough that results in a soft bread, you can also use tofu, for that matter.

Sour cream: Try to use low-fat sour cream in recipes, because sour cream is actually fermented heavy cream.

Heavy cream: Heavy cream has more butterfat, around 38% to 40%, Whipping cream has about 30% butterfat and medium cream has about 25% butterfat, Half and Half has about 10% to 12% butterfat and because of its low butterfat, you can't whip it. But you can use it for heavy cream in some of the recipes. One cup of heavy cream contains about 821 calories, 88g of fat (mostly saturated fat), and 326mg of cholesterol. So avoid using it, or use it in rare cases.

Yogurt: Yogurt is a nutritious and a low-cholesterol product. Try to use the low-fat yogurt; the taste is almost the same, but it has less fat. Yogurt has vitamin B, protein and a high level of calcium. You can also use yogurt cheese, which is actually drained yogurt (drained in several layers of cheesecloth overnight) where liquid is drained out.

Eggs: When buying eggs, check the date, open the egg carton and check out the eggs. Don't buy broken and unclean. Check out the eggs on all 4 corners make sure they are not stuck to the carton (they get banged around the edges). Eggs are loaded with protein, vitamins and minerals. The yolk is good for the eyes. They help in binding the batter, add texture and color. One large egg has about 75 calories and about 5.5g fat. Most of the fat comes from the yolk. The egg white has more protein, which is good for baking as well as for consuming.

Dr. Oz, on his show, suggested one egg with oatmeal for breakfast. Use them in moderation.

Egg safety is very important. Avoid using raw eggs and under-cooked eggs to avoid salmonella poisoning. Wash and clean cutting boards, utensils, etc. that had raw eggs. Store eggs in the refrigerator, away from the door.

Cream of Tartar

Cream of Tartar is an acidic white powder. It is produced by the wine industry. It is used in beating egg whites to stabilize, and also in making sugar syrup from crystallizing the sugar. You can also use lemon juice in to sugar to stop it from getting hard. With 1 cup of egg white, use 1Teaspoon of cream of tartar to stabilize the egg white.

Meringue (Egg white beaten to for peaks)

Beating egg white into meringue is easy. Make sure the whites are in room temperature. In the winter, I leave my eggs out overnight and in the morning, I separate them and make the meringue. To cover a 9-inch pie topping you will need the following to make meringue.

3 extra large egg whites in room temperature, pinch of salt, ¼ teaspoon cream of tartar, and 5-6 tablespoons of sugar.

Make sure the egg white and the bowl are at room temperature. Combine egg whites, cream of tartar and salt in a large, clean and grease-free mixing bowl. Using an electric mixer, whip the whites on medium speed until they are foamy. While beating, increase the speed to high, adding the sugar slowly. Keep whipping until they form a firm peak, making sure whites are not dry. Before stopping, check the whites between your fingers, making sure all the sugar has been dissolved.

When using on pie, spread out the topping, pulling whites on to the edges, making sure they do not shrink away from the edge during baking. Bake the topping about 10 to 12 minutes golden brown. Cool the pie on a wire rack, then refrigerate. This topping goes well on lemon meringue pie.

Grains

Grains are the vegetarian proteins that are very nourishing and important for the body. These are the seeds or fruits of plants. We use grains in many forms: whole berries, cracked, ground, boiled, milled and with the combination of other beans, rice, nuts, vegetables, fruits and dairy products to make a meal.

Store grain products in a dark and cool place away from light and heat, and in a bag and in a tightly sealed porcelain container if possible. A large porcelain container keeps it safe and preserved from weather elements (hot and cold). You can keep them up to a year; don't let any air escape in. Also, try to buy small quantities so you will be able to use it soon. When buying grains, check out the bags carefully. Any broken or old bag may sometimes have flour bugs. So buy a fresh and sealed bag and keep it airtight in the container.

Amaranth: These tiny little seeds have a nutty flavor and you can substitute it for the rice. Also, it cooks fast, almost like rice. Amaranth seeds are loaded with protein.

Bajara: This grain is found mostly in India. This is "poor-man's" food but is very nutritious. It has a small tear shape, round and silver-gray color. It is hulled and used mostly as a cereal and ground as flour for chapatti and deep-fried or spicy breads

Barley: This is a hulled product and can be whole grain or ground. It takes longer to cook. Barley comes in pearl, cracked and "Job's Tears" form. Barley is very good for the heart when used as whole grain cereal and in salad.

Buckwheat: These triangular-shaped kernels with a black shell outside and white starchy seed inside has more starch than protein. Buckwheat originally came from China and India. It has a mild and nutty flavor. When roasted, it gets more flavorful and is called Kasha. It does not take too long to cook. In about 15 minutes you can cook about two cups of it. It is used in breads, cereal, noodles, etc.

Bulgur: Bulgur is a processed or parboiled wheat. It is used as couscous or in place of rice, as flour used in bread and baking goods, etc.

Corn: Corn is an all-purpose grain. It can be used as corn meal to make polenta, a soft texture meal almost like cream of wheat; as a hominy (pesole) with a lightly sweet and firm texture; as a hominy grits that is ground. Polenta cooks very fast, but hominy pesole takes over two hours to cook three cups.

Farro: Farro is tan and oval-shaped, and has a nutty flavor. It can be whole and crushed grain. It can be used in place of rice.

Millet: Millet is a small and yellow grain with a small spot at one end. It is a chewy and nutty grain. After cooking it becomes fluffy. Coarse-ground, it can be combined and used with other flours to make a bread, etc.

Oats: Oats are used in so many forms: rolled oats, steel-cut, etc. Oatmeal whether quick or old-fashioned is very good for the heart and can reduce bad cholesterol.

Quinoa: This has a sweet flavor and a soft texture. It is light brown, with a flat shape, and is very small in size. It is very easy to cook. You can cook almost two cups of quinoa almost in fifteen minutes and that will yield to three cups.

Rye: Rye berries are used in a few forms: berries, rye groats that are rolled or flaked, and triticale. They have a nutty flavor. Rye flour is mostly used together with wheat flour. Rye has carbohydrates that helps absorb water more than wheat flour. So bread made with combination of rye flour expands and make you feel full easily.

Spelt: This is mostly grown and used in Germany and is called dinkel. Because of its high protein content, it is used in several different ways like in bread, cereal, soups and in baked goods, etc,

Wheat: Wheat comes in many forms. Wheat berries can be soft and hard; cracked wheat can be used as a cereal; bulghur can be used as a starch for rice; bran is the outer coating of wheat seeds; wheat germ is the seed of the wheat kernel and can be sprinkled over the cooked meal; couscous is ground durum wheat and can be substituted for rice. White couscous takes about ten minutes and whole one takes about fifteen minutes.

Pantry

It is very important to have a well-stocked pantry. You can buy things on regular basis but a pantry gives you freedom to cook all sorts of things in a matter of time.
Try to keep these items in stock:

For the Cupboard:
Flour: bread and all-purpose flour, corn meal, cereals, raisins.
Grains: rice, barley, millet, oatmeal, wheat germs, couscous.
Beans: canned, dry, lentils, chick peas, dry mushrooms, and other legumes
Meat: canned salmon, tuna, chicken, turkey, anchovies, etc.
Spices: whole and ground as per your cooking favorites; herbs, bouillon cubes.
Pasta: angel hair (fast cooking) and all other shapes and sizes.
Sauces: tomato sauce, tomato paste, capers, honey, salsa, peanut butter, cans of evaporated milk.
Fortified wines, low-sodium chickens and beef stocks, both instant and liquid.
Oils & Vinegar: Extra-virgin olive oil, canola oil and apple cider vinegar.
Baking needs: sugar, baking powder, baking soda, vanilla extract, yeast, semi-sweet and bittersweet chocolates, cornstarch, coffee and tea.
Crackers: low-salt, bread crumbs, graham crackers, etc.

In a Basket at Room Temperature:
Vegetables: Onion, garlic, potatoes, lemons, limes, dried mushrooms, bananas, ginger, sweet potatoes, apples, grapefruit, oranges, potatoes, etc.

For the Refrigerator:
Fresh meat, poultry, eggs, butter and spreads, vinegars.
Milk, yogurt, butter, juices, sauces, ketchup, mustard, fruit juices and water
Cottage cheese, buttermilk, cheeses, mayonnaise, white wines.
Vegetables fresh, fruits, herbs.
Bread, muffins.
Nuts and seeds.

For the Freezer:
Fruit juices, frozen fruits and vegetables, whole-grain breads, lean meats, fish and poultry, etc.

Food Safety

Food safety is something you have to pay attention to all the time. Buy food that is fresh, check the expiration dates, and at the time of cooking prepare right. Wash vegetables etc. especially greens in a few changes of water until all dirt is gone. Meat should be kept in its own package before cooking. Keep seafood in an ice bowl or an ice bucket. Wash all the utensils before and after using, there can be a danger of salmonella poisoning if proper attention is not given.
Wash vegetables like celery and leeks under running water before cutting and again after cutting. Never use soap as it may soak into the vegetable.
One rule we have in our house: before going out for a big food-shopping: We clean out our refrigerator. Anything open and spoiled (fruit and vegetables or opened food, leftovers) goes in the garbage, and we try to clean the refrigerator before we bring the new food home. This is a good habit that I learned from my mother.
In the same way, she taught us to brush our hair, take a shower and change clothes before walking in the kitchen in the morning. And have our hair braided or tied when cooking food, and always wear clean clothes when serving food. If you look sloppy, your food won't be appetizing either.
When serving, keep cold food cold and hot food hot. Be careful with partially cooked food like eggs and seafood, they may spoil fast. Even cookie and cake batter where raw eggs are used should not be consumed. Raw sprouts such as alfalfa and radishes, special care should be taken. Additionally, unpasteurized and untreated juices and raw meat, poultry, and seafood should not be consumed. For more safety tips check out the Food and Drug Administration website: www.fda.gov.

Rice

Rice is a universal, important and nutritious grain that is used almost on daily basis worldwide. It comes in many forms and sizes. The brown rice is more nutritious and wholesome than white rice. It contains carbohydrates, fiber, calcium, potassium, vitamin B & E. White rice is healthy as well, but when it is milled, most of the brans and hulls are taken out, leaving it more starchy than wholesome. When cooking rice, use the grains as it is. By washing water, you lose all the minerals and nutrients.

White rice cooks faster than brown rice. You generally need one cup of rice and two cups of water to cook it, but brown rice takes more water and longer to cook, depending on the type. In any case, soak the

82

brown rice at least two or three hours ahead of cooking, in a good, clean water, in a saucepan that you are going to cook rice in. Bring it to a boil, let it boil for about five minutes, stir well, lower the heat and let simmer covered until it is done. You can lightly brown the soaked rice in oil or butter, just save the soaking water and use it in cooking.

Basmati, Jasmine, Texmati, Royal, Gourmet, Delta Rose: These are aromatic, slim and long-grain rice. As rice ages it gets slightly aromatic. When you cook, the grain gets longer and gives a nutty and aromatic flavor. They come in white and brown, both varieties, and look very fancy to serve for company.

Long-grain: You can find both white and brown types. Both look pretty impressive and are good for daily use. If you make a fancy rice pilaf without spending too much money, the long grain rice will do a good job.

Medium grain: This is an all-purpose rice. We stock up on this when it goes on sale to substitute either small- or long-grain rice. This is the rice we never run out of stock because when we buy fancy rice, it's gone quickly by making fancy dishes.

Short-grain: Italian short-grain Arborio rice has a soft and creamy texture. You do not rinse this rice, just heat oil or butter, add the rice, sauté to coat with oil well, then slowly cook in liquid, adding more as needed.

Black: This rice comes from China and it has an impressive and unusual black color. It is flavorful and has a soft texture

Brown rice whole grain more nourishing, has vitamin B and B12.

Glutenous: This is a sticky rice mostly used in sushi, dim sum and desserts. The grains are a little shorter than Arborio rice.

Red: The most common red rice is the Bhutanese red rice. It is pretty looking and has a nutty flavor. Himalayan or Californian red or brown rice has almost same flavor, like brown rice. They have a more grainy texture and sometimes can be more chewy if cooked alone. Making a rice pilaf can be more flavorful.

Parboiled: This is partially cooked rice for fast cooking. Since it is steamed and pressurized, the grains stay separate.

Wild: This is the seed of a tall grass that is slim, grayish black, and long. This one you have to rinse well and then cook 1 cup rich in about three cups of water. It takes much longer to cook. I use 1 part wild rice and 2 parts brown rice and, at the end of cooking, drop a little oil or purified butter to give a smooth and sweet flavor.

Salt

Salts are not created, but are found naturally, mostly in bodies of water and in rocks. They are then refined and added with flavors. The National Academy of Sciences recommends only 2,400 milligrams, or about 6 grams, or about 1 Teaspoon, of salt to use on daily basis. Studies also have found that babies who are given a low-sodium diet in their first six months of life will be less likely to develop high blood pressure later in their lives.

You can make your own mixture of seasoning with or without salt by mixing dry herbs and spices.

Store salt in a glass or ceramic container. Add to table salt some dry rice grains and it will not absorb any moisture when it rains. Most of the salts are available in supermarkets, but for specialty shopping, you may have to go to a gourmet shop.

Salt is very important for bodily function. Lack of sodium can cause sleep disorder, less energy and even sexual performance. Salt is found in almost all kinds of prepared and preserved foods, so be aware of the added salt.

According to experts monitor and limit the salt intake in cases of Hyperaldosteronism (a disorder that involves increased secretion of the salt-retaining hormone), Cushing's disease (a disorder of the pituitary gland that causes high cortisol levels in the blood), Liddle syndrome (a form of high blood pressure that causes excess reabsorption of sodium in the kidneys), and Heart disease. Check with your doctor.

The bottom line is use salt in moderation, especially in cooking. Do not sprinkle extra salt over the food. Too much salt can cause excessive fluid build-up. This can lead to high blood pressure and, severe heart disease and stroke. Salt can also give problems with blood circulation. Blood carries nutrients and oxygen to the body.

There are many types of salt:

Black salt: Some people also call it Gray salt. This is not quite black, but is dark blackish gray salt. Be careful because sometimes you can get some pieces of rock in it. In India, they make a mixture of spices called churan, which is good to eat with yogurt to cure an upset stomach. We used to make churan a lot and used in yogurt almost on regular basis until my father read in a book that this salt is high in acid and can raise your blood pressure, so we stopped using it completely.

Flavored salt: You can find some of the common flavor salts, like garlic salt, celery salt, onion salt etc. in the supermarkets. We make our own green salt by grinding the cilantro leaves and Serrano peppers with the table salt. You can also add some fresh chop garlic cloves to this and use on eggs, grilled food and even on bread. This fresh-made salt is very flavorful, rich and aromatic.

Low-sodium salt: One nutritionist who was treating high blood pressure in my family has recommended this to use as a table salt. We love it. It's not too strong and you just have to get used to it.

Kosher salt: This is almost all-purpose salt used by Jewish dietary laws to bless and remove the impurities of meat. I mostly use it in brine and baking. It has a slight mineral taste, and less sodium.

Pink salt: This salt is of light pale pink color. It comes in a clear crystal rock form. When grinded, it turns in to an off-white color. It is believed that this has a low sodium content, therefore we used it when we want to eat less spicy vegetables on holy days.

Pink Himalayan salt: This salt come in a brick form. You can heat it in a baking tray in the oven, and serve cooked seafood on it, then wash out and reuse the brick.

Sea salt: You can use both coarse and powder form. It is mostly collected at the sea and then dried by evaporation. Some believe this is a pure salt and can lower the blood pressure, but it has same sodium content, the only difference could be that sea salt tastes better as it comes directly from the sea and there are no additives

Fleur de Sel: This salt comes from the coastal region of France. It has a little moisture and is tasty when used at the end of cooking, or as a garnish on final products.

Table salt (sodium chloride): This salt has Iodine. Iodine is very important nutrients for Thyroid function. This is a all purpose salt. It is widely used and is not expensive.

Rock salt: This salt is not for table use. It has a medicinal value. You can soak your feet in warm salted water if you have any pain or swelling. It is mostly used in chilling, curing and roasting.

Various Types of Tea and Making a Perfect Cup of Tea

Tea is used all around the world in one form or the other. Tea is a daily regular routine and a social event in India. The British, when they ruled India, had tea time, afternoon around 3 or 4 p.m., where they served tea with fancy biscuits, pastries and sometimes with cakes. Even today, drinking tea is a relaxing time. Tea has antioxidant properties and cancer-fighting benefits. Studies show that the green tea can soothe your body and mind as well as reduce your bad cholesterol. Try to drink tea in moderation as it contains caffeine.

Making a perfect cup of tea

There are a few secrets of making tea. We are told to pour a little hot water over the loose tea or tea bag first to soften the leaves and to get the extra caffeine out of tea:

1. First, use good water, preferably bottled water. Boil a little extra water, it may evaporate. Use hot tap water to warm up the cups.
2. Boil the water in a heavy-bottom pot, or teapot, covered, to a rolling boil and then let it boil for at least five minutes to 15 minutes, or just let it simmer on low for at least half an hour, until needed.
3. Rinse the cups with hot boiling water or hot tap water, pour in the hot water half way up the cups, let it stand a few minutes while you are making tea and then discard the water.
4. If using loose tea, after the water has boiled, turn the water off, place tea in the strainer or stir in the loose tea leaves in the hot water, (about ¼ Tsp. to ½ Tsp. of leaves for one cup of tea) cover, and pour the hot water over strainer or pour tea through a strainer into the prepared cups or from the tea kettle. If you are using a tea bag, pour the hot water in the cups or tea kettle over the tea bags, and hold the bag with the tags, keep on dipping the tea in the hot water a few times, to release the flavor and antioxidant. Always make a fresh pot or cup of tea just before serving. In the winter, cover the teapot with a cotton cover or a kitchen towel and place it on a hot tray to keep it warm.
5. When tea is prepared, take out the leaves from the liquid so it will not continue seeping and will not get stronger. Serve tea with milk, cream or lemon. In India, a study was done that drinking tea with milk protects your skin. Also, a study was done in America that if you add lemon to black tea, it has a double dose of antioxidants. In any case, use tea both ways, alternating with lemon and milk if you prefer. For guests, we always make tea with light heavy cream or milk tea, using low-fat or whole milk instead of water.
6. If you prefer, add about a hal-inch of fresh ginger in boiling water (for two people), it will give a very good taste, it is antioxidant-rich, and is good for colds and flu. The best of all, ginger can be used both with milk and lemon.
7. You can make your own flavored tea by adding mint, cardamom, ginger, lemon, black peppercorns, or any other flavor, or buy a flavored tea. To have a creamy flavor, use milk instead of water and you will love it. My father did not allow to use spices in tea for a prolonged time, although occasional use of spices with tea was alright. If you have flu or a cold, or aches and pain in the body, use spiced tea for specific conditions for a limited time.
8. Store loose tea in an airtight tin container in a dark and cool place for up 10 to 12 months. The tea bags can be stored in a cool place away from heat.

Ashwagandha: This is a herbal tea comes from the bushes in India. Mostly the roots are used in the tea, but leaves and berries are edible. It is an antioxidant, has iron, and is a tonic for your immune system. It also takes swelling away. It is rejuvenative and keeps your mind alert and young. This is an Ayurvedic medicine. You can also dry the leaves and make smoke to use as insect repellent.

Assam: This comes from the Assam region of India. It is an old and famous tea that has a rich and robust flavor. Tea is usually made with water and then some cream or milk added at end, but we made this tea with half water and half milk.

Ceylon: This comes from Ceylon, Sri Lanka. It has a delicate but original flavor.

Chamomile: Only the flowers of the plant are used in tea, and also in liqueurs like Benedictine and vermouth. The tea is made with dry petals of chamomile flowers. It has calcium, magnesium, potassium, iodine and some essential oils. It is believed to lower the blood pressure, repairs the tissues in the body, and wards off the E. coli and staph bacteria, helps arthritis, fever, headache.

Darjeeling: This comes from Darjeeling, India. This is a delicate and slightly sweet-tasting tea. When we were growing up, we were not allowed to drink tea. So, every now and then we added a few loose leaves in a strainer and lowered it in a pot of boiling milk, added sugar and we had a treat. You can also make a tea shake by adding the cream and sugar.

Earl Gray: This is a processed, fermented tea with a mild flavor.

Fenugreek: In India, people practicing Ayurvedic medicine use Fenugreek powder or seeds to make tea for longevity. Fenugreek is bitter so use very little and add lemon and jiggery (similar to brown sugar). Sip it slowly. When tea is lukewarm, you can also add honey. Do not use honey in hot water, it will turn to sugar and all nutrients will be gone.

Green: Green tea can be in dry-leaves form or in a green-powder form. Green tea is believed to be very beneficial for the bod. I can prevent dental decay and is used in meditation to keep peaceful and calm. It is made very light and used without any milk. The powder form is first diluted in warm water, then hot water is poured over it.

Gurukul Kangari: This is a herbal tea that looks like a coarse wood powder. It is used to cure flu and cold and is good for the immune system. When we were growing up, my father was transferred to another city. There was a flu epidemic and I and my two brothers got the flu right away. My grandmother, who was with us, started making this herbal tea, three times a day, and gave a large glass to all of us to drink. It took us over a week, but we all got over the bad flu.

Jasmine: This is a combination of two plants. The tea leaves are picked and mixed with the Jasmine flowers and then dried together to make the tea. It tastes almost like green tea and is partially fermented.

Oolong: This is partially fermented tea with a richness of a black and green tea.

Japanese green tea: The Japanese green tea, Hoji-cha, is very high flavored tea. It is roasted at high temperature to boost the flavor.

Tulsi: Tulsi is a plant you can grow indoors. This tea helps you calm down and relax the body. Most people who do daily Yoga drink this tea two or three times a week. It also supposed to cure common cold.

Ice tea: This form of tea is used in America all summer long. You can buy it made or make you own by brewing tea only with half of the amount of the water than for regular cup of tea, chill in the refrigerator in a pitcher, add apple, lemon, orange slices and some ice cubes, chill and serve. I always use half water to brew ice tea and then add apple or orange juices, crushed mint leaves and fruit slices, berries, and serve chilled overnight or with ice cubes.

Coffee and Making a Perfect Cup of Coffee

Just like Tea, coffee also has antioxidant properties. The tap water may contribute unhealthy chemical such as chlorine, calcium, lawn fertilizers and other minerals, so boiling the water on high for at least full five minutes, and then filtering through filter paper, or using a good bottle water, may protect you from all harmful chemicals. Also, to get the double dose of antioxidant, sprinkle a little cinnamon over the cup of coffee before serving. You can make coffee in a coffee machine, use instant coffee or grind your own beans and brew fresh cup of coffee. Whenever I go visit my brother in Berlin, he always makes a fresh pot of coffee with fresh-ground beans, and a fresh pot of tea with loose leaves. The aroma from both makes you want a cup of coffee or tea right away

Making a Perfect Cup of Coffee

Like you would for tea or any hot drink, first warm up the cups with hot water, discard the water and wipe out the cups with kitchen towels and immediately pour the fresh-brewed coffee. Coffee tastes better when it is fresh-brewed and served with cream or half and half. Choose any flavor or type of coffee that you like. If you want a strong coffee, use a little extra coffee, add a little grated chocolate, or some cocoa powder, so when milk or cream, is added it is still strong. Grind coffee beans only what you are going to use and store roasted coffee beans in an airtight container in a cool and dark place away from the heat.

1. Make sure your coffee maker is cleaned. After every 8 to 10 brews clean the coffee maker. Run the coffee maker with 2-3 Tbsp. of vinegar mixed in the water, and do not use any coffee with it. Then run one more cycle with plain water to rinse out.
2. Make a fresh pot of coffee just before using. Do not consume the coffee until the cycle is finished brewing. Because the first few cups are strong, and the rest of the coffee is a little weak. So let the process finished before using.
3. Follow the instruction of the manufacturer. Use a clean carafe and filtered water. Use a fresh clean filter. Grind fresh coffee beans at medium-coarse for each brew, or take out fresh coffee from an air-tight container and make fresh coffee.
4. While the coffee is brewing, fill the serving cups with the boiled water and let them sit for at least 5 minutes. Discard the water, wipe out the cups with a paper towel and pour the fresh-brewed coffee.
5. Use about 2 Tbsp. of fresh-ground coffee to make one cup of coffee. I do use, and stir in a little, (about 1 Tsp. per cup) dark grated chocolate, and add hot milk or cream. Do not use cold milk with coffee, it will not only ruin the taste of the coffee, it will cool down the coffee right away. You want a hot cup of the brew for the full effect.
6. Right after the coffee is brewed, transfer it to a hot-water washed, airtight, insulated coffee pot, to keep the coffee hot and the flavor intact.

Vinegars

Vinegars are made from wines, alcohol, fermented fruits like apples, berries, fruit juices, rice and cereals. Vinegar is used in cooking, mixed with oil for salad dressing and used on fruits and vegetables.

Some following combinations are very common:

White Vinegar is mostly for pickles. In India, we use white vinegar to separate whole milk from whey to make cheese (paneer).

Make Herbal Vinegar: Fill the bottle loosely with herbs and add vinegar to steep fruits like peaches, pears and fresh herbs like dill, tarragon, basil, coriander etc. and shake or turn over the bottle twice a week, or keep in the summer in the hot sun and shake every other day for 2 months; then you will have herbal vinegar. Depending on full or partial sun light you may get it even in one month.

Champaign or red wine vinegar used in moderation with sugar, sprinkled on the fruits and berries brings back the unique flavor of the fruits. You can serve it in dessert glasses topped with whip cream.

Balsamic vinegar goes well with grilled or roasted vegetables like Brussels sprouts and asparagus. Reduced balsamic vinegar with light brown sugar can be used on poached fruits.

Buying and Storing Commonly Used Food

Baking Powder and Baking Soda: When buying these ingredients buy them with a longer expiration date. Store them in a cool and dry place for up to 6 months. Buy double acting baking powder.

Butter and Butter Spreads: If they are in a plastic container, keep them in the refrigerator for up to a month. If they are in a carton, place the carton in a plastic bag and keep airtight in refrigerator about a month, or freeze them up to four months, thaw overnight before using.

Chocolate: Keep it wrapped in its original packing, then wrap the package in a plastic bag airtight, place in a cool and dark place for up to 6 to 8 months. The dark chocolate stores better. Milk chocolate and white chocolate should be stored for shorter periods of time.

Eggs: Check the expiration dates before buying. Keep in the original container for up to two months or up to the original date.

Flours: All-purpose flour, cake flour and Atta (Indian Bread Flour) should be kept in the bag they came in; just place the bag in a plastic zip-lock bag. Then transfer the double pack to an airtight container and store the container in a cool dark place, away from the light and heat.

Do the same for the whole wheat, chickpea, soybean, singhara, kuttu, urad, mung, rice and tapicoa flours. These flours can be stored for up to 3 months. For longer storage, freeze them in double packs up to one year. The general rule is if the package is not open it will last a little longer.

Herbs and Spices: Fresh herbs should never be washed ahead. Wash them just before using. Take out the herbs from the original package, wrap the bottom half, the root part, in lightly damp paper towels in batches and place them in a plastic bag, then fold over half of the bag and leave the top half exposed. Place the bag in the vegetable box. If the herbs have roots, you can place the herbs in a glass, half full of water, for up to 3 to 4 days. Just make sure you take out all the dead and yellow leaves from the package before storing them. The dry herbs and spices should be stored in a cool and dark cabinet away from heat up to a year.

Milk, Sour Cream and Heavy Cream: Always check the expiration dates before buying and use by the expiration dates. I have noticed if you do not open the container, the sour cream will last a couple of weeks pass the expiration date.

Nuts and Nuts Flour: When buying nuts, check the expiration date and also check the bottom of the bag (if it is a plastic bag). If the bottom has lot of crumbs, the nuts are old, so try to buy fresh ones. Keep them in the original packing, place the bag in an airtight container and freeze them up to one year. Or for opened ones, keep them in the refrigerator airtight in a plastic zip-lock bag.

Sugar, Honey and Molasses: Leave sugar in its original package (air can get in transferring to a new package) and store in a cool, dark place. Brown sugar may be placed in the refrigerator, in the original bag, in a large bottle or a plastic bag. Take out the bottle at least 1 hour ahead and to soften to room temperature.

For confectioner's sugar, buy in bags and keep it in a cool and dark place, but make sure you sift it just before using so there are no lumps left. Molasses and honey also can be stored in cool and dark place. In the winter the honey gets thick so I try to buy a larger bottle, where you can use a long spoon to take it out easily. Try not to heat the honey - it loses its nutrients.

Vegetables: There are certain vegetables, mostly roots, that you can buy and store in the refrigerator 3 to 4 weeks. But make sure they are not wet. If they are wet, take them out of the bag, dry with paper towels, discard the rotten and dry ones, wrap them in the paper towel across leaving the tops exposed, and then place in a clean plastic bag. This works for carrots, parsnips, yams, celery etc. If you are buying summer squash, buy with green stems and just spread them out loose over a paper towel in the vegetable box. Eggplant, asparagus and other greens should be used with a day or two. Mushrooms should be bought fresh, and when you open the package (within 2-3 days) use them right away or cover them airtight and use them next day. I love baby-bella mushrooms. I buy them fresh and keep the unopened package for up to 4-5 days. Fresh green onions or scallions can last 7-8 days if you discard the brown leaves and wrap them in a paper towel, then place them in a plastic bag. Leave the tomatoes outside in a basket in room temperature.

As far as fruits are concerned, most of the juicy fruits should be kept in the refrigerator, such oranges, grapes, peaches, apricot, berries etc. Keep the bananas, mangoes and apples outside in the basket in the room temperature.

Yeast: Check the expiration date before buying and keep in the refrigerator for up to 6 weeks or almost up to the expiration date. When using, if it does not foam discard and start with a new batch.

Substitutions

1. 1 c sour cream can be substituted by using 1 C Greek yogurt or yogurt cheese.
2. For 1 c whole milk, use ½ c of half-and-half together with ½ c of low-fat milk.
3. For 1 c cake flour, use 3/4c bleached all-purpose flour plus 1/4c corn starch. sift both together.
4. For 1 c packed light brown sugar, mix 1 c fine granulated sugar and 3-4 tablespoon of unsulfured molasses in a blender and store in the refrigerator.
5. For 1 c of buttermilk, use 1 c of low-fat or 2% of milk and add 1 tablespoon of lemon juice, stir well, cover, and let it stand 3-4 minutes, stir well and use.
6. For sour cream, use low fat Greek yogurt or yogurt cheese (drain out the liquid from the yogurt, in several layer of cheesecloth, overnight).

For eggs, use egg beaters and follow the instruction on the package. Also, you can use egg-white powder for the whites.

Breakfast

Healthy Breakfast Ideas

Breakfast: is breaking a fast after a long night of sleep. It is not only an important meal to start the day with, but a healthy breakfast nourishes your body, soul and mind. You are full of energy and ready for a long day ahead of you. Now, once you eat a healthy breakfast, you will not crave for junk food, or gain weight, or eat the wrong thing. So find some time and take care of your body.

Also, read the following doctor's message from Dr. Mandel, under Food and Health.

1. Start the day with some protein. Drink ½ cup coconut water or soy beverages with fresh berries, orange or pineapple.
2. Use oatmeal with fresh berries in place of syrup and one boiled egg.
3. Use whole-grain dry cereal with nuts and fresh fruits and berries.
4. Use coconut butter or soy butter on whole-wheat toasts with fruits on side and/or boiled or poached egg.
5. Have granola or dry cereal with low-fat yogurt and fresh fruits.
6. If having an omelet, make with lots of cooked vegetables and fresh herbs and whole-wheat toast.
7. No time for breakfast? Prepare a healthy snack bag (see snack chapter) and carry a bottle of low-sodium vegetable juice.
8. Have some protein on hand like: peanut butter, hard-boiled eggs, Greek yogurt, bean dip like hummus or edamame, cottage cheese, whole wheat bread and whole wheat cracker etc.
9. When ordering breakfast outside, stay with a protein (low-sodium ham and egg, or oatmeal, smoked salmon with eggs, etc.) breakfast with whole-wheat or mixed grain bread.

Eggs

Eggs are loaded with the nutrition. They have an average of 6 grams of protein. They are good for the brain and eyes, especially the yolk. Use more egg whites to reduce the cholesterol concern. Eggs, just like chicken, can give you salmonella poisoning. So use safety all the way. Wash the dishes before and after using.

Eggs can be stored in the refrigerator for 3 to 4 weeks, depending on how old they are. As they get old, eggs accumulate air, and the egg whites thicken. To find out how fresh the eggs are, place one egg in a cup full of water. The freshest egg will settle in the bottom of the cup sideways, and the older one will touch the bottom on its one end and will stand almost vertically.
When buying eggs, check out the carton (you have to move the eggs) and do not buy any cracked or broken ones. Avoid eating raw eggs. You do not need to wash the eggs before cooking, as they are washed already in the process, beside that you will remove the outer coating that protects them from bacteria. Keep them inside the refrigerator, not on the door. You can cook eggs for breakfast, lunch or dinner, it is a complete protein.
There are several varieties of eggs: organic – where chickens are given organic food (without pesticides); Free-range or cage-free – where chickens are raised to roam around outdoor in the fresh air; Omega-3 – these chickens are given omega-3 food, such as flax seed, to help reduce heart disease; low-cholesterol eggs – a special diet given to the chicken reduces the amount of cholesterol in the egg yolks.

Beside using the eggs in recipes, they are used for breakfast in many different ways.

Soft Boiled Eggs: These eggs have an egg white completely set and a yolk that is runny or soft. Take out the eggs from the refrigerator and leave them in the room temperature for 2 minutes. Bring a pot, half full of water, to a boil, let the water boil for a minute or two. Using a perforated spoon, place the eggs in the boiling water, bring the eggs to a boil, cover with the lid. Take off the heat and let them sit in the water for 4-5 minutes (depending on how soft you want).

Tap and crack the eggs in the middle with a knife, pull out the shells apart and pour the egg gently over the toast, or on a plate or in a bowl, and serve warm.

Hard Boiled Eggs: Leave the eggs in room temperature for 5 minutes in cold tap water. Change the water, cover the eggs two-inches higher with the cold tap water, in a heavy bottom pot with a tight-fitting lid, and place them on the stove on medium-high heat, uncovered, bring them to a rolling boil. Let them boil for 4 minutes covered. Take off the heat, and let them sit in the hot water covered with lid for 5 minutes. I call this 5-4-5 method.

Now crack the shells all around, and place the eggs in cold tab water, this will stop eggs from forming the skin inside and turning green, start peeling right away or peel a little and drop some water on the open space, and peel within 30 minutes. Once the cold water goes all over the egg it will peel right away. You can also crack the egg in the center and break it apart with hands or slice it in half with a sharp knife. Then scoop out the egg with a teaspoon.

Save the boiled egg water, cool it and pour in the house plants, they get extra vitamins, especially in herbs and spider plants.

You can also boil the eggs, just bringing them to a rolling boil, cover it with an air-tight lid, turn off the heat, and let it sit in hot water for about 15 minutes, peel and serve.

Tips: Before boiling the eggs turn them over (top side down) in the egg box at least 2hrs. before boiling. This way the yolk will move to the center.

Eggs are brain food and yolks are good for the eyes.

Poached Eggs: You can just serve poached eggs as they are or use them over toast with Hollandaise sauce (Eggs Benedict). Bring water in a large and wide pan, half full, to a boil, lower the heat to simmer, add about 1 tsp. of white vinegar (for 4 large eggs, and about 5-6 cups of water, about 1-1/2 to 2-inches deep). Break one egg in a lightly greased cup and carefully slide one egg at a time, in the simmering water, without breaking the yolk. If the white is running away, carefully move the white edges over the white egg to create a white circle and give them a round shape. Let them simmer until the white is set, about 3-4 minutes, and the yolk is set underneath (the yolk will be soft on the top). Using a perforated spoon, take them out of the water and place on a lightly damp, double paper towel, trim the edges with a knife and then serve immediately over toast, salad, fruits etc.

I want to tell you a little trick to make the poached egg fancy and thick-looking. Use one whole egg and one egg white for each poached egg. First separate the egg white and keep it in a cup. When the water is ready, keep it on medium heat. First drop the egg white in one place (like a pile) then break the whole egg over it. Keep the heat between medium and medium-high until the white is settled, about a half-minute, turning the pan around. This will keep the white in shape and it will not spread much. After about half a minute, cook the egg on medium heat for 3-4 minutes or until the yolk is settled, then lower the heat to low and just let the whole poached egg firm. Turn off the heat and let the egg sit in warm water 1-2 minutes, scrape the bottom, take out the egg. I poach all my eggs this way. These thick-poached eggs take about 15 minutes to settle, so give extra time.

Fried Eggs: These are fried eggs almost like sunny side up, but the yolk is broken and cooked well. These eggs go well with ham, bacon and other meat or cheese slices in sandwiches. If cooking 4 fried eggs: heat a large cast-iron pan on medium-high heat, take off the heat and spray with cooking spray or just add 1 tsp. of oil or butter, swirl around to coat the bottom of the pan. Put the pan back on stove halfway, tilted off the stove. Now break the egg on the lowered part of the pan, and poke the yolk to break it. Then break another egg same way, away from the first one. Now, put the pan back on the stove and break 2 more on the empty side (you can also break and whisk the eggs one at a time and pour in the pan). Cook eggs on medium heat until the whole egg is almost settled, about 3-4 minutes on medium heat. Take off the heat, cover with the lid half way and let the eggs sit in the pan for 4-5 minutes and serve warm, sprinkled with salt and fresh ground black pepper.

Scrambled Eggs: Heat a heavy-bottom skillet, large pan or a non-stick pan to medium. To cook 4 large eggs: whisk the eggs well in a medium bowl with about ¼ cup of light or heavy cream, whole milk or reduced milk. You can also use 4 tbsp. of almond or coconut milk. When the pan is heated, add 1tbsp. of oil or butter, swirl around to coat the bottom. Pour the eggs and immediately stir well with a fork, or a rubber or wooden spatula, for a minute. As soon as the eggs start thickening and settling down, and if there is any liquid left, move it to the middle of the pan and take the pan off the heat. Sprinkle a pinch of salt and pepper, and serve immediately. You can also add some fresh chopped parsley (1 tbsp.) or a little fresh oregano (½ tsp.) Serve with toasts and/or fruits, and over cauliflower bed, etc.

Sunny Side Up: These eggs have egg white settled and the yolk starting to thicken all around but is still liquid in the center. These eggs are better cooked when using an 8-inch skillet to cook 2 eggs at a time. This way the white expands up to the edges making a round attractive presentation. These eggs are a beauty and can be served over any food like corned beef hash, huevos rancheros, etc.
Heat an eight-inch cast-iron skillet or a heavy-bottom pan on medium heat. When heated, add 1 tsp. of clarified butter or oil to coat the bottom. When the butter starts sizzling, take the pan off the heat and carefully crack a fresh egg into the skillet, and place the pan back on the heat. Keep on cooking on low heat until the white is set well and lightly brown underneath and the yolk is slightly cooked on the edges, but still soft in the center, about 2-3 minutes, depending on the type of pan you are using. Take the pan off the heat, cover the pan about three-quarters with the lid, and let the pan sit slightly tilted off the stove for at least 5 minutes. Then loosen the edges with a spatula and carefully slide the egg circle on to the plate or over the food without breaking the yolk.

Bagel & Lox (Serves: 2)

This is a fancy as well healthy breakfast, and our favorite one. When buying smoked salmon, use it soon. Once the package is opened, it may go bad quickly. Be very careful with raw and smoked seafood.

Ingredients: 2 large fresh bagels of your choice; 4 ounces regular or light cream cheese; 4 ounces (113G) or about 4 large slices of good smoked salmon; 2 thin slices of a large fresh tomato; 1 ripe avocado; 1 large or two small bananas and some fresh blueberries or any other fruit to serve on side.

1. Slice bagels horizontally and toast them in the toaster, spread cream cheese equally on all four pieces. Top two of the pieces with smoked salmon.

2. Top two other pieces of bagel with tomato slices first then cut the Avocado in half, take out the pit with the knife and scoop out the pulp with a large spoon, butterfly or slice the pieces and place half avocado each on the tomato slices.
3. Serve with sliced banana and blueberries on side.

Tips
1. Bagels dry up very fast. So if you are not using them right away, place them in an airtight plastic bag in the refrigerator. Slice and toast, and spread cream cheese or butter right away before serving.
2. Also, avocado should be peeled just before serving so that it does not turn brown. You can also rub with lemon juice if delaying the serving, or mash with lemon juice, salt and pepper, parsley and diced red onion, and use it as a spread on toast.

Bacon, Ham & Eggs Benedict (Serves: 2)

You can make poached eggs and Hollandaise sauce a night before and just heat the eggs in the warm water and the sauce over the warm water.

Ingredients: 2 poached eggs (see recipe); 2 medallions of ham; 4 strips of bacon; 1 recipe of Hollandaise sauce (see recipe); 2 English muffins of your choice (we like cranberry muffins); ½ tbsp. butter; some fruits or salads to serve on side.

Make the Hollandaise sauce and keep it warm over warm water. Make the poached eggs (per recipe). Heat a cast-iron pan on medium heat and spread out the bacon strips, cook about 1 minute per side or until crispy, take out and place on a paper towel-lined platter. Take out the bacon fat and add 1 tsp. of butter, then cook the ham on medium heat for 1 minute each side. Lower the heat, cover the pan with a lid and cook another 1-2 minutes, depending on the thickness, until browned. Turn off the heat. Cut the muffins in half and toast them.

Assemble: Place the bottom slice of the muffin on a heated serving platter and drizzle some sauce or use butter on the muffin, top with the ham, poached egg, drizzle some sauce over the egg, place the bacon on the top, and place the top slice of the muffin on the side, serve warm with fruits or salad.

Chicken and Waffles (Serves: 2-4)

You need a waffle Iron to make waffles. You can make them ahead, freeze, and reheat directly from the freezer to a preheated 350 degree oven, directly on the rack, for about 8-10 minutes, in a single layer. You can make waffles with almost anything. I sometime use leftover stuffing, with mashed chickpeas, grated apple and some nuts; make 4 balls and close the lid and you get tasty waffles. Chickpea waffles cooked with lemon chutney taste very good. Try chocolate syrup or orange glaze for an extra treat. You can also serve chocolate-dipped bacon, instead of chicken, or serve with sausage gravy without any extra meat.

For the Chicken
Ingredients: About ¾ pound to 1 pound, or 2 boneless and skinless halved chicken breasts, all fat removed, sprinkled with ½ tsp. each black pepper and granulated garlic; batter mixture: 1 large egg

whisked in with about ½ cup buttermilk, 1 tbsp. hot sauce, salt and pepper to taste, ½ cup cornmeal to a thick and a dipping consistency; 1 cup panko (Japanese) bread crumbs; olive or canola oil to deep fry. To serve: orange slices and blueberries, 1 cup maple syrup heated with ¼ cup walnuts or pistachios, plus ¼ cup extra nuts to sprinkle on the serving platter.

In a medium frying pan, heat about 1-inch deep oil to 360 degrees. When hot, dip the chicken in the cornmeal batter, then press in the panko bread crumbs and deep fry in the hot oil, medium-high heat, about 3-4 minutes on each side on until golden. Keep them on a wire rack over a baking tray in a warm oven until serving.

For the Waffle

Ingredients: 1-1/2 cup whole milk; 2 large eggs; ¼ cup shredded coconut; ½ cup dry cranberries; 1 tbsp. chopped fresh parsley (op); 1 tsp. vanilla extract; the flour mixture: 1-1/2 cups all-purpose flour, 1 tbsp. baking powder, ¼ tsp. salt, 3-4 tbsp. melted butter for the iron.

Preheat the waffle iron per manufacturer instruction, or about 200 degrees. In a large bowl, whisk together eggs, herb, coconut and cranberries. Whisk in the milk, then the flour mixture, just enough to combine.

When iron is hot, spray or brush the grids with the butter up to the edges and pour in about 1 cup batter and spread out with a wooden spoon up to the edges. Close the cover and cook until crispy and browned or about 2-3 minutes. Serve hot, topped with the chicken, warm maple syrup heated lightly with nuts, with fruits, and more nuts sprinkled over the serving platter.
Tip: If you wish, instead of coconut you can add grated apple.
Also, if you prefer, serve drizzled with chocolate syrup.

For Sausage Gravy (about 3-1/4 cups)

This versatile gravy goes with almost any dish such as eggs, muffins, waffles, pancakes, greens, polenta, rice, roasted vegetables and meat.

Ingredients: 1 to 2 tbsp. olive oil; ½ cup each fine chopped onion and celery; ½ cup to 1 cup sliced baby bella mushrooms; ¼ tsp. each granulated garlic and dry oregano; 1 pound sausage meat or hot sausages out of casings; 1 tbsp. crushed fennel seeds; 2 tbsp. all-purpose flour; 2 cups 2% milk; salt and fresh ground black pepper to taste; fresh grated nutmeg.

Heat a large heavy-bottom sauté pan on medium heat. When hot, add the oil and cook onion for 5 minutes. Add the celery, garlic, oregano and cook another 5 minutes. Move the vegetables over on one side. Increase the heat to medium-high and cook mushrooms for 5-6 minutes or until their liquid has evaporated; take the vegetables out of the pan.

Add the sausage meat in the same pan and stir on medium-high heat for 2 minutes, reduce the heat and stir on medium heat for another 6-8 minutes or until it start turning brown. Lower the heat and sprinkle the fennel seeds and the flour all over, and mix them well for 1-2 minutes. Now, slowly add the milk, whisking constantly, and bring to a boil. Add the cooked vegetables, a little salt and pepper to taste, and simmer open on medium heat for 3-4 minutes, stirring until it is thickened. Grate the fresh nutmeg on the top and serve.

Old Fashioned Buttermilk Biscuits with Ham Gravy and Grilled Pineapple (Serves: 6-8)

Buttermilk biscuits are best when served warm, right out of the oven. You can grill pineapple slices a day before and just reheat in the pan or in the microwave oven.

1.   Grilled Pineapple

Ingredients: 1 golden (or annanas) pineapple cored, peeled and slice across into 6 rings (you can leave the center core, it is tasty and has antioxidant); all slices rubbed with a mixture of: ¼ cup sugar, 1 tbsp. salt, ¼ tsp. fresh ground black pepper and drizzled on both sides with 4 tbsp. melted butter.

Place pineapple slices on medium grill or in a greased grilling pan (with ridges) and grill slowly for about 6-8 minutes each side, or until pineapple has grill marks.

2.   Ham Gravy (M: about 4 cups)

Ingredients: 5 tbsp. unsalted butter, divided; 12 ounces (340g) or one or two, boneless and fully cooked ham steaks, rind taken out and then cut into ½-inch cubes; ½ cup dry cranberries; ½ cup chopped fine onion; ¼ tsp. each salt and pepper and 2 pinches granulated garlic; 4 tbsp. all-purpose bleached flour; 4 cups whole or 2% milk; ¼ tsp. each ground cloves and fresh grated nutmeg and some extra for garnish.

A. Heat a large, heavy-bottom sauté pan on medium heat, when hot add 1 tbsp. Butter and sauté the ham cubes and cranberries until they sizzle for about 6 minutes. Take all out in a bowl.

B. Use same pan, add 4 tbsp. butter, onion, garlic and salt and pepper and sauté onions on medium heat for 5 minutes, cover and let simmer on low heat for 5 minutes or until the onions are soft. Sprinkle the flour and cook on medium heat for 5 minutes. Now, take the pan off the heat and slowly whisk in the milk, breaking and whisking the flour into puree.

C. Put the pan back on medium heat, add sugar, ¼ tsp. each cloves and fresh grated nutmeg. Keep on whisking the gravy on medium-high heat, until the gravy starts bubbling. Now, reduce the heat to medium and keep on whisking until the gravy is thick, about 6 minutes. Add the ham and cranberry mixture, stir well, cover and turn off the heat. Reheat on medium heat just before serving.

3.   Buttermilk Biscuits (M: 15 large and 20 medium)

Ingredients: 3-1/2 cups bleached all-purpose flour plus extra for dusting; 1 envelope, about 1 cup instant nonfat dry milk; 1 tsp. baking powder; 3 tsp. baking soda; 1 tsp. salt; 1 tbsp. sugar; 2 sticks cold unsalted butter sliced into ½-inch slices plus extra butter softened for topping; 1 cup cold low-fat buttermilk; fresh baby arugula or watercress to serve (op).

A.   In a food processor, pulse all dry ingredients: flour, milk powder, baking powder, baking soda, salt, sugar and butter together until the butter is broken down into pea-size pieces (about 1 minute). Add the buttermilk and pulse 4-5 times just to incorporate the liquid, do not over mix. (Alternately, you can mix by hand: grate half of the cold butter over half of the flour mixture, sprinkle rest of the flour mixture and grate the rest of the butter again, then mix the grated butter into the flour mixture with a fork. Whisk in the buttermilk, and take out the dough on the counter.)

B. Prepare a large baking tray (12x18-inch) lined with aluminum foil and greased well with the butter. Dust a work surface with 2 tbsp. flour, and make an oblong disk of the dough, about 12-inches wide, 18-inches long, and 1-1/2-inch high. Do not roll the dough, just use your fingers, pressing from all around and from the top flattening into a disk. Using the biscuit cutter, dipping in the dry flour, cut out 3 inches (15 round) or 2 inches (20 round), using and pressing the trimmings again and again into biscuits. Place the biscuits in the baking tray as you go along.

C. Preheat the oven at 375 degrees. Brush and cover the top of each biscuit with about 1btsp. of softened butter, and bake at 375 degrees for about 18 minutes until biscuits are lightly browned on the top. Turn off the oven, take out the tray and let it rest on the counter for 5 minutes.

Serve, warm biscuits topped with warm ham gravy, on the side: pineapple, arugula or watercress, and a sprinkle of nutmeg and ground cloves on the top.

Chocolate Crepes (M: 8)

This is my Valentine's Day treat to my husband. He likes anything special, especially with chocolate. These crepes are very easy to make.

Ingredients:

Batter: 1 cup sifted all-purpose flour; 5 tbsp. unsweetened cocoa powder; ½ tsp. instant coffee; ¼ tsp. cayenne or black pepper; ¼ tsp. salt; 3 tbsp. melted butter plus more to cook; 2 large eggs; ½ to ¾ cup almond milk as needed to make a pourable batter; 1 tsp. vanilla extract. To serve: pineapple topping or maple syrup, and to garnish: whipped cream and chocolate syrup (bought) to drizzle.

Filling: chunky peanut butter or 1 cup drained ricotta cheese mixed with ½ cup chopped pineapple chunks.

1. In a blender, whisk together almond milk, eggs, cocoa powder, instant coffee, flour, salt and pepper well and pour into a bowl.
2. Heat a crepe pan or a non-stick pan on medium-high heat. When heated, brush or grease with a thick paper towel the bottom of the pan with 1/2 tsp. butter and pour in about a three-quarter ladle of batter in the pan. Pick up the pan, move around the batter to coat the bottom evenly. As soon as the top dries out, in about 1-1/2 minute, take the pan off the heat and with a greasy metal spatula, loosen the edges, then loosen the whole crepe and fold it in half. Now spread out 2 tbsp. of peanut butter or about ¾ tbsp. of cheese mixture and again fold in half into a quarter. Place on warm serving plates, Make the rest the same way and keep them on a wire rack in a warm oven. When ready to serve, drizzle with pineapple topping, top with a dollop of whipped cream and then drizzle the chocolate syrup.
3. Serve two per person.
4. Tip: If you have some mini chocolate chips, sprinkle them all over the platter – make it chocolaty all the way. I sometimes grate a chocolate bar over the crepes and add blueberries.

French Toasts: Plain or Stuffed (Serves: 2-4)

My husband's dream breakfast, which he would love to have every day! This recipe will make one plain and three stuffed French toasts.

Ingredients: 1 Italian loaf; about 1-1/2 cups milk (2% or whole); 4 large eggs; ¼ tsp. ground cinnamon. For filling and cooking: 1 tsp. olive oil and about 4 tbsp. butter; 2 tbsp. peanut butter; ½ medium banana; 1 thin slice of low-salt cooked ham; 1 slice provolone, Swiss or jack cheese; 1 slice smoked salmon, and 1 tbsp. roasted red bell pepper strips from a jar.
To serve: fresh fruits, syrup, some chocolate chips and sprouted chickpeas (op).

1. Cut one of the ends off the loaf and take out a wide 1-inch thick slice for the plain toast. Then slice three slices about 2 inches thick across for stuffed toasts. Whisk the eggs and cinnamon in a wider bowl first, then whisk in the milk. Preheat a heavy-bottom large pan or a cast-iron pan on medium heat.

2. For plain French toast: Dip 1-inch thick slice into the egg mixture for 5 minutes, turning over often to soak the egg mixture. When pan is heated, add the oil, swirl the pan to coat the bottom. Then add 1 tbsp. butter. When butter sizzles, add the toast, cover with the lid and cook on medium heat for about 2 minutes or until golden underneath. Turn the toast over and cook the other side for about 1 minute until golden. Keep them in a preheated 200 degree oven, tented with the foil until ready to serve.

3. For ham and cheese French toast: Take one 2-inch thick slice of the bread and cut the bottom side into two slices, making a pocket, leaving the other three sides intact together. If you wish you can slice the two bottom edges up to 1-inch deep to open the pockets a little wider. Then take half slice of the cheese (cheese slice should be smaller than the toast to fit in) wrap in single layer with the ham, push the pocket on the sides to open it wider, and insert the ham and cheese slice into the pocket with a fork. If the slice is sticking out a little it is alright. Cheese is wrapped in ham and will not come out. Soak the stuffed toast in the egg mixture for 5 minutes, turning over on all sides. Add in 1 tbsp. butter in the pan, cook covered with the lid, on medium heat, until golden, about 2 minutes. Turn over and cook other side open, until it is golden.

4. For smoked salmon: Just like ham and cheese above, make a pocket, wrap the other half of the cheese with the smoked salmon, and push in some pepper sticks in the pocket. Soak the toast in the egg mixture for 5 minutes, turning over on all sides. Add 1 tbsp. butter in the pan and cook covered, on medium heat until golden. Turn over and cook other side open until golden.

5. For the peanut butter and banana toast: Using the 2-inch wide toast, cut the pocket, spread out the peanut butter inside the pocket with a butter knife, then slice the half piece of banana into two slices and insert in the pocket; soak in egg mixture. Cook golden, covered on one side, and then cook open on the other side until golden.

6. Serve warm with fruits, berries, syrup, chocolate chips and chick peas (op).

Tip: Soak the bread well and cook one side covered with the lid, will make bread rise, heat the stuffing, and will make it soft. One large egg whisked into ½ cup of milk will yield 2 French toasts.

Cinnamon-Raisin French Toasts

If you prefer taste better than the texture, then use the Cinnamon-raisin bread to make plain or stuffed French Toasts. We love both ways.

German Breakfast (S:2)

In early seventies I lived in Berlin, Germany for a few months. My brother would do the shopping on Saturdays and cook this breakfast on Sundays. We ate almost a brunch, and then went out for a walk sometimes in the nearby forest, or sometimes took a long walk, and then sat down at a road side café, and had coffee with a little pastry. We had potatoes with eggs, cold cuts, sliced tomatoes, fancy brown bread that he sliced fresh every morning, marmalades, fruits, and orange juice with champagne, fresh grinded and brewed coffee, and tea for breakfast or brunch.

I. Potatoes with Eggs

Ingredients: 3 medium potatoes peeled, washed, cut into quarter lengthwise and thin sliced, then washed again and drained; 3-4 tbsp. olive or canola oil; 4 large eggs whisked with salt and fresh ground black pepper to taste. To serve: with brown bread (whole-wheat) and mini bread rolls.

1. Heat a large, heavy-bottom pan on medium heat. When hot, add oil and drained potatoes. Start stirring until potatoes are coated well, for about 5 minutes. Sprinkle a little salt and fresh ground black pepper, cover, lower the heat and cook on low for about 10 minutes. Then stir the potatoes, increase the heat to medium-high while stirring, then cover and cook again for another 10 minutes on low heat. Now, increase the heat high and stir the potatoes until they are a little crisp and brown.

2. Pour over the beaten eggs, increase to heat high and stir for 2 minutes, until eggs are settled. Serve warm sprinkled with salt and black pepper to taste, with brown bread, mini bread rolls and butter.

II. Cold Cuts, Tomatoes, Fruits, and Beverages

Ingredients: Medium-sliced (not too thick or too thin) German liverwurst, Swiss or other cheese and crushed black peppercorn salami (I buy large genoa salami and press in the crushed black peppercorn with a rolling pin between the plastic wrap, myself); fresh fruits such as purple grapes; 1 large tomato; olive oil to drizzle; orange or ginger marmalade; orange juice and champagne.

1. On a platter, arrange 2 slices per person of liverwurst, cheese, turkey and salami. Slice the tomato and immediately drizzled with the olive oil. Serve with orange or ginger marmalade.

2. Combine 2 parts orange juice with 1 part champagne and serve on side accompanying with fresh brewed coffee and tea in pots.

   Tip: Germans are very famous for smoked meat and you will find an enormous selection of it. This is a brunch so you can serve some pastries and slice of cakes.

Old Fashioned Indian Breakfast (Serves: 4)

My father loved the sweets. His four aunts, who lived in a joint family, had spoiled him so much that they would not cook a meal without consulting the only son. And what he wanted the most was the halwa (dried pudding). Even when we were growing up he will ask my mother to make semolina (sooji) and Moong Dal (beans) halwa with milk tea on Sundays. Also, he wanted his soaked and sprouted brown chickpeas with each breakfast. You can serve only one halwa with tea.

I. Semolina (Sooji) Halwa

Ingredients: 2 cups semolina (sooji); 6 tbsp. butter, 2 cups water mixed with 1cup milk; ¾ cup sugar; each ½ cup: slivered almonds, pistachios and dark raisins or cranberries.

1. Heat a large wok or a heavy bottom pan on medium heat. When hot, add 4 tbsp. butter and semolina. Stir 5 minutes on medium heat, then increase the heat and stir for 5 minutes on medium-high heat or until it is lightly browned. Take off the heat and add sugar, nuts, and water and milk mixture. Mix well, then cook on medium-high heat, stirring constantly until the mixture comes together, for about 5 minutes. Add rest of the butter and stir well to mix the butter for 2 minutes. The halwa should be leaving the edges and becomes a mass. Serve warm in a heated bowls immediately.

II.   Moong Dal (Mung Beans) Halwa

Ingredients: 1 cup split and peeled moong dal (found in the Indian grocery stores) soaked at least 3 hours in warm water, then ground in a blender or food processor with a little (about ¾ cup) water; can be done a day ahead; 5-6 tbsp. butter; ½ cup sweetened condensed milk; ½ cup soaked, slivered almonds; ¼ cup golden raisins.

1. Heat a large heavy sauté pan on medium heat. When hot, add 2 tbsp. butter, swirl around to coat the bottom, add the grinded moong beans, stir a little to mix the butter, then cover and let it cook on very low heat for 10 minutes. Open scrape the bottom, stir again and cover for another 10 minutes, until the beans are cooked and liquid is almost gone.

2. Now, increase the heat on medium-high, add rest of the condensed milk, stir and break the clusters, stir constantly until they are thick. Reduce the heat to low, add remaining butter, nuts, and raisin. Stir 1 minute just to heat through and serve warm.

III.   Egg Halwa

One of my friends told me that she makes egg halwa for guests, and it takes only a few minutes. So, every now and then I make the egg halwa.

Ingredients: 4 large eggs whipped; 4 tbsp. butter; ½ cup sweetened condensed milk; ¼ cup each pistachios, and dark raisins.

Heat a large heavy bottom pan on low heat. Add 2 tbsp. butter and the eggs and whisk together in the pan with a fork. As soon as the eggs start thickening, take it off the heat and whisk in the condensed milk. Now add the remaining butter, and put the pan back on the low heat. Start whisking again until it is completely dried up. Serve garnished with the nuts and raisins.

Serve breakfast with warm semolina and moong or egg halwa, milk tea (not water), fruits, and sprouted chickpeas.

Tips: Sprouted chickpeas - Soak the dark chickpeas overnight in cold water and they are ready to eat. To sprout them, put them in a damp cloth, take out all the water, cover from all around and place in a bowl in room temperature covered with a lid, for 3-4 days, washing them with cold water every day, until they are sprouted. Then refrigerate, but you have to wash with fresh cold water every day, and finish them within three-four days.

Irish Breakfast (Serves: 2)

Irish breakfast is famous for ham, sausage and egg. I like to serve with a little piece of a hard cheese and baked beans. Beans not only add flavor, but help digest the food.

Ingredients: 2 thick slices of soda bread or 2 soda biscuits; 1 cup baked pork and beans from a can; 4 strips of bacon; 2 extra-large or jumbo eggs and 2 egg whites to make poached eggs; 2 Italian sweet sausages or andouille sausages; 2 medallions of thick ham; 2 medium potatoes peeled and cut in to 1-inch pieces; ½ tsp. of granulated garlic, divided; salt and fresh-ground black pepper: 2 thick slices of any hard cheese such as gouda, cheddar etc., 2-3 tbsp. canola oil or clarified unsalted butter to cook; hot coffee to serve.

1. Heat a large heavy-bottom pan or a cast-iron skillet with about 2 cups of water, add the sausages, bring to a boil, simmer on low heat for 5 minutes, discard the water, and add 1 tsp. of oil or butter and brown the sausage on medium-high heat for 5 minutes all around. Take out the sausage and keep them warm and tented with aluminum foil in a platter. Wash and dry the pan, add 1 tsp. of butter and spread out the bacon strips and cook crispy, about 1 minute on medium to medium-high heat each side; drain on a paper towel. Take out all the bacon fat. Heat the same pan on medium heat and add the ham medallions and cook on low heat, 1 minute on each side, then cover and cook another 1 minute. Take out and set aside, tented with foil.
2. Heat the same pan on medium heat, add 2 tsp. butter, ¼ tsp. of garlic powder, potatoes, salt and pepper to taste; and stir potatoes to coat with the butter. Sprinkle 1-2 tbsp. of water on potatoes, cover, lower the heat and cook for about 15 minutes until they are soft, stirring once during the cooking (you can cook potatoes a day ahead and just reheat in the pan). When potatoes are done, move them over and add the cooked sausages and ham to keep them warm.
3. While potatoes are cooking, heat the beans in a small pot, until they are bubbling and heated through. Follow the recipe for poached eggs and cook the eggs and keep them warm in a heated serving platter. Heat the biscuit the last minute. Serve all in a heated platter. Place items clockwise: beans, bread, bacon, eggs, sausages, ham, potatoes and the cheese in the center.

Quinoa-Oatmeal Breakfast (Serves: 4)

Quinoa is a plant-based protein that can be used for breakfast, lunch and dinner. Buy whole-grain or natural seed quinoa.

How to Cook: bring 3 cups of water to a boil, add 1 cup old-fashioned oatmeal and ¾ cup quinoa, stir in 2 tbsp. flax seed powder (op), ½ cup slivered almonds, ¼ cup dry cranberries and ½ tsp. cinnamon powder, stir for 5 minutes, cover, and set aside for 20 minutes.

Peanut Butter and Honey:

Serve the hot quinoa-oatmeal in a bowl. Pour in about 1/4-1/2 c warm milk, top with 1 tbsp. peanut butter, ¼ cup grated coconut, ¼ c chopped walnuts, 2 tbsp. chopped pistachios; place a cherry on top, drizzle with 1 tbsp. honey and serve.

Yogurt and Orange Glaze:
Top the hot quinoa-oatmeal bowl with ½ cup non-fat yogurt, slices of half or whole banana, sprinkle with ¼ cup fresh blueberries, place fresh segments of orange, sprinkle with chopped glazed pineapple; place a cherry on the top, and drizzle with orange glaze or apricot jam.

Savory Cheese and Red Bell Peppers for Lunch:

Serve the warm quinoa-oatmeal in a bowl. Top with ½ cup cottage cheese, ¼ cup drained roasted red bell peppers from the jar; slice 4-5 cherry tomatoes on the top, garnish with shaved white cheddar cheese and almonds.

Shredded Chicken with Gravy for Dinner:
Serve the warm quinoa-oatmeal in a bowl. Top with about ½ cup cooked, heated and shredded chicken, pour in ½ cup hot chicken broth and garnish with avocado, fresh-grated radishes, and olives or capers.

Southern Shrimp & Grits Breakfast (Serves: 4)

This old-fashioned healthy meal is not only for breakfast, but you can use it any time of the day, just like we do. If you prefer, you can also serve it with some fruits on the side.

For Grits: 1 cup grits (not quick-cooking); about 4 cups chicken broth, milk or water; 2-3 tbsp. unsalted butter; ¼ tsp. each dry rosemary, salt and fresh ground black pepper or to taste; 1/3 cup grated cheese; orange-pineapple sauce to serve. To garnish: zest and juice of 1 lime.
For the shrimp: 1 tbsp. canola oil and 2 tbsp. unsalted butter; ¼ tsp. granulated garlic; 1 pound, peeled and deveined jumbo shrimp (20-24 count); ½ tsp. granulated garlic, divided; about ¾ cup thick chili sauce.
For the vegetables: 1 tbsp. canola oil and 2 tbsp. unsalted butter; 1 c fresh peeled pearl onion or shallots, whole or cut half in lengthwise; 1 dry pint grape tomatoes; 2-inch fresh ginger peeled and cut into match sticks; 4 fresh jalapeno peppers stemmed, seeded and cut into quarter lengthwise then cut across in half; salt and pepper to taste.

For the grits: Heat the chicken broth in a pot together with butter, rosemary, salt and pepper and bring it to a boil. Reduce the heat to low and slowly whisk in the grits, until it is thick. Keep on stirring for another 4-5 minutes. Whisk in the grated cheese and turn the heat off. Take out the grits into a heated bowl, cover and place the bowl over warm or simmering water.

For the shrimp: About 30 minutes before cooking, sprinkle the garlic over the shrimp and pour the chili sauce; mix well with a wooden spoon and marinate the shrimp. When ready to cook, heat a large heavy-bottom sauté pan over medium-high heat. When pan is hot, add the oil, move around and coat the bottom, add the butter, garlic and wait until the garlic is light brown. Immediately add the shrimp in a single layer (cook shrimp in batches) and cook them on high heat for about 1-1/2 minutes. Turn them over with the help of a knife and spatula and cook another 1-1/2 minutes. Take out the shrimp from the pan onto a platter, and set them aside, loosely covered with a foil.

For the vegetables: Heat the same pan (do not wash), add oil and butter and sauté the onion for 2 minutes, add jalapeno, ginger, tomatoes, garlic, salt and pepper, sauté a for 3-4 minutes, cover and cook vegetables on medium heat for about 5 minutes or until vegetables are soft. When ready to serve, add the shrimp back to the pan and stir together on medium heat for 3-4 minutes, until vegetables and shrimp are heated through.

Serve in heated platter, 2 scoops of grits, top with vegetables, then shrimp and a few more vegetables. Pour the orange-pineapple sauce all around and sprinkle with lime juice and zest and serve hot.

Stuffed Omelet with Cottage Cheese and Fruits
(Serves: 4)

This omelet is baked in the oven. You can prepare it a little ahead and just reheat it in the oven and serve.

Ingredients: 1 tbsp. olive oil; 3-4 tbsp. unsalted butter, plus extra for the baking tray; 1 medium onion, sliced; 1 large bell pepper, cored, seeded and cut into strips; 1 pkg., 12 ounces (340g) baby bella mushrooms cleaned with damp paper towel and sliced; salt and fresh ground black pepper to taste; 1 cup shredded cheddar cheese; 8 extra-large whole eggs or 5 extra-large whole eggs and 3 egg whites; ¼ cup each all-purpose flour and dry non-fat milk; 2 tbsp. fresh milk. To serve: 2 cups fresh baby arugula; 1 container, 8ounces (226g) large curd cottage cheese; 1 cup of pineapple-orange sauce; berries and fruits to serve.

Heat a large sauté pan over medium heat, add the oil and 1tbsp. butter and cook onion for 5 minutes; add little salt and pepper, cover and cook 5 minutes. Open the cover and stir until onions are light brown. Take them out and place in a platter. Add 1 tab butter and sauté red bell pepper strips on medium-high heat for 5 minutes or until soft, take them out over the onion. Add rest of the butter and sauté the sliced mushrooms on high heat, stirring constantly until the mushroom liquid has evaporated, then take them out and add to the onion platter.

Preheat the oven at 375 degrees. Line a 12x10x2 baking tray with parchment paper, grease the paper with the butter. In a large bowl mix together dry milk and flour, add the eggs and 2 tbsp. milk, and whisk together well. Pour the mixture in the prepared tray, moving the egg mixture to cover the tray evenly. Bake at 375 degrees for 12-15 minutes or until the eggs are set and puffed up. Take the tray out of the oven, sprinkle the cheese evenly on the top, then top with the pepper, onion and mushroom mixture. Put the tray back in the oven and heat for 5 minutes until the cheese is melted and the mushrooms are heated through. Take the tray out of the oven. Starting at one short end, lift up the parchment paper and roll the omelet with the help of the parchment paper into a log.

Assemble the platter: While the eggs are cooking, prepare 4 heated plates with some fruits, and serve one scoop of cottage cheese over the bed of arugula. When omelet is done, slice it into four and serve each piece drizzled with the pineapple-orange sauce.

Omelet Breakfast with Cheese Popovers (Serves: 4)

It takes only 40-45 minutes and you have a fancy breakfast.

Ingredients: for the popovers: 2 extra large eggs; 1 cup 2% or whole milk; 1 tab dry milk powder; flour mixture: ½ cup bleached a.p. flour, ¼ tsp. each dry rosemary, granulated garlic; 1-1/4 tsp. salt; 2 tbsp. melted and cooled butter, plus extra for the muffin pan; 2 very thin slices of hard cheese like sharp cheddar, Swiss or pepper-jack.
For the omelet: 3 tbsp. olive oil, butter or ghee; 1 cup each chopped: eggplant, mushrooms, red bell pepper, spinach; ½ cup chopped onion; 1-2 fresh hot pepper, seeded and chopped; 12 eggs; 2 tbsp. grated parmesan, grier or pepper jack shredded.

Sausages : 2 to 4 per person: fully cooked breakfast sausages.

Popovers : Preheat oven at 400 degrees. Spray well and drop about ½ tsp. of soft butter in each muffin cup. In a blender blend eggs, milk and milk powder. Add flour mixture, melted butter and blend just to mix. Pour into 8 muffin cups. Cut cheese slices in quarters, roll them up and push the cheese rolls in the center of the filling. Fill the rest of the empty slots halfway with the water. Bake at 400 degrees for about 35 minutes, or until golden. When done, make a ¼-inch deep slit with the point of a knife in each popover.

Sausages: Cover the frozen sausages with water, and bring them to a boil in a large sauté pan. Rinse out the water, wash the sausages under running water and put back on the stove. Add 1 tsp. of olive oil and cook on very low until browed all over.

Omelet : While popovers are baking, prepare rest of the breakfast. Heat a non-stick or heavy bottom large pan on medium heat add 1 tbsp. butter or olive oil and cook onion, sauté eggplant a little, cover and cook about 4 minutes, add mushrooms and red bell pepper, cook open for 3-4 minutes. Heat a small omelet pan on medium heat, when hot add oil and ¼ of the cooked vegetables and spinach; beat 3 eggs and pour over the vegetables, cook for about 4-5 minutes, tilt the pan and dry out all the juice and turn over and cook the other side, or put in a 400-degree oven (oven proof pan) and let the juice dry out for about 4-5 minutes. Repeat with the rest of the omelets. Serve omelets with warm sausages, popover and some fruits on the side.

Tips: You can make one large omelet with only 8-9 extra large eggs. Cook the vegetables in an ovenproof pan, in butter or oil; when vegetables are soft, pour the beaten eggs, top with cheese and cook 1 side for about 2 minutes. Then cook in a 400-degree oven for about 6-8 minutes, until all liquid has been evaporated; cut and serve.

Spanish Omelet (M: 2)

You don't have to be a genius, just make sure you use a little heavy cream, whip the eggs a lot to incorporate air, use a well-greased heavy-bottom pan or a non-stick hot pan; use a lot of caramelized onion, cooked ham, cilantro and cheese.
Ingredients: 1 tbsp. olive oil and about 4 tbsp. clarified, melted butter; ½ cup cubed ham; 1 medium onion thin sliced, ¼ tsp. granulated garlic and 1/6 tsp. salt; ½ cup each: sliced fresh mushrooms and chopped red bell pepper; ½ cup grated gruyere or aged Mediterranean parmesan cheese; 6 jumbo

eggs; 2-3 tbsp. heavy cream; ½ jalapeno pepper sliced (op); ¼ cup chopped cilantro; fresh fruits, Spanish olives (op), and toasts (your favorite bread) to serve.

1. Heat a large heavy-bottom pan on medium heat. Add 1 tbsp. butter and brown the ham cubes on medium-high heat for 2-3 minutes; cover and take off the stove. Let it rest 1 minute and take ham out in a medium bowl. Add 1 tbsp. olive oil, 1 tbsp. butter and onion. Sauté the onions for 1 minute on medium-high heat, sprinkle garlic, salt, cover and cook on low heat for 5 minutes. When onion is soft, take it out and place with the ham. Add 1 tbsp. butter and sauté mushrooms on medium-high heat until they release their liquid, add red bell pepper and sauté for 1 minute. Take them out and place with the ham.

2. Heat the same pan on low heat with 3 tbsp. of melted butter. In a medium bowl, whip the eggs foamy, add the whipping cream and ½ of the cilantro and whisk well. Now add half of the cheese, jalapeno, the sautéed vegetable, mix well and pour in the pan. Increase the heat to medium-high, whisk the egg mixture in the pan for 1 minute, reduce the heat to low, cover, and cook on low heat for about 3-4 minutes, until the eggs are settled. Sprinkle the cheese, take off the heat, and keep covered for another 3-4 minutes. Loosen the edge with a spatula, then loosen the center, shake the pan to move around the omelet and carefully slide it onto a heated serving platter. Keep warm and make the second omelet.

3. Serve sprinkled with more cheese and cilantro with fruits, Spanish olives, and toasts.

Tip: Do not wash the pan after sautéing the vegetables, you will get the flavors from the vegetable juices.

Italian Frittata (Serves: 4)

You can use this Italian omelet for breakfast, lunch or dinner. You can make with either with or without meat, or just with roasted vegetables. I like to serve with potatoes or toast, but you can use whatever your heart desires, it is that versatile.

Ingredients: 2-3 tbsp. olive oil; one of each medium: zucchini, Japanese eggplant cut in half lengthwise and then sliced ½-inch wide across; 1 medium onion sliced ½-inch wide; 2 garlic cloves chopped fine; 1 jalapeno stemmed, cut in half length, seeded and sliced thin; 8 extra-large eggs; ¼ cup heavy cream; 1 cup cooked ham cut in ½-inch cubes; ½ cup cooked quinoa or ¼ cup seasoned bread crumbs; ¼ cup grated parmesan cheese; 1/3 cup corn fresh basil; ¼ tsp. each salt and fresh ground pepper; ¼ cup dry cranberries (op); 1 medium plum tomato, blanch, peeled, seeded and chopped; to garnish: 1 tsp. fresh thyme or oregano.

Roast the Vegetables

Preheat the oven at 450 degrees. Grease a cast-iron pan with 1 tbsp. oil. Line a large baking sheet with aluminum foil, grease it well and spread out the eggplant, onion and zucchini. Sprinkle with salt, pepper and olive oil, shake the sheet to move the vegetable a little, then bake at 450 degrees for about 20 minutes or until they are soft. Take out of the oven and cool a little.

Preheat the oven at 375 degrees. In a bowl, whisk together eggs and heavy cream together, add garlic, jalapeno, cranberries, quinoa or bread crumbs, cheese, ham, basil, and about ¼ tsp. each salt and pepper and whisk all. Add roasted vegetables, whisk all and pour them in the prepared pan. Sprinkle all over with chopped tomato. Place the pan in the preheated oven and bake the frittata for about 15-20 minutes or until settled and cooked. During the baking turn around the pan half way around and make a cross in the center to let the liquid go to the bottom of the pan, to cook it completely. Let the pan stay in the oven for 5 minutes. Cut and serve hot sprinkled with thyme and a little olive oil, with toasted crusty bread.

Sausage and Eggs on a Bun (Serves: 2)

Comfort food any time of the day! You can celebrate an occasion, feed your soul or just do a simple and a satisfying breakfast.

Ingredients: 2 Andouille or any of your favorite sausages; 4 large eggs; 3 tbsp. butter or oil; 2 large breakfast buns; butter for the buns; roasted garlic and herb powder (McCormick); about 1 cup fresh, cleaned watercress; to serve: 2 roasted red bell peppers, seeded, peeled and cut into strips and some fruits.

1. In a heavy bottom pan add about ½ cup water and sausages, bring them to a boil on high heat. Reduce the heat and simmer on low heat for 5 minutes. Discard the water and wash the pan and the sausages under running water. Cut open the sausages lengthwise and cook them on medium heat in 1 tbsp. of butter or oil for about 15 minutes, or until they are browned on both side.
2. While the sausages are cooking, heat a small pan on medium heat, add 1 tbsp. of oil or butter; break 2 eggs in the pan, break the yolk with a fork, cover and cook on low heat for 5 minutes or until settled. Take off the heat, leave it covered for 1 minute and then scrape the bottom and take out the fried egg in one round piece. Cook and do the same with the other eggs.
3. Cut the buns in half, butter them well and sprinkle the roasted garlic mixture over the butter and heat the buns in a toaster oven or in regular preheated oven at 350 degrees 2-3 minutes or until browned lightly. Assemble the buns first with egg rounds, then sausages and then top with watercress. Serve immediately with roasted peppers and fruits.

Scrambled Eggs with Veggies and Fruits (Serves: 4)

This healthy breakfast can be served with veggies and fruits, alone or with toasts.

Ingredients: 8 extra-large organic brown eggs; 4 tbsp. low fat or 2% milk; 2 tbsp. grated parmesan cheese; 1-2 tbs. olive oil; about ½ pounds, or 12 thick green asparagus, tough bottom part peeled or discarded; 1 medium each of red and orange bell peppers, trimmed and sliced into ½-inch thick rings each; sweet red paprika; 4 slices of whole wheat grain bread; 2 large strawberries each per person or other favorite fruits to serve.

1. Bring about 2 cups of water to a boil in a non-stick or a heavy bottom pan, add the asparagus and cook them a little soft about 2-3 minutes. Discard the water and rinse them under cold running water and place them in a tilted platter to drain off all water. Wash the same pan and heat on medium high heat. When pan is hot, take off the heat, add 1 tsp. of oil and sauté the asparagus and pepper rings shaking the pan for just about 2 minutes, take them out on a heated platter and keep them warm in a low, on and off heated oven. Make the toast and keep them warm.

2. Wash the same pan and heat on the medium heat. Whisk together eggs, milk and grated cheese. When pan is hot, add 1 tbsp. oil, pour the eggs, wait for 1 minute, then start stirring the eggs, slowly scrapping the bottom; stir them for 3-4 minutes and eggs should be done. Take them off the heat, turn them over; if they look a little raw on the top, they will still be cooking off the heat, in the hot pan. Serve immediately: lay down the asparagus, top with pepper rings, and then top with scrambled eggs. Garnish with paprika. Serve with toast and fruits.

Oatmeal with Berries (Serves: 2)

The best breakfast you can have is oatmeal and one boiled egg in the morning.
Ingredients: ¾-1 cup silver-cut oatmeal or 1 cup quick-cooking oatmeal; 3 cups of water or milk or a combination of both; ¼ cup dry cranberries; 1 tbsp. flax seed powder (op); to serve: milk, fresh fruits, brown sugar or molasses, dark raisins (op); 1 hard-boiled egg or whole-wheat toast.

1. Bring water or milk to a boil, add the quick-cooking oatmeal, stir well, simmer on low heat for 5 minutes, add flax seed powder and cranberries. Turn off the heat, and add about ¼ cup of water or milk (so that it does not stick in the bottom). Let it sit for 5 minutes and serve with milk, fruits, brown sugar, egg and/or toasts.
2. To cook the silver-cut oatmeal. Bring about 3 cups of water to a boil, add the oatmeal, stir well, bring to a boil, lower the heat, and simmer for 25-30 minutes until oats are soft.

Tip: Oats are super food. They have protein, fiber, magnesium, potassium, zinc, copper, and thiamin etc. Silver-cut have whole-grain fiber.

Pancakes with Fruit (M: 8 pancakes)

We make pancakes for breakfast and even for lunch. The lunch one we eat with raita and chutney, and the breakfast one with fruits. When fresh blueberries and strawberries are in season, we splurge and make all sorts of things loaded with the berries.

Ingredients: 1 large egg; 1-1/2 cups buttermilk; 2 cups all-purpose flour; 1-1/2 tsp. baking powder; ¾ tsp. baking soda, ¼ tsp. salt; 1 tbsp. sugar (op); 1 tsp. celery seeds; ½ cup sliced green onions (scallions); ½ cup dry cranberries or 1 cup chopped fresh strawberries (or frozen; just lightly rinse fast under cold tap water), (unthawed) blueberries; 2-3 tbsp. melted butter; canola or olive oil to cook. To serve: either apple sauce, 1 recipe of apple filling, or maple, strawberry or your favorite syrup.

In a medium bowl, whisk together ½ cup water and the egg together then whisk in the buttermilk. Sift together the dry ingredients flour, baking powder, baking soda, salt and sugar, add the celery seeds, sliced onion and mix with a fork. Let it rest 20 minutes, then fold in butter and berries. Whisk just enough to mix the ingredients (don't over-mix it), leaving the small lumps in the batter.

Heat the oven at 200 degrees to keep the pancakes warm. Line a rack with aluminum foil. Heat a 12-inch cast iron skillet or a heavy-bottom pan over the medium-high heat for 2 minutes. When ready to cook, lower the heat to medium. Drop 3-4 drops of oil, spread it out with the metal spatula and then drop about a 3/4th ladleful (or about ½ cup) pancake batter into the hot skillet, spread it out with a fork to about 6-inches diameter. Cook for about 2-1/2 minute on the first side, light brown, turn over and cook the other side for about 2 minutes until light brown. Turn the pan around halfway during the cooking for even browning. Serve the pancakes right out of the pan for full flavor, or heat in a low oven and serve later when all are done. Serve either with apple sauce, apple filling, maple, strawberry or your favorite syrup.

Tip: Celery seeds are loaded with nutrients and taste very good with flour mixtures. The author H.K. Bakhru describes in his book: "Herbs That Heal," (page 59) "Celery is an excellent basic food. It is one of the best sources of mineral salts and vitamins ... healing power and curative properties, helps arthritis, rheumatism and gout, nervous system, blood disorders, respiratory disorders, kidney and gall stones, insomnia, etc."

Fruits and Protein Pancakes (M: 6, 4 inches)

These are flourless pancakes. You can prepare the batter a day ahead, keep covered, airtight with plastic wrap and then with a lid in the refrigerator. Just mix the protein shake powder or almond flour, and make hot pancakes just before serving.

Ingredients: 1 Granny Smith or a firm apples peeled, cored and grated; 2 extra-large eggs; about ¾ pound or 1-1/2 cups sweet potatoes baked and cut into ½-inch pieces (or cook in microwave for 5-6 minutes); ¼ to ½ cup dry cherries or cranberries; 1 ripe banana mashed; about ¾ cup protein shake powder or almond flour; ½ tsp. cinnamon; 2 tbsp. melted butter or canola oil for cooking; maple syrup or apple sauce to serving.

1. About 1 hour before cooking, mix the ingredients in the order they are listed.

2. How to cook pancakes: Heat a cast-iron pan on medium-high heat. When heated, add 1 tsp. butter or oil to the pan, and using a ladle drop in a ladleful of batter in the pan, spread out about ½-inch thick with a fork, cover with the lid and cook for about 2 minutes on medium-high heat, turn around the pan lower the heat to medium and cook about 2 minutes until golden brown; take off the heat for one minute. Drizzle 3-4 drops of butter or oil over the pancake, loosen all around and turn over the pancake. If you prefer, cover the pancake with a plate, turn over the pancake onto the plate and slide it back into the pan and cook the other side 3 minutes on medium-high heat and 1-2 minutes on medium heat until golden. Serve hot with or without syrup or apple sauce.

Energy Pancakes (M: 8, 4-inch, ½-inch thick)

You can prepare the batter a day ahead just as listed above.

Ingredients: 2 ripe banana mashed; 3 extra-large eggs; 1 sweet potato baked, peeled and cut into ½-inch pieces; ¾ cup wheat germ or cooked cup almond or walnut powder; 1 firm apple peeled, cored and grated; purified butter (ghee) or canola oil for cooking; ¼ cup slivered and toasted almonds, fresh pomegranate seeds and fresh blueberries and honey for serving.

1. Mix the ingredients in the order they are listed and Follow the procedure above.
2. Serve hot garnished with pomegranate, blueberries, almonds and drizzled with about 1 tsp. of Honey.

Cheeses

Cooking with cheese or serving cheeses at dinner parties is a personal preference. Soft or hard cheese can both be used in cooking or be served at the table.

Cheeses are rich in calcium. They are made both with raw and pasteurized milk, mostly cows, sheep, goats and buffalos. Cheese is made basically in three stages: 1. Heating the milk to certain high temperature, adding the rennet liquid (liquid extracted from the lining of the stomach of certain animal) to separate the curd from the whey; 2. Gathering the curd and concentrating it to prepare for cheeses; 3. The final stage is where the curd is put away and ripened for perfect flavor. For most of the soft cheese like ricotta, the final ripening stage is avoided. In India, the soft cheeses are made by separating the milk with white vinegar. The milk is separated and the curd is compacted and pressed under a heavy pressure, then cut it to blocks. Sometimes it is cubed, lightly browned and added to the dishes, or just used as it is in making sweets, where it is cooked further.

It is a matter of preference which one you like best. In the United States, the imported cheeses made with raw milk are allowed to be sold only if they are aged over two months. The aged cheeses mostly have more flavor. Try a few of them, the fresh cut, and the best tasting, before you buy them. Depending on the type of cheese, they have about 50% to 70% water and rest is mostly protein and solids. Cheeses are loaded with proteins, so use them at the end of the cooking and at a low temperature, to avoid the fat separating from cheese.

When buying American cheeses, you will notice the word IDM (In Dry Matter), and on most imported cheeses m.g. (matiere grasse) shows the actual percentage of butterfat content. The correct percentage of butterfat is hard to determine because cheese are constantly in the drying stage. The evaporation and ripen stages change the percentage.

Store cheeses in the refrigerator, mostly in the bottom boxes. I rub a little soft butter on the cut side, wrap them in foil, plastic wrap or wax paper for short period of time. For a longer period of time, or to wrap a large block of cheese, dip a piece of cheese cloth, to wrap cheese in a single layer, in ¼ C of vinegar, rinse out the vinegar completely, and wrap cheese cloth around cheese, then wrap cheese in another plain cheese cloth, put in a zip-lock bag airtight in a box in the refrigerator.

When slicing cheese from a wheel or a large piece, try to cut one side, and keep on slicing the same side every time you need to slice cheese. So that the rest of cheese is not disturbed, will not dry out, and will develop flavor. Hard cheese stays fresh longer. Hard cheeses are good for the heart if eaten one slice, raw, on daily basis with crusty bread, fruits and vegetables. Wine and cheese pair well when they are served with the same region. If I am serving French cheeses, I will try to pair them with French wines.

For leftover cheese either from a party or dried ends from the refrigerator, take out the rind, grate or chop them, season with you cooked garlic, onion and mushrooms and make a topping for vegetables, bread or make into cheese sauces and have macaroni and cheese. Sharp blue cheese, mixed and pureed with buttermilk and some other cheese, makes a good salad dressing.

Measurement: 1 cup grated cheese = 3 ounces, such as Parmesan.

1 cup shredded cheese = 4 ounces

How to Make Paneer (Indian Cheese)

(Makes about 1 pound, 16 ounces)

Indian Paneer is made for various types of cooking. It resemble feta cheese, and when stacked, pressed and chilled, you can cut into cubes, dust in flour and brown in 1-2 tbsp. butter, and then add to any meat, bean or vegetable dish. For sweets I use one gallon whole milk, and ¼ c vinegar; for the savory dishes I use lemon juice (1/3 c) or yogurt (2 c). Lemon and yogurt give a very soft texture that goes well with curries or kebabs.

Ingredients: 2-3 drops of oil or purified butter; 1 container, 1 gallon (3.78 litre) whole milk and ½ cup lemon juice, or 2 cups whole milk yogurt or 5 tablespoons cider vinegar.

Heat a large, heavy bottom pot on medium-heat. Add the oil or the butter, move around to coat the bottom. Take off the heat and add one gallon of whole milk. Place the pot on medium-high heat and, stirring occasionally, bring it to a boil. When milk starts to boil, lower the heat and add 2 cup yogurt or 5 tbsp. cider vinegar, stir well. Keep the heat on high until it starts to boil over again, then lower the heat to constant simmer, stir for about 15 minutes, until milk is separated and the curd starts floating on the top and the liquid (whey) is light lemon color. Turn off the heat, cover the pot and let it sit there for 15 minutes, until it is cooled slightly.

Have a large strainer ready with 3-4 layers of cheese cloth or a thin cotton kitchen towel, over a large bowl. Carefully with a large ladle, take out the curd and place on cheese cloth, then pour in the rest of the liquid. Shake the curd and place cheese cloth on a dinner plate. Now spread out cheese about 2 inches high in a square or a block. Wrap the towel around cheese tightly, place another dinner plate upside down over cheese and place some weight over the top plate (such as1 pound can of tomato sauce). Tilt the plate inside a large bowl or over a platter and leave there for at least 3-4 hours or until cheese is drained out. Discard the drained liquid. Now take out cheese cloth, place cheese carefully on the plate, cover with plastic wrap and refrigerate overnight to firm.

When ready to use just cut in cubes and add to the liquid. If making the kebabs, or salad, etc., cut cheese into 1-1/2-inch cubes, sprinkle with 2 tbsp. all-purpose flour. Heat a heavy bottom pan with 2 tbsp. butter and place the cubes in the butter on medium heat. When it is golden brown underneath, take the pan off the heat, let the pan rest for 5 minutes, sprinkle some melted butter on the top and carefully turn over the cubes and brown the other side. Use right away or refrigerate covered until needed. You can freeze cheese, wrap cheese well in plastic, and place in an airtight container and freeze up to three months. In India, these cheese cubes are used in fancy cooking.

Tip: The whey (liquid) that comes from making cheese is loaded with protein. I use lemon juice or yogurt to make cheese and save the whey for drinking or cooking.

Famous cheeses from around the world

These are some of the famous cheeses that I found are common, tasty and most of them are easy to find in most of the gourmet stores and/or supermarkets. I like to try them, especially when they are just arrived in the supermarkets, whether they are on sale or not, and find the tasty ones. Each time I buy a block of cheese, I try to find a new one. This is the only way you get to taste different types of chesses.

Abondance: This French cheese is buttery, mild, has a fruity and a nutty flavor.

Asiago Veccho: This is a sharp and various-stages cheese. The texture can range from soft to hard. It is made with cow's milk.

Beaufort: This French cheese is made with cow's milk and is made with cooked and pressed curd, and is creamy and fruity flavor.

Beemster Graskaas: This cheese is named after the Beemster cows. It is produced during the summer with a creamy milk so the flavor is unique and creamy. It has a medium firm consistency with a short maturing period.

BelGioioso: This round slicing provolone has a great taste.

Boerenkaas: This farmer's gouda cheese from Netherlands has a sharp and rich flavor with a nutty aroma.

Brie: This French pasteurized cow's-milk cheese has a soft, edible rind, a buttery and a nutty flavor. It is one of the best to serve on cheese platter.

Caerphilly: This is from Whales, and has a mild creamy and a lemony flavor.

Camembert: This is a cow's-milk cheese from France. It is similar to Brie but has a stronger flavor.

Cashel Blue: This is from Ireland, creamy, tangy and a little stronger than blue cheese. It is named after the Cashel Rock.

Cheddar: This is my favorite cheese for cooking. The American cheddar is softer but the British cheddar is firm and can be crumbly, with a sharp, nutty flavor. Low-fat cheddar is much lower in calories and fat.

Cinco Lanzas: This is from Spain. It has a blend of goat, cow and sheep's milk. It has the buttery flavor of an aged cheese and gives a rich flavor of nuts, and aromas of thyme and rosemary on the palate.

Colby Cheese: This is an American cow's-milk soft cheese with a mild flavor, and a very good melting cheese.

Cottage Cheese: This is a soft, fresh and an unripened cheese. It has small or medium lumps in cheese with a mild sour flavor. On an average it has about 4% fat. Low-fat cottage cheese has even less fat.

Cream Cheese: This is an unripened soft and fresh cheese. It is very common to use in cooking as well as for snacks. This cheese is made by boiling the milk and separating the curd from the whey. Then the cream and the milk are added and whisked together in the curd. The fat is taken out to make it low-fat cream cheese.

Danish Fontina: This is a semi-soft, smooth and partially skim-milk mild cheese.

Degli Sposi: This is a low-fat, fresh, very delicate and slightly creamy cheese.

Emmental: This Swiss cheese is semi-firm, smooth, mild and has a fruity and nutty flavor.

Feta Cheese: This cheese is found in various stages and textures. It is made with cow's, goat's or sheep's milk and is very common in Mediterranean countries.

Fol Epi Cheese: This is imported from France. It is lemon-colored and has a sweet and a nutty flavor.

Fontina: This is very tasty and creamy cheese. Use it in making creamy dishes.

Fontina Val D'Aosta: This is a firm-variety cheese with a nutty flavor from the Piedmont reign.

Goat Cheese: It has various stages from creamy to firm, with mild to pungent flavors.

Gorgonzola Dolce: This is a soft blue cheese with creamy texture and mild flavor.

Gorgonzola Naturale: This is an aged cheese and can crumble. It is more pungent and a little sharper than Gorgonzola Dolce.

Gouda: This is a cow's-milk cheese from Denmark that can be semi-firm to firm. Aged Gouda is crumbly with a sharp flavor, which is good to snack on. Some doctors advise to use the firm-type, which is good for the arteries.

Gruyere: American Gruyere and Fontina cheeses from Wisconsin are buttery, creamy and full flavor. The cow's-milk Gruyere from France and Switzerland can be strong and fruity.

Havarti: This cheese comes from Denmark, made with cow's milk, and is mostly flavored with herbs and caraway seeds. Besides giving the herbal flavor, the Caraway seeds in general help digest the food.

Jarlsberg Cheese: This is a Swiss cheese made with cow's milk. It is firm and has a sweet, fruity flavor.

La Pecora Vera: Pecorino cheese with white texture.

Locatelli Romano Cheese: Imported from Italy. You can grate it over finished dishes.

Mahon: This Spanish cow's-milk hard, creamy cheese melts in your mouth, and is very tasty for snacking, and thin-sliced is good for sandwiches. Try It, you will love it.

Manchego: This is a sheep's-milk cheese from Spain. It is a various-stage cheese from semi-firm to firm, with a nutty and salty flavor.

Marzolino: This Tuscan cheese is brushed with tomato concentrate for extra flavor and is soft and sweet.

Monterrey Jack Cheese: **This is one of my favorite cheeses. I serve as snacks and use in stuffing (like in stuffed shells) It is sharp** and you can see the red-pepper flakes in cheese.

Mozzarella: You cannot beat the taste of fresh-made mozzarella cheese. It is light with full cheese flavor. I use it with salad, on pizza, to stuff the Indian Paratha (bread), and use all over in place of Paneer.

Lioni Burrata Con Panna: A new locally made mozzarella cheese called came out in the market. It is a traditional mozzarella with a cream-filled center. You serve with prosciutto, and I also like it over the heirloom tomato salad. I found it in the Kings Supermarket in New Jersey.

Parmesan: It is a cow's-milk hard cheese. You can even find it grated in the supermarkets, which is very convenient to use in crumbs, dusting and mixing with other ingredients. It has a sweet, nutty and fruity flavor.

Parmigiano Reggiano: This is a hard and very dry cheese. You can grate this just before serving on pasta and vegetable dishes or use in stuffing, etc. It is salty but very flavorful.

Pecorino Romano: A white cheese packed with a strong pepper and salt flavors and is made of sheep's milk.

President: This fat-free Feta cheese is good to cut in cubes or crumble on a salad.

Provolone: This cow's-milk cheese from Italy can be found semi-firm and sliced and in firm version; salty, spicy and nutty.

Raschera: This is from Italy. It is a hard, pressed, raw cow's-milk cheese. The flavor is a little spicy. When it is aged, it can be a little salty with a soft, fine flavor.

Reypenaer: This is a Dutch made cheese. They are very good in making cheeses. Just like Gouda cheese it is hard, flavorful and takes one year to mature.

Ricotta: This is also a fresh, soft and an unripened cheese. The texture is almost like a thick yogurt with a soft and fine grains or clumps. Italian or American ricotta cheese is available in whole or part skim milk. This soft cheese is good for cooking, stuffing and serving with salad etc. I use this lot in Indian desserts:

first I dry out the water content by spreading out on an aluminum foil-lined tray in the oven, then mix it with other ingredients. It serves the purpose of reduced milk (Mava or Khoya).

Roquefort: This is a sheep's-milk blue cheese from France. It has a strong, salty and a mineral flavor. You can crumble it over salad, or puree with buttermilk and make salad dressing.

Stella Asiago Cheese: This is a great table cheese that has a mild flavor.

Toledo: This is from Portugal. This cheese has all three: sheep, cow and goat's milk, and in texture it is a semi-hard cheese. Cheese is creamy and mild.

Il Turtufo: With Tuscan full flavor, this cheese is infused with white truffles of San Miniato.

Urnsacher: This cheese is from Switzerland. It is dry and crumbly and good to snack on. The flavor is spicy but earthy.

Vermont Cheddar: The extra sharp Vermont cheddar is very special and we love it. This cheese is aged over two years and is good for snacking as well as for cooking.

Yancey Cheddar: This cheese is made in upstate New York; the Hot Wasabi or Horseradish cheddar is perfect for snacking.

Lunches, Soups, Salads, and Sandwiches

Burrito Bowl (Serves: 2)

You can either make the traditional burrito on a large tortilla or just serve in a bowl with quinoa or rice.

Ingredients: About 2 cups shredded romaine lettuce, about ½ cup vinaigrette: 1-1/2 cup cooked quinoa; 1 cup each cilantro pesto or cilantro chutney, sour cream and/or horseradish sauce, sriracha sauce and/or hot ketchup (see sauces and chutney section); 1 can 15 oz. (425g) black beans (frijoles negros) or 1 cup fermented beans; ½ pound roasted chicken sliced or cubes; 1 cup each: chopped fresh tomato cubes and hard cheese (jack, Swiss) cubes; 1 ripe avocado halved just before serving; cilantro springs; lemon wedges to serve.

Vinaigrette (about 1 cup)

In a bowl whisk together: 1/3 cup sherry vinegar with 1/3 cup e.v. olive oil, then grate in 1 large garlic clove, 1 tsp. sugar and 1 tbsp. prepared mustard.

Quinoa (M: about 1-1/2 cups)

Bring ¾ cup of water to a boil, add ½ tsp. turmeric powder or ¼ tsp. saffron threads, 1 tbsp. butter, a little salt and pepper to taste, then add ½ cup whole-grain quinoa. Stir well and let it cook for 5 minutes. Cover, turn off the heat, and let it rest for 15 minutes. Add 1 tbsp. butter, fluff with a fork and serve warm.

Assemble the bowl: Use two medium attractive serving bowls. Place the shredded lettuce evenly in two bowls, sprinkle with 1 tbsp. each vinaigrette. Top with quinoa, black beans, and sprinkle 2 tbsp. of vinaigrette; top with slices of chicken; then pour some pesto/chutney over the chicken, top with avocado, tomato, cheese, cilantro and pour 2-3 tbsp. of vinaigrette all over. Serve with lemon wedges and extra sauces on the side.

Tip: This is a very healthy, attractive and nutritional bowl. Just make sure you serve a lot of cilantro sauce.

Organic lunches

Organic food is very popular now-a-days. It is healthy and eye-pleasing when you get used to it. There are restaurants that specialize in organic food.

Organic Turkey Wrap (Serves: 1)

Ingredients: 1 large spinach tortilla; ½ cup hummus; about ¾ cup baby spinach leaves washed and pat-dried with paper towels; 2 large slices of tomato; ½ of a ripe hass avocado sliced in to 3 wedges lengthwise; 1 to 2 thin and long slices of low-salt roasted turkey; 1 slice (about 4-by-5-inches) of hard provolone, imported Swiss or your favorite cheese; 2 tbsp. lemon chutney or extra for dipping, or a few drops of lime juice; fruits and berries to serve on side.

Heat the tortilla over the stove lightly on both sides or follow the directions on the package. Spread out the hummus over the tortilla almost up to the edges, spread out the spinach leaves in the center, top with tomatoes, spread out the avocado wedges over the tomato, top with the half folded turkey slice, then cheese, squeeze lime juice or lemon chutney. Fold two sides over the ingredients tightly, fold remaining two edges one at a time, overlapping the first two sides, for a tight wrap about 6-inches long and 4-inches wide.

Slice the wrap on a diagonal basis in to two pieces. Serve with seasonal fruit like watermelon cubes and berries. You can also serve with some extra chutney on the side for dipping.

Quinoa and Grilled/Roasted Chicken (Serves: 1)

Quinoa is a grain, loaded with protein and amino acid, and cooked faster than rice.

Ingredients: 1 whole or half of the boneless and skinless chicken half, marinated with sprinkle of cayenne pepper and granulated garlic and 1 tsp. of canola oil for 30 minutes; 1 cup cooked quinoa with fresh herbs added; 1 plum tomato chopped in large cubes; 1 cup baby spinach leaves; ¼ medium red onion thin-sliced; cooking olive oil spray; 1/2 cup vinaigrette: a mixture whisked together of 2 tbsp. Champagne vinegar and 4 tbsp. extra-virgin olive oil, ½ tsp. Dijon mustard, and salt and fresh-ground black pepper to taste.

Spray the chicken with the cooking spray and salt and pepper lightly. Grill the chicken on high heat one side until browned, then turn over and grill the other side at medium heat until cooked to internal temperature of about 160 degrees. Or roast the chicken at 400 degrees in preheated oven, covered with loose aluminum foil, for about 10-15 minutes (depending on size of the breast) in a baking tray. Let the chicken cool slightly.

While chicken is roasting, heat a saucepan on low heat, spray with cooking spray and place the onion, tomatoes and spinach in it. Cover the pan and cook on medium heat about 5-6 minutes, until spinach is little wilted and onion is cooked slightly.

Assemble the platter: Place the warm quinoa on half of the plate and the tomato mixture on the other half. Top with the grilled or roasted chicken. Sprinkle with Vinaigrette, salt and fresh ground black pepper to taste.

Lentil Patties with Grilled Watermelon and Pineapple (Serves: 4)

Have you ever had the grilled watermelon and pineapple? If not, you should try them one day in the summer when the watermelon is in season.

(1) Lentil Patties (M: 4 large)

Ingredients: 1-1/2 cups whole green lentils (American) with skin on and picked over; ¼ tsp. turmeric powder (op); 1/4 cup soft cilantro stems and leaves, sliced thin; about 2 tbsp. canola oil for cooking; thick salsa (or ½ cup crushed tomatoes mixed with 3 tbsp. ketchup, ¼ tsp. granulated garlic and 1 tbsp. lemon-pepper mix); 1 large egg; salt and pepper to taste; 1/3 cup grated parmesan cheese; ½ cup roasted peanuts or almonds; for the crust: 1 large egg whisked for the egg wash; 4 tbsp. fine-grated coconut mixed with 2 tbsp. fine cornmeal. To serve: 1 cup plain yogurt and fresh cilantro or mint leaves; and grilled watermelon, pineapple and lemons.

In a medium pot add lentils and 2 cups water. Bring to a boil, add turmeric and the cilantro, cover, lower the heat to a constant simmer. Cook for about 25 minutes until they are soft. Stir a few times for even cooking. When done, dry out all the liquid over the heat. Take the pot off the heat.

Preheat the oven at 400 degrees. Line a heavy-bottom tray with aluminum foil. Grease the tray with 1 tbsp. canola oil. Mash the lentils in a pot with a potato masher. Add salsa, egg, cheese and salt and pepper to taste. Next, mash all together again, mixing it well. Fold in peanuts or almonds. Using a large cap of a jar about 3-inch diameter (from 3 pound peanut butter jar), line the cap with plastic wrap. Divide the lentil mixture into 4 portions. Take one portion at a time, press down over the plastic and make a thick and compact patty. Brush the patty with the egg wash, then sprinkle with the cornmeal and coconut mixture. Pick up the cap, turn over the greased baking tray and pull out the plastic carefully, inverting the patty over the foil. Make all same way. Brush the patties on the top with egg wash and sprinkle the cornmeal mixture. Drizzle some oil on the top. Place the tray in the oven and bake for 25-30 minutes, until they are browned underneath. Serve with a dollop of yogurt and garnished with cilantro or mint, serve together with grilled fruits.

(2) Grilled Watermelon and Pineapple

Ingredients: 4 slices of watermelon peeled (buy large melon and cut out smaller pieces, they are more tasty); 4 slices of golden pineapple peeled and cored; canola oil, salt and pepper to taste. To serve: 4 lemons halved and grilled over the grill; some other fruits or berries to sprinkle over the platter.

Prepare an indoor grill or a grill pan on medium-high heat. Grease it well with a thick and oily paper towel. Brush the melon and pineapple slices with oil on both sides then sprinkle with salt and pepper, and drizzle a few drops of lemon juice. Grill them on high heat about 2 minutes each side until they have grill marks. Do the same with the halved lemons to serve on the side. Serve warm in the warm platter with the lentil patties.

Tip: You can make bean patties with almost any cooked beans. I like lentils because they cook fast and are very healthy. You can make patties a day before and brown them in the oven or in a cast-iron pan with some oil, just before serving.

Vegetarian Cheese Baked Samosa (Pockets)

(M: about 18-20)

If you ever ate at an Indian restaurant or with an Indian family, you must have hard the Samosa. These are triangle-shape pockets filled with vegetables or meat, and then deep-fried. Here I will show you how to bake them easily.

Ingredients:

For the Crust: 3 cups (12 oz,) shredded sharp white cheddar cheese; 3 cups all-purpose unsifted flour plus ½ cup for dusting; ¼ cup corn starch; 1 stick (8 tbsp.) cold unsalted butter plus 2 tbsp. melted butter for brushing; 1 cup thick plain yogurt; ½ tsp. baking soda.

Ingredients for the Filling: About 1-1/2 to 2 pounds red potatoes boiled, peeled and mashed into about ½-inch pieces; fresh-ground spices: 1 large onion sliced thick about ½-inch wide; 4 large garlic cloves halved; 2-3 serrano peppers chopped, or to taste; 1-inch fresh ginger chopped; 2 tbsp. canola oil; 1 tsp. caraway seeds; ½ tsp. turmeric; 2tbsp. lemon-pepper mix or green mango powder (amchoor) to taste;1cup cooked peas; ½ cup dry cranberries;1 cup roasted and chopped peanuts or walnuts (op); ½ cup chopped cilantro or parsley; salt and pepper to taste.

For the Filling: Grind the spices first in the blender with very little water. Heat a large non-reactive frying pan on medium heat. Add the oil, and when it is hot, add the caraway seeds. Let the seeds brown lightly for 30 seconds, add the ground spices, turmeric, and little salt. Stir for 1 minute, cover and cook on low heat for 5 minutes. Open the cover and add the mashed potatoes, lemon-pepper mix, salt to taste. Increase the heat on medium-high and stir constantly for 6-7 minutes, until potatoes are a little brown and crispy underneath. Add peas and nuts, cranberries and cilantro, stir 5 minutes and take off the heat. Leave partially covered and let it cool.

For the Crust: In a large bowl combine flour and baking soda, and mix well. Grate the cold butter over the flour and mix well. Add the yogurt and mix well with a wooden spoon. Now slowly incorporate the shredded cheese. As soon as it is combined, use your hands and knead the dough for 30 seconds. Divide the dough into 3 portions.

Assemble the Samosas: Refrigerate 2 portions or keep covered with a dry kitchen towel, and work fast. Take out a large piece of plastic wrap. Make a long disk of the dough, dust the plastic with the flour well, and roll out the dough, about 8-inch wide and 12 inches long. Turn over the rolled-out dough (it is important so that it does not stick), and cut 4-inch squares, trimming out uneven edges. You will have 6 squares. Take about ½ cup filling in an ice cream scoop, place on each square, press it down, then seal the edges across with water, making a triangle. Press the edges with the tines of a fork. Place the prepared Samosa, on a well-greased aluminum-foil lined large (12 x 18-inch) baking tray, close to each other, in a row. Do the same with the rest. Then refrigerate the trays for 5 minutes. Brush with melted butter.

Bake the Samosas: Adjust the oven rack at upper-middle and lower-middle. Preheat the oven at 350 degrees. Bake Samosas in a preheated oven for 30 to 35 minutes. Rotate the baking trays after 15 minutes for even baking. Turn off the oven and leave the trays in the oven for another 10 minutes to crisp the crust. Serve warm with Chutney.

Meat Samosas

Follow the method above for vegetarian cheese Samosa. Instead of the potatoes, just brown about 1-1/2 pound, ground chicken or beef in 1 tbsp. oil, stirring constantly, on medium-high heat for about 15 minutes, or until the meat is cooked and browned, and then add to the ground spices. You do not need any lemon-pepper mix or mango powder.

Healthy Lunches

1.   Whenever possible, buy organic food and fresh food.
2.   Bring your own lunch from home and save money and calories.
3.   Make egg or tuna salad with low-fat mayonnaise, or yogurt and/or with diced or grated celery, onion, carrots, and walnuts.
4.   Make your own vegetable soup with beans and sprinkle grated cheese after heating the soup or whisked in 1 egg in the hot soup.
5.   Grill or broil chicken, salmon or lean steak, cut up in bite-size pieces, add cooked or grated vegetables and top with reduced balsamic vinegar or yogurt.
6.   You can make marinated tofu, tomatoes sandwiches with bean patties (rinse chickpeas from the can, mash them up, add garlic powder, oregano and a little ketchup or tomato paste, whisk in an egg and some bread crumbs, make patties and brown both side in a little oil In a cast-iron pan). Make open sandwiches, they look pretty and are easy to eat with knives and fork.
7.   Make quick, low-fat, cheese-grilled sandwiches and serve with a can of tomato soup or just with beef marrow broth.
8.   Serve low-sodium roasted turkey, chicken or roast beef with salad.
9.   The best way to prepare lunch is to prepare night before. This way you will have enough time to make a good lunch.

10. Use chutneys or low-fat yogurt as a dressing and topping for soups and sandwiches.

11. Use fresh fruits as desserts, drizzle some honey and peanut butter on halved bananas, it is loaded with protein and very satisfying.

12. For snacks, use fresh fruits, popcorn, roasted chickpeas mixed with some puffed rice, spelt pretzel sticks and mixed nuts with dry cranberries.

Secrets to Making Healthy & Tasty Soups

Add roasted vegetables: for 4 servings - Line a large baking tray with aluminum foil, grease it well then peel two medium onions and cut them in quarters; halve 2 medium plum tomatoes; cut and core 1 red bell pepper into quarters; halve 4 to 6 large button mushrooms and 10 garlic cloves and spread them all over the baking tray. Cover it airtight with foil and bake at 350 degree for 45 minutes. When roasted puree them with chicken, vegetable or beef broth; add to the soup at the end.

Serve soup sprinkled with two fresh herbs (such as parsley and thyme) and flavored toasts and/or grilled cheese sandwiches or vegetable wraps.

Tips for Making Salad

1. Make a colorful and nutritious salad by adding different items. If using bittermelon, slice it paper-thin and dip slices in lemon juice just before serving. If prefer add cheese cubes or chickpeas.

2. If it is your main meal, then add some dairy and protein such as cheese, almonds, walnuts, tofu, etc. If you wish you can also add sliced, grilled, seared, roasted or broiled steak, chicken, turkey or boiled eggs.

3. If it is a side dish to go with the meal, then add shredded or shaved hard cheeses, such as: parmesan, gouda, or Swiss, etc. You can also add crumbled blue cheese, cottage cheese or soft goat cheese, together with some sunflower seeds, etc. Sunflower seeds kill pollution. We love to use soaked or sprouted chickpeas and bean sprouts with some oil sprinkled on them. They are loaded with protein. Cooked quinoa, faro and purple rice are also healthy.

4. Lettuce is the base, so add the bite-size pieces of iceberg, or healthy romaine, or tasty butter lettuce. You can also add some other greens such as watercress, arugula a peppery taste, mesclun or a little shredded red cabbage or broccoli florets. If you want, you can brush some large kale leaves with oil, and roast them 4-5 minutes at 400 degrees, or until they are crunchy, and serve.

5. I like some roasted vegetables such as beets, sliced acorn squash, tomato and onions. You can bake 4 medium beets rubbed with a little oil, in a pie plate covered airtight, for about 1 to 1-1/2 hours; cool, peel and slice on the top. Beets are helpful for high blood pressure and are loaded with nutrients. You can also grill corn on the cob and use shucked in the salad.

6. If you can find some fresh okra, wash, slice and add to the salad. The silky part that you don't see much in raw okra is very healthy. Also, add thin-sliced kirby cucumber with skin on. Skin is the best part, and cucumber juice is heart-healthy. Add some fresh herbs such as parsley, cilantro, basil, etc.

7. Slice fresh tomatoes, and drizzle some olive oil before adding to salad. They have lycopene, good for the eyes. Sliced radishes and leaves are good too.

8. Use avocado whenever available, it has plant- based fat. If you prefer, add some fresh parsley or cilantro, too. When in season use some kiwi fruits, they are loaded with nutrition. In Australia, they make salad, soup, pies and cakes with it.

9. Make a simple dressing of 1 tsp. zest, 1 part lemon or lime or champagne or cider vinegar (about ¼ cup), and 2 parts of extra virgin olive oil (about 1/3 to ½ cup), together with 1-2 large cloves of grated or crushed garlic, and a tablespoon of prepared mustard (serves: 2). Have the dressing ready and pour in a thin stream just before serving. Lime zest and juices both are healthy, they have less acid and more nutrition. I also whip in a blender blue cheese with some buttermilk and a little salt and pepper to taste, and pour on the top, before serving. Also use pomegranate molasses as a dressing. You do not need any salt if using the shredded cheese.

10. Make salad in layers ahead, and sprinkle some green onion and cheese on each layer, top with tomatoes and refrigerate covered; pour dressing just before serving.

Beef Marrow Broth (M: about 2-1/2 quarts)

As you know, processed meat is very unhealthy. Also, too much red meat is harmful, so consume in moderation. To cut down the effect of the red meat I use a lot of vegetables in broth. If I am using about 6 pounds of bones with some meat on, then I like to use about 3 to 4 pounds of vegetables. I will use one-third celery – it takes inflammation away and helps reduce weight; one-third root vegetables that give vitamins and flavors such as carrots, beets, parsnips, etc.; and one-third leafy vegetables and herbs that cut down on pollution and give vitamins and minerals, such as kale, spinach, collard greens, beet greens, cilantro, rosemary, oregano, turmeric, tomato, onion, garlic and ginger. Turmeric powder or roots are antioxidants, and ginger takes care of the stomach against pollution, so they should be included.

Ingredients: About 2 pounds beef marrow bones; about 1-1/2 to 2 pound each bone-in beef chuck short ribs, and beef rib back bones; 2 medium carrots washed, peeled and sliced in one-inch length diagonally; 5-6 celery stalks washed and cut into one-inch pieces; 1 large onion trimmed and cut into wedges with skin on; 1 bulb of garlic cut across in half; 3-4 inch long ginger root split in half lengthwise; 2 large bay leaves; 1 tsp. turmeric powder; 1 tsp. crushed black peppercorn (op); 1cup chopped fresh spinach, collard green or kale; 1 cup mixed herbs chopped such as: cilantro, parsley, oregano and rosemary; about ½ tsp. kosher salt.

Toasted Whole Spices: 1 About 2-inch cinnamon stick; 2 tbsp. each: mustard seeds, cumin seeds, coriander seeds, black peppercorns; ½ of the star anise. Toast all on medium heat, in a cast-iron skillet for 3-4 minutes, shaking the pan constantly. Do not let them burn. You just need to light toast them.

Heat a large pot on low heat that is large enough to accommodate all the ingredients and liquid. Take out extra visible fat from the meat. Wash the meat under running warm water to wash out all the impurities. Then brown the meat in batches, in its own fat, on medium-high heat, for about 15 minutes per batch, or until all the bones are browned (they give more flavor). Now pour over about 3 quarts of water. The water should be about 2-1/2 inches higher than the bones. Add rest of the ingredients except the toasted whole spices. Add the toasted spices 1 hour before turning the heat off.

Bring the ingredients to a boil, stir well, lower the heat to a constant simmer, cover and simmer for 8 to 9 hours, stirring well, about every two hours. Turn off the heat, let it sit for 30 minutes, then take out the bones and large pieces, and strain through a large strainer. Cool completely, then refrigerate overnight, skim the fat from the top and use or freeze. I divide into 4 portions, leave one out and freeze three for next three weeks.

Beef Marrowbone Soup (Serves: 4)

Try to make a colorful soup by using different color of vegetables, it's more nutritious.

Ingredients: About 5 cups of beef marrow broth from above recipe; 1 cup each chopped fine: celery, asparagus or okra or brussels sprouts, red bell pepper; 2 cups chopped plum tomatoes; 1 cup frozen or fresh corn or ¼ cup quinoa; 1 apple cored and grated (op); 2 tbsp. lemon juice; ½ cup thin-sliced cilantro stems; ½ tsp. turmeric powder; salt and pepper to taste; to garnish: 4 medium kale leaves brushed with oil and roasted crispy, about ½ cup Greek yogurt, and ½ cup sliced green onion.

Combine all the vegetables, spices and the broth in a medium pot, and bring to a boil, lower the heat and simmer until soft, about 20 minutes, add some water if needed. Taste for the seasoning. Serve warm garnished with kale, yogurt and green onion.

Asian Style Beef Marrow Soup (Serves: 2)

This is a Vietnamese and Chinese-style soup that you serve layering the ingredients.

Ingredients: 1 cup fresh-cooked rice; 4 cups hot beef marrow broth; 6 paper-thin raw slices of a good boneless beef steak or roast beef; 1 cup fresh watercress; 2 tbsp. julienned fresh ginger; ¼ cup each: sliced green onion and cilantro. To garnish: 1 medium marrow bone split in half lengthwise; butter mixture: 3 tbsp. unsalted butter mixed with 1 tbsp. chopped fresh herbs, 1 garlic clove crushed, and 1 tbsp. chili powder: spread the butter mixture on the marrow side, and roast the bones in a preheated oven, over a parchment paper-lined tray for about 6-8 minutes in 400 degree oven, or until bubbly.

Heat two large and deep serving bowls (Chinese noodle bowls). Place in each bowl, the rice in the bottom, pour over 2 cups of hot marrow broth, drop 3 slices of the beef per person, adding one slice of the beef at a time on the top, sprinkle the watercress, green onion, cilantro and then ginger. Serve garnished with the marrow bone on the side of the bowl.

Tip: Just to get filled a little more, I serve the hot biscuits before serving the marrow soup.

Hearty Beef Stew (Serves: 6-8)

You can add all the aromatics and herbs, but to make a healthy and tasty stew you just have to go a little further. Here is what I call a hearty stew.

Ingredients: 5 ounces of slab bacon chopped up in ½-inch cubes; 4-5 tbsp. olive oil; 3 to 3-1/2 pound boneless chuck cut up into 1-1/2 to 2-inch cubes; 2 tbsp. all-purpose flour; aromatics: 1 cup each chopped: onion, celery, carrots, cabbage and cremini mushrooms – wiped, cleaned and halved; ¼ cup chopped cilantro or flat-leaf parsley soft stems and leaves; 1 tsp. each: granulated garlic and dry rosemary, divided; vegetables and flavors: ½ pound baby Dutch yellow or red potatoes cleaned; 1 can, 14.5oz. (2 c) whole beets; 1 cup frozen lima beans or peas; 2 tbsp. pearl barley; 2 cup red wine; 1 can, 14.5 oz. Italian style stewed tomatoes; 1can, 8 oz. tomato sauce; 2 tsp. Dijon mustard; 1 can, 14.5 oz. (2c) beef stock; salt and pepper to taste; to garnish: sour cream, roasted nuts, paprika and/or pickled pearl onions.

1. Heat a large heavy-bottom pot or a Dutch oven on medium-high heat. Pat dry the meat cubes and sprinkle with flour on both sides. Add 1 tbsp. of oil to the pot and brown the meat in single layer for 4-5 minutes or until it is browned underneath. Sprinkle another tablespoon of oil, turn

over the meat and brown the other side, (in batches if preferred). Take out the meat and tent with a foil.

2. Add 1 more tablespoon of oil and brown the slab bacon and onion for 5 minutes on high heat. Add celery, carrots, cabbage, mushrooms, half of the garlic and rosemary, a little salt and pepper, mix well, lower the heat to medium and cook covered for 5 minutes. Open the cover, add the meat back to the pot, pour in the wine, increase the heat to medium-high and let the wine evaporate for 5 minutes. Add potatoes, beets, lima beans, barley, stewed tomatoes, cilantro or parsley, tomato sauce, mustard, beef stock, bring to a boil, cover, and simmer on medium heat for 45 minutes. Add peas (if using), stir well, add rest of the garlic and rosemary, simmer for another 20 minutes or until vegetables are done and meat if soft.
3. Serve in warm bowls, garnished with sour cream, paprika, nuts and pickled onions.

Tips: Cabbage is healthy and gives very good flavor to soup and stews. Do not use too much barley, it will take over the flavors.

Cioppino (Seafood Stew) (Serves: 6 to 8)

We serve this for main meal with bread..Cioppino is like seafood stew. It is very tasty, thick and loaded with the seafood. It is very easy to prepare, you just need very fresh seafood.

Ingredients, for the Soup: 3 strips of bacon; 4 tbsp. unsalted butter; 2 cups white part of leek, washed well and sliced thin, or large onion chopped; 1 cup peeled and sliced thin carrots; 1 cup celery slice thin; 1 large red potato peeled and chopped fine; 1 large fennel bulb cored and sliced, 2 large poblano and 1 large red bell pepper; one can 28 ounces (794g) Italian crushed tomatoes; 2 cups chicken stock or as needed; 2 cups white wine: ¼ cup lemon juice; ½ tsp. red pepper flakes or to taste; 1 tbsp. old bay seasoning or lemon-pepper mix (Mrs. Dash); ¼ tsp. granulated garlic; salt and pepper to taste.

Seafood: 1 pounds each cleaned: sea scallops, jumbo shrimp; mussels or clams or a combination; 1 pound firm fish like cod, salmon or snapper fillets; to serve: garlic toasts or rye bread toasts: plain or with roasted red bell pepper aioli and to garnish: 1 cup pesto or lemon chutney, (or grind 1 cup packed flat-leaf parsley, with 4 large garlic cloves, and 1/3 cup lemon juice) use half in the soup and other half for garnish.

1. In a Dutch oven or a large and wide pot, on medium heat cook bacon for about 5-6 minutes until crispy, take out on the paper towel. Take out any bacon fat and add butter and leek or onion stir for 2 minutes. Move over the onion and add celery and carrots, cook 1 minute; add potatoes, sprinkle a little salt and pepper, stir the potatoes, cover and cook for 5 minutes. Add rest of the vegetable and Old Bay seasoning or lemon-pepper mix, fennel chopped, peppers, little salt, poblano and red bell pepper, do not stir; cover and cook for 5-6 minutes.

2. Add chicken stock, white wine, lemon juice, red pepper flakes, tomatoes, granulated garlic, stir well and increase the heat and bring to a boil and cook for about 15 minutes until all vegetables are soft. Eight minutes before serving, add fish, and cook 5 minutes, add mussels and or clams, shrimp, and scallops, a little salt and pepper, the mixture of lemon, garlic; do not stir, cover and cook 2-3 minutes until mussels are opened and shrimp are pink. Stir in half of the pesto, or chutney. Taste for salt and pepper. Serve immediately garnished with rest of the pesto or lemon chutney and sprinkled with bacon. Serve with garlic toasts or aioli rye bread on the side.

Warm Chickpeas (Garbanzos) Salad (Serves: 4)

This is our favorite salad. We eat this salad at least 4 times a week. Most of the time, we just use lettuce, tomatoes, onion, grated cheese, beans with oil and vinegar. If it is for dinner, you can use boiled eggs, chicken, fish, shrimp or even leftover meat heated well.

Ingredients:

For the Chickpeas: 1 can, 1 pound,13 ounces (822g) chickpeas, drained, washed and drained again then sautéed in 1 tbsp. olive oil on medium-high heat for about 8-10 minutes until heated through, then sprinkled with 1 tsp. each: onion, garlic and cumin powders, ½ tsp. dry oregano, and another 1 tbsp. olive oil. Heat for another 5 minutes, covered, on very low heat, without stirring. serve them warm.

For the Salad: 1 bag, 113G (4oz..) cleaned watercress; 1 medium iceberg lettuce; ½ pint grape or cherry tomatoes; 1 cup black olives; 1 small onion thin-sliced; about ¼ cup grated cheese from the bottle; about 1/3 pound hard cheese, such as: gouda or Swiss, shaved with potato peeler; for the vinaigrette: ¼ cup cider vinegar, whisked in with 1 tbsp. Dijon-type mustard, 2 fresh cloves of garlic grated fine, and ½ cup extra virgin olive oil. (no salt needed, cheese will give you enough salt.)

Assemble the Salad: Slice the lettuce into 1-inch-wide circles, dip them in the vinaigrette, place them on the serving plates and cut them carefully (keeping them in the circle) into 4 or 6 wedges. Now dip the watercress in the vinaigrette lightly and place around the lettuce, sprinkle grated cheese all over. Place the warm chickpeas in the center, and scatter onion, tomatoes, olives and shaved cheese all over. Serve immediately.

Tip: Watercress has over 18 vitamins and minerals. Instead of chickpeas you can also use cooked warm quinoa. Also, if you prefer, you can serve garlic bread to go with the chickpeas.

New England Clam Chowder (Serves: 4)

First, wash and scrub the clams, discard any cracked or open ones before cooking them and any clam liquid (liquor) should be strained. Line a strainer with a damp paper towel and strain through all the liquid into a bowl. I buy extra clams and after cooking and discard the black-stomach part, most of the time it is sandy.

Ingredients: 2 strips of bacon; 2 tbsp. butter; ½ cup each fine chopped onion and celery; 1 tbsp. fine chopped garlic cloves; 1 pound Yukon gold potatoes or new potatoes, peeled and cut into ½-inch cubes and soaked in cold water; 1-1/4 cup whole milk; ¾ cup heavy cream; ½ tsp. old bay seasoning; salt and pepper to taste; 15 unbroken and un-cracked littleneck clams scrubbed clean; 1 bottle, 8 fl. ounces (236ml) clam juice or chicken broth; 2 tbsp. lemon juice; ¼ tsp. cayenne pepper or tabasco sauce to taste; to garnish ¼ cup roasted almonds and pistachios; to serve, 1bag, 9 ounces, (255g) soup or oyster crackers, drizzled with 1 tbsp. olive oil, a little salt and pepper and heated in a 300 degree oven for 5 minutes and leave in the turned off oven for another 15 minutes, just to freshen them up.

1.   Heat a medium pot and spread out the bacon, cook on medium heat for about 2 minutes each side until crispy, take out the bacon and set aside for garnish. Add butter and onion to the pot and stir for 2 minutes, add celery and garlic and cook stirring and sweat the vegetable for 2-3 minutes without coloring them. Drain the potatoes and add to the pot, stir all together well. Add milk and bring it to a boil, stir well again, add salt and pepper to taste, cover, lower

the heat to constant simmer and cook until potatoes are soft about 20 minutes. Stir the potatoes during the simmering and make sure they do not burn or boil out.

2. While potatoes are cooking, heat a medium pot with clam juice, lemon juice and little fresh ground black or white pepper. Bring it to a boil, add the clams, cover and let simmer on low for 5 minutes. Then start taking out the clams that are opened, stir a little and let the rest of the clams open for another 1-2 minutes. Discard any unopened ones. Place the clams in a platter, open them and take out the clam meat with a knife, discard any blackened part and chop the clams into ½-inch pieces, strain the liquid.

3. When potatoes are done, turn the heat off. Take out half of the potato mixture and puree in the blender and add them back to the pot, add strained clam juice, heavy cream and bring to a simmer, add chopped clams, old bay seasoning and salt and pepper to taste, just heat through. Serve in heated bowls, garnished with bacon, and nuts, and with freshened crackers.

Chicken and Chickpeas Soup (S:6)

Ingredients: 1Can, 3LB (48oz.) low sodium chicken broth; 8oz can (1 cup) tomato sauce; about 1-1/2 pounds, 2 boneless chicken breasts or dark meat cut up into bite size pieces; 1bunch collard green (about 8 large leaves) each washed under running water and stem trimmed at the end then sliced across very thin; ½ cup chopped cilantro, 1Tsp. each: dry rosemary and turmeric powder; 2medium carrots peeled and sliced ¼-inch; 3 medium red potatoes scrubbed and cut into 1-inch cubes; 1 large onion chopped; 2Tbsp. garlic cloves chopped; 1cup fresh green chickpeas in the pod shelled or from the can; salt and pepper to taste; whole wheat toasts or grain bread to serve.

Heat a medium pot with 1cup water and bring it to a boil. Add collard green stir well, cover and let it cook on a constant simmer for about 8 minutes. Add carrots, onion, garlic, potatoes, and cook for 15 minutes until vegetables are soft. Add chicken, chickpeas, cilantro, rosemary, stir well, cover and simmer for 15-20 minutes until chicken is done. Add salt and pepper to taste. Serve with toasts or bread.

Tip: Green Chickpeas are available at the Indian grocery stores. Instead of chicken and chickpeas you can use half fresh shelled Peas and half Barley.

Chicken Supreme Soup (Serves: 6-8)

This is our favorite soup. You can make it either with a whole chicken, with chicken pieces or with boneless breast and chicken stock. If using chicken breast, just cut them in bite-size pieces, sauté them with the vegetables and add the hot chicken stock, cook just until chicken is done and vegetables are soft.

Ingredients: 1 (about 3 pounds) whole chicken, 2 tbsp. olive oil, 1 cup each chopped: carrots, onion, celery and mushrooms, 1 cup chopped potatoes (op), 1 cup diced fresh tomatoes, ½ tsp. dry rosemary, 2 cups washed and thin-sliced or whole baby spinach, salt & fresh ground pepper to taste, ½ cup chop fresh parsley or cilantro, ½ cup thin-sliced scallion for garnish.

Take out giblets and neck parts from the chicken, wash then put in a large pot or in a Dutch oven breast side up, cover with water about 8 cups, bring to a boil, cover with the lid and simmer constantly on medium heat for about 1-1/2 hour or until chicken is soft.

While chicken is cooking, heat another large pot on medium heat, add oil and sauté carrots, onion, celery for about two minutes, add mushroom, potatoes, salt and pepper to taste, add ½ cup water and simmer another 15 minutes or until vegetables are soft and potatoes are done, then add tomatoes and rosemary, stir well, then cover with the lid and turn off the heat.

When chicken is cooked completely, take the chicken out of the liquid and put on a cutting board. Skim some of the fat from the liquid and pour the liquid over the vegetable. Bring to boil then simmer on low. Now take out all the meat from the chicken, cut in bite-size pieces and add to the pot, add more warm water if needed, add spinach, parsley and rosemary, and bring to a boil, simmer 10 minutes, check for seasoning.

Serve hot soup, garnished with scallion or tomatoes or both, with toasted garlic bread on the side. This soup is so tasty and nourishing that it will cure all colds.

Chicken Soup with Nori (Serves: 2)

Nori is seaweed that is loaded with nutrients. My husband loves this colorful and tasty soup in the winter. You can prepare everything ahead, reheat and serve.

For the Stock: 3 cup homemade chicken stock (if bought then add the vegetables cook and strain); 1 cup beef broth; 1-inch fresh grated ginger; 1 large garlic clove chopped; ¼ cup chopped cilantro soft stems; 1 nori sheet 7 x 8-inch; 1 tbsp. lemon juice; salt and pepper to taste.

For the Soup: 1 cup 1-inch cubed mushroom sautéed in 1 tbsp. butter until their liquid has been evaporated; 1 fresh plum tomato chopped; ½ cup string beans cored and blanched for 3 minutes; 1 cup cooked, shredded or pulled chicken; to garnish: ½ cup roasted red bell pepper from the jar chopped; 1 avocado, halved, pitted and cut in large pieces; ¼ to ½ cup sauerkraut or kimchi.

1. In a medium pot on medium-high heat, bring all the stock ingredients, except the lemon juice, to a boil. Lower the heat and simmer for 10-15 minutes. Discard the nori sheet and keep the vegetables (if preferred). Add the lemon juice.
2. When ready to serve, ladle the hot stock halfway in the soup bowls. Then pile the mushrooms, tomatoes, beans and chicken all around. Place the roasted bell peppers in the center, top with avocado and sauerkraut or kimchi and serve.

Tip: Japanese cuisine is famous for using seaweeds. There are three types of seaweeds that are very common: nori, wakame, and kombu. Dry sheets of nori can be crumbled over the prepared dishes as a garnish. Some athletes munch on these dry sheets. We mostly use it making sushi and soups. You can also lightly warm it to release its flavor.

Chicken Tortilla Soup with Pepper Paste (Serves: 2)

There are so many variations of this soup depending on how you like it. This soup looks good as well as tastes good.

Follow the recipe above for the Chicken Soup with Nori. Just add pepper paste to taste (about ¼ c), to the soup and garnish with deep fried tortilla strips and Pepper Paste.

1. **Pepper Paste** (M: about 2 cups)

Ingredients: 1 can, 7 ounces (198g) chipotle peppers; 2 dry serrano and 2 dry pasilla peppers; 1 medium red bell pepper; ½ cup cilantro stems; 2 tbsp. tomato paste; 1 tbsp. fresh garlic cloves; 1 tsp. onion powder; 2 tbsp. cider vinegar; 3-4 tbsp. canola oil; salt to taste.

1. Place the red bell pepper directly over the stove, turn around all sides until it is blackened and charred. Place in a small bowl, cover tightly with the plastic wrap and then with the lid and place in the turned-off oven for 20 minutes, then peel and discard the seeds. Heat a dry skillet on medium heat, place the dry peppers and heat until they are light brown and fragrant, turn over and brown the other side, a total of 1 minute.
2. Now puree all ingredients in a blender together with the chipotle peppers into a fine puree. If needed, add a little extra oil and salt to taste. Store in a clean and dry jar in the refrigerator up to 2-3 weeks.

Cream of Asparagus Soup (Serves: 6)

Asparagus is loaded with nutrients. We start making this soup as soon as asparagus start selling in the supermarkets and we make this soup all year-round. While blanching, keep all the asparagus tips in the same direction so that it's easy to handle and they do not break.

Ingredients: 1-1/2 to 2 pounds fresh asparagus (about 5 cups cleaned and chopped), 1 medium chopped onion (about 1 C), 8 ounce (1 C) heavy cream, 3 Tab all-purpose flour, 4 tab butter, 1-16 ounce carton (2 C) chicken or vegetable broth, salt and fresh ground black pepper to taste, about 1/6 tsp. fresh grounded nutmeg, fresh chopped radishes or tomatoes for garnish.

Wash asparagus and break them off at the bottom where ever they break, taking off the white tough part. Soak them in cold water for 6-7 minutes. In a large skillet, bring about 6 cups of water to a boil, add asparagus and cook for 3 minutes, turning them over so they all cook evenly. Save about 2 cups of cooking liquid aside, then rinse asparagus off under the running cold water. Now take the tips off from about half of the asparagus and set them aside for garnish. Chop rest of the asparagus and blend them in a blender or food processor with 1 cup of cooking liquid.

Heat a large saucepan on a medium heat, add butter and chopped onion, stir and sauté for 5 minutes until onion are soft. Add flour and sauté until flour is bubbling and opaque, add chicken or vegetable broth, salt and fresh ground black pepper to taste, bring to a boil, simmer 5 minutes. Add asparagus puree and heavy cream and bring to a boil, then simmer on low heat for 5-6 minutes, add fresh-grated nutmeg and asparagus tips. Taste for seasoning. If needed, add more cooking water or heated milk.

Serve garnished with fresh chopped tomatoes or radishes.

French Onion Soup (Serves: 4)

This is very easy, tasty and fancy soup. I serve it with onion fritters as well as onion rings, both made almost same way. One is crunchy and the other has sweet and soft onion taste. Make soup first and keep it warm, then prepare the toasts with cheese, but do not bake until ready to serve, and then make onion fritters and rings at the end, to serve hot.

Ingredients: 1 tbsp. canola oil; 2 tabs unsalted butter plus extra for the toasts; 2 cans 14 oz. (396g) each beef broth, 1 bottle beer (about 1-1/2 c); 1 medium yellow and 1 medium red onion chopped; ½ tsp. granulated garlic; very little salt and fresh ground black pepper to taste; 1 tbsp. onion powder; 2 tbsps. instant sodium free beef broth; 4 rye bread slices (or any other bread); 2 tbsps. crumbled blue cheese; 2 cup shredded mozzarella cheese, 1 tsp. smoke paprika, ¼ tsp. dry rosemary.

1   In a medium pot, on medium to medium-heat, warm oil and butter, add chopped onion and sauté for 5 minutes, lower the heat, sprinkle a little salt and pepper, granulated garlic, stir well, cover and cook covered for about 5 minutes.
2   Add beef broth, beer, onion powder and fresh-ground black pepper, bring to a boil and simmer on low heat, covered for about 15 minutes until onions are soft. Turn off the oven but keep it warm by reheating every now and then till ready to serve.
3   Make 4 toasts, butter them, sprinkle a little blue cheese and then cover the top with lot of grated cheese (about ½ cup on each). Sprinkle each with paprika and rosemary. Keep the toasts in the refrigerator until onion rings are ready.
4   Make onion fritters and onion rings (see recipe: side dishes)
5   Broil, bake or microwave the toasts to melt the cheese. Cut each toast in to four pieces but keep them attached at center and gently place each toast on the soup just before taking the soup to the table.

Irish Lamb Stew (Serves: 6-8)

I am married to an Irishman and even for my own palate, I do like to make lamb stew every now and then. This is a hearty soup, good for lunch or dinner. Just have some crusty bread on hand. Beer makes food salty, so taste the stew at the end and add salt accordingly.

Ingredients: 2 to 2-1/2 Pounds boneless lamb, leg or shoulder meat cut into about 1-1/2 to 2-inch cubes; each 1 tsp. fresh ground black pepper or cayenne pepper, rosemary, granulated garlic divided; salt to taste; ½ cup all-purpose flour; 4-5 tbsp. canola or olive oil; each1/2 cup chopped: onion, celery and green bell pepper; 2 tbsp. flour and 2 tbsp. unsalted soften butter mixed and made into a paste; 1 bottle, 12 ounce Irish stout beer; ¼ cup to ½ cup fine red wine (op); 2 cartons, 32 ounces, 2 pounds (907g) each, fat-free, low-sodium beef broth; each peeled and cut into bite-size: 2 cup potatoes, 2 cup carrots, 1 cup parsnips; 1 pkg. 10 ounces frozen peas; 1 pkg. 10 ounces frozen, or 1 jar, 15 ounces (425g) pearl onions, 1 tbsp. lemon juice; 16 ounces, about 2 cup sour cream and sliced green onion or chives to garnish; crusty bread to serve.

1.   Heat a heavy-bottom pot or Dutch oven with oil on medium heat. Pat dry the meat cubes and sprinkle with a mixture of ½ tsp. of spices – pepper, rosemary and garlic. Roll the cubes in the flour, shake out the excess, increase the heat on medium- high and place the meat pieces in single layer, in batches, in the pot. Do not disturb, and let them cook for about 5 minutes or until they are golden underneath. Turn them over and cook the other side same way. When done, take them out with a metal spatula in a bowl. When all the batches are done, cook on medium heat onion, celery and bell pepper for about 8 minutes or until translucent. Move the vegetables all around and add the butter and flour paste in the center, break it up and cook a little until bubbly. Then mix with the vegetables. Move the onion mixture aside in the pot.
2.   Add the carrots, parsnips and potatoes, stir a little on medium-high heat. Take the pot off the heat and add wine and beer. Put the pot back on the heat, stir 5 minutes and add beef and chicken broth. All vegetables and meat should be covered with the broth. Bring to a boil, add the meat on the top, do not stir. Cover, lower the heat and simmer for 45 minutes to an hour or until vegetables and meat are tender.
3.   Add frozen peas and frozen pearl onion, stir well, add rest half of the spices – pepper, rosemary and granulated garlic and lemon juice. Simmer another 15 minutes or until vegetables are soft. Taste for seasoning and add salt and pepper to taste.

4. Serve garnished with sour cream and chives or green sliced onions, together with crusty bread.

Lentil Soup (Serves: 4-6)

(Indian Masoor Dal or Whole Lentil Beans)

This soup (eaten in India everyday with rice and bread) is my father's favorite. My father loved any dal (split or whole beans) with greens. It is very easy to make. Cook lentils a little, skim off the foam, add the spices and herbs and cook until soft. Lentils are loaded with iron, so tomato sauce help digest the iron. Here is our favorite recipe.

Ingredients: 1-1/2 cup whole green lentils (American green lentils cook fast) picked over for stones, etc., washed well in cold water then soaked in 2 cup water for about 15 minutes; 1 medium onion chopped; 1 tbsp. garlic cloves peeled and chopped; ¼ tsp. turmeric powder; about 4 c, 6 oz. baby spinach washed clean, keep the leaves whole and chop the stems; 1 cup cilantro leaves and soft stems chopped fine or ½ cup flat-leaf parsley chopped; ½ cup plain tomato sauce; 1 tsp. curry powder or cumin powder; ¼ tsp. dry oregano; about ½ tsp.salt and black pepper or to taste.

1. In a 5-quart pot, add soaked lentils and soaking water, plus 2 cups more water (total 4 cups of water). Bring it to a boil on medium-high heat. Reduce the heat to medium and cook simmering, partially covered until all the foam subsides; take out the foam with a spatula.
2. Add turmeric, salt and pepper to taste, onion, garlic and stir well. Then top with parsley/cilantro and spinach and cook simmering on low heat covered until soft, about 15 minutes.
3. When lentils are soft, add tomato sauce, oregano, curry or cumin powder and stir well. Taste for seasoning and add more salt and pepper if needed. Cook another 10-15 minutes.
4. Serve warm with rice or as a soup with toasts.

Matzo Ball Soup (Serves: 6-8)

I have family and friends who are Jewish and make a very good matzo ball soup. Following is an easy and a tasty version. I like to make soup with roasted chicken that I cook a day before, take out the meat and make a wonderful stock in the slow cooker with all the bones cooking overnight. You can also simmer a 3-4-pound chicken cut up in 8 pieces, with vegetables; pull out the meat and use the store bought chicken broth.
Ingredients:

For the Soup: 2 tbsp. olive oil; about 2 cups shredded or cubed chicken meat (buy a 3-4-pound chicken, roast at 350 degrees at 15 minutes per pound. Cool, take out the meat and make stock with the bones in slow cooker overnight, adding water, bay leaf, a little salt and pepper, 1 medium onion and 1 cup celery); 6 cup homemade or store-bought chicken broth; 2 medium bay leaves; 1 cup each chopped: onion, celery; 1 medium carrot peeled and sliced; 1 fennel bulb, trimmed and cut in quarters lengthwise, then sliced across; 1 red bell pepper, trimmed, seeded and chopped; fresh herbs: ½ cup green onion, ¼ cup chopped parsley, 1 tbsp. chopped fresh rosemary; salt and fresh ground black pepper to taste.
For the Matzo Balls:
3 large eggs separated and egg whites whipped to soft peak; ¼ cup chicken broth for matzo balls and 6 cup for cooking the matzo balls; ¾ cup whole wheat matzo meal; 2 tbsp. melted chicken fat (aka schmaltz, save your own or get from the butcher) 2 tbsp. (only) soda water; 1 tsp. each fresh thyme and rosemary; salt and fresh ground black pepper to taste.

1. Make the matzo ball mixture: In a medium bowl, whisk egg yolk, 1 tsp. salt and pepper to taste and soda water. Add matzo meal, chicken fat and ¼ cup chicken broth, thyme and the rosemary, whisk well. Now fold into the egg white, cover and refrigerate in the refrigerator for 30 minutes, until it is thickened.
2. To cook the vegetables: In a medium heavy-bottom pot, heat oil and increase heat to medium-high, sauté onion, bay leaves, celery, carrots and fennel for 6-8 minutes, add half of the parsley and green onion, rosemary, salt and pepper to taste, add 2 cups water. Bring to a boil and simmer for 25 minutes until vegetables are soft. Add the cooked meat and heat the meat through for about 10 minutes, keep warm.
3. To make the matzo balls: Heat a large pot with 6 cups chicken stock, the rest of the parsley and green onion. Bring to a boil, lower the heat and simmer. Using a small (1-1/2-inch diameter) ice-cream scoop or two tablespoons, take out the matzo mixture, round it up into balls and drop in the simmering broth. When all the balls are done, cover the pot, gently simmer the broth for about 15 minutes, just to firm the center. Do not overcook. Add the warm vegetable and chicken mixture, taste for the seasoning, and serve the soup in the warm bowls.

Mulligatawany Soup (Serves: 4)

(Lentil and Chicken)

This soup was very popular when the British were in India. This is made with the chicken thigh, vegetables and lentils. You can make it without chicken as well.

Ingredients: Four large chicken thighs (or drumsticks) about 1 pound total, washed, pat-dry and sprinkled with 2 tbsp. all-purpose flour; 4 tbsp. ghee (purified butter); ½ cup Indian brown or American green whole lentils (if using Indian lentils, then soak them in the water overnight); 1 tbsp. uncooked basmati rice; 1 cup each chopped fine: onion, celery, carrots; ¼ cup each fresh grinded garlic cloves, and ginger1/2 cup fresh grated coconut; ½ tsp. fenugreek seed powder, 1 tsp. curry powder; 1tsp. garam masala; 2 tbsp. lemon juice, 2 cups chicken stock or more as needed; ½ cup coconut milk (op). 1 cup diced tomatoes; salt and pepper to taste; fresh cilantro to garnish; garlic toasts to serve.

In a Dutch oven or a heavy-bottom pot, heat 2 tbsp. purified butter. Add the chicken thighs and brown them all sides on medium-high heat, then take them out. Lower the heat to medium, add rest of the butter, onion, celery, carrots, lentils, rice and brown them turning around for 5 minutes. Add garlic, fenugreek powder, coconut, ginger and brown for another 5 minutes. Add the stock, and put back the chicken on the top. Bring it to a boil, and simmer on constant simmer, for about 45 minutes to an hour, or until chicken is soft and the lentils are done.

With a perforated spoon, take out the chicken pieces. Take the meat off the bones and put it back in the pot. Add coconut milk, diced tomatoes, lemon juice, salt and pepper to taste, bring it to a boil. Serve garnished with the cilantro, and serve with garlic or plain toasts.

Sweet Potato Soup (Serves: 6)

Do you know that we watch Dr. Oz's show on TV every afternoon? On his show Dr. Oz has mentioned that sweet potatoes are very rich in vitamins and everyone should eat one cup of sweet potatoes every day. In India when we go on religious fast, sweet potato (shakerkand) is what we consume most. I love making sweet mashed potatoes and soup more often now than before. I bake a large bunch of sweet potatoes and beets and the first night, we eat baked vegetables on the side with meat. The next day, I make soup for everyone. It saves me a lot of time and we get two nourishing dinners in a matter of time.

Ingredients: 1-1/2 pounds (about 4 cups) peeled and chopped sweet potatoes, 1 apple peeled, cored and chopped, 4 cups skim or 2% milk, salt and fresh ground black pepper to taste, ½ cup grated parmesan cheese, ½ tsp. ground cinnamon, 1 cup small boiled or baked and sliced beets for garnish. Cinnamon and raisin bread and butter to serve on the side

In a large saucepan, cook apple and sweet potatoes in about 2 cups of water until soft. Mash the potato mixture well and add 3-4 cups of milk as needed, then stir in the grated parmesan cheese, salt and fresh ground black pepper, cinnamon and bring to a boil, lower the heat and simmer 10-15 minutes.

Serve warm, garnished with more cinnamon and sliced or chopped beets.

You can make this soup with half heavy cream and half milk. We simply like it with 2% milk. We also serve with cinnamon, raisin warm toasts.

Minestrone Soup (Serves: 6-8)

This is my favorite, fancy and nourishing soup. You can have it for lunch or dinner and left over, you can use in chili or mashed in dough to make the bread (Roti and Paratha), or over rice. We serve soup with chopped radishes that helps digest the beans better. If you prefer, you can use half tomato sauce and some lemon juice to taste.

Ingredients: 2 tab olive oil, 1 cup chopped onion, 3-4 anchovy fillets in oil or paste; 4 garlic cloves peeled and chopped; 1 cup chopped collard green (leaves only),1 14.5 ounce canned each chick peas, cannellini, and red kidney beans, 1 cup fresh cored and chopped string beans, 1 cup frozen peas, 1 cup diced red potatoes with skin on, 1C chopped cilantro or parsley, 14 to 16 ounces (about 2 cup) plain tomato sauce, 2 cups chicken or vegetable broth, ½ tsp. dry oregano, 2 tbsp. chop fresh or ½ tsp. dry basil, 1 tbsp. lemon juice, salt and fresh ground pepper to taste, ½ cup chopped scallion and ½ cup chopped radishes (op) for garnish. To serve, grated or shaved parmesan cheese and garlic toasts.

Blanch the collard green leaves in 2 cups boiling, salted water for 3 minutes, cool, then puree in the blender with ½ cup of chickpeas, and set aside.

Heat a large saucepan on medium heat, add oil and sauté onion on medium heat for 5 minutes; add anchovy and garlic, mash the fillet and stir well; add potatoes, string beans and garlic, sauté for 5 minutes. Add 2 cups of chicken or vegetable broth, cover and cook until potatoes are soft. Add cannellini and kidney beans, chick peas, green peas, cilantro or parsley, tomato sauce, oregano, thyme, salt and fresh-ground pepper to taste, and collard green puree. Bring to a boil, then simmer on low for 25-30 minutes. Taste the seasoning and add more spices or liquid (broth or water) as needed.

Serve garnished with scallion and/or chopped radishes, cheese, and with garlic bread.

Tips: Beans have low-fat protein, which is very good for diabetics. They also have magnesium, fiber, potassium, foliate, iron, vitamin B, etc.

Roasted Pumpkin, Butternut Squash and Parsnips Soup (Serves: 4)

This is a healthy soup and is very easy to make. If you want to make with protein, just add ½ cup washed and drained canned chickpeas while pureeing the ingredients.

Ingredients: About ½ pounds each of fresh butternut squash and parsnips (about 1 cup puree); 1 pound fresh pumpkin (about 2 cup puree); 1 large onion peeled and cut into 6 slices (wedges); about 3 tbsp. canola or olive oil; sprinkle of salt and pepper and 1 tbsp. of balsamic vinegar; 2 cups heated chicken broth; ¼ tsp. granulated garlic; 1 tsp. sugar; to garnish: 1 cup low fat plain yogurt in room temperature, chives or green onion, 1tbsp. dhana dal, or roasted coriander seeds in little butter, then seasoned with salt and pepper.

Move the oven rack in the center and preheat the oven 425 degrees. Line a large baking sheet with aluminum foil and grease it with a little oil. Cut the pumpkin and the butternut squash, scoop out the seeds, peel and cut the parsnip in half lengthwise and place all together with the onion on the baking tray, cut-side up, sprinkle with little oil, salt, pepper and then with the balsamic vinegar. Roast at 425 degrees for about 25-30 minutes or until vegetables are soft.

Place the onion and 1 cup heated broth in the blender and puree them together. Then add the vegetables to the blender, add another 1 cup of broth and puree all together, or puree in two batches. Pour the soup in a medium-size pot, add garlic, sugar, salt and pepper to taste, and heat on medium heat covered for 10-15 minutes or until heated through. Drain the liquid from the yogurt, then whip it well with a tablespoon. Serve the soup in heated bowls, top with the yogurt, then with chives and dhana dal.

Tip: Butternut squash has vitamins A and C, and it is sweet and tasty.

Split Pea Soup (Serves: 6-8)

This is a family recipe that comes from my husband's family. His mother learned it from her mother and passed onto us. You can use water or chicken/beef broth.

Ingredients: 2 tbsp. vegetable or canola oil; 1 bag, 1 pound (16 oz.) green split peas, looked over and soaked in cold water overnight; 1 large onion chopped; ½ tsp. granulated garlic. 2 garlic cloves peeled and chopped; 1 cup peeled and grated carrots; ½ cup sliced celery; 2 beef bouillons or 4cups chicken broth; 1 tbsp. mustard powder; ½ tsp. each dry thyme and tarragon, and rosemary; 1/2 cup chopped fresh cilantro or flat-leaf parsley; ½ tsp. fresh-ground black pepper; to serve: sourdough garlic croutons or garlic-cheese bread.

Heat a heavy-bottom large pot on medium heat. Add oil and brown the onion sprinkled with little salt and garlic powder for 5 minutes covered. Add carrots, garlic and celery, stir to coat the vegetables, then cover and cook 5 minutes. Wash and drain the peas. Add peas and cook stirring for 5 minutes. Add water about 2-inches above the peas, add all spices and bouillon, except the mustard powder, stir well, bring to a boil, cover and simmer on low heat for 1 hour, or until peas are completely mashed and disintegrated, stirring every ½ hour. Add mustard powder, stir well and cook for another 5 minutes. Turn off the heat. Just before serving, reheat again, check for seasoning, add more heated water if needed.

Serve topped with sourdough garlic croutons and/or garlic-cheese bread.

Tip: This recipe goes with almost any kind of beans. If you are using the whole beans like lima beans, just make sure the beans are cooked, but not falling apart.

Garlic-Sourdough Croutons

Ingredients: 4 cups sourdough bread cubes, crust removed and cut into 1-inch cubes; 2-3tbsp. olive oil; 1 tsp. granulated garlic powder; 1/ 2tsp. each dry oregano and rosemary; salt and fresh ground black pepper to taste. You can use any bread.

Preheat the oven at 350 degrees. Line a large baking sheet with aluminum foil and grease it well. Spread out the bread cubes in single layer. Sprinkle with garlic, herbs, salt and pepper to taste, then sprinkle with the oil. Bake at 350 degrees for about 20 minutes. Turn off the oven and leave the croutons in the oven for another 2 hours. Use right away or cool and store in an airtight jar in the refrigerator up to 3 months.

Hearty Vegetable Soup (Serves: 4 to 6)

My husband and I both love this vegetable soup. Try to use some root and some leafy vegetables. Also, use tomato sauce together with either mustard powder or lemon juice. It tastes better, and helps digest the iron from the leafy greens.

Ingredients: 1 can 48oz., 99% fat-free beef, or chicken broth or water; ¼ cup pearl barley; 1 cup each chopped: onion, carrots, celery, string beans; 1 tbsp. chopped garlic cloves; 1 to 2 cups chopped kale leaves or baby spinach; 1 large baking potato cubed; 1can 15oz. red kidney beans or black beans; 1 cup 8oz.. tomato sauce or fresh tomatoes; 1 tbsp. each: mustard powder, fresh oregano (or ½ tsp. dry), ¼ cup chopped cilantro or parsley leaves; fresh-ground black pepper to taste; garlic toasts to serve.

In a large pot, heat the broth or the water, add the barley, bring to a boil and simmer 5 minutes. Stir in the rest of the vegetables, stir and cook until they are soft, about 20 minutes. Add tomato sauce, kidney or black beans, and rest of the spices, simmer for 10 minutes. Serve garnished with cilantro or parsley, with garlic toasts on the side.

Avocado Salad (Guacamoli)

(M: About 2-1/2 cups)

You can have this healthy salad with almost any sandwich or side dish. I love to serve it over fish and roasted meat.

Ingredients: 2 ripe haas avocados, cut in half, pitted, scored in 1-inch pieces in the rind, and scooped out with a tablespoon and mixed with ¼ cup lime juice; ¼ cup diced red onion; 1 jalapeno seeded and diced or to taste; ½ cup diced plum tomatoes; ¼ cup diced pepper-jack cheese (op); 2 tbsp. diced sweet and sour cucumber pickles or relish; 1/3 cup chopped cilantro leaves; salt and fresh ground black pepper to taste;1 tbsp. e.v. olive oil.

Just before serving, mix all in order they are listed, in a non-reactive bowl. Or you can prepare all ingredients ahead, cut the avocado last and serve immediately. Keep it covered with the plastic wrap.

Tips for the Avocado

1. Avocado has monounsaturated fat, plant-based fat that is healthy for you. They have vitamins C and D, potassium, fiber, lower bad cholesterol and increases the good cholesterol in the body.
2. Avocados do not ripen on the tree. They are picked hard and they start turning soft in room temperature.
3. When buying the avocados, look for green stems (not dry), nice green color, make sure skin is not bruised, I like haas avocado the best, buy when they are a little firm and keep in room temperature for 1-2 days before using. Once they ripen (soft), store them in the refrigerator loose for 2-3 days.
4. Buy extra avocados. Sometimes they are brown inside, so you need some extra on hand.
5. If you want to use only half avocado, then save the other half with the pit in, and the skin on. Wash under running cold water. Pat dry with paper towel, rub with the lemon juice on the cut surfaces, wrap with the paper towel, and place in an airtight plastic container in the refrigerator, for up to 3-4 days.
6. If you want to make the salad ahead, place in an airtight plastic container, pour 1-2 tbsp. extra-virgin olive oil on the top, then cover with a plastic wrap, close with the lid and freeze right away in a plastic bag. Just thaw in the plastic container, overnight and serve.
7. If you want to freeze the avocado, peel it first, then puree with two tablespoons of lemon, little ¼ tsp. each black pepper and turmeric, and 1 tsp. olive oil, per avocado; do not use any salt. Transfer the puree in a glass or a plastic container, top with 1 tsp. vegetable oil. Making sure you leave about one-inch space on the top, cover the container with the plastic wrap, then with the lid, taking out all the air from the container. Place the container in a zip-lock plastic bag and freeze up to 3 months. Thaw overnight and serve. Of the top is brown, just skim off the brown part and serve.

Coleslaw (M: 3 cups)

This is a lightly creamy coleslaw.

Ingredients: ¼ of a medium (about 3 cup grated); ½ cup grated carrots; ½ cup grated purple cabbage (op); 1 tbsp. apple cider vinegar; 1 tsp. sugar; ¼ cup mayonnaise; ½ cup sour cream; 2 tsp. prepared mustard; 1 tsp. horseradish; ¼ tsp. celery seeds; salt and fresh ground black pepper to taste.

1. Cut and core the cabbage, slice it in two pieces lengthwise and put in the food processor sideways and shred it thin, or simply slice it thin by hand.
2. Prepare the dressing: In a medium bowl, whisk in vinegar and sugar together first, add mayonnaise, sour cream, mustard, horseradish, celery seeds and about ¼ tsp. (or to taste) salt and fresh-ground black.
3. In a large non-reactive bowl add the grated cabbages and carrots, sprinkle lightly with salt and pepper, toss well. Pour half of the dressing and mix well. Pour rest of the dressing mix well. Taste for seasoning and add salt and pepper if needed. Refrigerate to chill, uncovered, until needed.

4. Serve with grilled and fried food and sandwiches. Any left over, cover it loosely with a plastic wrap overnight and use with two days.

Colorful Salad with Ginger-lime Vinaigrette (S:2)

This salad is the main meal either for lunch or dinner. I make this after roasting turkey, chicken or ham.

Ingredients: 1cup each chopped: baby English cucumbers, red bell peppers, black olives, ripe mango, black/red beans from the can, fresh broccoli, grated fresh carrots, grated fresh beets, grape tomatoes, cooked shelled soy beans, fresh/frozen cooked corn, barley or faro cooked, roasted and chopped into ½-inch pieces turkey, chicken or ham, creamy goat cheese cut into 1-inch pieces, 1/2cup each: walnuts, cranberries; vinaigrette: 1/3cup lime juice, 1 large garlic clove grated, 1Tsp. fresh ginger grated all whisked in with 1/2cup extra virgin olive oil, and a little salt and pepper.

Arrange two serving plates, using a 2-inch biscuit cutter, fill in the rings with the salad items. First start in the center with large item such as tomatoes or cheese, then go all around. Make piles of one salad item in the ring, flatten out the top and carefully take out the ring, leaving the pile on the plate. Make 5-6 piles around the center pile. Then fill in rest of the space with a tablespoon of other items going all around. Whisk in the vinaigrette and pour over the salad just before serving; then sprinkle with cranberries and walnuts.

Nutritious Grain Salad (Serves: 8-10)

This salad is like the Mediterranean grain salad. It is not only good for the heart but helps high blood pressure and diabetes. You can omit or reduce the amount of honey for diabetic people. I cook faro and barley together, then cook quinoa in sautéed onion, hemp hearts coarsely-grinded, and they are ready to eat, just sprinkle them over the salad, cooked chick peas just rinse and drain, sprinkle the vinaigrette over the salad and top with garnishes. When we were growing up, my mother used to boil brown chickpeas, barley and black-eye peas and served them warm with raw oil and lemon juice and/or with at least 5-6 different garnishes like lemon, radishes, onion, chopped vinegar pickles, green onions and fresh-made cilantro and garlic salt. This was our lunch once in a while. She did the same with vegetables like string beans, potatoes and beets, boiled (baked veggies) and thin-sliced.

Hemp has Omega 3 and 6. Quinoa has higher protein contents than any other grain, also called mother grain. Chickpeas help lower bad cholesterol (LDL) and make you regular if eaten daily.

Ingredients : 1 cup farro soaked in 1c warm water at least 2 hours or in cold water overnight; ½ cup pearled barley; 2 tbsp. canola or olive oil; 1 medium onion chopped; 2 tbsp. garlic cloves chopped;1 cup whole grain quinoa; 1 can 15.5 oz. about 1-3/4 cup cooked chick peas rinsed and drained; ½ cup hemp heart; ½ cup sun-dried tomatoes in oil, chopped.

Vinaigrette: 3 tbsp. pure honey or maple syrup; 4 tbsp. cider vinegar; 3 tbsp. prepared whole-grain mustard; ½ tbsp. e.v. olive oil plus extra to drizzle over the salad. No need for salt (cheese and chickpeas are salted).

Garnishes: 1 fresh lemon both ends sliced off & discarded, then thin-sliced across and each slice cut into 6 to 8 pieces; 1 cup radishes chopped; 2 kiwi fruits peeled and chopped; 1 cup pomegranate seeds; 1 medium each yellow and red bell pepper, cored, seeded and cut into cubes; 1 cup pitted black olives; ¼ cup lightly toasted pumpkin seeds; 1pkg. 1-pound fresh mozzarella cheese cut in 1-inch cubes; about 4 c, 4 oz., (113.4g) washed baby arugula; 1 cup cherry or grape tomatoes halved (op).

136

1. In a 5-quart heavy-bottom pot or Dutch oven on medium-high heat, add 1-1/2 cup water, farro with its soaking water, and barley. Bring to a boil on medium-high heat, stir well, cook open for 5 minutes, skimming any foam that rises to the top. Reduce the heat to low, cover, and simmer for about 25 minutes until farro and barley are soft. Stir 2-3 times during cooking and add some warm water if sticking. If it has any liquid left, open the pot and cook out the liquid on high heat. Turn off the heat and leave it covered for 5-10 minutes.
2. In a sauté pan, on medium heat, add 2 tbsp. oil and sauté onion and garlic until soft, about 6-7 minutes, add the quinoa, stir and mix well. Add 1 cup water, stir again, cover, lower the heat and simmer for about 20 minutes until soft. Stir once during the cooking.
3. Prepare the vinaigrette: in a small bowl, whisk together honey or maple syrup, mustard with vinegar and whisk in the extra virgin olive oil. Take out farro and barley in a bowl and pour over half of the vinaigrette and mix well.
4. Assemble the salad: In a 9x12x2-inche glass or porcelain platter, make layers:
    First spread out the farro mixture, chopped sun-dried tomatoes, top with chickpeas, quinoa, sprinkle the hemp heart and pour over other half of the vinaigrette. Combine all the garnishes together, except cheese and arugula, and sprinkle all over the salad, then top with the arugula and then the cheese. Serve drizzled with some e.v. olive oil all over.
    Assemble the salad just before serving or serve the arugula separate in a bowl, next to the salad.
    Tips:
    •   The grain salad needs a lot of vinegar and/or lemon to taste, and extra oil to digest. Use them the last minute, just before serving you will have more flavor.
    •   Use quinoa or amaranth they both are high in protein. Amaranth, the tiny little gold, black-flecked seeds are high in vitamins and minerals. We dry toast on low heat in the pan and sprinkle over cooked dishes or make dessert.
    •   Barley is loaded with nutrition. It is high-fiber, high-protein and low fat grain with a nutty flavor. Hulled barley with the hull removed but the fiber-rich bran attached is higher in nutrition. Barley is good for the heart.

Lobster and Shrimp Salad (Serves: 4-6)

You can prepare everything ahead, just do not use salt, lime juice or vinegar until serving. Just before serving, put it all together. Cook shrimp any way you want.

Ingredients: 2 cup cooked quinoa or any other grain; ¼ cup cider vinegar; ½ cup extra virgin olive oil; ½ pound (about 1-1/2 cup cooked) lobster meat sprinkled with 1 tbsp. lime juice; 1/2 lb. or about 7 large shrimp (of 12-14 count) cleaned and deveined, then sautéed in 1 tbsp. butter, ¼ tsp. granulated garlic and ¼ tsp. cayenne pepper, on medium heat for 3-5 minutes or until cooked through and cooled; ¼ cup chopped sweet & sour cucumber pickles; ½ cup chopped tomatoes; ¼ cup sliced green onions (op); ¼ cup drained capers or olives; ¼ cup toasted sliced almonds and ½ cup dry cranberries; salt and pepper to taste; 1 cup shredded lettuce; garlic bread or wheat crackers to serve.

Have all the ingredients ready. Just before serving, place the shredded lettuce in a circle in a serving platter. In a nonreactive bowl whisk together oil, vinegar, a little salt and pepper and pour half over the quinoa, and mix together and spread out over the shredded lettuce.
Top with the mixture of tomatoes, capers, pickles, green onions, chopped pickles and a little salt and pepper. Then place the shrimps around the lettuce circle and mound the lobster meat on the top.

Sprinkle rest of the vinaigrette over the meat. Garnish with cranberries then with the almonds. Serve with garlic bread or the wheat crackers and lime wedges.

Potato Salad (Serves: 4-6)

Ingredients: About 1-1/2 pounds, or 5 medium red potatoes; salt and fresh-ground black pepper to taste; 2 tbsp. mayonnaise, 1 tbsp. prepared creole mustard; 1 tbsp. sugar; 3 tbsp. cider vinegar; 6 tbsp. olive oil; 1/4c chopped onion; ½ cup chopped red bell pepper, ½ cup chopped flat-leaf parsley (op).

1. Scrub and wash the potatoes well under running tap water, place them in a pot, cover with cold water and bring them to a boil, then cover with the lid and boil them for about 30 minutes or until soft (poke with a knife and it should go in easily). Drain out the water and let them cool covered.
2. In a large non-reactive bowl, whip mayonnaise, mustard, sugar and vinegar well, then whip in the olive oil slowly.
3. When potatoes are cooled, peel them or leave the skin on and cut them 1 to 1-1/2-inch cubes and spread out in a platter. Sprinkle salt and pepper to taste all over, then pour over the vinegar mixture, saving about 1 tbsp. of the mixture in the bowl. Carefully turn over the potatoes with a knife or a spatula and mix them a little. In the bowl, add chopped onion and bell peppers in the leftover vinegar mixture and pour the onion mixture over the potato salad. Slide the potato salad in the bowl, sprinkle with the parsley and refrigerate covered until needed.

German Potato Salad (Serves: about 6)

I lived for a short while in Berlin, Germany, and their potato salad seems to be mild; we make it more sharp here. But they both taste good. Bacon is salty, so be careful adding any additional salt.

Ingredients: About 2 pounds red bliss potatoes, small or large; boiled in first-cold water until soft, then cut into 1-inch cubes with skin on; about ¾ pound pork or turkey bacon cooked in a skillet both sides crispy, and crumbled; 2 tbsp. butter or canola oil; 1 cup chopped onion; ½ cup celery stalk, peeled on the back and then chopped fine; 1 tbsp. each grainy and Dijon (sharp) mustard; ½ cup cider vinegar; 1 tsp. sugar; salt and pepper to taste; to garnish: fresh flat-leaf parsley or fresh mint leaves chopped.

In a medium pot, on medium heat, add oil and cook onion and celery for 8-10 minutes until soft. Add sugar, vinegar, little salt and pepper, potatoes and stir well. Add mustards and about ¼ to ½ cup water and bring to a simmer. Add bacon and stir well, simmer for 5 minutes. Check for seasoning and serve garnished with parsley or mint.

Tip: Fry bacon first and take out all fat, it is health hazard. You have enough spices to give enough flavor.

Salmon, Quinoa, Broccoli & Chickpea Salad (Serves: 2)

You can serve this salad warm or cold. If warm, use blanched asparagus instead of lettuce. It is colorful, nutritious and easy to make.

Ingredients: ½ cup whole grain quinoa; 1 tsp. olive oil; 1 pound boneless salmon with skin on; ¾ cup chicken broth; 2 cup shredded romaine lettuce (for cold), or 2 cup trimmed and cut into 2-inch pieces asparagus blanched for 3 minutes (for hot); 1 cup cooked and drained kidney beans or chickpeas heated in 1 tsp. oil for 5 minutes, and then sprinkled with 1 tsp. cumin powder.1 cup grape tomatoes; vinaigrette: whisk 2 tbsp. sherry vinegar with 4 tbsp. olive oil, then grate in one large garlic clove and sprinkle ½ tsp. dry rosemary and salt to taste.

In a small pot bring to a boil ¾ cup of water add quinoa and 1 tsp. oil; stir well and let it cook on medium heat for 5 minutes, stirring occasionally. Cover the pot, turn off the heat, and let it rest for 15 minutes. Bring chicken broth to a boil in a large pan add the salmon skin side down, cover and simmer on medium heat for about 7 minutes or until the salmon flakes. Take out the fish and remove the skin, then sprinkle with 1 tbsp. vinaigrette and cut into bite-size pieces.

Assemble the plates: make layers - spread out the quinoa in two warm plates, top with asparagus or lettuce, then asparagus, tomatoes, salmon pieces, and kidney beans or chickpeas. Drizzle the vinaigrette all over and serve.

Heirloom Tomato Salad (Serves: 4-6)

To find heirloom tomatoes, you have to wait for the tomato season. This is perfect for the lunch and add 1 cup of chickpeas, or some snow peas, and some cubed ham or chicken, and you have a dinner ready without cooking. You can get about 2-1/2 pounds heirloom tomatoes of your choice.

Ingredients: 1 pkg. 4ounces (113.4g) watercress cleaned and spun dry; 1 container 16 oz. (453g) extra-firm tofu sliced in 4 thin layers; keep each type of tomatoes separate to make the design;1 large beefsteak tomato sliced in 4 slices; 1 box 8 oz. (227g) petite romas red and yellow mixed tomatoes on the vine, halved; 1 container 16 ounces (454g) unique brown kumato tomatoes each cut in 4 wedges; 1 container 16 ounces (454g) compari (about 2 inches in diameter) tomatoes each cut into 4 wedges; 4 fresh radishes cut in quarters (op); 1 container 8 ounces (227g) fresh mozzarella cheese medium balls; ¼ cup e.v. olive oil; ½ cup Champagne vinegar; 1 large crushed garlic clove; ½ tsp. dry or 1 tab fresh oregano chopped; 1 tsp. honey; salt and fresh-ground black pepper to taste. Garlic or cheese bread to serve.

Topping: ½ cup sliced green onion; ¼ cup each: grated parmesan cheese and toasted black sesame seeds; a little smoked sweet paprika.

1. Have 4 serving plates ready to make the layers of tomatoes. First whip together the vinaigrette: honey, oil, vinegar, garlic, oregano and a little salt and pepper.

2. Use about 1/3 of the vinaigrette, roll in the watercress and place in equal portions on 4 plates. Top with tofu, then with large slice of tomato on each plate. Now with 2/3 of the vinaigrette, dip the tomatoes and place the medium-size all around and little one over the large slice of tomato. Put some cheese balls and radishes with the small tomatoes. Sprinkle the topping and serve with tasty bread

Tips: Although the heirloom tomato salad is very famous, the cooked tomatoes have more nutrients. Tomatoes have lycopene which is good for eyes, has vitamins B and C, fiber, potassium, chromium, etc.

Stuffed Zucchini Blossoms served over Two Sauces (Serves: 2)

My friend Niki grows zucchini every year and gives out the flowers to her friends. They are hard to find in the market. You can order them at a farmer's market. If you grow your own, just pick them early in the morning, before bees get into them. I serve them over two sauces and/or salad.

The Fresh Tomato Sauce (M: about 2 cups)

Ingredients: 1 pint grape tomatoes or mini San Marzano tomatoes halved; 1 medium onion thick-sliced; 2 medium garlic cloves halved; ½ red bell pepper sliced; 1 tbsp. balsamic vinegar; 3 tbsp. olive oil, divided; 1 tsp. fennel seeds; salt and pepper to taste.

Preheat oven at 400 degrees. Line a large (12x18-inch) baking sheet with aluminum foil. Spread out the tomatoes, onion, pepper, and garlic in single layer, drizzle with vinegar and then with 1 tbsp. olive oil. Bake for about 15 minutes until soft. Then puree them with fennel seeds, a little water, 2 tbsp. olive oil, and a little salt and pepper to taste. Refrigerate covered until needed.

The Green Soy or Green Chickpeas Sauce (M: about 2 cups)

Ingredients: About 1-1/2 cup frozen green soy beans or fresh or frozen green chickpeas out of pod, cooked in a little water for about 10 minutes until soft; ½ cup flat-leaf parsley or cilantro; 1 tbsp. fresh or ½ tsp. dry mint; 2 tbsp. cider vinegar; salt and pepper to taste; about ½ cup cooking water; 4 tbsp. olive oil.

Puree all ingredients in a blender to a fine sauce consistency. Taste for seasoning and add as needed. Cover and refrigerate until serving.

For the Zucchini Blossom

For the Filling: About 10-12 zucchini blossoms: rinse with cold and slow running water and pour out the water, then dip each blossom in a bowl filled with cold water, shake well and place stems side up on a paper towel-lined platter; about 4 ounces mozzarella or goat cheese cut into ½-inch diameter and about

1-1/2 to 2-inches long sticks and then dipped into 1 tsp. lemon-pepper mix; 10-12 pieces of anchovy or sandwich salami cut into strips and sautéed fast in a hot pan to take out all fat,.

For the Dipping: 2 large egg whites whisked with ½ tsp. vinegar until foamy, then whisked in ½ of the yolk; for dusting: 1 cup almond flour mixed with ½ cup grated parmesan cheese; to shallow fry: olive oil.

Stuff each of the zucchini flowers with a stick of cheese and meat, then refrigerate for 5 minutes. Spread out two sauces, half and half, on each serving platters. Heat about 4 tbsp. oil in a large frying pan on medium heat. Flatten and dip the flowers on both sides, then hold in the middle and dip the opening (to seal the end as it cooks) in the egg white, press in the almond-and-cheese mixture; holding the stem, drop them in the hot oil, fry fast on medium-high heat, turning them over as soon as they are browned underneath, and cook both sides light brown. Take out on the paper towel lined platter. Serve warm over two sauces and some salad and/or crusty bread to soak up the sauces.

Tip: This is a healthy lunch all the way. Pick the blossoms early in the morning before bees get into them. Hold the stems and gently dip them in the bowl of cold water to get the dirt and bugs out, then tap them on the paper towels. I leave them there until I am ready to use.

Bacon, Lettuce & Tomato Sandwich (BLT)

(Serves: 2)

I think bacon is everyone's favorite. You can serve it for breakfast, lunch, snacks or with dinner over steak. We also like chocolate bacon on the side of a BLT. Or you can eat it as a dessert.

Ingredients: 1 tsp. olive oil; 4 slices of sourdough sandwich bread lightly toasted and cooled; about ½ cup horseradish cream or mayonnaise for toast; 2 slices of iceberg lettuce cut horizontally, about ½-inch thick; 1 large tomato, sliced horizontally in 4 slices; salt and fresh ground black pepper to taste; 4 strips of thick bacon or any bacon of your choice; 1 soft haas avocado ready to serve; 2 kiwi fruits peeled and sliced just before assembly; 4 slices of chocolate bacon to serve on side.

Heat a cast-iron pan on medium-high heat. When heated, add the oil and lay down the bacon strips, and cook the bacon about 2-3 minutes on each side, or until it is brown and crisp. Take out on a paper towel-lined platter.

Assemble the Sandwich: Spread the horseradish cream or the mayo over the toasted bread on one side. Place one slice of bread in each platter, top with lettuce, tomato, salt and pepper, then place two strips of bacon on the top, and finally halved the avocado, take out the pit with the edge of the knife, peel the avocado, and cut the wider end into strips, leaving it attached at the narrow end, and top the sandwich in a fan-like fashion. Place the second bread slice next to the sandwich, serve with kiwi and chocolate bacon on the side.

Tip: Kiwi fruit and avocado should be cut just before serving. Kiwi fruit loses its nutrients as soon as it is exposed to air. And the avocado turns brown. The best way to serve the avocado is cut and peel off the skin, scoop out the pulp and mash it with lemon juice, or wash the peeled avocado under running cold water, and then dip and leave in the lemon water. That way, it will stop from turning brown for 15-20 minutes.

Chocolate Bacon

Ingredients: 1 Pound thick bacon cooked; 1 bag, 12 oz., (340 G) semi-sweet chocolate morsels; 2 tbsp. unsalted butter; ½ tsp. instant coffee; ¼ cup milk.

Place the chocolate, butter, coffee and milk in a double boiler and melt chocolate over lightly simmering water, make sure the bowl does not touch the water; or in a microwavable bowl, heat the chocolate about 1 to 1-1/2 minute, stirring every 20 seconds, until the chocolate is melted. Cool the chocolate.

Dip the cooked bacon strips in the melted chocolate, halfway first, then brush with a pastry brush making sure the bacon is covered well. Cool in room temperature until the chocolate is hardened. You can make it a day before. Wrap the prepared chocolate bacon loosely with a paper towel, then with plastic wrap. Place in an airtight plastic container and place in the refrigerator. Bring to room temperature before serving.

Pulled Pork Sandwich with Caramelized Onion and Potato Chips (Serves: 2)

Ingredients: About 1 to 1-1/2 pound cooked pulled pork (see recipe under meat); ½ tsp. granulated garlic; salt and pepper to taste; about 1 cup vinegar sauce or heated barbecue sauce; ½ cup caramelized onions; prepared mustard or mayo for the bun (op); 2 Cuban or sandwich buns; 1 cup creamy coleslaw; fresh-made or oven-heated potato chips. Salt and pepper to taste; salad or 2 plum tomatoes and 2 kiwi fruits to serve.

Heat a medium pan, add 1cup barbecue sauce (I prefer vinegar and barbecue sauce mixture), bring it to a simmer on medium heat. Add meat, sprinkle with garlic, salt and pepper to taste stir a little just to warm the meat. Cut the buns in half horizontally. Heat the buns lightly, then spread the bottom with barbecue sauce and sprinkle with salt and pepper. Top the bottom piece of the bun with caramelized onions, then meat and coleslaw. Spread the mayo or mustard on the top piece of the bun. Serve with salad or fresh tomato and kiwi fruit, sliced, along with warm potato chips.

(1) Caramelized Onion (M: 2 cups)

Ingredients: 2 tbsp. unsalted butter or canola oil; 2 large yellow onions thin-sliced; ½ tsp. granulated garlic; salt and fresh ground black to taste; 1 tsp. balsamic vinegar (op); 2 tsp. light brown sugar (op); about ½ tsp. cayenne pepper (op).

Heat a heavy-bottom pan on medium heat. When heated, add butter/oil, move around to coat the pan. Add onions, stir for 5 minutes on medium-high heat to coat with butter. Add salt and pepper and stir well. Reduce the heat to low, cover, and cook for 8-10 minutes. Open the cover, stir in cayenne pepper and balsamic vinegar and sugar, stir open until it is soft and done.

(2) Potato Chips (Serves: 2)

You can make fresh potato chips: slice 2 peeled red potatoes thin on box-grater, bring 4 C of water to a boil, par-boil the chips, take out with perforated spatula, pat dry and then deep fry them at 350 degree heated oil. Or buy thick ones from the store and just heat at 300 degrees in the oven for a few minutes until warm.

Haddock Sandwich

With Avocado Sauce, Beet, Carrot, & Pumpkin Slaw

This is a fried-fish sandwich that takes only 7-8 minutes to cook. Use either haddock, cod or thick catfish fillets. Serve with avocado sauce, beet, carrot and pumpkin slaw.

(1) Avocado Sauce (M:1-1/2C)

Ingredients: ¾ cup Greek yogurt; 4 tbsp. lemon juice; 1 garlic clove grated over yogurt; 2 haas ripe avocado, cut in half, pitted and pulp taken out with a tbsp.; salt and pepper to taste; 2 tbsp. chopped cilantro.

Whisk all ingredients in a bowl, cover the bowl with plastic wrap, and then cover with the lid and refrigerate until needed.

(2) Beet, Carrot and Pumpkin Slaw (M:2C)

Ingredients: 2 medium fresh beets, (wear gloves, if you prefer) peeled and grated on the large holes of a box grater (about 2 c); 1 cup peeled and grated fresh carrot or julienned broccoli; ¼ cup roasted pumpkin seeds; ½ cup dry cranberries; 3 tbsp. cider vinegar; 3 tbsp. sugar; 3 tbsp. e.v. olive oil; salt (op).

Place the grated beets in a non-reactive bowl and press them down (pack them). Top with carrots and press it down, then top with a mixture of pumpkin seeds and cranberries and press it down. Just before serving, whisk together vinegar, oil and sugar and pour over the slaw. Take out stacked slaw in the layers and place on the serving plates.

(3) Fried Haddock

Ingredients: 1 pound boneless and skinless fillet of haddock cut across in two pieces; ½ cup all-purpose flour scattered in a platter; 1 large egg whisked in another platter; 1 cup panko bread crumbs (Japanese) mixed with 1 tbsp. paprika, 1 tsp. lemon-pepper mix, 1 tbsp. grated cheese scattered in another platter; about ½-inch deep canola oil to deep-fry; one large roasted red bell pepper halved from the jar.

Heat oil in a frying pan on medium heat. Wash, pat dry and check the fish for the bones by moving a finger all over the fish. Dip the fish first in the flour, then in the egg, and press down in the crumbs on both side. Increase the heat to medium-high, about 360 degrees. Carefully place the fish in the hot oil and let it cook for about 5 minutes or until it is golden underneath. Turn over once and fry on the other side golden brown. Take out and place on the paper towel-lined platter.

Assemble the Sandwich: While fish is cooking, heat two serving plates, cut the buns in half horizontally and toast lightly, then spread with the avocado sauce generously. On the bottom part, place the lettuce, and when the fish is fried, place it on the lettuce, and place the tomato and then halved roasted red bell pepper. Serve with the beet and carrot slaw on the side. If you prefer, serve with fruits or the chips as well.

Tip: Try to serve vinegar salad or slaw with fried food. It is healthy, tasty and attractive.

Salmon Sandwich (Serves: 2)

These sandwiches are tender, tasty and colorful. You can use long rolls or soft bread and smoked salmon, or 1 pound (16 ounces) fresh salmon rubbed with prepared mustard, salt and pepper; cook in a sauté pan in 1 tsp. butter, covered about 7 to 8 minutes or until opaque. Serve fruits, vegetables, and pickles etc on the side.

Ingredients: 2 soft long rolls (I prefer sweet Portuguese rolls); about 4 ounces (1/2 pkg.) or 4 tbsp. light cream cheese or light mayonnaise, 2 tbsp. sweet pickled relish; ½ cup shredded lettuce or baby spinach; 1 jar (6 ounces, about 1 cup) marinated artichokes drained; 1 red bell pepper cored, seeded and cut into thin strips; 2 tbsp. pumpkin seeds (op).

To serve with: 1 ripe Haas Avocado; 2 kiwi fruits and pitted black olives.

1. Heat the rolls in a toaster or regular oven, just 1 minute, to freshen them up and cut in half lengthwise. Spread cream cheese or mayo on all four pieces. On the top rolls, spread the smoked salmon or fresh cooked salmon, discard the salmon skin, then sprinkle with the pumpkin seeds.
2. On the bottom rolls, spread pickled relish, shredded lettuce/spinach, marinated artichokes and top with red pepper strips.
3. Serve with avocado and kiwi slices, and pitted black olives or any other pickles as you desire.

Tips: Smoked salmon sandwich is light, so load up with a lot of soft salad vegetables and tasty pickles.

Spinach Wraps (Serves: 6-8)

These are tasty, healthy and very easy to assemble. Just make sure you use two types of sauces or chutneys: sweet-and-sour and hot-and-spicy to taste, to give a lot of flavor. The meat is wrapped in the bread tortilla that can take extra spices.

Ingredients: 1 14 oz. pkg. (400g) spinach with garlic and pesto tortilla, burrito size; 1 8 oz. pkg. light cream cheese softened and/or 1 pound apple, raisin coleslaw; ½ pound thin-sliced provolone cheese; ½ pound thin-sliced Virginia ham; ½ pound thin-sliced roast beef; or 2 cups cooked and cubed barbecued or plain chicken, turkey or ham; 1 cup or to taste thick cilantro and lemon or mango chutney; pickled relish; or ½ cup peppercini (sliced and pickled peppers); to serve: olives, grape tomatoes, radishes and/or more coleslaw and fruits.

1. Heat the tortilla directly on the burner at medium heat, turning around until lightly-warmed, or use a dry cast-iron pan on medium heat and heat the tortilla, pressing down with the spatula and turning over until lightly heated.
2. On a large cutting board or trays, spread out a few tortillas; first spread with cream cheese and/or coleslaw, then with the chutney, leaving about a ½-inch border all around.
3. Now in the center of the tortilla, line up two slices of the cheese, top with the two slices of each type of meat or with the meat cubes.
4. Finally, top with a few slices of peppercini or about 1 tbsp. of the pickled relish.
5. Roll up the tortilla tightly, making a long roll of the cheese and the meat. Cut in half on a diagonal basis and serve with sides. You can make them one day ahead; do not cut, but roll each one separately in parchment paper, stack them in a platter cover with a paper towel and then place the platter inside a large plastic bag and refrigerate. Cut in half and serve later.

Fish Tacos with Avocado Pesto & Tomato Salsa (Serves: 4)

There is very little cooking here. Cook fish for about 5 minutes and blanche the asparagus, or any of your favorite vegetable.

Ingredients: 2 tbsp. canola or olive oil; country Dijon mustard; hot ketchup (ketchup mixed with hot sauce or cayenne); about 1 cup shredded iceberg lettuce; 2 red bell peppers seeded and cut into match sticks; about ½ pound asparagus, hard bottoms trimmed and blanched in hot water for 3 minutes, then cut to bite-size; 2 pounds salmon, cod or any other firm-flesh fish, boneless and skinless, each piece cut into 4 long pieces lengthwise; 1-1/2 tbsp. lemon-pepper seasoning mix mixed with 2 tbsp. dry seasoned bread crumbs; salt and pepper to taste; 2 whole lemons cut into small pieces and 1 lemon for sprinkling; tomato salsa and avocado pesto; 8 small or medium flour tortillas.

1. You can prepare everything ahead, just cook the fish the last minute and top the tacos. Sprinkle the fish with lemon seasoning mix. Heat a cast-iron pan or a heavy-bottom pan on medium heat.
2. Heat the tortilla according to the package directions or over the stove, on low heat for about 1 minute per side, turning the tortilla around. Place two tortillas on each serving plate. Make one row each of mustard and the ketchup in the middle. Top with the lettuce, bell pepper sticks, asparagus and then with tomato salsa.
3. When pan is very hot, add the oil and add the fish sticks flesh-side down, skin -side up, and cook on medium-high heat for about 2-3 minutes until golden. Take the pan off the stove for 1 minute. After 1 minute, turn each piece over and cook the other side for about 2 minutes or until fish is done and is flaky.
    Top each taco with 2 fish sticks, a squeeze of lemon juice and then top with the pesto and serve warm.

Cilantro, Almond and Avocado Pesto (M: 1 cup)

Ingredients: 2 cup cilantro leaves and very soft stems, chopped; 1-2 dry serrano peppers broken into small pieces; 1 large clove of garlic chopped; ¼ cup slivered almonds; 1/3 cup lemon juice; 1/3 cup extra-virgin olive oil; 1 haas avocado, cut in half, pitted and flesh scooped out with a large spoon; salt and pepper to taste.

In a food processor, pulse about 4-5 times: cilantro, dry pepper, garlic, almonds and lemon juice. While machine is running pour in a slow stream the olive oil and whisk until thick. Take out the pesto in a non-reactive bowl. Just before serving mash in the avocado with a fork. Add salt and pepper to taste.

Turkey Tacos (Serves: 4)

Make pepper relish a day before and prepare the turkey meatballs a day before; just bake the meatballs 20 minutes before serving.

Ingredients: 4 corn, flour or chickpeas (missi roti) tortillas; 1 cup pepper relish; 12 turkey meatballs; ½ cup sour cream, ½ cup thin slice red onion rings marinated in 2 tbsp. cider vinegar, 4 tbsp. extra virgin olive oil, 1/4t sp. each granulated garlic and oregano, salt and pepper to taste; to serve cucumber raita.

Heat the tortilla on a stove on medium flame, on both sides; keep them in a kitchen towel. Spread out ¼ cup of pepper relish, top with turkey meatballs, then sour cream and marinated red onion. Serve with cucumber raita, if wish.

Tip: You can also serve turkey meatballs in butter lettuce or over avocado. Fill the avocado with pepper relish, top with meatball and then with lemon chutney.

Tomato Salsa (M: 2 cups)

Ingredients: 2 cup chopped plum tomatoes (about 4-5 tomatoes); ½ cup thin-sliced green-onion stems or yellow onion; 1 tsp. garlic clove crushed fine; 1 tsp. lime zest; ¼ cup lime juice; ¼ cup extra-virgin olive oil; ½ tsp. dry oregano; salt and fresh ground black pepper to taste.

In a non-reactive bowl, mix together tomatoes, onion, garlic, zest and lemon juice. Sprinkle over oil, oregano, salt and pepper. Cover and leave in the room temperature up to an hour. Just before serving mix a little and serve.

Oyster Po'Boy Sandwich (Serves: 2)

You can make this sandwich with fried oysters or fried clams. We prefer a combination of oysters and scallops. To make the oysters more tasty and substantial, I coat them with coconut on one side and spicy dredging flour on the other side. We also have layers of flavors. On the bread, we use lemon or yogurt chutney, line the bottom of the roll with baby arugula or fresh watercress; on sautéed bell peppers and onions, we use cocktail sauce, and on the oysters we use tartar sauce. Also, we serve these sauces and/or coleslaw on the side.

1. For the Sauteed Onion and Bell Peppers:
   Ingredients: 1 tbsp. canola oil and 2 tbsp. butter; 1 large onion sliced ½-inch wide; 1 each of green, red and orange bell peppers, cored, seeded and cut into 1-inch wide strips; ½ tsp. granulated garlic; salt and pepper to taste; 2 long rolls; to serve: 1 cup fresh baby arugula or watercress, lemon or yogurt chutney, pesto or mayonnaise, tartar sauce cocktail sauce.

2. Heat a large sauce pan on medium heat. Add oil and the butter and sauté onion for 5 minutes. Add the pepper strips, garlic and about ¼ tsp. salt and fresh ground black pepper or to taste. Cover and cook on low heat for 8-10 minutes or until soft. Turn off the heat, but keep them warm, heating them on and off.

3. For the Oysters:
   Ingredients: About 1 dozen live oysters, scrubbed clean, shucked, loosened and kept on the half shell; for the batter: ½ cup pancake flour mix whisked with 5-6 tbsp. water to make a thick paste; 1 cup fresh-grated or frozen coconut; 1 cup Cajun or any spicy dredging corn flour mix; canola or peanut oil to deep-fry.
   A. Heat about 2-inch-deep oil in a wok or in a wide pot, or in a fryer at 375 degrees (medium-high heat). Pick up one oyster in the shell and paste it with the pancake batter on the top, then press in the coconut all over the batter. Carefully slide them into dredging flour mix, press down all over to coat with the flour. Then pick up carefully with a perforated spatula, shake a little to drop the excess flour from them, and drop them into the hot oil on one side. Fry them about 2 minutes on each side and take them out in a heated platter.
   B. To Assemble the Sandwich: Cut the rolls in half lengthwise, and heat them in the 350 degree oven for 3-4 minutes, until they are just warm.
   Spread inside the rolls lemon or yogurt chutney or pesto or mayo. Top the bottom roll with arugula or watercress, then with sautéed onion and peppers, drizzle the cocktail sauce, top with fried oysters and drizzle with the Tartar sauce and cover with the top of the roll. Serve with extra sauces and coleslaw on the side.

   Tip: The fresh herb-made chutneys are not only tasty and flavor-boosters, but they are healthy and are loaded with nutrients. Also, you will need less salt.

Cold Cut and Meat Sandwiches

Roast Beef Sandwich: Use soft butter buns, cut them in half horizontal, toast them lightly, top with horseradish, then pile up 2-3 slices of low-salt roast beef, top with stuffed jalapeno or marinated onion and then a thin slice of pepper-jack cheese.

Turkey Sandwich: Use low salt, Turkey is low in calories and high in protein. Use potato toasted buns or butter buns, top with coleslaw, pile up 2-3 slices of low-salt roasted turkey, then with any chutney.

German Liverwurst Sandwich: Use rye bread or onion or butter toasted buns, top with mustard, place cascading two slices of liverwurst and then top with sweet cucumber or hot pepper relish.

Meatball Sandwich: Use Italian long rolls, toasted; top with fresh tomato sauce, top with heated meatballs, sprinkle with grated cheese and top with sliced pickled cherry peppers or pepperoncino

Meat Handling, Food Poisoning & Cooking

I have a few secrets for handling and cooking meat.

If it is possible, before cooking I always wash and pat-dry the meat with paper towels. Then I rub it with turmeric, granulated garlic and cayenne or black pepper. This way the meat is cured, free of all germs and adds a healthy dose of spices. You can then sprinkle with coarse sea salt. Coarse salt will not melt or spread too much and will give some flavor to the meat. Use beer to marinade whenever possible, it is more healthy.

When cooking meat with liquid, such as making pot roast, add some greens (spinach, kale, broccoli rabe, etc.) that will take out some chemicals and also add some vitamins and proteins.

When marinating the meat, wash, pat-dry and sprinkle with garlic and cayenne pepper first, then marinate in citrus and/or beer together with other ingredients. Beer takes care of bad chemicals.

When cooking steak, salt and pepper just before cooking. If it is a thin steak, cook on high heat fast, turning over only once. But if it is thick, sear in a little oil in the pan on medium heat, and keep on turning over every minute or so for even cooking, and also slow cooking to make it more tasty. The slower you cook meat, the better it is for you.

Do not char or burn the meat. The burnt meat produces bad chemicals.

Serve meat and steaks with gravy or natural juices scraped with the beef broth, and top it with thin-sliced scallion and fine chopped tomatoes mixed with 1 part cider vinegar and 2 parts extra virgin olive oil. That's enough, but if you want you can add sliced radishes and cilantro or parsley leaves. I sometimes add ½-inch cubes of hard cheese, such as gouda, jack or Swiss. Always serve a little herbs and greens either with lemon juice and e.v. olive oil or with sherry or cider vinegar, and e.v. olive oil, or kimchi, or sauerkraut or horseradish. They all add flavor to the meat, and fermented food is good for the digestive tract.

As always wash everything: cutting board, knives, surface and dishes, after handling the meat.

Food Poisoning

Food safety is just as important as cooking the food. Sanitation, precautions, cooking food with the right temperature, and good hygiene is a must. To avoid foodborne illnesses, keep hot food hot, cold food cold, cook it right and handle it right. According to website of United States Dept. of Agriculture (www.FoodSafety.gov):

"**Food Poisoning**: Food poisoning (also known as foodborne illness or foodborne disease) is any illness that results from eating contaminated food.

Causes:

Each year, millions of people in the United States get sick from contaminated food. Symptoms of food poisoning include upset stomach, abdominal cramps, nausea and vomiting, diarrhea, fever, and dehydration. Symptoms may range from mild to severe. Harmful bacteria are the most common cause of food poisoning, but there are many other causes, including the following:

Bacteria and Viruses: Bacteria and viruses are the most common cause of food poisoning. The symptoms and severity of food poisoning vary, depending on which bacteria or virus has contaminated the food.

Molds, Toxin, Contaminants: Most food poisoning is caused by bacteria, viruses, and parasites rather than toxic substances in the food. But, some cases of food poisoning can be linked to either natural toxins or chemical toxins.

Parasites: Parasites are organisms that derive nourishment and protection from other living organisms knows as hosts. In the United States, the most common foodborne parasites are protozoa, roundworms, and tapeworms.

Allergens: Food allergy is an abnormal response to a food triggered by your body's immune system. Some foods, such as nuts, milk, eggs, or seafood, can cause allergic reactions in people with food allergies.

Long-Term, Effects:

Kidney failure, Chronic arthritis, Brain and nerve damage, & Death.

Keep Food Safe:

Check your steps: Following four simple steps – Clean, Separate, Cook, and Chill – can help protect your family from food poisoning at home.

What Government Does to Keep Food Safe:

The food industry is responsible for producing safe food. Government agencies are responsible for setting food safety standards, conducting inspections, and monitoring food products, including imports.

E. Coli

E. Coli is the name of a type of bacteria that lives in your intestines and in the intestines of animals. Although most types of E. Coli are harmless, some types can make you sick.

The worst type of E. Coli, known as E. Coli 0157:H7, causes bloody diarrhea and can sometimes cause kidney failure and even death. E. Coli 0157:H7 makes a toxin called Shiga toxin and is known as a Shiga toxin-producing E. Coli (STEC). There are many other types of STEC, and some can make you just as sick as E. Coli 0157:H7.

One severe complication associated with E> Coli infection is hemolytic uremic syndrome (HUS). The infection produces toxic substances hat destroy red blood cells, causing kidney injury. HUS can require intensive care, kidney dialysis, and transfusions.

Sources:

- Contaminated food, especially undercooked ground beef, unpasteurized (raw) milk and juice, soft cheeses made from raw milk, and raw fruits and vegetables (such as sprouts).
- Contaminated water, including drinking untreated waer and swimming in contaminated water.
- Animals and their environment: you could get an E. Coli infection.
- Faces of infected people.

What Do I Do?

Drink plenty of fluids and get rest. If you cannot drink enough fluids to prevent dehydration or if your symptoms are severe (including blood in your stools or severe abdominal pain), call your doctor. Antibiotics should not be used to treat this infection.

How Can I Prevent It?

- Avoid eating high-risk foods, especially undercooked ground beet, unpasteurized milk or juice, soft cheeses made from unpasteurized milk, or alfalfa sprouts.
- Use a food thermometer to make sure that ground beef has reached a safe internal temperature of 160 degrees F.
- Wash hands before preparing food, after diapering infants, and after contact with cows, sheep, or goats, their food or treats, or their living environment.
-

Salmonella

Salmonella, the name of a group of bacteria, is one of the most common causes of food poisoning in the United States. Usually, symptoms last 4-7 days and most people get better without treatment. But, Salmonella can cause more serious illness in older adults, infants, and persons with chronic diseases. Salmonella is killed by cooking and pasteurization.

Sources:
- **Food:** Contaminated eggs, poultry, meat unpasteurized milk or juice, cheese, contaminated raw fruits and vegetables (alfalfa sprouts, melons), spices, and nuts.
- **Animals and their environment:** Particularly reptiles (snakes, turtles, lizards), amphibians (frogs), birds (baby chicks) and pet food and treats.

Symptoms: Diarrhea, fever, abdominal cramps, vomiting.

What Do I Do? Drink plenty of fluids and get rest. If you cannot drink enough fluids to prevent dehydration or if your symptoms ae severe, call your doctor. Antibiotics may be necessary if the infection spreads from the intestines to the blood stream.

- Avoid eating high-risk foods, including raw or lightly cooked eggs, undercooked ground beef or poultry, and unpasteurized milk.
- Keep food properly refrigerated before cooking.
- Clean hands with soap and warm water before handling food. Clean surfaces before preparing food on them.

How Can I Prevent It?

- Separate cooked foods from ready-to-eat foods. Do not use utensils on cooked foods that were previously used on raw foods and do not place cooked foods on plates where raw foods once were unless it has been cleaned thoroughly.
- Cook foods promptly after serving and when transporting from one place to another.
- Wash your hand after contact with animals, their food or treats, or their living environment.

Botulism

Botulism is a rare but serious illness caused by a bacterium which occurs in soil. It produces a toxin that affects your nerves. Foodborne botulism comes from eating foods contaminated with this toxin.

Sources:

Infants: Honey, home-canned vegetables and fruits, corn syrup

Children and adults: Home-canned foods with a low acid content, improperly canned commercial foods, home-canned or fermented fish, herb-infused oils, baked potatoes in aluminum foil, cheese sauce, bottled garlic, foods held warm for extended periods of time.

Symptoms:

Infants: Lethargy, weakness, poor feeding, constipation, poor head control, poor gag and sucking reflex.

Children and adults: Double vision, blurred vision, drooping eyelids, slurred speech, difficulty swallowing, dry mouth and muscle weakness.

What Do I Do? Botulism is a medical emergency. If you have symptoms of botulism, contact your doctor immediately.

How Do I Prevent It?
- Be very careful when canning foods at home.
- Do not let babies eat honey.
- Get prompt medical care for infected wounds."

All Purpose Marinade (M: about 1-1/2 cups)

You can use this marinade for sauce, by reducing it in half, on medium to medium-high heat, in a large greased sauté pan, mostly covered, so it does not splash all over. Do not reduce the marinade after it is being used on the meat. If you don't have enough marinate then use only half as marinade and brush it over the meat. Then use other half with 1/4C of Teriyaki sauce and more fresh herbs, heat and reduce a little and use as a sauce.

Ingredients: ¼ cup Worcestershire sauce; 1 tbsp. crushed black peppercorns; 2 tbsp. cider vinegar; 2 tbsp. lemon juice; ¼ cup teriyaki sauce; 2 tbsp. chopped garlic cloves; 2 tbsp. chopped fine ginger; ¼ cup fine chopped onion or sliced green onion; 2 tbsp. fine chop fresh thyme; about ¼ cup olive or canola oil; 1cup beer or water.

Whisk all in a medium bowl and pour over the meat, refrigerate from 1 hour to overnight in the refrigerator. Take out the meat about ½ hr. before cooking.

Marinade for the Dark Meat (M: about 1-1/2 cups)

This marinade is for the dark meat such as: Beef, lamb and Pork etc.

Ingredients : 1 tbsp. each roasted and ground caraway and cumin seeds;1 tbsp. each fine chopped: garlic cloves, ginger; 1 tsp. crushed black pepper-corns; 1tbsp. agave nectar, honey or 2tbsp. light brown sugar; 2 tbsp. lemon juice; 1 tbsp. olive oil; 1 tbsp. Worcestershire sauce or dark beer. Experts have found that dark beer in the marinade cuts down on cancer-causing substances if you are going to grill or barbecue meat.

For the Lamb: Add 2-3 tbsp. fresh fine-chopped mint.

For the Beef: Add 1 tsp. each dry oregano and thyme.

For the Pork: Add 2 tbsp. fresh chopped or 1 tsp. dry rosemary.

Add to each marinade: 1 tbsp. lemon juice, 1 tbsp. olive oil, and 1 cup beer or water.

Chicken and Turkey Marinade (M: about ½ cup)

This marinade is good for about 3-4 pounds of meat. Combine and pour over the meat. Remember Cayenne pepper used as marinade does not give too much heat but it adds a good flavor.

Ingredients : ½ tsp. each: granulated garlic and cayenne pepper and fine-grated zest of lemon; 2 tbsp. each: olive oil; lemon juice, Worcestershire sauce, white wine; 1 tsp. coarse salt and ½ tsp. coarse black pepper.

Seafood Marinade (M: about ¾ cups)

Seafood does not need a long time to marinate. It will break the tissues too much. So marinate it briefly, about 10-15 minutes.

Ingredients: ¼ cup lemon juice; ½ cup orange juice; 1 tbsp. olive oil; ½ tsp. each granulated garlic powder and cayenne pepper and 2-3 pinches of salt and black pepper.

All Purpose Quick Marinade (M: about ½ cup)

This is for about 2-3 pounds of meat.

Lightly sprinkle the meat with granulated garlic and cayenne pepper, then brush over or pour over ½ cup of teriyaki sauce, mixed with some lemon juice or dark beer.

The Cuts of Various Meats

The Basic Cuts of Beef

Beef has 6 main cuts: starting from the shoulder are the chuck, ribs, loin, sirloin, round, and the brisket.

Chuck that has marble fat, is inexpensive and is excellent for burgers, pot roast and stews, etc.

Ribs are good for roasts. This is where the tenderloin is found, the most expensive meat. Also, most of the steaks like sirloin, porterhouse and T-bones are found. Ribs left attached to the meat are a rib roast.

The loin is the best and expensive meat. The shell steak or the New York strip steak comes from this part after the tenderloin is removed.

The round is the lean and tough meat.

The brisket, plate and the flank at the bottom are used for several different types of cooking like steak, pastrami and London broil, etc.

The tenderloin (about 2 feet) extends from the rib cage up to the hip. The filet mignon and tournedos both comes from this cut. Tenderloin has silver skin mostly on the wider part of the meat, it should be removed first before cooking by sliding a long boning knife or a sharp chef's knife underneath it and pulling out at both ends.

Precautions in buying Beef

1. Avoid buying the beef that is too fresh or deep red color.
2. Don't buy beef that has too much fat or no fat at all (marbling).
3. The fat should not be of grayish or yellowish color.
4. Buy beef with smooth texture.
5. Avoid damaged or leaky package.

Aging the Meat to Boost the Flavor

Take a roast or a large and thick steak and place it over a rack in a clean, dry, large glass platter, away from food (do not let anything touch it) for 3 to 4 days, turning the platter around daily (preferable in a 35-to-38-degree temperature). Then cut out or take a thick slice, brown it in a little oil or butter and oil mixture on both sides and then roast on low temperature (about 200 degrees), or pan fry on low heat for a good and juicy flavor and a tender meat. If the meat has freezer burn, then cut off that little slice and use the rest.

You can also age the meat by wrapping in 3-4 layers of fresh cheese cloth. Change the cloth each day and place it in the refrigerator on a dry platter. This way, meat will not have freezer burn, but you may lose some juices in the wrapping.

The Basic Cuts of Lamb

Lamb has five basic cuts: the shoulder, rib, loin, leg and the shank/breast. Lamb is best when it is purchased young — a leg of a young lamb should weigh around 4 to 4-1/2 pounds. Find the smallest one. The older and fatty meat can be chewy and can be tricky to cook.

Lamb that is over a year old is called mutton. In the famous mutton patties or kebabs, the meat is usually boiled with split chick peas, then ground with fresh and dry spices and seared on a large cast-iron griddle, then served with chutney and other condiments.

The shoulder is good for stew and soups or stuffed.

The ribs just behind the shoulder is the tender part called the rack of lamb, the tender lamb chops on the racks.

The loin the best and most-expensive, tender and flavorful. You can use for loin chops. The tenderloin is called the eye of the loin and is the most-expensive cut of the meat.

The leg, famous for roasting as whole, is the hind leg from the bottom to the hip. It can be boneless and butterflied, rubbed with spices and then grilled.

The shank, is from the forelegs and it can be stewed, braised, stuffed and roasted.

The Basic Cuts of Veal

Just like lamb, veal also has five basic cuts: the shoulder, rack, loin, leg and shank.

The shoulder has good fat that gives some flavor. After taking out the bones, it can be tied and roasted, or stuffed and roasted. The veal chops are part of the shoulder, loin and ribs. The meat is good enough for soups and stews as well.

The rack, just like lamb, has bones that can be frenched and roasted.

The loin, the best and tender of the meat, can be cut into chops or roasted boneless. The best chops are loin chops, thick, juicy and the flavorful.

The leg of the veal has eye round, top round, bottom round and top sirloin, just as found in beef. They all can be roasted or sliced into cutlets, etc.

The shank, or foreleg, is cut into ossobuco. The breast roasted stuffed or unstuffed.

The Basic Cuts of Pork

There are four basic cuts: the shoulder, ham, loin and spareribs.

The shoulder has two parts: the picnic ham or picnic shoulder is the part from the arm to the shoulder, and the Boston butt or Boston shoulder is the large part around the big muscle. It is good for roasts and cubes etc.

Ham comes from the upper part of the back legs. Ham is used in three different ways: fresh from uncooked, which takes a long time to cook. The wet-cured ham can be found in different products: "ham in water," dry-cured and the best type of ham, sold as ham "in natural juices." All of these hams are fully cured and cooked, therefore they take less time to cook. You can also find these hams pre-sliced and wrapped well. Be careful of the pre-sliced ham as it can be dry and less flavorful.

The loin, just like on other animals, is the expensive meat, tender and flavorful, and can be cut into chops or tied into crown roasts.

The shank is the mostly bony part of the back legs.

The spareribs are not called cuts, but they are part of the pig's belly.

Pork chops are mostly four types: the rib chops have little fat, are juicy and have a lot of flavor. The center-cut chops have some fat, are less juicy, but have good flavor. The sirloin chops are tough, dry and have less flavor. The blade chops have a lot of fat and look tough, but are juicy and have a lot of flavor.

Sweet and Spicy Bacon with Corn and Peas (S:2)

You will always find some bacon lovers who want to eat bacon almost any time of the day. Once in a blue moon we make this spicy bacon dish, and to feel not guilty we serve it with vegetables.

Ingredients: 1/2 Pound thick cut pork bacon, 1/4cup maple syrup; 1Tbsp. dry mustard powder; 2Tbsp. brown sugar; 4Tbsp. chili powder; 1tsp. black pepper; 1/2Tsp. garlic powder; 1Tbsp. onion powder; 1/4cup. sriracha sauce; to serve: 1cup cooked and shucked fresh corn, 1cup cooked frozen peas, pickles and bread to serve on side.

Cut bacon strips in half across. In a cast iron pan on a medium heat cook bacon half way and take out the fat by pressing down with a fork. Place the maple syrup in a plate. Make a mixture of the dry spices and place in a plate. In another plate place the sriracha sauce. Now dip each strip of bacon in the syrup, dry spices then in sriracha sauce place in a plate and again sprinkle a little dry spices all over. Place the bacon strips again in the clean cast iron pan or a baking tray, place in a 450 degrees preheated oven and bake about 10-15 minutes until they are brown and crisp, turning over once.

Serve bacon over the bread pieces, with corn, peas and pickles.

Roasting a Whole Beef Tenderloin (Serves: 8-10)

This luxurious meat melts in your mouth and is the best when you buy a larger piece, so you can have large and wide slices. It's OK to splurge once in a while. Buy at least 3 days ahead and leave it in the refrigerator. After roasting, I wrap the tenderloin in newspapers; it stays warm, cooks even, and melts in your mouth.

Ingredients: 1 trimmed beef tenderloin about 5 pounds, ask the butcher in the supermarket to trim it for you and then tie it with kitchen twine, folding the thin end underneath; 2 tbsp. canola oil; spice mixture of 1 tbsp. each: coarse sea salt, crushed black pepper and coffee granules; to serve: mashed potato, vegetables, and mushroom-wine gravy.

Take out the tenderloin and rub with oil, then with the spice mixture, and place in a large bowl or a baking tray open; refrigerate overnight or up to 2 days.

Take the tenderloin from the refrigerator and leave 3 hours in room temperature before roasting. Preheat the oven at 450 degrees for 10 minutes. Place the tenderloin in a heavy-duty roasting sheet with rims, in the oven, and reduce the temperature to 425 degrees. Roast for about 45 minutes and turn around the sheet halfway during the roasting. Insert the instant-read thermometer at the thickest part, it should read 120 degrees for rare, and 125 to 130 degrees for medium-rare. Take out the tenderloin and wrap in several sheets of plain paper or newspaper, then wrap in a kitchen towel for about 45 minutes to 2 hours. Open, slice thick and serve with gravy, mashed potatoes and vegetables.

Beef Tenderloin with Scallop Potatoes, Asparagus and wine gravy with mushrooms (Serves: 4)

This is our favorite Christmas or Valentine's dinner. Tenderloin or any good steak goes well with creamy potatoes, cream spinach or Indian pea curry called mutter paneer (creamy peas with cheese cubes).

(1)   Beef Tenderloin

Ingredients: 4 slices of trimmed beef tenderloin each about 3 inches wide, 4 inches long and about 2 inches high; some marble fat, coarse ground sea salt, fresh-ground black pepper, 2 garlic cloves peeled and slice half-lengthwise; canola oil to drizzle, and for the pan.

1. Preheat a cast-iron pan or a heavy-bottom pan on medium-high heat for 5 minutes or until it is very hot.
2. Rub the steak slices with cut garlic, press in the mixture of salt and pepper, drizzle some oil all over. Add 1 tbsp. oil in the pan, then press down the steak in the hot pan (it should sizzle), lay around the marble fat near each slice of steak. Cover the pan with the lid, leaving it open only about 1-inch for the steam to escape slightly. Immediately lower the stove temperature to medium and cook about 2-3 minutes until the steak is crusty and golden brown, turn over and cook steak the second side, only half-covered with the lid, and cook only for about 2 minutes on each side or until browned. Now place the steak in a preheated 250 degree oven for another 10 minutes, or until the internal temperature is 130 degrees for medium-rare.

3. Take out the steaks and let it rest on the warmed serving platters for about 5 minutes, slice diagonal or serve as it is with gravy.

(2) Scalloped Potatoes

Ingredients: 1-1/2 pounds new, fingerling or medium russet potatoes peeled and sliced slightly on bias about ¼-inch thick, washed and drained; 1 tsp. clarified butter; 1 packet low-sodium instant chicken broth; ¼ cup fine chopped mushrooms; 1 bay leaf; ½ cup fine chopped onion; ¾ cup heavy cream; ¼ tsp. dry rosemary; 1-2 pinches fresh-ground nutmeg (op); ½ tsp. granulated garlic (divided); 1 cup to 1-1/2 cups, about 4 to 6 ounces, sharp yellow, shredded, cheddar cheese; salt and fresh-ground white or black pepper to taste.

1. In a medium pot, on medium heat, heat the butter, move around to coat the bottom of the pot. Add mushrooms and cook on medium-high heat for 2 minutes, add the onion and cook for 5 minutes on medium heat. Add bay leaf and drained sliced potatoes, about 1/6 tsp. fresh-ground pepper, ¼ tsp. granulated garlic and instant chicken broth and brown the potatoes on medium heat for 5 minutes stirring with the metal spatula. Add about ½ cup water, increase heat to high, bring to a boil, then lower the heat and simmer for about 10 minutes until the potatoes are tender.
2. Take out the potatoes in a 8 x 8-inch baking dish and set them aside to cool a little.
3. In the same pot with left-over cooking liquid, add the heavy cream, nutmeg, rosemary, a little salt and pepper to taste. (potatoes need a little extra salt and pepper) and bring to a boil. Take off the heat, cool a little and slowly add half of the shredded cheese. Stir well to melt the cheese and immediately pour the sauce over the potatoes. Top potatoes with rest of the shredded cheese and bake at 425 degree oven for 5 minutes, increase the temperature and bake at 450 degrees and bake another 5 minutes or until potatoes are bubbly and light brown on the top. Serve warm.

(3) Asparagus

Ingredients: about 1-1/2 pounds fresh green asparagus with hard bottoms trimmed off; keep them together lengthwise in same direction so that it is easy to turn over and take them in and out of the pan. The cream sauce: 3 tbsps. each unsalted butter and flour; ½ cup to ¾ cup each water and heavy cream as needed; ¼ tsp. lemon zest; 1 tbsp. lemon juice or to taste; ½ tsp. prepared mustard; 1 egg yolk; salt and fresh-ground black or white pepper to taste; some butter (about 1 tab) to reheat the asparagus.

1. In a heavy-bottom large pan bring about 1-inch deep water with a little salt to a boil. Add asparagus in batches, move around with a tong and cook (blanch) for 2-3 minutes until they are a little soft and have a nice green color. Take them out in a platter and run the cold water on them to stop the cooking, or plunge them in a bowl of ice water. Set the platter a little tilted so that the water drains out. Reheat them in a little butter in a frying pan, just before serving. And if you prefer sprinkle a little granulated garlic, salt, pepper and a little lemon juice. Toss well and serve on a warm serving plate.

For the sauce: Heat a heavy-bottom pot on the on low heat. Whisk together water, yolk, a little salt and pepper, mustard, zest and lemon juice and set aside. When pot is heated add butter, shake around to coat the bottom of the pot, add flour and stir with a wooden spoon on low to medium heat for about 5 minutes, the flour should not get brown but it should be cooked well with the butter. Take the pot off the heat and slowly whisk in the egg and cream mixture. Put the pot back on the heat and whisking with a wire whisk cook the sauce to your desired consistency, adding more cream or the water. Taste and add salt, pepper or lemon juice as needed. Serve sauce across the asparagus or on the side in a gravy boat.

(4) **Wine gravy with Mushrooms** (M: about 2 C)

Ingredients: About 3 tbsp. clarified butter divided; 3 cups good red wine; 1 cup orange juice; 1 tbsp. lemon juice; 2 tbsp. corn starch; 1 tbsp. or packet low-sodium instant beef broth; salt and fresh-ground black pepper to taste; 1-1/2 to 2 cups, or 8 ounces, button or baby bella mushroom caps sliced about ¼-inch thick and stems chopped fine.

1. In a large and a heavy-bottom stainless steel pan add the butter, move around and coat the bottom of the pan. Off-heat, pour in the wine in the pan, increase the heat to medium-high and bring the wine to a boil. When wine starts boiling, cover with the lid, leaving about 2 inches open, so that you can see the wine reducing and will not bubble out. Reduce wine to 1 C (about 15 minutes). Add the orange and lemon juice, stir well, reduce by ¼ again and keep it warm on low heat. Add salt and pepper to taste.

2. Heat a separate small pot on low heat with about ¼ tsp. butter. Stir together cornstarch, 1 C water and beef broth and pour into the pot. Cook the gravy on medium-high heat, stirring constantly until thick, about 5-6 minutes. When gravy is done, pour into the reduced-wine mixture and heat a little.

3. While wine is reducing, heat a large heavy-bottom pan with 1 tbsp. clarified butter (mushrooms taste better in butter), add the sliced mushrooms caps, increase the heat to medium-high and brown for 2 minutes. Add the chopped mushroom stems and keep on browning the mushrooms until all the liquid has been evaporated and mushrooms are lightly browned. Take out the mushrooms and add to warmed gravy, whisk in remaining butter, and serve immediately.

Serve tenderloin with potatoes, gravy and asparagus or any other green vegetable.

Beef Wellington with Mashed Sweet Potatoes, Cream Spinach with Almonds, Cranberry Jelly and Wine Gravy with Mushrooms (Serves: 8)

Beef Wellington is a fancy Filet Mignon dinner where the whole tenderloin is wrapped in a flaky crust. I make cranberry jelly, sweet potatoes, spinach and wine gravy a day ahead, and cook the meat on the same day of serving. Refrigerate potatoes, place spinach in an oven-proof dish and heat at 300 degrees in the oven for about 30-45 minutes, or until heated through. Heat the gravy in a medium pot. Cranberry jelly settles well overnight, so just cut with a biscuit-cutter and serve in paper cups, or right on dinner plates. Follow the recipe for the wine gravy above.

(1) Mashed Sweet Potatoes

Ingredients: About 1-1/2 pounds sweet potatoes; 1 large carrot cored and peeled; 1 large parsnip cored and peeled; vegetable oil to sprinkle; ¾ cup heavy cream; ½ cup apricot jam; nutmeg; ¼ tsp. salt; to garnish: ½ cup dry cranberries.

1. **Preheat oven to 350 degrees. Line a large heavy-bottom** baking tray with aluminum foil, wash sweet potatoes and place them in the center of the tray, place the carrot and parsnip on the edges, sprinkle a little oil all over the vegetables, and cover with a large piece of aluminum foil, airtight, and bake them for about 1 hour and 15 minutes, or until soft.
2. When vegetables are cooled a little, peel the potatoes and process them in a food mill or grate them on the large holes of the box-grater. Heat the heavy cream in a medium pot on medium heat to simmer and whisk in the apricot jam; dissolve the jam. Add the baked and mashed potatoes and salt, stir well on medium heat, bring to simmer, add a little fresh-grated nutmeg. Serve warm sprinkled with cranberries.

(2) Cream Spinach with Almonds

Ingredients: 3 pkgs. each 10 ounces (283g) frozen cut-leaf spinach, 4 tbsp. unsalted butter; 4 tbsp. all-purpose flour; 1 cup milk plus more as needed; 1 cup heavy cream; ¾ cup toasted slivered almonds; ½ cup dry cranberries or raisins; ¾ cup chopped roasted red bell pepper from the jar; 3-4 tbsp. grated parmesan cheese; salt and pepper to taste.

1. In a medium pot, simmer the Spinach with 4 tbsp. water, on medium heat, covered, with a little salt and pepper, until it is soft, about 15-20 minutes, stirring occasionally.

2. In another pot on medium heat, heat the butter and flour and cook for 8-10 minutes until light brown. Take the pot off the heat and slowly whisk in the milk and heavy cream. Place the pot back on the heat and bring to a simmer, cook for 5 minutes; add the almonds, cranberry, red bell peppers and bring to a boil, simmer for 5-10 minutes until thickened. Add the cooked spinach, salt and pepper to taste. Add a little more milk if needed. Serve warm. We like thick spinach so it does not run in the plate.

(3) Cranberry Jelly cups

You can make this jelly a week ahead and freeze it covered. Defrost overnight in the refrigerator and serve.

Ingredients: 2 bags each 12 ounces (340g) fresh cranberries; 1-1/2 cups sugar; 1 box or 1.4 ounces (40g) strawberry Jell-O or pineapple Jell-O; 1 packet, about 1 tbsp., unflavored gelatin; zest of 2 oranges; juice of 1 fresh orange; 2 whole cloves; 1/6 tsp. salt.

In a heavy-bottom pan cook cranberries and sugar, stirring to dissolve the sugar, for about 25 minutes, or until half of the cranberries are cracked. Use a wooden spoon to crush some of the cranberries if they are not cracked. Take the pan off the heat and sprinkle the Jell-O and the gelatin on the top, stir well. Put pan back on the heat. Simmer for another 8-10 minutes until thickened, then pour in a greased 8 x 8-inch glass pan. Cool completely and refrigerate to harden. Use or freeze covered well. Defrost overnight in the refrigerator. Cut out with a biscuit cutter and serve in paper cups or directly on the serving plates

Beef Wellington

This is the whole Beef Filet Mignon, cooked, sprinkled with spices, wrapped in crust and baked again. I like this for dinner, you can cook about 2 hours ahead, wrap and it will be still warm. You can buy frozen puff pastry or make your own crust as follows.

Ingredients:

For the Crust: 4 cups all-purpose flour plus more for dusting; 2 sticks cold unsalted butter; 1 tsp. baking soda; 1 tsp. salt; ¼ cup plain yogurt; about 3-4 tbsp. ice water as needed.
For the Tenderloin: Buy at least 4-5 days ahead: one, about 6 pounds whole beef loin peeled tenderloin, sliver skin removed and tied (ask your butcher in the supermarket); sprinkle of onion powder, cayenne or fresh-ground black pepper, coarse salt; 2 tbsp. olive oil; 1 C pineapple topping; 2 egg yolks beaten with 1 tbsp water for egg wash; 2 tbsp. butter.

1. Buy tenderloin a few days before cooking and leave in the refrigerator for maturing. The night before cooking, unpack the beef, wash under running cold water, pat-dry, and sprinkle with cayenne or black pepper, onion powder, coarse salt and then rub oil all over. Cover with plastic wrap or place in a large zip-lock bag, and place on a baking sheet, refrigerate and marinate overnight.
2. Take the tenderloin out one hour before cooking. Preheat the oven at 500 degrees. Line a large baking sheet with aluminum foil and grease it lightly. Pat-dry the tenderloin, place on the baking sheet pointing the wider end toward the back wall. Roast the tenderloin for 5 minutes per pound (6 pounds will take 30 minutes) for medium-rare, turning around every 10 minutes to brown all sides. Take out the tenderloin and let it cool for 10 minutes.
3. While tenderloin is cooking, prepare the crust: In a large bowl mix the flour, baking soda and salt. Now grate the butter in the same bowl over the flour mixture. Then mix the butter and the four well with hand. Add the yogurt and half of the ice water and combine together to make a dough ball. Add more ice water by the tablespoon if needed.
4. Roll out the dough between two large sheets of plastic wrap, about 2-inches larger at the length, in a rectangle shape (about 18 x 10 inches). Trim off the ends of tenderloin to make them even. Take off the cord, pat-dry the meat all around, place on the rolled-out dough, brush with the pineapple topping, sprinkle a little black pepper and onion powder (do not use any salt); stretch the dough over the meat lengthwise and overlap the dough edges a little to enclose the meat. Then fold the ends over the meat. Put the seam down, and brush with the egg wash. Roast in a 425 degree oven, turning over once, until golden-brown crust, about 25-30 minutes, then reduce the temperature to 250 degrees and roast for 10 minutes. The internal temperature should be around 130-135 degrees for medium-rare. Take out of the oven, brush with butter all over. Set aside for 20 minutes, tented with foil before slicing. Serve with potatoes, spinach, cranberry jelly and wine gravy.

Roasted Tenderloin without the crust

Follow the instructions above and roast the tenderloin. When tenderloin is roasted for 30 minutes, turn off the oven, leave the tenderloin in the off oven for 5 minutes. Take out of the oven and roll in the double layer of newspaper, then in the kitchen towel. Set aside for 1 hour. The tenderloin is still cooking inside. Serve after 1 or 1-1/2 hour, sliced. It will be medium rare and still warm.

Tip: Wrapping in the newspaper does wonders. It keeps the steam inside, keeps it cooking, and keeps the meat warm for up to 1-1/2 hour.

Boneless Beef Brisket (Serves: 4-6)

At a very famous local restaurant from New York, now shut down due to Hurricane Sandy, we enjoyed the brisket sandwich very much, with gravy and coleslaw on the side. It forced us to make it at home now. You can make it smoky or plain. The secret is it should be steamed and sliced thin with an electric slicer.

Ingredients: About 2-1/2 pound beef brisket, thin-cut, boneless; salt and fresh-ground black pepper; 1 packet, 1.06 oz (30g) mesquite marinade mix and 1 tbsp. canola oil, or ¾ cup thick hoisin sauce, or any other smoky marinade. To serve: mashed potatoes and wine-mushroom gravy.

1. Wash the brisket under cold water, pat-dry with paper towels. Sprinkle the meat all around with salt and pepper, then on the fat side, sprinkle ½ packet on the top, then with oil (or sprinkle with half of the Hoisin sauce) and marinade open in a glass platter overnight.
2. When ready to cook, move the oven shelf in the middle, preheat oven at 325 degrees. Put large pieces of aluminum foil together to cover the roasting pan, air tight. Place about 2-inches hot water in the roasting pan, place the rack, fat side up, sprinkle with other ½ packet of marinate or sauce, cover air-tight with foil, pressing the foil against the rim well to seat the meat. Place in the pan, pointing the wider end of the meat toward the back wall, and steam the meat at 325 degree, or 30 minutes per pound, so it will take about 2-1/2 hours total steaming. Turn around the pan half-way around during the cooking. When done, take out the roasting pan on the counter and let it rest for 15 minutes, then open the foil away from you carefully. Let the meat rest in a heated platter for 10 minutes, loosely covered with foil.
3. Slice the meat very thin and serve with potatoes and gray, or make hot sandwiches on a large heated bun, with coleslaw and gravy on side. For sandwiches you need thin gravy made with beef broth, salt and pepper and a little onion powder (au jus).

Beef Brisket with Carrots, Potatoes and Fennel
(Serves: 4-6)

This is a easy recipe but make sure you roast the brisket for a long time. If you are roasting alone it will take about 1 hour per pound, and if you are adding vegetables, add another hour to it.

Ingredients: one beef brisket, about 3 pounds, even shape if possible; rub: 1 tbsp. each: black pepper, onion and garlic powders; 1 cup cola or seltzer; 1-1/2 cup beef broth; 3 tbsp. tomato paste; 1 tsp. garlic powder; 3-4 tbsp. sriracha sauce or hot sauce; vegetable: 1 large onion thin-sliced, 2 fennel bulbs sliced ½-inch thick, 1 pound baby carrots, about 1-1/2 pounds (24 ounces) baby red potatoes; coarse sea salt to sprinkle on the vegetables.

One or two days before cooking, pat-dry meat with paper towels and sprinkle with the rub all over, place in a re-sealable plastic bag or in a large platter covered with plastic wrap; refrigerate for one or two nights to marinate. When ready to cook, preheat the oven at 370 degrees. Line a non-reactive roasting pan or put together and fold 2 large pieces (larger than roasting pan) of aluminum foil together and make a large piece to cover the bottom, and another one for the top.

Place half of the onion in the bottom of one side of the roasting pan, then place the meat over the onion slices. Then in a bowl mix together: tomato paste, sriracha sauce, garlic powder; whisk together with ½ C beef broth and pour over the meat; top the meat with rest of the onion slices. Do not put anything over else over the meat. On one side of the roasting pan place the carrots, top with potatoes, then place the fennel slices all around the edges. Pour cola and the rest of the beef broth over the vegetables, sprinkle with coarse salt lightly. Cover the pan with large piece of aluminum foil, airtight, pressing the foil against the edges well. Roast meat and vegetable for 4 hours, turning around halfway every hour. Let meat rest in off oven for ½ hour, open, slice and serve with the vegetables and juices.

Tip: Do not put any salt on the meat, it will pull out all the water and will make it tough.

Dry Keema (mild Chili) with Quinoa Pancakes and Sour Cherries

(Serves: 4)

Traditionally the keema is made with lamb, but you can also make it with ground beef. Quinoa cakes or pancakes will go good with any Indian spiced meat. Sour cherries are a plus. You can make the cherries a day ahead. Make the keema first and reheat it later; make the pancakes last and serve warm.

Sour Cherries (Serves: 4-6)

Ingredients: 1 pound stemmed, halved, and pitted fresh cherries; 3 tbsp. frozen, concentrated orange juice, thawed; 2 tbsp. lemon juice; ¼ cup sparkling wine or champagne (op).

In a bowl combine all ingredients together, cover and refrigerate from 2 hours to overnight, and serve chilled.

Dry Keema (Chili)

Ingredients: 2-3 tbsp. olive oil; 1-1/2 to 2 pounds ground beef 80% lean; 3 tbsp. tomato paste; 1 tbsp. prepared mustard; 1 tsp. each garlic powder, cumin powder; ½ cup fresh cilantro stems and leaves thin-sliced, ¼ cup grated onion; 3-4 tbsp. dry bread crumbs; ⅓ cup raw shelled hemp seeds.

For garnish: 4 large eggs, ¼ cup thin-sliced green onion; ½ cup sour cream or ¼ cup shaved hard cheese, such as gouda or Swiss; sweet or hot paprika, hot sauce, such as tabasco to sprinkle.

Heat a large cast-iron skillet or a heavy-bottom pan on medium-high heat. When hot, add 1 tbsp. oil, and brown the meat on medium heat for 5 minutes, stirring constantly. Lower the heat to medium and brown the meat another 5 minutes, add tomato paste and stir well, add cilantro stems and leaves and stir well, add mustard, onion, garlic, grated cheese, cumin powder, bread crumbs and hemp seeds and stir well. Now pat down the meat mixture in the pan. If there is still some liquid, increase the heat and let all the liquid evaporate for 2-3 minutes. Take the pan off the heat, make 4 wells on 4 sides and break one egg in each hole. Reduce the heat to low, cover pan loosely with the aluminum foil or a lid, and cook on low heat for about 2 minutes or until the egg whites are settled. Take off the heat and just before serving sprinkle with rest of the garnishes, some olive oil, and serve warm.

Quinoa Pancakes (M:8)

Ingredients: 2 cups cooked quinoa; ½ cup packed (about 1 large potato) boiled and mashed potatoes or dry potatoes buds; 4 tbsp. grated onion; 4 tbsp. corn starch; 1 tsp. salt; ½ tsp. cayenne pepper or to taste; ¼ cup grated cheese; 1 tbsp. melted butter; 2 large eggs whisked in with about ¾ cup almond or coconut milk; ½ cup fresh blueberries or dry cranberries. Olive oil for cooking.

Combine all the dry ingredients in a bowl. Whisk the wet ingredients: milk, eggs and butter, onion and blueberries and pour over the dry ingredients. Combine just to mix.

Heat a large cast-iron skillet or a heavy-bottom pan at medium-high heat. When hot add 1 tbsp. oil, move the pan around to coat the bottom. Drop about 4-5 tbsp. of the batter each on 2 places, spread it out with a spoon in a ¼-inch thick circle, cover with the lid, lower the heat to medium and cook pancakes until golden brown underneath, about 2-3 minutes, sprinkle 2-3 drops of oil on each pancake, turn over and cook the other side golden. Take out and make rest of the pancakes, adding oil to the pan before pouring the batter each time. Keep the pancakes in a warm oven covered in foil, and serve warm with keema and sour cherries.

Tips: Cherries have vitamin C and potassium. Quinoa: is gluten-free and has all 9 essential amino acids.

Hemp seeds: are 100% whole grain, good source of iron, protein and omega 3's.

Bratwurst with Sauerkraut & Potatoes (S:4)

164

You can prepare this meal ahead, just reheat and serve.

Ingredients: 16oz. pkg. of bratwurst (about 5); 1 16oz. bottles of wine sauerkraut; 1tsp. caraway seeds; 1-1/2 pounds medium red potatoes scrubbed and boiled with skin on; to serve: prepared mustard and green salad/vegetable.

Pierce the bratwurst all around with a fork and boil them in simmering water for about 15 minutes turning them over every 5 minutes. Use a large glass platter or a stainless steel baking casserole dish: grease the dish with spray or butter then lay down the bratwurst in the center and boiled potatoes all around. Top with sauerkraut and sprinkle with caraway seeds. Cover airtight with a large piece of foil. You can refrigerate or leave out on the counter for up to one hour.

Take out of refrigerator 1 hour before baking. Bake covered in a preheated 350 degree oven for 45 minutes to 1 hr. until it is heated through. Serve with salad/vegetable and mustard.

Smoked Ham (S:15-20)

Ingredients: 1 Bone in Butt end about 8 to 10 pounds; 15-20 whole cloves; 4Tbsp. prepared mustard; ¼ cup brown sugar. To serve: 2cans, 16oz Pineapple chunks reduced on low heat (in half).

Take the ham out of refrigerator, and take out all the wrappings; pat dry. With a paring knife score the skin without cutting into the meat, slice through the fat and skin about 1-inch deep make diamond pattern. Rub mustard all over the ham, sprinkle the brown sugar, then push in the cloves into the cut parts. Place in a 13X9-inch baking sheet or pan, and cover tightly with aluminum foil. Let it rest in room temperature for one hour.

Preheat oven at 250 degrees. Bake the ham for 15 minutes per pound for about 2-1/2 hours until the internal temperature on an instant-read-thermometer registers about 110 degrees. Take it out of the oven and let it rest 20 minutes until internal temperature reaches 115 to 120 degrees. Carve and serve with reduced pineapple, potatoes and vegetables.

Calf Liver with Fruits and Vegetables (Serves: 2)

We serve pieces of liver with fruits, vegetables and a lot of chutney. It is so tasty with all the flavors that you forget you are eating the liver.

Ingredients: About ½ pounds, 8 oz calf liver; crumb mixture: 1/2 tsp. granulated garlic; ¼ tsp. cayenne pepper; ¾ cup dry and seasoned bread crumbs; 1 tbsp. grated parmesan cheese; ½ tbsp. lemon-pepper salt seasoning; and ¼ cup fine crushed almonds crumbs; 1 large egg whisked in with 1 tbsp. water; fresh-ground black pepper to taste; 2-3 tbsp canola oil or olive oil.

To serve: Baby arugula and green chickpeas or cooked peas, sprinkled with vinaigrette; 2 boiled potatoes, thick sliced, sprinkled with salt, pepper and granulated garlic, then sautéed in oil brown, your favorite fruits like ripe papaya, mango or pineapple slices; pumpkin and/or pomegranate seeds to sprinkle on the top; lemon or yogurt chutney.

1. Wash the liver, pat-dry with paper towels, then cut into about 3-inch pieces. Sprinkle a little black pepper all over, then double dip the liver, first in egg mixture, then in crumbs, again in egg and then in crumbs, and spread out each coated piece on a large platter. You can do this a few hours ahead and refrigerate.
2. Heat a large heavy-bottom pan on medium-high heat. Add about 2 tbsp. oil. When hot, place liver pieces in hot oil, immediately lower the heat to medium. Cook liver about 2-3 minutes until golden brown. Before you turn over, sprinkle about 2 drops of oil on each liver piece and then turn over and cook slow the other side until browned.

While liver is cooking prepare the plates. On lightly warm plates, place arugula in center, top with fresh green chickpeas or cooked peas, sprinkle the vinaigrette. Around the salad arrange the sautéed potatoes slices, fruits. When liver is done place it over the salad, sprinkle with pumpkin and pomegranate seeds and serve with chutney on the side.

Liver Mousse over Cauliflower Puree with Mint Chutney

(Serves: 2)

Some people are not crazy about liver. But this recipe is easy and tasty. You just have to cook and puree the liver and serve over the cooked and pureed cauliflower.

Ingredients:

For the liver: About 6 to 7 ounces veal liver; granulated garlic and fresh-ground black pepper; 1-2 tbsp. canola oil; 1 large onion thin-sliced; ¼ cup fine chopped celery; ¼ cup grated parmesan cheese, ⅓ cup sour cream. To garnish: roasted red bell pepper strips from the jar and hot chili sauce or tabasco. To serve: mint or yogurt thick chutney; 4 garlic toasts, 2 avocados.

For the Cauliflower: One small or half large cauliflower (about 5-6 cups); 2 tbsp. lemon juice; ½ cup grated parmesan cheese; ¼ cup sour cream; salt and pepper to taste.

1. Preheat the oven at 350 degrees. In a large aluminum foil place the liver, sprinkle all over with garlic powder and black pepper, top with onion and celery, drizzle 1 tbsp. oil, close airtight, place on a baking sheet and roast for 45 minutes, rotating the sheet halfway during the roasting. Take out of the oven and cool a little to handle.

2. While the liver is cooking, cut the cauliflower florets into 2-inch pieces and separate the stems, then slice the stems thin. Place them in a medium pan with about 3 tbsp. of water or chicken stock, sprinkle with a little salt and pepper and 1 tbsp. oil, cover bring to a boil, then lower the heat to a constant simmer, and cook for about 15 minutes or until soft, stirring once during the cooking. Puree the cauliflower in the blender with cheese, sour cream, and the lemon juice, then pour back on two warm serving plates. Keep the plates covered with foil or another plate.
3. Now chop the liver, taking out all the tough skin and fat. Puree the liver, onion, celery, cheese, sour cream and lemon juice in a blender.
4. Dollop the liver puree over the cauliflower, top with roasted red pepper strips, then drizzle some hot sauce all over. Place the avocado slices on the sides and serve with chutney in front and garlic toasts in the back.

Tip: Liver tastes good with chutney, so serve about ½ C of chutney per person.

Lamb Chops with Stewed Tomatoes, Sauteed Kale and Mashed Cheese Potatoes (Serves: 2)

You can make stewed tomatoes and blanch the kale a day ahead. Just reheat before serving. We serve this both with pan juices and with anchovy butter (See Spices and Spice Blends).

Ingredients: For the Kale: 5 ounces (about 4 cups Leaves) fresh kale; 1/4tsp. each granulated garlic and fresh-ground black pepper; 2 tbsp. butter divided; 2 tbsp. lemon juice or to taste; salt and pepper to taste; to serve 1 tsp. chaat masala or chili powder.

For the Stewed Tomatoes: 1 tbsp. canola or olive oil; 1 medium bay leaf; 2 large big boy tomatoes; 2 medium plum tomatoes; 1 cup each chopped: onion, red and green bell peppers; 1 tbsp. sugar or to taste; 2 tbsp. lemon juice or to taste; ½ tsp. dry oregano; ½ tsp. granulated garlic; salt and fresh-ground black pepper to taste.

For the Lamb Chops: About 1 pound, 4 loin lamb chops bone-in, about 1-1/2-inch thick; 1 tsp. each: fresh chopped mint leave, garlic cloves and fresh-ground black pepper; 2 tbsp. canola oil, divided; to serve: for pan juices1 packet beef broth and or anchovy butter.

For the mashed cheese potatoes: see Vegetables.

For the Kale: Wash each kale leaf, stem-down, under running cold water, then take out the leaves (going downward on the stem). Bring about 4 cups of water to a boil, and blanch the leave for 3 minutes, to get a bright color. Now chill them in a bowl of ice water or running cold tab water. Let them drain in a tilted platter, then slice them ½-inch wide.

When you are ready to serve heat 1 tbsp. of butter, garlic and some black pepper in a sauté pan, over medium heat; add the kale, stir until the kale is heated through. Serve sprinkle with lemon juice, salt and pepper to taste, chaat masala or chili powder and stir in some softened butter. I like to stir in some cilantro chutney or mango chutney just before serving.

For the Stewed Tomatoes: In a medium pot, on medium heat, heat oil, and sauté the onions and bay leaf for 5 minutes; add tomatoes, bell pepper, sugar and salt and pepper to taste. Bring to a boil, then lower the heat and simmer until onion and tomatoes are soft, about 15 minutes. Add garlic, oregano, lemon juice, sugar, salt and pepper to taste.

For the Lamb Chops: About half-an hour before cooking, take out the chops. Detach the meat from the bones at the center (leave the chops attached at the ends for easy handling) and rub them with garlic, mint, black pepper and 1 tbsp. oil. Let them marinate for ½ hour in room temperature.

When ready to serve, heat a large heavy-bottom pan with 1 tbsp. of oil, on medium-high heat. When oil almost start smoking add the chops and cook for 5 minutes, turn over and cook the other side for 3-4 minutes for medium rare. Take out the chops in a heated serving platter. Discard any fat in the pan, add about ½ cup water and the beef broth, scrape the bottom of the pan, if there is any foam, skim off the foam and pour the juices over the chops. If prefer top with a thin slice of anchovy butter and serve with kale, mashed potatoes and stewed potatoes.

Roasted Whole Leg of Lamb, Mint Potatoes, Glazed Carrots, Pineapple & mint Chutney (S:8-10)

My husband tells me, growing up in his family, they had lamb mostly on Sundays. I cook lamb 2-3 times of year, only when I get a smaller and semi-boneless leg of lamb. Buy the lamb about one week ahead and let it rest in the refrigerator; the meat will relax and will be much tender. Make mint chutney, potatoes and glazed carrots a day ahead and just reheat in a low 300 degrees oven until heated through. They will be loaded with flavor. Instead of pineapple chutney, you can use mint sauce.

(1) Pineapple-Mint Chutney

Ingredients: 1 cup packed fresh mint leaves; 2 cups cilantro leave and soft stems; ½ cup orange juice; about 2 cups fresh pineapple chunks or canned; 1 jalapeno cut and seeded or 3-4 serrano pepper chopped; 2 cups apple sauce; ½ cup frozen concentrated lemon-aid; salt and pepper to taste.

In a blender, first puree mint, cilantro, fresh peppers and orange juice. Add rest of the ingredients and puree well. Pour in a non-reactive bowl and serve. If making ahead, cover and refrigerate overnight.

(2) Mint Potatoes

When we were growing up, we used to eat these mint potatoes with yogurt chutney as a snack, all summer long. We couldn't wait until fresh mint started coming in the market.

Ingredients: 2 to 2-1/2 pounds red bliss potatoes; 2 tbsp. cider vinegar whipped with 4 tbsp. olive oil; 2 cups fresh mint leaves; 1 cup cilantro leaves and soft stems; 2 cups baby spinach blanched in boiling water for 3 minutes; about 2 tbsp. lemon-pepper mix (dash); salt and pepper to taste; 3 tbsp. olive oil; 1 tbsp. caraway seeds; 1/2 tsp. turmeric.

In a medium pot, wash potatoes, cover with cold water and boil until soft. Peel and immediately sprinkle with vinegar mixture. Cut into 1-1/2-inch pieces. Heat 3 tbsp. olive oil in a large sauté pan on medium heat. Add caraway seeds and cook to light brown for 1 minute. Add potatoes and stir to coat them.

While potatoes are cooking in a blender, puree mint, cilantro and baby spinach and pour over the cooking potatoes. Sprinkle with lemon-pepper mix, then with salt and pepper to taste. Increase heat high, and dry out the liquid for about 5 minutes. Serve warm or cold.

(3)   Glazed Carrots

Ingredients: About 1-1/2 to 2 pounds slim and long carrots, peeled and boiled in ½ cup water in a large pan, until soft; 4 tbsp. unsalted butter; 2 tbsp. lemon juice; 1 tbsp. ketchup; ½ tsp. each: onion and garlic powder, cayenne or tabasco sauce: 4 tbsp. maple syrup; fresh grated nutmeg; salt and pepper to taste.

Heat a large sauté pan on medium heat. Add butter, onion and garlic powder, cayenne, ketchup, lemon juice and drained cooked carrots. Increase heat to medium-high and turn over the carrots until they are sizzling and almost all the liquid is absorbed. Drizzle with the maple syrup, heat on low for 1-2 minutes, grate a little (¼ tsp.) fresh nutmeg, and turn off the heat. When ready to serve, heat them on low heat until heated through, check for seasoning, and serve.

(4)   Leg of Lamb

Ingredients: One (about 6 pounds) whole semi-boneless leg of lamb (Australian or American); spice rub: 1 tbsp. each onion and garlic powder, dry rosemary, 2 tbsp. dry mustard powder, 1 tsp. salt and 1 tbsp. cider vinegar, 4 tbsp. olive oil, ¼ tsp. turmeric (op); pineapple-mint chutney or mint chutney and/or extra virgin olive oil and lemon juice to sprinkle.

1. Preheat the oven at 450 degrees. Line a roasting pan with aluminum foil. Take the lamb out of the package, clean all over with the damp paper towels. Combine the rub spices mixture, set aside about 1 tbsp. for garnish, and rub rest of the mixture all over the lamb. Cover the end of the bone with aluminum foil and insert an instant-read thermometer at the thickest part of the leg away from the bone. Place the lamb in the roasting pan, wider end toward the back wall. Roast for about 10 minutes at 400 degrees, then reduce the temperature to 325 degrees and roast the lamb at 10 minutes per pound for medium. We like medium, it is softer and tastes better. Internal temperature at the wider part, away from the bone should be around 125 degrees for rare, 130 for medium-rare, and 135 degrees for medium.
2. Take the lamb out of the oven and let it rest for 25-30 minutes before slicing. Carve the lamb, holding the bone side (smaller end) up; make 2-3 cuts about 2 inches apart across first, then slice down thin against the grain. Rotate and repeat the carving. Serve meat sprinkle with lemon juice, a little olive oil and the rub mixture, Mint chutney, mint potatoes and glazed carrots.
    Tip: The best lamb curry is made with the fresh-roasted lamb. You can also make sandwiches with very thin-sliced lamb sprinkled with salt and pepper, on a toasted bun, with mint chutney on one side, and sweet India cucumber relish on the other side

Racks of Lamb with Roasted Cauliflower and New Potatoes (Serves: 4)

This is a fancy and expensive meal and you can become an expert just cooking it once or twice. You can prepare everything ahead, and cook the meat before serving. Serve with mint jelly, which you can make 2 days ahead.

(1) Mint Jelly (M: about 1-1/2 cup)

Ingredients: 2 cups packed fresh mint leaves; 2 medium pears (about ¾ pound), peeled, cored, paper-thin-sliced; ½ cup cider vinegar or lemon juice; ½ cup sugar; 1 tsp. grinded cardamom seeds (op); 1 packet, 14g,1/2 ounce, unflavored gelatin; ½ tsp. salt or to taste.

Puree the mint leave with ½ cup water in the blender, take out in a bowl and sprinkle the unflavored gelatin and set aside, covered. In a large heavy-bottom pan, cook the pears with 1 tbsp. water for 15 minutes or until soft. Mash the pears well, then add the sugar and vinegar. Increase the heat to medium-high and stir to dissolve the sugar. Now add the mint puree and the salt. Bring it to a boil, stirring constantly for 8-10 minutes until thick. Take off the heat, cool, and pour in a non-reactive bowl. Store in the refrigerator for up to 2 weeks in a dry and clean, airtight bottle.

(2) Frenched Mini Rack of Lamb

Ingredients: 2 small racks of lamb, frenched (tip of bones exposed) and vacuum-packed, about 1-1/2 pounds each with 8 chops in each rack (the lollipop chops); 2 tbsp. canola oil; a generous sprinkle of: granulated garlic, dried rosemary, salt and fresh-ground black pepper; for topping a mixture of: 3-4 tbsps. apricot jam, 1 tbsp. lemon juice, 2 pinches of salt, and 2 tsps. of dry rubbed mint or 3 tbsps. fresh chopped mint; mint jelly or mint chutney to serve.

1. Take out the racks of lamb 15-20 minutes ahead of cooking, trim off all excess fat on the top leaving a thin layer of the fat over the meat. Sprinkle each well with garlic, rosemary, salt and pepper. Cover the bones with aluminum foil and set aside in the room temperature for 15 minutes. Heat a cast-iron skillet on high heat, add oil and sear the racks for 2-3 minutes until bottom is browned; take them out with a tong. Prepare a shallow roasting pan or a broiler tray lined with aluminum foil. Preheat oven at 425 degrees.

2. Place the meat in the roasting pan, meat side up and bones facing the oven door. Bake in a preheated oven for 15-20 minutes. Take out the meat and spread the mint topping; put back the rack in the oven again and bake another 5 minutes. The internal temperature should be about 125 to 130 degrees for medium-rare, and 135 to 140 for medium-rare to medium. Take the rack out of the oven and let it rest at room temperature for about 8-10 minutes on the carving board, tented with a foil. Serve half rack per person (or buy 4 racks and serve one whole rack per person).

(3) New Potatoes with Taco Seasoning (Serves: 4)

New potatoes taste good even with salt, pepper and garlic. To make it fancy, use taco seasoning mix or chili powder mix.

Ingredients: 2 Pounds of medium new potatoes, fingerling or the small Yukon gold, scrubbed washed and cut lengthwise in quarters; 2-3 tbsps. canola oil; 1 tsp. cumin or caraway seeds; ¼ tsp. each about salt, fresh-ground black pepper and granulated garlic and 1 tbsp. or to taste taco seasoning mix or chili powder mix.

1. Heat a large cast-iron pan or a heavy-bottom pan on medium heat. When the pan is hot add 2 tbsps. of oil move around to coat the pan and add the cumin or caraway seeds on one side of the pan. When the seeds turn light brown, add the cut potatoes and sauté a little to coat with the oil. Sprinkle salt, pepper to taste, cover and let them cook on low heat. Stir once during the cooking and cook for about 20 minutes or until soft.
2. Open the cover sprinkle potatoes with garlic and taco/chili seasoning mix and then sprinkle about 2 tsps. of the oil over the top. Cover the pan with the lid and let it sit there. When ready to serve heat the potatoes on medium heat 5-6 minutes, stir and serve.

(4) Roasted Cauliflower over the Bed of Peas (Serves: 4)

I make this bed of peas one day ahead and use for almost everything: as a side vegetable, under fish, with eggs, under roasted vegetables or over bread for sandwiches. You can also serve the cauliflower over balsamic vinegar-reduction or any of the chutneys.

For the Peas: 1 pkg., 10 ounces, about 2 cups frozen or fresh peas cooked for about 5-10 minutes in a little water; ¼ cup lemon juice; 1 cup fresh cilantro leaves and soft stems; salt and pepper to taste.

1. In a blender, puree cilantro with lemon juice and a little water (if needed). Add the cooked peas and puree well. Take out in a nonreactive bowl and leave covered, in room temperature, until needed or refrigerate for the next day.

For the Cauliflower: 1 medium cauliflower cut in half, leaves removed and saved for soup. Take out all the florets with about half-inch stems; ½ tsp. granulated garlic; salt and fresh-ground black pepper; 1 tsp. of lemon-pepper seasoning mix; ½ tsp. turmeric (op); 2-3 tbsp. canola oil, ½ cup pomegranate seeds for decoration.

1. Preheat oven at 450 degrees. Line a heavy-bottom tray with aluminum foil and place the cauliflower in the center. Sprinkle with garlic turmeric, lemon-pepper seasoning, salt and pepper to taste and then oil all over, do not stir. Bake in a preheated oven for 20 minutes covered.

Serve the cauliflower over the bed of peas, then sprinkle the pomegranate seeds all around the peas. Serve with new potatoes and the meat with mint jelly or with cilantro-mint chutney (op).

The Perfect London Broil with Stewed Sweet Peppers and Tomatoes, Orange-Hoisin Glaze, and Garlic Roasted Red-Bliss Potatoes (Serves: 4)

Buy a good cut of meat, I like Angus beef round, top London broil boneless, and serve with some sauce. I serve my London broil with orange-hoisin glaze, stewed sweet peppers and tomatoes and garlic-roasted red bliss potatoes. They all are very easy to make.

(1) Stewed Sweet Peppers and Tomatoes

Ingredients: 2 tbsps. butter; 1 to 1-1/4 pound sweet red, yellow and orange peppers, trimmed, seeded and cut into 2-inch pieces; 1 can, 14.5 oz., (411g) stewed tomatoes; 1 tbsp. ketchup, ¼ tsp. each granulated garlic and oregano. ¼ cup chopped fresh cilantro or parsley.

Heat a large, non-reactive pan over medium heat. When heated, add the butter and sauté the peppers on medium-high heat, stirring constantly until they are a little soft, about 5 minutes. Take the peppers out of the pan into a bowl. Now add the juice of the stewed tomatoes in the pan and cut the tomatoes pieces into 1-inch pieces. Add the pieces to the pan and cook on medium-high heat, open, until juice is reduced in half. Add the sautéed peppers, spices, and cilantro/parsley, bring to a boil, stir well, and turn off the heat. When ready to serve just warm and serve.

(2) Orange-Hoisin Glaze (M: 3/4 C)

Ingredients: 2 cups orange juice; ¼ cup hoisin marinade and sauce (can be purchased in a supermarket or an Asian store) or use your own hoisin type of marinade and sauce; a little salt and fresh-ground black pepper.

In a large, non-reactive pan, heat the orange juice on medium-high heat, Bring the juice to a boil, partially cover it with the lid and stir occasionally, scraping the sides and the bottom. Reduce, switching the heat to medium and medium-high. Reduce the juice to almost ½ cup.

Add the hoisin marinade and sauce, a pinch of salt and pepper, simmer a little, about 5 minutes. Pour in a non-reactive small bowl or a gravy boat and refrigerate until needed.

(3) Garlic Roasted Red-Bliss Potatoes

Ingredients: About 2 pounds, or about 5 large red-bliss potatoes cut into about 2-inch cubes; 1 head of garlic, cut in half across, drizzled with 1 tsp. of oil, covered with an aluminum foil and roasted tender, for about 15 minutes at 350 degrees preheated oven; ¼ tsp. dry rosemary (op); ¼ cup canola or vegetable oil; salt and pepper to taste.

Bring a large pot of water (about 6 cups) to a boil, add potatoes, stir a little, cover half way with the lid, lower the heat to medium and boil the potatoes until just tender, about 15 minutes. Drain the potatoes and leave in the open pot or a bowl. In a large bowl add oil, rosemary about ½ tsp. each of salt and pepper and squeeze in the roasted garlic. Stir well and add the warm potatoes, toss the potatoes with a spatula.

About 20 minutes before serving preheat the oven to 400 degrees. Line a baking tray with aluminum foil, grease the tray lightly with cooking spray and spread out the potatoes in a single layer. Bake for 10 minutes, take out the tray and turn over the potatoes with a metal spatula and bake for another 5-10 minutes, or until they are browned. Keep them warm in the oven until serving.

(4) London Broil

Ingredients: About 1-3/4 to 2 pound piece of certified Angus beef round, top London broil boneless; about ¼ tsp. each granulated garlic and cayenne pepper or fresh-ground black pepper; 4 tbsp. thick hoisin marinade and sauce;

About 4-5 hours before serving, take out the meat, wash it under the running cold tab water, pat-dry with paper towels, rub with garlic and pepper, place in a large platter and let it dry out in the refrigerator for 3-4 hours. Prepare the both broiler trays and cover with them with aluminum foil. Make some slits on the top tray for grease and juices to drip down. One hour before cooking, take out the meat cover with 2 tbsp. of hoisin marinade and sauce; on each side spread out the marinade covering the meat completely, and then leave in the room temperature for 1 hour on a prepared broiler-top tray or an aluminum foil-lined baking tray to marinate.

When ready to broil the meat, first preheat the oven for baking at 400 degrees for at least 5 minutes. Turn off the baking and heat the oven on broil for 5 minutes. Place the broiler tray together with the meat under the broiler, about 5-6 inches away from the heating source, and broil the meat for about 8 minutes, placing the trays vertically. Then turn around the trays horizontally (holding with gloves), and broil for another 6 to 8 minutes, a total of 12-14 minutes for medium-rare or an internal temperature about 130-135 degrees. Take the trays out of the oven. Take the meat out and place on a cutting board and let it rest for at least 15 minutes. Slice meat across the grain, on a bias angle, very thin. Serve with the glaze drizzled over the meat, stewed peppers and red-bliss potatoes..

To Reheat the Meat

After cooking, slice only the meat that is needed. Refrigerate the unused meat in one piece wrapped with single layer of plastic wrap. Just before serving, slice the meat thin again and pick up all the slices with one or two spatulas and place directly over low heat, cover with the lid and heat low for 6-8 minutes, just to take the chill out of the meat and steam the meat lightly. This way you are just steaming the meat.

Meatloaf with Wine Gravy (Serves: 6 to 8)

This is my husband's favorite comfort food. He likes it with mashed potatoes, gravy and vegetables. The leftovers he prefers in a sandwich, on the toasted and buttered bread or soft buns. We like to make with beef, but you can make with 2 parts beef and 1 part pork and or turkey, or both. This is tasty enough, so no need for bacon. It is very important to use a wooden or plastic spatula to mix all ingredients together; mixing by hand will turn the salty mixture watery with the heat of your hands.

Ingredients: About 2-1/2 pounds lean ground beef; 2 tab canola oil, 1 cup each chopped fine: mushrooms, onion, green or red bell pepper; ½ cup chopped celery; 4 thick slices of Italian loaf broken in to very small pieces, ¾ cup hot milk, ¼ cup dry bread crumbs (op); a paste mixture consist of: ½ cup ketchup, 1 can, 6 oz. (170g) tomato paste, 4 tbsp. prepared mustard; 1 tsp. lemon juice, 2 tsp. sugar, ¼ tsp.each salt and pepper or to taste, mixed together and set aside until needed; ½ cup dry cranberries; ½ tsp. each granulated garlic and cayenne pepper; ¾ tsp. dry oregano; 1 tsp. dry rosemary; 1 packet (1 tbsp.) instant chicken broth and ¼ cup to ⅓ cup grated parmesan cheese. Mashed potatoes and/or vegetables and gravy to serve.

1. Place the pieces of bread in a large bowl, and pour hot milk over; soak the bread covered for 10 minutes, pressed down and moisten it well with a fork. In a large sauté pan, on medium heat, heat 2 tbsp. oil; when hot, add mushrooms and sauté on high heat 2 minutes; move over one side, add onion, celery and sauté on medium heat for 5 minutes, add bell peppers and sauté until onion is soft about 1 minute. Take off the heat and cool.
2. Preheat oven to 350 degrees. Line a large baking tray with aluminum foil, grease the foil and set it aside.
3. In the same large bowl over the bread, layer all ingredients: break the meat with a rubber/wooden spatula, sprinkle cayenne and garlic, ½ of the ketchup, and paste mixture, mustard, cranberries, sprinkle the cooked vegetables and dry bread crumbs, oregano, rosemary, chicken broth, the beaten eggs, grated cheese, and salt and pepper or to taste. Mix with spatula and form in to two loaves, each about 5 inches wide and 4 inches high. Pat down the loaves from all four sides in to compact loaves. Spread out the other half of the ketchup paste mixture on the top and an extra 1 tbsp. of ketchup over the mixture on each loaf.
4. Bake about 1 hour until golden brown and well done. Turn around the tray once halfway during the baking. Take out of the oven and let it cool for 5 minutes before slicing. Slice into about 1-inch thick slices with a sharp knife and serve with mashed potatoes and gravy.

Quick Wine Gravy (M: about 1 C)

Ingredients: 1 cup dry red wine; ¼ cup ketchup; ½ cup teriyaki sauce; ¼ cup orange juice; ½ tsp. cayenne pepper; salt and fresh-ground black pepper to taste; 2 tbsp. thin-sliced cold unsalted butter.

1. Heat a large, heavy-bottom sauté pan, on medium high heat. When hot add butter, move around to coat the pan. Immediately take off the heat, add wine, covering the pan halfway so that it does not splash all over. Reduce the wine in half on high heat, in about 10 minutes. Add orange juice, ketchup, teriyaki sauce, salt and fresh-ground black pepper to taste. Cook on medium heat, until heated through, about 5 minutes.
2. Take off the heat and whisk in the remaining, 1 tbsp. butter.
3. Serve on mashed potatoes and/or meatloaf.

Super Healthy Meat Loaf (Serves: 6-8)

This Meatloaf has mushrooms for cold and flu, oats for fibers and lowering blood pressure, lime zest and juice that contain hesperidin for fighting cancer, sesame seeds for magnesium and zinc to help the immune system, black pepper that has anti-inflammatory qualities, oregano for immunity (and the fresh leaves of oregano have an oil that is antiviral); sage helps with memory, it is very close to wisdom; apple sauce to give flavor and add iron in the diet, cranberries for urinary tract infection and antioxidants, garlic tomato paste for heart and eyes, spinach for iron, lutein and vitamin E that helps arteries prevent from plaque buildup, instant beef broth and eggs to give a little extra protein, grated cheese to give dairy and calcium, cilantro and parsley for calcium.

Ingredients: About 2-1/2 pounds fresh-ground beef 80% lean; 1 can, 6 oz. (170 G) about ⅓ cup roasted garlic tomato paste; 1 can, 8 oz. (1 cup) tomato sauce with herbs; 2 tbsp. prepared mustard; about 1-1/2 tbsp. lime juice and 1 tbsp. lime zest; ½ tsp. gran. garlic (op); 1 tbsp. fresh chop or 1 tsp. dry oregano; ½ tsp. dry sage; ¼ cup fresh chopped parsley or cilantro; 1cup unsweetened apple sauce; ½ to 1 tsp. fresh-ground black pepper or to taste; 1cup cooked quinoa (add ½ cup whole-grain quinoa in 1 cup boiling water stir well, turn off the heat, let stand 15 minutes, it is ready) and ½ cup quick cooking oats grinded into powder; ¼ tsp. salt or to taste; 1 packet or 1 tbsp. instant beef broth; 1 cup fresh baby spinach without stems chopped; 2 large eggs; ½ cup grated cheese; 2 tbsp. dry onion flakes; ½ cup grinded into powder dry mushroom caps (op); ½ cup lightly crushed black sesame seeds; ½ cup to 1 cup dry cranberries; to serve: 1 tbsp. fresh chopped oregano leaves or thin-sliced ½ cup green onion (scallion), and mango BBQ sauce and salad.

1. In a large bowl combine together: tomato paste, tomato sauce, mustard, lime juice and zest, fresh-ground black pepper, oregano, little sprinkle of salt, parsley, apple sauce stir well with a wooden or rubber spatula. Take out about a quarter and set aside for the topping.

2. Now add eggs and whisk well, add quinoa, oats and broken ground beef and mix well. Add rest of the ingredients except the ¼ cup of the tomato paste mixture that is set aside and leaving oregano or green onion for garnish.

3. Line a large baking tray with double aluminum foil, grease it lightly and make a compact (about 4 inches diameter) roll of meatloaf. Top with tomato paste mixture (set aside) and chill in the refrigerator for about 1 hour. Bake in the preheated oven at 400 degrees for 10 minutes and at 350 degrees for about 30 minutes.

4. Let it rest for 10 minutes and serve sprinkled with fresh oregano or scallion, and mango sauce with salad on the side.

Stuffed Meatloaf (Serves: 6-8)

You can stuff meat with ham and cheese thin slices (cold cuts) or any other cooked and very thin-sliced meat. We like it with salami and cheese. Leftover meatloaf can be heated in the microwave for 2-3 minutes. Make meatloaf sandwiches with a lot of pesto, chutney or sweet cucumber relish, it is delicious.

For the Crust: About 2-1/4 pound lean ground beef (80%); 1 tbsp. each: mustard powder, onion powder and paprika; 1 tsp. each: granulated garlic and oregano; ¾ cup fine grated parmesan cheese;1cup panko (Japanese) dry bread crumbs; 2 large eggs beaten; 3 tbsp. sriracha sauce; 2-3 tbsp. melted butter.

For the Filling: 5 slices provolone cheese, about 6 ounces: 6 slices, about 2 ounces, genoa salami; ¾ cup roasted red bell peppers from the jar, cut into strips; ¼ cup drained capers. To serve: 1 bottle, 23.7 ounces (673 g), merlot marinara Prego sauce or mango BBQ sauce; salad, and/or mashed potatoes.

1. In a large bowl, mix together meat and spices. Mix together grated cheese and the bread crumbs; save about 3 tbsp. of the mixture and mix rest of the cheese mixture in the meat, then mix in the eggs.

2. Preheat oven at 350 degrees. Line a half-sheet baking tray with plastic wrap and spread out the meat in the tray about 15 inches wide, leaving about a 2-inch-long border empty. Now place the slices of the provolone cheese on the 2-inch empty border, half of the slices touching the meat and other half of the slices touching the empty border. Place the salami slices over the cheese. Now slice one of the cheese slices into ½-inch slices and place on the top of salami; place the red bell pepper strips, then top with the capers. Brush rest of the ground meat with sriracha sauce and sprinkle the set aside cheese and crumb mixture.

3. Fold the provolone half way off the meat, then roll over the meat and start folding and rolling the meat, with the help of the plastic wrap, into a 15-inch tight roll. Pinch the end of the roll inside, so that cheese does not flow outside. Brush with the butter and bake at 350 degrees

for about 1 hour turning the tray around halfway. Serve warm with salad and/or potatoes and gravy.

Meatballs with Tomato Sauce (M: 20 large; Serves: 8-10)

These are our old fashioned favorite meatballs, baked, soft and very delicious. This very famous sauce goes well with any pasta dish, sausages and even with stuffed shells, etc. More mushrooms, onion and fresh herbs give you more flavor. If you prefer, you can add one peeled and grated apple as well.

Ingredients:
For the Sauce: 2 large can 289 oz. san marzano tomatoes milled; 1 bottle, 16 oz. tomato sauce; 2 tbsp. canola oil; 1 cup each chopped: 1 large onion, red and green bell pepper, mushrooms or mushroom stems, celery, carrots; ½ tsp. each oregano and granulated garlic; salt and fresh-ground black pepper to taste; pinch of red pepper flakes or to taste; 4 tbsp. fresh basil torn into small pieces; ½ cup to 1 cup water as needed according to the amount of the vegetables added to the sauce; ½ cup red wine (op), ½ cup orange juice.

1. Heat a large pot on medium heat, when hot add oil and sauté the mushroom-onion for 5 minutes; add rest of the vegetable and sauté another 5-8 minutes or until soft. Add tomatoes, sauce, salt, fresh-ground black pepper, red pepper flakes, oregano, granulated garlic, water and the wine and orange juice. Bring to a boil, lower the heat and simmer for 15 minutes. Add the meatballs and fresh basil, then bring to a low simmer until meatballs are heated through.

For the Meatballs: About 2-1/2 to 3 pounds lean ground beef; 2 tbsp. canola oil; 10 oz. (283g) mushrooms, caps chopped and save the stems for the sauce; 1 large onion chopped; 2 medium plum tomatoes peeled and chopped; ½ tsp. each of dry oregano, granulated garlic; ¼ tsp. dry rosemary; 1 tbsp. fresh torn basil (op); 1 tbsp. ketchup; 1 tsp. prepared mustard; 4 thick slices (about 1-inch thick) of Italian loaf cut into small pieces; ¾ cup hot milk; 1 extra large egg; 1 packet beef broth; a little salt and fresh-ground black pepper; ½ tsp. granulated garlic; ½ cup hot water.

1. Line a heavy-bottom large tray first with aluminum foil, then with parchment paper. Grease the parchment paper well.
2. In a large bowl add bread pieces and pour over the hot milk, cover and let it stand for ½ hour.
3. Heat a sauté pan on medium heat, add some oil and sauté mushroom on high heat until all the moisture has evaporated about 10-15 minutes. Take out the mushrooms from the pan, add a little more oil and sauté the onion; sprinkle a little salt and fresh-ground black pepper, sauté a little, cover and let it cook on low heat for 5-8 minutes until soft.
4. Mix the bread well with a fork and mush around to dissolve the bread pieces. Add ground beef on the top, egg, then ketchup, mustard, spices, salt and pepper, chopped tomatoes and then sautéed and cooled vegetables. Slowly add hot water. Mix all the ingredients well with a wooden spoon. Do not mix with your hands.
5. Using an ice cream scoop, take out a scoopful of mixture on lightly wet hands. First make a roll shape of the mixture, then slowly turn it into a ball while pushing the bread pieces and the vegetables in the center. Place the balls on the prepared tray. Chill the meatballs for ½ hour.

6. Preheat the oven for 450 degrees. Take the tray from the refrigerator and turn over the meatballs, lightly reshaping them in the tray. Drizzle a little oil over the meatball and bake in preheated oven for 10 minutes. Reduce the oven to 350 degrees, turn around the tray halfway and bake meatballs for about 25 minutes until they are sizzling in the bottom. Take out the tray out of the oven and let them rest over the stove for 15 minutes.
7. Bring the sauce to a boil, add the meatballs and the fresh basil. Then reduce the heat to simmer and heat the meatballs for another 15 minutes or until they are heated through. Do not boil or overcook the meatballs.
8. Serve meatballs over pasta, with salad and Italian bread or the garlic bread on the side.

Perfect Rounded, Large Meat Balls

Every now and then I make these meatballs for a party. The only thing you have to do is deep-fry them in order to make large and then keep their shape. Once I had deep-fried over 140 meatballs to take them to my brother-in-law's house. It took me about 7 hours from start to finish. But everyone enjoyed them very much. They are soft inside and very fancy looking.

Follow the meatball recipe above. Just when mixture is ready, sprinkle on the top ½ cup seasoned, dry bread crumbs, mix a little and make large meatballs. Do not refrigerate, just deep fry them in about 3-inch deep hot oil (about 375 degrees) in a wok, wide pot, or in a deep fryer. Do not crowd, fry each batch about 8-10 minutes, depending on the size, until they are lightly browned. Turn the meatballs over half way through cooking. Make gravy as above and add meatballs to the warm gravy, simmer 15 minutes and serve. Always sprinkle some fresh basil in the sauce and fresh grated parmesan cheese over the meatballs. Serve with crusty bread or garlic bread.

If you have to fry more than 1 batch, then scoop out the foam or any burnt pieces from the oil with a perforated spatula or a spider. You can also strain the oil, through a paper towel-lined strainer, from one pot to another pot. Just be careful handling the hot oil.

Large Baked Meatballs (M:about 30 large)

These are our favorite ones. We make these when we have many people over or just for ourselves and freeze half of the them without adding the sauce. Very easy to make, and a lot less work.

Ingredients: In a large pan with 2Tbsp. oil cook 1cup each: chopped onion, celery and mushroom for 8-10 minutes until soft, cool; 3 pounds ground beef 80/20 fat; 4 slices whole wheat or Italian bread made into crumbs in the food processor and soaked in 1/2cup milk; 1/3cups rolled oats grinded into powder in the food processor; 3 large eggs; 1/4cup grated cheese; 1/2cup dry cranberries; 1/4cup ketchup; 2Tbsp. wet or dry mustard; 1/2Tsp. salt; black pepper to taste; 1Pkg. about 1Tbsp. instant beef broth; hot sauce (tabasco) to taste; 1Tbsp. dry oregano; ½ to 1/3cup hot water as needed to make soft balls. For the sauce: 2 bottles each 16oz. spaghetti or marinara sauce, 1/2Tsp. granulated garlic; 1/2cup fresh torn basil, salt and pepper to taste.

Preheat oven at 450 degrees. Prepare a large lasagna pan (12X14-inches). In a large bowl combine all ingredients with a wooden spoon then add the hot water and form with light hands large meatballs (about 1/2cup of mixture), just rolling between the palms for 2-3 times. Place the meatballs all around the edges, then in the middle. Bake them in a preheated oven for about 15 minutes light brown. While meatballs are baking heat the sauce ingredients in a large and wide pot, and bring it to a boil. Now lower the heat and submerge the meatballs starting from the edge going to the center. Simmer them in single layer (in batches) for about 30 minutes, turning over once. Serve warm, sprinkled with grated cheese and fresh herbs over pasta with Italian bread and some salad.

Tip: Make meatballs 1 to 2 days ahead so that they will have more flavor. Even the frozen one have more flavor.

Swedish Meatballs with Egg Noodles and wilted Kale
(Serves: 4)

Swedish meatballs are very tasty. We make both the small (about 1-1/2-inch diameter) ones for the cocktail, and the medium (about 2-1/2-inch diameter) ones for the dinner. Traditionally you scrape the drippings and add to the sauce, but I do not want to add more fat, so I use Worcestershire sauce.

Ingredients for the Meatballs: About 1-1/2 pounds 80% lean ground beef; 5 tbsp. butter, divided; 1 cup diced onion; ¼ tsp. granulated garlic; ¾ cup diced baby bella mushrooms; ¾ cup heavy cream mixed with ¼ cup milk; 1 large egg; 1 packet, about 1 tbsp. instant beef broth; 4 tbsp.dry bread crumbs; 2 tbsp. flour; ½ tsp. dry oregano; salt and pepper to taste; 4 tbsp. oil, divided. To serve: wilted kale and egg noodles, prepared per package direction, cooked about 7 minutes in a salted water and drained.

For the Sauce: 1-1/2 cups heavy cream; ½ cup milk; ½ tsp. onion powder; 4 tbsp. Worcestershire sauce; little salt and pepper.

To make the Meatballs: Heat a heavy-bottom skillet on medium heat. Add 1 tbsp. butter and cook onion. Sprinkle with little salt and garlic powder. Cook stirring on and off for about 8-10 minutes until soft. Take them out in a large bowl. Add 1 more tbsp. butter to the pan and cook mushroom on high heat, until their liquid has evaporated and they start turning light brown, about 5 minutes. Take out the mushrooms in the same bowl. Cool the mixture, and then add to the bowl meat, heavy cream mixture, egg, beef broth, bread crumbs, flour, oregano, salt and pepper to taste, 2 tbsp. oil; mix well with a fork. Then knead with the hand for about 2 minutes, until the mixture is smooth. Wash your hands, and drop about 3 tbsp. mixture onto a platter. Wet your hands, moisten with little oil and start rolling the meatballs; place them in a single layer on a greased platter. Refrigerate and chill them for about 1 hour.

Heat a heavy-bottom skillet with 2 tbsp. oil and 3 tbsp. butter on high heat. Brown the meatballs, and turn them over only when the bottom is browned, scrapping the bottom and turning all around until they are cooked, browned, and crispy outside, about 10 minutes per batch. Keep them warm in a 200-degree oven. Make platter ahead with noodles and the kale; place the meatballs and serve over the sauce.

For the sauce: In a medium pan, bring all the sauce ingredients to a simmer. Simmer 10 minutes on low and pour into the serving platters.

Wilted Kale

Bring a large frying pan half full of salted water to a rolling boil. Add 1 bunch (about 8 oz.) kale leaves stripped off the stems and washed. Simmer for 3 minutes. Discard the water, add 3 tbsp. butter, ½ tsp. each garlic and onion powders, and dry oregano. Increase the heat high and stir for about 8 minutes, until the kale is wilted; serve warm, squeezed with some lemon juice.

Tip: Kale is loaded with calcium and has some iron. It also has vitamin K.

Hot Dogs (Serves: 4)

Since franks are loaded with sodium, we eat them only a few times a year. We like them with everything on and with a lot of salad and pickles on the side. To make them healthy, they are boiled in water and then sautéed in little olive oil to get most of the salt out; served with salad, fermented beans, and with both beets and sweet potato fries.

Ingredients: 8 beef franks; 2 tbsp. olive oil, divided; 1 cup grated cheddar cheese; ½ cup diced red onion; prepared mustard; 1 package (½ pound 277 g) crispy or wine sauerkraut; 4 large long rolls.

For the Chili: 1 pkg. 1-1/2 to 2 pounds lean ground beef; 1 large red onion chopped; 2 garlic cloves chopped; 1 cup chopped mushrooms; ½ cup chopped celery; 1 can, 14.5 ounces tomato sauce; ½ tsp. prepared mustard; 2 tbsp. pomegranate molasses or ketchup; ½ tsp. dry oregano; ¼ tsp. dry basil; 1/2tsp. granulated garlic.

To Serve: daicon (white radish) slices, 4-kiwi sliced, 1cup fermented sweet beans; lettuce; beets and sweet potato fries, ketchup, mustard, sweet and sour pickles.

1. To make the Chili: Heat a medium pot on medium heat. When heated add 1 tbsp. olive oil and sauté onion and celery for 2 minutes, add mushrooms, garlic and sauté for 5 minutes until soft, take out and set aside. In the same pot add beef and brown for 8-10 until browned. Now add tomato sauce, molasses, mustard and half of the dry spices: oregano, basil, and granulated garlic. Stir well and add sautéed vegetable mixture, cover, bring to boil, reduce heat and simmer for about 30 minutes. Add rest of the herbs and taste for the seasoning. Turn off the stove and reheat again at serving.

2. To cook the franks: While chili is cooking, poke the franks with the point of a knife and boil them covered with the water for 5 minutes. Discard the water and wash the franks under the running water well. Put the pan back on the stove, dry out all the water and add 1 tbsp. olive oil and brown franks, all around, on low heat.

3. Assemble the hot dog: Slit each roll and heat in the oven, right on the shelf at 250 degree oven for about 5 minutes or until crisp. While roll are heating, arrange daicon,

4. kiwi slices and fermented beans together with beets and sweet potato fries on one side of the platter. Then spread the mustard inside on all 4 warmed rolls, squeeze out the liquid of sauerkraut and spread inside the rolls, top with hot franks, chili, grated cheddar cheese and diced red onion.

5. When serving make sure, rolls are warm, franks are hot and chili is warm. Heat everything again just before serving. Serve with Ketchup and Mustard and pickles on the side.
   Tip: In our family we all like hot dogs with everything on them: mustard on one side of the roll, ketchup on the other side, topped with chili, sauerkraut, sliced pickled cherry peppers and finally chopped onion. I bet you can use one of those too!

Layered Hot Dogs (Serves: 2)

We lived in Long Branch, New Jersey, at the shore. The Windmill , famous for the hot dogs, was just 2 blocks away from us. So we got into eating the hot dogs and developing our own flavors. These hot dogs have tasty layers of all sorts of flavors.

Ingredients: 2 brioche buns or Cuban rolls or light long rolls, about 3 tbsp. butter, divided; mustard and ketchup; ½ cup hot or mild pepper relish; 4 slices (4 x 4 inchs) of sharp cheddar cheese; 2 long or 4 regular-size beef hot dogs;1 cup crunchy sauerkraut squeezed out of the liquid; 1 cup beef chili (sauté ½ cup onion in 1 tbsp. oil 2 minutes, then add 1 pound ground beef. Brown for 8-10 minutes on medium-high heat, add 1-1/4 ounces can of Italian stewed tomatoes, and salt, pepper to taste. Add 1 tbsp. chili powder, simmer 5 minutes: makes 2 cups); ½ cup fresh chopped yellow or green onion. To serve: cole slaw, and/or fries on the side.

Lightly poke the hot dogs all around with the point of the knife, cover with water and bring them to a boil, and simmer for 5 minutes turning them around. Heat a heavy-bottom pan with 1 tbsp. butter, and sear the hot dogs on low heat until browned all around, about 8-10 minutes. Butter the buns inside with soft butter and just before assembling, place the butter side down and brown them in a heated skillet until light brown.

To assemble: Open the buns and spread mustard on one side, and the ketchup on the other side. Spread out the pepper jelly, and top with cheese. Now heat the buns under the broiler for 2-3 minutes or until the cheese is melted halfway. Take out and top the cheese with hot dogs, sauerkraut, chili, and then with fresh onion. Serve immediately with sides.

Tip: You can make the toasted buns flat or hold them in double foil wrappings.

Beef Teriyaki (Serves: 4)

This is the best Japanese comfort food that we like. Meat is served on the soba noodles with steamed or sautéed veggies.

Ingredients : 1-1/2 pounds boneless sirloin or club steak, partially frozen, then cut against the grain, into 1-inch wide strips, and again cut diagonally into about 2-inch pieces (you can also use 80% lean ground beef); about 3 tbsp. sesame seed or canola oil; ¾ cup teriyaki marinade or sauce (divided); 2 medium kirby (pickling) cucumber thin-sliced; about 6 medium tomato wedges to decorate the edges; 1 cup thin-sliced mushrooms, 2 cups thin-sliced Napa cabbage, 1 cup broccoli florets; ½ cup grated carrots; 4 servings of soba noodles; 3 tbsp. toasted sesame seeds or nuts to garnish.

For the Marinade: 2 tbsp. red wine vinegar; 1 tsp. light brown sugar; 2 tbsp. olive oil; 2 tbsp. grated fresh ginger; 1 tbsp. chopped hot pepper or to taste; 1 tbsp. corn starch; ¼ tsp. each salt and black pepper.

1. Sprinkle beef with little salt and pepper then pour over ¼ C teriyaki sauce and marinade for at least ½ hour. Steam or sauté the vegetables in 2 tbsp. oil for about 10-15 minutes until soft and keep them warm. Decorate the edges of 4 serving plates with cucumber slices and tomatoes slices or wedges and set them aside. Fill a large pot halfway with water, add 1 tsp. salt and 1 tbsp. oil, bring to a boil, add noodles, stir and cook, al dente about 8-9 minutes. Heat a large sauté pan with 1 tbsp. oil, little salt, pepper and ¼ C Teriyaki sauce and add the noodles right after taking them out of the boiling water; stir well and keep them warm. Add some cooking liquid to keep them a little moist and warm.

2. Take out the meat from the marinade on a plate, pat-dry with paper towel. Have the serving plates ready with warmed vegetables and noodles. In a large sauté pan on medium-high heat, heat 2 tbsp. of oil; when oil almost start smoking, add the meat, cook for about 1 minutes, pressing it down with the metal spatula; turn over and cook the other side fast, stir in ¼ C of teriyaki sauce, stir well and immediately serve over the noodles. Garnish with sesame seeds or nuts and serve immediately.

Perfect Steamed Corned Beef, Cabbage and Roasted Potatoes (Serves: 4)

We have a very famous deli in our town, and their steamed corned beef is the best that I have ever eaten. The steamed corn beef does not fall apart even when you slice thin. It takes about 40 minutes at

350 degrees to steam 1 pound of Corned Beef Brisket, and about 15 minutes to rest. But if you are adding the cabbage in the roasting pan, it will take about 45 minutes per pound.

Ingredients:
For the Meat: About 4-1/2 to 5 pounds premium corn beef brisket; 5 tbsp. pickling spices or 1 tbsp. each: coriander seeds, caraway and black mustard seeds; 2 broken bay leaves and black peppercorn crushed on the cutting board with the bottom of a cast-iron or heavy pan or coarsely grinded; 1 tbsp. red pepper flakes; ½ tsp. granulated garlic; 1 tbsp. olive oil; mustard to serve.

For the Cabbage: 1 medium red or green cabbage, stem out and cut in quarters or into four wedges; salt and pepper; 2 tbsp., or to taste chili powder (op); 1 tsp. granulated garlic; 1-2 tbsp. olive oil.
For the Mustard Potatoes: About 2-1/2 pounds or about 7-8 large red potatoes scrubbed clean, covered with cold water and boiled about 25 minutes, until soft; 4 tbsp. cider vinegar; 2 tbsp. Dijon mustard; 3 tbsp. ketchup; about ½ tsp. salt and pepper or to taste; 1 tsp. granulated garlic; 5 tbsp. olive oil; for garnish: ½ cup chopped parsley or cilantro leaves chopped (op).

(1) Mustard Potatoes

1. Preheat oven at 450 degrees. Cut potatoes into quarter lengthwise then cut into 1-1/2-inch pieces across. In a large non-reactive bowl, whisk together vinegar, mustard, ketchup, salt and pepper, garlic and about 3 tbsp. oil. Add potatoes and toss together with a large spoon. Then spread them out on a heavy and large baking sheet lined with aluminum foil and greased well with 1 tbsp. of the oil, cut-side down. Drizzle rest of the oil on the top all over. Bake potatoes until golden underneath for about 15 minutes, take the sheet out of the oven, let it rest 5 minutes, then carefully turn over the potatoes and roast on the other side until golden. Keep them covered with foil until serving.

(2) Corn Beef and Cabbage

1. Preheat oven at 400 degree. Prepare a large roasting pan with 1-1/2-inches deep hot water (up to the grades). Put 2 large pieces of aluminum foil together, a little larger than the roasting pan, and put them together by folding two long edges, three times together (3 folds), to cover the roasting pan airtight.
2. Take the meat out from the package, save the spices, and wash the meat under running cold water. Place the meat on the grade the fat side down. Then spread the pickling spices all over on the top of the meat, sprinkle the red pepper flakes, garlic powder, and drizzle the oil on the top. Cover the pan airtight, pressing the foil, inside and outside of the rim. Carefully place pan on the middle self. Steam meat 30 minutes at 400 degrees. Then reduce the temperature to 350 degrees and roast for 3-1/2 hours, a total of 4 hours. Turn the roasting pan around halfway during the roasting. Take the pan out of the oven and let it rest for 15 minutes, then open the foil carefully on the other side, away from you (stay away from the steam) just before slicing. While the meat is resting, you can reheat the potatoes on low heat in the oven.

3. Take off all the fat from the meat and slice warm meat thin across the grain and serve with roasted potatoes, cabbage and mustard.

   Tip: Red pepper flakes are necessary to give unique flavor; you can always scrape them off after roasting, if you do not want any spices.

Variation

(3) Sauteed Cabbage

We like sautéed cabbage, it has more taste and gives natural sweet flavor with the meat. The secret is in the slicing and sautéing of the cabbage.

Cut the cabbage in half and take out the stem. Cut each piece into 3 wedges, then take out the core from each wedge. Now take one wedge at a time and, starting at the stem end, slice the cabbage across at about 45 degree angle, about ½-inch wide.

Heat a large, heavy-bottom pan, add 2 tbsp. of canola or olive oil, add the thick (bottom) part of the cabbage first, then rest of the sliced cabbage and sauté cabbage on medium-high heat for 5 minutes; reduce the heat and sauté 10 minutes at medium heat. Sprinkle 1 tsp. of granulated garlic, ½ tsp. each turmeric and fresh-ground black pepper, and sprinkle 1 tbsp. oil on top of the spices, cover the pan and simmer for 15-20 minutes, stirring every 10 minutes, about 3-4 times, until cabbage is soft. No need for salt but if you prefer, you can sprinkle some lemon juice and a little salt and serve warm.

Steamed Pastrami

Follow the direction of the steaming the Corned Beef Brisket; just marinate the brisket for 3 days, dip meat in the spice rub and steam-roast the meat in aluminum foil.

Brine: 3Tbsp. each caraway seeds, mustard seeds, 4 large bay leaves broken, red pepper flakes, black peppercorn, coriander seeds, fennel seeds all crushed, 2Tsp. turmeric.

Ingredients: One piece 4-1/2 to 5 pounds premium corn beef brisket; lightly roast in a dry pan: 2 tbsp. each caraway seeds, cumin seeds, black mustard seeds, black peppercorns and fennel seds. Take out the veins and crumble 2-3 bay leaves (for about 1 tbsp. powder) and lightly toast in the pan. Grind the spices coarsely in a coffee grinder or a blender dry, without adding any water.

Take out extra fat from the meat and wash it well. Place the meat in a large platter /bowl sprinkle brine spices and cover with the cold water. Place the platter/bowl in the refrigerator for 3 days, turning the meat over twice a day.

About one hour before roasting, take out the meat out of the refrigerator and let it sit in the room temperature. Pat dry the meat with paper towels. Press the meat all over in the grinded spices, wrap the meat in a large aluminum foil in a single layer. Steam in a roasting pan large enough to hold the meat, fat side up for about 55 minutes per pound. Turn around the roasting pan halfway roasting during the roasting. When done, take out the meat and let it rest in a platter or a cutting board, for at least 30 minutes covered. Open the foil and slice the meat thin across the grain just before serving.

Pierogis with Fresh Tomato Sauce (M: 18, 3 inches diameter)

The name may be different they are called pierogis but the process is the same for dal gujhiya. These gujhiyas are filled with soaked, ground and spice-sautéed beans that we make in India. You can also fill

182

them with samosa filling. You can serve them with fresh tomato sauce, cucumber raita (yogurt salad), or with chutney, sauces and relishes.

For the Dough: 1 extra large egg beaten with ½ cup Greek yogurt; 1-1/2 cups all-purpose flour and 2 tbsp. semolina mixed with 6 tbsp. butter softened lightly; ¼ tsp. salt; extra flour for dusting.

For the Filling: 2 tbsp. canola oil; 4 tbsp. butter; 2 cups chopped onion, divided; 1 cup broccoli florets chopped, and blanched in hot water for 3-4 minutes; 1 cup seeded and chopped red bell pepper;1 cup cooked ham cut in ½-inch cubes; 1 pound drained ricotta cheese; 1 extra large egg; 1 tsp. dry oregano; ½ tsp. granulated garlic; ½ tsp. dry rosemary; salt and fresh-ground black pepper to taste

To make the dough: In a bowl rub butter with the flour, semolina and salt then add the yogurt mixture and stir in with a fork and make a dough. Knead the dough for a few minutes. If needed add some water by teaspoons. The dough should be soft and pliable. Set the dough aside in a bowl covered with lightly damped kitchen towel.

To make the filling: Place the ricotta cheese in a paper towel-lined strainer and let it drain 3-4 hours over a bowl. Heat a large sauté pan on medium heat, add oil and 1 tbsp. butter, cook the onion, sprinkled with a little salt and garlic, cover and cook onions for 5-6 minutes, take out and put aside half of the sautéed onion. Add red bell pepper and sauté for another 5 minutes. Pour everything in a bowl, add ham, ricotta cheese, beaten egg, and spices. Mix well with a wooden spoon.

Divide the dough in to two parts. Dusting the counter and the rolling pin, roll out one part of the dough into about 1/8-inch thick and about 6 inches wide and 11 inches long. Cut out 3-inch circles with a biscuit cutter, dusting the cutter in the flour. Pick up one circle in hand, fill in 2 tbsp. of filling, wet the edges with water, then fold in half and seat the pierogi. Place on the cutting board, press down the edges again to seal then well, then press down the edges with the tines of a fork. Do the same with the other part of the dough. Reroll the scrapings and roll out some extra rounds to stuff.

Bring a large pot half full with salted water to a boil, drop the pierogis in batches and cook in boiling water about 8 minutes, until they start floating.

Heat a large, heavy-bottom pan on medium heat. Add 1 tbsp. butter and cooked onions sauté the pierogis in batches for about 5-6 minutes until they are light brown. When all the pierogis are browned take them out and serve with fresh tomato sauce, sprinkled with fresh or roasted herbs and/or roasted cumin powder.

Tip: You can also use the Samosa filling either the potatoes or the meat.

Fresh Tomato Sauce (M: about 3 C)

You can make this sauce a day before, just heat and serve.

Ingredients: 1-1/2 pounds fresh plum tomatoes blanched in water 1 minute, peeled and cut into 1-inch cubes; 1 tbsp. olive oil; 2 tbsp. butter;
1 cup chopped onion; ½ cup each chopped fine celery, carrots, green bell pepper; 1 tsp. each dry oregano and granulated garlic; about ½ tsp. salt and pepper or to taste; 2 tbsp. sugar; 2 tbsp. fresh basil.

In a large, heavy-bottom pan, heat oil and butter and sauté onion with a little salt and garlic powder for 5 minutes. Add carrots, celery and bell pepper mix well, cover, reduce heat to low and cook for 6-8 minutes. Add the tomatoes and remaining ingredients; bring to a boil then reduce the heat to low and simmer open for 30 minutes. Mash the sauce with potato masher and check for seasoning. Serve or cool and refrigerate covered until needed.

Stuffed Pork Chops in Cider Gravy with Corn and Asparagus
(Serves: 4)

Pork chops have to be cooked right, so watch carefully. The temperature should be around 145 degrees to 150 degrees. The temperature will go up a little even after they finish cooking.

1. Asparagus Ribbons

Ingredients: About ½ pound thick fresh asparagus; 3-4 tbsp. lemon juice; salt and pepper to taste; extra virgin olive oil to drizzle.

Wash and pat-dry the asparagus then trim off the hard bottom. Using a potato peeler, peel one asparagus at a time, lengthwise, into ribbons. Just before serving place the ribbons with two forks on the warm serving plates, drizzle with lemon juice, little salt, pepper and olive oil.

2. Corn with Marinated Red Bell Peppers

Ingredients: 2 tbsp. butter; 3 fresh corn on the cob, peeled and scraped off the kernels or one package, 10 ounces (284g) of frozen corn; about ½ cup marinated red bell strips from the jar chopped; little salt and pepper to taste.

Five minutes before serving, heat a large heavy-bottom pan on medium-high heat. Add butter, move around and coat the bottom. Immediately add the corn and stir on medium-high heat for 6-8 minutes until corn is heated through and is little soft. Take off the heat mix in the red bell pepper. Serve sprinkled with a little salt and pepper.

3. Stuffed Pork Chops
Ingredients:

For the Stuffing: One gayla or golden delicious apple peeled, cored and grated; 2-3tbsp. grated cheese from the bottle; 1/2cup each dry cranberries and pistachios.

For the Coating: 4, about 1-1/4- to 1-1/2-inch thick, (total about 3 pounds) pork loin center cut chops for stuffing with pockets; 5 tbsp. butter; coating mixture: ¾ cup all-purpose flour mixed with 1 tsp. each garlic powder, onion powder; rosemary and fresh-ground black pepper.

(4) Cider Gravy (M: about 1cup)

For the Gravy: 1 Large onion sliced about ¼-inch thick; 1 cup hard cider; 1 cup concentrated frozen orange juice thawed; salt and pepper to taste. Combine all and pour over the pork chops. After the chops are done, serve with pan gravy.

(5) Pork Chops

Preheat oven to 400 degrees. Grease a 9X9-inch or 9X13-inch baking platter.

If pork chops do not have pockets, them slit them on inside edge in half (leave the fat side out) in the middle first, then insert the knife inside, make the pocket going around, do not take them apart. Now using a fork mix the stuffing ingredients and fill the chops evenly with the mixture. Then press and flatten them. If you wish you can close the opening with the toothpicks. Dredge each pork chop well in the coating mixture on all sides, including the opening. Heat 3 tbsp. butter in a large pan on medium-high heat, and lightly brown the chops fast, in the butter for about 2 minutes on each side, total of 4 minutes per chop. Take out the chops and cook the onion in 2 tbsp. butter, stirring constantly until they are soft, about 8 minutes. Take out the onion and heat the cider in the pan, bring it to a boil.

Place the chops in the baking pan, sprinkle the onion all around, then pour the cider all around. Bake the chops in a preheated oven at 400 degrees for 10 minutes, then at 350 degrees for 5 minutes, or until it has reached an internal temperature of 145 degrees, checked in the center of the chops with an instant-read thermometer. Take out the chops in a warm platter, and tent them with aluminum foil. Pour the juices back in the pan, add the orange juice and reduce them about ¾ C on medium-high heat, boiling constantly until thickened about 6-8 minutes. Add salt and pepper to taste.
Serve chops immediately drizzled with gravy, corn and asparagus on the side.

Fresh Pork Spare Ribs (Serves: 8-10)

If you are a rib lover, you will love these spare ribs. They are loaded with meat. Country ribs are also have enough meat, but for me, the baby back ribs do not have much meat. Spare ribs take about 1-1/4 hours per pound to cook. So a 5-pound piece will take about 6-1/4 hours, and another 15 minutes to rest in the oven covered, and another 15 minutes to rest on the counter. You just need coarse salt and a lot of coarse black pepper to marinade overnight. We like them with the vinegar-based barbecue sauce.

Ingredients: About 5 pounds fresh pork spare ribs, ask the butcher to slice off the bottom bone to separate them later; ¼ cup each coarse salt and coarse black pepper; 3-4 tbsp. canola oil, plus extra for the foil; 1 bottle (about 2-3/4 c) vinegar-based barbecue sauce; salt and fresh-ground black pepper to taste. To serve: fries, coleslaw and/or potato salad or the grain salad, biscuits or your choice of side dish.

1. Pat-dry the pork with paper towels and rub both sides with the coarse salt and pepper, drizzle with the oil, place in a glass platter or in a large bowl, and marinate open, overnight in the refrigerator.
2. Place the oven rack in the middle, and preheat to 325 degrees. Prepare a large roasting pan or a heavy-bottom large baking sheet with double layer of aluminum foil put together in to one piece, and grease the foil well. Wrap the meat in a single layer, in large foil, airtight and place in the roasting pan or baking sheet, pointing the wider end of the meat towards the back wall.
3. Roast for 3 hours then turn around the pan half way and roast another 2 hours. Open the meat, pull out the foil and sprinkle the salt and pepper on the meat; brush heavily with the barbecue sauce and roast extra 20-30 minutes, basting with the sauce. Turn over the meat with a spatula and a tong, sprinkle with salt and pepper and brush heavily with the barbecue sauce, and roast another 15-30 minutes. Turn off the oven and take out the meat; let it rest, tented with foil for 15 minutes Cut separating the bones, and serve with extra barbecue sauce for dipping. The meat is very soft, so you can pull it out with your hands. Serve with coleslaw and/or fries.

Barbecued Spare Ribs

Follow the recipe above. Soak the wooden chips overnight in water, drain, and place the chips in a large double piece of aluminum or in a metal container, then place them on the grill in indirect heat. Preheat the grill for indirect cooking at 225 degrees with meat thermometer attached. Grill meat at 225 degrees for about 5 hours, turning around the meat, then cook directly on the heat brushed well with sauce on both side for about 1 hour or until the ribs almost fall apart, but still intact.

Quick BBQ and Grilling Sauce (M: 1-1/2 cups)

Ingredients: 2 small cans, each 8 oz., (227g), 2 cups plain tomato sauce; ½ cup ketchup; ¼ cup apple cider vinegar; 2 tbsp. light brown sugar; ½ tsp. granulated garlic; ¼ tsp. dry oregano; salt and fresh-ground black pepper to taste, ¼ tsp. cayenne pepper or to taste.

Combine all ingredients in a medium pot, bring to a boil then simmer, covered, on low heat for 15 minutes.

Herbed BBQ and Grilling Sauce (M: about 2-1/2 cups)

Most of the tasty sauces are made with fresh herbs and spices. So go to a little extra effort and grind the fresh spices.

Ingredients : 1 tab roasted cumin or caraway seeds (roast about 8 minutes on medium heat in a dry skillet); 1 tbsp. canola oil; ½ cup fresh chopped onion, 1-2 fresh stemmed and seeded and chopped jalapeno; 1 tab chopped garlic cloves; ¼ cup chopped ginger, ¼ cup fresh chop cilantro or flat-leaf parsley, ¾ cup apple cider vinegar, 1cup ketchup; 1 can, 8 oz. (227g) 1 cup plain tomato sauce; 4-5 tbsp. brown sugar; 1 tsp. cayenne pepper or to taste; salt and fresh-ground black pepper to taste; 1-2 ounces semisweet chocolate chopped.

1. In a blender or food processor, grind the roasted cumin or caraway seeds without water, then add some water (about ½ c) and grind and puree together onion, garlic, jalapeno, ginger, parsley or cilantro.
2. To make the Sauce: Heat a medium pot on medium heat. When hot add 1 tbsp. oil and cook the pureed and fresh-ground spices, stirring for 10 minutes. Add tomato sauce, ketchup, cayenne, brown sugar, vinegar, salt and pepper to taste, and cook, stirring every few minutes. Bring to a boil, lower the heat and simmer about 15 minutes. Stir in chocolate. Add about ¼ cup cooking liquid from the pan, if using the pan. Take off the heat and use warm sauce on the ribs or any other grilled meat.

Pot Roast with Wine Gravy (Serves: 8-10)

This pot roast doesn't require too much work, is very tasty, impressive and serves a small party. Order your meat through a butcher or at your local supermarket. I go to ShopRite and order most of my meats. You can freeze it cooked, wrapped in the plastic in a plastic container for up to 3 months, thaw overnight in the refrigerator and reheat in the gravy. Chuck bottom roast takes longer to cook, so I cook half hour per pound, and then extra 30 minutes to soften it. Use an electric knife to slice it. If you can make it a day ahead, heat slowly in the gravy, it will be tastier and softer, and will melt in your mouth.

Ingredients: 4 tbsp. canola oil, divided; 2 tbsp. butter; 1 piece 6 pounds boneless bottom chuck roast, about 4-inches high and even shape; 2 tbsp. all-purpose flour mixed with each ½ tsp. granulated garlic and fresh-ground black pepper; 2 large onions sliced paper-thin; 1 cup very thin-sliced celery stocks; 3-4 bay leaves; 1 tsp. dry rosemary; ½ tsp to ¾ tsp. granulated garlic; 1 apple peeled, cored and sliced; 1 orange peeled, seeded and quartered; 1can 16 oz. (about 2 c) beef broth; 1 can (1cup) tomato sauce; 1 tbsp. Worcestershire sauce; 1 tbsp. hot sauce or to taste;12 ounces baby bella medium-size mushroom, left whole and cleaned; ½ pound (2 cups) baby carrots cleaned; salt and pepper to taste; 4 tbsp. corn starch for the gravy.

Wine Reduction for the gravy

Ingredients: 2 tbsp. butter; 3 cups red wine and ½ cup concentrated frozen orange juice thawed.

1. In a large heavy-bottom pot for the stove or in a large Dutch oven for the roasting in the oven, heat 2 tbsp. oil on medium heat. Sprinkle the meat all over with the flour mixture then sear (brown) in the hot oil on medium-high heat on all sides. Add bay leaves, carrots, apple, orange, rosemary, garlic, tomato sauce, Worcestershire sauce, hot sauce, beef broth and bring to a boil. Then reduce the heat and bring it to a constant simmer on medium heat. Roast the meat in the Dutch oven at 350 degrees, covered for the same amount of time, or on the stove. The total roasting time will be about 30 minutes per pound of the meat. So 6 pounds of meat will take about 3 hours, then let it simmer another 30 minutes. Turn over the meat every hour.

2. While meat is cooking, heat a heavy-bottom sauté pan on medium heat, add rest of the oil, add onion, a little salt, pepper and garlic powder; stir a little, cover and let it cook for 5 minutes. Open the cover, add the celery and sauté onion and celery for another 5 minutes until onion is caramelized, and then add to the meat. Add the butter to the same pan and sauté the mushroom on high heat for 7-8 minutes until all the liquid has evaporated; take them out and add to the meat.

3. **For the Wine Gravy:** Use the same pan, add the butter, coat the pan and add the wine and the orange juice. Reduce it, without stirring, for about 20 on high heat, to about 1 cup. Turn off the heat.

4. When meat is fork-tender, take it out on the warm serving platter, arrange the mushroom and carrots all around. Tent the platter with the foil. Use about half of the liquid from the pot to the reduced wine then whisk in the corn starch to the wine, stir well. Heat the wine sauce over high heat stirring constantly. When it is bubbling and thickened, add rest of the cooking liquid, taste for the salt and pepper. Pour some gray over the sliced meat and serve some on the side in a gravy boat.

Old Fashion Pot Roast (Serves: 6)

We love to make a good pot roast with less fat and more flavorful meat and we make it double so that we have for next day, if we are not having any guests. The best meat we liked is a thick slab of London Broil for pot roast. After cooking for 3 hours, you can cut the meat with the fork; it will melt in your mouth.

Ingredients: 3-1/2 to 4 pounds boneless chuck roast (I prefer chuck, it melts in your mouth) or beef London broil for pot roast or beef loin boneless sirloin steak; flour mixture: 5-6 tbsps. all-purpose flour, ½ tsp. granulated garlic and ½ tsp. cayenne pepper, each 2 cups chopped: onion, celery, button mushrooms; 2 tbs. canola oil; 2 pieces of vegetable per person each peeled: large carrots, whole potatoes, parsnips (you can cut across carrots and parsnips into 2-3-inch pieces); 2 cans, each,14.5 oz. (411g) beef broth 99% fat-free; 2 bay leaves; 5-6 ginger snaps crushed fine; 1 tbsp. Dijon mustard; salt and fresh-ground black pepper to taste.

1. Heat a large Dutch oven or a heavy-bottom pot on medium-high heat when hot add 1 tbsp. oil. If meat is too big cut in half across, to make two pieces. Dip the meat both side into the flour mixture, pat out excess (save any left- over flour mixture), and brown the meat in the pot on both sides, about 2 minutes each side. Take out the meat in a platter and tent it loosely with an aluminum foil or keep it partially covered with a plate. Add 1 tbsp. more oil and sauté mushrooms, onion and celery until soft, about 6-8 minutes.

2. Add 2 cans of beef broth and about 1 cup of water, bay leaves, carrots, parsnips and potatoes, sprinkle a little salt and pepper. Make sure liquid is almost covering the vegetables. Place the meat on the top of the vegetables. Cover and bring to a boil. Reduce the heat and simmer for about 1 to 1-1/4 hour or until vegetables are soft. Turn the pot around half way during the cooking.

3. Take out the vegetables to a platter and keep them covered. Now put the meat in the bottom of the pot over the chopped onion, celery and mushrooms, add any leftover flour mixture and crushed ginger snaps, Dijon mustard and a little salt and pepper if needed, stir a little, and simmer the meat on low heat for 1 hour more until it is fork-tender and most of the chopped onion has cooked down. Put the cooked vegetables back over the meat and simmer another 15 minutes more. Serve warm with mustard on the side.

Slow Roasted Pulled Pork: Cuban Style (Serves: about 8)

A few years back I saw Emeril Lagasse, cooking Picnic Roast Pork on the Martha Stewart show. It was a large piece of meat and looked very appealing. Pork takes spices well, so marinate it first.

Ingredients: 1 large piece about 7 pounds, bone-in, with skin on picnic roast; for the rub in a bowl combine: 2 tbsp. each canola oil, red pepper flakes, kosher salt, crushed cumin seeds, crushed black peppercorn, 1 tsp. each dry oregano, granulated garlic, onion powder; ½ cup lime juice; ½ cup orange juice; to spread on top: 1 can 6 ounces (about ½ cup) tomato paste; 2 medium bay leaves; 1 tsp. coarse salt; to serve: about 2 cups your favorite barbecue sauce.

1. Score the skin 1-1/2-inches apart and about 1-1/2-inch deep, then rub the spices all over the skin and under the skin as much as possible and marinate the pork overnight in a large sealable plastic bag or a large bowl covered. Bring out the pork at least two hours into room temperature before roasting.

2. Preheat the oven at 450 degrees for 10 minutes. Spread the tomato paste on the top of the pork, and top with bay leaves and coarse salt. Place the pork in the roasting pot with skin side up.

3. Roast the pork at 425 degrees for 30 minutes. Lower the temperature to 250 degrees and roast for about 8-1/2 to 9 hours. Turn around the roasting pan half way during the roasting at least 3-4 times. Pour over and baste the pork with cooking juices at least twice during the roasting while you are turning the roasting pan around. After roasting for about 8-1/2 to 9 hours, the pork should fork-tender. The internal temperature on an instant-read thermometer

at the thickest part should be around 175 to 180 degrees. Take out of the oven and let it rest on the cutting board, tented with a foil, for 20-30 minutes.

4. Take out the skin and cut into small manageable pieces. Discard fat and the bone. Slice the pork against the grains into thick slices or pull it apart with 2 forks. Pour over some cooking juices and mix with some heated barbecue sauce, and serve with sides or make pulled-pork sandwiches.

Boneless, Skinless Pulled Pork (Serves: 6-8)

Ingredients: 1 boneless and skinless about 6 pounds roast pork; rub: 2 tbsp. each crushed black peppercorns; crushed cumin seeds; 1 tsp. each dry oregano; granulated garlic; onion powder; fennel powder; 3 tbsp. olive oil; ¼ cup lime juice; ½ cup orange; 1 cup chicken broth; 1 cup barbecue sauce; 1 cup each chopped: onions, celery and red bell pepper.

Rub half of the spice mixture all over the pork and place the pork in a large bowl or a zip-lock plastic bag and then in a bowl and marinate pork overnight or at least 6 hours
Heat a large pan on medium heat, add oil, pat-dry the meat and brown all sides on medium-high heat, about 8-10 minutes on each side. Take out the meat, add the vegetables, and cook for 8-10 minutes soft.

Move the oven shelf at the middle. Preheat the oven at 400 degrees. Heat a large Cast-iron Dutch Oven or a heavy-bottom Pot with tight-fitting lid. Place the pork in the bottom, sprinkle with rest of the spice mixture, and place the chopped onion, celery and pepper all around then pour over the chicken stock, orange and lemon juices over the vegetables, and then the barbecue sauce over the meat. Cover the pot with the lid, and bring it to a boil over the stove, then place pot in the preheated oven. Roast the meat at 400 degrees for ½ hour, then reduce the temperature to 325 and roast for another 4 hours until it is fork tender. It will take about 40 minutes per pound. Take out of the oven and let it rest for 15 minutes. Slice the pork and serve with roasting juices, barbecue vinegar sauce, mashed potatoes and vegetables or pull it apart with 2 forks and serve with vinegar sauce or make pulled pork sandwiches.

Pork Sliders (Serves: 6-8)

Make enough of these sliders; they will disappear in a minute. I make 2 sliders per person.

Ingredients: 1 recipe (above) of boneless, skinless pulled pork; 2 slider rolls per person; 1 pound bought or home-made coleslaw; 1 cup heated your favorite barbecue sauce; salt and pepper to taste; to serve: sweet potato fries or salad.

Heat the rolls and the barbecue sauce just before serving. Pull the cooked pork with 2 large forks, and shred it

Place the barbecue sauce on the bottom bun, and sprinkle with little salt and pepper. Top the sauce with pulled pork, then coleslaw. Serve with fries or salad on the side.

Pork Tenderloin on Apple Bed with Roasted Vegetables (Serves: 4)

We are also using fingerling potatoes, which come in various shapes and sizes. They are slim and long, and cook fast, have a unique and a soft taste. Try to buy them all in same size. We also serve this with Brussels sprouts, snow peas and pickled pearl onions (op), and roasted red bell pepper to give some color.

(1)   The Pork Tenderloin

Ingredients for the Tenderloin: About 1-1/4 pound 18.4 ounces trimmed pork tenderloin (trimmed of all excess fat and the silver skin with a boning knife); 2 tbsp. canola oil; 2 tbsp. crushed black pepper; 1 tsp. crushed fennel seeds; 1 tsp. granulated garlic. To serve: about ¼ cup warmed hoisin sauce and vegetables.

1.   Prepare a large baking sheet with rim about 10-1/2 x 14-1/2 x 2 inches, lined with aluminum foil (or a 13 x 9 x 3-inches aluminum foil lasagna pan). Preheat the oven at 425 degrees.
2.   Heat a large, heavy-bottom, dry pan on medium heat and roast the garlic, shaking the pan until it is light brown. Spread out all the spices in a large platter. Pat-dry the tenderloin, rub with 1 teaspoon oil, then roll in the spices. Fold the pointed and thin end of the meat underneath and tie the tenderloin four places with kitchen twine, making it round. Now heat rest of the oil in the same large pan over medium-high heat. Add the tenderloin and brown all 4 sides for about 5-6 minutes.
3.   Place the tenderloin in the baking pan and roast at 425 degrees for 15-16 minutes, until internal temperature on an instant-read thermometer is around 135 degrees, and tenderloin is firm to touch. Turning the tenderloin over, halfway through roasting. (If one end of the tenderloin is wider, place that end facing the back wall of the oven for extra heat.) Take out the pan and let the tenderloin rest 5 minutes in the pan. Pick up the aluminum foil together with tenderloin and place on the cutting board, and let it rest another 6-8 minutes, while you are preparing the serving platter. Slice it slightly diagonally, about 1-inch thick slices just before serving, and drizzle with warm hoisin sauce and serve with the roasted vegetables.

(2) Apple Bed

Use one recipe for apple-pie filling or buy a can of cooked apples: 1 can, 20 oz. (we prefer Duncan-Hines, Comstock, no sugar added). Also use a few prunes, fresh from a can, all around the apples on the serving platter.

(3)   Roasted Fingerling Potatoes

Ingredients: 1 to 1-1/4 pound same size fingerling potatoes; 2 tbsp. canola oil; 2 tbsp. chili powder; ½ tsp. granulated garlic; salt and pepper to taste; 1 large red bell pepper, trim, seeded and sliced in wide strips.

Line a large baking sheet with aluminum foil. Place the potatoes in a medium pot, cover with about 3 cups of cold water, bring to a boil, and boil covered for about 15 minutes, or until soft. Using a spider or a perforated spoon, take out the potatoes and save the water for other vegetables. When they are still warm, cut them in half lengthwise, place in a platter, together with the red pepper strips and sprinkle with chili powder, garlic and salt and pepper to taste, then drizzle the oil.

Preheat the oven at 425 degrees, place each piece of the potatoes and pepper, cut side down in the baking sheet and bake together with Brussels sprouts for about 20 minutes or until they are golden.

(4)   Brussels Sprouts

Ingredients: About 3/4 to 1 pound Brussels, trimmed of the stems and stem split in half, ¾ way up, but still attached on the top; 1 tbsp. ketchup, ½ tsp. each granulated garlic, salt and fresh-ground black pepper; 1 tbsp. canola oil.

Blanch the Brussels sprouts in same potato boiling water for 3-4 minutes or until a little soft, cool them in a bowl of ice water or just run cold tab water over them and place them in a platter to drain. Pat-dry them, then toss them in a bowl with ketchup, garlic, salt, pepper and oil. Spread them out on a baking sheet and roast with potatoes about 15-20 minutes.

(5) Snow Peas

Wash and trim about 15 fresh snow peas. Blanch them in the potatoes water for about 3 minutes or until they are a little soft, run the cold tab water on them and place on a paper towel-lined platter. Keep them warm and covered and serve within 10 minutes drizzled with a little extra-virgin olive oil.

(6)   Pickled Pearl Onion

You need only about ½ cup of pickled onions, you can buy them in the jar or make your own in the pickle brine. Just peel the raw pearl onions, poke them, a few places with the toothpick and submerge in the brine; keep in an airtight jar in the refrigerator for about 2-3 weeks and they will be ready to serve. I pickle them with the raw garlic cloves so they have a very good garlic taste.

Assemble the Platter: Make sure you prepare all the vegetables first and keep them warm, in the warm oven, covered with the aluminum foil. Roast the meat last. While the meat is resting (after roasting), assemble a large platter or make 4 individual platters. Then slice the meat place over the apples and drizzle with the warm hoisin sauce.

Tips: Tenderloin can dry very fast so slightly undercook it and roast in a light metal baking sheet with rim or in an aluminum foil platter, to reflect the heat from all around.

Apples, prunes and fennel seeds help digest the pork.

Perfect Standing Rib Roast with Scalloped Parsnips, Bell Peppers & Gravy(Serves: 6)

One of the key here is to rub the meat with seasoning one day ahead, and then bring the meat in room temperature for at least 2-1/2 to 3 hours before roasting. You roast for 10 minutes at 450 degrees, leave in the oven for 2 hours and then roast 10 minutes per pound until internal temperature is around 125 degrees. This is a fancy dinner. Usually, rib roast is served with baked or mashed potatoes and some green beans or salad on the side. We like something new to go with it. Do not serve with a thick gravy. The natural juices taste much better with the delicate meat.

1. Standing Rib Roast

Ingredients: Buy at least 4-5 days ahead: One 2 bones, about 6 pounds, USDA choice beef rib prime rib roast, ask the butcher to slice off the bottom bone, put back in its place, then tie the roast with kitchen twine; 1 tbsp. hot sauce mixed with ½ tsp. garlic power. For the rub: 4 tbsp. fresh garlic chopped and 2 tbsp. fresh rosemary chopped then crushed or grinded fine; 4 tbsp. spicy Montreal steak mix; 1 tsp. coarse salt; 1 tbsp. cider vinegar; 2 tbsp. canola oil; for the gravy: 1 cup heated beef stock mixed with natural juices; to serve: horseradish cream.

Take out the rib roast from the refrigerator a night before cooking and rub the hot sauce and half of garlic and rosemary mixture all over, place in a plastic zip-lock bag or a large bowl tented with a large foil, and refrigerate overnight. About 3 hours before roasting take it out and let it sit in the room temperature. Preheat the oven at 450 degrees. Line a medium shallow broiler tray or a shallow heavy-duty roasting pan with aluminum foil, place the meat standing up (or hold with an aluminum foil ring) and roast the meat for 10 minutes. Turn off the oven and let it rest in the off oven for 2 hours; do not open the oven because the meat is still cooking inside.

After 2 hours, take out the meat and rub both sides with the remaining rub mixture. Insert the thermometer in the meat at the thickest part. Roast the meat at 350 degrees, or about 5 minutes per pound. So the meat will take about 30 to 35 minutes to roast, or internal temperature should be around 115 degrees for rare and 120-125 degrees for medium-rare. Take out the meat and let it rest on the carving board with a trough, or place the carving board inside a rimmed baking sheet, tented with the foil, for 20-30 minutes. Slice the meat thin and serve with the natural juice gravy, collecting the juices from all over to make the gravy and just add heated beef broth. Serve horseradish cream on the side.

Tip: In place of Montreal steak mix, you can put together: 2 tbsp. onion powder, 1 tbsp. red pepper flakes and 1 tbsp. lemon pepper mix (Dash).

2. Scalloped Parsnips

You can bake these a day ahead and bring out to the room temperature and reheat while the meat is resting after roasting.

Ingredients: About 2 pounds parsnips peeled, sliced ¼-inch thick; custard: 3 large eggs, whisked with 2 cups of milk; spice mixture: 2 pkgs. instant chicken broth, 1 tbsp. onion powder, 1 tbsp. paprika, ½ tsp. each salt and pepper or to taste; ¼ cup dry bread crumbs, ¼ cup grated parmesan cheese; 4-5 tbsp. unsalted butter.

In a large pot bring about 4 cups of lightly salted water to a boil, submerge the parsnips and bring to a boil. Boil for about 8-10 minutes until they are just soft. Drain out the water. In an 8x8 or in a 9x12 glass greased pan, pour in half of the slices, top with half of the custard and dot with 1 tbsp. butter, then sprinkle half of the spice mixture and then repeat again with rest of the custard and spice mixture. Then dot the top with 3 tbsp. of butter. Cover the dish with the aluminum foil and bake in a preheated 350 degrees oven for about 25 minutes; open the cover and increase the oven temperature to 450 degrees and bake for about 10 minutes, golden brown.

Tip: In place of custard, you can use 1-1/2 cups of heavy cream mixed with ½ cup milk.

3. Bell Peppers

Ingredients: 1 tbsp. olive oil; 2 tbsp. unsalted butter; 3 medium onion sliced; ½ tsp. each granulated garlic, salt and pepper; 1 of each large: green, yellow and red bell pepper, sliced, seeded and chopped into 1-inch cubes and kept separate; ½ cup tomato-basil sauce or ½ cup drained crispy sauerkraut.

Heat a large sauté pan on medium heat. Add oil and 1 tbsp. butter and sauté the onion for 2 minutes. Sprinkle the garlic, salt and pepper, cover with the lid and cook for 5 minutes on low, until soft. Open the cover, move over the onion on one side, add rest of the butter and sauté the green bell pepper for 2 minutes. Top with the yellow and red pepper cubes, cover and cook on low for 6-8 minutes or until soft, stir all together.

Just before serving add tomato-basil sauce and sauerkraut and heat on medium heat and serve warm. In place of tomato sauce you can use ¼ cup juice of the sauerkraut.

4. The Natural Juice and the Beef broth Gravy

In a medium pot heat about 2 cups of beef broth, 1 cup red wine, 1 tbsp. lemon juice,1 tsp. of onion powder, 2 pinches of granulated garlic, fresh-ground black pepper to taste. Add the natural juices from the pan, bring to a boil, strain and serve.

Spaghetti Squash Bowl with Beef Chili
(Serves: 4-6)

About a month ago, on New York news, I heard that Taylor Swift, the singer, visits a restaurant where she ordered spaghetti squash. So, I tried and liked it very much. You can bake whole squash a day before or several hours before serving. If you prefer, serve two bowls in the rind and scooped out spaghetti directly in the bowls.

Ingredients: 1 medium (about 1-1/4 lb.) spaghetti squash; 1 cup mango or any other favorite sauce; salt and pepper to taste; 1 cup heated prepared chili, or about 1 pound lean (80%) ground beef browned in pan on medium heat for 10-15 minutes move it on one side. Add 1 tbsp. olive oil, ½ tsp. each: garlic and onion powders, and dry oregano, mixed with 1 cup tomato puree and 1 tbsp. prepared mustard; heat and stir in with the beef on medium-high heat for 5 minutes. Add salt and pepper to taste. To garnish: 1 cup shredded cheddar cheese, drained capers and/or roasted red bell peppers from the jar; ½ cup sour cream.

1. Preheat oven at 350 degrees. Wash, pat-dry and rub the whole squash with little olive oil, wrap in the aluminum foil, leave the top open, place in a large pie plate, and make 2-3 about ½-inch cuts on the top with the knife. Bake the squash for about an hour, turning around halfway once. Leave the squash in the turned-off oven for another hour to soften and cool down.
2. When ready to serve, cut the squash in half and scoop out all the seeds from the center. Then scoop out the spaghetti from the squash in a spiral motion with a fork. Heat a large pan with the sauce on medium heat. Carefully place the spaghetti over the sauce in the pan, sprinkle with salt and pepper to taste, turn over lightly with the spatula and place on the heated bowls. Top with the warm beef chili and garnish with shredded cheese, sour cream, roasted peppers and capers.

Spaghetti Squash Bowl with Veggies (Serves: 4-6)

Follow the recipe above for the spaghetti squash bowl with beef chili, just omit the chili and add the vegetables.

Veggies: Heat a large pan with 1 tbsp. olive oil, add 1 large diced onion, ½ tsp. garlic powder, salt and pepper to taste, stir for 2 minutes, move it over on one side. Add each: 1 cup peeled and diced carrots, cored and chopped green beans, and chopped plum tomatoes, sprinkle with 2 tbsp. water; cover and cook for 10-15 minutes or until soft. Add 1 can 15.5 ounces (439G) drained chick peas (garbanzos) or butter beans, stir well until heated through. Serve as above.

Steaks

You know that beef needs to be aged. I buy it 3-4 days ahead, and night before cooking I leave it open in a large bowl uncovered. There is another trick that works very well, which is to freeze the steak for 1-2 nights, defrost overnight, then cook. Also, cook the large and thick steaks slowly, in a heavy-bottom pan, over the stove, or grill, turning them over almost every 2 minutes for even cooking.

Beef Boneless Rib Club Steaks (Serves: 2)

We love rib club steaks or a good sirloin steak. It's so simple. If the steak is thin, cook on high heat fast, and if it is thick, cook on medium heat slowly, turning over every 2-3 minutes, until it is done to your taste.

Ingredients: About 3 tsp. olive oil; 2 each about 8 oz., boneless rib club steaks, about 1-1/4-inch thick; coarse sea salt and cayenne pepper to taste; ½ tsp. each: granulated garlic and onion powder; 1cup beef broth.

Heat a cast-iron skillet on medium-high heat. Sprinkle the steak with salt, pepper and a little oil on both sides. When the pan is hot, add a little oil and cook the steaks halfway covered with the lid, for about 3-1/2 minutes, or until the bottom is browned. Turn over and cook the steak open for about 1-1/2 minute until light browned, for medium-rare.

Take out the steaks and place them in a warm serving platter. Pour out extra fat, and add little salt, pepper, granulated garlic, onion powder, and the beef broth, bring it to a boil on medium-high heat, scrape the skillet, and pour over the steaks, serve with sides.

Thick Cut Filet Mignon Steaks (Serves: 2)

This is a 3-inch-high steak, just like you see in the steak houses. Serve with gravy, pan juices, bacon, or steak sauce and sides.

Ingredients: 2, about 1-1/2 to 2 pounds, thick and round, about 3-inches-high Filet Mignon steaks, sides tied with the kitchen twine. Rub: 1 tbsp. each, chopped roasted or fresh garlic cloves, black peppercorns, and coarse sea salt; canola oil to brush on.

As mentioned before, always buy the beef a few days earlier, and let it sit in the refrigerator for 2-3 days to mature. Take out the steaks from the refrigerator 1 hour before cooking. Rub with the spices on both sides, then drizzle with some oil.

Preheat the oven at 200 degrees. Heat a large cast-iron pan on medium-high heat, and sear steaks on each side for about 2 minutes, or until a nice brown crust forms. Take the skillet and place in the preheated oven and cook for about 8 to 10 minutes for medium-rare, or until it is done to your liking.

Take out the steaks, drizzle off any extra fat from the pan. Add ½ tsp. granulated Garlic, 1 tbsp. Instant Beef Broth, Salt and Pepper to taste. Bring to a boil and pour over the steaks, and/or serve with the sides and gravy.

Porterhouse Steak (Serves: 1 to 2)

Porterhouse steak has strip and a nice portion of filet mignon. Try to buy at least 1-1/2-inch thick and the bone in the middle so you have generous portions of both meat. T-Bone steak is similar to Porterhouse but it has a smaller portion of tenderloin. It comes from between porterhouse and the club steak. Usually, Porterhouse is broiled, but you can pan-bake as well. To broil the steak cook underneath, almost halfway, in the skillet and then cover with the butter and broil on the top. Each method takes average 8 to 10 minutes.

Ingredients: 3 tbsp. hoisin garlic marinade and sauce or asian marinade; 1 about 1.3 pound and 1-1/2-inch thick beef loin Porterhouse steak- bone in, dry aged steak; 1 tsp. canola oil; 2 tbsp. unsalted soft butter; mashed potatoes and vegetables or salad to serve on side.

1. To dry age the steak: Place the steak in a dry, clean, large glass or porcelain platter or a bowl, tent loosely with a large aluminum foil and place on the side of a shelf in the refrigerator, undisturbed, for 1 to 2 days.
2. Bring out the steak in room temperature at least 1 hour before cooking. Pat-dry the steak with the paper towel, place in a dinner plate, and spread 1 tablespoon of marinade on each side, tent with the foil and leave in the room temperature for 1 hour.
3. When ready to cook, preheat the oven to 400 degrees. Heat a cast-iron skillet on medium-high heat, then grease the skillet with the oil. When the skillet starts smoking, pick up the steak, place it in the skillet and brown it 1 minute on each side.
4. Take out the browned steak on the cutting board and separate it on both sides from the bone leaving about one-inch attached, about two-thirds of the way down for easy handling. Rub 1 tbsp. softened butter on top and place the steak back in the pan, the butter side down; spread another 1 tbsp. butter on the top. Pull away the meat from the bone so that the heat can get in, all around the steak. Place the pan in a preheated oven, the wider part of steak facing the back wall. Roast the steak for 7-8 minutes for medium-rare. Take the pan out of the oven, add another 1 tbsp. marinade to the pan, sprinkle coarse salt and pepper on the steak and then drizzle the pan juices with a spoon over and serve right in the pan.

Perfect Rib-Eye Steak with Bacon, Blue Cheese Topping, served with Whipped Potatoes, Cheese stuffed Tomatoes and Snow Peas over Orange-teriyaki Sauce (Serves: 4)

I think rib-eye steak is the easiest one to cook and the best one to eat. Prepare all the items first and cook the steak just before serving

(1) Rib-Eye Steak

Ingredients: 4 each 10 to 12 ounces boneless rib-eye steaks, about 1-inch thick; a little salt, cayenne pepper and granulated garlic; 8 bacon strips; 4 tbsp. canola oil. To serve: orange-teriyaki sauce or mushroom-wine gravy, stuffed tomatoes, snow peas and whipped garlic potatoes.

1. The night before serving the steak, place the steaks in a large platter in a single layer, cover with the platter with plastic wrap, leaving the two sides open about 1-inch on both sides for air to circulate.

2. Take out the steak about 30 minutes before cooking. Sprinkle first with cayenne, then garlic, then with some salt on both sides. Heat two large heavy-bottom pans or cast-iron pans on medium heat and cook the bacon half-and-half in each pan until browned and crispy. Take out the bacon on a paper towel to drain.

3. Leave the bacon fat in the pans and add about 2 tbsp. of canola oil in each pan. Heat the oil on medium-high heat until it almost starts smoking. Carefully place two steaks in each pan and cook on high heat exactly 4 minutes on each side, turn off the heat and let the steak stay in the pan for another 1 minute for medium-rare. Take out and let rest on warm platter for 8 minutes and serve, topped with bacon and blue cheese ball, over sauce or gravy.

(2) Roasted Garlic Whipped Potatoes (Serves: 4)

Ingredients: 4 large russet (baking) potatoes; 6 tbsp. butter; 1 cup heavy cream; 1 fresh garlic bulb; 2 tsp. oil; gravy to serve

1. Preheat oven at 350 degrees. Scrub-clean the potatoes then rub all around with some oil and place directly on the oven rack. Bake about an hour until soft. Cut the garlic bulb across in half and place in a piece of aluminum foil, sprinkle some oil, cover and bake in the oven for about 20-30 minutes soft.

2. When potatoes are cool enough to handle, peel, slice and place in the blender. In a small pot, heat heavy cream and butter together. Pour half of the liquid over the potatoes, add the roasted garlic, hold the cover with a kitchen towel and whip to puree them. Add rest of the butter mixture as needed. Take out the potatoes in a warm bowl and keep them covered and warm over simmering water until serving or heat in the microwave.

(3) Cheese Stuffed Tomatoes (Serves: 4)

Ingredients: 8 campari tomatoes (serve:1 or 2 tomatoes per person); 2 tbsp. seasoned bread crumbs; 1 tbsp. grated parmesan cheese; ¼ cup fine shredded sharp white cheddar cheese; ½ tsp. lemon-pepper seasoning mix; salt and pepper to taste.

Blanch the tomatoes, stems side down, for 1 minutes in the boiling water. Wash them under the cold running water and let them cool. When tomatoes are cooled, make a cut on the top half way. With the point of the knife cut only the inside of the tomatoes a little, for easy stuffing. Mix breadcrumbs, chesses, lemon mix, salt and pepper and stuff each tomato, leaving some cheddar on the top. Just before serving, microwave 1 minute, or cook in a lightly greased pan covered for 4 minutes until cheese is melted.

(4) Snow Peas (Serves: 4)

Ingredients: About half a pound of fresh snow peas; 1 tbsp. butter; sprinkle of granulated garlic, salt and pepper.

Blanch the peas for 1 minute in the boiling water, then wash under running cold water. Drain and keep in the refrigerator. When ready to serve just heat in a pan with the butter, garlic, salt and pepper and serve.

(5) Blue Cheese Topping

Ingredients: 2 sticks (½ pound) unsalted butter softened; ½ cup crumbled blue cheese or ½ cup fine grated aged white cheddar cheese; ¼ cup mayonnaise; 1 tbsp. diced raw onion; 1 tbsp. diced cilantro; cracked black pepper and salt to taste.

Mix all ingredients together in a bowl with a fork, drop on a parchment paper-lined baking sheet with small ice cream scoop, or with two tablespoons, making into balls; freeze until hard. Store in a plastic bag in refrigerator until needed.

(6) Orange-Teriyaki Sauce (M: 1 cup)

Ingredients: 1 tsp. butter; 2 cups orange juice; ¼ cup teriyaki sauce or to taste; salt and cayenne pepper to taste.

In a heavy-bottom, non-reactive pan, on low heat, add the butter, move around to coat the bottom. Add the orange juice, increase the heat to medium-high, stirring occasionally, reduce the orange juice to half (1 cup). It will take about 10-15 minutes. Add the teriyaki sauce, salt and cayenne pepper, simmer 5 minutes and pour in a gravy bowl; keep in room temperature, covered until needed.

Grilled Rib-Eye Steak

Prepare the grill for medium-high heat, follow the cooking process as above. Cook the rib-eye steak 3 minutes each side, until they are browned. Place them on the indirect heat and cook for another 5-6 minutes each side for medium-rare. Let them rest 6-8 minutes and serve.

Strip Steak with Roasted Vegetables, Purple Potatoes and Chimichurri Sauce

(Serves: 2 to 4)

Chimichurri Sauce (M: about ¾ cups)

Ingredients: 2 tbsp. chopped fresh mint leaves; ½ cup chopped cilantro leaves or flat-leaf parsley; 1 tbsp. garlic cloves minced; ⅓ cup thin-sliced green onion; 1-2 serrano peppers thin-sliced or to taste; ⅓ cup fresh lemon juice; salt to taste.

Prepare all ingredients ahead, and just before serving (or about 1 hour ahead) combine all ingredients in a bowl, cover the sauce surface with the plastic wrap, then cover with the lid.

For the Roasted Purple Potatoes: 1.5 pounds (24 oz., 680g) baby purple potatoes; 2 tbsp. canola oil; 3 tbsp. minced fresh garlic cloves; 2 tbsp. fresh chopped thyme or rosemary, salt and pepper to taste. Move an oven rack in the center and preheat the oven at 350 degrees. About two hours before serving, scrub-clean the potatoes and cut them in bite-size, about 1-1/2-inch pieces. Toss them with the mixture of oil, garlic and thyme or rosemary and spread them out in one layer, cut-side down and skin-side up, on a heavy baking sheet lined with aluminum foil. Roast them at 350 degrees for about 40 minutes, then at 400 degrees for about 10-15 minutes until potatoes are done. During the roasting take out the tray, drizzle a few drops of oil and move the potatoes, and still bake them cut-side down and skin-side up. Keep them covered and warm, in the tray until ready to serve.

For the Red Bell Peppers and the Green Onions: 3 large red bell peppers; 2-3 tbsp. canola oil; ¾ tsp. granulated garlic; 1 tsp. dry rosemary; about 8 thick, whole green onions (scallions), very bottom of the roots removed and washed, any wilted or bad leaves removed.

Core and seed the bell peppers, then slice them into 1-inch-wide rings. Brush the scallions with the oil, garlic and rosemary mixture. Then toss the pepper rings in the mixture, in a large bowl. Prepare a large baking sheet lined with aluminum foil. Spread out the rings and place the scallions on one side of the baking sheet.

For the Roasted Asparagus: About 1 to 1-1/2 pounds thick green asparagus, the hard bottom removed, washed; 1 tbsp. canola oil, ½ tsp. granulated garlic, and ½ tsp. dry rosemary.

Bring about 2 cups of water to a boil in a large sauté pan with rims. When water starts boiling, submerge the asparagus, stir a little and blanche them for 1 minute. Rinse out the water, wash them under running cold water, pat-dry the asparagus, and toss them in the oil, garlic and rosemary mixture. Place them one side on the baking sheet next to the red bell peppers.

Roast red bell pepper rings, scallions and asparagus in 400 degree oven for about 20 minutes, until soft. After 15 minutes, check on vegetables and take them out as they are done.

Ingredients For the Steak: Two about 14 oz. each, and about 1-1/2-inch-thick New York strip steaks, bone in; 2 to 3 tbsp. Grill Mates: roasted garlic with herb seasoning; salt and black pepper; 3 tbsp. olive oil or canola oil; 2 to 4 tbsp. unsalted butter. Take out the steaks from the packing, place them in a rimmed, dry, glass platter and place them in the vegetable box, or loosely cover with a piece of the aluminum foil and place the platter on one side of the refrigerator to age the steak overnight.

For the Steak: About 45 minutes before cooking, take out the steaks from the refrigerator. When ready to cook, heat the broiler first for 5 minutes turn it off, then heat the oven at 375 degrees.

Heat a large cast-iron skillet on medium heat. Now sprinkle the steak with the roasted garlic seasoning, and salt and pepper all over, or press the steak down in the spices then sprinkle little oil all over. Increase the heat to medium-high, place the steaks in the skillet and sear steaks until browned on both sides about 2-3 minutes each side.

Once the steaks are browned transfer them to the preheated oven, and roast for about 5 minutes, then spread out one tbsp. of the butter on the top on each steak. The internal temperature on instant-read thermometer for rare should be around 120 degrees, and about 125 for the medium-rare. While in the oven, baste the steak with the pan juices.

Serve steak topped with the chimichurri sauce or on the side, with roasted purple potatoes, red bell peppers rings and long green onions.

Salisbury Steak (Serves: 4)

This steak is named after the creator of the steak. It is actually a spiced, long burger that is good for the elderly who want to have a soft and a tasty steak with a fancy gravy.

Ingredients: 2 tbsp. canola or olive oil; about 1-1/2 pounds 85% lean ground beef; ½ cup seasoned bread crumbs; 2 tbsp. grated parmesan cheese; 1 tbsp. ketchup; 1 tbsp. Worcestershire sauce; 3 tbsp. hoisin sauce; 1 tsp. granulated garlic; 1 tsp. yellow mustard powder; ½ tsp. dry oregano; ½ tsp. fresh-ground black pepper; ⅓ cup warm heavy cream or half-and-half; mushroom-wine gravy, mashed potatoes, cranberry sauce (op); and vegetables to serve.

Heat the oven at 350 degrees. Heat a heavy-bottom oven-proof large pan on low heat. In a large bowl spread out the meat and sprinkle all spices then bread crumbs and ketchup, Worcestershire and hoisin sauces, mix well. Then mix in the warm heavy cream. Now knead the meat with the heal of the hand for 1 minute. Using some warm water, make 4 long, oval and even-size patties about ¾-inch thick.

Increase the heat to medium-high and add the oil to the pan. Brown patties golden brown on both sides. Then place the pan in a preheated oven and roast about 5 minutes each side for medium-rare. Serve with thick mushroom-wine gray, mashed potatoes, cranberry sauce and vegetables.

Tip of Sirloin Steak (S:2)

Sirloin is my favorite steak. Get a 1.25 to 1.50 Pound boneless steak and serve it with mashed potatoes, green beans/vegetable and mushroom wine gravy.

Ingredients: About 1.50 pound boneless Tip of Sirloin with all excess fat removed, leave the steak open in a clean bowl loosely tented with foil; a spice mixture: 2Tbsp. fresh crushed garlic cloves, 1Tsp. instant beef broth, 1Tbsp. lemon-pepper mix, 1Tbsp. canola oil.

Rub the steak with the spice mixture and let it stand in room temperature for 30 minutes tented with a foil. Preheat the oven at 400 degrees.

When ready to cook, heat a cast iron pan on medium-high heat. When the pan is hot, add oil and brown the steak all around for about 1 minute per side. Place the pan in the preheated oven and cook for 4-5 minutes for medium-rare or to your liking. Pour the pan juices over the steak. Serve with sides and some gravy in the bottom and some on the top of the steak.

Tips for the steaks: I brown all my steaks on high heat, in the cast iron pan in a little oil, on all sides fast, then finish in the oven at around 400 degrees (depending on the thickness). If the steak is too thick around 2-inches high, use a stainless-steel large pan, keep on turning the steak every minute over and over until it is browned (about 5 minutes on each side), then finish in the oven to your liking. We prefer wine gravy or mushroom-wine gravy with steak.

Sauerbraten - German Pot Roast) (S:6)

In seventies, I lived in Berlin, Germany, for about 4 months. My brother, who was a student and living in a student hostel, gave me coupon books to have my lunch at the cafeteria. Each coupon was for one German mark. With that, they gave me a thin slice of sauerbraten with some gravy and potato dumplings and purple grapes. So whenever I make this dish, I always think of good old days in Berlin. I serve this meal with potato dumplings and purple cabbage. Traditionally, the meat is marinated for 6-7 days, but I do a quick marinate only overnight. You can make dumplings and cabbage one day ahead just heat and serve.

(1) Sauerbraten

Ingredients: One, about 4 pounds, boneless, rounded piece of sirloin tip or chuck or bottom round roast tied; rub mixture: ½ tsp. each onion powder, garlic powder, cayenne pepper; a marinade mixture of: 1 cup cider vinegar, 1-1/2 cup red wine, ½ cup water, 2 large bay leaves, 1 cup sliced carrots, 1 cup sliced celery, 1 cup sliced onion, 2 large chopped garlic cloves, 1 tbsp. brown sugar, 4 whole cloves, 1-inch chopped ginger, 2Tbsp. butter to brown the meat. For the gravy: 2 tbsp. light brown sugar; 6-8 gingersnaps; to serve: fresh flat-leaf parsley.

Rub the meat all around with rub and set aside for 10 minutes. Place the meat in a nonreactive or a glass bowl and pour the liquid mixture, and then top with the vegetables, cover, and refrigerate for 2 days turning it over once halfway, so that the meat is in liquid.

Take the meat out of marinade, pat-dry all around with paper towels. Heat a large nonreactive pan or a stainless steel pan and brown the meat all around in butter evenly for about 15 minutes. Place the meat in a casserole or roasting pan then heat the marinade in the pan (where you had browned the meat), bring it to a boil, and pour over the meat. The liquid should be about 2-1/2 cups. Place the meat in a preheated 350 degrees oven, tented with a large piece of foil. Roast the meat about 45 minutes per pound, turning over every hour until it is very soft. It will take about 3 hours to cook.

Now take the meat out of cooking juices. In a blender puree the warm vegetables with some liquid, holding the cover down with a kitchen towel. Add sugar, gingersnaps as needed and add more liquid or some warm water to make a nice gravy. Heat the gravy and serve over thin-sliced (about a half-inch wide) meat and potato dumplings and purple cabbage.

(2) Potato Dumplings (M: 16)

Ingredients: About 2 pounds, or 4 large potatoes boiled with skin on, peeled, and mashed fine or processed in a food mill; ½ tsp. each: onion powder and garlic powder and salt and pepper to taste; 4 tbsp. semolina or cream of wheat; 5 tbsp. all-purpose flour plus extra for dusting; 2 large eggs beaten; croutons:1 large slice of Italian loaf crust removed and cut into 1-inch cubes, sprinkled with salt and pepper and then browned on medium-high heat in a cast-iron pan for 8-10 minutes in 2 tbsp. butter.

Bring a large pot half full of salted water to a boil. Mashed potatoes and then mix in a bowl with salt, pepper, garlic and onion powders. Add semolina and the flour and mash well with hands. Add the beaten eggs with a fork and mix well. Now, dusting hands with flour, take out about 2 tablespoons of potato mixture, flatten a little, place one bread cube in the middle, roll potato mixture all around it, and roll into a ball. When all the balls (dumplings) are done, in two batches drop them in the boiling salted water. Either stir them with a perforated spoon or just move them around holding one handle of the pot carefully, and move them in a circular motion. Cook about 12-15 minutes on medium-high heat. When done, take them out in a heated platter. Serve them immediately with some gravy or serve later heated in a pan with some butter on low heat. I make them a one day ahead and heat them in the oven and serve with warm gravy.

(3) Purple Cabbage (Serves: 6)

Ingredients: 2 tbsp. canola oil; 1 medium purple cabbage, cut in half lengthwise, cored and then each half cut in 3 wedges. Now take one piece at a time and slice them across shredding it; 2-3 tbsp. cider vinegar; 3-4 tbsp. brown sugar or as needed; 1/ 2cup dry cherries or cranberries; salt and pepper to taste.

Heat a medium pot with oil, on medium-high heat. Add the shredded cabbage and sauté for 5 minutes. Lower the heat, add about ½ cup water, vinegar, sugar, cranberries or cherries, little salt and pepper to taste. Bring to a boil, cover, then cook on constant simmer for about 25 minutes or until cabbage is soft. Serve warm or cold.

Shell Steak in Natural Juices (Serves: 2-4)

Open the package and age the steak in the refrigerator 2-3 days in a clean and dry bowl or a platter, loosely covered with an aluminum foil.

Ingredients: About 1-1/4 pound, 2 beef loin shell boneless steaks, each about 1-inch thick; 3 to 4 tsp. Montreal steak seasoning (McCormick) or make your own: each granulated or crushed dry ½ tsp. ginger, ½ tsp. roasted garlic, 1 tbsp. black peppercorn and ¼ tsp. salt; ¼ tsp. granulated garlic; ¼ tsp. cayenne or black pepper; 3 tsp. oil; to serve: mashed potatoes and vegetables.

Take out the steak 30 minutes before cooking, press spices into the steak and drizzle with a little oil. Leave in room temperature about 30 minutes.

Heat a cast-iron pan on medium-high heat; when the pan almost starts smoking, add about 1 tsp. of oil in the pan and add the steaks. Cover the pan halfway with the lid and cook steaks on medium-high heat for about 4 minutes or until the bottom is browned. Take the pan off the heat and keep it tilted 30 seconds, then drizzle 2-3 drops of oil on each steak. Using a metal spatula, scrape the bottom and turn over the steak. Place the pan back on medium high heat and cook the steak open for about 3 minutes or until browned, for medium-rare. Take the steaks out of the pan and place on the serving platter. Wipe out all the oil from the edges of the pan with a paper towel. Take the pan off the heat add granulated garlic and cayenne, ½ cup water a little salt or 1 package dry beef broth, scrape the pan and pour the hot juices over the steak and serve.

Pepper Shell Steak (Steak au Poivre) (S:4)

This is a French-style steak. I add onion and garlic powder for extra flavor. You need to marinate the steak overnight. The cognac and wine gravy gives a very good flavor.

Ingredients: 4 boneless shell, rib-eye or strip steaks, about 1 to 1-1/2-inch thick; ¼ tsp. granulated garlic powder; ¼ tsp. onion powder; 4 tbsp. black peppercorn crushed evenly in a food mill; 4 tbsp. olive or canola oil, divided; 1 can, 10-1/2 ounce, (298g) about 1 cup beef consommé, ¼ cup orange juice; 1 cup red wine; ½ cup cognac or brandy; 3 tbsp. unsalted butter cold and sliced; to garnish: 2 tbsp. fresh flat-leaf parsley; to serve: mashed potatoes and buttered peas.

1. Spread the crushed peppercorns in a large platter. Pat-dry the steaks with paper towels. Rub garlic and onion powders on the steaks, then press the steak in the peppercorn mixture, so that each steak is coated with the spices. Drizzle about 1 tsp. of oil on each side of the steak and rub the oil with the back of the spoon pressing down the pepper mixture. Place the steaks in a large platter with the rim, tent with aluminum foil and marinate overnight in the refrigerator.

2. Take out the steak 1 hour before cooking, in room temperature. Heat a large cast-iron or a heavy-bottom pan on medium-high heat, add 1 tbsp. of oil, and when the pan almost starts smoking, add the steaks and cook about 3 minutes or until browned. Drizzle another 1 tab of oil, turn over the steak and cook another 3 minutes on the second side to seal the juices. Now keep the heat still medium-high and cook the steak the other side for 3 minutes each. So you need to cook a total of about 7 minutes on each side for medium rare and if the steak is about 1-inch thick. You can also cook steaks in batches (two at a time).

3. Take the steaks out on a warm platter and tent them with the aluminum foil. Now rinse out any extra oil from the pan and off the heat, add beef consommé, orange juice, cognac or brandy and the red wine to the pan. Put the pan back on the medium-high heat, scrape the bottom, and reduce the sauce in half, rapidly, stirring occasionally. (You can reduce the sauce a day before, and just reheat in the steak pan.) Take the pan off the heat and whisk in the butter slowly, with a wire whisk until all the butter is melted in the sauce. Serve the steak garnished with parsley, mashed potatoes and buttered peas. Pour some sauce over the steaks and serve rest of the sauce in a gravy boat.

The Perfect Roast Beef (Serves: 6-8)

Roast beef thin-sliced with an electric slicer, and mushroom-wine gravy is my husband's favorite. You can slice ahead and use up to 3-4 days. To cook perfect Roast beef, you need to age the beef from 3-4 days to 1 week. Buy a boneless, unpack and place in a clean, dry, glass/porcelain bowl or a platter with sides, loosely cover the bowl with a piece of plastic wrap on the top, refrigerate near the side wall, undisturbed, and nothing touching, just overnight.

Ingredients: About 3 pounds boneless chuck roast or tri-tip roast (triangle: no need to tie) or sirloin tip roast, or certified Angus bottom roast; try to buy an even and a high piece; the rub: ¼ tsp. each granulated garlic and rosemary, 1 tsp. each coarse sea salt and cracked black pepper, about 1 tsp. canola oil; to serve: mashed potatoes, vegetable and mushroom-wine gravy.

1. Rub the meat with half of the rub and place it in a large bowl tented with the aluminum foil. Take out the meat from the refrigerator about 2 hours ahead of cooking, and leave in room temperature. Prepare a medium roasting pan: line the bottom with the aluminum foil, and top with the flat wire rack.
2. Preheat oven at 400 degrees for 10 minutes. Rub the meat with the remaining rub. Tie the meat with the kitchen twine, at about 1-1/2-inch intervals. Place the meat fat-side-up over the wire rack.
3. Roast the beef at 400 degrees about 10 minutes per pound. Turn around the roasting pan half way during the half of the cooking. So 3-1/2 pounds of meat will take about 35 minutes, or 120 degrees for rare, and 125-130 for medium-rare, on an instant-read thermometer. Then take out the meat out of the roasting pan, place on a wooden cutting board with a trough, tent loosely with an aluminum foil and let it rest for 20-25 minutes. Slice the beef thin in an electric slicer against grains. To slice it very thin, refrigerate overnight or freeze a little until it is little hard. Add all the drippings to gravy, then simmer for 5 minutes and serve drenched with gravy.
4. If you are roasting a tri-trip, place the point of the meat pointing at 3 o'clock. Because the grains in tri-tip roast runs horizontally. So slice the meat starting from the tip and moving to the wider base, and slicing the meat vertically.

Pork Loin, Boneless, Center Cut Pork Chops with Roasted Sweet Potatoes, and Asparagus with Lemon Sauce (Serves: 4)

These thin boneless pork chops are very tasty and cook fat. This dinner for four takes only about 1-1/4 to 1-1/2 hours

Ingredients for the Pork Chops: About 1-1/4 to 1-1/2 pounds, 8 boneless, ½-inch to ¾-inch thick loin, center cut, pork chops; 3 tbsp. tapioca flour; ¼ tsp. each: ground cayenne pepper, fresh-ground black pepper; 1 tsp. smoked or regular paprika; 2 pinches kosher salt; 1 extra large egg; 1 cup dry, seasoned, Italian bread crumbs; about 4 tbsp. each canola oil and unsalted butter.
For the Lemon Sauce: ¼ cup each mayonnaise, sour cream; 1 tbsp. prepared mustard; 2 tbsp. lemon juice; salt and pepper to taste.
For the Sweet Potatoes: 2 large sweet potatoes, about 1-1/4 pounds; 2 tbsp. canola oil; ¼ tsp. each granulated garlic and dry rosemary; salt and pepper to taste (op).
For the Apple Sauce: 2 red Delicious or other little firm, red apples; 1 tbsp. lemon juice; ¼ cup dry cherries; 2 tbsp. light brown sugar; 2 tbsp. corn starch; pinch of salt and pepper.
For the Asparagus: 1 pound (16 ounces) thick, fresh, green asparagus; 1 tbsp. unsalted butter.

(1)   Lemon Sauce

Combine and cream with a spoon, all sauce ingredients in a small bowl and refrigerate, covered.

(2) Sweet Potatoes

Line a large sheet pan with aluminum foil, grease well with canola oil and set aside. Preheat the oven at 400F. Bring to a boil about 6 cups of water in a medium pot. Wash the sweet potatoes, scrubbing with a paper towel, trim the ends; depending on the thickness, cut them lengthwise into 5-6 large wedges. When water starts to boil, cook the potatoes in boiling water for about 5 minutes until they are parboiled (cooked partially). Drain out the water carefully and pour the potatoes on to the foil lined baking sheet. Sprinkle about 1 tbsp. oil, garlic, rosemary over the potatoes, shake them well and keep away from the edges, roast them in a 400F oven for about 15-20 minutes until golden. During the baking, shake the baking sheet or turn over the potatoes once. When done, turn off the oven and leave them in the warm oven until ready to serve.

(3)   Apple Sauce

Heat a large sauté pan on low heat. Core the apples and slice thin across. Sprinkle the lemon juice. When pan is hot, add the 2 tbsp. butter and cook them on medium-high heat, for 1 minute. Reduce the heat to medium, add cherries, pinch of salt and pepper, cover and cook them for 6-8 minutes until they are soft. Whisk the corn starch, with ¾ cup of water, increase the heat high, and pour over the apples, cook stirring until thick. Add the brown sugar and cook 1 minute. Turn off the stove, keep the apples warm off stove.

(4) Asparagus

In a large sauté pan, bring about 2-3 cups of water to a boil. Bend the asparagus towards the bottom and break off the white bottoms, keep only the soft, green part. Add them to boiling water (keep them in the same direction for easy turning) and boil them on high for 3-4 minutes, turning all around. When they are nice green color, and soft, discard the water and wash them under the running cold water and spread out on a kitchen towel or pat-dry in a platter. Put the asparagus back in a cold, dry sauté pan, uncovered. When ready to serve, add 1 tab butter, heat the asparagus on high heat for 1-2 minutes, sprinkle a little salt, fresh-ground black pepper, a little granulated garlic, toss well and serve with the lemon sauce or lemon juice. (Most of the greens have Iron, so blanch and serve them with extra virgin olive oil and lemon juice, to help digest them well.)

(5)   Pork Chops

On a dinner plate, mix the tapioca flour with spices and make 3x3-inch piles of the mixture. In a medium bowl beat the egg. On another dinner plate make 3x3-inch piles of the bread crumbs. Heat a large non-stick pan on low heat. Wash, pat-dry the chops with the paper towel, and make two long slashes on each of them, diagonally, across the grain, one side. Now dip each one of them, both sides in the tapioca flour, pat them between both hands, to shake off the extra flour and pile them up in a dry plate. Take one chop at a time, dip both sides in the egg, wipe it out against the edge of the bowl and dip both sides in the bread crumbs, and leave them on a wire rack or a dry plate in a single layer.
When pan is hot, add 2 tbsp. butter and 2 tbsp. oil, increase the heat to medium-high and cook the chops in two or three batches in single layer in the hot oil. Cook 3-5 minutes first side (depending on the thickness), golden brown. Turn over, add 1 tbsp. of oil all around the edges and cook 2-4 minutes (second side will take less time) on the second side golden. The internal temperature of the pork chops should be 140F. When done take them out on a paper towel-lined platter. Keep them warm in a baking tray, on a low heat (about 200F), until all are done.

Serve warm Pork chops with apple sauce, potato wedge and asparagus with lemon sauce.

Tip: Tapioca flour Is very high in starch. It sticks well to the meat. Even after the final coating of the bread crumbs, the rest will stay on the chops.
Tapioca flour needs a lot of seasoning to give flavor. Here, all 3 types of the peppers used, they all give different types of flavor in the crest.

Lasagna with steamed Eggplant (Serves: 8)

I lived in Berlin, Germany, for a few months, and some of my brother's friends were crazy about eggplant, I used to cook Eggplant a lot. When I got married and visited my brother again, I had made this eggplant lasagna, and people went crazy. This is made with steamed eggplants. I had to go back and pick up the cheese wrappers etc. from the garbage to show them the ingredients that I had used. You can prepare and assemble this dish a day ahead, refrigerate covered, and bake before serving.

Ingredients:

For the Steamed Eggplant and Sauce: 3 jumbo (about 4 pounds) royal purple eggplants; 1 can, 29 ounces (822g) tomato puree; 4tbsp. tomato paste; 1 bottle, 23.7 ounces (673g) merlot marinara or just plain marinara sauce; spice mixture: 1 tsp. each: granulated garlic, onion powder, dry oregano, and little salt and pepper or to taste. Combine all ingredients, bring to a boil and simmer 10 minutes.

For the Filling: 1 tbsp. olive oil to grease the pan and foil. 1 pound (about 2 cups) non-fat ricotta cheese whipped with 1 large egg and ¼ cup fresh parsley; 1 pound shredded white cheddar or Monterey Jack cheese blend or Mexican cheese blend; for the meat: 1 to 1-1/2 pound, 80% fat-free ground beef and ½ pound sausage meat browned in the pan on medium-high heat for 15-20 minutes and then sprinkled with about ½ tsp. salt, pepper and granulated garlic, add 1 cup frozen thawed peas at the end; 1cup panko bread crumbs mixed with 1/2tsp. basil or parsley; 1 cup grated parmesan cheese. To serve: green salad and/or garlic bread.

Steamed Eggplant

Preheat the oven at 350 degrees. Line a large and heavy-bottom baking sheet with the aluminum foil. Wash and dry the eggplants. Take one eggplant at a time, cut off the stem, stand the eggplant (stem side up), and thin slice the eggplant about ¼-inch thick, into 6-7 slices. Immediately sprinkle each slice lightly with salt (before it turns brown), and stack it back in its original shape. When all the eggplants are sliced spread out in single layer on the foil, now cover the layer with the parchment paper and spread out another layer, then cover with parchment paper again and spread out the third layer. Finally, put two pieces of foil together and cover the tray air-tight. Bake at 350 degrees for about 90 minutes. Let rest 15 minutes and open the tray carefully, away from the steam.

To Assemble the Lasagna:

In a glass or a lasagna pan 10-1/2x14-1/2 inches, grease the bottom and sides well with oil. Now make the layers: spread 1/3 of sauce in the bottom, top with 1/3 slices of steamed eggplants (about 6 slices), overlapping slightly, spread with ⅓ of the ricotta and ½ of the meat on top, then 1/3 of shredded cheese. Repeat layers one more time. Top with tomato sauce, ricotta cheese, shredded cheese, bread crumbs and parmesan cheese.

Cover the dish airtight with foil. Place the dish in a large baking sheet, and bake in a preheated 350 degrees oven for about 90 minutes, bubbling, turning the tray around half way during the baking. Serve with salad and garlic bread.

To make vegetable lasagna all the way: substitute the meat with cooked vegetables, such as cauliflower and broccoli mixture or any other cooked vegetable mixture.

Lasagna with Meat (Serves: 6-8)

We both like Italian food very much. This meat lasagna, which we eat with salad, is filling. I bake a whole pan and once it is cooled, I freeze half in a glass dish for future use so that my husband can enjoy a delicious meal again. We just heat and eat.

Ingredients For the Meat Sauce: 2-3 tbsp. olive oil; ½ cup each fine chopped: onion, carrots, celery, and red or green bell pepper; 1 pound ground lean beef; 1 pound lean ground turkey or veal; about ½ cup red wine; 1 tsp. each: granulated garlic and dry oregano; 1 tbsp. each chopped fresh: parsley, sage and rosemary; 2 tbsp. tomato paste; 1 can 28 oz. crushed tomatoes.
ingredients for the pasta: 1 box, 10 oz. frozen chopped spinach, defrosted and squeezed out of all the water; 2 pounds low-fat ricotta cheese whisked with 1 extra large egg, ½ cup grated parmesan cheese, ½ tsp. dry oregano; 16 sheets no-boil lasagna; 4 cups, 16 oz. shredded mixed cheeses or sharp cheddar cheese. 1 cup seasoned dry bread crumbs lightly browned for 5 minutes in 2 tbsp. butter and then mixed with ½ cup grated parmesan cheese; about 1-1/2 pound plum tomato thin-sliced to cover the top (op). Sweet paprika and dry oregano to garnish.

For the Meat Sauce: Heat a large heavy-bottom pan on medium heat, add oil and brown onion with little salt and pepper for 5 minutes. Add carrots, celery, and cook for 5 minutes. Add the pepper and cook another 5 minutes until vegetable are soft. Take out the cooked vegetables. Now add the meat and brown the meat on medium-high heat, stirring constantly, until it is browned for about 8-10 minutes. Add the tomato paste and brown for 2 minutes. Add the wine stir and let it evaporate for 5 minutes. Add the garlic and oregano and stir well. Add the tomato sauce, the cooked vegetables and bring it to a boil. Add the fresh rosemary, sage, and parsley, simmer for 8-10 minutes and turn off the heat, let it cool.

To Assemble: Boil a large pot half full of water. Preheat oven at 375 degrees. Grease a lasagna pan (11x16x2) well. Pour in about 2 ladles of meat sauce. Dip the lasagna sheets in the hot water, one at a time and holding with two tongs, take it out right away, shake a little and lay down over the sauce covering the entire sauce with the sheets. Making 3 layers of the sheets, divide the ricotta mixture and spinach, into two parts. Spread out half of the ricotta, and half of the spinach, ⅓ of the shredded cheese, over the sheets ladle ⅓ of the sauce. Repeat one more time with sheets, ricotta, spinach, cheese, and sauce. On the top spread out the rest of the sauce all over, then sprinkle shredded cheese, bread crumbs, and cover with the sliced tomatoes. Cover the pan with a large aluminum foil airtight.

Bake in the preheated oven about 45 minutes to an hour, until it is bubbly. Take off the aluminum foil, and bake another 10-15 minutes open, until the top is browned. Serve garnished with paprika and oregano.

Lamb Curry (Serves: 6)

I like to make lamb curry a little thick, just like you get in the restaurant. Instead of lot of spices, I use spices and vegetable puree.

Ingredients: 4 tbsp. Canola Oil; about 2-1/2 to 3 pounds (about 1-1/4 kilogram) boneless leg of lamb with all extra fat trimmed, and cut in to 2x2-inches cubes; ¼ cup (4 tbsp.) garlic-ginger paste; 1 tsp. turmeric powder; 1 tbsp. caraway seeds; 1 large onion sliced; ½ cup fresh soft cilantro stems chopped; about 2 fresh hot green serrano peppers or 1-2 jalapeno seeded or to taste; 1 tsp. each granulated garlic and cayenne pepper; ½ cup a.p.flour; 1 tbsp. cardamom seeds grinded; 1-1/2 cups plain yogurt; 2 cups tomato pasta sauce; 2 tbsp. chat masala or 1 tbsp. curry powder and ½ tbsp. garam masala; 1 tbsp. fresh chopped rosemary or ½ tsp. dried; 1 tbsp. lemon juice; salt and pepper to taste; to garnish: chopped fresh mint or cilantro leaves.

1. Heat a sauté pan on medium heat, when hot add1 tbsp. oil and lightly brown the caraway seeds then add the onion and sauté until transparent. Add tomatoes, hot peppers and sauté until soft, about 5-6 minutes, cool and puree with cilantro stems, in the blender.
2. Heat a Dutch oven or a large, heavy-bottom pot, on medium heat. When pot is heated, add 2 tbsp. oil. Sprinkle the meat pieces with granulated garlic and cayenne pepper, lightly sprinkle the flour and brown the meat on medium-high heat in the oil, in two batches. When meat is lightly browned underneath, turn over once, and brown on both sides, and take out in a platter. Now add the garlic-ginger paste, pureed onion mixture, Turmeric and ¼ tsp. salt and pepper, stir well, cover, lower heat and cook for 5 minutes. Open the pot, add the meat, stir well, add yogurt, pasta sauce, cardamom seeds; stir, bring to a boil, lower the heat to constant simmer and cook for 45 minutes until soft. Add chat masala or curry powder and garam masala, lemon juice, ½ tsp. each salt and fresh-ground black pepper, stir well, cover and simmer on low for about 10 minutes. Taste for seasoning and serve garnished with mint or cilantro leaves with rice or bread.

Lamb with Spinach (Serves: about 6)

Lamb Saag

This is a traditional Indian lamb curry. Saag is a dish made with greens. Remember, a complete Indian dinner is served with meat or vegetables, rice, bread, raita and chutney. At the end you should serve thin buttermilk sprinkled with dry mint powder and roasted caraway seed powder and/or sweets.

Ingredients: About 6 tbsp. canola oil, divided; about 2-1/2 pounds boneless leg of lamb or the shoulder meat cut into 2x2-inch cubes, all fat taken out and sprinkled with: 1 tsp. each garlic powder and cayenne pepper and ½ cup all-purpose flour. For the fresh-ground spices: 2 tbsp. coriander seeds, 1 tsp. caraway seeds, 1 tbsp. bay leaves veins taken out and crumbled into small pieces, 1 tbsp. cardamom seeds, and grind them first, dry, in a blender or food processor into powder, then add 2 cups fresh chopped onion, ½ cup chopped garlic cloves, ½ cup chopped cilantro stems, ¼ cup fresh chopped ginger, puree all in about ½ cup water; 1 tsp. turmeric, 1-/12 cups tomato sauce; 2 tbsp. lemon juice; ½ c heavy cream; salt and 1 tsp. cayenne pepper or to taste; 1 pkg. 10 ounces cut frozen spinach; to garnish: ¼ c cilantro leaves, to serve rice or bread.

1. Heat a medium, heavy-bottom pot on medium heat, when hot add 2 tbsp. oil, and brown the meat on medium-high heat in batches. When meat is browned underneath, turn it over once and brown the other side. Take the meat out in a platter. Add 2 tbsp. oil to the pot and stir in the spice mixture. Sauté for 1 minute, add a little salt, cover and cook for 12-15 minutes, stirring occasionally. Leave about a quarter of the spice mixture in the pot and take out three-quarters of spice mixture and set aside. Add the meat, tomato sauce, turmeric, and salt and pepper to taste. Bring all to a boil, then lower the heat and cook on constant simmer for about 50 minutes or until soft.
2. While meat is cooking, blanch the spinach for 3-4 minutes in boiling water, take out with perforated spoon, and drain. When meat is done heat a large sauté pan with 2 tbsp. oil, add the spinach and 2 tbsp. cooked spice mixture (set aside), sauté the spinach well in the spices for 5 minutes and move the spinach on one side. Then take out the meat with the perforated spoon and add to the pan add rest of the spice mixture and sauté the meat and spices together on medium-high heat for 10 minutes, adding about ½ cup of cooking liquid and then dry it out then add the lemon juice and heavy cream stir well together with the spinach, and simmer everything together for 5 minutes open. If needed add more cooking liquid. But the dish should be a little juicy, not runny.
3. Serve over rice or with the bread, garnished with the cilantro.

Tips: Instead of spinach, you can use kale or broccoli rabe.

Chorizo with Pasta (Serves: 8-10)

Chorizo sausages are hot so use either all chorizo or half chorizo and half sweet Italian sausages. It's up to you how hot you prefer. You can also use Japanese eggplants instead of Brussels sprouts.

Ingredients: 1 tbsp. olive oil; 1pkg., 16 ounces, (1 pound) fresh chorizo, casings removed; 1pkg., about 1-1/2 pound sweet Italian sausages casings removed; 1cup each chopped – onion, celery and green bell pepper; 1 bag, 8.8 ounces (250g) three cheese tortellini; 1 bag, 32 ounces (907g) fresh or frozen Brussels sprouts; each ½ tsp. dry rosemary and granulated garlic; 3 large red bell peppers roasted, peeled and cut in to 1-inch pieces or from the jar; 1 cup dry cranberries; ¼ cup tomato sauce mixed with 2 tbsp. lemon juice; salt and pepper to taste; ¼ cup plus more grated cheese to garnish and to serve; garlic bread or any of your favorite bread to serve.

1. Wash and take out the yellow leaves from the Brussels sprouts. Slice off the wilted part of the stem then cut the stem and make a deep cross. If they are small leave them as-is; if they are medium or large then cut them in half or in quarter. Bring a 5-quart pot half full, and lightly salted water to a boil and cook (blanche) the Brussels sprouts for 4-5 minutes. This gives them a nice green color and helps them cook faster later on. Take them out of the water with a perforated spatula and drain.
2. In a wok or in a large sauté pot heat oil on medium heat. Add chopped onion, celery, green pepper, stir a little and then add the drained Brussels sprouts on the top, cover and let them cook 5 minutes. Open the cover, increase the heat to medium-high, add granulated garlic, rosemary and salt and pepper to taste. Stir on high heat for about 15 minutes or until they are soft, but still crunchy. Take the vegetables out of the pan and keep warm in a bowl covered. Use the same boiled water, just add little more salt and about 1 tsp. of oil, and cook the tortellini, per package direction, or about 15 minutes in the boiling water, until they start floating. Drain the pasta and keep covered in the same pot or in a covered bowl.

3. Add the meat in the pan and break the sausages with a metal spatula, stirring for 10 minutes on medium heat. Increase heat to medium-high and stir for 15-20 minutes until meat is done and is in small pieces. Add cranberries, cooked vegetables, tomato sauce mixture, tortellini, salt and pepper, if needed and cook another 5 minutes on high heat stirring constantly.
4. Serve warm with the toasts, sprinkled with the grated cheese and extra cheese on the side.

Veal Parmigiana (Serves: 4)

In the past I have enjoyed veal parmigiana in a few restaurants, but in the summer of 2012, while visiting the beach at the Wildwood Crest, NJ, I had the best veal parmigiana at an Italian restaurant. This dish is so easy and so tasty that once you make it, you will make it over again. The key is to buy good veal cutlets, not too fatty and even-cut, and brown them fast.

Ingredients : for the sauce: 2 tbsp. olive oil; ½ cup diced onion; ½ cup diced celery; 1can 28 oz, (794g) crushed tomatoes with tomato puree; 3 tbsp., about 3 oz. (85g) tomato paste; 1 tsp. lemon juice; 1 tsp. sugar; ¼ tsp. each granulated garlic and dry oregano; 1 tsp. dry or 1 tab fresh torn basil leaves; salt and pepper to taste.

For the Veal: 1 pound or 4 slices of veal cutlets pounded ¼-inch thick, between two large pieces of plastic wraps; ½ cup all-purpose flour; 2 eggs beaten; 1 cup each Italian seasoned dry bread crumbs and panko (Japanese); ¼ tsp. gran. garlic; ¼ tsp. dry oregano;1/2 cup grated parmesan cheese; 16 oz. (454g) sliced mozzarella cheese; dry or fresh basil to sprinkle on the top; canola oil to deep fry the veal

1. Sauce: Heat a non-reactive, heavy-bottom pan on medium heat. When hot add the oil and sauté onion and celery until soft about 7-8 minutes. Add crushed tomatoes and tomato paste and stir well. Bring to a boil add granulated garlic, oregano, lemon juice, sugar and basil; simmer, covered, on low heat for about 10 minutes, until sauce is thick.
2. Beat the eggs in a shallow bowl, spread out the flour in a platter, and mix the bread crumbs with ¼ cup parmesan cheese, granulated garlic and oregano and spread out in another platter. Heat a large skillet or frying pan with 1-1/2-inches deep oil on medium-high heat or to 375 degrees. Dip one cutlet at a time, first dust with flour and shake out the excess, dip in the beaten egg and drip out the excess, then dip well in the bread crumbs; carefully drop in the hot oil from the side. The oil temperature will go down a little, but maintain it at least 350 degrees and cook cutlets on medium to medium-high heat, golden brown about 2-3 minutes each side. Take the veal out on a paper towel-lined platter and finish rest of the veal.
3. Preheat the oven to 400 degrees. Take four heated serving plates, top each with the sauce in the center, sprinkle with 1 tbsp. grated parmesan cheese, then top with the fried veal and cover with the mozzarella cheese; sprinkle with the basil and bake in a preheated oven for 8-10 minutes until cheese is melted and bubbly on the edges.
4. Serve with extra cheese on side, stuffed artichokes and warm cheese bread and/or salad.

Veal Schnitzel with Mushroom Sauce (Serves: 4)

When I lived in Berlin, one thing I found out that my brother wants most of his meat served with a sauce. Now I am used to sauces from Germany, and the chutney from India. Traditionally this meal is served with German Potato Salad, and Red Cabbage.

Ingredients:

For the Sauce: 1 can 8 oz. condensed cream of mushroom soup; ¼ cup good white wine; 1 tbsp. lemon juice, ½ tsp. dry thyme; salt and pepper to taste.

For the Veal: About 1 pound, 4 thin slices of Veal for scaloppini, pounded thin between two layers of plastic wrap; 2 tbsp. canola oil; ½ cup unsalted butter; seasoned flour: ½ cup all-purpose flour mixed with ½ tsp. each garlic and onion powder, 1 tsp. cayenne pepper; 2 large eggs whisked; for the crumb mixture: 1 cup dry seasoned bread crumbs mixed with 1 tbsp. paprika, 2 tbsp. grated parmesan cheese, 1 tbsp. fresh chopped basil, 1 tsp. dry oregano, salt and pepper to taste; to serve: German potato salad, red cabbage (follow the recipe in the book), and mushroom sauce.

The Mushroom Sauce (M: about 2 cups)

Combine all sauce ingredients in a medium pot, whisk in about 1 cup water or as needed for a sauce consistency. Bring to a boil, lower the heat and simmer for 5 minutes. Reheat just before serving.

For the veal: Heat a large, heavy-bottom skillet on medium heat. Take 1 slice at a time, dip in the flour mixture, shake out the excess flour. Dip in the beaten egg, then dip in the bread-crumb mixture. When pan is hot, add the oil, move around to coat the bottom, then add the butter. Increase the heat to medium-high. When the butter is foaming, add the veal in single layer and cook golden about 2 minutes per side. Take out the veal and serve warm over the sauce, potato salad, and cabbage on the side. I also like to add a little kiwi, avocado, or tomatoes, for color and nutrition.

Veal Chops with Orange Sesame Glaze, Stuffed Zucchini and Polenta Cakes

(Serves: 2 to 4)

This is a fancy dinner that you can prepare all items a day ahead except the veal chops; reheat in the sauté pan or in the microwave oven until heated through and serve. Serve with purchased, marinated artichoke hearts (1 jar, 6.5 oz., (184G). I cook the veal chop just like chicken-fried steaks, on medium heat. See Pasta, Rice and Grain section for Polenta Cakes.

Orange Sesame Glaze (M: 1 cup)

Ingredients: 1 tbsp. peeled and finely grated fresh ginger; 4 tbsp. soy sauce; 4 tbsp. ketchup; ¾ cup concentrated frozen orange juice, thawed; 2 tbsp. lemon juice; about 1/5 tsp. salt and fresh-ground black pepper or to taste; 2 tbsp. lightly roasted and crushed sesame seeds.

Heat all the ingredients except the sesame seeds, in a nonreactive sauté pan. Bring to a boil then reduce the heat and let it simmer on low until it is reduced by a third. Add the crushed sesame seeds and take off the heat. Cool and serve or store in an airtight glass bottle, in the refrigerator up to a week.

Stuffed Zucchini with Chickpeas Patties (Serves: 2 to 4)

Ingredients: 2 tbsp. canola oil; 2 tbsp. butter; 1cup chopped onion; ½ cup fine chopped plum tomato;1/4 tsp. each granulated garlic and dry oregano; ½ cup thin-sliced soft cilantro stems; ¼ cup grated cheese; 4 tbsp. ketchup; ½ cup dry cranberries; 1 can, 15.5 ounces, about 2 cup chickpeas (garbanzos) drained, washed and drained again and mashed potatoes; 1 large egg; 2 tbsp. all-purpose-flour; salt and pepper to taste.

Heat a sauté pan on medium heat. Add oil and sauté onion for 1 minute. Sprinkle garlic and a little salt and pepper, cover and cook for 5 minutes until onion are soft. Add chopped tomatoes, stir on high heat for 1 minute and take off the heat. In a large bowl add the onion mixture, chickpeas, cilantro stems, cheese, ketchup, cranberries, egg and mix well with a wooden spoon. Sprinkle the flour on the top and mix well. Make 4 patties and cook them in oil, in the same sauté pan, on medium high heat, until the patties are browned both sides, about 3 minutes on each side.

Wash and trim the ends of zucchini and cut them in half lengthwise. Leaving a ½-inch border, scoop out the pulp about ½-inch deep (and save for the soup etc). Now cut the patties in half and stuff each zucchini pieces with two pieces of patties each. Heat a large skillet, on medium heat, add the butter, carefully add the zucchini, filling side up, cover with the lid and cook zucchini until they are soft, about 25 minutes, turning the pan around halfway during cooking.

For the Veal Chops

Ingredients: 2 veal chops round bone-in, about 1-inch thick; 2 tbsp. canola oil and 4 tbsp. butter; ¼ tsp. each granulated garlic and dry rosemary and fresh-ground black pepper; 4tbsp. all-purpose-flour; 1extra large egg beaten, ½ cup seasoned bread crumbs.

Take out the veal chops about 45 minutes before cooking. Pat-dry the chops and sprinkle with garlic, rosemary, and pepper, and leave in the room temperature. When ready to cook, heat a large, heavy-bottom skillet (not cast-iron skillet), on medium heat. Dust the veal chops with flour on both side and shake out the excess, dip in beaten egg and then in the bread crumbs both sides. Add 2 tbsp. of oil and 2 tbsp. of butter in the pan, add the chops to the pan in single layer. Sear the chops in the butter for about 6 minutes first side, or until light brown. Drizzle 2 tbsp butter on the top, turn over the chops, and sear about 5 minutes on the second side, until light brown. Serve drizzled with orange glaze, zucchini, polenta cakes & artichoke.

Poultry

Home Made Chicken Stock (M: about 6 cups)

The best chicken broth comes out of roasted chicken bones and brown meat. You can also use cooked chicken parts and bones.

Ingredients: Bones, skin, and leftover brown meat from one about 5-pound chicken broken into pieces; 1 cup each chopped onion, celery, green bell pepper, and carrots; 2 large bay leaves; 8 cups of water or enough to cover the bones; ½ tsp. each salt and pepper (op).

In a pressure cooker or slow cooker, place the bones, vegetables, bay leaves and water. Cook in the pressure cooker for one hour and then let it sit for another half hour. Line a large strainer with paper towel, open the cooker, stir it well, then take out the large bones with a tong and strain rest through the strainer while stock is still warm.

If using the slow cooker cook at least 8 to 10 hours and then strain, the stock will be much richer.

Chicken and Rice (Serves: 4)

This chicken dish is good to use over rice or over the cooked grain. It tastes good as well as is easy to make. You can make your own sauce or you can buy sweet and sour sauce, pomegranate molasses or any other of your favorite sauce. More sauce you have better it tastes.

Ingredients: 4 cup orange juice and 4 tbsp. lemon juice; 1-1/2 cup brown rice or wild rice soaked in 3-1/4 cup warm water with ½ tsp. turmeric (op), ½ tsp. caraway seeds for 2 hours, in a medium pot, covered; 2-3 tbsp. canola oil; 1 to 1-1/2 pounds boneless, skinless chicken breast cut on bias, into strips and sprinkled with each ¼ tsp. pepper and granulated garlic; 1 large onion thin-sliced; 1 large bell pepper, cored, seeded and cut into strips; 1 tbsp. fresh ginger cut into thin strips; ½ cup each: dry cranberries and slivered almonds or pumpkin seeds; salt and pepper to taste.

1. Heat a sauté pan on medium heat, add a few drops of oil, move around the oil to coat the pan and add the orange juice and lemon juice. Bring to a boil on high heat, reduce the heat a little and leave it to a constant simmer, open, until it is reduced to about 1-1/2 cups. Add a little salt and pepper to taste. Pour the sauce in a bowl and keep it warm. You can boil the sauce to reduce, but lower the heat every now and then, to avoid burning.
2. While the sauce is simmering cook the soaking rice with the soaking water and 3-4 drops of oil, almonds and cranberries. Bring the rice to a boil, lower the heat, cover, and simmer on low heat until it is soft, about 25 to 30 minutes. When rice is done fluff the rice with a fork.
3. Heat a sauté pan on medium heat, add 1 tbsp. oil. When oil is hot, add the onion and little salt and pepper and sauté for 5 minutes, add bell pepper strips and sauté 6-8 minutes. Take out the onion and bell pepper and add little more oil and the marinated chicken strips and ginger. Brown the chicken stirring on medium heat, for about 10-12 minutes or until done, season with salt and pepper to taste. Now add the onion mixture back to the pan and pour in 1/2 of the reduced orange sauce. Cook a little to heat.
4. Serve warm rice topped with the chicken and remaining sauce.

The Best Steamed Roasted Whole Chicken with Vegetables (Serves: 6)

This is a healthy dinner of what we call a healing food. The chicken comes out almost like butter. The secret is no salt. Just use herbs and fruits, inside and outside the chicken, and steam for 20 minutes per pound without vegetables and 25 minutes with vegetables. Put 2 large pieces of foil together, with about aluminum foil 6 inches longer than the roasting pan. You will be amazed at the easy and tasty dinner you have created.

Ingredients: 1 large roasting chicken about 8 to 9 pounds (I prefer a plump Perdue one); herbs for under the skin: 2 tbsp. unsalted butter softened; 2 tbsp. pickling spices crushed; fresh garlic cloves crushed, rosemary and thyme chopped fine. For the cavity: 1 tsp. salt, 1 each peeled and sliced: orange, lemon and apple; for the outside: 2 tbsp. olive oil, and lot of fresh crushed black pepper, and 1 tsp. granulated garlic.

Vegetables: 6 medium carrots peeled, cored and blanched for 3-4 minutes in boiling salted water; 6 medium red potatoes scrubbed; 6 medium zucchini scrubbed and cored; 6 medium red bell peppers; spices to stuff the vegetables: 2 tbsp. cumin powder, 4 tbsp. grated parmesan cheese; 1 tsp. salt, ½ tsp. fresh ground black pepper, ½ tsp. turmeric (op), 1 tbsp. olive oil; low-fat sour cream or gravy to serve (op).

1. Preheat oven at 350 degrees. Prepare aluminum foil (put 2 pieces together) to cover the roasting pan air-tight.
2. Prepare the vegetables: mix together cumin powder, grated cheese, salt, pepper, oil and turmeric. Make a long slit in the zucchini and hold it open with fingers or a spoon and sprinkle about 1 tsp. of spice mixture inside. Take out the stems and seeds form the bell peppers and sprinkle a little spice mixture inside.
3. Prepare the chicken: take out the neck and liver pieces, wash the chicken under running cold water, pat dry and sprinkle the cavity with 1 tbsp. salt, and then insert the orange, lemon, and apple slices. Push under the breast skin the butter and herb mixture. Rub the olive oil outside all over the chicken, then sprinkle with the garlic powder and fresh cracked black pepper.
4. Fill the roasting pan with about 1-1/2 cups of tap water or up to the wire rack. Place the chicken on one side on the rack, so that the legs are touching the roasting pan. Then place the hard vegetables like carrots in the bottom, and then potatoes; place zucchini on the top, then the bell peppers. Cover the roasting pan with large aluminum foil air-tight, pressing the foil on the inside and outside of the edges. Place the roasting pan so that the legs are facing slightly the back wall of the oven. Roast 25 minutes per pound. So a 9-pound chicken will take about 4 hours. Take the

roasting pan out of the oven and let it rest for 5 minutes, then open the foil slowly, away from you, so that hot steam escaping from the pan stays away from you.

5. Scrape the chicken off the bottom then take out the chicken with folded towels and place on the cutting board. Serve the vegetable in heated plates. Cut off one leg, and one wing off the chicken first, and then slice the breast thin on an angel and serve with sour cream, gravy or just plain pan juices or thickened with the 2 tbsp. corn starch per 1 cup of juices.

To Reheat: Any left over chicken or vegetables, just reheat in a foil or in a baking tray, covered, in a 300-degree oven until it is heated through.

Chicken Cacciatore (Serves: 4-6)

When my brother came to visit us from Berlin, Germany, his two little girls loved this dish so much that we start making extra all the time.

Ingredients: 3-4 tbsp. olive oil; about 3 to 3-1/2 pounds chicken thighs and separated wings (save tips for the broth) mixed or just thighs alone; 1/3 cup flour mixed with ½ tsp. each garlic powder and pepper for dredging; 1 cup each chopped: onion, Portobello, celery, and green bell pepper; 1 tbsp. garlic cloves sliced; ½ tsp. dry oregano; 1 can 28 oz. diced tomato or puree; 1-1/2 cups red wine; 1 cup chicken stock; 2 tbsp. honey; 1 tbsp. lemon juice or to taste; 1 tbsp. fresh minced thyme leaves; salt and pepper to taste; grated parmesan cheese to garnish; to serve: extra virgin olive oil, pasta or bread and salad.

Preheat the oven at 350 degrees. Heat a large Dutch oven or heavy-bottom pot on medium heat. Add 2 tbsp. oil and cook onion, mushrooms, celery and sauté for 5 minutes add the bell pepper and sauté for another 5 minutes. Take out the vegetables, and add another 2 tbsp. oil and cook on medium to medium-high heat to brown the chicken. Dredge the chicken pieces in the flour, shake out excess flour, and add to the oil. Let the chicken get light brown underneath, then turn over once and cook the other side until light brown. Add wine to the meat, stir, and let it evaporate for one minute. Now add tomatoes, chicken stock, sautéed vegetables, stir and bring it to a boil. Place the pot in a preheated oven and simmer for 30 minutes or until chicken is soft. Add honey and lemon juice, thyme, salt and pepper as needed. Let the chicken rest for 15 minutes. Serve garnished with olive oil, and cheese with pasta, bread, and salad on the side.

Chicken Jambalaya (S:6)

This is a southern meal. My brother-in-law loved this at lunch time.

Ingredients: About 3 pound fryer chicken cut up into pieces; 2 strips of bacon; 2tbsp. olive oil; 1/2 cup each chopped onion, green pepper, celery; 2 medium bay leaves; 4 garlic cloves chopped; 1 can 16 oz. crushed tomatoes; 1-1/4cup long grain rice; 1cup cooked ham cut into ½-inch dice;1/2cup mixed fresh herbs parsley, shallots; 2 pinches each rosemary and thyme; 2-3 drops of tabasco or to taste.

In a heavy bottom pot cook bacon until crisp. Take out the bacon and add the olive oil to the pot. Season chicken pieces with salt and pepper add to the pot and brown until golden. Take out the chicken. Add onion, green pepper and celery and brown lightly. Add garlic, bay leaves, tomatoes, 1cup water, and chicken. Bring it to a boil and add rice. Lower the heat and cook on constant simmer for about 1 hr.

When rice is almost done add ham, crushed bacon, herbs and tabasco sauce. Cover and cook 5 minutes and serve.

Coq Au Vin (Chicken in Wine Sauce)
(Serves: 4-6)

This is a classic French dish that became popular around 1960. If you do not want to use wine, then use 2 parts of beef stock and 1 part chicken stock, and stir in some lemon chutney or pesto.

Ingredients: **For the reduced wine**: 1 bottle, 750 ml. fruity red wine such as zinfandel or pinot noir, 1 cup chicken stock, ½ cup orange juice, 1 tbsp. lemon juice; simmer all together in a large non-reactive saucepan and simmer on high, partially covered, for about 30 minutes, or until it is reduced to about 4 cups (you can reduce one day ahead and refrigerate.).

For the Chicken: ½ pound bacon slices, or about ½ cup cooked minced ham; 3-4 tbsp. clarified butter or as needed; 1 cup each chopped fine: onion, celery, carrots, green bell pepper; about 3 pounds chicken thighs and drumsticks, excess fat removed; ¼ cup all-purpose flour mixed with each: 1 tsp. granulated garlic and cayenne pepper for dredging; 1 pkg. frozen pearl onions; 8-10 oz. small whole button mushrooms; 1 cup frozen peas; 2 tbsp. tomato paste; ½ tsp. each dry: rosemary, and oregano; salt and pepper to taste; to serve: pasta, or small boiled potatoes or mashed potatoes.

Heat a large Dutch oven or a large heavy-bottom pot. Add bacon and fry on high heat until brown and crisp about 5-6 minutes take out on a paper towel-lined platter. Discard all the fat. Add 2 tbsp. clarified butter and onion, carrots, celery, and bell pepper and cook on medium heat, stirring for 5 minutes, then covered for 5-6 minutes, until soft, and take out. Now add 2 tbsp. of butter to the pot, dredge the chicken in the flour, shake out excess, and brown the chicken pieces, in single layer, on medium to medium-heat, until they are browned underneath, about 5 minutes. Turn over the chicken and brown the other side.

Add the tomato paste, and stir for 5 minutes, add the cooked vegetables, reduced wine, and little salt and pepper to taste. Bring to a boil, and simmer on low heat for about 20 minutes. Add all the raw vegetables, bacon or ham, herbs, and simmer another 25 minutes or until chicken pieces are soft. Serve with potatoes or pasta.

Roasted Cornish Game Hens (Serves: 2)

When I was working at the bank, the whole office, together with other branches, used to take our bosses out for the Boss Night. We mostly went to the Town and Campus, in West Orange, N.J. After a long cocktail hour, we had a very nice dinner of stuffed hen. Since that time I started making the easy recipe of Cornish hens. You can also stuff it with cooked stuffing, and it will take about another 15-20 minutes longer to roast.

Ingredients: 2 Cornish game hens, about 1-1/2 to 2 pounds each; herb mixture: 1 tbsp. each chopped fresh rosemary, garlic cloves, unsalted melted butter; 1/3 cup thick original hoisin sauce or marinade. To serve: vegetables and potatoes.

Preheat the oven at 400 degrees. Prepared a shallow roasting pan lined with foil. Wash the hens inside out and pat dry with the paper towels. Sprinkle with salt all over and let it sit in room temperature for 20 minutes; then wash out the salt and pat dry again.

Rub the mixture all over, place the hens in the prepared pan, facing the legs towards the back wall; tent loosely with a piece of aluminum foil, and bake for 20 minutes. Take the hens out and brush all over with the hoisin sauce, and bake open for about 10 minutes, or until the internal temperature on an instant-read thermometer on the thickest part of the thigh is around 165-170 degrees. Let it rest for 15-20 minutes and serve with pan juices and the sides.

Roasted Duck with Sriracha-Hoisin Sauce (Serves: 4-6)

Most of the ducks found in the supermarkets are called Long Island duck, also known as Peking duck. Some people also call it duckling. After roasting, the fat that is rendered in the roasting pan is a golden fat you can use in cooking greens, vegetables, etc. You can roast the duck a day ahead. About 30 minutes before reheating, leave it in the room temperature. Just before serving, cut it into pieces, heat in a 350 degree oven for about 10 minutes in an aluminum foil-lined baking tray. Then glaze with the sriracha-hoisin sauce, heat about 5 minutes and glaze and heat again. Keep on glazing and heating for about 15 minutes until it is heated through and serve with sides, and with extra sauce on the side.

Sriracha-Hoisin Sauce (M: ¾ cups)

Ingredients: 1 tbsp. butter; 1 tsp. each cumin and fennel seeds crushed; ¼ cup sriracha (hot) sauce; ½ cup thick hoisin sauce or marinade; 1 tbsp. ketchup; salt and pepper to taste.

Heat a medium pot on medium heat. When hot, add the butter, cumin and fennel seeds, cook for 1 minute, add rest of the ingredients, stir well. Bring to a boil then lower the heat and simmer 15 minutes. Cool and store in a clean jar in the refrigerator for about 1 week.

For the Duck

Ingredients: 1 frozen or fresh duckling or duck, about 5 pounds; if frozen, leave in the refrigerator for about 3-4 days until it is defrosted. For the rub: 2 tbsp. each: cumin powder, mild chili powder, chopped fresh thyme, fresh grinded ginger and garlic cloves, sea salt, black pepper, fine grated lemon zest, olive oil; 1 tbsp. light brown sugar. 1 recipe of sriracha-hoisin sauce.

One day before roasting, take out the giblets from the cavity (save for the soup), wash and pat dry duck, and rub half of the spice mixture all over the duck and refrigerate it overnight (duck takes spices well). Just before roasting, heat oven to 350 degrees. Boil about 2 cups of water with brown sugar. Line a roasting pan with aluminum foil. Score the duck skin, about 2 inches apart, about 1/3-inch deep all over; do not touch the flesh. Place the duck in a platter and pour hot water all over. Now place the duck in the roasting pan, breast side down and roast duck for 1 hour at 350 degrees. Take out the pan and pour or carefully take out the fat with a large spoon. Place the duck back in the roasting pan breast side up and rub with the remaining rub mixture, and roast at 325 degrees for about 30-40 minutes, or until the internal temperature at the thickest part, on an instant-read thermometer registers around 170 degrees.

Now take out the duck and place into a rimmed baking sheet, brush the duck with the sauce, increase the oven temperature to 500 degrees and roast for another 5-6 minutes until it is glazed and browned. Let the duck rest for 10-15 minutes, carve or cut into quarters, take out the backbone and serve with potatoes and vegetables and/or salad, and fancy pancakes, and extra sauce on the side.

Roasted Duck Breast with Broccoli Rabe, Potatoes, Roasted Red Bell Pepper and German Wine Sauerkraut (Serves: 2)

You can buy the duck breast fresh or frozen. Defrost them completely before cooking. They are also called magrets, and are about 12 ounces each.

Ingredients: 1 duck breast about 12 ounces; salt and pepper to taste; to serve: about 10 ounces fresh broccoli rabe blanch in the boiling water for 3 minutes then sautéed in the little duck fat until soft; about 8 mini potatoes boiled soft and then sautéed in the little duck fat to light brown; store bought: roasted red bell pepper and original German sauerkraut in the wine, and sriracha-hoisin sauce.

Preheat the oven at 300 degrees. Score the duck breast on the fat side into 1-inch diamonds. Then place it in the dry, heavy-bottom pan on medium heat and sizzle the fat side down, until it is golden brown underneath for about 15-20 minutes. Place the breast in the oven fat side up, and slow roast it for about 15 minutes or until it registers 135 to 140 degrees at the thickest part. It should be rosy-red or rosy-pink (slow roasted). Serve sliced across with broccoli rabe, potatoes and drizzled with the above sriracha-hoisin sauce, and roasted pepper and sauerkraut on the side. Serve extra sauce on side.

Tip: If you cannot find the wine sauerkraut, then buy the crispy sauerkraut (or any other), place in a clean glass jar, drain out almost all the liquid leaving the sauerkraut a little moistened, and fill with the good white wine about 3-inches above the sauerkraut. Let it soak for 2-3 days in the refrigerator, and serve.

Steam Roasted Turkey Breast with Walnut-chocolate Sweet Potatoes, Turkey Gravy, and Sugarless Cranberry Sauce (Serves: 6)

You can close your eyes and steam this turkey breast. It won't get dry or burn. Just set a timer and turn around the roasting pan once during halfway of roasting. Make sure turkey is defrosted completely. We like to serve with cream spinach (see index).

1.   Steamed Turkey Breast

Ingredients: About 6 pounds bone-in Butterball turkey breast defrosted completely in 3-4 days; ½ stick, 4 tabs melted unsweetened butter; ½ tsp. granulated garlic powder or 4 large cloves fresh garlic chopped; ½ tsp. dry or 1 tbsp. fresh-chopped rosemary; 1tbsp. fresh chopped thyme, about 1 cup rough chopped celery leaves; 1 tbsp. coarse sea salt, and fresh ground black pepper.

1-14.5 ounces (411G), about 2 cups low-sodium chicken stock heated with ½ cup water; 2 oranges: one peeled and one unpeeled sliced into ½-inch thick slices; 2 lemons: one with the thick ends trimmed out and sliced and the other to save for the juice; 1 apple, cored and cut in to wedges; coarse ground black pepper to taste.

In a large roasting pan, add heated water and chicken broth, orange and lemon slices and apple wedges. Put the wire grade over the stock. Take out two large pieces of the aluminum foil, big enough to cover the roasting pan airtight, put them together, then fold over twice lengthwise, on the long side, to make one large piece, and set aside.

Preheat the oven at 400F and arrange the middle rack for roasting turkey.

Wash and pat dry the turkey. Sprinkle the cavity all over with black pepper, then stuff the turkey with celery leaves. Rub the lemon juice all over the turkey. Mix butter, garlic and rosemary, thyme, and rub all over the turkey, sprinkle with little coarse sea salt and pepper all over. Put the turkey over the wire rack in the roasting pan, cover with aluminum foil, air-tight, pressing the foil against the edges well. Place the roasting pan in the hot oven.

Roast turkey for 30 minutes at 400F, turn around the roasting pan halfway, reduce the temperature to 350F and roast about 50 minutes or until turkey is done and internal temperature at the thickest part of the meat is 160F. Take out the breast and rest on a cutting board, loosely tented with aluminum foil for about 15 minutes; collect the juices from the pan and make gravy. Slice the turkey against the grain with an angle, thick or thin, and serve with the warm gravy, cranberry cups, mashed potatoes and stuffing.

2.   Walnut-chocolate Sweet Potatoes

Ingredients: About 2-1/2 pounds slim and long sweet potatoes or yams, peeled, cut across to 2-inch pieces, then soaked in water; 4 tbsp. butter; salt and pepper to taste; for the syrup: 2 tbsp. lemon juice, 1cup brown sugar, 2 tbsp. butter; ¾ cup orange juice; ½ tsp. each: cardamom seeds crushed fine, and ground cinnamon; to sprinkle: ½ cup toasted walnuts or pistachios, and 2 ounces grated semi-sweet chocolate.

Preheat oven at 350 degrees. Melt butter in a 9x12-inch baking dish. Spread out the potatoes in the dish, in single layers, cut side down, and cover air-tight with foil. Bake for about 30 minutes, or until they are fork-tender, turning the dish around once during the baking.

In a small pot, bring all the syrup ingredients to a boil. When the potatoes are done, turn each piece over and sprinkle the toasted walnuts, and bake at 400 degrees for about 10 minutes, until half of the syrup is absorbed, Serve warm sprinkled with grated chocolate.

3.   Turkey Gravy (M: 2 cups)

Ingredients: 2 cups thick strained turkey roasting liquid (rinse out the fat from the top); 1 packet instant chicken broth; 4 tabs cornstarch; ½ cup water; ½ cup good white wine (op); salt and pepper to taste; ½ cup each dry cranberries and dry prunes chopped; ½ cup white wine; salt and fresh ground pepper to taste.

Whisk the corn starch and chicken stock in ½ cup water in a medium pot, add 2 cups thick cooking liquid, bring to a boil on medium heat until thick, about 4-5 minutes. When it starts bubbling and is thickened, take off the heat, add wine, cranberries, prunes, salt and pepper to taste, simmer on low heat 5 minutes. Turn down the heat and keep it warm on very low heat, or heat it again and serve it later. If it is too thick, add some orange juice or lemon juice with some water. Pour in a gravy bowl and keep it warm.

Tips: The secret to steaming turkey or chicken is not to brine or salt the turkey or chicken. You can also steam in a flavorful broth.

Buy a frozen Butterball turkey breast (that's the one we prefer), defrost for three days in the refrigerator, sprinkle spices inside-out to have enough flavorful liquid in a roasting pan. Cover the pan with the foil airtight, even though you have a cover. Turn around the roasting pan halfway during the roasting. Don't open the foil until meat is almost done. First roast the meat on high temperature for two-thirds of the time, Turkey will be heated and cooked halfway through by now, reduce the temperature slightly, just to steam. This meat is so flavorful and cooked just right that you can slice very thin or freeze into large pieces wrapped in the plastic, in a container, up to three months. For best results before freezing, dip the meat in the cooking liquid before wrapping in plastic and leave the skin on. We freeze turkey all the time and enjoy later with the fresh gravy.

4. Sugarless Cranberry Sauce

Ingredients: 2 Gayla or Red Delicious apples, peeled, cored, and cut into 1-inch cubes and washed; 1 tsp. orange zest; 2 oranges peeled, seeded and chopped; 1 bag, about 2 cups (340g) fresh cranberries washed; 1 cup dry cranberries washed; 1 cup orange juice; pinch of salt; ½ tsp. cardamom seeds crushed.

In a heavy-bottom, large stainless steel pan, cook apple chunks on medium heat covered for about 15-20 minutes until they are soft. Then mash them with a potato masher.

While the apples are cooking, in a food processor or a blender puree oranges, orange juice cardamom seeds and the dry cranberries first. Then add the fresh cranberries in 2-3 batches and grind them coarsely. Pour all the ground items over the apples, add the zest, salt, the orange juice, and stir well. Bring all to a boil. Cook on a constant simmer for about 45 minutes, stirring often, or until they are very soft and taste sweet. Serve warm with the turkey or chicken, sweet potatoes, cream spinach, turkey gravy and cranberry sauce.

Tips for the Perfect Roasted Turkey

1. **Defrost the Turkey**: I like the Butterball turkey. It has a lot of meat and does not dry up easily. Keep the turkey in the freezer and take out only 5 days before roasting if the turkey is about 20 pounds. Take out 4 days before if the turkey is about 15 pounds. Defrosting too far ahead will cause losing out on the liquid.
2. **Brining the Turkey:** Brining the turkey will take a little less time to cook, because the salt has gone into the meat.
    To Brine the a 20-pound Turkey: Heat 4 cups of water, 4 tbsp. of kosher salt, ½ cup pickling spices (or 1 tbsp. each: coriander seeds, black peppercorn, mustard seeds, all crushed, 2 large dry bay leaves), 2 large garlic cloves crushed and 1 red dry serrano pepper broken (or red pepper flakes). Bring all to a boil, pour in a large platter, cool completely. Submerge the turkey in a pale of cold water and pour over the brine, leave in the room temperature for 1 hour. Take out and pat dry. I just sprinkle with spices.
3. **A covered Turkey takes about 15 minutes per pound at 350F to roast.** So a 20-pound turkey will take 5 hours to roast. In the beginning I use higher temperature: 400F for ½ hour (turkey breast

facing the back wall) to get the turkey started. Because of the higher temperature for ½ hour, I reduce the roasting time by ½ hour So instead of 5 hours it will take only 4-1/2 hours altogether to roast.

Next, I reduce the temperate to 350F, and roast turkey 3 hours, the legs facing the back wall, loosely covered with aluminum foil.

Then I turn around and roast the turkey open (to get color) for 1 hour, now with the breast facing the back wall.

By now the turkey should be done. Legs have tough bones and muscles, so they take longer; breast meat is tender and takes less time. The perfect temperature should be between 160F-165F. While the turkey is resting, the temperature will go up, so do not overcook. Let the turkey rest 20 minutes in a warm platter (not in the roasting pan).

In the meantime, take out the cooking juices and make the gravy.

Perfect Roasted Turkey (Serves: 8-10)

I prefer Butterball turkey that has lot of meat and less bones, and after roasting it is plump, golden and juicy It takes about 15 minutes per pound.

Ingredients: One about 20 pounds (10 kg.) Butterball turkey defrosted in the refrigerator for 5 days, no more; 2 tbsp. clarified butter (has high smoke point), salt, pepper, granulated garlic and dry rosemary.

1. Take out the turkey from the refrigerator about ½ hour ahead of roasting. Preheat oven to 400F. Line a large roasting pan with aluminum foil. Also, prepare a large piece of aluminum foil, well-greased with oil, to cover loosely the whole turkey.
2. Wash and pat dry turkey, sprinkle the cavity with salt and pepper and let it sit on the counter for 10-15 minutes. Rub the clarified butter all over the outside of the turkey and sprinkle with garlic, rosemary, salt and pepper all over. Place in roasting pan with wings tucked in underneath, and the legs are tied together or tucked in the skin.

3. Now here is the trick: Place the turkey in the oven, breast side toward the back wall, and roast for 30 minutes at 400F.
Open the oven, cover loosely with aluminum foil and turn around the turkey, the legs toward the back wall, roasting pan slightly to the right or left, and roast for 1-1/2 hour.
Open the oven and carefully turn around the roasting pan a little to the other direction (left or right), still with legs toward the back wall, and roast 1-1/2 hours. Open the oven, take off the aluminum foil, turn the turkey breast towards the back wall and roast for 1hour.
Check the turkey with instant-read thermometer, 2-3 places, at the thickest part of the breast, away from the bone; it should be about 160F-162F. Turn off the oven, let the turkey sit in the oven for 5 minutes. Then take out the turkey, and transfer to a large, heated platter on the counter, cover with foil, and let it rest for 20 minutes, until all the juices are back in to the meat. Now carve the turkey: take out 1 wing and l leg and from a diagonal angle and slice the breast. Serve with gravy, stuffing, wine mushrooms and vegetables, etc.

Roasted Turkey Breast Sandwich (Serves: 4-6)

Your own roasted breast will be full of nutrients and less salt.

Ingredients: 1-3/4 to 2 pounds boneless, skinless, organic turkey breast; 1 tbsp. whole-grain Dijon mustard; crumb mixture of: ½ cup crushed pistachios, 2 tbsp. grated parmesan cheese; ¼ cup seasoned bread crumbs or quick-cooking oatmeal, ¼ tsp. each salt and pepper, 1 tsp. lemon-pepper seasoning mix.
8 to 10 slices of grain bread or 4 to 6 whole-wheat buns lightly toasted at the end; ½ cup your favorite chutney and/or light mayonnaise; 4 to 6 slices of tomatoes; salad or pickles to serve on side
.

1. Preheat oven to 400 degrees for 5-10 minutes. Line a heavy baking tray with aluminum foil, then lightly spray the foil with the cooking spray.
2. Wash and pat dry the turkey breast, spread the mustard on both sides, then dip well in the crumb mixture. Let it sit in room temperature on a baking tray for 5 minutes. Spray with cooking spray both sides, place the tray in the oven and bake at 400 degrees for 10 minutes. Reduce the temperature and bake at 375 degrees for 15 minutes, loosely covered with aluminum foil; turn the tray around halfway and bake open another few minutes or until turkey is done about 160 degrees internal temperature (when checked on the thickest part on an instant-read thermometer). Take out the tray and the breast and let it rest on a cutting board for 15 minutes.
3. Toast the bread or buns, then spread the chutney and/or mayonnaise and a little salt and pepper on the bread. Slice the meat against the grain in to thin slices and place on the bread, top with tomato slices and serve warm with salad or pickles.
Tip: You can roast chicken or firm fish this way, just reduce the baking time.
Tips: Turkey has a low-fat protein, vitamin B, iron, zinc, selenium, etc.

Tasty Turkey Meatballs (M: 15 large)

You can use just ground turkey, or half turkey and half ground chicken meat. You can freeze them in an airtight plastic bag, placed in a plastic container, for up to 3 months. Thaw overnight, heat in a 200 degree oven for about 20 minutes; serve with chutney or in heated tomato sauce.

Ingredients: 2 slices, about 1-inch thick Italian loaf cut into ½-inch pieces and soaked in ½ cup milk; about 2 pound ground turkey; 2 extra large eggs; 1 cup baby spinach or kale leaves, blanched in water for 3 minutes and chopped fine; 1 medium onion cut in half and grated or grinded; 4 large garlic cloves grated; 1 cup mushrooms chopped and cooked in 1 tbsp. butter on high heat until liquid is evaporated; 1 cup fresh tomato, blanched, peeled and chopped fine; 2 tbsp. ketchup; 1 tbsp. fresh bil chopped; 1 tsp. dry rosemary; 1 tbsp. dry mustard powder; 1 tsp. salt and black pepper to taste; 1 tbsp. smoked paprika; 1 cup roasted peanuts or other nuts; 1/3 cup grated parmesan cheese; 1 cup fresh grated white cheddar cheese; about 2 tbsp. melted butter; to serve: lemon, mango or yogurt chutney.

1. In a large bowl with a wooden spoon (do not use hand, it will get watery), mix together bread crumbs, ground turkey and eggs. Then add rest of the ingredients except the butter.
2. On a parchment paper lined heavy-bottom tray, drop the meatballs with an ice cream scoop and shape them round with the wet fingers. Chill the meatball in the refrigerator from 30 minutes to an hour. Drizzle with the melted butter and bake in 400 degrees preheated oven for about 15-20 minutes. Turn off the oven and let stay in the hot oven for another 5 minutes to get golden.
3. Serve warm with your favorite chutney.

Chicken Meatballs with Sauerkraut
(Serves: 4)

When I was an underwriter at the Weichert Financial Services, I met another underwriter, Cathy. She told me that she makes meatballs in sauerkraut. Since I like the fermented food, I loved making these meatballs.

Ingredients:

For the Sauce: 1 bottle, 16 oz. herb spaghetti sauce or mushroom tomato sauce; 1 cup packed: crispy or wine sauerkraut; 2 cups chicken stock, salt and pepper to taste.
For the Meatballs: 1 pound ground chicken; ½ cup fresh bread crumbs mixed with each: ½ tsp. dry oregano, and granulated garlic; red pepper flakes (op); 4 tbsp. milk; 2 tbsp. grated parmesan cheese; parsley to garnish.

In a large, wide, and in a non-reactive pot heat the tomato sauce, chicken stock, bring it to a boil and simmer for 5 minutes.

In a large bowl mix together all the meatball ingredients, and form walnut-size meatballs. Add the meatballs to the simmering sauce, and cook for about 10-12 minutes, turning them over 3-4 times, until the meatballs are cooked through. Stir in the room-temperature sauerkraut, taste for seasoning, simmer for another 5 minutes or until it is heated through, and serve warm in a soup bowl, sprinkled with parsley. Serve with crusty or garlic bread, or over pasta.

The Best Fried Chicken (Serves: 6-8)

This chicken is marinated, steamed, and then deep-fried. So it takes less oil to fry. Serve with potato salad, biscuits, and coleslaw.

Ingredients: 1 whole chicken about 5 pounds cut up into 8 pieces, or 4 pounds drumsticks (I like Perdue brand); oil to deep-fry.

For the Marinade: 2 large eggs whisked into 1/2 cup water; 1 quart (946 ml.) buttermilk.

For the Flour or Fresh Bread Crumbs Mixture: 2 tbsp. each – onion powder, garlic powder, cumin powder; 1 tbsp. each: cayenne pepper, dry oregano, paprika; 1 tbsp. salt.
1 cup all-purpose flour or 2 cups fresh bread crumbs, ½ cup mung bean flour (found in Indian grocery stores) or corn meal, 4 tbsp. corn starch; 1 tsp. baking powder; 2 tsp. salt; 1 tsp. fresh-ground black pepper; extra salt and pepper; 2 eggs whisked with 2Tbsp. water.

Whisk the marinade ingredients in a large bowl. Pat dry the chicken pieces with the paper towel and marinate the chicken overnight in the refrigerator covered with the plastic wrap, or in a zip-lock bag, placed in a bowl. Take out 1 hour before steaming.

Preheat the oven at 375 degrees. Or use a pressure cooker to steam the chicken. Line a large baking sheet (12x18x1-inch) with aluminum foil and grease it lightly with oil. Pick up the chicken pieces from the marinade with a tong, shake a little and place on the baking sheet, larger pieces outside and smaller ones inside. Bake about 12 minutes per pound, covered air-tight with foil. Turn the tray halfway around once during the steaming.

When baked, take out the pieces, draining out the liquid (save for soup). Sprinkle pieces with some salt and a lot of black pepper. Dip each piece in egg mixture, then in to flour/crumbs mixture well. Shake out excess flour, and place the chicken pieces in a large platter, in a single layer.

Heat the oil in a fryer, wok (I prefer) or in a wide pot, about 2-inches deep, at 375 degrees, or on medium-high heat. Fry the chicken in batches in a single layer, about 1-1/2 minute per side, or until golden, a total of 3-4 minutes. When the pieces are golden, turn them over fast once more, to crisp them. Take out the chicken pieces on a paper towel-lined platter and serve warm with the sides.

Tip: Mung flour gives good flavor, also it's light protein.

Baked Chicken Pieces (Serves: 6-8)

This is my favorite baked-chicken recipe. It is very flavorful, and low in calories. I buy a larger chicken with lots of meat.

Ingredients: 1 large chicken about 8-9 pounds cut up into 10 pieces (see instruction), or cut up pieces such as drumsticks, all the same size, and bring to room temperature; salt to sprinkle on; marinade mixture: 1 cup good white wine, ½ cup fresh orange juice; 4 tbsp. olive oil; ½ cup lemon juice, 2 tbsp. Dijon type or sharp Chinese mustard; 2 tbsp. Tabasco-type hot sauce; spice mixture1 tbsp. each crushed: fennel seeds, cumin seeds, granulated garlic, ginger powder, turmeric powder; 1 tbsp. celery seeds, salt to taste (about 1-1/2 tsp.). To serve: ½ cup green onion sliced, potato salad, dipping sauce or chutney, and/or slaw.

Preheat the oven at 350 degrees. Line a large baking tray with sides (12x18x1 inches) with aluminum foil and spray or grease it well.

Pat dry the chicken pieces with the paper towel then sprinkle generously with the salt all over, and set aside for 15-20 minutes. Wash the chicken pieces under the running water, rinse, and pat dry well.

Spread out the spice mixture in a platter. In a large bowl whisk together the marinade ingredients. Dip each chicken piece into the marinade, and then roll lightly into the spice mixture, and place on the baking tray, skin side up, placing the dark meat outside and light meat inside the circle. Tent the tray with the foil, and bake at 350 degrees, about 15 minutes per pound. Turn the chicken over halfway with the tong during the baking. When the chicken is done, take out the foil and let it cook open at 400 degrees, for about 5-10 minutes or until it is lightly browned. The internal temperature on an instant-read thermometer, at the thickest part, away from the bones, should be around 170 degrees for the dark meat, and about 160 for the light meat. Serve sprinkled with green onion, and with dipping sauce or chutney, potato salad and slaw.

Chicken Pot Pies or Turnovers
(M: 8 large turnovers or 2 8 inch pies)

These turnovers can be frozen and used whenever you are in a hurry or unable to cook. Just defrost in the microwave and heat them in the oven at 350 degrees for about 20 minutes until heated through.

Ingredients:

For the Filling: 2 halved, about 1 pound, boneless, skinless chicken breast, all fat removed and cut up in 1-inch cubes; 3-4 tbsp. olive oil; flour mixture: 3 tbsp. all-purpose flour mixed with each: ½ tsp. cayenne pepper, garlic and onion powders, ½ tsp. oregano; 1 cup each ½-inch cubed: onion, celery, carrots and frozen peas; 2 tbsp. tomato paste; 1 tbsp. lemon juice; 1 tbsp. fresh chopped dill (op); ¼ cup heavy cream or whole milk; ¼ tsp. fresh grated nutmeg; salt and fresh ground black pepper to taste. To serve: salad or coleslaw, and yogurt or lemon chutney.

For the Crust: 2-1/2 cups all-purpose flour mixed with 1 tsp. salt, ½ tsp. baking soda; 1 tbsp. baking powder; 6 tbsp. cold butter; ½ cup cold sour cream; 3-4 tbsp. cold water or as needed to make a firm dough; for the topping: 2 tbsp. melted butter, 2 tbsp. grated cheese, dry rosemary.

To make the Filling: Heat a heavy-bottom pan on medium heat. Pat dry chicken cubes with paper towel and sprinkle with the flour mixture. Heat about 2 tbsp. oil in the pan and spread out the chicken in single layer. Let the chicken cook for about 3 minutes or until it is lightly browned underneath, then turn over once and brown the other side for 2 minutes.

Lower the heat to medium, and add tomato paste, lemon juice, and stir well then move over the chicken on one side. Add the chopped onion, celery, carrots, dill, little salt and pepper and drizzle 1 tbsp. oil over the vegetables, and sauté for 1 minute. Move the chicken cubes over the vegetables, add heavy cream, nutmeg and peas, bring to a boil. Simmer on low heat for about 20 minutes or until chicken and vegetable are soft.

For the Crust: In a large bowl place the flour mixture and grate the cold butter over the flour, dusting the grated butter with the flour. Make a well in the center add the sour cream and little water and mix all with a fork. Then try to make two equal balls, do not knead the dough. As long as dough comes together in a ball, it is ready. Put the dough ball on the board and start rolling, dusting with the flour between two plastic wraps. Roll out each ball in a 10x10-inch square. Cut each square in to 4 pieces.

Working with one piece at a time, lightly wet the edges with the water, pick up one piece in the hand, place about 2 tbsp. filling (do not use any liquid), and fold two opposite corners together, making a triangle. Place it on the board; press down the edges to seal well. Then dip the tines of a fork in to the flour and press down the edges with the fork. Place them on a parchment paper lined and well-greased baking tray. When all are done, brush them well with the melted butter, sprinkle the cheese, then dry rosemary; place them in the refrigerator for 10 minutes to chill.

Preheat the oven at 375 degrees. Bake the turnovers for about 25 minutes, turning the tray around halfway during the baking. The last 5 minutes, increase the oven temperature to 450 degrees and bake for another 5 minutes until the bottom is light brown. Serve warm with salad and chutney.

To make the pies: divide the filling into two 9-inch pie plates. Roll out two round crusts about 1-inch larger than the pie diameter (about 10-inches). Break one large egg and whisk with 1 tbsp. water, brush the edges of the crust about 1-inch wide all around with the egg wash, then cover the pie plate, pressing the crust to the edges, brush the top, sprinkle cheese and rosemary, then make an X on the top and bake as above.

Spicy Chicken Wings (Serves: 6-8)

These are our favorites, they are so tasty that you can eat them hot or cold with fries or potato salad and celery sticks or thin-sliced celery stalks. You need to marinate them overnight.

Ingredients: About 4 to 4-1/2 pounds whole chicken wings cut up at the joints, washed and pat dry with paper towel; save the tip ends for the soup or broth; salt to sprinkle before and after marinating and 1 tbsp. cayenne pepper, or to taste; canola oil to deep-fry.
For the Marinade: 2 large eggs; ¼ hot sauce; 4 cups buttermilk or 2 cups plain low-fat yogurt whipped with 1 cup water.
For the Flour Mixture: ¾ cup all-purpose flour; ¾ cup dry bread crumbs; ¼ cup almond flour or grated parmesan cheese from the bottle; ½ tsp. baking powder; ¼ tsp. baking soda; 1 tsp. salt; 1 tsp. fresh-ground black pepper; 2 tbsp. lemon-pepper mix; 1 tsp. dry oregano; 1 tsp. dry rosemary' ½ tsp. granulated garlic; 2 tbsp. chili powder mix or taco seasoning; salt and fresh ground black pepper to taste; to serve: pepper relish and fries.

1. Sprinkle the wings with salt all over and place them in a large bowl. Whip up the marinade ingredients and pour over the wings, cover with a plate and marinade them overnight in the refrigerator.
2. Take out the wings from the refrigerator 1 hour before cooking and leave them covered in room temperature. Just before cooking, heat a wok or a wide pot with about 2-1/2-inch deep oil on low heat. Then take out the wings from the marinade and place them on large platters, slightly tilted so that some liquid drains out. Discard the liquid and sprinkle the wings with salt and cayenne pepper to taste.
3. Mix the flour mixture in a medium bowl. Take one wing at a time and press down in the flour mixture and place them in a large baking tray in single layer. Increase the heat to medium-high or about 350 degrees. When oil is hot, slide one wing at a time in the hot oil from the side, flesh side down and skin side up. Do not crowd the pan. Fry the wings about 8 minutes or until golden underneath then turn over and fry the other side about 5 minutes or until golden. Now turn the wings over one more time to crisp them in the oil. Take out a few wings with the metal spatula and hold them on the side of the pan to drain

a little then take them out on a paper towel lined baking sheet. Keep the wings warm in a 200-degree oven until all are done. Serve warm with relish and fries.

Barbecue Chicken Wings (Serves: 4-6)

You can make these wings a day before and reheat in a 350-degree oven about 15 minutes, covered in foil, or heat about 3-4 minutes covered in the microwave oven.

Ingredients: 2 pounds chicken wings cut off at the joints and tips saved for soup; salt to sprinkle the wings. To bake: 2 tbsp. olive oil. To serve: fries or potato salad, and/or celery stick with blue cheese dressing.

For the Marinade: ¼ cup lemon juice; ¼ cup Worcestershire sauce; ¼ cup orange juice; 1 cup dark rum or red wine; 1 tsp. granulated garlic; 2 tbsp. coconut powder (op); 1 tsp. cayenne pepper or 1 tbsp. hot sauce; 1 tbsp. sugar; ½ tsp. salt.
.

For the Sauce to brush on the wings: 2 tbsp. lemon-pepper mix; ¼ cup ketchup; 1 tsp. cayenne pepper;1/2 tsp. salt; 2 tbsp. butter.

1. Sprinkle the wings all over with salt and set them aside for 10 minutes. Then wipe out all the liquid and salt with the paper towels. Place the wings in a non-reactive bowl or a zip-lock bag. Whisk the marinade ingredients and pour over the wings. Refrigerate 4 to 6 hours.
2. Take out the wings ½ hour before baking. Preheat the oven at 325 degrees. Line a baking tray with foil. Grease it with 1 tsp. oil, take out the wings with a tong and lay them on the foil, skin side up. Drizzle the remaining oil on the top and bake at 325 degrees for 30 minutes. Turn them over once half way through baking.
3. Sauce to baste on the wings: while wings are baking, heat a large heavy-bottom pan on medium-high heat, grease it with a few drops of oil. Pour in the marinade and reduce in half, to about ½ cup, Whisk in ketchup, lemon mix, cayenne, salt and butter. Prepare an indoor grill or use the broiler, brush the wings with the sauce and grill or broil for about 5 minutes each side. Serve hot with potato salad or fries, celery stalks and blue cheese dressing.

   Tip: Lemon-pepper mix or lemon mix (I prefer Mrs. Dash), gives instant lemon flavor and makes the sauce thick.

Chicken Tikka Masala (Boneless Chicken pieces in Cream Sauce)

(Serves: 6)

(Boneless Chicken pieces in the Cream Sauce with Mild Spices)

I read in the AAA magazine, Dec. 2016, under Culinary Tours, "Robin Cook, the U.K.'s late former foreign secretary, declared chicken tikka masala a national dish in 2001 because of its popularity and reflection of how British citizens absorb and adapt to external influences."

This is a very famous and easy dish that goes well with rice and deep-fried breads. This dish comes out very good with the boneless beasts of a baked chicken. Just make and cook the gravy, add the chicken pieces, simmer about 15-20 minutes and serve. It freezes very well, too.

Ingredients: 2 tbsp. canola/olive oil; ½ cup milk; 2 pounds boneless chicken breasts with skin on; ½ cup ginger-garlic paste; 1-1/2 cup heavy cream;1 tbsp. sugar; 1 can 15 oz. (425 g) tomato sauce; 4-5 tbsp. lemon juice or to taste; 1 tsp. fenugreek seed powder (op); 1 tbsp. cardamom seed powder; salt and pepper to taste; 1 tab chopped cilantro/parsley.

1. Sprinkle a little salt and pepper on the chicken both sides. Simmer the chicken in a large sauté pan with ½ cup milk and ½ cup water, until soft, about 20 minutes, skin side up. Take out the chicken, when cool to handle, cut into bite-size pieces (about 1-1/2 inches).
2. Wash and dry the same pan. Heat the pan on medium heat, add 2 tbsp. oil. When oil is heated, take the pan off the heat. Add fenugreek powder, stir well, add ginger-garlic paste, stir well and put the pan back on the medium-high heat, add ½ cup water, ¼ tsp. each salt and pepper, stir well, bring to a boil, and simmer, covered for 10 minutes until reduce at least in half.
Add tomato sauce, heavy cream, sugar, lemon juice, stir well and add chicken pieces. Bring it to a boil on medium-high heat, lower the heat and simmer 10 minutes, open. Taste for seasoning: this dish should be a little sour, a little hot and a little sweet. Add seasoning as needed.
Serve right away, sprinkled with parsley or reheat for 5 minutes and serve later.

Tip: This dish is the best when whole roasted chicken breasts are used. It just melts in your mouth.

You can make extra gravy by adding more spices and half-and-half.

Chicken Kiev (Serves: 2)

Kiev is a chicken roll stuffed with creamy spinach and served with baked or boiled vegetables. Baked or boil the vegetables with their skin on. You can prepare a day ahead and take out of the refrigerator 30 minutes before baking. Reheat the vegetables with their skin on, peel and serve.

Ingredients; 2 tbsp. canola oil and 1 tbsp. butter; 2 halved, large boneless and skinless chicken breasts (I prefer Perdue); 1 pkg. 10 ounces chopped frozen spinach, thawed and squeezed out of all water; 4 ounces, ½ package cream cheese or silken tofu; ¾ cup grated parmesan cheese (divided); 1 packet or 1 tbsp. instant chicken broth; 2 tbsp. lemon-salt seasoning; salt and pepper to taste; ½ cup walnut or almond fine crumbs mixed with ¼ cup plain flour, ½ tsp. dry rosemary, ½ tsp. granulated garlic, a little fresh-ground black pepper; 2 large eggs.

Vegetables: All vegetables preferably should be the same size: 2 kiwi fruits, 2 medium tomatoes blanched and peeled; 1 Belgium endive; each baked or boiled medium 2 beets, 2 red potatoes, 2 white turnips, 1 or 2 sweet potatoes; vinaigrette mixture to pour over the vegetables: 1 tbsp. red wine vinegar; 2 tbsp. e.v. olive oil; 1 fresh garlic clove mashed; salt and fresh-ground black pepper to taste. To serve: red or white wine sauce; horseradish sour cream; garnish: pumpkin and pomegranate seeds.

1. Prepare the spinach: Heat a medium sauté pan on medium heat. Add butter and sauté the squeezed-out spinach for 5 minutes on medium high heat. On low heat add the cut-up small pieces of cream cheese or tofu. Mix well, take off the heat and then add ¼ cup grated parmesan cheese. Divide the spinach mixture in two and make 2 rolls of spinach, and refrigerate on a plate.
2. Wash and pat dry the chicken breasts. With a meat pounder, pound the chicken between two large pieces of plastic wrap to about ¼ to ½ inches thick (about 8-inches in an oval shape). Mix remaining 1/4 cup parmesan cheese and lemon-pepper seasoning and sprinkle all over on the flattened chicken breast. Place the spinach roll in the center of the pounded chicken breast, fold

the sides over the spinach then fold over other two edges on the chicken overlapping slightly if possible, making sure the spinach is covered completely with the chicken. Tie the two ends of the chicken roll with the kitchen twine, then tie the middle in two places. Do not make the rolls too tight.

3. Preheat the oven at 350 degrees.

4. Heat a medium cast-iron pan on medium heat. When hot, add the oil. Spread out the mixture (flour, nut fine crumbs, rosemary, gran. garlic and rest of the ¼ cup grated parmesan cheese) on a plate and whisk well 2 eggs with 1 tab water in a shallow bowl. Double dip the chicken rolls first in egg wash, then in crumbs mixture, then again in egg wash and in the crumbs. Brown the chicken in a hot skillet on all sides, stand the rolls on the sides and brown the sides as well. While browning the chicken, wait until it is browned completely before turning over to the other side, so that the crumbs stay on.

5. When chicken rolls are browned well on all sides, cover loosely with aluminum foil and bake in the oven for about 40-45 minutes until the chicken is done. Make a cut into the chicken to test the doneness. Let the chicken rest for 5 minutes before serving.

6. Serve the chicken Kiev in the center of a large platter and arrange the colorful vegetables all around; pour the vinaigrette over the vegetables and salad items.

7. Serve with wine sauce and horseradish sour cream on the side. Sprinkle the platter with pumpkin and pomegranate seeds if you prefer.

Tip: Pound the chicken between 2 large sheets of plastic wrap, over a cast-iron skillet placed on the thick layers of a cotton towel. It pounds fast and flattens into a large piece.

Shallow Fried Boneless Chicken
With Lemon Chutney and Strawberry Sauce
(Serves: 4)

This chicken takes a very little oil and tastes almost like deep-fry chicken. The trick is to slice into long and thin pieces and cook on high temperature in the beginning until it is browned, then cooked on very low heat so that it cooks inside.

Ingredients: 1-1/4 to 1-1/2 pound chicken tenders or boneless, skinless chicken breasts split in half lengthwise; if they are large chicken breasts then cut into three pieces lengthwise; 1-2 tbsp. canola oil or safflower oil; about ¾ tsp. granulated garlic; ½ tsp. cayenne pepper; ¼ tsp. salt or to taste; 2 tsp. grated parmesan cheese; about ½ cup pancake mix (I prefer Aunt Jemima).

1. Wash and pat dry chicken pieces and sprinkle generously all over with garlic and cayenne pepper, and set them aside.

2. In a medium bowl whip together pancake mix, ¼ tsp. granulated garlic, ¼ tsp. cayenne pepper, about 2 pinches of salt and about 1 tbsp. less ½ cup water. Sprinkle a little salt on each piece of the chicken. Dip the chicken in the batter, wipe out the excess on the rim of the bowl and line it up in a dinner plate. Sprinkle 1 tsp. of cheese on the top, all over the chicken.

3. Heat a large heavy-bottom pan or a large non-stick pan on medium heat. When pan is hot add 1 tbsp. of oil and increase the heat to medium-high. As soon as oil is very hot (the oil start moving, but not smoking), starting from the edge carefully lay down the chicken pieces, sprinkle the rest of cheese on the top, cover the pan with the lid (about ¾ covered) and cook chicken for about 1 to 1-1/2 minutes (depending on the thickness) until it is golden, then immediately lower the heat to very low and let the chicken cook, ¾ covered with the lid, for about ½ to 1 minute.

Take the pan off the heat and put it tilted against a cold burner for about 1 minute, to loosen the chicken in the bottom. Then sprinkle 3-4 drops of oil on each piece and turn over the chicken and cook ¾ covered on medium-high heat, for about 1-1/2 minutes or until golden.

Take out the chicken in a paper towel=lined platter, serve right away or keep it warm in a low-heated, turned-off oven for 15 minutes. Serve with lemon chutney and strawberry coulis, rice pilaf and a vegetable.

Strawberry Sauce

The fruit sauce goes well with almost any sweet or savory dish. I even use it as a decoration on the plate, garnish and in the fruit salad.

Ingredients: 2 pints about 4 cups washed, hulled and halved strawberries; 2-3 tbsp. orange juice; pinch of salt; 3-4 tbsp. sugar or to taste; 1 tbsp. lemon juice or to taste.

1. Save about ¼ cups of sliced strawberries. Put rest of the strawberries, lemon juice and sugar in a nonreactive medium pot and bring them to a boil. Stir well with a wooden spoon to dissolve the sugar on the low heat and cook for about 5-6 minutes. Take off the stove and leave uncovered. Cool strawberries completely.
2. Pureed them in a blender with rest of the raw strawberries, orange juice. Add salt and a little more sugar as needed.
3. Store in a nonreactive bowl, covered in the refrigerator. Last for 2-3 days. If kept frozen in a plastic container can be kept up to 2 months. Thaw overnight and serve.

Turkey and Shrimp Gumbo (S:10-12)

Ingredients: 2tbsp.flour; 8tbsp. butter; 2 cups each chopped: onion, celery, green pepper, okra, tomatoes; 2 tbsp sliced garlic cloves, ½ tsp.dry thyme; 1tsp. salt and fresh ground black pepper; 1/2cup fresh parsley; 1 pound smoked turkey sausage sliced ½-inch; 4 cups chicken stock heated; 2 pounds medium shrimp peeled and deveined (25-30 count); 2 tsp. lemon juice; 1 tsp. Worcestershire sauce; ½ tsp. cayenne pepper; 4 cups cooked plain rice.

In a heavy bottomed skillet melt butter on medium heat add flour and stir for 8-10 minutes until it turn to brown color. Add onion, celery, pepper, okra, sausage, Worcestershire sauce, tomatoes, salt and pepper, thyme, and stock. Bring to a boil, lower the heat and simmer for about 1-1/2 hours. Add parsley, lemon juice, shrimp, cayenne and simmer for 6-8 minutes until shrimps turn pink. Taste for seasoning. Serve hot over a small mound of rice.

Egg Curry with Chicken and/or Cheese (Serves: 4)

The South Indian coast of Malabar is very famous for egg curry and adding the homemade cheese (paneer) is a royal treat.

Ingredients: For the fresh curry paste: 1 tbsp. caraway seeds; 2 tbsp. coriander seeds; ¼ cup fresh garlic cloves chopped; ¼ cup fresh ginger chopped; ½ cup fresh onion chopped; 2-3 serrano (hot) peppers chopped; ½ tsp. turmeric powder; 1 tbsp. canola oil; 2 tbsp. clarified butter; salt and pepper to taste.

Other Ingredients: 1 tbsp. fresh crushed black cardamom seeds; ½ cup fine chopped soft cilantro stems; ½ cup fresh grated coconut or ¼ cup coconut powder; 4 tbsp. lemon juice; 1 cup 8 oz., (227g) tomato sauce; 1 cup heavy cream; ½ cup water; 8 hard-boiled eggs; 1 package 12 oz. (350g) browned and cubed paneer (homemade Indian cheese, made or bought). To garnish: ½ cup cooked peas or chickpeas; rice or bread, and chutney to serve.

1. In a blender, first grind caraway and coriander seeds to a powder, without any water. Add onion, garlic, ginger, fresh pepper and about ½ cup water and puree all.
2. Heat a heavy-bottom, wide sauté pan with about 2-inch sides, on medium-high heat. When hot, add oil, butter and pureed spices, turmeric and a little salt, sauté the spice mixture for 5 minutes add coconut and stir well. Cover, lower the heat and simmer, covered for 10 minutes. Open the cover, increase the heat and sauté another 5 minutes, or until the spices are cooked and the oil starts separating from the spices.
3. Add cardamom powder, tomato sauce, water and cilantro stems; bring to a boil. Lower the heat, cover and simmer on low heat for 5 minutes. Open the cover, add heavy cream and lemon juice, increase the heat to medium-high and bring to a simmer; cut the eggs in half lengthwise, add them to the pan, add cheese cubes and simmer on low, covered 5 minutes. Serve warm garnished with peas with bread, or rice and chutney.

Seafood

When you walk in a seafood store, it should not smell fishy. If this is the case, just walk right out of the store. The key to buying seafood is use a good and reputable dealer whose stock turns over quickly. Store seafood with ice in a bowl and use it within a day or two. While preparing it, wash and prepare it right. Any utensil used, even the cutting board, should be washed thoroughly. Seafood is low in calories, full of protein and has good fat, minerals and vitamin B. Uncooked and undercooked seafood can cause a lot of food-related illnesses.

Caviar

There are several varieties of fish eggs produced at farms or from the wild-caught fish. The most expensive seafood, caviar, or the roe of the sturgeon, is luxurious among seafood. They even can be more nutritious than the fish itself. Do not use the ones that are not mature as they are small and hard and less flavorful. Also do not use those that are fully matured, either. The right ones are soft, lightly salted and medium-size, just poach them slightly to give a firmer look, good taste and protein. Use them for garnishes, on toasts, on crackers and other cooked dishes.

Cooking the Fish

Fish has light protein, Omega-3 fatty acids that fight inflammation, and helps reduce the risk of a stroke. It is quick and easy to cook. Sprinkle some salt and pepper, drizzle with olive oil or canola oil, cook in a pan over high heat or place on a foil-lined baking sheet and bake at 400 degrees, or broil under the broiler about 5-6 inches away from the heat source. Just serve with lemon juice, relish, vegetables, salad or over beans, etc. In general, the fish takes about 10 minutes per one-inch of thickness. If you are using the tail part, fold the thin end underneath before cooking. Cook fish with the skin on and it will stay moist and give you healthy fish oil. You serve with or without skin on, if you have a deep-water fish like salmon.

Catfish with Celery, Fennel & Pumpkin Seed Slaw, and Herbal Sweet Potatoes (Serves: 2)

Fish is a light protein, and almost any kind of slaw gives it a very good flavor. Sweet potatoes are a plus.

(1) Celery, Fennel, and Pumpkin Seed Slaw (Serves: 2-4)

Ingredients: 2 cups heart of celery (center) sliced very thin diagonally; 1 large fennel bulb, leaves and stems removed, cored, quartered and sliced across thin into match sticks (about 2 cups); 1vtsp. lime zest; 3 to 4 tbsp. fresh lime juice; 2 tsp. champagne vinegar; 1 tsp. prepared mustard; 1 tbsp. honey; 1 tbsp. fresh mint leaves sliced thin; 5-6 tbsp. extra virgin olive oil; 2 tbsp. roasted pumpkin seeds or walnuts; ¼ cups dry cherries or cranberries; salt and pepper to taste.

In a large bowl whisk together all the ingredients, except the celery and the fennel. Place the sliced celery and the fennel on the top and refrigerate. Just before serving whisk all together and serve.

(2) Herbal Sweet Potatoes

Ingredients: 2 tbsp. canola oil or clarified butter; 1 tsp. caraway seeds; about 1 pound (2 medium) sweet potatoes peeled and cubed (or just scrubbed and cubed unpeeled) into 1-inch pieces; 1 cup chopped fine onion; salt and fresh-ground black pepper to taste; 5-6 ounce fresh baby spinach leaves stemmed, washed and pat dry; 1 tbsp. each chopped fresh: garlic cloves, thyme, oregano; ½ cup chopped cilantro leaves and soft stems; 1 tsp. lemon zest; 1 tbsp. lemon juice.

Heat a large skillet or a heavy-bottom pan on medium heat. Add oil and caraway seeds. Cook seeds for 30 seconds light brown, and move them on one side. Add the onion and stir well and cook for 8 minutes, add the cubed sweet potatoes, garlic, stir well to coat with oil or butter, sprinkle with 2 tbsp. of water, then with little salt and pepper, top with the spinach leaves, cover and cook on low heat for 20 minutes or until soft. Stir the potatoes once during the cooking. Add the fresh herbs and lemon juice and salt and pepper to taste, turn off the heat. Reheat on low again just before serving.

(3) The Catfish

Ingredients: About 1 pound, 1 thick slice of boneless and skinless catfish, washed pat dry. checked for bones, and then sliced into 2 equal pieces; 2-3 tbsp. canola oil or olive oil; 1 tsp. Tabasco-type hot sauce; a mixture of dry spices: 1 tbsp. each: granulated garlic, onion powder, light brown sugar, fresh-ground black pepper, chili powder, sweet paprika, mustard powder, grated parmesan cheese, mixed together well; ¼ cup almond flour; salt to taste.

Combine all spices, cheese, and almond flour together and spread out in a large platter. Brush the fish with the hot sauce, then press into the spice mixture on both sides. Heat a large skillet on medium-high heat. When hot, add 2 tbsp. oil, and then the fish pieces, lower the heat to medium, and cook fish until it is golden underneath. Take the pan off the heat. Sprinkle 2-3 drops of oil on the top, turn over the fish and cook golden on medium-high heat on the second side. Serve with sweet potatoes, and slaw.

Gluten-Free Seafood Ravioli (Serves: 4)

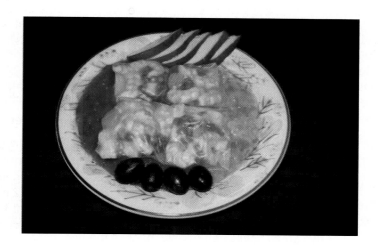

This is made with the rice pancakes. We like with the shrimp and lobster meat, and fermented beans or sauerkraut, and pickled veggies. You can use your favorite filling as you like. It is served with fruit sauce and mild salsa, with some fruits on the side.

Ingredients: 1 pound large shrimp (38-40 count) peeled, deveined; 2 tbsp. butter; 1 tbsp. chili powder, ¼ tsp. granulated garlic; 2 tbsp. lemon juice; salt and pepper to taste; 1 cup cooked frozen peas; 1 can 8oz. (227g) sliced water chestnuts drained; 1 cup drained sauerkraut; 1 bottle, 6oz. (170g) marinated artichoke hearts drained; 1 bottle, 32oz. (op) (946ml) giardiniera (mixed pickled veggies); 1 pkg. 4.5 oz. (134g) rice pancakes (rice spring roll wrappers).

Sauce Bed: 1 bottle 19 oz. (539G) Saucy Susan sauce with peach-apricot; 1 bottle, 16oz. (454G) mild tomato salsa.

Fruits to serve: 2 large Anjou pears thin-sliced, then cored; 4-5 large black grapes per person.

Heat a large sauté pan on medium heat, add butter and shrimp and sauté for 1 minute. Increase the heat to medium-high and sprinkle chili powder, garlic powder, and salt and pepper to taste. Cook shrimp constantly turning over for 3 minutes or until they turn pink. Take off the heat, sprinkle the lemon juice and place in a bowl. In the same pan add the water chestnut and the peas, just warm them on medium heat, and take out in a bowl. Up to this point you can prepare ahead or overnight and just warm again before assembling.

Prepare 4 serving plates, make half bed of fruit sauce and other half of salsa; using a plastic knife, neatly spread it out in half moons, making a circle of both.

Place some water in a shallow bowl or a dinner plate. On a cutting board place a moistened, double paper towel. Now dip the rice paper in the water on both sides, holding it with both hands drip out the water, and place it on the wet paper towel. First place in the center 3-4 shrimp, then water chestnut and peas, artichokes, 1 tbsp. pickled drained vegetables, top with 1 tbsp. sauerkraut. Shape the filling into a square. Fold the bottom (near you) first, then sides, and then the top over the other folds. Pick up the ravioli and place over the sauce bed, in the serving plates. Make 4 ravioli per person. Serve with sliced pears and black grapes immediately.

Coconut Fish with Coconut Rice (Serves: 2)

This recipe is from South India, where coconut grows all over. People do wonders with coconut being a part of their daily life.

For the Fish: About 1-1/2 pound boneless, skinless, haddock or cod or any other firm-flesh fish; 1 tsp. canola oil and 2 tbsp. butter; ½ cup grated onion, 2 tbsp. grated ginger; 1 tbsp. grated garlic cloves; ½ cup to ¾ cup fresh grated or frozen and thawed coconut; ¼ tsp. turmeric powder (op); 1 tsp. sugar; ½ tsp. fresh-ground cardamom seeds; salt and pepper to taste; 1can, 13.5 ounces unsweetened coconut milk, divided. To serve: some fruits and snow peas blanched for 3 minutes in boiling water, drained and tossed with butter and a little salt and pepper.

For the Coconut Rice: In a medium pot soak: ½ cup basmati, Jasmin or long-grain rice, in ½ cup water and ½ cup whole milk, for ½ hour; 1 tbsp. butter plus extra for the bowls; ½ tsp sugar; pinch of salt.

1. **For the Rice:** Place the soaking rice and the liquid pot over the medium-high heat, bring it to a boil. Add the butter, reduce the heat to low and cook rice until it is done, for about 15 minutes. Turn off the heat. Just before serving add the coconut milk, sugar and pinch of salt, and heat on low and serve. Butter two small bowls generously, pack in the rice, cover with foil and set aside. When ready to serve, turn over the bowl, run a little hot water on the bottom, then move a knife around the inside edge of the bowl to loosen the rice, and just invert onto the serving plate.

2. **For the Fish:** Heat a heavy-bottom frying pan on medium heat. Add the oil and the butter, move around and coat the pan; add grated onion, ginger, garlic, turmeric, a little salt and pepper and stir 1 minute; add on the top the grated coconut, cover and cook on low heat for 5 minutes. Open the cover and stir, move the mixture on one side of the pan. Add the fish and cook flesh side down for 2 minutes, on low heat, turn over the fish and add cardamom, 1 cup coconut milk, and the sugar, stir all around the fish. Simmer the fish in simmering liquid for 10 minutes open. Turn off the heat. Keep covered. When ready to serve, reheat the fish on low heat.

3. Serve fish topped with the sauce, with coconut rice, snow peas and fruits.

Lobster and Shrimp Curry (Serves: 4-6)

This is one of the traditional prawn curry found mostly in South India, which is surrounded by the ocean. I have added lobster tails and made with the jumbo shrimp. This is a feast that is made for special occasions.

Ingredients: 2 lobster tails, about 8 ounces; 1 pound jumbo shrimp, peeled, deveined and tail left on; 1 tsp. each cayenne pepper. granulated garlic and 1 tbsp. lemon juice; fresh-ground spice mixture: 2 tbsp. coriander seeds, 1 tbsp. cardamom seeds, 1 tbsp. caraway seeds, ground together in a blender first, then chopped and add: 2 cup onion, 1/3 cup garlic cloves, ¼ cup serrano peppers or to taste, ¼ cup ginger, 1/3 cup cilantro stems all pureed in about ½ cup water grind all together and set aside; about 7 tbsp. canola oil, divided; 1 tsp. turmeric; 1/3 cup lemon juice; 3 tbsp. tomato paste; 1/2Tsp. cayenne pepper or to taste; salt to taste, lemon juice to squeeze before serving. To garnish: about ½ cup chopped sliced green onion and tomatoes. To serve: rice, or bread, chutney and raita.

1. Place the shrimp in a platter and sprinkle cayenne, granulated garlic, pinch of salt, and then with 1 tbsp. lemon juice; set aside in room temperature to marinate. Tie the two lobster tails together on the wider side with a thick rubber band or kitchen twine. Bring a medium pot half full of water, with a pinch of salt, to a boil. Add the lobster tail, cover and cook for 7 minutes on medium heat on constant simmer. When the lobster tails have changed their color, take them out of the water and let them cool. When they are cooled enough to handle, cut the shell lengthwise on both side, peel off the shells and the membrane underneath, and take out the meat.

2. Heat a large and a heavy-bottom non-reactive pan on medium heat. Add the 6 tbsp. oil and fresh-ground spices; cook spices, stirring for 1 minute, cover with the lid and let it cook for 15 minutes, stirring occasionally. Open the cover, add turmeric, 1/3 cup lemon juice, tomato paste, and about ½ tsp. salt and pepper or to taste; stir, cover and cook another 5 minutes on low heat. Move over the spices on one side, add 1 tbsp. oil in the pan, and cook shrimp for 3 minutes until they turn pink underneath; turn the shrimp over, add the lobster tails and then top with the cooked spices. Stir a little just to warm the meat. Cover with the lid, and turn off the heat. Serve warm, squeezed

with lemon juice and garnished with tomatoes and green onions. Serve with rice or bread, chutney, and raita on the side.

Tips:

1. This dish should be hot and spicy. If you prefer, instead of tomato paste, add 1 cup of tomato sauce to give more liquid.

2. Cook shrimp only on one side, turn them over, stir 2-3 times, turn off the heat, cover, let it stand 1 minute and serve warm sprinkled with lemon juice.

3. Cayenne pepper has a substance called, 'capsaicin,' works as a pain reliever for arthritis, headaches, and other chronic problems. According to experts capsaicin inhibits the release of P-protein, which interrupts the transmission of pain signals to the brain. We also use garlic, turmeric and cayenne to cure the food such as seafood and chicken etc. Even a small amount of cayenne pepper, about one sixth of the teaspoon can give you health benefits. Drink milk to calm down the effect of the chili pepper. Caseins in milk blocks the heat of the chili pepper.

Lemon and Pecan Mackerel over Red Pepper Sauce and Celery Root Puree

(Serves: 2)

According to experts, salmon, mackerel and tuna are high in Omega-3 fatty acids. You can substitute any firm-flesh fish here. This red, white and green dish is nutritious and attractive.

(1) For the Pepper Sauce (M: about 2 cups)

Ingredients: 2 large bell peppers, one red and one orange, cut in half, take out seeds, rub outside with oil; 1 large onion peeled and cut into 1-inch thick slices and drizzled with little oil; bake on a sheet at 400 degrees for 15-20 minutes until charred lightly; put in a bowl, cover, then peel and seed the peppers; 1 fresh garlic clove, 1 tsp. cider vinegar; 4 tbsp. olive oil; salt and pepper to taste.

Puree all ingredients in a blender then slowly pour the olive oil while machine is running and mix just until thick. Add salt and pepper to taste by hand.

(2) Celery Root Puree (M: about 2 cups)

Ingredients: 1 medium, about 1 to 1-1/4 pound celery root, washed, cut in half, peeled, and then cut into 1-inch cubes; about ¾ cup low fat milk; 3 tbsp. butter; ¼ cup grated cheese; salt and pepper to taste; ½ cup chopped green onion.

Put the celery root cubes in a pot, cover a half-inch over with water. Bring it to a boil for 5 minutes, stir well, cover with the lid, lower the heat and simmer on low until it is fork-tender, about 25-30 minutes. Drain, add 2 tbsp. butter, cheese, milk, a little salt and pepper to taste, and puree in the blender or with the potato masher. Serve with butter, just mix in on the top and sprinkle the green onion all over the fish and puree.

(3) For the Fish

Ingredients: 1 pound boneless, skinless mackerel; 2 tbsp. fresh lemon juice; 1 cup shelled but unroasted pecans crushed fine and mixed with ½ tsp. garlic powder, ½ tsp. fresh crushed black pepper, and 1 tsp. lemon zest; salt and pepper to taste; 2 tbsp. melted unsalted butter or cooking butter spray.

Preheat the oven at 350 degrees. Wash and pat dry the fish and check for the bones by moving the finger all over. Spread out the pecan mixture on a platter evenly. Drizzle the lemon juice all over the fish and press down both sides in the pecan mixture. Place the fish on a piece of the parchment paper or greased aluminum foil; drizzle the melted butter or use the butter spray. Bake the fish in the center of a preheated oven, until it turns opaque, about 12 minutes. To serve, place the red pepper sauce all over the plate, place in the center the celery root puree, spread out a little larger than the fish piece; top with the fish and sprinkle with the green onion.

Roasted Pomfret (Serves: 4)

This recipe is very popular at the coastal area in India. In Bengal, it is cooked with mustard oil and in South India, it is cooked with tamarind. You can also wrap with banana leaves and secure with toothpicks and cook on a griddle, or just bake in the oven.

Ingredients: About 2 to 2-1/2 pounds whole pomfret or butterfish scaled, gutted, head and fins cut off, then washed under running water and pat dry; for the rub: 2 tbsp. mustard oil or canola oil mixed with 1 tbsp. dry mustard, 1 tsp. lemon zest, 3 tbsp. lemon juice, 1 tsp. turmeric, 1 tsp. fresh crushed garlic cloves, mixed all together; for spice mixture: 1 tbsp. cardamom seeds ground fine, 1 tbsp. madras curry powder, 2 tbsp. crushed black peppercorns, 1 tsp. sugar, ½ tsp. cinnamon powder, 1 tsp. fennel seed ground fine, 2 tbsp. tamarind pulp, ½ tsp. salt or to taste, 1 lemon sliced paper thin. To serve: quinoa or rice pilaf and chutney.

Spread out 1 tsp. of the rub inside the fish, then rub the remaining mustard mixture all over the fish, and set aside for 15 minutes. Preheat oven at 350 degrees.

Combine the spice mixture, make 3-4 slashes across on the body of the fish, then rub the fish with tamarind paste, and sprinkle the spice mixture all over; place 4-5 lemon slices inside the fish. Place the fish in a large banana leaf and seal with toothpicks, or in the aluminum foil; fold and seal the foil airtight, then place in a baking tray and bake in a preheated oven for about 10 to 12 minutes until opaque. Serve with pilaf and chutney.

Roasted Tile Fish with Black Beans (Serves: 2-4)

You do not find this fish very often in the market. We bread it and then roast it on a wire rack. Beans can be cooked a day ahead and reheated just before serving. You can make a salad ahead and leave in the refrigerator without adding any salt and citrus. Same with the quinoa cakes: make ahead and reheat before serving.

Ingredients for the Black Beans: 1bag 16oz. (454g) black turtle beans (frijoles negros) picked over and soaked overnight; 2 tbsp. olive oil; 2 bay leaves;1 cup each chopped: onion, celery, and carrot; 1 bottle 16 oz. (454g) mild or hot tomato salsa (or make your own); 1 cup cooked and chopped Taylor ham (brown ham for 5 minutes on medium heat, and chop in ½-inch cubes); 16 oz. beef broth; salt and pepper to taste; to garnish: grated cheese and cilantro.

For the Fish: 4 pieces, about 1-1/2 to 2 pounds tile fish fillets, 1 tsp.each: lemon-pepper mix (Mrs. Dash); granulated garlic; cayenne or black pepper (divided); ½ cup corn or rice flour; 1 cup panko bread crumbs;

½ cup grated parmesan cheese; salt and pepper to taste. Cooking spray or olive oil to sprinkle. To serve: black beans or salad, and quinoa cakes with chutney.

For the Beans: Heat a heavy-bottom medium pot, add oil, and bay leaves and brown the leaves. Add onion, and cook for 5 minutes. Add carrots and celery and stir for 6-8 minutes and cook until soft. Now add the drained beans and mix well. Add beef broth and water to come up to about 2 inches higher than the beans. Bring to a boil, then lower the heat to a constant simmer and cook for 90 minutes or until beans are soft. Add the salsa, bring to a boil, and cook for 10 minutes; add ham and cook for 5 minutes or until heated through. Check for seasoning. Serve garnished with cheese and cilantro.

Heat the oven to 400 degrees. Spray a cooling rack that fits in a baking tray with sides, (rack is for heat to circulate). Pound the fish pieces slightly between two pieces of the plastic wrap, just to make them thinner, but do not break them. Sprinkle the fish with half of the spices and set aside for 10 minutes.

On a platter, combine flour, the rest of the spices and panko bread crumbs. Press down and dredge the fish pieces in the mixture, then spray with cooking spray or drizzle lightly with olive oil on both sides. Place the pieces carefully on the wire rack with a spatula and roast in a preheated oven for about 10 minutes. Turn off the oven and let the tray sit in the oven for another 2-3 minutes. Serve warm with beans or salad, quinoa cakes and chutney.

Tip: You can make fish sticks and use almost any kind of fish, just adjust the timing according to the thickness of the fish (1-inch of thickness will take about 9-10 minutes to cook with the crust on).

Steamed Fish with Fermented Beans, Grilled Honey Dew Melon & Papaya Salad, and Orange-pineapple Sauce (Serves: 2-4)

This colorful dinner is light, tasty and healthy. The only thing you have to prepare is the sauce (make one day ahead) and the fish, which will take about 10 minutes per inch of thickness. Always buy the fish with skin on. It cooks perfect and keeps the fish moist. Grill the fruits a day ahead but do not add any salt; refrigerate covered. The fermented beans are available at Asian grocery stores. Fermented beans can be served without cooking. They are salty, so if you prefer, you can serve them with a regular can of black beans; drain, wash and just sauté them in a little butter to heat them.

Ingredients: 1 to 1-1/2 pounds of salmon filet or any other firm-flesh fish such as cod, haddock etc.; ½ tsp. each: dry thyme and no-salt lemon-pepper mix (I Prefer Mrs. Dash) 1-2 tsp. olive oil; 1 cup per person fresh baby arugula; one small can fermented beans drained and/or 1 can 10.5 ounces (297g) premium black beans, washed and drained, then sauté in 1 tbsp. unsalted butter just to heat; to serve: honey dew and papaya salad; pineapple and orange sauce (see below).

Orange-pineapple Sauce (M: about 1-3/4 cups)

Ingredients: 1-1/2 cups pineapple juice (take out the juice from the fresh pineapple or buy one can 20 ounces (1lb. 4 oz.), 567g crushed pineapple. Place a double paper towel in a bowl, pour the crushed pineapple in the paper towel, bring together all the four corners, make a ball, and squeeze out the juice in the bowl (save the pulp for the cakes etc.); 1 tbsp. butter; ¼ cup each diced onion and fresh mushrooms; 2 pinches of granulated garlic; 1 cup frozen, concentrated, thawed, orange juice; 2 tbsp. ketchup; 2 tbsp. corn starch; 2 pinches of salt and pepper or to taste.

Heat a large, heavy-bottom sauté pan on medium heat. Add butter and onion, sprinkle with garlic and salt and pepper, sauté for 5 minutes, then add the mushroom and cook until the liquid has evaporated. Whip together the pineapple juice with ketchup, and corn starch and add to the pan. Increase the heat and whisk until it comes to a boil and thickens. Add the orange juice and salt and pepper to taste, lower the heat and simmer for 5-8 minutes or until bubbly. Turn off the heat and keep the sauce covered and stir every now and then, as needed, or pour in a jar and refrigerate overnight and reheat again in the pan or microwave oven; strain the heated sauce or just serve as it is.

Grilled Honey Dew Melon and Papaya Salad

Ingredients: 1 medium honeydew melon; 1 medium ripe papaya; 1tbsp. olive oil to brush the fruits before grilling; little salt to sprinkle for grilling; juice of 1 lemon; about ½ cup dry cranberries.

Cut the melon in quarter or cut in half and slice each half into 3 pieces. Scoop out the seeds, Move a knife underneath the pulp, above the rind, go all around each piece and take out the melon pulp in one piece. Brush the melon on the skin side lightly with oil, sprinkle on the top with a pinch of salt on each piece and grill on medium heat skin side down, grill just to mark the grill mark about 5-8 minutes. Do the same with the papaya. When grilled, cut the fruits in 1-1/2-inch cubes, sprinkle with the lemon juice and a little salt to taste, serve top with dry cranberries.

For the Fish: Heat the steamer, or place the steaming basket in a pot, or use a large strainer, place the fish in the strainer, over the boiling water in a pot, do not let the strainer touch the water, and cover airtight with a double aluminum foil. First, wash the fish, pat dry with the paper towel, check out for the bones, and pull out the bones with the tweezers, sprinkle with thyme, lemon-pepper mix, then drizzle a few drops of oil. Place in the steamer, cover airtight with the lid or the foil, and cook over boiling water for about 10 minutes per inch of thickness. Take the pot off the heat, but leave it covered for 5 minutes, then open the lid away from you. Remove the fish skin, cut and serve sprinkled with a little more salt and pepper and lemon-pepper mix.

Assemble the Platter: Place the arugula on the heated plates, top with the beans and fish, then top with the fruit salad; drizzle the sauce all over and serve.

Blackened Flounder or Catfish with Papaya Slaw, over Hummus and Peas

(Serves: 2)

You can blacken the fish just with the spices. That's what we prefer, to stay away from dangerous substances. Or you can char the fish over the flames. Either way the fish is blackened. I use thin fillets of fish such as flounder, or whiting. They are easy to char. This is very healthy and attractive platter.

Ingredients:

For the Peas: 2 tbsp. butter; 1 pkg. 10 oz. frozen peas.

For the Papaya Slaw: 2 cups, peeled, seeded and julienned, half-way ripened yellow papaya; about 8-10 grape tomatoes halved; 1 tbsp. fresh lemon juice; 2 tbsp. orange juice; 2 tbsp. extra virgin olive oil; to garnish: ½ cup dry cranberries; 2 tbsp. green onion sliced; salt and fresh-ground black or white pepper to taste.

For the Fish: 2 fillets, about 1 to 1-1/4 pound of flounder or Lemon Sole; about 4 tbsp. lemon herb mix; 1 tbsp. cumin power; 1-2 tbsp. fresh-ground black pepper or to taste; 1 tbsp. light brown sugar; 1 tbsp. each dry: oregano, basil and thyme; ½ cup melted butter; salt to taste; ½ cup to 1 cup hummus (chickpea spread).

1. **Peas:** Heat a large, heavy-bottom sauté pan on medium heat. Add the butter and let the butter bubble for 3-4 minutes until it turn light brown. Add the peas, stir with a spatula and cook for 5 minutes, or until the peas are soft. Turn off the heat and leave them partially covered in the pan. Reheat them just before serving.

2. **Papaya Slaw:** In a non-reactive, medium bowl, mix together papaya, tomatoes and chill them together. Just before serving toss in lemon and orange juices then olive oil. Garnish with cranberries and the green onion. Serve the slaw in the serving plates and sprinkle a little salt and pepper.

3. **For the Flounder:** Marinate the flounder with lemon-herb mix, rub it all over, on both sides of the fillets, set aside for 10 minutes. Heat an indoor grill or a cast-iron skillet, on medium-high heat. Just before cooking, grease it well. If you are using the outdoor grill, use the fish rack.

   Combine all remaining spices together and spread out on a platter. Dip the fish in the butter then press down in the spices. Place the fish carefully on the grill or skillet. Cook the founder only about 4-5 minutes on the direct heat, or until it is blackened or charred. Turn over and cook the other side if needed.

Tip: I cook thin fish only on one side, until it is charred, or blackened, to avoid the cancerous substances. Flounder cooks in about 4 minutes. on high heat. There is no need to turn it over. Catfish will take about 8 minutes, and turn it over after 2-3 minutes.

To Assemble the platter: Before you start cooking, arrange some salad ingredients such as papaya, bell peppers or small sweet colorful peppers, radishes, green onion, and cherries on one side of the platter in an attractive fashion. Then place the hummus, peas on the other side, and top with the fish, sprinkle with salt and pepper, to taste. Pile some papaya slaw on one end of the fish. Serve immediately.

Lobster Roll (Serves: 2)

Don't forget to get the soft rolls such as brioche or potato rolls. Soft rolls go well with the tender lobster. If you wish, you can just heat them in the oven or brush them with soft butter and heat them in the pan before using.

Ingredients: 2 lobster tails cooked for about 6-7 minutes until they turn red, then cut the shell and take out the meat, and peel off the thin membrane from over the meat, then sprinkled with 1 tbsp. fresh lemon juice. You can also use cooked lobster meat from two lobsters, each weighing about one pound each (1 pound lobster takes about 7 minutes in boiling water until it turns red). 2 brioche or potato rolls; for the dressing: ¾ cup light mayonnaise mixed with ¼ cup diced celery, ½ tsp. lemon zest, 2 tbsp. lemon juice, 2 tbsp. diced cucumber pickles, 2 tbsp. chives or capers, and salt and pepper to taste; to serve: grilled corn, salad, and horseradish cream.

Heat the buns with or without the butter inside out. While the lobster is still warm sprinkle with the lemon juice (or heat the lobster meat on low heat in some butter, then sprinkle with the lemon juice. Make the dressing, save a third for the buns and mix two-thirds with the lobster meat. Spread the dressing inside the rolls, then place half of the lobster salad in each bun. Immediately serve the rolls with horseradish and the salad.

Mango Fish (Serves: 4)

This is a green and sour mango fish, which is prepared with green mango chutney. You can use this chutney with the potatoes, rice, chicken, etc. Green mangoes are found in Indian grocery stores mostly. But now, you can buy at some of the supermarkets. Here you cook fish one minute on each side, then place the thick chutney on the top and cook on high heat fast, then and serve.

(1) Green Mango Chutney (M: about 3 cups)

Ingredients: 1 large green mango (about ¾ pound); 1 tsp. canola oil; 1 cup canned chickpeas washed and drained; 2 cup packed cilantro soft stems and leaves chopped; 4 large garlic cloves chopped; 2-3 serrano peppers or 1 jalapeno, seeded and chopped; 1 tsp. sugar or to taste; 1/4cup lemon juice or to taste; salt and pepper to taste.

Preheat oven at 350 degrees. Wash and dry the mango, then rub all around with oil, wrap in the aluminum foil and bake in a pie plate, for about 75 minutes or until soft. Cool the mango, then peel and slice off all the pulp and juices.

In a blender, place garlic, cilantro, chopped peppers, chickpeas, mango pulp and juices, sugar, about ½ tsp. salt and pepper to taste, and about ¼ cup to 1/3cup lemon juice as needed. Puree all together. Taste for the seasoning and add more salt and pepper as needed. Pour in a non-reactive bowl and refrigerate until needed. You can make this chutney a day ahead. Chutney will last in the refrigerator for 6-7 days and frozen for up to two months.

(2) Mango Fish

The key here is the green Mango should be sour, if not add some lemon juice.

Ingredients: 4-5 tbsp. canola oil; ½ of the recipe of green mango chutney mixed with 2Tbsp. lemon juice; ¼ cup all-purpose flour; 2 pounds salmon or cod fillet (or any firm-flesh fish); 1 tbsp. fresh-ground black pepper or to taste; ½ tsp. salt or to taste; ½ tsp. granulated garlic; ½ tsp. turmeric (op).

Wash, pat dry fish and check for the bones. Heat a large heavy-bottom pan on medium heat. Cut the fish in 4 serving portions. Sprinkle the fish with little salt and pepper then dip in the flour and shake out extra flour.

When the pan is heated, add 1 tbsp. oil and brown the fish, on high heat, first flesh down, then on the skin side just for 1 minute each side; take it out of the pan, keep tented with the foil. Add 1 tbsp. oil in the pan and the chutney and reduce it on high heat for 6-8 minutes until it is very thick. Take the pan off the heat.

Just before serving, with the spatula place the chutney on the fish on the flesh side. Now add 1 tbsp. oil in the same pan, over medium heat, place the fish with skin side down and chutney side up, cook for 1 minute. Sprinkle 1-2 tbsp. oil over the chutney, and carefully turn over the fish- the chutney side down, cook on high heat for about 1-2 minutes (a little skin will form over the chutney and it will turn brown) and fish will turn opaque. Take the fish out of the pan sprinkle with some lemon juice all over, and serve immediately.

Steamed Red Snapper in the Wine Sauce (Serves: 2)

Steamed fish is tasty when it is served with a good sauce. This wine sauce and other accompaniments are not only tasty, but are very attractive.

(1) Wine Sauce (M: ¾ cups)

Ingredients: 1 tsp. canola oil. 6 tbsp. butter, divided; ½ cup chopped shallots; 1 tsp. fresh thyme; 1 tsp. orange zest; 4 tbsp. fresh orange juice, 4 tbsp. lemon juice; 1c up white wine; 2 tbsp. fish sauce or chicken broth; ¼ tsp. salt and fresh-ground black pepper.

In a heavy-bottom large frying pan, heat oil and 1tbsp. butter and sauté the shallot on medium heat, for 6-8 minutes until soft. Add wine, lemon juice, orange juice, zest, thyme and salt and pepper. Bing to a boil, reduce the heat and simmer open for 20 minutes until sauce is reduced to ¾ cup. Take off the heat and whisk in the butter 1 tablespoon at a time. Keep covered until needed.

(2) For the Fish

Ingredients: 1 pound, one long fillet piece of red snapper; ¼ tsp. granulated garlic; 1tsp. Old Bay seasoning or lemon-pepper mix; marinated cucumber: 1 Kirby cucumber thin-sliced and added to a mixture of, 2 tbsp. cider vinegar, 3 tbsp. e.v. olive oil, ½ tsp. each salt and fresh ground black pepper or to taste; to serve: 1-2 radishes thin sliced; lemon wedges.

1. Check out for the bones, and sprinkle fish fillets with salt, pepper and garlic. Steam the fish in a steamer per manufacture's direction. You can also use a metal steaming basket in a large pot. Fill the pot about 2-inch deep with boiling water. Place the fish in the basket over a parchment paper, cover and let it steam for about 10 minutes or until fish is done.
2. Just before serving, heat the wine sauce on medium heat. Place the fish in the sauce and heat on low, until it is warmed through.
3. Place the fish in a warm serving platter. Trim off the fish from all around to make it look like a whole fish. Pour the wine sauce all around. Then place two of the trimmings at the tail. Place black sesame seeds or small olive for the eye. Decorate the body with the marinated cucumber. Sprinkle with the Old Bay seasoning and black pepper. Serve with radish and lemon wedges.

Quick and Easy Salmon Meal (Serves: 2)

This dish is quick, easy, tasty, healthy and very colorful. You can use any other firm-flesh fish, such as cod, halibut, snapper etc. We are crazy about salmon, as advised by our physician. It is deep-water fish and has less mercury.

Ingredients: 1 medium zucchini cut into 2x1/4-inch strips (cut zucchini in quarter lengthwise, take out the center pulp, leaving about ½-inch skin and flesh together, then slice into strips. Slice and cook the center pulp into thin strips); 1 red and 1 yellow bell peppers, cored and cut into 2x1/2-inch strips; 1 lemon cut across into two pieces; 1 pint cherry or grape tomatoes; about 1 pound boneless salmon with skin on and checked over for the bones; ½ tsp. each: garlic powder, onion powder, paprika, salt and fresh-ground black pepper, seafood seasoning mix or Old Bay seasoning mix; olive oil to sprinkle; thyme sprigs to garnish (op).

Preheat the oven at 450 degrees. Grease a 9x12-inch platter with olive oil. Layer the platter with zucchini, peppers strips, place the lemons on the corners. Cut the salmon across into two steaks and place over the vegetables in the center, then place the tomatoes around the fish. Sprinkle garlic, onion, salt and pepper all over the vegetables. Sprinkle paprika and seafood seasoning over the fish; sprinkle platter generously with olive oil. Place the platter in the oven, reduce the temperature to 400 degrees and roast for about 15 minutes, until fish is opaque. Serve on heated platters, placing the fish over the vegetables. Sprinkle fish with salt and pepper to taste, garnish with thyme sprigs and serve immediately.

Tip: Cooking fish with skin on keeps it very moist. Fried salmon skin is a delicacy in some Asian cuisines.

Swordfish with Pepper Relish, Beets Greens, and Sweet Potatoes
(Serves: 2)

The best part of this meal is that you can almost cook everything a day ahead; just cook the fish before serving. Swordfish is like meat, so you can use spices and relish both. Back in '80s, we (me, my boss, his boss and his secretary) used to go to a restaurant called "Don's 21" in Newark, N.J., right behind our bank. Very often we ordered this famous dish. It was so good, it just melted in your mouth.

Ingredients: 1 tsp. canola oil; 3 tbsp. butter; 1 to 1-1/4 pound swordfish, about 1-inch thick, and no blood line going through; 2 tbsp. pickling spices; 2tbsp. pumpkin seeds; salt and fresh-ground black pepper to taste; vine-ripe cherry tomatoes; 1 large sweet potato (about ¼ pound); about 1 tbsp. butter; 2 tbsp. honey; and cinnamon to sprinkle.
To serve: beets greens (see instruction under vegetables); pepper relish (see instruction under relishes).

1. Heat beets greens in a sauté pan and keep them warm.

2. **For the Sweet Potatoes:** Wash the potato, pierce with the point of the knife 4-5 places, about ½-inch deep, and bake in the microwave oven 1-2 minutes at a time, a total of 5 minutes until soft. Or bake in the oven, at 350 degrees, for about 45 minutes. Or reheat again if cooked earlier. Just before serving slice thick, place on the warm serving platters, drizzle with butter, then with the honey, and sprinkle with cinnamon. While fish is cooking, make the platters, place the greens and sweet potatoes.

3. **For the Fish:** Heat a large cast-iron pan on medium-high heat. On a platter, spread out the pickling spices and then pumpkin seeds on the top. Check out for bones and then wash the fish; press down the spices on one side only. When the pan is hot, add oil and coat the pan, then add the butter. Carefully place the fish in the pan, spice side down. Let it cook for 4-5 minutes until it is golden brown. Take the pan off the heat, let it rest 1 minute and then use 2 metal spatulas to turn over the fish, keeping the spices intact. Cook fish on medium-high heat for another 4-5 minutes. The total cooking time will be about 8 minutes. Immediately take out the fish and place on the serving platters.

4. Place the tomatoes in the hot pan, drizzle with some oil and cook on very low for about 1 minute. Sprinkle fish with salt and pepper, and pour any butter from the pan and serve with pepper jelly; place the tomatoes carefully on the serving plates and serve immediately.

Tilapia or Cod with the American Flag (Serves: 4)

My older sister Saroj and her husband taught at a military school (Sainik School). He was the head of the Physics Department. Whenever they entertained their friends on a patriotic day, my sister made rice pudding with an Indian flag on the top. People loved it. So I started making American flag every now and then for special occasions. The base of the flag is made with cauliflower puree, topped with roasted red bell pepper strips from the jar, and halved purple grapes are topped with toasted sesame seeds for the stars.

1.   American Flag

Ingredients: 1 tbsp. canola oil; 1 large cauliflower; ½ cup heavy cream; 2 tbsp. lemon juice mixed with 2 tbsp. olive oil to sprinkle; 1 cup purple grapes; about 1 cup roasted red bell pepper strips from the jar bought (or roast red bell pepper and cut out in thin strips); about 2 tbsp. white sesame seeds roasted for 5 minutes in dry pan.

Cut cauliflower in half, take out the core, slice the stems very thin, and cut the florets into 2-inch pieces. Heat a cast-iron pan, on medium heat, add 1 tbsp. oil and sauté the stems 5 minutes; add the florets and sauté another 5 minutes, sprinkle with 2 tbsp. water, cover, bring to a boil. Lower the heat to a simmer and cook for about 10-15 minutes. Stir once during the cooking. When cauliflower is little soft, puree in the blender with heavy cream. If needed, add another 3-4 tbsp. milk.

Take out the puree and spread out in 4 dark serving plates in 5x3-1/2-inch rectangle on one side of the plate. Even out all edges with a knife. Chill for 1 hour until it is firm. Take out and drain about 1 cup of the red pepper strips and place them on double paper towels. Now pick up one strip at a time and trim them with a scissor, if necessary, and lay them down from the bottom of the flag over the puree with the help of a fork and a pointed knife. Lay down 4 strips, up to almost halfway of the flag, then cut and take out top left corner in square with a knife. Place another 3 short strips up to the top. So you will have 7 red pepper strips. Now slice the grapes in half and cover the corner square, sprinkle a little water over the grapes, then sprinkle the sesame seeds for the stars; place some sesame seeds on the outer edge of

244

the grapes for the border. Refrigerate for 3-4 hours until you are ready to serve the dinner. Sprinkle the oil and lemon juice mixture over the flag, sprinkle a little salt and serve with the fish.

2.   Orange-Hoisin Glaze (M:3/4 cups)

Ingredients: 1 Cup frozen concentrated orange juice thawed; 3 tbsp. lime juice; 1 level tablespoon thick hoisin sauce; 2 tsp. ketchup; sprinkle of salt and pepper or to taste.
In an non-reactive or a stainless steel pan combine all ingredients, bring to a boil, and simmer on medium-high heat, bubbling for about 10 minutes, or until it is thickened and reduced to ¾ cup. Pour in a serving boat, leave in the room temperature covered until serving.

3.   Tilapia or Cod Fish

Ingredients: 1 tbsp. canola or olive oil and 3-4 tbsp. butter; 4 pieces, totaling about 2 pounds, boneless, skinless tilapia or cod fillets; sprinkle of garlic powder and fresh-ground black pepper; about 4tbsp. Dijon type mustard; crumb mixture: ½ cup fine cornmeal, ½ cup almond flour, ¼ cup grated cheese from the bottle, 2-3 tbsps. lemon-pepper mix (dash); to serve: 2 slices, about 1-inch thick each of watermelon and cut out 8 small stars from the cookie cutter; to garnish: herbs or sliced scallion.

Pat dry the fish with the paper towel. Check out for bones by moving the finger all over the fish. Sprinkle the fish with garlic powder and black pepper, then brush both side with the Dijon mustard. Dip each piece of the fish in the crumb mixture on both sides. Heat a large, heavy-bottom pan on medium-high heat. When hot add oil, coat the bottom and then add the butter. Lay down the fish in the pan and cook about 3 minute on each side or until it is browned and flakes easily.
Assemble the Platters: Take out the serving plates from the refrigerator ½-an hour before serving. When fish is cooked place it on the plates, drizzle with the glaze, garnish the fish with herb, place the melon stars opposite to flag and serve with extra glaze on the side.

Lobster in Cream Sauce (Serves: 4)

This is an easy and a tasty dish. Once you eat lobster in cream sauce over buttery angel hair pasta, linguini or with the rice pilaf on the side, you will cook this dish over and over again.

Ingredients: 2-3 tbsp. unsalted butter (divided); ¼ cup minced onion; ¼ tsp. granulated garlic; 1-1/2 to 2 pounds of cooked lobster meat (buy at the supermarket or fish store); 1 cup peeled and fine chopped plum tomatoes; ½ cup good white wine; 1 cup heavy cream; ½ tsp. fine-grated lemon zest; 1 tsp. lemon juice; ¼ cup fine-ground peeled almonds; sea salt to taste; ¼ tsp. white pepper or to taste; garnish with 1 tsp. fresh thyme, parsley or chives.

1.   Heat a heavy-bottom, non-reactive, large pan on medium heat. When heated add 1 tbsp. butter and onion, and a little salt and garlic powder. Stir well and cook the onion until soft about 5 minutes. Add wine and the heavy cream, bring to a boil, lower the heat to medium, and cook on constant simmer until it is reduced by a quarter. Add the minced tomatoes, almonds and simmer until reduced another quarter, about 5 minutes on medium-high heat. Turn off and take off the heat until ready to serve.
2.   Heat the sauce on low heat, add the zest, lemon juice, 1 tbsp. butter, white pepper, salt to taste. When the sauce is heated through for about 5 minutes, add the lobster meat, stir for 2-3 minutes or until the meat is heated through and is coated with sauce. Serve in a pretty dish sprinkled with chopped fresh thyme or parsley or chives.

Note: Cook pasta al dente per package direction. Do not add any oil or butter (the sauce will not stick to the pasta). Just add some sauce from the lobster (for extra sauce: add ¼ cup heated cream), salt, pepper, mix well, then add 1 to 2 tabs of butter in the warm pasta, and serve the creamy lobster over the pasta.

Scallops in Cream Sauce (Serves: 2)

You can use bay scallops in this recipe, but the large sea scallops are the best. They just melt in your mouth.

Ingredients: ½ tsp. olive oil just to grease the pan; ½ pound about 8 sea scallops, touch mussels removed on the side; ¼ cup white wine (op); 2 medium plum tomatoes peeled, seeds removed and diced; ¼ tsp. each granulated garlic; sprinkle of fresh-ground black or white pepper to taste;1 tbsp. lemon juice; 1 packet about 1 tbsp. instant chicken broth; ¼ tsp. Old Bay seasoning or 1/4tsp. dry thyme.

Heat a large heavy-bottom, nonreactive sauté pan on medium heat. Add oil and move around with a piece of paper towel to grease the bottom and wipe out the excess. Place the scallops cut side down in the pan and cook golden brown for about 1-1/2 to 2 minutes. Off the heat add the wine, and let the wine evaporate for 30 seconds.

Take out the scallops from the pan in to a plate, and add tomatoes, lemon juice, chicken broth and pepper and bring to a boil. Add the scallops in the liquid, the uncooked side down. Simmer on low for 5 minutes and taste for seasoning. Serve sprinkled with Old Bay seasoning or dry thyme in a bowl and with pasta, rice, or salad on the side.

Scallops in Almond and Orange Sauce (Serves: 2 to 4)

This is my favorite dish. It is loaded with protein and vitamin C.

Ingredients:

For the Scallops: 1 tsp. melted butter; 1 pound large sea scallops, feet removed (the tough mussels that was attached to the shell); ½ cup dry white wine.

For the Sauce: 2 tbsp. butter; 1 small can 6.5 ounces (184g) mushrooms pieces; ½ cup fine chopped each: onion and celery; ¼ tsp. each: granulated garlic, cayenne pepper and dry thyme, salt and pepper to taste; ¾ cup whole almonds with skin on, soaked overnight in cold water, peeled and pureed in the blender with 1 cup whole milk or almond milk; 2 tbsp. amaretto liqueur (op); ¼ cup concentrated frozen orange juice, thawed; 2 tbsp. lemon juice; 1 tsp. fine grated tangerine zest on microplane zester or 2 tbsp. Grand Marnier liqueur; ½ cup heavy cream or 2 tbsp. cornstarch diluted in ½ cup water (slurry); salt and fresh-ground white or black pepper.

To Garnish: Fresh green watercress; tangerine slices, radishes (op); roasted 4 to 6 whole almonds. To serve: plain rice or quinoa, amaranth and wild rice pilaf.

To Make the Sauce: Heat a medium pot on medium heat. Add 2 tbsp. butter and sauté onion for 1 minute; add the celery and sauté for 2-3 minutes just to sweat the vegetables, do not color (brown) them. Add half of the almond puree, amaretto, and cornstarch mixture (or add the heavy cream), increase the heat to medium-high, whisk the mixture until it is bubbling and thick. Add rest of the almond puree, orange juice, lemon juice, drained mushrooms, garlic, cayenne and the thyme, zest or the Grand Marnier, salt and pepper to taste, bring it to a simmer, simmer on low for 5 minutes and reduce the heat very low just to keep it warm.

To make the Scallops: Heat a large heavy-bottom stainless steel pan or a nonstick pan. Dip a paper towel in butter and lightly grease the bottom of the pan with butter. Increase the heat to medium-high. When pan is hot (not smoking), place the scallops all around in the pan, against the side of the pan, and cook about 2 minutes per side until golden brown. Off heat, pour the wine over the scallops, take out the scallops and deglaze the pan with wine, for 3-4 minutes, then pour the wine in the sauce.

To assemble the plates: While the sauce is cooking, decorate the two serving plates with the sides with watercress, tangerine, radishes and whole almonds in a creative fashion. When ready to serve, divide the sauce among the plates and place the scallops in the sauce. Serve the rice on the side.

Broiled Scallops with Roasted Vegetables (Serves: 2)

This is my husband's favorite meal. It only takes about 20-25 minutes to prepare

Ingredients: For the Vegetables: 2 cups each broccoli and cauliflower florets, sliced ¼-inch thick; ½ to ¾ pounds medium or small Yukon gold potatoes sliced paper-thin on the box grater; 1-2 pints grape tomatoes; salt, pepper, garlic powder, and 1-2 tbsp. fresh rosemary; olive oil to drizzle. For the scallops: 6 to 8 dry, jumbo sea scallops; granulated garlic and onion, salt and pepper, olive oil; 1 to 2 ounces smoked salmon or prosciutto to decorate the plates. To serve: ¼ cup to ½ cup mango BBQ sauce or hot sauce or hoisin sauce.

1. Preheat the oven at 400 degrees. Line a large baking sheet with foil and grease it well. Spread out in single layer potatoes, broccoli, and cauliflower. Sprinkle with salt, pepper, and garlic. Take the rosemary leaves off the stems by pulling them backward off the stem and sprinkle over the potatoes, then sprinkle with the olive oil (about 1-2 tbsp.) Roast vegetables for 10 minutes, turn them over with a metal spatula, place the tomatoes in the center, and bake another 10 minutes, or until soft.
2. Heat the broiler. Pat dry the scallops with paper towels, pull out any tough muscle from the side and place on a foil-lined baking sheet. Roll and coat the scallops in 2 tbsp. olive oil, and place them on foil. Sprinkle the scallops with garlic, onion, salt, and pepper to taste. Broil the scallops about 6 inches from the heat source for about 6-7 minutes, until they are light brown. Serve on warm dinner plates with roasted vegetables, broiled scallops, decorate with prosciutto or salmon and drizzle the sauce over scallops.

Lobster - Tandoori Style or Broiled (Serves: 2)

Tandoori lobster is cooked in the clay oven (Tandoor) on the long metal skewers with Tandoori spices (at Indian groceries). To make it easy, I steam it first for 4-5 minutes, plunge in ice water and then drizzle Tandoori mixture, and broil or grill it, just until heated through.

Ingredients: 2 live lobsters, each about 1-1/2 pounds; 1 stick unsalted butter; 3 tbsp. tandoori masala (or ½ tsp. cayenne pepper, dry roasted: 1 tbsp. caraway seeds. 1 tsp. fennel seeds and 1 tbsp. coriander seeds, 1 tsp. cardamom seeds from the pods; grind all seeds, and add 1 tbsp. sweet paprika); salt and fresh-ground black pepper to taste; 1-1/2 to 2 tsp. lemon pepper salt; ½ tsp. granulated garlic; 1 tbsp. instant beef broth (op), 2-inch piece of fresh ginger thin-sliced; 1/3 cup white distilled vinegar, ice bath: a large pot or bowl filled halfway with ice and water; 2 tbsps. each slivered almonds and pumpkin seeds for garnish; 2 tbsp. chat masala homemade or from the Indian grocery store; lemon chutney to serve.

1. Heat and melt the butter in a small pot. Take off the heat and stir in all the spices except ginger and vinegar, set aside to cool.
2. In a large pot with a metal basket or a rack or in a steam pot, bring water, ginger and vinegar to a boil, add the lobster in the basket or over the rack, cover with the lid. Hold down the lid with gloves on and let the lobster steam for about 4 minutes or until it turns pink. Take the pot off the heat, let it sit covered for 1 minute, take out the lobster with tongs and plunge in the ice water. Turn over the lobster to cool and leave it in the bath for about 2 minutes. Take out of the bath, pat dry, place in a large plastic bag and refrigerate until needed for up to 3-4 hours.
3. When ready to cook, start the broiler, grill, or clay oven on high. Clean out all green stomach waste up to the tail, wash under running water, pat dry. Then put the lobster on the cutting board. With the point of the sharp knife, cut and make a long slit on the top, in the shell, push in some almonds to hold open the slits and pour in half of the butter mixture and sprinkle ½ of the chat masala in each lobster over the meat. Then place the lobsters on an aluminum foil-lined baking sheet; broil, grill, or put on the long metal clay oven skewers and cook lobster in the shell just until heated through for 2-3 minutes. Serve warm, sprinkled with chat masala and with a lot of lemon chutney for dipping, fermented black beans, roasted red bell peppers, blanche and pan roasted red potatoes and Brussels sprouts.
4. Fermented Black Beans: ½ cup fermented black beans, just serve on the side. Available at the most supermarkets and Asian food stores.

5. Roasted Red Bell Peppers: You need 2 medium red bell peppers(sweet) per person (4 in total), 1 tsp. canola oil.

   Wash, pat dry and rub the peppers all around with the oil, place them in a rimmed baking sheet and place them in a preheated 400 degree oven, on the base of the oven, underneath the bottom rack. Roast peppers turning around all sides until they are charred for about 25 minutes. Take out of the oven, cover with aluminum foil and leave on the counter, away from any draft, for 1 hour, until cooled completely. Place each pepper on a plate and peel off the charred skin; make a slit and take out and discard all seeds; save the juices.

6. Pan Roasted Potatoes and Brussels Sprouts:

   Ingredients: Use 2 medium red potatoes per person and about ½ cup cooked Brussels sprouts per person; 2 tbsp. canola oil; 1 tsp. caraway seeds; ½ tsp. granulated garlic; salt and fresh-ground black pepper to taste; 2 tbsp. fresh chop cilantro or parsley; 1 tbsp. lemon juice or a little balsamic vinegar or to taste.

   Bring a medium pot half full of water to a boil. Lightly salt the water, cut potatoes in half and add to the boiling water. Blanche potatoes for 3 minutes, then take out of the water with a perforated spatula.

   Heat a large cast-iron pan on low heat. Add 2 tbsp. of canola oil, increase heat to medium high, pat dry potatoes and add to the oil. Sauté the potatoes for 1 minute all sides, then sprinkle with salt and pepper and caraway seeds, put cut side down; cover and let roast on low heat for about 15 minutes or until soft. Sprinkle with granulated garlic, stir well, take off the heat and sprinkle with cilantro or parsley and serve.

   Wash, trim, blanch and cook Brussels sprouts same way as potatoes; it will require less time, about 5 minutes in the oil to roast; roast just until soft, then sprinkle with salt, pepper and balsamic vinegar and serve warm.

Fillet of Flounder Pan Fried (Serves: 4)

This is an easy, fast and a tasty way to cook almost any fish. Flounder fillets are thin and light so they cook fast. For the thicker fish like cod, you will need more spices and a longer cooking time. Usually one-inch-thick fish takes around 6 to 7 minutes. I start each side in a little butter or olive or canola oil, on medium-high heat, for a few minutes to give a golden color, then reduce to low heat to cook through, then turn it over and cook fast.

Ingredients: 4 flounder fillets about 1 pound (boneless and skinless); 1 extra large egg whipped well; ¼ cup seasoned dry bread crumbs; 1 tbsp. grated parmesan cheese; 1 tsp. packed lemon-pepper seasoning; about 2-3 tsp. purified butter (ghee) or canola oil.

1. Wash, pat dry fillets with a paper towel and check for bones; pull out any leftover bones from the fillets, set the fillets aside.

2. Mix the dry ingredients: bread crumbs, cheese, and lemon seasoning. Spread out half of the bread crumb mixture in a large platter. Dip the fish in the beaten egg on both sides, then press down in the sprinkled bread crumbs on one side. Now sprinkle the other side with the rest of the bread crumbs. At this point cover and refrigerate the fish or go ahead and cook right away.

3. When ready to cook, heat a heavy-bottom large sauté pan on medium-high heat. When pan is hot add about 1 tsp. oil or purified butter, move the pan around to coat the bottom, then immediately add the flounder fillets (2 or all 4 fillets, according to the size of the pan), cover the pan with the lid, leaving about 1-inch opening for steam to get out. Cook fish golden underneath, about 2 minutes, reduce heat to low and cook another 1 minute until fish is opaque on the top. Take the pan off the heat and leaving it still covered for a little while, about 1 minute. Now drizzle about 2

drops oil on each piece of the fillet, scrape the bottom and turn over the fish. Put the pan back on medium-high heat and cook fish uncovered, golden on the other side, about 2 minutes. Fish should then be done. Take the pan off the heat and serve warm right away with tartar sauce, horseradish sauce and lemon wedges, etc.

Linguine in Clam Sauce (Serves: 4)

This easy, light and healthy dish is loaded with nutrients: Clams have Vitamin B-12 that gives you energy, Tomatoes have lycopene, which is good for eyes and prostate health, and avocado has a good healthy fat.

Ingredients: 2 tbsp. olive oil; 24 littleneck clams (about 2 pounds) soaked in ¼ cup corn meal for 10 minutes and scrubbed clean under cold tab water; 1 bottle 24 oz. 68 g pasta sauce with herbs; 3 tbsp. lemon juice; 16 oz. 453g spinach, I box linguine; 1 cup chopped onion; about 2 large garlic cloves chopped; ½ tsp. granulated garlic; salt and pepper to taste; 6 oz. (170g), about 2 cups fresh crimini mushrooms wiped clean with lightly damped paper towel and stem ends trimmed; 1 cup good white wine, about ½ cup clam juice or pasta cooking water as needed; for garnish: ½ cup grated parmesan cheese or to taste, 1 red bell pepper cored, seeded and chopped, 2 green onions sliced.

1. In a large pot bring salted water to a boil and cook pasta al dente (with a little bite to it) per package direction. Drain pasta in a colander and keep it warm, over the pasta water, until the clams are ready.
2. Heat a Dutch oven or a wide and a large pot on medium heat. When hot, add 1 tbsp. oil and sauté the onion for 5 minutes. Move over the onion on side and add 1 tbsp. oil and the mushrooms. Increase the heat medium high and sauté mushroom for 5 minutes. Add garlic, sauté a little then add the pasta sauce and bring it to a boil. Off the heat add wine, lemon juice, fresh-ground black pepper, gran. garlic and clam juice or about ½ cup pasta water; bring it to a boil. Lower the heat to medium, add the cleaned clams, in a single layer if possible; cover, and let them steam for about 6 minutes. The clams should be open by now, if not then cover again for a minute. Discard any unopened clams. Take out the clams with a tong and arrange all around in the warmed serving plates. Then add the warm pasta to the sauce, stir a little and serve in the middle of the plate, nestled with the tong. Pour over the sauce evenly. Garnish with cheese, red bell pepper and green onion. Serve ½ pitted and peeled avocado with each serving.

Stuffed Mussels

These stuffed mussels are very easy to make and are very tasty. It takes only 15 minutes to prepare. Buy cleaned mussels, and have the stuffing ready ahead.

Ingredients: 1 pound cleaned (beard out) mussels; ¼ cup corn meal; 2 cups white wine; ½ cup tomato sauce; 1 tbsp. unsalted butter; each chopped:1/2 cup pepperoni, bacon or pancetta; 1 medium onion; ½ cup red bell pepper; ½ cup fresh tomatoes; ¼ tsp. granulated garlic, salt and black pepper to taste; 2 tbsp. fresh chopped oregano (or dry ½ tsp.); 1 tbsp. fresh chopped thyme (or dry ¼ tsp.); 1 tsp. lemon salt seasoning or Old Bay seasoning; 3 tbsp. white wine; about 2 tbsp. lemon juice.

1. Mix corn meal in a quart of cold water and soak the mussels for about 10 minutes, then clean out the mussels under cold running water. Prepare a serving platter, either sprinkle about ½ cup of coarse salt or just double-line it with parchment paper in the center.
2. In a sauté pan on medium-high heat, cook pepperoni, bacon or pancetta for 5-6 minutes until crispy. Take out of the pan and add butter and sauté onion with a little granulated garlic and salt

and pepper, for 3-4 minutes until translucent. Add tomatoes, red bell pepper, cover for 2 minutes, open and sauté for 4-5 minutes until peppers and onion are soft. Sprinkle the lemon salt or bay seasoning, thyme and oregano and keep them warm on low, on and off heat.

3. In a wide pot add the wine and the tomato sauce, place the mussels on the top, cover, bring to a boil, and as soon as the mussels are opened, take them out of the pot. Discard any unopened ones. Take off the top ½ shell of each mussel and leave them on only on half shell; place them on the prepared platter. First sprinkle about ½ tsp. of wine on the mussels, then top with onion mixture and sprinkle 2-3 drops of lemon juice on each and serve immediately.

Shrimp with Coconut and Pineapple in Cream Sauce (Serves: 4)

I had this dish in Las Vegas, in a very crowded restaurant. It is tasty, easy and very attractive dish.

Ingredients: 3-4 tbsp. butter; 2 tbsp. ginger-garlic paste; 2 tsp. sugar; 1 can 13.5 ounces (480 ml.) unsweetened coconut milk; ¼ cup tomato sauce; ½ cup heavy cream (whipping); 2-3 tbsp. lemon juice; 3-4 drops tabasco sauce or ¼ tsp. cayenne pepper; ½ tsp. cardamom seeds crushed (op); 6 slices pineapple, cut into 1-inch pieces; ½ pound snow peas; 1 pound large shrimp (36-40) peeled and deveined; 6 cups cooked plain rice; salt, pepper to taste.

1. Cook about 2 cups rice in about 3-1/2 cups cold water, let it come to a boil, add 1 tsp. butter, stir well, simmer on low until soft. Line 4 flour-measuring metal cups or regular cups with plastic wraps, grease the wrap well, and press in the cooked rice; leave in the off oven to keep it warm.
2. Trim the ends of the snow peas by pulling the thread on the thicker edge of the peas. Heat a large sauté pan on medium heat, add 1 tbsp. butter and sauté on high heat 1 minute; take out into a bowl.
3. Heat the same pan back again with 1 tbsp. butter on medium heat. Sprinkle the Shrimp with Tabasco sauce/cayenne and add shrimp to the pan. Cook shrimp for about 2 minutes each side, until pink. Take out the shrimp in a small bowl.
4. Heat the same pan again on medium heat, add 1 tbsp. butter, ginger-garlic paste, and ¼ cup water, ¼ tsp. each salt and pepper, and cook covered, on low, for about 6-8 minutes, until most of the water is gone. Stir in tomato sauce, coconut milk, heavy cream, lemon juice, cardamom seed powder, increase heat to medium-high and bring back to a boil, reduce the heat and simmer on low for about 10 minutes, add the shrimp and just reheat the shrimp for 1 minutes. Taste for seasoning.
5. Serve in large platters: first turn over the rice cup in center, pour over the juice, arrange the shrimp and peas all around, open the cup and plastic wrap, and add pineapple all around the rice and serve.

Baked Coconut Shrimp (Serves: 2-4)

These are baked light, tasty and easy to make. It is a light protein. They taste best with the yogurt chutney.

Ingredients: 1 pound jumbo shrimp (14 count) peeled and deveined; spice mixture: 1 tsp. each garlic powder, cayenne, and lemon-pepper mix; 2 jumbo egg whites whisked until foamy; bread crumb mixture: ½ cup unsweetened grated coconut, ½ cup panko (Japanese) bread crumbs, 2tbsp. grated cheese (from the bottle), ½ tsp. kosher salt and 1 tbsp. fresh cracked black peppercorns; to sprinkle on the top: 1 fresh lemon to squeeze the juice, little salt and pepper. Shrimp to serve: cilantro and mint chutney, or cilantro yogurt chutney, or vinegar barbecue sauce.

Sprinkle the shrimp with the spice mixture all over and set them aside for 10 minutes. Preheat the oven at 425 degrees. Line a baking tray with aluminum foil and spray it with the cooking spray.

Take the shrimp and pour them into the whisked and foamy egg white. Place the bread crumb mixture in a bowl. Pick up one shrimp at a time with the tong from the egg and dip into the bread-crumb mixture, and place on the prepared tray in a row. Spray the shrimp lightly with cooking spray. Bake in a preheated oven for about 15 minutes, or until golden. Take the shrimp out of oven, sprinkle with the lemon juice, salt and pepper. Serve with the sauce or chutney.

Surf & Turf (S;2)
You want to be creative: make a design with the salad ingredients. Make sure they all are bright colors and different varieties. This meal is steak and shrimp. You can have any seafood that your heart desire.

(1)   Steak
Follow one of your favorite steak recipe under meat, and serve with the shrimps.

(2)   Garlic Shrimps
Ingredients: 1pound small shrimps peeled and deveined (35-40 count); 6Tbsp. unsalted butter melted and cooled; 1/4c fresh garlic cloves; 2Tbsp. fresh ginger peeled and chopped; 1Tsp. cardamom seed crushed (op); 1/4tsp. granulated garlic; 1tbsp. lemon-pepper seasoning mix; tabasco or hot sauce to taste; salt and pepper to taste; to serve: 1lemon cut in wedges and 1 lemon for juice.

In a blender or food processor puree together all spices then add the butter and pulse 3-4 times to mix well. Make your salad design in the serving platters and set aside.

Prepare the steak and keep it warm.

Heat a large stainless steel or non-stick pan on medium heat. Add the pureed spice mixture and cook for 8 minutes covered. Open the cover, add the shrimp and cook for 3 minutes on high heat stirring often. Reduce the heat and stir for 2-3 minutes until they turn pink. Serve shrimps squeezed with lemon juice, steak, lemon wedges and salad.

Barbecue Shrimp with Chickpeas, Quinoa, Hemp, and Zucchini Cakes (Serves: 4-6)

These shrimp take only 4 minutes to grill. You can use indoor grill or as I do very often, cook in a large, very hot grilling pan. I like these shrimp on a buttered hot dog bun with some tartar sauce or serve over deviled eggs, and/or serve with chickpeas, quinoa, hemp, and zucchini cakes, which you can make indoors, or grill, heat and serve.

(1) **Shrimp**

Ingredients for the Shrimp: 1 pound jumbo shrimp (24-26 count); peeled, deveined and tail left on; to serve: lemons, green salad or fries.

First Marinade: 1 tbsp. each: granulated garlic, cayenne; 2 tbsp. lemon juice, and 1 tsp. salt.

Second Marinade: ½ cup yellow onion; 1 tbsp. each fresh grated ginger and garlic cloves; ¼ c lemon juice; 1 tbsp. fish sauce; 1 tbsp. sugar; 1 cup coconut milk, ½ tsp. salt.

Sauce to Baste: 1/3 cup chili sauce mixed with 1 tbsp. lemon mix or lemon juice; 1 tbsp. melted butter; ½ tsp. salt.

1. Peel the shrimp, take out the vein, wash under running cold water; when done pat dry the shrimp with paper towels. Sprinkle with garlic, cayenne, salt, and lemon juice; set aside for 5 minutes.

2. Place the shrimp in a non-reactive bowl and grate the onion over the shrimp. Whisk in the second marinade ingredients and pour over the shrimp, cover the bowl, and marinate the shrimp for 1 hour in room temperature. If you need more time to cook, refrigerate the shrimp.

3. Soak the wooden skewers at least ½ hour in water and thread 4 shrimp, 1-inch apart, on two skewers to cook. Prepare an indoor grill very hot or prepare a large grilling pan very hot and grease the grades very well with the oil.

4. Place the shrimp on very hot pan or grill. Grill on medium-high heat. each side for only 1 minute. Baste with the sauce generously and grill shrimp again for another one minute on each side. Serve hot, sprinkled with lemon juice and sides.

Tips: Use a large bowl, and grate the onion right over the shrimp. It saves all the nutrients and the essential oil from the onion that may escape in the air. Stir in the grated onion with the shrimp right away. Garlic, too, loses its nutrients in contact with the air. So slice, chop or grate the garlic right over the food and mix in the food right away.

(2) **Chickpeas, Quinoa, Hemp, and Zucchini Cakes**
(M: about 8-10)

Ingredients: 1 cup chopped onion; 1 tbsp. fresh garlic cloves chopped; ¼ tsp. salt; 1 cup cooked quinoa, ¾ to 1 pound thin and slim (about 3-4) fresh zucchini washed trimmed and grated; for thick batter: 1 cup chickpea flour (from Indian grocery stores) mixed with 1 tsp. celery seeds, pinch of salt and pepper, and whisked in with 10-12 tbsp. water. 3-4 tbsp. canola oil; mint chutney or barbecue sauce to serve.

Heat a large cast-iron skillet on medium heat add 1 tbsp. oil, chopped onion, garlic and salt, stir for 30 seconds, cover and cook until soft about 8 minutes. To the batter whisk in the zucchini, onion and mix well; then add the quinoa and mix. Sprinkle hemp on the top. Heat the same skillet on medium heat, add 2 tbsp. oil, and with an ice cream scoop, drop about ¾ cup mixture, spread out with the back of the scoop about 1-1/4-inch thick cake; cover and cook about 5-7 minutes, or until it is light brown underneath. Take the pan off the heat for 1-2 minutes, keep it covered, then open and drop 2-3 drops of oil on each cake; then turn over and cook the other side for 4-5 minutes until browned. Serve warm, or heat and serve later with chutney and/or sauce. These Vegan cakes have amino acid, protein, iron and vitamins.

Mango Barbecue Shrimp

Follow the barbecue shrimp recipe above, just baste the shrimp with barbecue mango sauce, and serve extra sauce for dipping.

Pineapple Rice in Pineapple Shell with Shrimp or Lobster (Serves: 2)

This is a very tasty and attractive dinner. Tasty wild pineapple rice is served in the pineapple shell. You can use shrimp or two lobster tails, boiled for about 6-7 minutes, until they turn pink. Cut open the top of the tail, loosen the meat, and drizzle the warm melted butter immediately.

Ingredients: 1 large golden pineapple with healthy green crown.
For the Shrimp: ½ pounds jumbo shrimp (12-15 count) deveined shrimp with tails attached; about 1 tsp. cayenne pepper;1 tbsp. butter and 1 tbsp. olive oil; 2 chopped tomatoes; 3 tbsp. lemon juice; 1 tsp. granulated garlic; 1 tsp. sugar; salt and pepper to taste.

For the Rice: ½ cup wild rice; 1-1/2 cups to 2 cups water or chicken stock as needed; 2 tbsp. chopped onion; 1 large garlic clove chopped; 1 tsp. butter.

salad: 1 tbsp. sugar; ½ cup frozen peas: cooked 5 minutes in boiling water and drained; ½ of each red and orange bell pepper seeded and chopped; ¼ cup sliced green onion; ½ cup (about 4) blanched asparagus, cut into 1-inch cubes; ¼ cup dry cranberries; 6 ounces of marinated artichoke hearts or 1 cup halved black or green olives.

For the Dressing: 2 tbsp. red wine vinegar; 1 tbsp. e.v.olive oil.
To serve: lemon wedges and 4 to 6 medium salad tomatoes, skin peeled on the top and sprinkled with grated cheese; cocktail sauce.

1. In a large heavy-bottom pot, on medium-high heat, add 1-1/2 cups water or chicken stock. Wash the wild rice a few times, until the water is clear, then add to the water. Bring to a boil, cook open for 5 minutes, stir well, add chopped onion and garlic, butter; cover and simmer on low heat until soft, stirring 1-2 times during cooking; cook for about 50-60 minutes, until soft and all the water is gone. If needed add 1-2 tabs more water.

2. Wash and dry the pineapple, put on the cutting board. With a serrated steak or bread knife, cut the body of the pineapple in half, then use a chef knife to split it in half (do not take it apart). Use the same steak or bread knife, split the crown in half carefully, starting from the body of the pineapple, going in up and down motion, toward the crown. Cover the crown with a lightly wet paper towel so it stays fresh until it is ready to serve. Leaving about ¾-inch edges all around, cut the pineapple about 1-2-inches deep, separating the skin and the flesh. Then cut the flesh into 3-4 strips lengthwise and hollow out the pineapple with the help of a spoon and a knife.

3. Sprinkle the pineapple chunks with some salt, let it sit 5 minutes and wash out the salt under the running cold water, this way all the acid will be gone. Cook about 1 cup of pineapple cubes, in a pan, for about 15 minutes in 1 tbsp. sugar, until almost dried out and tasty. Add to the salad ingredients.

4. When the rice is done, move the rice all around and add 1 tbsp. butter in the middle; add all salad ingredients and warm on low heat.

5. Sprinkle the shrimp with half of the granulated garlic and cayenne pepper. Heat a large sauté pan on medium heat. Add 1 tbsp. butter and 1 tbsp. olive oil, chopped tomatoes, 3 tbsp. lemon juice, rest of the ½ of the granulated garlic and cayenne pepper, 1 tsp. sugar; stir well and add the shrimp. Leave the shrimp alone for 1 minute; when they are pink in the bottom, turn them over and cook all around pink, a total of 3-4 minutes. Sprinkle with salt and pepper to taste.

6. Assemble the platter: In each hollowed pineapple, sprinkle the salt and pepper, fill with the warm salad. Top with half of the shrimp in each. Whip the red wine vinegar and olive oil and pour all over the salad. Serve with cocktail sauce, salad tomatoes, and lemon wedges on the side.

Shrimp Paneer (Shrimp with Cheese)
(Serves: 2-4)

In India, the cheese (paneer) dishes are considered the fancy cooking. You just have to make the sauce and add the cheese to it. Make cheese at home or buy at Indian grocery stores.

Ingredients: 1 Recipe of Indian cheese: paneer (from cheese section, or 1 pound toasted paneer cubes bought); 1 pound jumbo shrimp, 20-24 count, peeled and deveined; and sprinkled with ½ tsp. granulated garlic and cayenne pepper, and 1 tbsp. lemon juice, about ½ hour before cooking; 2 tbsp. unsalted butter; 2 cans each: 13.5 ounces (480 ml.) unsweetened coconut milk; ½ cup cashew nuts ground into powder; 1 tsp. fresh-ground cardamom seeds; 2 tbsp. lemon juice; salt and pepper to taste. To garnish:

1 tbsp. salt-free lemon-pepper seasoning mix (I prefer Mrs. Dash); cilantro to garnish, and any type of rice pilaf to serve.

Bring the cheese cubes (paneer) to room temperature about a half hour before cooking, then heat them in the microwave oven for 2 minutes on high, or in the regular oven on a greased aluminum foil-lined baking tray at 350 degrees for 10 minutes, or until heated through. Heat a large, heavy-bottom sauté pan on medium heat, add the butter and sauté the shrimp for 2 minutes each side or until the shrimp are cooked and turn pink. Place the shrimp in the heated serving platters. Now add the cheese cubes with the shrimp in a single layer. Keep the platters loosely covered, or place them in a heated but turned-off oven.

Make the sauce: Heat the same shrimp pan on low heat. In a bowl whisk together coconut milk. cashew powder, cardamom, lemon juice, and little salt and pepper to taste. Pour the coconut mixture in the pan, increase the heat to medium-high and cook the sauce until thickened. When it is bubbly and cooked through, simmer it on low heat for 2 minutes and then pour over the shrimp and cheese platter. Garnish with salt and pepper and lemon-pepper seasoning mix and serve immediately with rice pilaf.

Lobster Paneer (Serves: 4)

Follow the recipe above, just replace the shrimp with cooked Lobster meat and sprinkled with lemon juice. You can also use 1 lobster tail per person, boiled for 7-8 minutes until it turns pink; cut the shell with a pair of scissors and slice the tail meat, then drizzle with the hot sauce.

Skate and Squash (S:4)

This is a fancy fish dish. It is tasty and colorful.

Ingredients: 1 medium (about 1 pound) acorn squash with yellow and green color; 4 tbsp. olive oil; salt and pepper to taste; 1/2tsp. turmeric powder; 1tbsp. pumpkin spices; 2- 16oz. can Italian style stewed tomatoes pureed then heated; about 3 pound skate wing, bone in and skin taken out; 1/2tsp. each old bay seasoning, garlic and onion powders; 3tbsp. butter; 1/2cup toasted pumpkin seeds; 2 large red potatoes boiled with skin on. To serve sliced radishes, yellow cherry tomatoes and 1 lemon.

Preheat the oven at 400 degree. Wash, core and slice the squash in half lengthwise. Scoop out all seeds with a spoon then slice across 1/4-inch wide semi-circles. Line a large baking sheet with foil, grease it then spread out the squash slices in single layer. Slice potatoes in quarter lengthwise and place cut side down on the baking sheet. Sprinkle salt, pepper, 1 tsp. turmeric, pumpkin spices and olive oil and bake for 25 minutes until squash is soft. Take out of the oven, keep it covered and warm.

Using a paper towel dry the skate wing and sprinkle bay seasoning, salt, pepper, onion and garlic. In a oven proof skillet heat 2tbsp. olive oil. Now brown the wing on medium-high heat on one side. Add butter to the pan and let the butter get brown then spoon the butter over the fish, it should take only1-1/2 to 2 minutes. Turn over the wing and place in the oven and bake at 350 degree for about 7-8 minutes until it is just opaque. Serve immediately in a heated platter: place the skate over heated stewed tomatoes, squash, potatoes, tomatoes and radishes on side and garnish with pumpkin seeds. Sprinkle little bay seasoning and lemon juice on warm skate, and pumpkin spices over the squash.

Salmon En Papillote (Steamed Salmon in Parchment Paper)
(Serves: 2)

Salmon or any other fish cooked "wrapped in paper" is En Papillote. Here you will have whole meal steamed in paper. Bake just before serving.

Ingredients: 1 pound skinless, boneless salmon fillets or any other firm-flesh fish such as cod, haddock, halibut, etc.; salt and pepper to taste; 1 cup cooked quinoa or any other grain, mixed with ½ cup each chopped roasted red bell pepper from the jar, and dry cranberries; 4 paper-thin slices of fresh lemon; cheese mixture: ¼ cup goat cheese mixed with 2 tbsp. sliced green onions and 1 tsp. lemon zest; 2 large circles of parchment paper cut out about 12-inch diameter; ½ cup white wine (op).

Preheat oven at 400 degrees. On a large baking tray (12x18x1 inches) place the parchment paper in the center place the quinoa, top with salmon, sprinkle with salt and pepper, then spread out the goat cheese mixture; top with lemon slices. Fold the parchment paper in half (semi-circle). Now start folding the double layer of the parchment on the edges, forming an airtight pocket and still keeping the shape of the semi-circle, enclosing the ingredients for steaming. Just before the end of the fold, pour in about 2 tbsp. of the white wine; fold the semi-circle all the way, then tuck in underneath the last fold. Place on the baking tray, and place in a preheated oven. Bake until parchment is puffed up, for about 12 minutes.

Serve the packets as-is, hot out of the oven, with some extra salad on the side, if you prefer.

Tips: According to some experts Salmon, Mackerel, and Sardines have a substance called: Coenzyme Q10. This substance helps heart disease, high blood pressure, and helps mental function associated with Alzheimer's disease and Schizophrenia etc.

Baked Salmon Sticks (Serves: 2)

For this recipe you can use any firm-flesh fish instead of salmon. This is an easy, fast, tasty and healthy way to cook the fish.

Ingredients: 1 pound boneless, skinless salmon fillet; ½ tsp. each granulated garlic and lemon-pepper seasoning mix; salt and pepper to taste; to dip: 3tbsp. all-purpose flour, 1 large egg beaten and ½ cup wheat germ or a mixture of ½ cup dry bread crumbs mixed with ¼ cup fine crushed almonds; 2 tsp. canola oil or cooking oil spray; 1 tbsp. lemon juice to sprinkle over the sticks and 1 lemon cut into wedges; salad, vegetables and potatoes to serve with the fish.

1. Line a large baking sheet with aluminum foil and grease it well in the center. Preheat the oven at 400 degrees.
2. Wash, pat dry fish, look for any bones then cut across into about 1-inch wide strips.
3. Mix all the spices together and sprinkle on the sticks on the flesh side. Dip the sticks into the dry flour, shake out the excess flour, then into the beaten egg and finally press the flesh side into the wheat germs or nut crumbs. Any leftover crumbs sprinkle on the skin side. Spray the sticks on the flesh side with the cooking spray or drizzle a little oil on a

platter and drag the fish sticks, flesh side into the oil to grease them. Line the fish sticks on the greased tray, flesh side down. Bake in a preheated 400 degree oven for about 10-12 minutes until opaque.

4. Heat the serving platters, arrange with the side dishes and lemon wedges. Serve warm fish sticks, squeezed over with some lemon juice.

Tips: The wild salmon has Omega-3 fatty acids, protein, vitamins B and D, calcium, potassium, etc.

Tips: Salmon contains omega-e fatty acid, that helps the heart, and vitamin B-12 that produces chemicals in the brain for good mood, and it takes away depression.

Salmon, Cod or Haddock over Chickpeas Puree with Tahini, and Apple, Date & Ginger Relish
(Serves: 4)

You can use any firm-flesh fish with this recipe. We mostly use salmon, the heart-healthy deep-water fish. I prefer to make the relish a day before and just add the cilantro, scallion, salt and pepper just before serving.

Ingredients: For the Fish: 1 tbsp. canola oil; 1-1/4 to 1-1/2 pound salmon filet with skin on; 1 tbsp. lemon-pepper seasoning mix; 1/4, tsp. each granulated garlic and onion powder; salt and pepper to taste.

For the Relish: 1 Gayla or Red Delicious apple, cored and chopped into 1-2-inch pieces; 1/2cup medjool or regular dates pitted and chopped ½-inch pieces; 2 tbsp. grated fresh ginger; ½ cup orange juice, 3-4 tbsp.fresh lemon juice; 1 tbsp. soy sauce (op); ½ cup sliced green onion; ¼ cup chopped cilantro, plus extra cilantro leaves for garnish; salt and pepper to taste.

For the Chickpeas Puree: 1 can, 15 oz. (425 g) chickpeas (garbanzo beans) drained; 3 tbsp. canola oil; ½ cup tahini (or ½ cup sesame seeds lightly roasted and ground, mixed with 1 tbsp. canola oil, 1 tsp. lemon juice and salt and pepper to taste); to serve: some fruits and watercress.

Prepare the relish: Mix together apple, dates, ginger, lemon and orange juice in a small bowl cover and refrigerate. Just before serving, add scallion, cilantro, soy sauce and salt and pepper to taste.

Prepare the Chickpeas Puree: In a blender, puree the chickpeas with 1 or 2 tbsp. of water as needed, then pour in the oil through the feed tube and whisk well. Take out and stir in the tahini by hand.

Prepare the Fish: Prepare the serving platters before cooking the fish. Spread out the chickpea puree on one side of the platter, and top with tahini. Place the fruits and the watercress on the other side. Heat a large heavy-bottom pan on medium heat. Wash and pat dry the salmon, move the finger on the flesh. Check for the bones and take them out. Sprinkle the lemon-pepper mixture. garlic and the onion powder and the fresh-ground black pepper on a platter then press down the flesh of the fish into the spice mixture. Increase the heat to medium-high and cook the fish flesh side down for 5 minutes or until golden. Take the pan off the heat, cover halfway, tilt the pan, and let the fish rest 3-4 minutes. Now turn the fish over and cook the skin side down for another 3-4 minutes or until the fish is just opaque. Take out the fish, sprinkle a little salt over it, and serve topped with the relish and cilantro leaves.

Salmon Bouquet

When we got married, every now and then, we used to go out and meet with my husband's Japanese friends. They always went to a Japanese restaurant. One of his friends, Bill Kochiyama, ordered a seafood tray where they made a nice scenery with seafood, salad, tofu and sauces, etc. So, I started doing the same at home. This is a colorful bouquet with salmon and salad ingredients.

Ingredients: 3 ounces sliced smoked salmon; 1 large sweet potato boiled; 6 radishes; chives; 2 kiwi fruit; ¼ pound firm silken tofu cut in a flower or small round slices, small tomatoes; 1 Kirby cucumber sliced, black and green olives, some cilantro springs, scallion; sautéed snow peas, lemon juice, soy sauce, tartar sauce, and chutney to serve.

Take two large serving platters. Peel and slice the sweet potato in the shape of a basket and place it on the platter about 1/3 of the bottom. Place some green onions, about 2 and 3 inches long, to make several stems connecting to the basket. Now with the smoked salmon, take one slice at a time, roll it up, then open the top like a rose and place on the platter, making a bouquet. Place the kiwi slices top with cucumber and then top with the radishes (large slices in bottom and smaller on the top), and place them all over. Connect all flowers with the stems and leaves made of cilantro, scallion and chives. Also outline the basket with the stems and herbs. Now you can decorate or add olives and the tofu in empty spaces. Just use your imagination.

Prepare it about 1 hour ahead, cover with the plastic and refrigerate. Just before serving, sprinkle lemon juice all over, and serve with your favorites sauces, and chutney for dipping.

Fish and Chips with Apple Slaw, and Potato Rolls (Serves: 2)

This English tradition is not only our favorite, but we make it fancier each time. We make a crunchy fish with potato rolls and apple slaw.

1.   Apple Slaw

Ingredients: 1 Granny Smith apple washed and sliced 1/10 of an inch thin lengthwise, into round slices, then cored and slice 1/10 of an inch-wide strips (like matchsticks) washed under cold water and pat dry; ¼ cup dry cranberries; ½ cup about ½ celery stock peeled on the back and cut into matchsticks; ¼ cup baked or raw beet peeled and cut into matchsticks (op). For the vinaigrette: 1 tbsp. Champagne or rice wine vinegar; 3 tbsp. e.v. olive oil whisked together with a little salt and crushed black pepper to taste.

Prepare slaw ahead, and keep it covered with the plastic wrap and the lid. Just before serving drizzle the vinaigrette and serve.

2.   Fried Fish

Ingredients: About 1 pound boneless and skinless cod fillet; ½ tsp. each: cayenne pepper and granulated garlic; lemon juice; canola oil to deep fry. To serve: lemon wedges, tartar sauce, cocktail sauce.

Fish Batter and Crumbs: ¼ cup all-purpose flour; 1 large egg; ¼ cup seltzer water; ¼ tsp. each onion and garlic powders; salt and pepper to taste; bread crumb mixture: ½ cup dried bread crumbs, ¼ cup grated parmesan cheese, ¼ cup almond flour, ¼ cup corn meal, ¼ tsp. each salt and pepper.

Marinate Fish: Wash and pat dry fish and chick for the bones. Cut fish into 4 pieces and sprinkle with cayenne pepper, garlic powder and a little lemon juice; set aside to marinate for 15 minutes.

Prepare the Batter: In a bowl, whisk the egg and the flour together, add seltzer water and whisk well. Add salt, pepper and garlic and onion powders and whisk all together. Combine the bread crumbs mixture together.

Heat a medium pot with 1-1/2-inch deep oil, on medium heat. Pat dry the marinated fish, dip in the batter on both sides, pick up with forks and drop on the bread crumb mixture. Turn over the fish and coat well with the crumbs. When oil is hot (360 degrees) drop the fish pieces in batches from one side in the hot oil and deep fry on medium-high heat for about 2 minutes on each side. Turn the fish over only when it is browned underneath. When the fish is golden brown turn it over again, in the hot oil, to crisp it. Then take out with a perforated spatula, on the paper towel lined platter. Keep the fish in a low heated oven until potatoes are ready.

3.   Potato Rolls

Ingredients: 2 large potatoes (about ½ pound) washed and boiled in cold water until they are almost done, but not overdone; ½ tsp. each onion powder, garlic powder; 1 tsp. dry mint crumbled or 1 tab fresh mint chopped; 2 tbsp. grated parmesan cheese; salt and pepper to taste. For spicy look and taste: sprinkle 2 tbsp. chaat masala (found in Indian grocery stores) after they are fried.

1. Peel and grate the potatoes while they are still warm. Mix onion, garlic and mint, and sprinkle with the cheese, salt and pepper. With oily hands, make balls with light hands, do not press hard, then turn them into rolls (long).
2. Fry them in 350 degree hot oil. Turn them over, scraping the bottom carefully, only when they are golden in the bottom. Once they are golden brown all over, turn and roll them in the hot oil to crisp. Serve warm with the fish.
4. **Tarter Sauce:** Mix ½ cup mayonnaise with 1/3 cup sweet pickle relish), stir well. Yields ¾ cup.
5. **Cocktail Sauce:** Mix ¾ cup tomato sauce, 1 tbsp. ketchup, ¼ cup hot sauce (op), ¼ cup prepared horseradish. Stir all ingredients together and add salt and pepper to taste. Yields 1-1/4 cup.

Assemble the heated platters: serve warm fish, potato rolls, apple slaw, lemon wedges with tarter and cocktail sauces.

Tips: The secret of fried food is the crispiness. After the fish is cooked light brown, turn it over twice in the hot oil to crisp the outside. After that, put the fried fish on a wire rack, in a very low heated oven, to warm while it is also getting crispy. Do not let it dry or burn. Take it out within 15 minutes. Do not use microwave, it will get soft.

Fried Seafood Platter (Serves: 2)

When we were growing up we had a lot of fried food pakauri (fritters). But my father made sure that we have raita (yogurt salad) and/or yogurt chutney. It tastes good, is healthy and cuts down on the greasy food. Here I have fried sea scallops, spicy crab cake, coconut shrimp, flounder, sweet potato fries and drunken oysters. Serve with cocktail sauce, tartar sauce, Greek yogurt and ketchup.

When you bring seafood home, fill a large bowl with ice cubes, place the seafood containers on the ice and keep them chilled until cooking. Cook them the same day. Make all the batters and dredging flours, sauces ahead of frying and serve fried seafood hot, or heat the oven at low, about 200 degrees, for 5 minutes and shut it off. Do not keep the oven on; it will dry up the seafood.

1. **For the Coconut Shrimp:**
   Ingredients: Pancake batter: ½ cup pancake flour mixed with about 5-6 tbsp. of water; 2 cups fresh-grated coconut or fresh-frozen coconut thawed overnight, mixed with 2 tsp. of sugar; 8 jumbo shrimp clean and peeled, but leave the tail on; canola or peanut oil to deep-fry. To serve: Greek yogurt or raita, cocktail sauce, tartar sauce and ketchup.

A. Line a large baking tray with aluminum foil and cover half of the tray with paper towels. Just before deep-frying, make the batter. In a bowl, whisk pancake mix and the water and make a thick batter. Place one shrimp on the plastic wrap at a time, score inside (on Leg side) up to the tail, then pound them with a mallet or a cast-iron pan and flatten them just like butterflies open wings. Spread out the fresh coconut on a platter. When ready to fry, heat a wok, a wide pot or a deep fryer with about 2-inch-deep oil at 375 degrees.

B. Hold a shrimp in one hand and using the other hand, paste the shrimp on both sides with the pancake batter, then drop in the coconut, press down firmly on both side to coat with the coconut. When a batch is ready, hold the tail and slide them into the hot oil, from the edge of the oil. Let it cook about 4 minutes or until light golden underneath, turn over and cook the other side and take them out on the tray on aluminum foil.

2. **For the Crab Cakes:** Follow the recipe for the crab cakes. Make them a day ahead and just deep-fry them in hot oil for 1-2 minutes to refresh them.

3. **For the Scallops:**

   Ingredients: ½ pound about 6-8 sea scallops, side muscle removed; dredging flour mix: 1 bag, 10 ounces, (263g) Cajun crispy fish fry, or make your own.

   A. Spread out the dredging Cajun flour mix in a platter. Drop the scallops in the flour, press down and coat the scallops with the flour on all sides. Drop them in the hot oil and fry about 2 minutes each side or until light brown color. Take them out on a paper towel-lined sheet.

4. **For the Fish:**

   Ingredients: 1 pound filet of flounder, check out for the bones by moving a finger over the fish. I prefer filet of flounder, light and crispy.

   A. Just like scallops, press the fish pieces into the dredging flour on both sides, shake out excess and slide into the hot oil from one side of the oil. Cook fish about 2-3 minutes on each side or until golden. Then turn over and cook each side for about 2 seconds to crisp the fish, and take out on the paper towel lined tray.

5. **For the Drunken Oysters:** 4 live and scrubbed clean oysters; Tabasco or hot sauce or lemon juice, and Champagne.

   A. Just before serving shuck the oysters, loosen them from the shell, and keep them on half-shell. Drizzle lightly with the Tabasco sauce or lemon juice. Then fill the shell with the Champagne and carefully place them on the serving platter directly, or over the chopped herbs, and serve.

6. **For the Sweet Potato Fries:**

   Ingredients: 1 large sweet potato scrubbed clean and partially boiled (par-boil) in hot water and chilled in the refrigerator; 1 tbsp. chili powder mix; salt and pepper to taste.

   A. Peel the sweet potato or leave the skin on. Cut the potato into 1-inch wide slices lengthwise. Then cut each slice into 1-inch wide strips. Drop them in hot oil, in single layer and cook them in batches, about 4-5 minutes per side or until they are browned and crisp. Once they are browned, turn them over again to crisp. Take them out on an aluminum foil-lined tray. Sprinkle with spices and serve hot.

   Assemble the Platter: Use a large heated platter, place the fish in the center, and rest of the seafood all around. Serve with raita (yogurt salad) or Greek yogurt, cocktail sauce, tartar sauce, and ketchup.

Seared Tuna in Black Sesame Seed Crust with Remoulade, & Garlic Aioli (Serves: 4)

Every now and then I like to prepare some of my meal ahead and cook the meat or seafood just before serving. Here you can make polenta cakes ahead and reheat or make fresh polenta. The Remoulade can be made ahead, just keep the liquid and the vegetables separate. covered in the refrigerator. Tuna takes only 15 minutes to marinate and 5-6 minutes to cook.

Ingredients: For the Polenta, see under Rice, Pasta & Grain.

For the Remoulade: 1 tbsp. canola oil; 1cup chopped yellow onions; 2 fresh garlic cloves peeled and chopped fine; 2 cans, each 14.5 ounces, (411g) Italian style stewed tomatoes; ½ tsp. each dry oregano and thyme; 2 tbsp. fresh squeezed lemon juice; 1 tbsp. sugar; salt and fresh-ground black pepper to taste; 1 Gayla or Red Delicious apple; bell pepper one of each red, orange and green colors, cored and cut into ½-inch cubes (if preparing ahead, wash the cubes, drain out the water, cover with plastic wrap and refrigerate).

For the Aioli: 2 tbsp. fresh squeezed lemon juice; 3-4 large garlic cloves peeled and grated over lemon juice; ¼ to ½ tsp. fresh-ground white or black pepper; 1 tsp. tangerine or lemon zest fine-grated. Mix all together well, then fold into ¾ cup mayonnaise. Cover with plastic wrap and refrigerate until needed.

For the Tuna: One large piece, about 1-1/4 to 1-1/2 pound sushi-grade tuna steak; ¼ cup canola oil; to marinate tuna: ½ tsp. each granulated garlic and fresh-ground black or white pepper, 1 tbsp. tangerine or lemon fine grated zest, 2 tbsp. canola oil; for the crust: ½ cup roasted black sesame seeds; to serve: 1 cup fermented beans (op).

To make the Remoulade: Heat a medium pot on medium heat, add oil and move around to coat the bottom. Add the onions and stir for 5 minutes; add garlic, salt and pepper, cover and cook another 5 minutes on low heat. Add stewed tomatoes, oregano, thyme, sugar, cover and simmer on low heat for 15-20 minutes until onions are soft. Now cut the apple and core it, then slice it into 16 wedges, and then slice each wedge into ½-inch slices across; squeeze the lemon juice all over the apple. When tomatoes are done add the apples to the pot. Turn off the heat and let them cool, then place in a non-reactive bowl and cover with the plastic wrap. You can prepare up to this point a day before.

One hour before serving, add the pepper cubes, stir a little with the wooden spoon (do not use any metal spoon) cover with plastic wrap and refrigerate until serving.

For the Tuna: While you are preparing the peppers, marinate the tuna. Whisk together all marinade ingredients in a medium bowl, slice tuna into 4 equal pieces across, dip tuna pieces on both side, cover with a lid and leave in the room temperature from 15 minutes to ½ hour. Refrigerate for an hour.

When ready to prepare the dinner, take out the tuna slices from the marinade, pat dry with the paper towels, Place the sesame seeds on a plate. Heat a large, heavy-bottom pan over medium-high heat. When oil is very hot, but not smoking, carefully place the tuna in the pan and cook each side only about 45 seconds, take the pan off the heat, wait about 15-20 seconds and carefully turn over the tuna on the next side. Put the pan back on the heat and again cook that side only for 45 seconds, take the pan of the heat, wait for 15 seconds and turn the tuna over to the next side. Do the same until all the sides are cooked. Tuna will be raw in the center.

Prepare 4 heated platters: place the polenta about 2-3 ice-cream scoopfuls, top with the remoulade. Wait 1-2 minutes, then slice each piece of tuna into 1/2-inch thick slices, dip the edges in the sesame seeds and serve around the remoulade and polenta. Scatter the fermented beans all around. Serve with aioli alongside.

Side Dishes

Cheese Balls (M: 15 balls)

These cheese balls are good over salad, with soup, for snacks or in buffets with chutney.

Ingredients: 2 cups grated white sharp cheddar cheese; 1 cup grated fontina cheese; ¾ cup thick ricotta cheese (or drained overnight in a strainer lined with paper towel), 1 tsp. lemon pepper salt seasoning; 1 tsp. fine grated lemon zest; ¼ cup chopped walnuts; canola oil for deep-frying.

For the Coating: 1 cup all-purpose flour; 2 pinches of salt; 1 large eggs beaten with 2 tbsp. milk; 1 cup seasoned bread crumbs.

In a medium bowl mix: cheddar, fontina and ricotta cheeses, then sprinkle lemon seasoning salt, lemon zest and mix well with a fork. Take out some mixture (the size of a walnut roll) into a ball, slightly firmly so it does not fall apart, then put them on wax paper in a tray and chill in refrigerator for at least 30 minutes.

Use 3 platters, one each for flour, eggs and bread crumbs.

Take out the cheese balls and dip them first in flour, then in eggs all around, finally in bread crumbs, pressing them slightly to coat well. Refrigerate them again on wax paper for 10 minutes.

In a frying pan heat 1-1/2-inch-deep canola oil on medium high heat.

When oil almost starts smoking, then drop a few cheese balls in hot oil, sliding them from the edge of the pan, and cook about 40 seconds, turning all around, cooked light brown; take them out fast on paper towel-lined tray. Make sure you cook them in batches and take them out of oil before cheese starts melting.

Serve them warm, or reheat them fast in microwave oven.

Vegetable and Bean Chili (Serves: 4-6)

Ingredients: 1 tbsp. vegetable oil; 1 cup each chopped fine: onion, celery, red or green bell pepper; 1 can each: (15.5 ounces 439g) black chili bean and cannellini bean; 1 can 15 ounces (425g) chickpeas (garbanzo bean); 1 pkg. 10 ounces frozen, or fresh corn; ½ cup cilantro or flat leaf parsley: soft stems and leaves chopped; 1 cup fresh string beans, blanched 2-3 minutes then cooled under running cold water; 2 cans (each 15.5 ounces) stewed tomatoes, 1 can pureed in the blender and 1 can chopped if chunks are too big; 2 tbsp. ketchup; 1 tsp. granulated garlic; 1 tbsp. chili powder; a few drops of Tabasco sauce or red pepper flakes to taste, salt and pepper to taste. To garnish: low-fat yogurt or sour cream, shredded cheddar cheese, sliced scallions and cilantro or parsley, 1 tbsp. warmed smoked or regular paprika.

Place paprika in a piece of aluminum foil, fold the foil from all around and heat over the stove 1 minute, let it rest 1 minute, then sprinkle over the garnish.

Heat a Dutch oven or a large, heavy bottom pot with oil. Sauté onion for 5 minutes, then add the celery and sauté for 5 minutes, now add the green pepper and stir in for 1-2 minutes until it is cooked a little. Add all the beans and corn, stir a little, add half of the garlic and half of the chili powder. Add stewed tomatoes, tomato puree, cilantro or parsley and bring to a boil. Cook on medium heat for 15-20 minutes, simmering. Add rest of the garlic powder, chili powder, tabasco or red pepper flakes, and ketchup, taste for seasoning and add salt and pepper. Turn off the stove. When ready to serve, heat through again, until simmering. Serve garnished with cilantro or parsley, yogurt or sour cream, topped with cheddar cheese and green onion and a little smoked paprika.

Lentils in Cream Sauce
(Dal Makhani) (Serves: 4-6)

In India, beans either split or whole (Dal) are cooked every day. This is a main meal and is served with bread, rice, raita (yogurt salad), and or chutney. Dal Makhani is a fancy and juicy lentil dish.

Ingredients: 2 cups picked-over brown Indian whole lentils soaked in water overnight or green American lentils unsoaked; 3 tbsp. oil or clarified butter (ghee); the puree of 1 cup chopped onion, ½ cup chopped fresh ginger, ¼ cup chopped garlic cloves, 2-3 serrano peppers, pureed in a blender with about ¾ cup water; add ½ tsp. turmeric powder, ½ cup soft cilantro stems, 1 tsp. fresh cardamom seed taken out of the pod,1 tbsp. curry powder or cumin powder and ground a little to incorporate; ½ cup almonds ground into powder; salt to taste; about 1 cup plain tomato sauce; 1 cup heavy cream; 3 tbsp. lemon juice.

1. In a large pot over medium-high heat, bring lentils and 4 cups of water to a boil. Add salt and pepper to taste, reduce the heat and simmer on low. Cook American green lentils for about 15-20 minutes until just soft. Cook Indian brown lentils for about 35-40 minutes until soft. During the cooking, take out all the foam from the top. Then add turmeric and cook soft.

2. In another large pot heat butter or oil on medium heat. Add the onion and spice puree and a little salt and stir well for 2 minutes, add a little salt cover and cook on low heat for 8-10 minutes until it is lightly browned. Add tomato sauce, and lemon juice, almonds and cooked lentils, stir and bring to a boil, then lower the heat to medium and let simmer 10 minutes. Add the cream, stir well and taste for seasoning. Bring to a boil. Lower the heat and simmer 10 minutes. Turn off the stove. When ready to serve simmer on low just to heat through and serve.

Gnocchi (Serves 4 to 6)

I love Italian food just as much I like Indian food. Anything prepared with cheese and sauce is my favorite. This is very easy to make and once you master the technique, you will do it with a snap.

Ingredients: 2 pounds ricotta cheese drained overnight in a strainer lined with double paper towels; 1 medium baking potato boiled and pressed through a potato ricer or mashed well with a fork; 1 extra large egg white; 1/3 cup all-purpose unbleached flour (plus extra for dusting) and 1 teaspoon salt (divided)

1. Boil water in a large pot half filled (about one gallon) and add 1 tsp. of salt, lower the heat and let it simmer.

2. In a medium bowl with a wooden spoon whip ricotta, potato and egg white. Sprinkle the flour and mix it well. Fill the mixture in a medium ziplock bag taking out all the air.

3. Sprinkle about 2 tabs of flour in 4 dinner places, cut one of the corner of plastic bag about 1-inch diameter; twist the bag and squeeze out about a 1-inch piece on a plate over the flour, hold and cut off with a knife with the other hand. Fill one place at a time. Then dust the hands with flour and roll one piece of Gnocchi at a time and put back in the same plate. When one batch is ready (one plate full) carefully drop them in the simmering water. Let them cook for about 8 minutes until they all come up and start floating on the top. Then take a perforated spatula and scrape the bottom, make sure there are none left in the bottom, and then take out of the water onto a tray lined with paper towels. Repeat and cook rest same way.

4. Serve the gnocchi now (or wait until all batches are done) with roasted vegetables or with flavored olive oil and/or with your favorite sauce such as marinara or mango bbq and even with lemon chutney.

Flavored Olive Oil

In a small sauté pan heat ¼ cup of olive oil and 1 large clove of garlic, thin-sliced. When garlic is light brown, add ¼ tsp of red pepper flakes and one thin-sliced scallion (green part only). Take off the heat immediately and pour over the gnocchi and serve. You can prepare this ahead and reheat and serve.

Yogurt or Buttermilk Dumpling (Kadhi) (Serves: 4-6)

This is a vegetarian dinner. This dish has chickpea (garbanzo beans) dumplings, which are very tasty with yogurt. Dumplings alone are so tasty that when we make them, half of them are gone right away. So here I am making a little extra. You can freeze them wrapped in a plastic container for the next time. It is very easy. Instead of dumplings you can also use chopped, cooked or cubed: ham, franks, turkey or chicken, if you prefer with meat.

Ingredients:
Dumpling: 2 cups chickpea flower (besan), ¾ cup water; salt and pepper to taste; canola oil to deep-fry.
Gravy: 2 cups plain low-fat plain yogurt or 2-1/4 cup buttermilk; 1 cup chickpea flour; 2 tbsp. canola oil; 1/2cup chopped onion; ¼ tsp. celery seeds; 1/4tsp. turmeric, 1 tsp. fenugreek power (op); 1 tsp. curry powder or cumin powder; 1 tsp. pani-puri masala or ½ tsp. lemon-pepper mix; ½ tsp. granulated garlic; ¼ cup chopped cilantro stems (op); salt and pepper to taste; 1 cup frozen peas; 1-2 tbsp. grated ginger; 2 tbsp. chopped parsley or cilantro to garnish

Dumplings:
1. In a large non-reactive bowl whisk together chickpea flour, water, salt and pepper and set aside for at least 15 minutes.
2. Heat a large wok or large and shallow pot with about 2-inches deep oil on medium-high heat. When oil almost starts smoking, then using a small ice cream scoop or a tablespoon, very carefully fill in the scoop half way and drop the batter, in a ball, in the oil, starting near the edge. Continue to drop the batter into the oil, wiping the bottom of the scoop against the rim of the bowl. When the wok is full, in a single layer, wait until they are lightly brown underneath. Stir the oil in the middle with a metal spatula, so that most of the dumpling will turn over by themselves; the rest you can turn them over with the spatula and cook the other side golden. Using the large perforated spatula, take the dumplings out on a paper towel-lined platter and repeat the process for the rest of the dumplings.

Gravy:
1. To make the gravy: use the same bowl and whisk together chickpea flour, salt and pepper to taste and 2 cups water; then slowly whisk in the yogurt/buttermilk, then whisk in the another 3-1/2 cups of water. The mixture will be watery.
2. Be careful and pour out all the oil from the wok into another pot (extra oil) saving only about 2 tbsp. for the gravy. Now add the chopped onions and sauté on medium heat for 5 minutes. Push the onions aside and sauté the celery seeds light brown. Sprinkle turmeric, fenugreek powder, curry/cumin powder, gran. Garlic and a little salt and pepper over the onion and sauté for 5 minutes, until transparent.

3. Now pour in the watery yogurt mixture, increase heat high and stirring and scraping the bottom, bring the mixture to a boil. Add cilantro stems and when mixture start boiling, reduce the heat to medium and keep it on constant simmering; stir on and off for about 30 minutes cooking open. Add the frozen peas, lemon-pepper mix or pani-puri spices, ginger, and again bring the mixture to a boil. Boil for 5 minutes, lower the heat and let it cook for 15 minutes, open on medium heat, stirring every- occasionally until the gravy is cooked. It should go down about 1 inch on the edges. Taste for salt and pepper.

4. Turn off the heat, wait for about 5 minutes and then add the dumplings (or cooked and heated meat), dipping them lightly and covering them with the gravy. But let them float on the top. Cover wok almost all the way, leaving about 1 inch open with the lid; wait for 15 minutes and serve in a bowl garnished with parsley or cilantro with rice and vegetables.

5. Reheat on low heat next day. Pani-puri spices are found in Indian grocery stores, which is almost like chili spices.

Yogurt Salad (Raita) S:6-8

This yogurt salad, or raita, can be served with almost any meal, leftovers, grilled or baked food or snacks. We make sure we serve with fried food to cut down the effect of the fat. Although the black is high in acid, it tastes good with the yogurt.

Ingredients: 2 pounds plain low-fat yogurt, ½ cup diced red bell peppers, ½ cup diced fresh tomatoes, 2 med. Kirby cucumbers, one cored and grated and one cored and diced; ½ cup sliced green onion (scallion), ¼ cup peeled and grated fresh ginger, 1 tab fresh and soft cilantro (coriander) stems thin sliced, ¼ tsp. granulated garlic, salt and fresh-ground black pepper to taste, 1 tab clarified butter (ghee) or canola oil, 1 tsp. caraway seeds, 1 tsp. black mustard seeds (op), 4 dry serrano peppers broken in half, stems and seeds taken out (op), ½ tsp. black salt (op); 1 tab fresh chopped or 1 tsp. dry crumbled mint for garnish.

Whip the yogurt in a large bowl with 1 cup of water. Add all chopped vegetables, herbs and spices except oil, caraway and mustard seeds, serrano peppers and mint.

Heat a small sauté pan, add caraway and mustard seeds, shake a little, then pour oil on the top. When caraway seeds get a shade darker and mustard seeds start cracking, drop the pieces of the serrano peppers, cover right away, shake a little and pour the contents onto the yogurt cover and set the yogurt aside.

Just before serving, stir the raita, garnish with the mint.

Eggplant Parmesan (Serves: 8-10)

This vegetarian dish is everyone's favorite. You can use for lunch, dinner or as snack, with or without garlic bread. This tastes better the next day. You will need a large lasagna pan or a 14-1/2x9-1/2x2-inch glass pan.

Ingredients: 4 large royal purple eggplants or large even shape eggplants without big heads (large-head eggplants are matured and have tough seeds); 3 large eggs; about 2 cups seasoned dry bread crumbs (divided); canola or olive oil to shallow fry; 2 pounds ricotta cheese mixed with 1 large egg and 2 tbsp. chopped chives or fresh basil; 1 cup grated parmesan cheese or 2 cups fresh shredded parmesan cheese; 2 bottles each 24 ounces 680 g, tomato-pasta sauce; 1-2 tbsp. butter; to serve on side: garlic bread and roasted red bell peppers or green salad.

1. Heat 2 large, heavy-bottom pans on low heat. Spread out 1-1/2 cups bread crumbs in a large platter. Beat 3 large eggs in another large platter.
2. When pans are heated, add about 2 tbsp. of oil in each. Take one eggplant at a time, cut off the stem, peel the skin off on two flat sides and stand it up, with stem side up, head side down. Now slice thin, the peeled side, into about ¼-inch slices. Large eggplant will give about 8 slices. Sprinkle each slice lightly with salt.
3. Increase the heat to medium to medium-high, do not let the oil burn. Dip each slice of eggplant in egg, then lightly in bread crumbs, and add to the pan, about 3-4 slices as they fit. Brown the eggplant slices about 2 minutes on each side or until light brown on both sides. Take them out on a large tray lined with paper towels. Cook rest of the eggplants same way. If there are any burned bread crumbs, wipe out the pan with paper towel before adding new oil each time.
4. Assemble the platter: Preheat the oven at 400 degrees. Grease a large pan with 14-1/2x9-1/2x2-inch sides. Pour over ½ of the bottle of the pasta sauce (about 1 cup) all over. Line a layer of eggplant slices (about 10 slices) overlapping about ½-inch. Pour over another ½ bottle of tomato sauce, sprinkle 1/3 of the parmesan cheese, then top with 1/3 of the ricotta mixture all over. Repeat, making 3 layers of the eggplants. Finally, on the top, spread tomato sauce, parmesan cheese, ricotta mixture, and mix about 1/3 cup of bread crumbs with 1 tbsp. of butter and sprinkle all over on the top. Pour about ½ tsp. of either tomato sauce or tomato water in each corner (so corners don't burn).
5. Cover platter airtight with aluminum foil. Bake in a preheated oven at 400 degrees for 15 minutes, and at 350 degrees for about 30 minutes, until bubbly. Open the platter and bake about 30 minutes until lightly brown on the top. Turn off the oven and let it rest in the oven for 15 minutes before serving.
6. Serve with garlic bread and roasted red bell peppers or salad.

Tips: When you cut the eggplant it turns brown and gets bitter as soon as it is exposed to air. So immediately after cutting or slicing, sprinkle lightly with the salt. If you are not going to use the slices right away, put the slices back in the shape of the eggplant. This way salt will get on both sides of the slices and air will not get between them.

Eggplant parmesan tastes better when reheated. So either make it a day ahead and reheat it or just make 1 or 2 hours ahead of serving and reheat it a few minutes covered, until bubbly, then reheat it open; do not let it burn on the sides.

Black-eyed Peas and Rice (Serves: 6-8)

This is the New Year's Day "Hoppin' John" dinner to bring good luck throughout the year is a famous southern dinner with beans, greens, rice and corn bread. You can choose any of your favorite greens recipe to go with the dinner. Fennel gives a good flavor and helps digest the food.

For the Black-eyed Peas – Ingredients: 1 cup dry black-eyed peas picked over and washed; 1 cup each chopped: onion, carrots, celery, fennel (or ½ cup fennel frongs); 1/3 tsp. turmeric (op); 1 can 8 ounce (227g), about 1 cup tomato sauce; salt and pepper to taste; ½ tsp. granulated garlic; 1 tbsp. ketchup and 1 tsp. lemon juice. To garnish: ½ cup chopped cilantro or flat-leaf parsley and ½ cup grated fresh ginger.

1. In a medium pot add about 4 cups of, water add the beans, then top with the chopped vegetables and turmeric. Make sure water covers all the vegetables. Bring it to a boil, lower the heat and simmer covered for about 30 minutes or until beans are cooked well, but not mushy.

2. Add tomato sauce, granulate garlic, salt and pepper to taste add ketchup, lemon juice, and simmer for 5 minutes. Serve with rice and garnished with cilantro and ginger.
3. If you do not want to use the tomato sauce and ketchup then use half water and half chicken broth in cooking, and add about ½ cups chopped, soft cilantro stems and about 1 tbsp. fresh ginger in the beginning with the beans.

Plain Rice

This is plain nourishing rice with some flavor. You can use brown rice with a little more water and it will take a little longer to cook. But white rice works very well.

Ingredients: 1 cup aged (about 6 months old) long-grain white rice; ½ tsp. black mustard seeds; ½ tsp. caraway seeds; 1/3 tsp. turmeric powder; about 3-4 drops vegetable oil or ghee (clarified butter).

1. In a medium pot (about 5 quart) soak rice, 2 ups water, turmeric, black mustard and caraway seeds for about 2 hours. Just before cooking add oil or ghee, cover and leave the pot on medium heat for 5 minutes. When rice starts boiling, stir it well, lower the heat and simmer, covered for about 12-15 minutes or until all the water is gone and the rice is ¾ soft. Turn off the heat and leave it covered for another 10-15 minutes. By this time rice should be cooked completely. Fluff the rice with a fork, add some butter for flavor, if desired, and serve with beans.

Chickpeas or Garbanzo Beans (Serves: about 15)

These fancy chickpeas or cholay go very well with deep-fried bread called bhature. This is one of the famous dishes from Delhi. These freeze very well in the containers, so make a large batch and serve with the bhature (puffy bread) or rice pilaf. You can use these for lunch, dinner and even for snacks.

Ingredients: 1 recipe of all-purpose fresh-ground spices, or you can buy cholay or chickpeas spices from Indian grocery stores; ¼ cup canola or olive oil; 1 large can, about 6 lb.,14 oz., (3.12 kg) cooked chickpeas or garbanzo beans drained and rinse well with the water; 3 to 4 tbsp. or to taste lemon juice; 1 bottle 24 oz. (680g) Italian tomato sauce with basil and garlic (or Prego sauce); 1 cup, 8 ounces plain tomato sauce; 1 cup chopped fresh cilantro leave and stems, plus extra chopped leaves to garnish; salt and cayenne pepper to taste; vegetable, bhature (puffy fried bread) or rice pilaf to serve.

Heat a large pot (about 10 pounds) on medium-high heat. Add oil and fresh spice mixture and sauté for 8-10 minutes. Reduce the heat, cover and simmer for 15 minutes, stirring once during cooking. Add chickpeas and cilantro stems, stir well, bring to a boil, cover and simmer on low heat for 30 minutes.

Add tomato sauces, lemon juice, salt and cayenne pepper to taste and simmer another 30 minutes. When ready to serve heat again and serve in a bowl sprinkled with fresh cilantro, with vegetables, bread or rice.

BBQ, Grilling, Sushi, Burgers and Kebobs

Barbeque is slow-cooking and grilling is fast and direct cooking on the grill. I like to do most of my seafood cooking on the indoor grill or the grilling pan; it is controlled and fast. Buying grills depends on your budget and type of cooking you will be doing. If you are an entertainer and having a large number of people, you sure need a large grill; otherwise no reason to go overboard. A charcoal or gas grill is also the consideration. To my experience, gas grills are easier to handle, clean and within a few minutes they are ready to grill. A charcoal grill will need a starter, briquettes and some patience.

When using a grill make sure you have necessary tools to do the cooking: heat-resistant gloves, a long-handle fork, tongs, a spatula, basting brush, metal and wooden skewers, a hot-coal poker, meat thermometer, drip pan, etc.

For healthy grilling, buy a lean cut of meat, trim all excess fat and precook most of the meats and poultry indoors; then just partially cook or heat outdoors. The burned meat and fat produces hydrocarbons that cause cancer, and it is believed the prolonged use of burned and charred meat increases the risk of cancer by a large percentage. So why not enjoy the grilling as well as taking care of the health? Also, try to grill more vegetables and fish than meat. Always use an aluminum drip pan right under the food and over the coals so the fat that drips from the meat will end up in the pan and will not produce any cancer-causing elements.

Prior to grilling on a charcoal grill, make sure grill is hot enough to do the job; place your hand about four inches above the center of coals; if your hand can take the heat for 2 seconds, it is hot; four seconds for medium and about six seconds for low heat. I first wash my hands with water and dry well just before placing four inches above the coal. This way your hand will not burn, especially if you have to do grilling for a long time.

Grilling Tips

1. Make sure you take out the meat from the refrigerator 30 minutes to an hour before grilling so that the meat is almost at room temperature.
2. Heat the grill first and then turn it off; scrub clean the grill with a metal brush or a damped rag, dipped in oil.
3. Trim the excess fat so that it does not drip down or cause fire while grilling.
4. Use both direct and indirect heat. Direct heat will be for shorter cooking and for tender cuts that cook under 15-20 minutes, such as fish, steak, kebabs etc. Indirect heat is for longer and larger piece of meats, like roasts and whole chickens.

Start the Grill: Use a gas or charcoal grill. For the charcoal grill, use a chimney starter. Open the bottom vents. Fill the chimney starter ¾ with charcoal briquettes, pour lighter fluid all over the briquettes lightly; close and put the fluid away. Then light the briquettes and let them burn on high heat to full intensity. Pour the briquettes in the grill and top with the grates.

For direct grilling, wait till briquettes are fully red and glowing. Place the grate about 6 inches above the heat source and grill directly on open fire fast. Turn the meat over only once when it is cooked almost half way. For indirect heat, push out the coals on one side of the grill, making room on the opposite side for indirect barbecuing. Open all the vents and cook covered.

Barbecuing is low, slow, smoke cooking. Maintain a steady temperature. Add about 1-2 handfuls of coals every 20 to 30 minutes to keep the fire going. Keep on turning the food over and around to keep it from burning, every half hour or so. If food starts burning, cover it loosely with foil and cook until it is done. When the meat is done, take out in a serving platter and let it rest 5 to 8 minutes before slicing.

Skillet Beans (Serves: 4-6)

These are grilled beans that you can cook in the oven or on the grill. We make extra beans, and if there is any leftover you can serve them over rice.

Ingredients: 2 tbsp. canola or olive oil; 4 strips bacon; 1 cup diced onion; ¾ cup or to taste thick ketchup-style hot sauce; about 3 tbsp. molasses; 2 tbsp. Worcestershire sauce; 1 tbsp. brown mustard; 1tsp. dry oregano; salt and cayenne pepper to taste; 2 cans 14.5 oz. pinto beans drained; 1 cup chunk pineapple from the can.

You can bake these beans indoors in the oven and later heat on the grill, or cook on the BBQ grill. Prepare a barbecue grill at medium heat or around 350 degrees. In a large cast-iron skillet, cook bacon strips until they are crispy; take out and set aside. Pour out the bacon fat and add the canola oil, and fry onions for 6-8 minutes until transparent. Add rest of the spices and sauces. Bring to a simmer, add the beans stir well, cover and simmer for 25-30 minutes covered with the foil. Add the pineapple, crumbled bacon and salt to taste, heat to warm ingredients. Take off the heat and serve, or keep covered reheat and serve little later.

Grilled Whole Beef Tenderloin (Serves: about 8)

Beef Tenderloin is the king of grilling. Everyone loves a juicy and tender beef. Take out the silver skin and trim off the ends to make it almost an even thickness. In my opinion tenderloin should be cooked medium or medium-rare; you want it juicy.

Ingredients: One beef tenderloin, about 4 to 5 pounds trimmed with even thickness; rub: 1-2 seeded jalapeno ground with 4 large garlic cloves, 2 tbsp. fennel seeds, 2 tbsp. cumin seeds, 1 tsp. kosher salt, and 4 tbsp. olive oil; spices to sprinkle: 1 tbsp. dry mustard powder, 2 tbsp. onion powder, and 2 tbsp. dry rosemary.

Prepare the charcoal or gas grill on high heat, about 500 degrees. Pat dry the tenderloin and rub all around with the jalapeno mixture, then sprinkle the spice mixture; set aside for 5 minutes on a rack in a shallow roasting pan. Place the roasting pan on the direct heat, cover the lid, and grill the tenderloin for about 35 to 40 minutes. The internal temperature should be around 135 degrees for medium-rare. Take out the roasting pan and let it rest for 15-20 minutes tented with an aluminum foil, before slicing. Serve with wine gravy and sides.

Barbecue Ginger Chicken (Serves: 4-6)

This is boneless, skinless chicken and can dry out very easily. So be careful in cooking, use medium direct heat halfway then move chicken to indirect heat or cook open without covering the grill, so that the juices stay in, while the chicken is cooked. If you are crazy about the smoky flavor, add to the prepared sauce:1tsp. Liquid Smoke, take it out from the bottle without shaking it and do not use the bottom residue.

Ingredients: For the Chicken – 3 to 3-1/2 Pound boneless, skinless big and plump Chicken Breast; 1/2tsp. each: granulated Garlic & Cayenne Pepper; 1tbsp. Smoked Paprika; to brush the chicken at the end: 2tbsp. soften Butter mixed with 1tbsp. Lemon Juice.

For the Marinade: 1C Dark Beer, 1tbsp. crushed Ginger; 1tsp. crushed Black Pepper; 1tbsp. Vegetable or Canola Oil, (No Salt: beer is salty).

For the B.B.Q Sauce: 3/4Cup Orange Juice; 3/4cup Ketchup; 3tbsp. fine grated or ground fresh peeled Ginger; 3tbsp. Tomato Paste; 1/2tsp. each: granulated Garlic, Onion Powder, fresh-ground Black Pepper, dry Rosemary; 1/4tsp. each dry Oregano, salt or taste; 3tbsp. light Brown Sugar.

For the Sauce: Heat a large sauté pan on medium heat add the orange juice, increase the heat to medium-high and reduce the juice to half. Add rest of the ingredients bring to a simmer and simmer 12-15 minutes, set aside, covered to cool. You can make the sauce a day before and reheat just to warm the sauce.

For the Chicken: Wash the chicken pieces under the running cold water. Trim out all the fat and then cut each halved chicken breast across in to two pieces. Whip together the marinade ingredients in a platter and coat the chicken pieces both side and refrigerate for 2-3 hours.

When ready to cook, take out the chicken from the refrigerator. Clean the grill and lightly dampen a cloth or a few layers of paper towels, squeeze out all the water, fold and dip well in the canola oil then generously grease the grades. Prepare the grill for medium heat.

Take the chicken pieces from the marinade and place in a large platter in single layer. Sprinkle the chicken with granulated garlic, cayenne and then with the smoked paprika, turn over and sprinkle the other side. When the grill is ready place the larger pieces of the chicken in the center and smaller pieces outside, the skin side down and flesh side up. Cover the grill halfway with the lid and grill the chicken on medium heat for 8-10 minutes (depending on the thickness of the breast). The chicken should be done half way.

Take out the chicken and drop in the sauce pan, coat both sides with the sauce or brush the sauce both side and place on the grill again, flesh side down and grill uncovered for 6-8 minutes, until you have grill marks and the chicken is almost done. Turn over and cook the other side for another 1-2 minutes or until done. Now brush the chicken with lemon butter one side and place on the warm serving platter, loosely tented with the aluminum foil or serve it right away. Serve warm with green salad, potatoes and/or garlic toasts, etc.

Tips:

1. The best way to use chicken breast is fresh. If you have frozen chicken breasts, defrost them for 2-3 days in the refrigerator; make sure they are completely thawed.

2. If you have any doubt that chicken is not done inside, leave the chicken on indirect heat (the cool side of the grill) for a few minutes, but do not let the chicken dry.

3. While grill is still warm, scrape the grades with a metal spatula. Use damp paper towel and clean out the grades as much as possible when the grill is completely cooled, then do the rest of the cleaning.

B.B.Q. Chicken Wings (S:4-6)

These easy and tasty wings are party favorites. Serve with salad or for appetizers.

Ingredients: About 2 pounds chicken wings separated and tips removed; 1Tsp. each granulated garlic and cayenne pepper; marinade mixture: ½ cup tomato ketchup,1/4 cup honey, 1/2 cup sour cream, 1Tsp. curry powder, 1Tsp. onion powder, 2Tbsp. soy sauce, 1/2Tsp. tabasco sauce, whisk all together and set aside about 4Tbsp. marinade for brushing later; to garnish: 4Tbsp. each toasted sesame seeds and scallion.

Wash and pat dry the wings and sprinkle with cayenne and garlic powder lightly all over. Dip the chicken wings in the marinade with a tong to coat all sides. Refrigerate for about 45 minutes.

Clean and oil the grill well and prepare it at medium heat about 350 degrees. Drip dry the wings and place them on the grill with a tong; cover and grill the wings for about 15-20 minutes, turning them over every 10 minutes, until they are done and crisp. Brush with the reserve marinade and serve with salad. Alternately, you can bake them indoor in the oven. Preheat oven at 350 degrees. Use a large baking tray with sides, line it with the aluminum foil. Place the wings in a single layer, then cover top with the aluminum foil. Bake wings for 30 minutes turning the tray around halfway once. Then open the tray, turn the wings over, increase the temperature at 400 degrees and bake 8-10 minutes until they are crisp.

Grilled Fresh Corn

We grew up on grilled corn. The more dry spices and lemon juice you use, the better it tastes. And if you are chutney lover, almost any kind of sour and spicy chutney can be brushed on as an extra bonus. My father needed a little bowl of spicy and sour cilantro-mint chutney all the time. He will use a tablespoon and as he eats the corn, he will keep on layering the corn with extra chutney.

The Basic Grilling of the Corn (Serves: 4)

Buy 4 fresh corns, take out the outer dark green husk, twist the top silk and take it out. Then slowly peel one upper layer at a time and turn over backward. At the end, pull out all the silk covering the kernels. Now, soak for 2 hrs. in the cold salted water.

Scrub clean the grill, grease it with a rag or the wand of paper towels. Prepare a charcoal or gas grill at medium heat or use the gas stove indoors; place the corn over the grill, making sure the husk is away from the heat. You will hear popping noises while the kernels are cooking. Cook each side about 30 seconds or until it is browned or charred lightly. Keep on turning around the corn until it is browned on all sides. It should take about 5 to 8 minutes, depending on the thickness of the kernels and the heat intensity. Rub the corn with the flavor you want, and also serve extra spices and lemon wedges on the side.

The Lemon Flavor: Right after grilling the corn, rub the half-cut lemon all over the grilled corn, then brush with the melted butter, sprinkle with salt and pepper or with the lemon-pepper seasoning mix (Mrs. Dash).

The Cilantro Flavor: After grilling the corn, rub with the half-cut lemon, then brush with the butter, and sprinkle with the cilantro salt to taste, or brush with some cilantro and mint chutney.

Cilantro Salt (M: about ¼ cup)

In a mortar and pestle (or in a blender, you can double or triple the recipe), crush well: 1/4 cup cilantro leaves, 4 large garlic clove diced, 1serrano pepper chopped and 4 tbsp. table salt. If you prefer. You should make it the day you are going to use, and keep it wrapped in a plastic wrap, in a covered bowl. The flavor and color go away very fast.

The Spicy Tandoori Flavor: Grill the corn as above, rub with the cut lemon, brush with the melted butter, then dip or sprinkle about 1-2 tbsp. of chat masala (make your own or buy at the Indian grocery stores) or Montreal steak seasoning (found in most of the American supermarkets).

The Cheese Flavor: On the fresh-grilled corn, you can always use some lemon juice for extra flavor. Or just rub in about 1-2 tbsp. of feta or soft goat cheese first, then sprinkle or dip in grated parmesan cheese. Serve some soft cheese and grated cheese on the side.

Lamb Kebob (Serves: 4)

These are spicy and tasty with fresh herbs and dry spices.

Ingredients : l-1/2 pounds (about 3 cups packed) ground lamb; 3-4 tbsp. canola oil; each chopped and pureed together: 1 medium onion, 4 garlic cloves, 4 tbsp. fresh ginger, 2 serrano peppers, ½ cup soft cilantro stems and leaves; ½ cup seasoned bread crumbs; ½ tsp. salt or to taste; 2 extra large eggs beaten; 2 tbsp. pomegranate molasses or ketchup; ¼ tsp. baking soda; 1 tbsp. curry powder; 1 tsp. fenugreek powder (op); 1 tsp. granulated garlic; 1 tbsp. lemon juice. Serve with lentil pilaf, raita (yogurt salad), lemon chutney, hummus, pita bread, lemon wedges, and fresh ripe grape or salad tomatoes.

1. Heat a large cast-iron pan on medium high heat or start an outdoor grill with well-greased grades on medium-high heat. Spread out the ground lamb on a large platter, then top with herb puree, bread crumbs, salt, baking soda, molasses or ketchup, eggs, curry powder, fenugreek powder, garlic powder, and lemon juice. Mix a little with a wooden spoon. Do not mix with the hands.
2. Divide meat mixture in to 8 pieces. When pan is hot, add 1 tbsp. of oil and make 4 meatballs with light hands; roll them long and drop on the edge, against the side of the pan, drizzle with 1 tsp. of oil on top, cook about 1 minute on medium-high heat, until browned underneath, then turn over with a metal spatula. Cook all 4 sides dropping a little oil over, for easy turning, until all sides are browned. It will take about 6-7 minutes in the hot pan. Cook in 2 batches.
3. If cooking on the grill, take 1 meatball at a time, press all around the metal skewer to hold the meat well, drizzle some oil and cook on direct high heat, about 2 minutes, until browned well underneath, then scrape with the metal spatula, loosen the kebab and turn over the meat; drizzle a few drops of oil for easy turning. Brown all 4 sides and serve hot on skewers in a large platter over rice pilaf.

Shish Kebobs (Serves: 4-6)

Traditionally, shish kebabs are made from lamb. These Mediterranean kebabs are threaded with the lamb meat and grilled. There are a few layers of spices to give a robust flavor.

Ingredients: About 2 to 2-1/2 pounds shoulder or leg of lamb meat cut into even size, about 1-1/2-inch cubes (cut meat into slices first, then cut into strips and then cut into cubes.); the rub: 1 tbsp. dried mint leaves (take out the mint leaves, place them in a platter and dry them out on the refrigerator top for 4-5 days; crumble just before using.), 2 tbsp. dried marjoram, 1 tbsp. ground cumin, 1 tsp. granulated garlic, 1 tsp. cayenne pepper, combine all together; the marinade: 1-1/2 cup red wine (or ½ cup cider vinegar mixed with 1 cup water) mixed with 1 tbsp. lemon zest, 2 tbsp. canola oil; spices to brush on: ¼ cup melted butter mixed with ¼ cup lemon juice, 1 tbsp. cayenne pepper, and 1 tsp. salt; 2 tbsp. chat masala to garnish (op); metal skewers to thread the meat on. To serve: lemon wedges, pita bread, mint chutney and yogurt raita etc.

Place the meat cubes in a bowl, add half of the rub to wine mixture and other half to butter mixture, and pour over the wine mixture over the meat; marinate the meat from 2 hours to overnight. Drain the cubes, thread tightly in the same direction on the metal skewers. Prepare the grill with medium-high heat, about 390 to 400 degrees.

Place the skewers directly over the grades, brush lightly with butter mixture, and cook the meat until light brown underneath, then turn around each side until they are lightly browned, about 7 to 9 minutes total. Brush them with the butter mixture again, sprinkle with the chat masala and serve warm with sides.

Grilled Pork Shoulder (Serves: 8-10)

My friend Maria, from Cuba, always cooked the whole pig outdoors on each Father's Day. They roasted pork shoulder and smoked ham. They always served that with black beans, corn and potato salad. This pork you can serve on buns, or sliced or pulled with the sides.

Ingredients: One bone-in about 5 to 6 pounds pork shoulder; for the rub: 2 tbsp. each: garlic powder, onion powder, ground cumin, and 1 tbsp. black pepper; 6 oz. tomato paste, 1 tbsp. coarse sea salt; sauce or the glaze: ½ cup cider vinegar, ¼ cup brown mustard, ½ cup ketchup style hot chili sauce, ½ cup marmalade, salt and pepper to taste; heat all sauce ingredients and strain.

Pork takes seasoning well, so about 1 hour before cooking or the night before, rub the pork with the rub, place in a zip-lock bag and marinate overnight. Soak about some apple, pecan or hickory chips in water for 2-3 hours, drain and place them in aluminum foil and close from all around. Make some holes on the top, and when ready to grill, place them directly on the heat on one side of the grill. Place a water pan under the indirect heat side

Prepare a barbecue grill for indirect heat at medium heat about 350 degrees. Sprinkle the salt on top of pork, then spread out the tomato paste on the top. Place the pork above the water pan and smoke the pork at medium-low heat of about 275 to 300 degrees until the internal temperature reaches around 142 to 145 degrees, for about 3-1/2 to 4 hours. When the pork is done, take out the roasting pan, tent with a foil and let it rest for 15 minutes. Then slice, or pull apart with 2 forks, drizzle some sauce over, and serve with extra sauce or glaze on the side.

Barbecue Pork Skewers (Serves: 6 to 8)

Buy about 3 pounds, boneless pork butt (shoulder) and cut into 2-inch cubes. Marinate overnight as above. Prepare the indirect grill, thread the soaked skewers with about 4-5 pieces of the pork on each; cook on the indirect heat with lid down at 300 degrees for about 30 minutes. Open the lid, increase the heat to medium about 350 degrees, and grill open, turning them all around until they are done and you can pull them apart (internal temperature should around 145 degrees). When they are almost done, brush them with the glaze generously all over, heat a little all around, and serve. Serve over the beans or salad.

Baby Backs Ribs (Serves: 4)

Ribs need to rest after partial cooking. So plan ahead. Use a glaze or your favorite barbecue sauce for brushing and serving. I like these ribs because the hard work is done earlier. You just have to heat, glaze and serve.

Ingredients: 4 slabs, each about 1-1/2 pound pork baby back ribs, a total of 6 pounds; pull out the clear skin with a point of a knife from the bottom, then pull back with a paper towel; to brush: ½ cup brown mustard; the rub: 1tbsp. each: cayenne pepper, roasted and ground cumin and cilantro seeds, granulated garlic, onion powder, 1 tsp. kosher salt, and 2 tbsp. ground fennel seeds, mixed together; about 1-1/2 cup favorite thick barbecue sauce; to garnish: ½ cup green onion sliced.

About 30 minutes ahead of cooking, bring the ribs in the room temperature. Brush the ribs with the mustard and sprinkle the rub; do not use any salt. Preheat the oven at 275 degrees. Place the ribs in a double layer of aluminum foil, wrap the foil from all around airtight, and bake them for about 2 hours. Take out the ribs and after 15 minutes open the foil; cool the ribs in the foil. Again wrap them and refrigerate for at least 2 to 10 hours.

Half an hour before grilling, take out the ribs in room temperature. Prepare a barbecue grill with medium heat about 275 to 300 degrees. Cook ribs in foil for 1 hour until heated through. Then place the ribs directly over the grades and heat for about 15 minutes, turning them all around. Brush well with barbecue sauce, and heat again for another 8-10 minutes or until the sauce start glazing the ribs. Serve hot with slaw, fries and extra sauce on the side.

Hoisin Glazed Cedar Plank Salmon (Serves: 4)

This is a fancy way to cook and present salmon. Make sure you serve with fresh herb-vegetable vinaigrette. You need to buy a cedar cooking plank, unpolished, about ¼ to 1/3-inch thick, and soak it in clean cold water for about 3 to 4 hours before using.

(1) Herb-vegetable Vinaigrette (M: about 2 cups)

Ingredients: ½ cup thin sliced scallions; 1 cup fine chopped plum tomatoes; 2 tbsp. drained capers; ½ cup fine chopped red bell pepper; 2 tbsp. sherry vinegar; 4 tbsp. extra-virgin olive oil; 1 tbsp. peeled and fresh grated ginger; salt and pepper to taste.

Prepare all vegetables and herbs ahead, place them in a non-reactive bowl, cover and refrigerate until serving. Just before serving whisk together oil, vinegar, ginger, capers, and add salt and pepper to taste. Pour over the herbs and vegetables, and garnish the fish.

(2) For the Grilled Salmon

Ingredients: 1 panel untreated cedar plank soaked in water for about 3 to 4 hours; about 2 pounds boneless salmon with skin on (I prefer the tail part that has more meat and less bones); the rub: ½ tsp. cayenne pepper mixed with 1 tbsp. lemon-pepper mix (Mrs. Dash); marinade and sauce: ¾ cup thick hoisin sauce and marinade (original) mixed with 1 tbsp. lemon juice, ¼ tsp. salt, and ½ tsp. granulated garlic powder; 5-6 tbsp. olive oil.

Prepare the grill for direct cooking at about 450 degrees. Heat the marinade mixture with 1 tbsp. of olive oil, and set aside to cool. Wash and pat dry the salmon, and check out for bones by moving a finger over the surface. Sprinkle with the rub mixture first, then pour over about a quarter of the marinade mixture, spread out with a wooden spoon and set aside for 15-20 minutes.

Take out the plank, pat dry and brush well with about 3-4 tbsp. of oil on the top surface where you will place the salmon. Place the salmon on the plank, and carefully place the plank on the heated grill. Close the lid. Cook the salmon for about 15 minutes, or until it turns opaque and flakes easily, but the center can be a little firm and rare. If the plank catches on fire, spray some water and put out the flames. Take out the plank, place it on a folded kitchen towel over the serving platter. Brush again with more hoisin sauce mixture. Then spread out the herb-vegetable vinaigrette and serve with extra sauce and the sides.

Seafood Kebobs (Serves: 4)

You can do this on indoor or outdoor grill. Oil the grill well and have the grill ready on medium to medium high heat. If using wooden skewers soak them in the water 2-3 hrs. or overnight.

1. **Ingredients:** 2 tbsp. Old Bay seasoning or lemon-pepper salt mix with ½ tsp. ground cumin; salt and pepper to taste; 2 lemons sliced and 1 lemon to use for juice; 1 pound each: large sea scallops, center-cut salmon fillet or other firm fish, cleaned jumbo shrimp, olive oil or canola oil to brush on the skewers; to serve: grilled corn, watercress, marinated beets, radishes, lemon slices, yogurt chutney, cocktail or any other sauce.

2. Heat grill on medium-high for direct heat and brush well with the oil. Using two skewers (holds seafood better), thread three scallops each on the skewers. Check for any bones and cut salmon in to 8 large pieces. Thread on two skewers, alternating 3 shrimps and 2 pieces of salmon across the grain. Push salmon tightly between the shrimps so they don't fall apart.

3. Sprinkle skewers both sides, first with Old Bay seasoning, then salt and pepper and finally brush with olive oil. Place the skewers with an angle on the medium heat. Cook scallops about 4 minutes first side and about 3 minutes on the second side. The shrimp will be ready to turn in about 3 minutes on the first side and about 2 minutes on the second side; when shrimp turn pink and salmon turns opaque and have good grill marks they are done. Each seafood cooks differently, depending on the cut and thickness. Use a metal spatula from left and right to scrape off the grill and loosen the skewers before turning over. Brush lightly again before turning over to second side. Turn skewers over only once.

4. When done, sprinkle skewers lightly with all the spices again while they are still hot. Serve on the lightly heated platter and sprinkle all kebobs with the lemon juice. Serve with grilled corn, fresh watercress, marinated beets, fresh radishes, lemon slices, yogurt chutney (healthy with grilling) and cocktail or any other sauce.

Burgers

Comfort food is getting more common all around the United States, especially here in New Jersey. Burgers are famous for meat and toppings. Also, burgers and cheeses go together very well. As a matter of fact when the cheese is filled inside a burger, it helps cook it faster and tastier. I like cheese both inside and outside. Inside cheeses taste better when you use sharp and flavored ones like pepper-jack, cheddar and blue cheese. Blue cheese is a sharp one, so use it in moderation. Outside cheese can be both sharp and soft. Just make sure after burger is done, you top it with a slice of cheese, cover or cook a little longer and melt the cheese. Our secret to burgers is Cilantro Chutney on the bun and Pepper Relish on the top (the last item), and now you are in heaven. Try to use two different type of sauces, and chutney made with the herbs a must.

Making a Burger: You can use a 100% USDA meat. Just make sure you use good meat. As far as fat is concerned, you can always add some melted clarified butter, a little warm milk or a little heavy cream. Just do not mix too much. Use a wooden spoon and mix lightly the added ingredients.

You can make patties by hand. Divide the meat evenly among burgers. Roll meat into patties, make a depression in the center, make sure they have even thickness. Just remember to handle the meat with light hands and as little as possible.

You can also use a large lid of a bottle, like for a 4-pound peanut butter jar, that makes very good large burgers in a minute. Just line the lid with plastic wrap and press in the meat. Then make a depression in the center. To make 4 large beef burgers, you need around 1-1/2 pounds ground beef. Turn over the lid and place the patty on a platter. You can also fill them with cheese etc. Make one at a time, fill with cheese etc., press down the cheese evenly, then cover the stuffing with the meat. Do all the same way.

Cooking the Burger: Burger should be cooked on high heat and in a heavy-bottom pan. I prefer the cast-iron pan, for the crusty burgers. You can also grill them on medium-high heat, about 5 to 8 minutes per side, depending on the thickness. To cook in the pan, first heat a large cast-iron pan on medium heat until it is hot. Add 1 tsp. Canola Oil or clarified butter move around to coat the bottom, increase the heat on medium-high and place the burgers. Let the burgers cook undisturbed on medium-high heat for about 5-6 minutes (depending on the thickness), and when the bottom is browned then drizzle 2-3 drops of oil or the butter on the top and turn over the burger and cook until browned about 3-4 minutes or to your taste. Burgers should be cooked well and should be turned over only once, otherwise they can dry up. Cooking with the oil or butter it browns better and retains it shape, they do not shrink all over.

To make a juicy burger: To the meat add about 1-2 tab of warm water or heavy cream for each burger; do not add any salt because it will pull out all the juice. You can use fresh-ground pepper or fresh or dry herbs. Cook in omelet pan (non-stick) with some oil or butter or in a well-greased stainless steel pan. Cook the burger first, then melt the cheese on the top. serve over a tasty and thick sauce like wine sauce, hoisin sauce or pomegranate molasses etc., then top with relishes, more sauces or coleslaw and other toppings. The more toppings you have, the better it tastes.

Toppings for the Burger

Toppings are the best part of the burger. But remember burger and the melted cheese on the top is the main taste that you get from a burger.

1. **Melted Cheese:** Once the burger is cooked, cover it with a thick slice of a cheese like, cheddar, jack, mozzarella, provolone, etc. If you are stuffing with a sharp cheese, then use a mild cheese on the outside. Place the cheese and cover the burger with a lid, or just cook a little longer and melt the cheese a little. Do not melt too much, it will run out and all the taste will be gone.

2. **Fresh vegetables and Fruits:** You can place a thick slice of raw onion, tomato, kiwi fruit, apple, mango, pear, etc. Make sure it is not too soft. You can use shredded or torn lettuce leaves. The iceberg and butter lettuce go very well. Baby arugula, baby spinach, watercress, etc. and sliced avocado go very well, too.
3. **Fried snacks:** Fresh and hot fried onion rings, fries, and/or bought vegetable chips, especially BBQ, go very well.
4. **Fried Bacon strips, Ham and Egg:** always tastes good.
5. **Pulled Pork:** One restaurant I know serves beef burger with melted white cheddar cheese, topped with pulled pork and coleslaw. It is a heavy meal, but tastes good.
6. **Onion in the Wine Sauce:** You can thin-slice the large onions. Cook them on high heat for 5 minutes stirring them constantly. Add salt and pepper to taste and sprinkle a little granulated garlic, stir well, cover and cook on low heat. When onions are soft, take the pan off the heat, add some white or red wine (2 large onion can use about ½ cups wine). Increase the heat to medium-high, burn out the alcohol, stirring the onion; add a little lemon juice. Taste for the seasoning and add salt and pepper to taste and serve over the burger. You can also serve onion marmalade as well.
7. **Sauces and Chutneys and Relishes:** Burgers can use a lot of sauces. You can use horseradish, horseradish mayo, mayonnaise, mustard, hot sauce, ketchup and red wine sauce. You can make wine sauce plain or with the mushrooms. Chutneys, like lemon and mango, go very well. Relishes of all kinds go very well. These you can top on the burger and also serve on the side.
8. **Coleslaw and Salads:** Cole slaw of any kind and salads, especially made with vinaigrette, go very well. Use cilantro-lemon or yogurt chutney on bun.
9. **Pickles:** All sorts or pickles taste very good with the burger. You can make fresh ones or buy from the market. Deep-fried pickles taste good both on the burger and on the side.
10. **Hot Peppers:** Fresh, pickled, fried or stuffed go very well. My favorite ones are the stuffed Jalapeno peppers with cheese. I serve them both ways, on the burgers and on the side. Remember, the more toppings you have, the better it tastes.

Beans Burgers (M: 4)

This is a big burger with layers of beans and eggplant patties and two types of cheeses together with other vegetables. These are actually two burgers (beans and eggplant) put together for a great taste. Instead of mayo and chutney, use 1 cup (1 roll) of softened goat cheese and mix with 2 tbsp. lemon juice and 1 tbsp. each: fresh diced onion and parsley; salt and pepper to taste, and spread on the buns.

Ingredients: ½ package, 8 ounces, (272 g) frozen soy beans cooked in little water for about 8 minutes and mashed; 1 can 15 ounces (425 g) cooked chick peas mashed; 1 royal purple eggplant; 2 tbsp. canola oil and 2 tbs. unsalted butter; 1 cup frozen spinach thawed and squeezed out of all water; ½ cup fine chopped red onion; ½ cup red bell pepper seeded and chopped fine; 2 tbs. fresh-grated ginger; about 4 serrano peppers chopped or 1 jalapeno pepper seeded and chopped fine; 1 large egg; 3 tbsp. grated parmesan or mixed grated cheese(from bottle); 2 tbsp. ketchup divided; ½ cup chopped parsley or cilantro; 1/4 tsp. granulated garlic; 3 tbsp. lemon juice divided; salt and fresh grated black pepper to taste; ½ cup seasoned dry bread crumbs.

To serve: 4 large cracked wheat buns; 4 slices of a large tomato; 4 thick slices of sharp cheddar cheese; 4 slice of provolone or any other light cheese; 4 lettuce leaves, stems out; ½ cup light mayonnaise; ½ c green mango or any other sour chutney; coleslaw and pickles, etc.

1. Slice the eggplant 1-inch thick and sprinkle each slice both sides with salt and pepper. Heat a large heavy-bottom on medium heat and brown the eggplant slices both sides, sprinkle with 2 tabs of water and granulated garlic, cover and cook about 10 minutes until soft.
2. In a large bowl combine mashed soybeans, chickpeas, chopped onions, both peppers, spinach, ginger, beaten egg, grated parmesan cheese, 1 tbsp. ketchup, 2 tbsp. lemon juice, parsley/cilantro, (no salt needed, cheese is salty enough) about 2 pinches of fresh grated black pepper or to taste; combine with a wooden spoon and form 4 patties; dip the patties in the bread crumbs and chill in the refrigerator for about 5-10 minutes.
3. Heat a large heavy-bottom pan, when hot add 1 tbsp. butter and 2 tbsp. oil, heat on medium high heat and brown the bean patties about 4 minutes on each side, top with thick slices of the cheddar cheese and melt the cheese when ready to assemble the burger
4. In the meantime heat the eggplant again, sprinkle with 1 tbsp. lemon juice and 1 tbsp. ketchup, turn over each slice and when heated, pile 2 slices together and make four piles, top with the soft cheese (provolone), cover melt the cheese when ready to assemble the burger.
5. Assemble the burger: Slice the buns and heat in the toaster oven or regular oven lightly on both sides.
   Spread the mayonnaise on the bottom buns, and spread mango chutney on the top buns. Start with the bottom bun: top with lettuce, tomato, bean patties with melted cheddar, then eggplant slices melted with provolone cheese and finally the top bun.
   Serve on the side, coleslaw and pickles or any leftover tomato slices.

Burger and Hash Brown (Serves: 4)

A few years ago, we lived in Las Vegas, in an apartment. Every now and then when we went out to eat and when my niece ordered a burger, she loved it with no buns but with a lot of toppings. This is how I got this idea. Here I have 3 burgers: beef, bean a veggie, and a turkey burger, with toppings and hash brown and olives and stuffed peppers on the side. This is a big meal, so you can serve only 1 or 2 burgers of your choice, if you prefer.

Since there are so many items assembled together, you can make most of them ahead. You can make hash browns, sauces and stuffed pepper a day before and just heat them in the microwave or regular oven. Prepare onion rings ahead and deep-fry before serving; they can be kept warm in a lightly heated oven. But the burgers you can prepare night before and cook them just before serving.

To Serve: Use mango chutney, coconut chutney and hot sauce (follow the instructions under chutneys.). You will need 4-5 tbsp. of hoisin and wine sauces, olives and fresh grape tomatoes to serve on side. Or you can serve with pickles of your choice. You will need 2 cups prepared coleslaw, ketchup and about 1 cup fresh baby arugula.

(1) Hot Sauce

Ingredients: ¾ cup ketchup; 1 tab or to taste Tabasco sauce; 2 pinches granulated garlic; a little salt to taste; ¼ cup water.

Heat all ingredients together, bring to a boil and pour into a non-reactive bowl. Cool and refrigerate until needed. Reheat again and serve in room temperature.

(2) Hash Browns

Ingredients: You will need 1 large red or Yukon gold potato per person; 2 tbsp. canola or vegetable oil; 1 tsp. cumin or caraway seeds; salt and pepper to taste; 1 tbsp. chili powder (or 1 tsp. each: cayenne, sweet paprika and ground mustard powder.).

Heat a large cast-iron or a heavy-bottom pan on medium heat. Scrub clean the potatoes under running water. Cut the potatoes in 4 portions lengthwise then slice ½ inch thin across. Increase the heat to medium, add 1 tbsp. oil, the cumin/caraway seeds on one side in the pan; then add the potatoes, move around the potatoes right away so they do not stick in the bottom. Cover with a lid and cook on medium heat for about 5 minutes. Open the cover stir the potatoes well then sprinkle with salt and pepper on the top, cover, reduce the heat to low and cook another 15 minutes or until potatoes are soft (you can do this a day before.) Stir the potatoes sprinkle with the chili powder, then sprinkle rest 1 tbsp. oil, cover and turn off the heat. Reheat on high for 5 minutes just before serving.

(3) Stuffed Peppers

Ingredients: You can use 4 to 6 peppers per person, either hot Jalapeno or sweet peppers; 1 tsp. oil or butter; 1pkg. 8 ounces, (227g) whole milk mozzarella cheese; 1 tbsp. lemon-pepper seasoning mix; 1 tbsp. seasoned dry bread crumbs; ¼ tsp. granulated garlic; salt and pepper to taste.

Heat a large sauté pan on low heat. Wash and pat dry peppers. Make a long slit on each pepper. With a potato peeler, detach the vein inside the peppers and take out the seeds if using the Jalapeno, or leave the seeds in if you prefer. Mix all the dry spices together. Cut the cheese in ½-inch wide and about 2-3 inches long sticks (according to the length of the peppers) to fit into the peppers. Press the cheese stick into the dry spices and coat the cheese with the spices.

Increase the heat to medium and add the oil or butter to the pan and sauté pepper (unstuffed) on medium heat for 2 minutes, then on the low heat for about 5 to 8 minutes as needed, until they are a little soft. Turn off the heat, cover pan with the lid and let the pepper cool off for about 20-30 minutes in the pan. Now take out one pepper at a time and place one cheese stick into the slit of the pepper and place a little dry spice into them, then close the slit pressing the cheese inside the pepper. When ready to serve, microwave the pepper for 1 minute and melt the cheese. Serve warm or cold. They are very tasty.

(4) Onion Rings

Ingredients: 4 medium onions; ¼ cup plain yogurt; ½ cup pancake flour mix; 1-2 tbsp. water as needed; ¼ tsp. granulated garlic; salt and fresh-ground cayenne or black pepper; canola oil to deep-fry; ½ cup seasoned dry bread crumbs;

Peel and slice each onion across in to ½-inch thick slices. Peel off and take out 2 layers of onion rings together. Up to this point you can soak onion rings in extra yogurt or buttermilk, overnight, in the refrigerator. When ready to deep-fry the rings, prepare the batter for the onion rings: whip pancake mix, yogurt and a little water (about 2-3 tbsp. as needed) to make the batter. The batter should be a little thicker than pancake batter, so that it sticks together and coats the onion rings well. Then dip each ring into the batter first and then press into the bread crumbs (you can do this a few hours ahead and leave the rings in the refrigerator.)

Heat the oil in a large sauté pan about 1-1/2-inch deep on medium-high heat. When hot, drop the onion rings carefully from the side of the pan and cook until rings are golden. You may have to reduce and increase the heat to cook rings on high and the same time not to let them burn on high heat. After rings are cooked on both sides, turn them over 2 more times into the hot oil. This will make them crispy.

(5) Chickpea, Veggie and Cheese Burgers

Ingredients: 2 cups cooked chick peas; ½ cup chopped onion; 1 tbsp. chopped parsley or cilantro; 2 tbsp. ketchup; 1 tbsp. lemon-pepper mix; ½ cup washed well and fine chopped baby spinach or kale leaves; salt and pepper to taste; ¼ tsp. granulated garlic; 2 large eggs; ½ cup seasoned dry bread crumbs; canola oil to deep-fry. cheese topping: combine 4 ounces cream cheese, 1cup shredded sharp cheddar cheese, 2tbsp. fresh grated onion, 1/4tsp. granulated garlic, 1tbsp. lemon-pepper mix (dash seasoning) mix all place in the plastic wrap, make a 4-inch long roll, refrigerate, then slice in 4 slices.

After you have fried the onion rings, you can use the same oil to fry these burgers. Mash the chick peas with the fork. Sprinkle salt, pepper, garlic, ketchup and lemon-pepper mix and mix well. Add kale or spinach, herbs and break 2 eggs on the top. Mix all well. Sprinkle 1/4C bread crumbs on the top and divide mixture into 4 portions. Line a 3-4-inch diameter bottle cap with plastic wrap. Press in the chickpea mixture and make 4 Burgers. Then spread out the rest of the crumbs and turn over the prepared burgers on the bread crumbs. (you can refrigerate and deep-fry these later when onion rings are done.) Heat about 1-inch deep oil in a large sauté pan/frying pan, on medium-high heat (about 375 degrees) Pick up the burgers with a metal spatula and carefully place them in the hot oil and cook on high heat for about 8 minutes until they are golden. Carefully turn them over on the side of the pan and cook the other side the same say. When done, top with the slice of the cheese, cover with the lid and melt the cheese lightly and Serve warm with or without buns.

(6) Beef Burgers

Ingredients: 1-1/2 pounds 85% fat-free ground Angus beef; 3 tbsp. heavy cream or steak sauce; ¼ tsp. each granulated garlic and fresh-ground black pepper; ½ cup shredded pepper jack or sharp cheddar cheese; 4 thick and large slices of mozzarella, Swiss or provolone cheese to top the burger; about 2 tsp. oil or clarified butter.

Take the burger meat, flatten it out, then sprinkle the heavy cream, pepper and garlic, fold over with a wooden spoon making a log. Divide and cut the meat into 2 parts, one a little smaller and the other a little bigger. Then take out each part and cut again each portion into 4 parts. Line a 4-inch-diameter jar cover with plastic wrap. Starting with the smaller portions, press one piece of the meat on the plastic wrap, flatten it out thin, make about 1-inch sides (upward) all around and then turn over onto a plastic wrap-lined platter. Do this with all four small portions. Then take out one large portion at a time, flatten out, make 1-inch sides (upward) and stuff them with the Jack or cheddar cheese. Press down the cheese, even out and then place a cover of the smaller portion of the meat on the burger; seal the sides together, turn over on your hand and press the two edges together to seal; now the burger is stuffed and ready to cook. Do this with all the burgers (up to this point you can refrigerate the burgers until you are ready to cook).

Heat a large cast-iron pan on medium heat. Add 1 tsp. oil or butter in the pan, increase heat to medium-high and cook burgers for 4-5 minutes on each side until golden. Drizzle 2-3 drops of oil or butter on each burger, turn them over and cook the other side about 3-4 minutes, or until they are browned or to taste. When they are done, top with a slice of mozzarella or provolone cheese, cover with the lid and melt the cheese; and take pan off the heat. Serve warm.

(7) Turkey Burgers

Follow the procedure for beef burgers. Use the ground turkey meat and sprinkle a little salt and pepper or hoisin sauce inside the burger before filling with the cheese. Do not mix any salt in the meat; it will pull out all the liquid and will make the burger dry.

Assemble the Platter

In a large platter, in the center, place 1 tbsp. of wine sauce or your favorite sauce in the bottom, then place the beef burger with cheese, turkey burger with cheese, col slaw, then bean and veggie burger, top with ketchup, arugula and then onion rings.

On the side of platter, place hash browns on one side, and olive and grape tomatoes on the other side. Place stuffed peppers near the burgers.

Serve mango and coconut chutney and hot sauce next to the platter.

Note: If you prefer you can serve only one meat burger, either beef or turkey together with the rest.

Chutneys are made with the fresh herbs. They are not only healthy but they are loaded with flavor and go very well with the burger. You can make chutneys 1-2 days ahead and serve whenever needed.

Lamb Burger (Serves: 4)

50 billion! That's how many cheeseburgers Americans eat every year. This was the headline in a newspaper. Whether it is beef, pork, turkey, salmon, they all taste good with a lot of sauce and cheese. I think cheese tastes good on burgers period!

Ingredients: 1-1/2 to 2 pounds ground lamb; 1 large egg; ½ tsp. each dry rosemary and granulated garlic; ¼ cup each thin sliced fresh cilantro stems (op), grated fresh ginger and fresh mint leaves; 2 tbsp. lemon juice; ¼ tsp. each salt and fresh-ground black pepper; 1 tbsp. melted unsalted butter; oil to brush on the burgers; 4 slices cheddar cheese; 4 brioche or soft buns; 4 large tomato slices; 4 large red onion slices or 4-1/2-inch-thick slices of yellow onion, brushed with oil and sprinkled with a little salt, and grilled on medium heat 2-3 minutes each side until transparent; lettuce (op); ½ cup cilantro and mint chutney, ketchup and/or mayonnaise for the buns; salt and pepper to taste.

1. Prepare a grill with medium-high heat. In a large bowl place the meat, break the egg whip a little and pour on the top, add rosemary, garlic, cilantro, ginger, mint, lemon juice, salt and pepper and melted butter and mix well with a fork. Spread out in a 3-inch diameter lid and make 4 burgers, each about ½-inch thick. Make a depression in the center. Refrigerate the burgers for 15 to 30 minutes.
2. When ready to cook, brush the burgers lightly with oil and place them on the grill and grill for about 7-8 minutes or until browned underneath; then turn over and grill the other side for about 5 minutes or until browned or about 155 to 160 degrees on an instant-read thermometer for medium done. Top each with the cheese slices, cover with a lid and melt the cheese on the grill.
3. While burgers are grilling, slice and heat the buns. Spread out chutney on the bottom and mayonnaise on the top, then sprinkle with a little salt and pepper. On the bottom piece, place lettuce then burger with cheese, onion, tomato and a little ketchup on the top, and serve warm with some salad on the side.

Tip: Lamb tastes better with both fresh and dry herbs and fresh ginger. Cheddar cheese also goes well with burgers.

Umami Type Burgers (Serves: 4)

Besides, salty, hot, sweet and sour tastes, there is a fifth savory taste that Japanese called it Umami, the "delicious." You can buy a umami paste or put together your own blend by adding naturally rich and protein-building amino acid food for delicious taste. The natural glutamate vegetables like tomatoes, olives and mushrooms, dashi that is made with seaweed, grated cheese and fermented soybean powder, etc. give a lot of Umami taste. I use some Indian spices (available at the Indian grocery stores and in some supermarkets) such as turmeric, celery seed, fennel seeds, fenugreek powders. They not only give a good taste, but cure a lot of diseases.

Ingredients:

For the Burger: About 1-1/4 pounds ground certified angus beef 85% lean; sprinkled with: ¼ cup fresh bread crumbs (op) ¼ cup whole milk or half-and-half; about 1 tbsp.tomato paste; ¼ cup nori powder (about ½ sheet of dry nori, or seaweed ground into powder); 1 tbsp. fermented soybean powder; ½ tsp. each of the powders: turmeric, fennel seeds, celery seeds, fenugreek seeds; ¼ tsp. dry oregano; 3-4 tbsps. chopped fresh cilantro or flat leaf parsley; 1 tbsp. low-sodium instant beef broth powder; 1 tbsp. grated cheese from the bottle; ¼ cup fine chopped or grated onion; and ¼ cup dry shiitake mushrooms caps, ground into powder, or ½ c cooked and diced mushrooms. To cook: 3-4 tbsp. purified butter or olive oil.

To serve: 4 toasted sesame seed buns, umami paste or cilantro chutney or horse radish sauce, lettuce and tomato and/or coleslaw.

1. Heat a large heavy-bottom pan or a cast-iron skillet on medium heat .
2. Spread out the ground beef in a platter and sprinkle with the burger spices, mix in 2-3 strokes and make 4 patties about ½-inch thick, with a little depression in the center. When the pan is hot add 2 tsp. butter or olive oil, increase the heat to medium-high, add the burgers to pan and cook halfway covered with the lid for about 4-5 minutes, or until golden brown underneath. Drizzle 1 tbsp. butter on the top and turn over the burger and cook the other side for about 2 minutes uncovered until light browned underneath; or to your taste.
3. Serve burger on a toasted sesame seed or whole wheat bun with umami paste, or chutney or the horse radish sauce, over the lettuce and tomatoes and/or coleslaw.

    Tip: According to Indian ayurvedic medicine, there are six different types of tastes (rasa):

    1. Sweet (Madhur), 2. Sour (Amla), 3. Saline (Lavana), 4. Pungent (Katu), 5. Bitter (Tikta), 6. Astringent (Kashaya).

    Each taste has a series of properties, functions and effect s on the body.

Salmon burgers (M: 4)

These salmon burgers are tasty, colorful and healthy. You can serve them with salad, on the buns or with potatoes and greens for the dinner.

Ingredients : About 1-1/4 pounds boneless salmon fillet; salt and fresh-ground black pepper; about 2-3 tbsp. canola or olive oil; ½ cup each: chopped onion, red and green bell peppers; ¼ tsp. garlic powder; 2

tbsp. each chopped fresh thyme and flat leaf parsley; ½ cup seasoned dry bread crumbs; 1 large egg; 2 tbsp. unsalted butter.

For the Sauce: 1 cup sour cream; ½ cup mayonnaise or ¼ cup grated parmesan cheese; 2 tbsp. lemon juice; salt and pepper to taste (if using cheese, do not need any salt); ¼ tsp. cayenne pepper (op); ½ cup drained and fine chopped cucumber pickles in vinegar.

1. Heat oven to 400 degrees. Wash, pat dry and place the salmon on aluminum foil, in a baking tray. Make a long slit in the center of the salmon, lengthwise and sprinkle salt, pepper and little oil all over. Bake salmon in a preheated oven for about 10 minutes, until it is opaque. Cool and break the salmon in to about 1-inch lumps.

2. While salmon is cooking, heat a heavy-bottom sauté pan on medium heat. When hot add 1-2 tbsp. oil and sauté onion 1 minute, sprinkle with salt, pepper and garlic; mix well, cover and cook about 4 minutes until onion is soft. Add chopped bell peppers, increase the heat and sauté on medium-high heat for about 2 minutes until soft. Take off the heat and cool.

3. To make the sauce: in a large non-reactive bowl mix all ingredients, stir well and take out 2/3 of the sauce for serving.

4. Use the same bowl with leftover 1/3 of the sauce. Sprinkle the cooked vegetables over the sauce, then salmon, bread crumbs, fresh herbs, beat the egg and pour all over the salmon. With a wooden or rubber spatula, mix the salmon a little (just 2-3 strokes scraping the bottom), divide mixture in to fours. Pick up 1 portion at a time, drop on a clean and dry platter, and just round it off. Chill the burgers for 15-30 minutes.

5. Heat a clean heavy-bottom pan on medium-high heat, add butter and cook burgers 2-3 minutes each side, golden brown, turning them over gently with a metal spatula. Serve with the sauce.

Lobster Skewers with Corn on the Cob (Serves: 2)

These skewers take only 4-5 minutes to grill because most of the work is done ahead. I serve one lobster tail per person; if you wish you can serve extra.

Ingredients: 2 lobster tails; 4 wooden skewers soaked in the water; 2 sticks salted butter softened and mixed with 1 tbsp. each: lemon-pepper mix, chili powder, fresh thyme leaves chopped, and ¼ cup thin-sliced fresh chives; 2 fresh corns on the cob; 1 fresh lemon cut into wedges; 1tbsp. chili powder. To serve: coleslaw, horseradish cream sauce (¼ cup prepared or fresh horseradish mixed with ½ cup sour cream, and salt and pepper to taste), and some salad.

Lobster Skewers: Tie two lobster tails flat-side together with thick rubber bands on the top and the bottom of the tail. Bring a medium pot of water to a boil. Place the tails in the boiling water and boil for only 4 minutes. Take out of the water and cool. When cool to handle, take one tail at a time and move a utility knife around inside the shell and over the meat, going in a circle to loosen the meat. Then with a sharp knife, cut them in half lengthwise on the inside. Now push in two skewers on the tail side in the meat. Immediately place about 1 tbsp. of herb butter on each piece, wrap them in a large piece of foil and refrigerate. When ready to serve, just grill them on the shell side, on medium heat, about 3-4 minute, until heated through and serve again with herb butter over the meat.

Corn on the Cob: Grill the corn over high heat, turning around slowly until the kernels start popping and are charred all around. Immediately rub with lemon juice, sprinkle with the chili powder, and rub with herb butter. Serve with horseradish cream, coleslaw and salad.

Skewers for Appetizers (M: 10)

These are colorful cheese skewers we make them around Christmas and 4th of July. You can put more cheese if you wish.

Ingredients: 10 long (about 10-inches) bamboo skewers, washed, pat dry and rubbed with damp and oily paper towel, or sprayed with cooking spray; 1 pint fresh grape tomatoes, ½ cup pimento stuffed Spanish olives; 1 cup cubed cooked ham or browned spam; ½ cup black olives; 1 cup cubed double-cream brie cheese marinated with a mixture of: 1 tsp. olive oil, 1 tbsp. crushed fresh garlic cloves, ½ tsp. each lemon and orange fine grated zest, 1 tbsp. lemon juice, 1 tsp. each Dijon mustard and fresh chopped rosemary, ¼ tsp. cayenne pepper and pinch of salt.

A few hours before serving make the skewers: thread black olive, grape tomato, cheese cube, ham cube, grape tomato and Spanish olive. Place in a large platter with sides, lined with parchment paper and loosely tented with the foil.

Surf and Turf Kebobs with Quinoa Pilaf, Cauliflower and Broccoli

(Serves: 4)

These kebabs are made with steak and shrimps. While cleaning the filet mignon I take out the thin long strip of the meat that is almost separated by the fat. You can also use the rib-eye, which takes less than a pound of beef. You can prepare everything ahead; heat before serving and just cook kebabs hot and serve. I serve with quinoa pilaf, cauliflower and broccoli vegetable, lemon wedges and heated seafood BBQ sauce on the side for dipping.

(1) Quinoa Pilaf

Ingredients: 1 tsp. olive oil; 2 large egg whites; ½ cup roasted red bell pepper from the jar; 1 cup whole grain quinoa; ½ tsp. turmeric (op); salt and pepper to taste; 1 tbsp. butter; 1 tbsp. fresh herbs (parsley, thyme, oregano, etc.).

Heat a medium pan on medium heat, when hot add olive oil and drop the egg white. Cook on low heat for about 5 minutes, or until it is settled. Cover and take off the heat and set aside until it is needed; cut in to cubes and mix with the pilaf.

In a medium pot bring 1 cup water to a boil, on medium-high heat. Stir in turmeric, quinoa and salt and pepper to taste. Stir for about 30 seconds, cover and turn off the heat. Set aside for 20 minutes. Then stir in butter, egg white cubes and roasted bell pepper just before serving.

(2) Cauliflower and Broccoli Vegetable

Ingredients: Each half of the medium cauliflower and broccoli cut into 2-inch pieces and stem split into four but still attached; sprinkle of salt, pepper, granulated garlic and canola oil.

In a medium-large pot, bring about 2-inch-deep water to a boil; add cauliflower and broccoli florets and blanch for 3 minutes. Take them out of water and set aside in a bowl, sprinkle with salt, pepper, garlic and little oil all over. Reheat on the grill just before serving.

(3) Steak and Shrimp Kebabs

Marinade: 3 tbsp. Worcestershire sauce; sprinkle of granulated garlic and cayenne or black pepper;

For the Kebabs: 1 of each: green and orange bell pepper, cored, seeded and cut into 1-inch cubes; 1 pound large shrimp (24 count) cleaned and the tail left on; abut ¾ pound fillet mignon or rib-eye steak cut into 1-1/2x2-inch flat cubes (flat cubes about 1-inch wide cook fast); 1 red apple cored, and cut into 1-1/2x2-inch cubes or 8 grape tomatoes; 8 long wooden skewers, soaked in cold water for 30 minutes; 1 cup heated seafood BBQ sauce (see Sauces). To brush on the spice mixture: 6-8 tbsps. butter, 2 tbsp. lemon pepper seasoning blend (dash), 1 tsp. salt, heat together to melt the butter. To serve: quinoa pilaf, cauliflower and broccoli vegetable and lemon wedges.

A day before or at least 6 hours ahead of cooking, marinate the steak in Worcestershire sauce. Sprinkle a large platter with salt, pepper and garlic lightly, wash, pat dry the shrimp and place the shrimp on a platter, then sprinkle the shrimp heavily with salt, pepper and garlic on the top. Refrigerate both loosely covered with a foil.

Clean and heat an indoor grill on medium-high heat. When heated, brush it well with the oil and spread out the cauliflower and broccoli on it to heat through. Heat 4 serving platters and while the kebabs are almost at the end of cooking, place the quinoa pilaf and cauliflower and broccoli and lemon wedges on the heated platter. Place some warm BBQ sauce in small cups on the side.

While grill is heating, thread the kebabs: first curve a shrimp in U shape and thread on the skewer, head-first, then the tail, then 2 pieces of the orange peppers together, steak lengthwise, shrimp, 2 pieces of green peppers together, steak, orange peppers, shrimp, and apple or tomato piece the last. Brush on top with the BBQ sauce, then heavily with butter mixture and place on a heated and oily grill, butter-side down. Press down on the steak and shrimp with fingers on the grill, and cover loosely with a piece of foil. Let the shrimp cook for 5 minutes or until they are golden underneath. Then brush the top again with the sauce and butter mixture; turn over and cook the other side for about 3 minutes covered with foil. When turning the skewers over, scrape the bottom with the spatula with one hand, holding the skewer with the other hand, and when done, place on the serving platter. Serve immediately.

Tip: This is a light but a filling meal. I make two skewers per person, but you can make extra. Quinoa is a super food, has protein and all essential amino acids that body requires. Seafood is a light protein. The combination of the vegetables such as cauliflower and broccoli gives you another combination of the super food.

Vegetable, Cheese and Fruit Kebobs (Serves: 4)

I call it a gluten-free meal. It is served over rice, spinach and chickpeas. Kebabs are: Paneer (Indian cheese, found in Indian grocery stores or make your own a day ahead), vegetables and fruits.

Ingredients: If using bamboo skewers, soak them in water for 1-2 hours.

For Cheese Kebabs: 1 pkg., 12 oz., all-natural paneer cut into large cubes about 1-1/2 by 2-inches, or make your own paneer (see cheese: how to make paneer); sprinkles of cayenne, granulated garlic and a little salt.

For Veggie Kebab: Seasoned oil to brush on: a mixture of 3-4 tbsp. canola oil, 1 tbsp. cumin or curry powder, 1 tsp. granulated garlic, 1 tbsp. smoked paprika or cayenne pepper to taste, 1 tbsp. lemon-pepper mix, ¼ tsp. salt; 1 can 14.5 oz, (411 g) tiny whole beets drained; half a medium head of broccoli cut into 2-inch florets and boiled for 1 minute (blanched); 4 scallions with thick stem parts cut into 1-1/2-inch pieces; 1 large red bell pepper, seeded and cut into 1-1/2-inch squares.

For the Fruit Kebabs: 2 cups pineapple chunks or buy fresh pineapples, peel and cut into 6 slices lengthwise, then cut across into 1-1/2 cubes and sprinkle with a little salt; 4 peaches cut halved or into three pieces lengthwise; 2 tbsp. light brown sugar; canola oil to brush on.

To Serve: 4 cups cooked rice; 4 cups chickpeas cooked with 1 cup spinach with cheese vegetable (palak paneer; just use cooked spinach without cheese); coriander and mango chutneys.

To make the veggie kebab: Grease an indoor grill or a grilling cast-iron pan with some oil and heat the pan on medium heat. Make the seasoned oil. On a cutting board, line up the veggies the way you want on the skewers: beet, red bell pepper, broccoli and scallion, repeat 3 times. Then start threading on the skewer, making a tight skewer for easy turning. Just before cooking, brush the veggies with the seasoned oil all around and place them on the grill or grill pan, across the grates. Let them get brown underneath about 1 minute; scrape with a metal spatula and turn over the other side.

To make the Cheese Kebab: You can thread the paneer cubes on the skewer, brush lightly with seasoned oil and cook on low heat about ½ minute per side, scrape the bottom and turn over. If you are making your own cheese (paneer), cut the strips of the cheese, dip in ½ cup of coconut flour or almond flour, and cook strips in the regular cast-iron pan, in 1 tbsp. butter ½ minute per side; take off the heat, wait a while, then drizzle some melted butter over and turn over the other side; cook on low to medium heat. When cheese strips are cooked, place them on a cutting board with a large metal spatula, cut each strip in 2-inch cubes and carefully thread on the skewer and place on the rice. This are very tasty and fancy-looking cheese cubes.

For the Fruit Kebabs: Simply place the fruit in a row on the cutting board, thread them on skewers, lightly brush with oil and sprinkle a little brown sugar and place on the grill, cook 1 minute per side or until browned, scraped with the metal spatula to turn over and serve.

Keep all the cooked kebabs warm on the aluminum foil, off the heat on the grill or in a lightly heated oven or in a large pan, and serve over the heated rice and heated chickpeas with chutneys.

Fruit Skewers (M: 10)

These skewers we make for large crowds on holidays. You can make them any time of the year. Kids love them.

Ingredients: 10 long skewers (10 inches) washed, pat dry and lightly greased with cooking spray or with a damped oily paper towel; 1 container 16 oz. (454g) fresh strawberries hulled and wiped cleaned with damp towel; 1 fresh pineapple peeled and cut in 6 slices lengthwise, cored, and then sprinkled with salt; wash out the salt under running cold water and pat dry, then cut 1-inch wide pieces across; 10 jumbo purple grapes; ½ cup fresh blueberries.

A few hours before serving make the skewers: thread strawberry, pineapple pieces lengthwise, jumbo grape, then a few blueberries. Place on a parchment paper-lined large platter with sides, and tent loosely with the foil.

Tip: Sprinkling salt on the fresh pineapple takes the acid away and it tastes better. Try to buy golden pineapple when it is in season.

Sushi

If you are a sushi lover, you need a passion and a pallet, not much of the skills, to make sushi. You can make them with meat, fish, and with vegetables, tofu, cheese, almost anything that is ready to eat. As far as other ingredients, you need the basics: a sushi mat, nori sheets, sushi rice, light sauce (dressing sauce) to mix with the cooked rice, ingredients for filling; and to serve: miso and/or wasabi paste, and/or pickled ginger, dipping sauce, kimchi, fermented beans and/or fermented vegetables, etc. Buy them at the Asian or specialty stores so you will have chance to buy fresh stuff.

Sushi Rice (Serves: 2)

Sushi rice is low-starch, short-grain rice. You can buy sushi rice or small-grain Japanese rice.

Ingredients: 1 cup sushi rice or Japanese short-grain rice, (you can also use brown short-grain rice, just use 1-1/3 cup of water in cooking) washed in a few changes of cold water, then soaked in water for 30 minutes and drained; about 1-1/4 cup water; 1 piece of dried kelp, kombu or 1 tbsp. raw hemp seeds or 2 tbsp. cooked quinoa (op).

In a medium pot bring the water to a boil, add the rice, stir well; bring to a boil and let it boil for 5 minutes; skim the foam that rises on the top. Add the kombu (if using) and stir well. Lower the heat and simmer, covered for 10 minutes or until rice is soft and the liquid is almost gone. Turn off the heat and let it sit for 10 minutes to puff.

Move a wooden spoon or a rubber spatula all around the edge and loosen the rice, break it up gently, and puff it up, take out the kombu piece, if using. Transfer the rice to a large and wide wooden bowl and spread it out. Cool the rice only, then sprinkle the dressing sauce in a thin stream, evenly, over the rice. Sprinkle the hemp or quinoa on the top evenly, and with a plastic fork just stir the top gently, without damaging the grain. If you need to use the rice immediately, fan the rice to evaporate the liquid and cool the rice first before adding the sauce. Cover the rice bowl with a lightly damp and squeezed-out double cheese cloth or cotton cloth, over the surface, and use within two hours. Do not refrigerate, it will get tough. Any leftover rice wrap in the plastic wrap, then in a paper towel, and place in a plastic container; freeze or refrigerate, and reheat in a steam pot or microwave covered just to heat through.

Dressing Sauce

You can make the dressing sauce or buy a bottle of Saucy Susan, 19 ounces (539G). This sauce comes very handy. I mix it with any rice dish and sprinkle and serve with seafood.

Ingredients: 3 tbsp. rice vinegar; 1 tbsp. honey or 2 tsp. sugar; about 1-1/4 tsp. kosher or low-sodium salt.

In a non-reactive bowl, whisk all ingredients well until they are dissolved.

Pickled Ginger (M: about 1-1/2 cups)

You can buy or make your own pickled ginger. We make it mostly in the winter and use as a pickle and a garnish over the dishes.

Ingredients: About 9-10 ounces young ginger peeled (or less fibrous ginger); ¾ cup rice vinegar; 6 tbsp. sugar; about ¼ cup thin-sliced, raw fresh beets, or ½ tsp. red food color (op); 1-1/2 tsp. sea salt or low sodium salt; 1 tsp. white peppercorns crushed lightly.

Peel the ginger, take off the little knobs, and slice thin in long slices, with vegetable peeler or a mandolin, about 1/10-inch thick. In a large non-reactive pot, bring all the ingredients, except the ginger, to a boil; stir well, add the sliced ginger, stir well, and simmer for 10 minutes, until ginger is almost soft. Turn the ginger slices over once halfway through cooking. Take off the heat, cover the pan with the lid. Let the ginger cool completely for about one hour or so. Take out the beets, and serve as a pickle. Pour the pickled ginger mixture into a clean, dry, airtight jar. Serve or leave on the counter overnight, then refrigerate.

Dipping Sauce (Serves: 2)

The most common and readily available sauce is soy sauce. But you can make your own dipping sauce. Soy sauce is made with soybeans and few other ingredients. You can buy the regular soy sauce or the **lighter version. The lighter one is more salty.**

Ingredients: ½ cup low sodium soy sauce; 1 tsp. lime juice; ¼ tsp. lime zest; 1 tbsp. thin-sliced green onion; ½ tsp. toasted sesame seeds.

Whisk and combine all ingredients together, except green onion, in a small non-reactive bowl. Pour into two serving bowls. Sprinkle with the green onion and serve.

Wasabi Paste (Serves: 2-4)

Buy wasabi powder from an Asian grocery store, you will have better chance of getting the pure wasabi. **Wasabi is also known as Japanese horseradish.**

Ingredients: 1 Container, 1.06 ounces (30G) Wasabi Powder.

In a non-reactive bowl mix together 5 tsp. of wasabi powder and 3 tsp. water. Mix together, cover, and refrigerate until needed.

Nori Sheets

Nori is a seaweed that is used to make the sushi rolls. It should be dry and flexible. I like to buy a package of 10 sheets, full size, net weight: 1 ounce (28G). These square sheets are sufficient to make about 4 to 5 pieces of sushi in one sheet.

Sushi Mat

Sushi Mats are important to roll the sushi. If you are using the Nori sheets, buy a 10-1/2x10-1/2-inch square thin bamboo mat, tied together with cotton strings. Wash the mat after each use, drip-dry first, then place on a kitchen towel, turning over back and forth to dry it completely.

Salmon Sushi

This is the most easy, and colorful sushi. I serve it with salad on the side.

Ingredients: 1 pkg. about 3 ounces smoked salmon or fresh raw salmon sliced paper-thin and marinated in citrus marinade; about 4 cups cooked rice mixed with dressing sauce. To serve: wasabi paste, dipping sauce, pickled ginger and some watercress to serve on.

Take individual attractive serving platters, and spread out some watercress on half of the platter and set aside.

Take out a few pieces of the smoked salmon and lay them down in a clean and dry plate. Damp your one hand lightly with water, and with a plastic spoon or a rubber spatula carefully take out about ½ cup of rice in a wet hand. Make a ball of rice in one hand, place the ball over the watercress. Then pick up the smoked salmon and wrap over the rice ball. Now press down the salmon piece and make it elongated, pressing lightly from all sides. Repeat and make a few more. Serve with dipping sauce, wasabi paste, and pickled ginger, and chop sticks.

The Egg Sushi (Makes: 8 pieces)

Try to buy jumbo brown eggs. These eggs have bright yellow yolks. These sushi are not wrapped in rice, but rice is placed between the eggs.

Ingredients: 4 jumbo brown eggs, hard-boiled and peeled (cover the eggs with cold water, bring them to a boil for 5 minutes, cover, turn off the heat, let them sit in the water for 5 minutes. Take them out, crack all around, then submerge in cold ice water for 5 minutes; peel and let them cool completely.); about 1-1/2 cup cooked sushi rice mixed with dressing sauce; 2 nori sheets; sushi mat. To serve: dipping sauce, fermented beans and kimchi.

Place a sushi mat over the cutting board. Place the nori sheet on the top. Now place two eggs on the nori sheet in a row, almost touching each other, leaving about 2 inches of border near you. Hold down the eggs with one hand. Take out some rice (about ¼ cup) with a wet hand, make a fist and insert the rice under and over the eggs where they meet (between two eggs). So you are really making a row of rice and egg.

How to Roll Sushi

Wet the other end (away from you) about 1-inch wide with the water. Roll the mat end over the eggs. Now holding the eggs, carefully roll the nori sheet together with the mat with both hands, pressing the roll; make a tight roll of the nori sheet. Remove the roll from the mat, keeping the seam side down. Spray a sharp knife with nonstick cooking spray first, then peel the eggs and cut the eggs in half, going back and forth for clean edges. Now cut the roll again where the egg ends. Again, peel the second egg, and cut it in half again. So you will have four pieces. Serve the cut side up to show the yolk. Serve with dipping sauce, fermented beans, kimchi and chopsticks.

Shrimp Sushi (M: 8 pieces)

You can make all-vegetarian, using quinoa cakes or tofu sticks. Here we use jumbo shrimp and vegetables.

Ingredients: One Kirby cucumber cut in half, scooped out of all seeds, then thin sliced lengthwise; 1 long red bell pepper, trimmed, seeded, washed and thin-sliced lengthwise; 4 thick asparagus stalks, tough end trimmed, blanched in boiling water for 3 minutes then cooled; 4 jumbo shrimp, peeled, deveined, then cooked threaded on two skewers, in a mixture of: 1 cup water, 1 tbsp. chopped ginger, ½ tsp. turmeric, and 1 tbsp. lemon juice; bring to a boil and simmer for 5 minutes, take out and cool. To serve: dipping sauce, wasabi paste; kimchi, fermented beans or vegetables, and chopsticks.

On a cutting board, lay down the sushi mat, top with about 1 cup cooked rice mixed with the dressing sauce, leaving about a 1-inch border away from you and leaving about 1-inch of border near you; top the rice with 2 asparagus, 2-3 sticks of each bell pepper and the cucumber, then top with 2 shrimp. Wet the farther end with the water, roll the sushi as above. Serve with dipping sauce, wasabi paste, fermented beans, kimchi and the chop sticks.

Sushi Tips

Use fresh vegetables and the seafood and cook them just before making sushi. Sushi rice also should be cooked fresh or no more than two hours ahead.

Keep the fresh seafood in a bowl of ice, drain out any liquid as ice melts, and cook the same day or within 24 hours.

Spray a sharp knife with cooking spray and slice the sushi rolls and seafood etc. with clean and smooth edges (not rough edges).

Wet your fingers with water in working with the rice and soon after wipe your fingers. Work with clean fingers thereafter.

When rolling the sushi rolls, hold the large items such as the eggs, shrimp and other meat, while pressing down and firmly rolling the nori with the help of the mat.

Always try to make the platter colorful using some salad items such as avocado, red bell peppers, kiwi slices, fermented beans, kimchi, and even pickled red, green and yellow peppers.

Appetizers and Snacks

Healthy Snacks (M: 7 servings)

This mixture mostly comes from my father's daily snacks. Chickpeas are almost like nuts; the only thing you need is to add some good fat. So coconut plays a good part here. You can buy both from an Indian grocery store or just add shredded coconut to it.

½ cup roasted, unsalted chickpeas with skin on; ½ cup shelled dry coconut, cut into small pieces (about ½ inch); ½ cup shelled unsalted pistachios (toasted or untoasted); ½ cup shelled, peeled, unsalted and whole toasted almonds; ¾ cup dry cranberries.

Toss them together and store in an airtight glass jar, or portion them in seven servings in re-sealable plastic lunch bags, and use them on the go.

Tips: Chickpeas have protein and fiber, and help you keep regular. Nuts help you reduce coronary heart disease and give protein and good fat. Cranberries are antioxidant, helping to reduce urinary tract disease, and also to add some sweetness to the snacks.

Antipasto Platter (Serves: 6-8)

You can make one large platter or keep the meat and other ingredients separate. We have some guests who do not eat any meat. You can also serve some crackers or mini bread slices on the side. You can choose any meat or pickles you want, just try to make it colorful.

For the Vegetables and Pickles: 1 bag 10 oz. mini San Marzano fresh tomatoes; 1 bottle 16 oz. sweet gherkins; 1 jar 8 oz. mixed pickled vegetables; 1 can, 6 oz. pitted black olives; 1 can 8oz. grade A fancy, mini whole beets; fresh fruits or berries, about 2 cups; 2-3 celery stalks, cut about 2-1/2-inch long sticks; about 2 cups coleslaw or cheese spread.

Place each ingredient in a separate bowl and place them all around the meat platter. Keep all ingredients chilled in the refrigerator until served.

For the Meat: Buy thin-sliced cold-cut meat ½ pound each: honey-cured ham, roast beef, and/or roast turkey. I also like to buy 1 pkg. 6oz. (170g) sandwich pepperoni, and ½ pound thin-sliced Swiss cheese. On a circle, about 8-inch diameter, ad about 2-inch-high peeled watermelon ring or honey dew melon ring.

On a large glass platter, over a Lazy Susan wheel (op), place the platter. Place the melon rind in the center. Take 2 slices of the pepperoni fold in quarter, hold in the bottom with a toothpick and insert the toothpick into the melon to create a flower look. Place all the pepperoni in the center, then fold the roast beef in quarters and lay down on the edge of the melon ring. Now take the cheese and roll it and place on the edge of the platter. Fold the ham in quarters and place between the cheese rolls.

You can also make a large platter: Wrap the meat and cheese slices into separate rolls; slice them into 2-inch long pieces, place in the platter, refrigerate and just before serving, sprinkle rest of the vegetables and pickles, and pour about ¾ cup of vinaigrette made with: 1/3 cup e.v. olive oil, ¼ cups champagne vinegar, 1 tbsp. Dijon type mustard, 1 tsp. sugar, 1 tbsp. fresh-grated garlic clove, 1 tsp. dry oregano; whisk all and pour over the meat and vegetables.

Sesame Crackers (M: about 4 dozen)

Fresh-baked crackers are tasty by themselves. You do not need any fancy dip or topping for these crackers. The taste of the sesame seeds will take care of everything. You can replace sesame seeds with cheese or nut flour, etc. Store them on the counter or on the shelf between paper towels in a plastic or glass container.

Ingredients: 1-3/4 cups all-purpose flour plus more for dusting; 1 tsp. salt; 1/2 tsp. baking powder; ½ cups lightly toasted and crushed white sesame seeds, plus 2 tsp. whole to sprinkle on the top; 4 tbsp. lightly softened butter; 1 large egg; ½ cups whole milk, plus little extra if needed.

1. Preheat the oven at 400 degrees. Line a large sheet tray with the parchment paper. In a large bowl combine 1 cup flour, salt, baking powder and softened butter; rub and mix well by hand. Add the crushed sesame seeds and mix well. In a small bowl whisk together the egg and ½ cups milk and pour over the flour mixture. Whisk to combine well. Using a wooden spoon, add rest of the flour and slowly combine into a dough. Using your hands, knead the dough about 4-5 minutes until it is elastic and smooth. If needed, add little more flour or a little more milk to make it the right consistency to roll out very thin.
2. Divide the dough into two portions. Keep one wrapped in plastic and refrigerated. Using a large sheet of plastic wrap, and dusting with the flour, roll out the dough over the plastic wrap, into a very thin sheet.
3. Sprinkle with 1 tsp. of whole sesame seeds, then roll over the sesame seeds firmly with a rolling pin. Carefully pick up the rolled dough and turn it over the parchment paper-lined tray. Peel off the plastic. Using a ruler and a sharp corrugated knife, cut the sheet of dough into 2-inch squares, pressing and holding the dough on both sides of the cut.
4. Bake in a preheated 400-degree oven for 18-20 minutes, until light brown. Repeat with the other piece of the dough. When all the crackers are baked, put them back again in the tray and leave them in the turned-off oven for another 10-15 minutes to crisp.
   Tip: If you like salt, sprinkle each sheet of cracker with 1/2 tsp. of coarse sea salt just before baking and press in the salt pieces by rolling over with the rolling pin. If you like butter, brush the crackers with the melted butter just before baking.

Variations: After rolling out the dough brush with the egg wash (1 whipped egg) and sprinkle 1/4cup pumpkin seeds, 1tbsp. each sunflower seeds, quinoa, black sesame seeds and bake.

Roasted, Tasty Pistachios and Nuts(M: 1 cups)

These snacks are not only healthy but are tasty as well.

Ingredients: 2 tbsp. unsalted butter or melted ghee; 1 cup pistachios; 1cup mixed nuts; 1tbsp. worcestershire sauce; 4 tsp. fresh minced parsley or ¼ tsp. dry fine grind rosemary; 1 tbsp. chat masala or chili powder; salt and fresh-ground pepper to taste.

Heat a heavy-bottom pan or a skillet on medium heat. When heated add butter, nuts and stir for 5 minutes or until light brown and aromatic. Add Worcestershire sauce stir 1 minutes until sauce is absorbed, then add spices and herbs and stir 1 minute. Take out and cool completely before serving. You can also roast in the oven: mix together melted butter, spices and spread out on a piece of aluminum foil, and roast at 250 degrees for about 10-15 minutes, or until light browned and aromatic. Leave in the turned-off oven for extra 15 minutes for crunchy taste; cool and serve as snacks.

Guacamole (Avocado Salad)

(M: about 3 C)

Buy a ripe Haas avocado, a little soft, without spots, if you need right away. Otherwise, buy a Haas avocado that is dark green, hard and unblemished. Leave in room temperature for 2-3 days to get a little soft and then they are ready to use. Try to make salad close to serving as it turns brown.

Ingredients: 3 to 4 Haas avocados; 1 jalapeno or serrano peppers, to taste, seeded and chopped fine; 2 tbsp. each yellow and red onion minced; 1/ 2c fresh cilantro leaves and soft stems chopped; 1 large plum tomato chopped fine; 1 tsp. lime zest; 2 tbsp. lime juice or to taste; 1 tsp. extra-virgin olive oil; salt and fresh-ground black to taste.

1. Make the cut all around the pit in the avocado lengthwise; twist the two parts to take them apart. Place the blade of the knife into the pit, twist and take out the pit. With a large spoon, scoop out the pulp into a bowl; immediately pour lime juice over the avocado and mash the pulp with a wooden spoon in the bowl. Add all herbs and spices and mix well. Add the oil and cilantro and mix well. Cover with plastic wrap, then with the lid, and refrigerate. Serve as soon as possible.

Tips: Avocado has good monounsaturated fat, folate, fiber, magnesium, vitamin E, lutein, etc.

Calamari with Peach Salad

(Serves: 2-4)

This is a very tasty and colorful dish. Calamari are high in protein. You can make either one large platter or make individual small plates for each person. Cook calamari rings, dusted with corn starch, and deep-fried in hot oil, light brown, for less than ½ minute.

Ingredients:

For the Salad: 3 very ripe peaches, blanched in boiling water for 3 minutes, then peeled, sliced ½-inch thick and sprinkled with 2 tbsp. of lemon juice and little salt and pepper to taste; 3 tbsp. canola oil; 1 bag 8 ounces (227g) pearl onions, trimmed, peeled and sautéed in 2 tbsp. butter on low heat, until soft (you can also buy marinated pearl onions in a jar); about ½ cups or to taste pickled sliced cherry peppers.

For the Calamari: 12 ounces (340G) cleaned calamari sliced into ½-inch wide rings, then dipped in 1 cup buttermilk; flour mixture: 1 tbsp. all-purpose flour; 1 tsp. sugar, and about ¼ tsp each salt and pepper or to taste. For the garnish: cook 4 tbsp. garlic cloves chopped on medium heat in 4 tbsp. butter in a large pan, until light brown; 1 container, 4.2 ounces (113g) feta cheese to sprinkle on top.

Heat a large, heavy-bottom pan with 3 tbsp. oil on medium-high heat. Take out the calamari with a strainer, shake out the extra buttermilk and sprinkle flour mixture on top. Shake off the extra flour and drop them in the hot oil in a single layer. Cook for about ½ minute, or until light brown. Now add the cooked pearl onions, cherry peppers and stir all together with the calamari.

To assemble: Place half of the peaches and salad mixture in the warm serving platter. Top with calamari mixture, and finally pour over the cooked garlic and butter. Serve immediately, garnished with feta cheese.

Tip: Cook calamari in very hot oil only for 20-30 seconds, stir two times with rest of the cooked ingredients, and serve.

Barbecued Calamari (Serves: 2 to 4)

These Calamari are very tasty. If you wish you can sprinkle with fresh shredded Fontina cheese. Place under the broiler for 5 minutes, and when the cheese is melted, serve sprinkled with green onion. Fontina is a very creamy cheese, and when it is melted it tastes superb.

Ingredients: The Rub: about 4 whole squid cleaned; 1 tbsp. each paprika, lemon-pepper mix, and onion powder; 1 tsp. each: granulated garlic and cayenne pepper; 1 tbsp. olive oil; about 1 cup vinegar-based barbecue sauce. To garnish: thin-sliced green onions.

Sprinkle the calamari outside with the rub and drizzle olive oil all over; set aside for 5 minutes. Prepare an indoor or outdoor grill at medium heat. Spray the grill well, then line the grill with a large piece of perforated aluminum foil; spread out the calamari in single layer, press down with a weight or aluminum foil-wrapped brick. Cook for 2-3 minutes until golden brown underneath. Take out and slice about ½-inch thin rings, drizzle with the BBQ. sauce and sprinkle with salt and pepper to taste. Serve garnished with green onions and extra sauce, and lemon wedges on the side.

Cheese Platter (Mini) (Serves: 4-6)

I find any occasion to make these mini cheese platters when cheeses are on sale. With fruits and vegetables and especially with ham, I like sharp cheeses. You can use your favorite one. You can also serve without ham or prosciutto.

Ingredients: 1 pkg. 8 oz. (226G) Vermont, premium naturally-aged white cheddar cheese; Virginia ham, round and thin slices, or aged prosciutto, about 2 slices per person; 1 med. Kirby cucumber thin-sliced; 2 plum tomatoes thin-sliced; 2 star fruits; purple grapes, crackers any kind.

1. Use an oblong platter and line up cucumber, tomato and star fruit (a little thicker) slices; place grapes in center.
2. On the other side, stack up your favorite crackers, then take one slice of ham at a time, fold in quarter, twist the bottom and open up the edges like a flower, and place them by the crackers in a row.
3. Open cheese halfway and serve on a marble cutting board with a sharp knife if possible. I leave the wrapping on the cheese so that people can read the name and if they like the cheese, they will use it again.
4. Serve with wine or beer.

Tips: When you are serving cheeses, use a marble cutting board that keeps the cheeses cold.

Use plain crackers with spicy and strong cheeses to get the full flavor of the cheese.

Deviled Eggs (M: 16 Egg Halves)

These eggs are so good, as soon as you put them out they are gone within 5 minutes. I use jumbo eggs and good amount of topping, so they are very tasty as well as very attractive.

Ingredients: 9 jumbo eggs (you need 2 extra yolks); 2 tsp. cider vinegar; 1 tsp. prepared mustard; 1 tbsp. olive oil; 3 tbsp. mayonnaise; 1 tbsp. horseradish cream sauce; 1 tsp. Worcestershire sauce (op); 2 tsp. grated yellow onion; ¼ tsp. turmeric (op); salt and pepper to taste; ice bath. For the topping: 4 thin slices of smoked salmon; 4 pieces of cornichons (mini pickled cucumbers); 4 pieces of marinated artichoke hearts; 4 cooked and marinated or spiced shrimp; and/or fermented beans. For the salad: salad tomatoes and 2-3 kiwi fruits, peeled and quartered.

1. About 1 hour before boiling take out the eggs from the refrigerator, turn them upside down and keep in the box, in room temperature.
2. Place the eggs in a large pot in single layer and cover with 2-inch-deep cold water. Bring the eggs to a full boil, cover with the lid, and boil for 5 minutes. Take the pot off the heat, let the eggs sit in the hot water for another 5 minutes. Prepare an ice bath: in a large bowl, place about 1 quart of cold water and add 1 tray ice cubes. After 5 minutes of soaking in the hot water, place the eggs for another 5 minutes in the ice bath. Then crack the eggs all around and peel them. If they are hard to peel, peel them under running cold water.
3. Carefully cut them in half lengthwise, wiping the knife after each use with a damp paper towel.
4. Hold one egg at a time at the ends, slightly bend them backward, and the yolk will loosen. Mash all the yolks with a potato masher. Add oil, mustard and vinegar and mash again. Then fold in mayo, horseradish cream, Worcestershire sauce, turmeric, onion and little salt and pepper to taste. Take one teaspoon of filling at a time and slide into the egg-white shells with a knife. When done, shape the filling with wet fingers, and top with the toppings.
    Tips: Turning the eggs about 1 hour before boiling, the yolk moves to the center. If you do not have a deviled egg dish, use a shredded lettuce bed for the eggs. Serving salad with the eggs is appealing and healthy.

Hot Pizza Pockets (M:9)

These are puff-pastry triangles filled with pepperoni, cheese and tomato sauce. Make them ahead, chill and bake just before serving. For a vegetarian treat, make them without pepperoni and add ½ cups sliced and sautéed mushrooms, or any other cooked vegetable or beans.

Ingredients : 1 pkg. 17.3 ounce 490g puff pastry sheets; about ½ cups all-purpose flour; ¼ cups grated parmesan cheese; 4 ounces about 25-30 slices of pepperoni cut in half, heated 4-5 minutes on medium heat in a pan, all fat soaked away with paper towels; 1 small can 8 ounces, (227g) plain tomato sauce, heated 10 minutes with ¼ tsp. each granulated garlic and dry oregano, and cooled; 4 ounces, about ½ cups shredded fresh mozzarella cheese, 1 egg beaten well, 1 tbsp. melted butter to brush the triangles.

1. Defrost the puff pastry in the refrigerator overnight. Prepare 2 large baking sheets and line them with parchment paper.
2. Take out 1 sheet at a time and dusting well with the flour the rolling pan and the cutting board, roll out the pastry into 11x11-inch squares. Using a large ruler as a guide, mark the pastry on two edges about 3-1/2-inch squares. Keep the ruler on the pastry sheet, use a pizza wheel or a sharp knife, and cut out 9 squares (each about 3-1/2 inches square).
3. Preheat the oven at 400F.
4. Move each square a little far apart (about ½ inches) so that you can work on each square well. First brush the egg wash on one corner and two adjoining sides, place 2 pieces of pepperoni in the corner; top with 1 tsp. each grated parmesan cheese and tomato sauce, then finally with about 1 tbsp. shredded mozzarella cheese. Hold the filling with one hand, fold that corner across with the other hand, making a triangle. Keep the fold about ½ inch away from all sides, in case any of the sauce leeks out. Dip a fork in flour and press the edges of the triangle with the fork, making a little design. Brush the top with the melted butter.
5. Bake one sheet at a time at 400F for about 12-15 minutes golden.

Vegetable Tempura (Serves: 4)

After we got married, we used to meet some of our Japanese friends in New York. They loved going to Japanese restaurants. We always ordered vegetable tempura, where they have fried broccoli crowns, fried sliced onion, string beans, etc. Once in a while it is alright to treat yourself with the fried food.

Ingredients:

For the Tempura Batter: 2 cups all-purpose flour mixed with 1 tbsp. corn starch, 2 tsp. baking powder; 2 cups ice-cold water; 3 tbsp. roasted sesame seed oil.

For the Vegetables: 1 medium broccoli crown taken out from the top (florets), and all stems attached cut into quarters and left attached to the crown; 1 large sweet onion sliced into ½-inch wide wedges; about 1 cup string beans, washed and cored; 1 red bell pepper, washed, cored, seeded and cut into ½-inch slices; canola oil to deep-fry; salt and pepper to sprinkle. To serve: any dipping sauce or yogurt chutney.

To make the Batter: In a medium bowl, whisk together flour mixture and ice water well; add the sesame oil and whisk to combine. Refrigerate for at least for 15 minutes.

When ready to cook, heat a wok, a fryer or a medium pot with about 2-inch-deep oil, on medium-high heat. Dip the vegetable pieces in the batter, shake out the excess and carefully drop in the hot oil away from you. Wait until it is golden in the bottom, turn over with the spatula or tongs, and fry the other side golden, about 6 to 8 minutes total. Keep the heat from medium to medium-high, about 360 degrees; do not burn the vegetables. Take the fried vegetables out on a paper towel-lined platter, sprinkle with salt and pepper and serve with sauce or chutney.

Tip: Try to serve fried food with yogurt or yogurt chutney; it will cut down on the fat.

Spreads

Tofu Spread (Serves: 4-6)

This is a low-calorie healthy spread. You do not need to add any salt if you prefer. Use it with almost any fruit and vegetable, over almost anything.

Ingredients: 1 pkg. 12.3 oz. (349g) firm silken tofu, 3 tabs sweet orange marmalade, ¼ tsp. cayenne pepper, 2 pinches salt, 1 tab each diced fresh red and green bell peppers, ½ cup Spanish olives with pimentos, 2 kiwi fruits or 2 star fruits, sliced.

1. On an oval platter in the center, slide carefully the drained tofu and place Spanish olives on one side and star fruits or kiwi fruits slices on the other side.
2. In a small saucepan, heat the marmalade with salt and cayenne pepper, just to dissolve it; set aside to cool. When marmalade is cool completely, pour it over the tofu and immediately sprinkle it with red and green bell peppers or with extra fresh-ground black pepper.
3. Chill in refrigerator at least 15 minutes and serve.

Tips:
When serving tofu spread, you can make it more colorful by adding more spices like paprika and more fresh vegetables and fruits like pomegranate and radishes. You can also sprinkle with fresh-diced parsley and other herbs in moderation.

Tips: Tofu has protein, vitamin B and E, potassium, iron, magnesium, etc.

DIPS

Onion Dip (M: 1 Cup)

Onion dip is very common. You can just make it plain with sour cream, mayo, diced onions and diced jalapeno or little distinctive flavor. Any leftover, I serve it with seafood.

Ingredients: ½ cup each mayonnaise and sour cream, 1 tsp. lemon juice, 3 tab sweet India relish, 1/3 cup diced fresh onion, salt and fresh-ground black pepper to taste.

1. In a medium bowl with a fork, mix mayonnaise, sour cream, lemon juice and sweet relish well.
2. Fold in diced onion and add salt and fresh-ground black pepper to taste. Chill for 15 minutes before serving.
3. Serve mostly with chips, cracker and fresh vegetables.
4. If you prefer you can sprinkle scallion on top and serve.

Yogurt Dip (M: 1 Cup)

Yogurt dip can be used with fresh vegetables for snacks and with sandwiches over the bread. I like to use with rice dishes as garnish.

Ingredients: 1 cup Greek yogurt or yogurt cheese (yogurt drained overnight in a few layers of cheese cloth); 1 tbsp. lemon juice, ½ tsp. lemon zest; ¼ cups green onion (scallions) thin sliced; jalapeno or serrano peppers seeded and minced to taste; 1 tbsp. India sweet cucumber relish or ¼ cups minced plum tomato; 1 tsp. caraway seed, dry toasted and ground in to powder; salt and pepper to taste.

Mix all ingredients, taste for seasoning and serve immediately, or cover and refrigerate until needed.

Tips: Greek yogurt or yogurt cheese has more protein. Yogurt also has live active cultures that helps the digestive tract. It has calcium, vitamin B, magnesium, potassium, zinc, etc.

Raw French Oysters (Serves: 4)

The French Oysters are rounder and the shells are deeper. It is a cute and interesting experience to have Oysters the French way, with wine or champagne.

Ingredients: 16 French oysters opened with oyster knife and placed on an ice-lined platter or a bamboo steamer basket; about 1 tbsp. lemon juice; 1 tsp. tabasco sauce or any other hot sauce; a chilled bottle of fine champagne.

Open the oysters just before serving, save the oyster liquor inside. Drizzle about 3-4 drops of lemon juice and 1-2 drops of Tabasco sauce or to taste on each oyster, and serve on the ice. You can pick up one oyster at a time and fill about 2 tsp. of chilled champagne, and swallow it down in one shot. If preferred, fill the oyster shell again with the chilled champagne and wash down the oyster.

It is a unique experience that you want to share with your friends and family.

Tip: Oysters are rich in zinc. Body needs this mineral daily because it is not stored in the body. Beans, cashews and beef also contain zinc.

Wine-Steamed Oysters with Garlic Potatoes and Bacon (Serves: 2)

You can use raw oysters or steam them in wine sauce. But serve with rest of the ingredients. This is our favorite and healthy way to serve oysters.

Ingredients: 4 strips of bacon; 2 large potatoes boiled and sliced in to wedges (about 6 pieces each); 6 to 8 oysters per person; ½ tsp. granulated garlic; 2 tbsp. unsalted butter; sea salt and cayenne pepper to taste;1 cup white wine and 1 cup chicken broth; 1 large fresh garlic clove crushed; 4 sprigs of fresh thyme; 2 sprigs of fresh oregano; 4 sprigs of parsley; plus extra herbs and about 2 cups of blanch and sautéed-in-garlic kale leaves for the base; 2 kiwi, peeled and cut into 4 wedges each; 2 plum tomatoes, cored and cut into wedges; horseradish sauce and tabasco to serve.

1. Heat a cast-iron pan on medium heat. Spread out the bacon strips and cook for 1-2 minutes per side until crunchy (depending on the thickness). Take out the bacon on a paper towel. Drain off all the fat. Place the pan on the medium heat and heat until warm. Take the pan off the heat, sprinkle the garlic and a little salt and cayenne; add the butter and potatoes cut side down. Cover and cook on medium-high heat for 3-4 minutes until browned. Take the pan off the heat and let it rest 1 minutes covered. Open the pan and sprinkle more salt, pepper and garlic, turn over the wedges and cook again 2-3 minutes covered on medium heat or until browned. Turn off the heat.

2. Prepare two serving platters with some extra herbs or blanched and sautéed kale leaves and set aside. In a large pan with rims, heat wine, chicken stock, crushed garlic, thyme, oregano and parsley; bring to a boil, lower the heat, place the oysters in the pan, cover and let the oysters open in the steam for 2-3 minutes. After 5 minutes, discard the unopened ones.

   Assemble the Platter: Take out the top shell from each oyster and place the oysters on the herb or kale bed; spoon 1-2 tsp of wine sauce over the oysters. Place the potato wedges on both sides of oysters in the bottom; place tomato and kiwi wedges at the top of the platter. Place the bacon strips on the sides. Sprinkle the Tabasco sauce over the potatoes and oysters. Then sprinkle the horseradish sauce over the oysters and serve.

   Tip: Seafood and fresh herbs go together very well. In some countries it is customary to serve an herb platter with the meal. They not only help digest the food, but work as an anti-oxidant. So munch on some fresh herbs with the food.

Salmon Hors d'oeuvre (Serves: 8)

We love smoked salmon and vegetables. You can buy salmon, and bake and peel vegetables, and assemble 1-2 hours before serving.

Ingredients: 8 ounces (226G) smoked salmon; 2 medium beets and 1 large and long baking potatoes; 1 long sweet potato baked in a 350F oven for about 1 hour; 1 yellow apple cored, sliced and rubbed with lemon and sautéed in 1tb of butter for 5 minutes; ¼ cups sour cream; 2 tbs. chopped chives or garlic greens for garnish.

1. Slice all vegetable about ½-inch thick, cut in half all apple slices and top each with about 2x1-inch salmon pieces. Drop about half tsp. of sour cream on top and garnish with chives or garlic greens.

2. If you are making these ahead, assemble them in the serving tray, cover with plastic wrap and refrigerate until serving.

3. If sweet potatoes and beets are too soft, you can place them just before serving, on barbecued potato chips or herbal crackers.

Quinoa, Oat and Cheese Fritters
With Asparagus & Jalapeno Aioli
(M: 12 large and 18 medium)

We also call these fritters protein fritters. Quinoa is a seed harvested from a plant in the broccoli, spinach and Swiss chard family. It has all amino acids that are essential for the body. Quinoa is loaded with plant-based protein.

How to Cook Quinoa: Bring ¾ cup plus 2 tbsp. water to a boil, add a pinch of salt, and 1 tsp. oil, ½ cups old-fashioned quick oats, and ½ cups whole grain quinoa. Stir for 5 minutes for even cooking, cover, turn off the heat, and let it sit for 15 minutes. Yields: 2c.

Ingredients:

For the Batter: 1 cup chickpea flour (besan); 1 tsp. celery seeds; 5 tbsp. water; ¼ tsp. each salt and pepper.

For the Filling: 2 cups about 10 ounces frozen peas; 1 cup packed cooked quinoa with oatmeal; 1 large egg; 1 cup packed part-skim ricotta cheese; ½ tsp. onion powder; about ¼ tsp. each salt and pepper, or to taste; ¼ cups drained roasted red bell peppers from the jar, chopped, or capers (op); ¼ cups chopped cilantro or parsley; ¼ cups grated parmesan cheese; 1/3 cups dry cranberries; 1c all-purpose flour to coat; oil to deep-fry; chutney: yogurt, lemon, mango or coconut, or asparagus and jalapeno aioli to serve.

For the Batter: Whisk together all batter ingredients together in a medium bowl, and set aside at least 30 minutes to overnight to rise. The batter should be thick enough to coat the fritters.

For the Filling: Place the frozen peas in a small pot and wash them under cold water, drain, and place on medium heat. Stir the peas for 5 minutes and dry out all the liquid. Turn off the heat, and mash with the potato masher.

In a medium bowl, whisk the egg, add the quinoa mix, and whisk together. Add the ricotta and parmesan cheeses and whisk. Mix in peas, cilantro or parsley, onion powder, cranberries, salt and pepper well. With a fork, fold in red bell peppers. Just before cooking, spread out half of the flour in a large platter; using an ice cream scoop, scoop out the filling and drop over the flour, then sprinkle rest of the flour on the top. Roll the balls in the flour.

Heat a wok, medium frying pan or a medium pot with about 2-inch-deep oil to 375 degrees, medium-high heat. To coat the balls with the batter: place your hands over the batter, then take about 2 tbsp. of batter in left hand; place a ball over it and using the right, hand drizzle about 3-4 tbsp. of batter with a spoon over the ball; wipe the dripping batter against the bowl, and drop the ball in the hot oil, on the edge, with the left hand. If you prefer, pour the batter right over the balls into the platter where they were coated with the four. But make sure all sides are covered with the batter. Let the balls (fritters) get brown underneath before turning them over. Make sure the temperature of the oil is 355 degrees all the time so that fritters brown evenly without burning. Fry them in batches. Once they are browned all sides, keep on turning them over in the hot oil for an extra minute to crisp them. When golden brown, take them out on a paper towel-lined platter and serve warm with chutney or aioli.

Asparagus and Jalapeno Aioli (M: about 2 Cups)

This is a hot sauce that goes with lots of recipes. Just make it hot according to your taste.
Ingredients: 2-3 jalapeno, seeded and chopped; 1 cup trimmed soft asparagus, blanched in hot water for 3 minutes and then cooled under running cold water and drained; 2 large egg yolks; ¼ cups prepared brown mustard; zest or 1 lime; juice of 1 lemon and 1 lime; salt to taste; ½ cups extra virgin olive oil to drizzle.

In a blender, puree all ingredients in the order they are listed; then while machine is running, drizzle the olive oil in a slow stream through the feed tube. Check seasoning; add more lemon juice or the salt to taste. Pour in a bowl chill or serve.

The Basic Fritter Batter (Pakaura) (to dip about 30 pieces)

Following is the basic batter that can be used for all kinds of fritters.

Ingredients: 1-1/2 cup chickpea flour; 1 tbsp. celery seeds; 1 tbsp. milk; 1 tbsp. canola oil; about ½ cup water or as needed to make batter (a little thicker than pancake batter) for dipping; ½ tsp. each: salt and cayenne pepper; ½ tsp. turmeric powder.

In a medium bowl, whisk together all ingredients; cover and set aside for 30 minutes. When ready to cook, heat about 2-inch-deep oil in a wok, heat to about 360 degrees; dip each piece of the vegetable in the batter, then lightly wipe out the batter against the rim of the bowl, and drop on the edge of the hot oil. Fry for 2-3 minutes (depending on the cut and type of the vegetable), until it is golden underneath; turn over and deep-fry on the second side until golden.

Onion Fritters (Serves: 4)

Onion Fritters are very tasty and go well with almost any kind of soup. You can serve them with any sour and hot chutney and/or soup.

Ingredients: 2 medium onions; 1 recipe of basic fritter batter (above); canola oil for deep-frying; chutney to serve.

1. Peel and slice each onion across into 1/3 inch round slices.
2. To make the batter: In a large bowl whisk chickpea flour, water, oil, celery seeds, salt and fresh-ground black pepper until light and fluffy and set aside for 15 minutes to 2 hours to rise.
3. Heat oil in a wok or heavy-bottom skillet with sides, about 2 inches high, on medium-high heat (about 375 degrees). To test the oil, drop a little piece of bread and it should sizzle and float on the top right away. When oil is ready, put half of the onion slices, standing up, on the side of the bowl into the batter. Take one slice of the onion, dip both sides in the batter, then wipe out excess batter on the edge of the bowl and very carefully drop in the hot oil pan on the side (not in the middle, or it will splash). Fill the pan in a single layer about ½ inch away from each piece. Wait about 1-1/2 minutes or until underside is golden, then with a metal spatula (prefer a perforated one) turn over and fry on the other side. Even though the fritters are done, turn over one more time on each side fast to crisp. When done, hold 3-4 fritters on the spatula against the side of the pan, take them out on a paper towel-lined platter, and serve hot or keep warm on a baking tray in a low heated oven.

Fresh Vegetables, Herbs & Nut Fritters (M: 25-30 Balls)

These are the party favorites. You can prepare them ahead and deep-fry a few hours before serving. You can serve, hot, or at the room temperature.

Ingredients: 3-1/2 to 4 pounds red potatoes, boiled in cold water until soft, cooled, peeled, mashed and sprinkled with 1 tsp. of lemon-pepper seasoning mix, ½ tsp. turmeric powder, salt and cayenne or black pepper to taste; 1 medium cauliflower cut in half, florets cut out with ½-inch stems, sautéed in 1 tbsp. oil and ½ tsp. gran. garlic until soft; 1 can 15oz., (425g) chick peas drained, washed and sautéed in 1 tsp. oil for 10 minutes on medium heat to dry out all water, then add 2 cups baby spinach leaves; sauté a little to wilt; 1 cup slivered toasted almonds or roasted peanuts; 1 cup washed and pat dry cranberries; ½ cups fresh grated ginger; 1 cup fresh chop cilantro leaves and soft stems; oil to deep-fry and yogurt chutney to serve.

The Batter to coat with: 4 cups chickpeas flour (besan) plus extra; 1 tab celery seeds; salt and cayenne or fresh-ground black pepper to taste.

1. In a large sauté pan on medium heat, heat 2 tbsp. oil, add caraway seeds, light brown for 5 minutes; add onion, increase the heat high and cook onion until soft, about 5 minutes. Lower the heat to medium again and add the mashed potatoes, stir well scraping the bottom until potatoes are heated through, about 6-7 minutes. Pour potatoes in a large bowl, add cooked cauliflower, sautéed spinach, chickpeas, almonds, cranberries, ginger and cilantro. Mix all with a metal spatula. Take out some mixture in the hand and make golf ball-size balls, pushing the nuts and chickpeas inside the balls while potatoes are still warm. Now you can cover with plastic wrap and refrigerate until the next day (take out balls and leave in room temperature, then heat in microwave for 2 minutes or in the oven for 10 minutes at 350 degrees), or proceed and leave the balls in room temperature.
2. Make the thick batter: add 4 cups of chickpea flour, celery seeds, salt and pepper to taste and ¾ cups to 1 cup of water as needed.
3. Heat oil at medium-high heat about 375 degrees. Hold 1 meatball at a time over the batter with left hand and pour about ½ cups of batter with a ladle with the right hand over the ball; let it drip out a little, coating the balls completely, then wipe the bottom of the fork against the rim of the bowl, and turn over the coated ball into the hot oil, starting from the edges. Do not over-crowd the oil. When the balls are golden brown underneath, turn over in the oil, cook golden the other side. When the balls are completely golden, move them around in the oil to crisp a little, and take out

with a slotted spoon or spider, on a paper towel-lined platter. Adjust the heat and keep a steady temperature of 375 degrees.

4. Serve with yogurt or lemon chutney, or with ketchup.

Tip: Use more potatoes than vegetables to for form a ball. Also, use the firm-cooked vegetables so the mixture does not turn watery. Push in all the nuts and chickpeas inside the ball. The vegetable balls should be covered with batter; then let the batter drip out, leaving a thin coating of the chickpea flour, before you place the coated ball, bottom side up, carefully in the hot oil.

Green Chickpeas Fritters or Pancakes (Serves: 4 to 6)

My mother used to make these fritters and pancakes with fresh shelled chickpeas. Since I don't get them here, I started using the dry ones. You can also use the regular chick peas. My father's favorite beans were chickpeas. They purify the blood and give protein and fiber as well as keep you regular. Be careful not to add too much of the pancake flour, because of the baking soda and baking powder will soak up a lot of oil in deep-frying.

Ingredients: 1 cup dry green chickpeas, soaked overnight; 1 large onion chopped; 4 cloves of garlic chopped; 2 inches of ginger chopped; ½ cup chopped soft cilantro stems (washed well before and after chopping); 1 cup of chickpea flour or pancake flour, or a mixture of both; salt and Black Pepper to taste; 1 cup rice flour and canola oil to deep-fry.

1. First puree onion, garlic, cilantro and ginger in a blender with a little water (just enough to grind). Heat a heavy-bottom sauté pan on medium high heat; add 1 tab of oil. When oil is hot, pour the ground onion mixture; stir well, cover and let it cook on medium while you are grinding chickpeas. Use as little water as possible to grind the chickpeas and puree them well. Now open the cover of the sauté pan add little salt and pepper, stir onion mixture well then pour over the chickpea mixture; cover and let it cook 15 minutes on medium. After 15 minutes, turn off the stove and let it cool.

2. When the mixture is almost cool, whip 1 cup of rice flour and 1 cup of pancake flour or chickpea flour with 1 ½ cup water; make a thick batter, then add chickpea mixture to it. It should be a thick batter, like a paste; add salt and pepper to taste. Do not add too much pepper.

3. Heat about 2-inch-deep oil in a frying pan to 350F and drop 1 tab full of batter or one small ice cream scoop full of batter in hot oil. Let it cook until it is brown underneath, about 2-3 minutes, then turn them over and cook the other side. Once fritters are brown, turn them again all over just to make sure they cook all around and make them crispy. Take fritters out of oil with a perforated metal spatula on a tray lined with a paper towel.

4. Serve then hot with yogurt chutney.

Green Chickpea Pancakes

Heat a cast-iron skillet on medium high heat, add 1 tab of canola oil and when oil almost starts smoking, take a ladle full of batter, drop in the skillet in center, and from the back of the ladle, spread it out in a circle as thin as possible. You can also spread it out with wet fingers. Remember the first pancake you cook should be a little thicker than the rest of the pancakes. When it is brown underneath, drop a few drops of oil on top and turn it over and cook the other side. Serve hot with any chutney or salsa.

Mixed Vegetable Fritters (M: about 55 large fritters)

These are very easy, nutritious and loaded with fresh vegetables and herbs. The best part of these fritters is that you can make them ahead, reheat in the oven and serve with yogurt chutney. You can also freeze in a plastic bag and placed in a plastic container up to at least three months. The trick for these fritters is sprinkle about 1 tbsp. of pancake flour over the chopped vegetables as you chop them, and at the end, divide into four sections. Take one section at a time, sprinkle about 2 tabs water and 2 tabs of pancake flour, mix little to bind them, scoop out about half an ice cream scoopful, round it up and carefully drop them on the side in the hot, almost-smoking oil about 350 degrees; let them cook about 4 to 5 minutes until golden underneath, and then turn over and brown the other side. Chop soft vegetables like squash thin, about ¼-inch wide and about ½-inch long; hard vegetables like carrots and potatoes should be grated.

Ingredients: 2 cups split and peeled mung dal (beans) soaked in lightly warm water for 3 hours, and ground in blender/food processor with about 1 cup water; 1 cup chickpea flour; about 2 cups pancake flour; 1 tsp. celery seeds; 1 cup chopped baby spinach; all fresh vegetables chopped fine about ¼-inch wide and ½-inch long: 1 red bell pepper seeded, 1 long and slim zucchini, 1 long Japanese eggplant, chopped and sprinkled with salt; 2 red onions, 6 large garlic cloves, 3 tbsp. ginger, about 4 serrano green peppers (op), 1 large baking potato; peeled and grated (sprinkle each chopped vegetable with 1 tab of pancake flour as you go); 1 cup soft stems and leaves of cilantro chopped; salt and fresh-ground black pepper to taste; canola or olive oil to deep-fry; yogurt and/or any chutney to serve on side.

1. Grind half of the mung dal with about 1 cup water to puree, then add the other half of the Dal and grind with the pureed Dal, using as little water as possible. Take out the ground beans (Dal) and add 1 cup chickpea flour in a large bowl. Now add the chopped vegetables and herbs and sprinkle about ½ cups of pancake flour over; salt and pepper to taste, and mix all vegetables with the batter (down below) by hand.
2. Heat about 2-inch-deep oil to fry the fritters in a large wok, or wide heavy-bottom pot, on low heat.
3. Divide the mixture in to 4 portions in the same bowl. Sprinkle about 2 tabs of water and 4 tbsp. of pancake flour on one portion; mix it well with a wooden spoon. Heat the oil on medium heat and when oil is hot and almost smoking, about 350 degrees, drop about three heaping tablespoon of mixture with a large ice cream scoop neatly on the edge of the hot oil. Cook fritters until golden on underside, about 4 to 5 minutes, then turn over with a metal spatula and cook the other side golden. When fritters are done, turn them over one more time to crisp, and take them out on a paper towel-lined baking tray. Do not crowd the oil, just cook 5-7 fritters at a time. Keep fritters in a lightly warm oven (200F) if serving soon.
4. Serve with yogurt or tamarind chutney while they are hot.

Tasty, Spicy, Cruncy Snacks with Chutney (Serves: 4)

Snacks (Chat)

Chat is a general term for the tasty snacks. It is a very famous snack that can be served for lunch or snack almost any time of the day. It is layered meal, put together just before serving. These layers are various flavors of beans, vegetables, herbs and spices. They are crunchy, soft, sweet, salty, hot and spicy. The garnishes are fresh chutneys, spices and herbs that are antioxidants and full of nutrients. I even garnish with dry cranberries and fresh pomegranate seeds that look like jewels. You can also use crunchy French fried onions (that you use in a bean casserole) on the top. These vegetables, spices and noodles can be found at the Indian grocery stores and in some supermarkets. Make separate plates for each person, up to four, and make a large platter for the group. Heat all the crunchy food: papdi and noodles in a low (200F) oven to crisp and heat the food.

Ingredients: 4 cups papadi (crunchy bread in large round shape, sticks or cut about 2-inches in diamond shape); 1 can 14 ounces about 2 cups cooked chickpeas with salt and pepper to taste and mixed with 1 tbsp. ketchup and heated to a boil; 2 cups baked or cooked peeled potatoes; fine chopped: 2 cups fresh cucumbers; 1 cup onions; 1 cup daicons or radishes, 1 cup fresh red bell pepper cored, seeded and chopped; 1/ 2c fresh cilantro or coriander; 1 cup fresh tomatoes; 2 lemons cut in to wedges; about 2 tbsp. lemon juice; ¼ cups grated fresh ginger; 1-1/2 cups coriander-lemon chutney; 1 cup tamarind sweet chutney; 2 cups plain yogurt; 1 cup fine chickpeas noodles; 8 vegetarian samosas, heated; salt, cayenne pepper to taste; ¼ cups roasted caraway seeds powder; ¼ cups chopped fresh serrano peppers; 1/2 cups dry cranberries and/or pomegranate seeds for garnish.

1. On 4 separate dinner plates, make layers in a circle. Save half of the chutney, herbs, garnishes and lemon wedges to serve on the side.
2. First spread out crunchy papadi on bottom, top with chickpeas and potatoes, top with lemon juice, onion and cucumber, top with sweet and sour coriander and tamarind chutneys; sprinkle yogurt all over, then sprinkle salt, cayenne, caraway powder and finally top with crunchy fine chickpeas noodles and/or crunchy French fried onions, Serrano chopped peppers, cranberries and pomegranate seeds. Put samosas on top and bottom of the plate, whole or cut in half.
3. Serve, with half of the chutneys, lemon wedges, daicons, onion, caraway seeds powder, salt, cayenne, yogurt on side.

Bean Fritters (Vada) (M: 35 Bara)

This is a big hit among the snacks. They look like doughnuts. These bean fritters are very popular in South India, traditionally served hot with coconut chutney and the sambhar (thin bean stew). In the North, they are served topped with yogurt, tamarind chutney and sprinkled with the spices. We soak them 3 days in water to for fermentation. Fermented protein is a lot better than animal protein. I prepare the batter and freeze half, airtight, in a plastic container; thaw overnight in the refrigerator, mix the spices and herbs and it is ready to deep-fry. These fritters are made with a hole in the center (like doughnuts).

Ingredients: 2 cups whole and peeled urad beans (gotta), picked over for stones etc.; ½ cup plain yogurt; ¼ cups chickpea flour; ¼ cup corn starch; ½ cups chopped each: cilantro soft stems; peeled and grated ginger; ¼ cups crushed black peppercorns; 1 tbsp. crushed fennel seeds; salt to taste; oil to deep-fry. To serve: coconut or lemon chutney, and/or sambhar.

1. Place the beans in a large bowl, wash with cold water, then fill the bowl with about 2 inches cold water above the beans; cover with a plate and soak them for 3-4 hours. Tilt the bowl in the sink and slowly take out the water from the beans and replace with fresh water, or use a strainer to wash the beans. Grind the beans in the food processor, in batches, without little or no water. Add all the spices and yogurt, mix well. Place the mixture in a wide non-reactive bowl, and place in the refrigerator overnight, covered.
2. When ready to cook, heat a wok or large, heavy-bottom frying pan with 2-inch-deep oil on medium-high heat, about 370 degrees. Take out the batter from the refrigerator, sprinkle the top lightly with the salt. Wet your fingers lightly with water, then using an ice cream scoop, take about ½ cup of the mixture, round it up, and make a 1-inch diameter hole in the center with a wet finger rotating in the circle. Drop the fritter in the hot oil, near the edge. Wait for about 3-4 minutes or until the underside is lightly browned, then turn it over with a metal spatula. When almost browned, turn each side of the fritters 2-3 times in hot oil to crisp. Take them out on a paper towel-lined platter. Do not crowd the oil and fry in batches. Serve warm with chutney and sambhar if desire.
3. Any leftover fritters can be stored in the refrigerator; reheat in the microwave or in the regular oven at 350 degrees about 10 minutes or until warm and serve.

Yogurt and Beans Dumpling (M: 12-15)

(Dahi Gujiya/Bada)

Traditionally these are called stuffed Vada, the Yogurt Gujiya. They are shaped like pierogis (semicircle). It can be tricky to make them if the beans are ground with too much water. The batter should be very thick-ground in a food processor. Follow the recipe above of the Vada. Just fill them with the filling.

The Filling: ¼ cups soaked silvered almonds; ½ cup dry cranberries; ½ cups grated soft ginger; 1 tbsp. sliced thin fresh serrano peppers or to taste (op); 2 tabs chopped cilantro or parsley; 1 tbsp. crushed cardamom seeds; 1 tbsp. small fennel seeds and mix all together. One recipe of plain bean fritters (vada) without mixing any spices. To serve: red hot sauce, and yogurt sauce, and ¼ cup chat masala.

Red Hot Sauce: ½ cups ketchup; ½ cups tomato sauce; ½ tsp. cayenne/tabasco; ¼ tsp. salt or to taste;1 tbsp. unsalted butter. Combine and simmer on low for 15 minutes and set aside covered.

Yogurt Sauce: 1-1/2 pounds plain yogurt, mixed with 4 tbsp. sugar, 1 tsp. rose water, and whipped well.

Heat about 2-inch-deep oil in a wok or deep-frying pan, or in a wide pot on medium heat. Take a 12x12 cotton cloth, wet it well and spread on the cutting board. Now take about ½ cup of plain bean mixture with a scoop (from Vada recipe), spread it out on the corner of the cloth; using a wet finger, about ½-inch thick. Place about 1-2 tbsp. of the filling in the center. Lift up the corner of the cloth and fold the bean circle in half, making a semi-circle, and press the edges to seal. Now wet the fingers of one hand, lift up the cloth and drop the Gujhiya (semi-circle on the wet fingers), then drop the bean fritter in the hot oil on the edge carefully. Cook each fritter for 5-6 minutes each side at medium-high heat (about 370 degrees), until golden and crisp, turning them over and over again, until they are lightly browned. Repeat with the rest. When all are done, soak them in a bowl covered with the water for 15-20 minutes. Take out of the water and holding one piece at a time between fingers of two hands, squeeze out some of the water carefully. Then mix them with half of the yogurt sauce.

To serve, place two stuffed fritters on each individual plate. Sprinkle with salt and pepper. Top with more yogurt sauce, then pour hot sauce across, and sprinkle with chat masala.

Breads

Brioche Bread (1large Loaf)

Breads always taste good when they are hot and fresh-baked. But this one tastes good all the time. This is an easy recipe to make buns or bread.

Ingredients: ¼ cup warm water, about 90 degrees; 1 envelope 7g ¼ oz. active dry yeast; 2 tbsp. sugar; the flour mixture: 4cupsifted all-purpose flour and 1tsp. salt; extra flour for dusting; 1-1/2 sticks, ¾cupunsalted melted butter, room temperature; 4 large eggs, beaten then whisked with ¾ cup whole milk; 2 tbsp. softened butter for folding; 1egg whisked with 1tbsp. water for brushing. To serve: butter, jelly and jam etc.

1. Place the yeast, then sugar, in a large bowl, and pour the warm water, cover and set aside for 6-8 minutes until yeast is bubbling.
2. In another large bowl add flour, salt, and half of the butter. Rub the flour with the half of the butter by hand to incorporate the butter. Add the yeast mixture to the flour mixture with a rubber spatula, then add the eggs mixture and mix well. Now add the rest of the butter and mix well by hand. Cover with greased plastic wrap, then with the cotton towel, and place in the turned-off cool oven for one hour, or until it is double.
3. Take out the dough and knead in the bowl for two minutes, dusting with the flour. Place the dough in a greased plastic wrap, then place in the large bowl, cover with a large plate and refrigerate for 6 hours to overnight.
4. Prepare a 9-inch loaf pan, line the bottom with parchment paper, and grease well both the paper and the pan. 2 hours before baking, take out the dough and leave on the cutting board, covered with a towel. Knead the dough, on and off, to make it pliable (or you can leave for 2-3 minutes, in a lightly heated but turned-off oven to soften it). Knead it again; when the dough is pliable, spread it out to 6x8 inches by hand; spread the softened butter. Roll the dough loosely in a cylinder, from top to bottom. Shape it in a loaf. Place in the prepared pan and let it rise for 30 minutes in room temperature.

5. Move the oven rack to lower third from the bottom, and preheat the oven at 375 degrees. Brush with egg wash all over, make 2-3 diagonal slashes, about half inch deep, on the top. Place the pan on a baking tray. Bake at 375 degrees preheated oven for about 50 minutes, golden brown. If bread starts getting dark on the top, tent it with foil. Take the pan out and cool over a wire rack. Serve warm or at room temperature.

Tip: You can bake a large loaf or bake 12 buns. Bake the buns at 400 degrees for 12-15 minutes, in batches, until they are browned. Take the buns out of the tray as soon as they are baked and keep them warm in a towel or foil until serving. With leftover bread, make bread pudding or croutons, yummy!

Brown Grain Bread (M:1 Loaf)

This is German Brown Bread with lots of grains and very tasty. When we visit my brother in Berlin, we always buy this bread and slice it on the meat slicer.

Ingredients: Grain mixture – 1/2cup black sesame seeds, ¼ cup each sunflower seeds, flax seeds, quinoa, 1Tsp. celery seeds, mix all well and take out 2Tbsp. grain mixture for the topping roast remaining and cool; 1-1/2 cups lukewarm water; 2Tbsp. cider vinegar; 1-1/2Tsp. coarse sea salt (tiny crystals); 2Tsp. baking soda; 1-1/2cups protein bread flour; 1cup brown whole wheat flour.

Preheat oven at 375 degrees. Line the bottom of a 9.25 X 5.25 X 2.3/4-inch Loaf Pan with parchment and grease it well.

In a large bowl whisk together water, vinegar, and salt, then sprinkle baking powder. Add toasted grain mixture and flours and mix well with a large wooden or plastic spoon. Pour the thin and sticky batter into the prepared pan and even out the top. Lightly wet your hand and even out the surface, sprinkle the topping mixture then press it down lightly. Let the batter sit in the room temperature for 30 minutes. Bake in a preheated 375 degrees oven, place the pan over the aluminum foil, and bake for about 45 minutes. When done take the pan out of the oven, cool 5 minutes, loosen the edges with a dinner knife and place the bread right side up on a wire rack. Cool for 1 hr. and put it back in the pan cover, or wrap with foil. When ready to serve slice thin, toast it lightly and serve with butter, jam etc. Keep the bread wrapped in a plastic bag, in the bread box for up to a week.

Tip: To roast the grain – line a baking sheet with aluminum foil, spread out the grains and seeds roast in a preheated 350 degrees oven for about 5 minutes or until light brown.

Chickpeas (Garbanzo) Bread (1 large Loaf)

My father loved chickpeas. He said, "It keeps you regular and makes new blood in the body."

Ingredients: 4 jumbo or 5 extra large eggs; 1 large banana; 1 cup dry cranberries; 1 cup cauliflower puree (cook cauliflower with 1 tbsp. water on low heat until soft, then puree in blender with 2-3 tbsp. heavy or light cream); 1 cup about 2 medium potatoes, boiled, peeled and fine-grated on the small holes of a box grater; 1 cup buttermilk; a mixture of: 1 cup chickpeas flour (called besan or graham flour, found in Indian grocery stores or health food stores), 1 cup almond flour, 2 tsp. baking powder, ½ tsp. baking soda, 1 tsp. salt, 1 tsp. ground cinnamon; to fold in: 1stick melted and cooled butter.

Preheat oven at 375 degrees. Spray or butter a 9-1/4x5-1/4x2-3/4-inch loaf pan, then line the bottom with the double parchment paper.

In a large bowl, whisk the eggs; cut banana in quarter lengthwise then thin-slice across; whisk in cranberries, cauliflower puree and potato puree well. Add the buttermilk, whisk well; add flour mixture and whisk to incorporate. Fold in the melted butter. Pour in the prepared loaf pan. Bake for 20 minutes at 375 degrees. Make a long cut on the top lengthwise in the center for steam to escape, turn around halfway, and bake another 40 minutes or until golden. Cool in the off oven.

Serve: slice and toast it first in the toaster or regular oven, then butter it and serve. This bread is very soft so handle it carefully.

Gluten-Free Chickpea Skillet Bread (Paratha)

(M: about 14, 6-inch diameter)

This is a cast-Iron skillet (tawa) bread. It is like a pita bread, but much thinner, and is cooked in about 2-3 drops of oil, on each side, to give the nutty taste.

Ingredients: 3 baking potatoes scrubbed cleaned, boiled, peeled and mashed, about 2 cups packed; the flour mixture: 3 cups chickpeas flour (plus ¾ cups for dusting); ½ cup fine corn meal or rice flour; ½ cup lightly toasted and crushed sesame seeds; 1 tbsp. each: celery and caraway seeds, salt; 1 tsp. each: red pepper flakes (op), turmeric powder; 2 tbsp. canola oil; ½ cup buttermilk, about 1/3 to ½ cup water as needed; oil to cook. To serve: raita, chutney, greens, and/or curry.

In a large bowl with a wooden spoon, whisk all ingredients except the water. Slowly add about 1/3 cup of water to make a firm dough. Now using the hands, make a dough ball; cover and set aside for 30 minutes for dough to rise.

Heat a cast-iron skillet on medium heat. Knead the dough; it should be a little sticky. If needed, sprinkle 1-2 tbsp. of water to knead the dough. Scrape off the hands with a dinner knife. Wash and dry the hands, dusting the hands and the cutting board with the flour; make about 14 portions of the dough.

Pick up one portion at a time, dust with the flour, make a ball, then a patty, dip again in the flour and roll out, about 5-6-inches. Scrape off the bread with a knife if it is sticking on the board. You can also roll out the bread over well-dusted plastic wrap. Increase the heat to medium-high, slap the bread on the hot skillet, cook for 1 minute, turn over, and over and cook on both sides on medium heat (about 2 minutes on each side); do not let the bread burn. When the bread is almost done (brown specks on both sides), then drop 2-3 drops of oil over the bread, in a circle, spread out the oil with the back of a large spoon, cook for 30 seconds on each side, and place in a large paper towel-lined bowl. Repeat with rest of the breads. Serve hot right out of the skillet with raita, and/or greens or Juicy Curry.

Tip: Grain breads are sticky, so when rolling the bread, use a bread knife, to scrape off the cutting board. Try not to make too thin or too big.

To make a regular bread (not a gluten-free): use 2 cups of bread flour, instead of the mashed potatoes. Also, use the bread flour to roll out the breads.

Irish Soda Bread (M: 1 Loaf)

We don't wait for St. Patty's Day, so we bake this soda bread several times a year, for our pallet and our heritage.

Ingredients: Dry: 2-1/4 cups all-purpose flour; 1 tsp. salt; 1-1/2 tsp. baking soda; 1-1/2 tsp. baking powder; 3 tbsp. sugar; 1 tbsp. vegetable oil and 6 tbsp. softened butter. Wet: ½ cup milk; 2 ext. large eggs; 1 tsp. lemon zest; ¾ cup dark raisins. To sprinkle on the top: 1 tbsp. melted butter and 1tsp. sugar.

1. Preheat the oven at 350 degrees. Grease and line the bottom of a 9-inch Loaf Pan.

2. In a large bowl combine flour, baking soda, baking powder, salt and rub in the oil and the softened butter to dry ingredients. In a medium bowl, whisk together milk, zest and the eggs; add the raisins and pour over the dry ingredients, whisk just to combine. Do not over-mix. Scrape the batter into the prepared pan with a spatula and even out the top. Brush the top with melted butter and sprinkle the sugar.

3. Bake in the preheated oven for 35 to 40 minutes, until the bread has risen to the top and the top is light brown. Turn around the pan halfway during the baking. Cool the bread in the pan for 10 minutes. Use a dinner knife and loosen the edges, then invert on a platter, right side up. Serve warm with butter, jam and jelly.

Foolproof Naans (M: 10 large)

Naan is an Indian bread. It is very soft and goes well with the meat and vegetable curries, or raita (yogurt salad), etc. It is cooked in the tandoori oven, over open fire. But you can cook one side in the very hot skillet and the other side under the broiler; it takes about 3 minutes per bread. Keep the cooked naan wrapped in foil and/or a kitchen towel in the cold oven up to 24 hours If you cook Naans on daily basis, have two cast-iron skillets, one for the stove and the other for the broiler. Wear long ovenproof gloves when baking the bread, and take your time, do not rush.

Ingredients: 1 packet, 7g, (1/4 ounces), rapid-rise active dry yeast; 1/3 cup warm (90 degrees) water; 2 tbsp. sugar; flour mixture: 4 cups all-purpose bleached flour (not bread flour) mixed with ¼ tsp. baking soda, 2 tsp. and baking powder; eggs mixture: 2 large cold eggs whisked first, then with 1 cup cold half-and-half; 1 tbsp. kosher salt 2 tbsp. melted but cooled butter, plus extra (about 2 tbsp.) for brushing on the top; about ½ cup extra flour for dusting.

In a large bowl, place the yeast, and sugar, pour the warm water, and whisk for 30 seconds to dilute the yeast (if the yeast doesn't dilute and stays grainy, discard the mixture and start again with the live yeast). Now add flour mixture and mix with the hands. Slowly pour in the egg mixture and mix by hand to incorporate completely. Sprinkle the salt and melted butter all over, and mix all in the dough with the hand. Take the dough on the counter and knead for 2 minutes, dusting with flour. Cover the dough with the damp cloth and let it rise in a cold oven for 45 minutes to 1 hour, or until it is almost doubled. Dust your hands and knead for 1 minute on the cutting board. The dough will be loose.

Preheat the broiler. Also heat a cast-iron skillet on low heat over the stove.

Divide the dough into 10 large balls. Take one ball at a time, flatten it dusting with the flour, roll out to about 7 inches diameter, about 1/10 inch thick. Place the naan in single layer on the large clean and dry towel. When all are rolled out, increase the stove heat to medium-high. Dusting hands with the flour, take one naan at a time, stretch it a little, slap on the hot skillet, shape it round and even by pressing down with the fingers over the edges. Cook for about 1-1/2 minutes or until the bottom is browned. Do not turn over. Pick up the naan with tongs and place it under the broiler on the hot broiler tray; cook the top for about 2-3 minutes until it is puffed up, and has brown specks. Repeat with rest of the naans. Brush the baked naan with the butter on top, and stack them in aluminum foil or in a paper towel-lined large bowl. When all are done, cover them with the kitchen towel to keep warm.

Tip: To make the garlic naan, just add 2 tbsp. crushed garlic cloves, and 2-3 tbsp. chopped cilantro with the 4 tbsps. melted butter, and spread the butter mixture with a tablespoon on one side, right after they are baked.

Famous Indian Deep-Fried Bread - Poori

Poori is deep-fried bread traditionally served at parties with fancy vegetables and meat. I make plain poories and with the eggs. Poories made with eggs have protein. They are tasty on their own and go very well with fancy curries. Just serve raita (yogurt salad) on side to ease the deep-fried effect. Add any salt add at the end, just before you are dividing the dough into portions.

Basic Poories (M: 18-20)

Ingredients: 3 cup atta, the Indian bread flour, plus about ½ cup extra for dusting (I prefer Golden Temple flour); ½ cup plain yogurt; 4 tbsp. melted butter or oil; ½ to ¾ cup warm water (about 100 degrees) as needed; canola oil or sunflower oil to deep-fry.

In a large bowl, mix together flour and 4 tbsp. oil first with the hands. Add yogurt and ½cupwarm water and start mixing by hand, trying to make a ball. If needed, add little more water by teaspoons just to bring the dough together into a ball. Remember, the dough for the poori should be hard. If the dough is soft, the poories will be chewy. After the dough comes together into a ball, start kneading the dough by pressing your knuckles into the dough, to make into a pliable, for about 2 minutes. Make a smooth log of the dough, cover with a lightly damp cloth towel, place inside the cold oven and let it rest for 1 hour.

When ready to make poories, use a wok or a heavy-bottom rimmed medium sauté pan with about 1-1/2 to 2 inches of oil. Start kneading the dough again for another 1 to 2 minutes. The dough should be pliable, but still thick and dense. Divide it into 18-20 portions. Pick up one portion at a time, make a roll, then make into a ball and flatten into a patty, about 2-1/2 to 3-inches. Dip and dust the patty both sides in the flour, shake out the excess flour and roll one side 2-3 times; turn over, pat it down on the board (so it does not move) and roll in the middle first, then on all four edges, to make an even poori about 4-1/2 to 5 inches in diameter. Roll out all the patties first and keep the last rolling side up in a paper towel-lined baking sheet.

Heat the oil on medium-high heat, about 375-degrees. When the oil starts moving in the wok or pan, pick up one poori at a time and drop it into the hot oil, from the edge and halfway into the oil, the last rolled side down. Let the poori cook on its own for 1 minute, then move the poori around in the oil just once and turn it over with the help of a spoon and a metal spatula. The poori should puff up. Turn each side 2 times in the oil, until light brown on both sides. Take the poori out with the spatula, stand it up on the side of the pan to rinse out the oil; then place it first on a paper towel-lined plate and then arrange them standing up in the baking sheet. Keep the baking sheet in the off oven to keep them warm (away from the draft). Repeat with rest of poories.

Khasta Poories (Crispy Poories) with Eggs (M: 36)

These poories are everyone's favorite. You can make them plain or stuffed. I make double dough and freeze half of it. Whenever your heart desires to have these delights just defrost overnight and deep fry in oil. I make double so as to give them to neighbors. These poories can be served just with yogurt salad (Raita) or chutney alone.

Ingredients: 3 whole extra-large eggs; 1-1/2 cups water at room temperature; ½ cup plain yogurt at room temperature; 2 sticks (1cup) melted butter; 6 cups atta, the Indian bread flour; 1Tsp. salt, 1cup (1packet) dry milk powder, ½ cup flour for dusting; canola or sunflower oil or ghee to deep-fry.

In a large bowl whisk together water and egg well. Then add the yogurt. In a large bowl hand mix atta, salt, milk powder and butter. Pour over the egg mixture and mix well with a wooden spoon. Knead the dough 5 minutes, cover with a damp towel, and set aside for 30 minutes to 1 hr. to rise. When ready to cook, divide the dough into 2 parts and knead each part for 5 minutes until pliable. Now divide each portion in half again, roll out each portion into a cylinder and divide the dough into 9 equal portions; then roll each piece into a ball and flatten into patties. Dusting lightly with the flour, roll out each patty 3 times on one side, dip into the flour and roll on the 2nd side into a 5-inch poori. Spread out a large clean towel on the table and line up the poories on the towel. Keep poories covered with another clean towel. Do the same with each piece of dough.

When all the poories are rolled out, heat a wok or wide pot with about 2-inch deep oil on medium-high heat. When oil start moving, and reaches a temperature of about 375 degrees, carefully slide one poori from the side into the hot oil. Wait about 10 second when it starts floating, turn it over and drop 2nd poori the same way. Cook poories until they are light brown on both sides, about 2 minutes total. Hold the poori on the side of wok with the metal spatula to drain, and then carefully take it out carefully and place it on the paper towel-lined platter. Proceed same way. Serve hot.

Waterchestnut, Kuttu or Quinoa Poori (M:10)

These gluten-free, salt-free poories are used for fasting day in India in Hindu families. This herb-and-whole-grain bread is made with fruits. Kuttu is a small grain, a little bigger than sesame seed and is known as a fruit.

Indredients: 1 cup water chestnut flour; 1 cup kuttu flour, or you can grind regular quinoa into flour and use that (available at the Indian grocery); 1 large potato boiled, peeled and mashed; ½ cup each dry non-fat milk, sesame seeds, and coconut flour; ½ cup chopped soft cilantro stems; 1 tbsp. celery seeds; 4 tbsp. canola oil; ½ tsp. fresh-ground black pepper; ½ cup plain yogurt; ½ cup water.

In a large bowl mix all ingredients together and knead into a ball. If needed add a little more water one teaspoonful at a time. Let it rest 1 hour covered with a damp kitchen towel. Divide the dough into 10 portions. Grease two pieces of plastic wrap. Place one portion at a time between greased plastic and press down into a 3-3-1/2-inch diameter round. This bread should be a little thick and the edges should be neat and round and even. Fry each bread like a basic poori in 375-degree hot oil, until golden on both sides. Serve with chutney and raita.

Bhature (Deep-fried, soft, stuffed bread) (M: 14)

This is a very famous and my favorite fried bread. You can make it plain or stuffed. Traditionally it is served with spicy chickpeas (garbanzo beans) as chole and bhature in Northern India, especially in Delhi. It is good to serve plain yogurt mixed with salt and pepper, or yogurt salad (Raita), with the fried food, it cuts down on the fat and helps digestion.

Ingredients:

For the Dough: 1 package ¼ ounce (7g) active dry yeast, ¼ cup warm water about 90 degrees, 2 tbsp. sugar; 2-1/2cupall-purpose unbleached flour, plus extra for dusting; ½ cup semolina (sooji); 1 tsp. baking powder; ¼ tsp. baking soda; ½ cup to ¾ cup (as needed) yogurt at room temperature; 2 large eggs at room temperature; 4 tbsp. butter melted; 1-1/2 tsp. salt.; 2 tsp. oil to grease the dough,

For the Stuffing: 2 tbsp. canola oil; ¼ tsp. each: garlic, methi powder (op), turmeric powders, salt and pepper to taste; ½ cup urad bean flour (or moong or lentil flour); 1 tbsp. peeled, fine grated fresh ginger; 1 tbsp. crushed fennel seeds.

Make the Dough: In a large bowl, add yeast and sugar, then pour the warm water, cover and set aside for 5 minutes, until the yeast is bubbly. Add semolina, butter, eggs, yogurt and salt and whisk well. Add the flour mixed with the baking powder and baking soda, and combined by hand to make a ball. Dust the counter with some dry flour and knead the dough for 2 minutes then make a ball. Sprinkle 1 tsp. oil all over in the bowl, move the dough around in oil to grease all sides. Wet a kitchen towel with warm water well, then squeeze out the water, cover the dough and let it rise in the cool oven for 1 hour or until it is doubled.

To make the Stuffing: Heat a heavy bottom sauté pan with oil on medium heat. Add garlic, methi, turmeric, salt and pepper and when it starts sizzling, add the urad bean flour. Keep on stirring the mixture until it is light brown for about 8-10 minutes then take off the heat, cover, and let it cool stirring on and off. When the stuffing (powder) is cooled, add the fine-grated ginger and the crushed fennel seeds, and set aside.

To make the bread: Knead the dough again for 5 minutes, divide into 2 pieces, make each piece into a log and cut with a knife into 7 equal portions, dusting with the flour. Spread out each portion on a platter or a cutting board. With a spoon, spread out about 2 drops of oil on each dough piece, add a little sprinkle of salt, then top with about 1 tsp. of filling on the top; spread the filling with a spoon over the oil on each piece, leaving a ¼ inch edge for folding; then press down the stuffing powder with the back of the spoon into the dough. Carefully gather the dough from all around the edges, keeping the filling in the center, and enclose the filling, making sure no air is trapped inside; twist the top of the gathered dough and press down the seam. Make a flat disk with each portion and, dusting with the flour, make each disk flat and bigger, about 3-4-inches diameter. Then dusting with the flour, carefully roll out each disk a little larger; turn over, dip in the flour and now roll out into about 5-6-inch circles. Bread should be rolled on both sides to make it puff, and rolled evenly and carefully so that the stuffing is not exposed. Make all the bread ahead and keep them covered under dry kitchen towels, in a single layer.

Deep-frying the bread: Heat about 2-inch-deep oil in a wok or pan, on medium-high or about 375 degrees. Pick up one bread and from the edge of the oil, slide it in the hot oil carefully. At this point do not touch the bread until it puffs up and floats in the oil. If bread does not puff up, then carefully pour some hot oil with spatula over the bread to make it puff all over, and just before it becomes round and fully, turn it over with the spatula. If you prefer, you can use a large spoon and a spatula to turn the bread over carefully. This bread browns very fast, so keep on turning over and over until it is lightly browned on both sides takes about 1 minute to cook each bread. Pick up the bread with the spatula and hold on the side of pan or wok to rinse out the oil, then place on a paper towel-lined platter. Serve hot with raita, chickpeas or any curry.

Buttermilk Cornbread (Serves: 6-8)

Fresh-baked corn bread is very tasty. If there is any leftover, you can always use in stuffing.

Ingredients: 1-1/2 cup fine ground yellow cornmeal; 1 cup unbleached all-purpose flour; 1tbsp. baking powder; ½ tsp.salt; 8tbsp. melted and cooled butter; 1/3 cup. sugar; 2 large eggs and 1 egg yolk; 1 tbsp. canola or olive oil; 1-1/2cup whole milk; 1 tsp. lemon or tangerine zest; 2 tbsp. black or white sesame seeds.

1. Preheat oven to 400 degrees. Line a 9X5X3-inches loaf pan with parchment paper, then spray the paper with cooking spray.
2. In a large bowl, whisk together all dry ingredients. In another medium bowl, whisk together eggs, , zest, butter and milk. Pour the wet ingredients into dry ingredients and mix them together until smooth. Pour the batter in the prepared pan and top with the sesame seeds. Bake in the preheated 400 degree oven for about 40 minutes until a toothpick inserted in the center comes out only with a few crumbs on. Take the bread out of oven and cool on the wire rack.

Baking the Breads

Before baking any bread, follow the recipe and get all the ingredients that are needed for that particular recipe. All dairy products should be in room temperature. I use a clean, dry, and lightly warm bowl for yeast dough. The water for the yeast should be around 110 to 115 degrees. Sprinkle the yeast first and then sprinkle the sugar on the top of the water. Usually, 3 cups of flour (depending on the recipe) takes about 1 packet, 7g, ¼ ounce of yeast and 3 teaspoon of sugar. Cover the bowl and leave in a warm place, or in room temperature away from the draft. When yeast starts bubbling, add the flour and stir either with hands or with a wooden spoon. If yeast does not bubble at all, it is not active one. Throw out the water and start all over with the active yeast. Beside the warm water, other liquid like oil, yogurt, butter and milk are also added in the bread dough. So be careful and follow the recipe as instructed.

Banana, Raisin & Nut Bread (or Muffins)

This is an easy, tasty and a healthy bread. Serve warm or in room temperature. You can make about 15 large muffins with the same batter and bake in a muffin pan lined with paper cups; grease the cups, bake at 350 degrees for 12 to 15 minutes. Keep in room temperature covered for 2-3 days. Keep refrigerated, well covered, up to 2 weeks. Heat each serving in the toaster oven or microwave and serve.

Ingredients: 2 medium ripe bananas; 1 cup sugar; 2 large eggs;1/3 cup canola or vegetable oil; 1/3 cup 2% milk; 1 cup dark raisins; 1 cup chopped walnuts; Dry ingredients mixture: 2 cupss all-purpose flour, 1 tsp. baking powder, 1 tsp. baking soda, ¼ tsp. salt,1 tsp. ground cinnamon; 1 tbsp. lemon juice; 1 tbsp. melted butter; ¼ cup pumpkin seeds. To serve: apple sauce or butter and/ milk, coffee or tea.

1. Preheat the oven at 350 degrees. Use a 9-1/4x5-1/4x2-1/4-inch loaf pan. Line the bottom of the pan with parchment paper, then grease the paper well with the butter or oil.
2. In a large bowl, thin-slice the bananas, add the sugar and beat well with the electric mixer, into a cream. Add the eggs and beat well. Add milk, oil and mix well. Add raisins and walnuts mix well. Add the flour mixture and beat on low speed to mix. Do not over-mix. At end, add the lemon juice

and fold it in the mixture by hand. Then fold in the melted butter. Pour in the prepared pan. Even out the top with the spatula. Sprinkle the pumpkin seeds on the top.

3. Bake in a preheated oven for about 50-60 minutes until the toothpick inserted in the center come out with only 2-3 crumbs on. Cool in the pan over a wire rack. Serve warm or room temperature with apple sauce or butter with milk, coffee or tea.

Energy Bread (Healthy Stuffed Potato Paratha)
(M: about 12)

Believe it or not, my husband is crazy about these breads. You can serve these with or without vegetables just with chutney and/or yogurt. You can also make these without filling.

Ingredients: 2 Cups bread flour (Atta) plus extra for dusting; 1cup almond flour; 1/2cup grinded sesame seeds; 1/2Tsp. salt; 2 large eggs whisked; 3/4 cup potato boiling water, or as needed, to make a sticky dough; filling mixture: 4 cups packed boiled, peeled and mashed red potatoes, 1/2Tsp. celery seeds, 1/2Tsp. each salt, cayenne pepper (or to taste), garlic power, and turmeric powder; canola oil to cook.

In a large bowl mix together bread flour, almond flour, sesame seeds, and salt; add eggs and potato boiling water and mix with a wooden spoon to make a sticky dough. In a medium bowl mix the filling ingredients together. Now dusting your hands with flour divide the dough into 12 pieces. Dip each piece in the flour, flatten it, and place on the cutting board. Then divide the filling into 12 pieces and place over each piece of dough. Pick up one piece at a time in the hand and dusting with the flour cover the potatoes with the dough making a ball. Flatten the ball and roll out into about 7-inch round; place each rolled paratha on a clean cloth towel.

Heat a cast iron pan on medium-high heat. When hot, place one rolled bread in the pan and cook for about 30 second, turn over and cook the other side, until brown specks are all over. Now drop about 1/2Tsp. oil in a circle on the surface, spread the oil around with the back of a large spoon. Turn over oil the bread on the other side. Cook another minute or so until bread is puffed, cooked and has brown specks on both side. Repeat with the rest or the bread. Serve warm.

Sesame Seed Buns (M: about 15)

I use these buns all day long. They are small, easy to make and tasty. Make sure you lightly roast the sesame seeds.

Ingredients: 3 Cups unsifted all-purpose flour plus extra for dusting; 4Tbsp. melted unsalted butter; 1/2Tsp. salt; 1Tbsp. sugar; 4Tsp. baking powder; 4 large eggs; 1/2cup plus 2Tbsp. milk; 1 cup lightly toasted sesame seeds; egg wash: 1 egg whisked with 2 tbsp. water.

Preheat oven at 325 degrees. Prepare two large baking sheets (each: 12x18x1-inch), line with the parchment paper and grease them lightly with butter or cooking spray.

In a large bowl whisk together flour, salt, sugar and baking powder. Add butter, mix with hands. Whisk eggs and milk together and add to the flour mixture. Using a wooden spoon mix it well. The dough should be sticky. Spread out the sesame seeds in a large platter. Using two tablespoons take out about 2 heaping tablespoons of dough and drop it on the sesame seeds. Dust your hands with flour and pick up one piece at a time, round it slightly then roll into the sesame seeds and place on the prepared sheets, about 1-1/2-inches apart. With a sharp knife or razor blade make a ½-inch deep cross on the top. Brush the buns on the top and all around with egg wash. Bake at 325 degrees for about 25 minutes until buns are light brown and puffed up. Turn around the tray half way during the baking. Serve warm with butter or jelly.

Soy, Waterchestnut, Cranberry and Nut Bread (Serves: 8-10)

This bread is considered the fruit bread. In India, when Hindu families go on fasts, they eat only fruits and vegetables and no salt. This bread is made with soybeans and water chestnut flours. Both these flours can be found at Indian Grocery stores. It is tasty, very healthy and can be eaten any time of the day.

Ingredients: 1 pkg. quick-rising active dry yeast; 1 cup warm water (110-115 degrees); 3 tsp. sugar; 1 cup soybean flour; 1 cup water chestnut (singhara) flour; 2 medium ripe bananas; 1 cup sugar; 1 cup vegetable oil; each ½ cup: dry cranberries, grated coconut; ¼ sesame seeds (op); 1 cup chopped walnuts; ¼ cup slivered almonds, 1tsp. cinnamon; 1 tbsp. lemon juice; 1 tbsp. unsalted melted butter plus extra for greasing the pan. To serve: apple sauce, jelly, jam, or butter, and milk, coffee or tea.

1. Use a 9-1/4x5-1/4x2-1/4-inch loaf pan. Line the bottom with parchment paper and grease the paper well with butter. Preheat the oven at 350 degrees.
2. In a large lightly heated bowl add the warm water; sprinkle the yeast on the top, then sprinkle the 3 tsp. sugar. Cover and let it stand for 5 minutes. When yeast bubbles, add the soybean and water chestnut flours and mix well by hand or a wooden spoon. Cover the bowl and place in a warm place.
3. In another medium bowl, thin-slice the bananas and add 1cupsugar; beat well with the electric mixer into a cream. Add oil, walnuts, cranberries, 2 tbsp. sesame seeds and coconut, and mix well. Now pour this mixture over the flour mixture. Mix well with a wooden spoon. Fold in lemon juice and melted butter. Pour into the prepared pan, even out the top, and sprinkle the almonds and 2 tbsp. sesame seeds on the top; press down with a dry spatula. Leave in the room temperature, covered with a kitchen towel, for 15-20 minutes.
4. Bake in a preheated 350-degree oven for about 45 minutes or until the center is done (toothpick inserted in the center comes out with only 2-3 crumbs on). Cool in the off oven for 5 minutes, then place the pan over a wire rack and cool.
5. Serve warm or room temperature with apple sauce, jelly, jam, or butter, and milk, coffee or tea.
    Tip: The water chestnut flour turns a light gray color after cooking because of the several nutrients, including Iron.

Healthy Sandwich Bread (M:1 Loaf)

Ingredients: 1Cup water and 1/2 cup whole milk heated to lukewarm (110 degrees) ; 1-1/2Tbsp. (1Pkg.) instant rise active dry yeast; 3Tbsp. sugar; 3Tbsp. melted butter; 3cups unbleached protein bread flour (such as: King Arthur) 1/4cup chickpea flour; 1/2cup almond flour; 1-1/2Tsp. salt; 1Tbsp. vegetable oil; topping: 1/4cup white or black or a mixture of both sesame seeds.

In a large bowl add sugar then pour over the lukewarm water and milk mixture and sprinkle the yeast. Cover and set aside for 8-10 minutes until the yeast foams. Whisk in the butter then add the mixture of flours and salt whisking by hand until dough comes together, then take out and knead on the counter for 10 minutes (or in a stand mixture with dough hook for 10 minutes, until dough comes together) until smooth and elastic.

Clean and dry out the bowl place the oil in the bowl, and roll the dough ball in oil to grease it on all sides. Cover dough with damp towel, place in the off oven (away from draft) and let it rise until doubled about 1 hour. Take the dough and punch down and knead for 5 minutes. Now line the bottom of a 9X5-inch loaf pan with parchment paper, grease the paper then place the dough in the pan. With lightly wet hands even out the surface, sprinkle the sesame seeds, make 2 slashes with a sharp knife across for steam, place the pan back in the warm place and let the dough rise for 30 minutes, until it reaches to the rim. Preheat the oven at 350 degrees (180 C). Place the pan on the middle oven rack and bake for about 30 to 35 minutes, until it is puffed and browned, rotating the pan halfway during the baking.

Take the bread out of the oven and loosen the bread on the edges with a dinner knife, transfer the loaf to a wire rack to cool. Then wrap the bread in plastic and place in a plastic bag airtight for up to 3-4 days. Slice and serve and again secure it airtight. You can freeze the wrapped bread, just cover with paper towels and place in a plastic bag and then in a plastic container freeze up to 2 months, thaw overnight wrapped and serve.

Zucchini Bread (2 loaves)

Make sure you buy soft, unbruised, slim and green zucchini for this recipe and shred them with skin on.

Ingredients: 3 cups all-purpose flour mixed with 1/2Tsp. salt, 1Tsp. baking soda, 3/4Tsp. baking powder, 2Tsp. cinnamon and 1/2Tsp. celery seeds; 3 large eggs; 3Tsp. vanilla extract; 1-1/4cup sugar; 1cup vegetable oil; 2cups shredded zucchini (2 medium); 1/2cup dry cranberries; 1cup chopped walnuts.

Preheat oven at 350 degrees. Grease and line the bottom of two 9X5X3-inches baking pans with parchment paper and grease it well.

In a large bowl beat the eggs until light and foamy about 5 minutes. Add vanilla, sugar and beat well. Then add oil and beat well, whisk in the zucchini and mix well. Sprinkle flour mixture then nuts and berries on top and whisk well. Pour evenly in two pans and even out the top. Bake in a preheated 350 degree oven for about an hour or until browned. Serve warm.

Pasta, Pizza, Grain & Rice

Pasta Dishes

You do not want cold or a soggy Pasta. So cook pasta the last minute, just before serving. When cooking pasta, bring a large pot of salted water to a boil. Let the water boil for 5 minutes, add the pasta and cook about 6-8 minutes, al dente (a little bite to it) per package direction; drain in a colander and immediately add the pasta in the hot cooking sauce. Serve immediately sprinkled with fresh-grated Parmesan or your favorite cheese. If you do not want pasta to stick, add a few drops of oil after it is drained. To keep it warm for 5-10 minutes, drain the pasta in a colander and place the colander over hot the pasta pot, cover with the lid and let it drain and stay warm.

Cook only the pasta you going to serve, and cook at the last minute. Pasta will swell up in the water, so drain it immediately after cooking. Adding to the hot cooked sauce, it will get flavorful immediately. You can sprinkle fresh herbs, cheese, vinaigrette or other toppings.

Tips: Pasta gets flavor from tomato sauce, fresh herbs, or just a sprinkle of garlic powder and oregano. Try to buy pasta that are more healthy such as, whole wheat, spinach, and spaghetti made with Jerusalem Artichoke Flour etc.

Ham or Shrimp Fettuccini Alfredo (Serves: 4)

One of my friends, Blanche, loved this dish so much that she ordered it almost all the time at Italian restaurants. I like it with lots of shallot, peas, and diced red bell peppers, as something healthy to munch on.

Ingredients For the Sauce: 2 tbsp. olive oil; 1 cup each chopped fine: shallot, red bell pepper, sliced or crushed drained tomatoes, and frozen peas; 1 pkg. 8 ounces low-fat cream cheese at room temperature; 1 cup 2% milk (or whole milk or half-and-half) or as needed; 2 packets instant chicken broth or salt and pepper to taste; 1 pound medium shrimp (25 count) peeled and deveined; ¼ tsp. each: granulated garlic and cayenne pepper; salt and fresh ground black pepper to taste; 1 cup, about 4 ounces, grated pecorino Romano cheese.

Ingredients For the Pasta: 1 pound fresh or dry fettuccini; 1 tsp. fresh oregano or 1 tbsp. fresh parsley to garnish.

To make the sauce: Sprinkle the shrimp with the garlic and the cayenne pepper. Heat a large heavy-bottom pan on medium-high heat, add 1 tbsp. oil and add the shrimp in single layer. Cook for 2 minutes until the bottoms turn pink. Turn over and cook only 1 minute; take them out, and keep tented with the foil.

Use the same pan, reduce the heat to medium, add 1 tbsp. oil, and shallot. Cook shallots stirring for 1 minute. Add bell peppers and cook 1 minute; add peas and cook 2 minutes, stirring. Now add the drained tomatoes and stir well for 2 minutes. Move the vegetables on one side, cut up the cream cheese into 1-inch pieces and add to the pan; add milk and chicken stock. Whisk in the cheese to dilute it in the milk. Lower the heat and let sauce simmer covered 6-8 minutes on low heat until it is heated through.

To make the Pasta: Follow the instructions on the package and cook the pasta al dente. Or bring about 8 cups of salted water to a boil, and boil the fresh pasta for about 1-1/2 minutes, or dry for about 6 minutes al dente.

Take the pasta out with a slotted spoon and add to the simmering sauce. Add about ½ cup of pasta water or as needed, bring to a simmer add half of the cheese, salt and pepper to taste, and serve mixed or topped with the warm shrimp, sprinkled with herbs and the rest of the cheese.

To make with ham: You can use either fresh peas, or fresh chopped watercress. Also, in place of shrimp, use 1 cup cooked and cubed ham or browned Spam slices, then cube and add to the dish. Either garnish on the top or mix it in.

Tips: Traditionally, this dish is made with 2 cups of Heavy Cream, no cream cheese. You can also use this recipe with the orzo (the rice shaped pasta).

Macaroni & Cheese (Serves: 8-10)

Mac and Cheese is very easy to make, it is tasty, and you can serve almost any time of the day, with or without side dishes.

Ingredients:

For the Crumbs and Garnishes: 1/3 cup dry bread crumbs; 2 tbsp. unsalted butter; ½ tsp. each dry oregano and paprika: ¼ tsp. each dry marjoram and fresh ground black pepper; ¼ cup fresh chopped basil; ¼ cup grated cheese (any kind of hard cheese); for garnish: 1 cup frozen peas cooked in ¼ cup water boiling water for 5 minutes; 1 cup frozen, shelled, green chickpeas cooked (op) (cook peas and take them out, then cook the chickpeas in the same water for 4-5 minutes); 1 c grape or cherry tomatoes.

For the Macaroni: 2 tbsp. all-purpose flour; 2 tbsp. butter; 2 cups milk; 1 box 12 ounces elbow macaroni; 1 tbsp. butter plus extra for the baking pan; 1 extra-large egg; 1container 16 ounces sour cream; 1 tbsp. yellow mustard powder; ½ tsp. cayenne pepper or to taste; ¼ tsp. each salt and fresh-ground black pepper or to taste; 2 pounds, about 7 to 8 cups, shredded sharp cheddar cheese; ½ cup pasta cooking water.

To make the Crumbs: Heat a heavy-bottom skillet on medium heat, add the butter, move around to coat the bottom. Add the crumbs and stir on medium heat until they are light brown for about 6-8 minutes; add oregano, paprika, marjoram and black pepper. Take off the heat, cool and mix in the grated cheese and basil; transfer to a small bowl.

To make the Macaroni: Grease a 9x13x3-inch baking pan with butter and set aside. Bring a large pot of water to a boil, add 1 tsp. salt, stir and add the macaroni for a few minutes, until macaroni stops sticking in the bottom. Cook open for about 9 minutes, al dente (or follow the direction on the package). Drain the pasta, saving ½ cup pasta water.

In a pot, on medium heat, heat the butter and the flour, stirring constantly, until the mixture (the roux) is light brown; off the heat, slowly whisking add the milk. Put the pot back on the heat and, stirring constantly, bring the mixture to a boil and keep on stirring until the mixture is thick, for about another 6-8 minutes.

Move an oven shelf in the center and preheat the oven at 350 degrees. In a large bowl beat the egg and add the flour mixture, whisking slowly. Then whisk in the sour cream, pasta water, mustard powder, cayenne pepper, salt and black pepper. Stir in 7 cups of the cheddar cheese (saving about 1 C for the topping) and mix it well. Add the macaroni in two batches, mixing together well with a large wooden spoon. Pour the mixture in the prepared pan, even out the top, and sprinkle leftover shredded cheddar cheese on the top all over. Sprinkle the crumbs in the center, and top with the peas and chickpeas. Bake covered with aluminum foil, at 350 degrees for 15 minutes, open the cover and bake another 20-25 minutes until it is bubbly and lightly browned. It will take about 40 to 45 minutes total. Turn around the baking pan halfway during the baking. Take out of the oven and let it rest for 10-15 minutes, top with cherry tomatoes and serve.

Macaroni & Cheese with Lobster and Shrimps

Follow the instruction as above. You will need 1 pound large shrimp, deveined and tail end trimmed, and meat from two 1-pound lobsters. Use cooked lobster tail or lobster meat (lobster takes about 7-8 minutes per pound to boil) or lightly cooked shrimp (sauté with garlic and butter for 2-3 minutes, light pink). Pour the cheese mixture into the prepared pan, push in and submerge the large pieces of lobster meat and whole shrimp into the cheese mixture; top with rest of the grated cheese, bread crumbs and peas and chickpeas. Bake as directed above.

Low-Calorie Vegetarian Mac & Cheese (S:8-10)

This Macaroni and Cheese has half of the calories per serving.

Ingredients: 1 Box 12 ounces (340G) medium shells or macaroni; 2 pounds, about 5 cups peeled, seeded and about 1-1/2-inch cubed butternut squash; 1 cup 2% milk; 1 lb, (454g) silken tofu; 1 cup, 4 oz. fresh grated fontina cheese; 1 cup about 4 oz. gorgonzola (blue cheese) crumbled; 1 tbsp. yellow mustard powder; ¼ tsp. each salt and pepper or to taste; 2 tsp. lemon-pepper seasoning mix: 1 tsp. sweet paprika; to garnish: ½ cup blanched and sliced thin broccoli florets, 2 medium plum tomato, blanched, peeled and chopped and ½ cup red cabbage very thinly sliced; and/or green salad on the side.

1. Bring the milk and the squash in a medium pot to a boil. Cook the squash in the milk, covered, for about 25 minutes, stirring 2-3 times and be careful not to let it boil out. (or roast the squash: cut the squash in half lengthwise, rub with salt, pepper and oil all over, bake at 350 degrees in a tray open for about 50 minutes, fork tender).
2. Cook pasta per package direction and drain out the water and keep it covered. Mash the squash with potato masher, add the tofu, mustard, salt and pepper, and mash all well. Add the gorgonzola and only ½ cup Fontina cheese; if needed add a little hot pasta and mix well. Pour in a greased 9x12-inch baking dish, spread out evenly. Sprinkle the rest ½ cup Fontina cheese and top with lemon-pepper and paprika all over.
3. Bake in a preheated oven at 400 degrees for about 18-20 minutes, until bubbly. Serve garnished with broccoli, red cabbage and chopped tomatoes, and/or fruit salad on side.

Variations

With Bacon: Cook 4-5 strips of bacon crispy, slice into 1-inch pieces. Add ½ of the bacon in the mixture and sprinkle the rest on the top before baking.

With Ham: You need 1c up of cooked ham, cubed; mix it in before baking. You can do the same with almost any cooked vegetable.

Red Wine Bucatini with Spam (Serves: 4-6)

We love wine pasta and bucatini, the thick pasta that gives you more flavor. This is a full meal. Serve with more salad if you prefer.

Ingredients: 1 box 12 ounces bucatini pasta; 2 tsp. canola oil; 1 bottle 1.5 liter full-body red wine (we prefer merlot); 1 cup concentrated frozen orange juice defrosted; ¼ tsp. each salt and fresh-ground black pepper; 1 can (340g) 25% less-sodium spam (or cooked ham cubed); 1 can 8 ounces (227g) tomato sauce; ¼ tsp. granulated garlic and fresh-ground black pepper. To serve: ½ avocado per person; 1 kiwi fruit peeled and sliced per person; seeds from one medium pomegranate, grated cheese on the side.

To make the Wine Sauce: Heat a large, heavy bottomed sauté pan with 2-inch rim; on medium heat, add 1 tsp. oil and move around to coat the bottom. Take the pan off the heat and stir in concentrated orange juice, 2 pinches of salt and pepper and whole bottle of the wine, filling up 1-1/2 inches below the rim. If the pan is not large enough, then use only half of the bottle at a time, reduce it and then add the other half of the bottle. Place the pan over the medium-high heat. Stir occasionally in the first half hour; let it come to a full simmer, and then let it simmer until the wine is reduced to 1 cup. Turn the heat off and keep it covered; reheat again before adding the pasta.

While the wine is reducing, cook the Spam. Heat a large heavy-bottom pan on medium heat. Add the 1 tsp. oil, move around to coat the pan. Cut the spam into 8 long slices, about ¼-inch thick, and then cut each slice into 4 sticks (slice Spam lengthwise in half, then each half in half again for 8 slices.) When the oil is hot, add the Spam in single layer, pour the sauce on the top, add granulated garlic and some fresh ground black pepper. Cover the pan with a lid halfway and simmer on low heat, bubbling for 10 minutes. Turn over the slices with a metal spatula, and simmer the other side on low for another 8-10 minutes, or until all the sauce is absorbed.

When the sauce and the Spam are almost ready, bring a large pot of salted water to full boil, add the pasta, stir well and cook about 7-8 minutes or per package direction, just a little more than al dente. Drain the pasta and add to the warm wine sauce all at once. Stir the pasta with tongs or a large spoon, heat it through and serve warm, on heated dinner plates with sliced and pitted avocado, kiwi and pomegranate seeds. Serve grated cheese on the side.

Tip: To make the wine pasta, it is good to cook pasta just a little more than al-dente, about 30 second more than the regular pasta.

Pomegranate Bucatini with Roasted Vegetables (Serves: 2-4)

You can buy either pomegranate molasses or make you own sauce.

Ingredients: ½ box 6 ounces, bucatini pasta; 1 tbsp. butter; 3 cups pomegranate juice (about 4-5 large pomegranates); 4 tbsp. ketchup; 2 tbsp. hoisin sauce and marinade; 1 medium zucchini, washed, cut in half lengthwise, then sliced across ½-inch thick; 1 medium beet, peeled, cut in quarter, then sliced ¼-inch thick across; 2 tbsp. canola oil; salt and pepper; to garnish: 1 cup cooked frozen peas, ½ cup peanuts, roasted in pan, on medium heat, in 1 tbsp. butter for 5 minutes or until light brown; ½ cup pomegranate seeds; grated cheese.

Heat a heavy-bottom large pan, with 2-inch rim, on medium heat; add the butter, move around to coat the bottom. Add the pomegranate juice, increase the heat to medium-high and bring to a boil. Stir a little and let the juice reduce to 1 C, stirring on and off and reducing the heat a little, as needed.

While the sauce is cooking, preheat the oven to 400 degrees. Line a baking sheet with aluminum foil. Toss the zucchini with little salt, pepper and oil and spread out on one side of the prepared sheet. Do the same with the beets. Roast the vegetables in the oven for about 15-20 minutes, or until soft. Turn the heat off, tent with a foil, and leave in the oven to keep warm.

Bring a large pot of salted water to full boil, add bucatini, stir well and cook for 7-8 minutes, al dente or per package direction. Drain the pasta and add to the warm pomegranate sauce, stir well with tongs to heat through. Serve on heated dinner plates, sprinkle the warm roasted vegetables all over, and garnish with cooked peas, roasted peanuts and pomegranate seeds. Serve grated cheese on the side.

Grain and Grain Dishes

Chart for Cooking Grains

For: 1 cup grain: Bring water, chicken or vegetable broth to a boil, add grain, stir well, bring back to a boil, lower the heat, cove, and simmer on low, follow the cooking time or until all the liquid has evaporated, and grains are soft, stir well, add a little butter (op), cover and let it stand few minutes and keep warm until needed. Add herbs and serve as a side dish, salad, or as a main meal; add fresh cooked chicken, turkey or steak. A little butter (about 1 tablespoon for 1 cup uncooked grain) gives very good flavor and keeps the grain separated. But if you are going to add sauce, omit the butter.

Type of Grain	Liquid,	Cooking Time: minutes	Yield:cups
Amaranth	3cups	25-30 Mts.	3-1/2
Pearl Barley	3"	30 Mts.& let stand 10Mts.	3-1/4
Buckwheat	2 "	15 Mts.& let stand 10Mts.	3
(Groats or Kasha)			
Bulgur Wheat	2cups: pour boiled water over grain &stand 30Mt, 2-1/2		
Farro	1-1/2cups	30 Mts. & let stand 8 Mts	1-3/4
Millet	3cups	30 Mts. & let stand 10Mts.	3
Quinoa seed	1-1/4	Boil 5 Mt, let stand 20Mts.	3
Spelt	2-1/2	50	2
Wheat Berries	2	55	2-1/4
(soaked overnight and drained)			

Grain Dishes

Baked Chickpea Patties (M: 10)

This is our favorite recipe. We use these patties over salad, in burgers, in sandwiches with avocado and tomatoes, and over rice. Make them ahead, heat and serve.

Ingredients: 1 can 13 ounces (822g) chickpeas washed, drained and mashed; 2 large eggs; ¼ cup each seasoned bread crumbs, grated parmesan cheese, chopped cilantro, lemon juice; ½ tsp. powder or 1 tbsp. fresh garlic cloves; salt and pepper to taste; 2-3 tbsp. canola or olive; chutney or raita (yogurt salad) to serve.

Heat the oven at 400 degrees. Line a large baking tray with aluminum foil and grease it well. In a bowl, mix together all the ingredients except the oil, and make 10 balls; then using a plastic wrap over the cutting board, press them down, shape the edges and make about 1-inch high patties. Sprinkle 1 tbsp. of oil all over the foil, place the patties 2-inches apart, then drizzle the top of each patty with little oil and bake in a preheated oven for 30 minutes. Take the tray out of the oven carefully turn the patties over and bake the other side for another 20 minutes or until golden brown. Serve with any sauce, chutney or yogurt salad (Raita).

Quinoa with Spinach (M: 3 cups)

Quinoa is the most healthy grain. It tastes somewhat like rice. You can also add berries, toasted nuts, fresh herbs and serve with chutney or with the pomegranate molasses. We like it even with the plain low-fat yogurt.

Ingredients: 1c quinoa seeds quinoa (large grains); 1 tsp. canola or olive oil; ½ cup chopped onion; ¼ tsp. turmeric (op); about 1-1/2 cups fresh baby spinach, stems removed and chopped; ¼ tsp. granulated garlic; ¼ cup cilantro or parsley leaves and soft stems chopped; 1 cup chicken broth or water; ½ cup dry cranberries; salt and fresh-ground black pepper to taste; to garnish: about 1 tbsp. lime zest (about 1 large lime); to serve: pomegranate molasses, raita (yogurt salad) or any green chutney.

1.   Heat a large heavy-bottom pan on medium heat. When heated add oil and sauté onion until transparent, about 5-6 minutes. Add quinoa stir for about 5-6 minutes until lightly roasted. Add granulated garlic, turmeric, cilantro leaves and soft stems; stir well, then add cranberries, water or broth, and top with spinach. Cover, bring to a boil, lower the heat and simmer for 20 minutes, until all the water is gone and quinoa is soft. Sprinkle lightly with salt and pepper.
2.   Take quinoa out in a bowl, keep warm and covered, or serve right away sprinkled with lime zest and chutney or pomegranate molasses

Quinoa Pilaf (Serves: 4-6)

You can make this ahead or make extra and freeze for the future use. Just thaw overnight, heat with a little butter and serve.

Ingredients: 2 tbsp. canola or olive oil; 1 cup chopped onion; ¼ tsp. each: granulated garlic and salt; 1 cup chopped celery; 1 cup quinoa seed quinoa (large grains); ½ cup each: dark raisins and shelled pistachios; 1 tbsp. butter (op), ¼ cup chopped parsley or cilantro.

1.   Heat a large sauté pan on medium heat. When heated add 1 tbsp. oil and celery and sauté for 5 minutes. Move the celery on the side, add onions and sprinkle with garlic and salt; cover with lid and cook 5 minutes.
2.   Move the celery and onion on one side, add 1 tbsp. oil in the pan and add the quinoa; stir a little for a minute to coat the quinoa with oil, and pour 1-3/4 cup water all over the vegetables; bring to a boil, cover and simmer on low heat for 20-25 minutes or until done. Stir the pilaf halfway during the cooking and add the raisins and nuts on the top after stirring.
Take off the heat, add the butter, fluff with a fork and serve warm sprinkled with parsley.

Amaranth, Quinoa and Wild Rice Pilaf (The Protein Pilaf)
(Serves: 4)

I call this dish the Protein Pilaf, loaded with protein and very tasty. I use large quinoa seeds, and small wild rice that is gluten-free and very light; cook it separate so it doesn't color the other grains. To make it a main meal, just serve it with yogurt or raita.

Ingredients: 1 tbsp. canola or olive oil; about 3 tbsp. butter, divided; 1-1/2 tsp. caraway or cumin seeds; 1 cup each fine chopped: onion, celery and cauliflower (op); ¼ cup wild rice, soaked in the water for about 1 hour; ½ cup each quinoa and amaranth; about 2-1/2 cups chicken or vegetable broth as needed; ½ cup each: dry cranberries, pistachios and peeled whole or slivered almonds; ½ tsp. granulated garlic; ¼ tsp. dry rosemary; 2 tbsp. lemon juice; salt and fresh-ground black or white pepper to taste; to garnish: ½ cup each diced red bell pepper and sliced scallions.

For the Rice: Heat a small saucepan over the medium heat, add ½ tsp. caraway/cumin seeds and 1 tbsp. butter, and the soaked and drained rice; stir a little, add ¾ cup water or the broth. Bring it to a boil, cover, and lower the heat to constant simmer. Cook rice for 20-25 minutes or until soft. Stir rice once during the cooking.

For the Pilaf: Heat a medium saucepan over medium heat. When hot add 1 tbsp. oil, spread out the onion, celery and cauliflower; cover and cook 2 minutes. Open the cover and stir well and add 1 tbsp. butter, quinoa and amaranth and stir together for 5 minutes; add cranberries, pistachios and almonds and stir well. Increase the heat to medium-high, and add 1-1/4 cup broth; Bring the mixture to a boil. Lower the heat to a constant simmer and cook for 15-20 minutes when all the liquid is absorbed and grains are soft. Stir the mixture once during the cooking and check the liquid, adding 2-3 tbsp. broth if needed. Now sprinkle with granulated garlic, rosemary, little salt and pepper to taste, lemon juice, and fluff the grains with a fork. Keep it warm over simmering water. When ready to serve, stir in 1tbsp. butter and serve garnished with scallions, red bell pepper etc.

Tips:

Amaranth: These are cream-colored little seeds. It is gluten-free and a protein powerhouse. It has cholesterol-lowering properties, contains potassium, calcium and vitamin C. My mother used this with oatmeal for cereal and dry-roasted and popped in the wok.

Quinoa: It is gluten-free, known as the "Mother Grain" and pronounced keen-wah. It has higher protein contents than any other grain, contains all eight amino acids, a complete protein grain. Buy pre-washed quinoa that has removed the naturally occurring bitter coating called saponin. It comes in various colors, but I like the natural grain.

Bulgur (Serves: 4)

Bulgur is actually the cracked wheat. It is whole grain loaded with fiber and protein. Grains cooked with nuts and chopped vegetables give more flavor, more nutrients, and are more appealing. The caraway seeds give good flavor and help digestion. You can add herbs like parsley and a little lime zest or fresh oregano to make it more nutritional.

Ingredients: ¾ cup bulgur; 2 cups water; ½ tsp. caraway seeds; ½ cup chopped onion; 1 tsp. chopped ginger (op); ½ cup slivered almonds; ½ cup chopped red or green bell pepper; to garnish 1/2c pomegranate seeds and 1 tbsp. butter.

1. In a medium pot, on medium heat, dry-roast the bulgur and caraway seed for just 5 minutes without browning them.
2. Add onion, ginger, almond, and water, stir well and bring to a boil. Sprinkle the chopped peppers on top and add ½ of the butter; cover with the lid and let it simmer for about 15-20 minutes, or until all the water is gone and the bulgur is soft. Fluff with a fork and keep it warm.
3. Just before serving add rest of the butter, stir it well. Serve garnished with pomegranate seeds in place of rice.

The Basic Pizza Dough

"350 Slices Per Second. That's how much Pizza America eats!"

This was in an article that appeared in Parade magazine on Sept. 4, 2016. I know, I like Pizza, and people all around me like Pizza very much.

Ingredients: 1 packet 7g, ¼ ounces quick-rise active dry yeast; 1/3 cups warm (90 degrees that doesn't burn your wrist) water; 4 tsp. sugar; 4 cups high protein, unsifted bread flour such as: King Arthur, All Trumps, or Indian chapati flour (white whole grain); 2 tbsp. semolina; 1-1/2 cups ice water; 1 tsp. fine salt; 1 tsp. olive oil; 1 tsp. butter (op).

Place the yeast in a bowl, pour over the warm water, sprinkle the sugar, and whisk for 30 seconds until the yeast is dissolved and foamy. If yeast doesn't dissolve and stays grainy then discard the mixture and start again with the live yeast.

Now add the flour and the semolina and mix with fingers (the heat from the hand helps the dough rise). Add 1-1/2 cups ice water, ½ cup at a time, and mix with fingers. Scrape the bottom and bring the dough together into a smooth ball. Stretch the dough a little, sprinkle salt and mix it well into the dough by folding from all around, and make a smooth ball. Pour the oil all over the ball, then move the ball around in the bowl. Now take out the dough on the counter and knead for 2 minutes, until it is smooth. Divide into two equal balls. Work with one and refrigerate the other in a pizza pan (bowl) wrapped airtight with the plastic up to 24 hours, or freeze it for up to 3 months, placed in a large greased zip-log bag inside a plastic container.

Place the other dough ball in a bowl, wet a kitchen towel with warm water, squeeze out water, and cover the dough. Place the bowl in a draft-free place (a cold oven, etc.) for about 45 minutes, until the dough is almost doubled. Proceed with making the pizza.

Alternately, use a stand mixer. Place yeast, warm water, and sugar in the stand mixer bowl, and with dough hook attached mix the yeast foamy. Add the flour and semolina, and mix the dough for 1-2 minutes until the dough comes together into a ball. Take the dough off the hook, scrape the bottom, sprinkle the salt and mix again. Now sprinkle the oil and mix a little. Take the dough out and knead on the counter for 2 minutes into a smooth ball. Let dough rise covered with a damp cloth for about 45 minutes, and make pizzas.

The Basic Pizza (M: 1 large)

Ingredients: 1 dough ball from above basic pizza dough recipe; 1 tsp. olive oil; 4 tbsp. bread flour mixed with 2 tbsp. semolina for dusting; 1 can 8 ounces tomato sauce heated with 1 tbsp. fresh basil and 1 tsp. crushed fresh garlic clove; ½ pound shredded or sliced fresh mozzarella cheese; 1 red bell pepper, cored and cut into 1-inch pieces; 1 cup cooked ham or chicken or ¼ pound thin-sliced pepperoni; 1 tsp. butter (op); pizza pan (perforated pan) lined with parchment paper, or pizza stone and a wooden peel.

Preheat oven at 450 degrees for 25-30 minutes. If using pizza stone, heat the stone for 30 to 40 minutes in the oven.

Place a large plastic wrap over the cutting board, and dusting with the flour, roll out the dough evenly, about 10-inch diameter. Pick up the plastic wrap and turn the dough over the pizza pan, or a wooden peel sprinkled with the semolina. Shake the peel often to move the pizza. Now stretch out the dough up to the edges, making sure the edge of the pizza is a little thicker than the center. Drizzle the oil all over, then tomato sauce; sprinkle the red bell peppers and meat, then cover with the cheese. Slide the pizza from to the heated stone, or just place the pizza pan in the oven. Bake the pizza in a very hot oven for 5 minutes, if using the pepperoni, place them on the top, rotate the pizza and bake another 5-6 minutes, until top is golden and the bottom is browned and crispy. Take the pizza out of the oven and rub the butter on the open edge (makes the crust tasty). Cut with pizza wheel into six wedges, and serve sprinkled with red pepper flakes and/oregano, if preferred.

Tip: The ice water, and very hot oven (heat at least ½ hour at 450 degrees) makes pizza rise well and crispier. If you are making a few pizzas for a company, then use 2 pizza stones and heat them at 500 degrees for 1 hour before baking. First bake the pizza on the top stone at 500 degrees for 5 minutes, then move to the lower stone for another 5 minutes, until golden brown top, and crisp bottom.

Gluten - free Protein Pizza (M: 1 large)

This pizza is made with whole-grain quinoa, you can grind the quinoa in the coffee grinder or use as whole seeds.

Ingredients:

For the Crust: 1 cup whole-grain quinoa, whole or ground; 1 cup low-fat buttermilk; 1 large egg beaten; 1 tsp. baking powder; ½ tsp. baking soda; ½ tsp. salt; 1 cup almond flour (meal); 2-3 tbsp. olive oil or as needed.

For the Topping: 1-1/2 cups plain or pasta sauce; 1 large clove of garlic; ¼ tsp. dry oregano; about ¾ pound to 1 pound sliced fresh mozzarella cheese; 1 red and 1 green bell pepper, seeded and cut into match sticks; some thick-sliced ham or salami or your favorite meat, and fresh watercress or baby arugula, to garnish.

1. Preheat oven at 450 degrees for 30 minutes. Line a pizza pan or a large baking sheet with parchment paper and grease it well.
2. In a blender, puree quinoa and buttermilk for 2 minutes. Add beaten egg, baking powder, baking soda, salt and 1 tbsp. olive oil and pulse 5-6 times. Take out the mixture and pour over the almond flour in a bowl and mix all together with a rubber spatula.
3. With the rubber spatula, spread out the crust in a pizza pan, then with the wet hands even out the crust. Drizzle 1 tbsp. olive oil on the top. Bake the crust in a preheated oven for about 10-12 minutes until it is light brown underneath. Take the pan out of oven, let it sit for 1 minute, then scrape the bottom with a metal spatula; carefully holding by hand, turn the crust over.
4. Put all the toppings on the browned side: spread out tomato sauce, sprinkle oregano, grate the garlic all over, spread out the cheese slices, sprinkle the bell pepper sticks. Bake pizza for another 10-15 minutes or until it is lightly browned underneath. Take out of the oven, drizzle with some extra virgin olive oil, and garnish with meat, watercress or arugula and serve.

Pizza with Sausage Ragu and No-Salt Coleslaw (Serves: 4-6)

This is a regular cheese pizza topped with sausage ragu, has much more flavor because the sausages are cooked in whole, and mashed after, so the flavors stay inside the meat. We use no-salt coleslaw, it is very light and healthy.

Ingredients:
For the Pizza: 1 large cheese pizza with sauce, and extra cheese, and not topping, cooked and heated warm.

For the Sausage Ragu: 4 tbsp. olive oil; 2 medium bay leaves; 2 tbsp. fennel seeds; one cup each chopped: onion, celery and carrots; 1 pkg. 16 ounces about 5 large andouille, regular or Creole sausages, or Italian hot or sweet sausages; 1 bottle 24 ounces 680g any pasta sauce with herbs; ½ tsp. each: granulated garlic, dry oregano, and basil; salt and pepper to taste, ¼ cup grated cheese.

For the No-Salt Coleslaw: About 2 cups fine shredded cabbage; ½ cup each thick sliced: red onion, cucumber and red bell pepper; ¼ cup toasted slivered almonds; 1/3 cups e.v. olive oil, 2 tbsp.; champagne vinegar mixed with 3 tbsp. water.

Toss all the vegetable and almonds with the olive oil and refrigerate them uncovered. Just before serving, sprinkle the vinegar mixture over the slaw in each individual plate and serve.

For the Sausage Ragu: Heat a large pot with 1 tbsp. olive oil on medium-high heat, add the sausages and brown them on all sides, stirring constantly for about 8-10 minutes. Reduce the heat to medium and take out the sausage in a bowl. Add 2 tbsp. of the olive oil and sauté bay leaves, fennel seeds for 1 minute; add the onion, carrots and celery and stir for 4-5 minutes, just to sweat them. Add the sauce and heat until it is bubbling. Add the sausages back, increase the heat to high and bring them to a boil. Then lower the heat to a constant simmer for about 1 hour. Turn off the heat and let them cool a little; slice them with a knife and fork in 1-inch pieces. Then pulse them in a food processor to about ¼-inch pieces (this way they will have some bite).

Heat a large heavy-bottom sauté pan on medium heat. Add 1 tbsp. oil, garlic, oregano, basil, and then the sausage mixture; stir well, bring to a simmer and simmer in the open pan until all the liquid is almost gone and the sausage are heated through. Taste for seasoning.

Serve hot on the prepared heated pizza, with coleslaw on the side and some fruits, if you wish.

Polenta (Serves: 4 to 6)

Polenta takes only 10 minutes to cook. Use coarse corn meal (not quick-cooking) or corn grits. This is a basic polenta. To make creamy add 4 oz. mascarpone cheese.

Ingredients: 1 cup medium-grain corn meal; 2 cups whole milk; 1 cup water or chicken broth or a mixture of both; 6 tbsp. butter, divided; salt and white pepper to taste; ½ cup grated parmesan cheese.

In a medium, heavy-bottom pot bring the liquid to a boil; add salt, pepper to taste, and 4 tbsp. butter, whisk well. Use a large wire whisk, slowly in a thin stream pour the polenta into the hot liquid while constantly whisking. Put the pot back on the heat and keep on whisking a few minutes until polenta is thick. Cover the pot and keep it warm over simmering water. Just before serving, stir in a grated cheese and 2 more tbsp. butter.

Polenta Cakes (M: 12-18)

Grease a muffin tin very generously with 1-2 tbsp. of softened butter. Right after polenta is done and while still warm, add ½ cup of any nut flour, such as Hazelnut or Walnut, lightly toasted and ground. Using an ice cream scoop, drop the polenta in the muffin tin. Smooth the top with wet fingers. Then drop a little melted butter on the top and sprinkle with little grated cheese. Let the polenta cool for about ½ an hour. Bake in a preheated oven at 400 degrees for 12-15 minutes until settled and light brown. Cool completely, loosen with a dinner knife all around, and take out with a tablespoon.

You can make stuffed cakes: You can pour only half of the scoop of polenta in the muffin tin, then top with the filling, about 1-2 tbsp. of cooked onion and garlic, or bacon or the cooked frozen peas; cover with the other ½ of the polenta, and bake until light brown.

Creamy Polenta

Cook polenta in the whole milk or half-and-half. When done, stir in warm heavy cream and some shaved parmesan cheese. Serve warm. Garnish with more fresh-grated cheese.

Brown Rice (Serves: 6-8)

This cooked brown rice looks almost like a rice pilaf. You can cook it in chicken/vegetable broth for more flavor.

Ingredients : 2 cups brown rice, soaked in 2 cups warm water, ½ tsp. caraway seeds (op) for about 1 hour; 1 medium onion chopped fine; 1 garlic clove crushed fine or grated; 1 about 2-inch stick of cinnamon; about 8 thick asparagus, tough bottoms peeled; ½ of each red and yellow bell pepper cut into 1-inch cubes; 1 tbsp. butter; ¼ cup each pumpkin and sunflower seeds lightly toasted in a dry pan.

1. In a large, heavy-bottom pan, bring about 2 cups of water to a boil, add the asparagus, boil for 2-3 minutes, then rinse out under the running cold water and place the asparagus in a platter.
2. Wash the pan, place the soaked rice and soaking water in same pan and cover with the warm water, about ½-inch above the rice. Heat the rice on medium-high heat and bring to a boil; add onion, garlic, cinnamon stick and drop 1 tbsp. of butter in the center; cover, lower the heat and simmer for about 45-50 minutes until rice is soft. Stir the rice during cooking 1-2 times, add a little more hot water if needed. When rice is done, move it all around and add the yellow and red bell peppers and asparagus, cut up in small pieces, in the center, and turn off the heat.
3. Serve warm rice, sprinkled with pumpkin and sunflower seeds.

Tips:
1. Do not wash the rice. The white powdery substance all around the rice has a lot of nutrients.
2. The brown rice cooks fast if soaked 1-2 hours covered in warm water.
3. Also, you can dry-toast the rice in a heavy-bottom pan or brown in oil or butter for fast and tasty cooking.
4. When the rice is done, fluff it with a fork or add 1-2 tbsp. of butter to separate.
5. Add 2 cups cooked green peas to above cooked brown rice, and serve with yogurt salad. It will make a complete meal.

Lentils and Brown Rice Pilaf (Serves: 4)

This pilaf is rich and substantial; just serve with cottage cheese or raita (yogurt salad).

Ingredients: 2 tbsp. olive oil or purified butter (ghee); 1 cup good brown rice; ½ cup whole green lentils; 1 large onion chopped, 4 garlic cloves chopped, 2-inch fresh ginger chopped; 1-2 serrano peppers chopped; ¼ tsp. each salt and pepper or to taste; ½ c tomato sauce; ½ cup chopped fresh spinach; ¼ cup cooked chickpeas or green peas (op); ½ cup chopped red bell peppers, ¼ cup pumpkin seeds; ½ cup raisins or dry cranberries, 1 tbsp. butter.

1. Heat a large heavy-bottom pot or Dutch oven on medium heat. When hot, add the oil or ghee, onion, garlic, ginger, serrano peppers, and cook on medium-high heat for 4-5 minutes until transparent. Wash out the lentils with warm tap water, drain and add to the oil. Add about 2 tbsp. of warm water to the rice (do not wash) and add to the pot. Slowly stirring, cook the rice in the pot for about 1 minute. Add about 2-1/2 C warm water, bring

to a boil, cover, lower the heat and simmer about 45 minutes until lentils and rice both are soft. Stir the rice once during cooking and add more warm water if needed.

2. When rice is done, add tomato sauce, chick peas or green cooked peas, spinach, red bell peppers, raisins and cranberries, pumpkin seeds, 1 tbsp. butter; stir well and keep covered and warm until serving.

Boiled Rice Pilaf or Poha (Serves: 4)

Poha is made with boiled and flattened Indian rice. But you can use quick-cooking or just boiled rice. This dish is very light, colorful and tasty. We use 1 cup of rice and about 4 cups of vegetables. You can use more rice if you prefer. Cook vegetables and rice in separate pans and at the end, just mix and serve.

Ingredients: 3-4 tbsp. canola, olive oil or butter, divided; 1 tsp. granulated garlic and 1-1/2 tsp. turmeric powder divided; 1 tsp. caraway seeds; 1 medium potato, quartered lengthwise and thin-sliced across; 1 pkg., 10 oz. (284g) frozen peas; 1 large red bell pepper cut into small strips; ¼ cup cilantro soft stems and leaves; salt and pepper to taste; ½ cup to 1 cup unroasted peanuts; 1 cup poha or quick-cooking rice; 2 tsp. lemon juice; 1 c chopped plum tomatoes; yogurt or yogurt salad to serve (op).

Heat a large sauté pan on medium heat, add 1 tbsp. oil and sauté the peppers for 5 minutes. Add peas and sauté 5 minutes. Cover for 5-6 minutes until soft, take out in a bowl. Add 1 tbsp. of oil in the same pan, add caraway seeds brown lightly and add potatoes; sauté 5 minutes, sprinkle half garlic, turmeric and 1 tbsp. water, cover and cook until soft. When done, add tomatoes stir 1 minute and turn off the heat.

While potatoes are cooking, heat rest of the oil in another large pan, and brown the peanuts on medium heat for 2 minutes; add rice and sauté 5 minutes. Add turmeric, garlic, lemon juice and about ½ C water. Stir well, cover and cook until rice is soft and done.
Now pour cooked rice over the vegetables and garnish with peppers and peas. Serve warm with plain yogurt or yogurt salad (Raita).

Tips: Brown rice is only husked and keeps most of its nutrients. White rice is husked and germ and bran are removed. So, it looks more pleasing and cooks faster. Rice is made up of endosperm, germ, bran, and husk. To get most out of it, buy brown rice even though it takes a little longer to cook. You will gain less calories, less starch and more nutrients.

Vegetable Cuts, Handling & Cooking

Wash all fresh vegetables under running cold water (except the mushrooms: clean with a damp cloth) to get the dirt out before cooking. Some of the vegetables and herbs like lettuce, cilantro, spinach, etc., you may need to wash in a few changes of water to get all the dirt out.

Various Vegetable Cuts

Peel: You can peel some of the small vegetables and fruit like kiwi and apples with the utility knife. For the bigger jobs, use a vegetable peeler. If you have a peeler that is stationary curved, peel the vegetables by pulling toward you. If you have swivel-blade peeler, use it in strokes away from you.

Core: To take the small cores out of vegetables you can use the pointed top end of the peeler by inserting into the vegetable and moving all around the core. For the larger cores like lettuce, endive, fennel, etc. use a small sharp knife and cut around the stem at an angle; when the core is loose, pull it out with your fingers. In some cases, cores can be large and tough like cabbage. So cut the cabbage in half, then in a quarter, and work all around the stem to cut it off on an angle.

Bias: You cut the vegetable on a slight angle (about 45 degrees) so the inner part of the vegetable is exposed more to heat. This way they cook fast as well as look decorative, especially in case of zucchini and Japanese eggplant.

Mince: To cut herbs or vegetable in very small pieces, about 1/8 to ¼-inch pieces. These pieces are not precise, but are small.

Chiffonade: This cut is used mostly for the delicate vegetable and herbs like fennel, chives, basil etc. Use scissors to snip off the tender leaves into fine, decorative pieces.

Chop: Chopping can be coarse or fine. Chop the vegetables by holding the large chopping knife in one hand and pressing the point of the knife with the other hand while cutting (chopping) the vegetables. Do not lift the point of the knife; it should stay on the chopping surface all the time; while chopping, move the blade of the knife up and down over the vegetables.

To fine-chop the vegetable: gather the cut vegetable with the blade of the knife into a long pile and go over and chop again, chopping until desired size of the vegetable are cut.

Dice: This cut makes a precise size of pieces used for cooking or garnish etc. First you julienne them evenly, then take a handful of the sticks at a time and cut them crosswise to dice. To cook with beans, I dice most of my vegetables to make them the same size as the beans, potatoes, onion, carrots, etc.

Slice: You can slice vegetables small or large. Hold vegetables firmly with one hand and cut vegetable into thin pieces with the other. Make sure you are holding the vegetable with fingers curved under away from the cutting end so you do not get hurt in slicing. Always leave enough vegetable exposed away from the fingers. If you have a round vegetable like melon, first thin-slice a piece on the side, then use that side as a base to proceed slicing across into desired slices.

Julienne: Julienne is cutting vegetables into fine sticks. First cut the vegetable into two -inch length, then take one piece at a time, and slice each piece into thinner slices. Now put two or three slices together and cut into thin and long sticks. You can julienne small or large sticks as desired. Julienned vegetables are good for stir-fry as they cook fast.

Paysanne: This cut has a bias cut at both ends to make a triangle shape, and the pieces are about two inches long. The shape of the cut looks almost triangular. I like these pieces for soup or stir-fry.

Shred: Shred or chiffonade is mostly for the leafy vegetables. For instance, to shred romaine lettuce, wash and clean the leaves, then pat dry with paper towels; hold leaves in the same direction with one hand pressing the leaves with the tips of the fingers and hold a sharp knife with the other hand, and slice very thin slices across to shred it. You can also roll herb leaves lengthwise then cut them into thin slices for long, thin and attractive threads. I like to shred almost all my leafy vegetables, the way my grandmother used to do almost every day. After you clean, wash and pat dry the vegetables put them together with stems on the same side (all soft stems together). First, thin-slice all the stems on the bias. Then cut the leaf pile in half, turn around and make one large bundle putting the cut part together; hold and press down firmly the bundle with folded fingers under with one hand and slice thin on a bias with the other hand. You can shred very thin and in no time you will slice off all the leaves. You can shred in batches if there is too much to slice. Soft stems (like baby spinach) do not matter if they are mixed up with the leaves.

Snip: You can snip off the herbs with sharp kitchen shears to avoid bruising them if they are very thin. I snip some of my herbs, like chives and cilantro, right over the serving plates as a garnish. They look attractive, you get a fresh flavor, and a little goes a long way.

Vegetables

Indian cooking is known for fancy vegetables and vegetarian food. I came from the northern part of India, which is famous for vegetables and dal (beans) and breads. The southern part of India is known for rice dishes and dals, and northwest region (Kashmir and Panjab) has good meat dishes of mostly Moghul cuisine. In Hindu families, vegetarian food is the main meal and tasty flavorful vegetables are a must to go with breads, rice and yogurt dishes. Tasty vegetables and beans take place of the meat and make you full and happy. You can smell a tasty meal just entering the house.

The Basic Vegetable Cooking

Make any soft vegetable such as cauliflower, zucchini, eggplant, okra, potatoes etc. If making cauliflower, take out the stem, peel it and then slice thin across, Slice zucchini slice, cut eggplant and potatoes into about 1-1/2-inch cubes. Fenugreek seed powder helps digest the food, takes inflammation away and gives very good taste to the food. It is hot in reaction, so use in small quantities

.

The Basic Eggplant Vegetable (Serves: 2-4)

Ingredients: 3 tbsp. canola or olive oil; 1 medium onion chopped; about 1-1/4 to 1-1/2 pounds or 1 large or 2 small purple eggplants; salt and pepper to taste; ¼ tsp. to ½ tsp. fenugreek powder (op); ½ tsp. turmeric powder; 1 tsp. granulated garlic; 2 medium or 1 cup chopped plum tomatoes; ½ cup cilantro or flat-leaf parsley chopped.

Heat a heavy-bottom pan on medium heat, add 1 tbsp. oil and onion, sprinkle with little salt, pepper, turmeric, garlic and fenugreek powders; stir well, cover and steam for 5 minutes. While onions are cooking, cut the eggplant in half lengthwise, put cut side down, make about 1-1/2-inch wide strips, then cut across into 1-1/2-inch cubes. Move the onion aside, add the eggplant cubes to the pan, sprinkle salt and pepper and 2 tbsp. oil; stir well, then spread out onion on the top and spread out the tomatoes pieces all around (not on the top); cover and cook on low heat for about 20-25 minutes, until soft. Stir the eggplant after 15 minutes and mix all ingredients together. When done, taste for seasoning and add as needed; sprinkle with cilantro or parsley and serve hot with bread, rice, quinoa and meat etc.

Tip: Eggplant gets bitter very fast, so cut it just before cooking, or sprinkle lightly all the cut surfaces with salt, and cook immediately.

Potato and Cauliflower (Alu Gobhi) (Serves: 8)

This traditional Indian vegetable is very versatile. Follow this technique and the spices and you will be amazed how tasty and flavorful it will turn out. It is easy to cook: Sweat and brown cauliflower and potatoes separate, cook fresh-ground spices separate and pour over the vegetables; cook everything together for about 10-15 minutes.

Ingredients: 5-6 tbsp. canola oil; 4 large red potatoes (about 4cups) peeled and cut into 1-1/2-inch cubes; 1 medium head of cauliflower cut into 2-inch diameter pieces and stems split into four, but still attached to the florets; ½ cup (8 tbsp.) ginger-garlic paste; 1 tbsp. fenugreek (methi) powder; ½ cup peeled and ground green mango or 2 tbsp. mango powder (amchoor); 1 tbsp. garam masala, divided; 1 tsp. turmeric, divided; salt and ½ tsp. cayenne pepper or to taste; ½ cup chop fresh cilantro or parsley.

1. Heat a large heavy-bottom sauté pan on medium heat; when hot, add 2-3 tbsp. oil and cauliflower. Shake the pan to move around the cauliflower. Stir the cauliflower to coat with oil, cover and let it steam for 4-5 minutes; stir again, cover and let it steam again until cauliflower is cooked at least halfway.
   When it is done, take out cauliflower and use the same pan to brown the potatoes the same way, adding a little more oil. When potatoes are done, leave them in the pan, sprinkle salt and pepper to taste and top with the layer of steamed cauliflower.

2. Heat a cast-iron pan or a heavy-bottom medium-size pan on medium heat, add 1 tbsp. When oil is warm, take the pan off the heat and add the fenugreek powder in the oil; stir a little (do not let it burn) and immediately add ginger-garlic paste, mango powder, half of each garam masala and ½ of turmeric, cayenne; put the pan back on medium heat, stir a little, add ¼ tsp. salt, ½ cup water; cover, bring it to a boil and let it simmer on medium heat about 10 minutes, until it is reduced in half and spices are cooked. If the water is gone, add 3-4 tbsp. of water and stir it well; when heated, pour over the cauliflower. Sprinkle rest of the garam masala and turmeric, salt and pepper to taste; on cauliflower, do not stir, just cover and cook another 15 minutes until potatoes and cauliflower both are soft. If there is any liquid left in the pan, let it simmer, open, on medium heat until all the liquid has evaporated. Do not add any water or cover the pan; when they are done, just cover halfway with the lid while vegetables are still hot. When ready to serve, heat it again uncovered, sprinkle the cilantro and serve with deep-fried bread, paratha or bread.

Potato, Peas, and Cauliflower (Alu, Mutter, Gobhi)
(Serves: 8)

This is a juicy vegetable dish mostly served with rice or bread. All ingredients and methods of cooking are the same as above: just add 1 extra tbsp. of garam masala together with one to 1-1/2 cup of water in the spices; cook and pour over the cauliflower. At the end add 1 pkg. 10 ounces frozen peas, and 4 medium plum tomatoes (about 2 cups) chopped in the last 10 minutes of cooking. The vegetables should be juicy.

Tips:
1. Cauliflower is full of water, so sauté a little in the oil, cover and let it cook on medium heat, and keep on stirring every 10 minutes until cauliflower is done.
2. Red Potatoes are the brain food. There is a substance called 'choline' that helps make brain cells healthy. Scrub wash the potatoes and leave the skin on, use very little or no water in cooking, and cook on low heat they will be very healthy.
3. When adding fenugreek powder, heeing powder and even granulated garlic, heat the pan first, add a little oil (about 1 tbsp.); when oil is warm (not hot), take it off the stove and add the spice powder, sprinkling over the oil on one side of the pan (in about 1-2-inch area) stir a little with the spatula, and when it starts bubbling add other spices, stir well and put it back on the heat. Dry spices tend to burn fast and lose their flavors, so add them in warm oil, and off the heat.
4. Peas are loaded with protein, just add them last minutes.

Stuffed Artichokes (Serves: 2-4)

Artichokes are known to help digest the food well. Buy them firm and with green stems.
Ingredients: 2 large and firm globe artichokes; 2 large lemons: 3 tbsp. butter plus extra for brushing; ¼ tsp. turmeric powder (op); 1/2cup dried seasoned bread crumbs; ¼ cup parmesan cheese; ½ cup crumbled blue cheese; 1 tbsp. drained capers;1 tsp. granulated garlic; ¼ tsp. dry rosemary; salt and fresh ground black pepper to taste.

1. Peel the stems, cut artichokes in half and rub the lemon juice all over on the cut part. Scoop out the fuzzy center with a potato peeler and discard. Now with kitchen scissors, cut off the top 1/3 of the artichoke (the hard leaves) and rub with the lemon again. In a large pot or a Dutch oven, lay down the artichoke halves, cut side down, cover with cold water, sprinkle 2 tbsp. lemon juice, ¼ tsp. of turmeric, salt and pepper, all over on the artichokes; add all the cut-off leaves back to the pot. Bring to a boil, cover and simmer on low heat for about 25 minutes, until inside of the artichoke is soft. Drain out all the cooking water and save it for the soup etc. and let the artichoke cool in the covered pot for about ½ hour.
2. Now carefully pull out, upward, the outer hard leaves (about l5 leaves) of the artichoke. Brush the boiled artichoke with melted butter. In a bowl combine bread crumbs, 3 tbsp. butter, parmesan cheese, gran. garlic, rosemary, 2 tbsp. lemon juice, salt and pepper to taste, and mix well by hand. Add capers and blue cheese and stuff the mixture evenly over the cut artichoke. Brush the artichokes with melted butter again.
3. Place them on the foil and brown them under a heated broiler for about 5 minutes until top is golden. Serve warm with the meal.

Artichoke Fritters (Serves: 4-6)

I like to buy the baby artichokes for fritters. They usually come in the market by the end of the summer season, around November and December. You can also ask the growers to pick them early for you.

Ingredients: 2 pounds fresh baby artichokes; 2 tbsp. white vinegar; 1-1/2 cups pancake mix or chickpea flour; 1 tsp. celery seeds; ½ tsp. each: cayenne pepper, garlic powder, turmeric powder (op); ¼ cup milk;

about ¼ cup to ½ cup water as needed; canola or olive oil to deep fry; chutney or any favorite sauce to serve.

Place the whole artichokes in a large and wide pot, cover with the water about 1-inch higher, add the vinegar, and bring them to a boil. Cover and boil for 20 to 25 minutes, depending on the size, until they are soft. Drain, cool, then working with one artichoke at a time, cut off the pointed top, about ¼ on the top; take off the stem, split the artichoke in half lengthwise from the stem. Now take off the outer dark 4 to 5 leaves and leave on the lighter leaves attached to the stem. Baby artichokes do not have chokes (fibers at the center). Do the same to all artichokes.

For the Batter: In a medium bowl, whisk pancake mix or chickpea flour, celery seeds, cayenne, garlic powder, turmeric powder and salt to taste if using the chickpea flour. Add the milk, then slowly add the water, whisking until it is a little thicker than the pancake-batter consistency.

Heat the oil in a wok, or a deep-frying pan about 1-inch deep, to 375 degrees. When the oil is hot, take one piece of the cut artichoke, hold the stem, dip both sides into the batter, then wipe out the batter slightly on the rim of the bowl, and drop the artichoke cut side down into the hot oil. Cook fritters in batches, in single layers; do not crowd the oil. When browned underneath, turn it over once. Cook about 2 minutes on each side or until browned. Take them out with a perforated spoon on a paper towel-lined tray. Serve hot with sauce or chutney.

Marinated Artichokes (M: about 4 cups)

I like to buy the globe, firm and medium-size artichokes for marinating. Make sure the stems are green.

Ingredients: 2 pounds medium but firm artichokes; 2 tbsp. lemon juice; marinate mixture: ½ cup each: Champaign vinegar and olive oil; 2 tbsp. lemon juice; 2 large garlic cloves, grated; 1 tsp. dry oregano; 2 tbsp. fresh-chopped flat leaf parsley; ½ tsp. each salt and fresh-ground black pepper.

Place the artichokes in a large and wide pot, cover with the cold water about 1-inch higher, add the lemon juice, and bring them to a boil. Boil for 25-30 minutes covered until they are soft, drain out the water, and cool. Now working with one artichoke at a time, trim off about 1/4th of the top, take off the stem, and split the artichoke in half lengthwise from the stem. With a potato peeler take out the choke (fibers) from the center, take out all the (about 5-6) tough and darker outer leaves, slice the softer leaves together with the stems lengthwise into about 1-inch wide slices. Place the slices into a large, dry and clean jar.

Heat the marinating mixture, bring it to a boil, and pour over the artichoke slices. Wait until the liquid cools down slightly, then close the jar with the lid, keeping it slightly loose. Bring to room temperature, then refrigerate or serve.

Oven Roasted Broccoli (Serves: 6)

Broccoli cooks fast whether you cook it in a pan or in the oven, but tastes better when roasted.

Ingredients: 2 medium, thick, fresh heads of broccoli, florets cut almost same size, with only about 1-2 inches of stems attached, and all stems split in half in the bottom for fast cooking; 2 tbsp. olive oil mixed with 2 tbsp. lemon juice; 1 tsp. granulated garlic; 1 tsp. dry oregano; about 1 tbsp. balsamic vinegar; salt and pepper to taste.

1.   Preheat oven at 450 degrees. Line a large tray with aluminum foil. Wash the florets under cold water. Line up the florets, stem side outside toward the edge of the tray. Sprinkle with oil and lemon juice mixture all over. Then sprinkle with granulated garlic, oregano, and salt and pepper all over. Roast in the preheated oven for about 15 minutes. Sprinkle balsamic vinegar halfway through roasting. Turn off the oven and leave in the oven for another 5 minutes. Do not let the broccoli burn. Serve immediately.

Tips: The secret to roasting broccoli is split the stems all the way to the bottom, but keep them attached on the top at the florets; wash the florets so it cooks in some moisture.

Red and Green Vegetables (Serves: 4)

We cook this for Christmas and other holidays. It is quick and tasty.

Ingredients: 3-4 tbsp. butter; 1 pkg. 10 ounces (284g) frozen peas; 2 large red bell peppers cored, and cut into 2-inch long strips; ½ tsp. granulated garlic; salt and pepper to taste.

Heat a heavy-bottom pan on medium heat and sauté peppers in butter for 5 minutes, or until soft. Add peas, stir well; sprinkle spices, cover for 5 minutes until peas are soft and serve warm.

Quick Curry of Jackfruit or Kathal (Serves: 4)

You can usually find this large green, watermelon-type of vegetable cut-up in pieces at the Indian supermarkets. If you are using a fresh one, wear rubber gloves and/or rub a lot of oil on your hands to cut it into pieces. After cutting into pieces, peel the rind, and boil the pieces until they are soft. Peel off the brown skin of the jumbo seeds after boiling.

Ingredients: 1 can, 20 ounces, (565g) young green jackfruit in brine; 4 tsp. canola oil; ½ tsp. each fenugreek powder (op), granulated garlic, madras curry powder, turmeric; 1 tsp. lemon-pepper seasoning mix or 1 tbsp. lemon juice; salt and fresh-ground black pepper to taste; 3 tbsp. chopped fresh parsley or cilantro.

Drain and pat dry the pieces of the jackfruit. Heat a large sauté pan on low heat. Add the 1 tbsp. of oil and fenugreek and curry powder, and cook in oil for 30 seconds, or until it starts bubbling. Add the jackfruit pieces and stir well, then spread out the pieces in single layer. Increase the heat to medium, sprinkle with turmeric, garlic, salt and pepper, and a few drops of oil over the spices; cover and let it cook until it is brown underneath, about 5 minutes. Turn over and cook the other side covered for 5 minutes or until brown. Turn off the heat.

When ready to serve, heat again on low and sprinkle with parsley and serve as a side dish.

Fancy Jackfruit (Kathal) Curry (Serves: 4-6)

This curry is so tasty that you can eat it as a fritter. It is made with ripe (light yellow), fresh jackfruit. Wear rubber gloves and rub hands well with oil. Peel off the rind, cut the jackfruit into large pieces, about 5-6-inches in diameter, cover with the cold water add ¼,tsp. salt and boil until soft, drain well.

Ingredients: About 1 pound (500g) peeled and boiled jackfruit cut into 2-3-inch pieces and brown skin peeled off the seeds, then put the seeds back in its place (to fill in the hole); 1 tbsp. black cardamom seeds; 1 cup chopped onion; ¼ cup chopped garlic cloves; ½ tsp. turmeric, about ¼ cup canola oil; 4 tbsp. madras curry powder; ½ cup chickpea flour; 1 cup plain yogurt; about ½ tsp. each salt and cayenne or black pepper or to taste.

In a food processor, grind the cardamom seeds, add onion and garlic and grind all together well, with 1-2 tbsp. of water if needed. In a large bowl, whip together chickpea flour and yogurt, then add all dry and wet spices and whip well. Add the pieces of jackfruit and coat well with a wooden spoon.

Heat a large, heavy-bottom sauté pan on medium-high heat. When hot add about 2 tbsp. oil, and add the coated jackfruit pieces in the pan in a single layer. Cook the pieces until browned underneath. Sprinkle 2-3 drops of oil on each piece and turn each piece over with a metal spatula and cook another 3-4 minutes or until browned. Take out in a serving platter. Repeat with rest of the pieces and oil. Serve warm as a side dish.

Tip: You can make a large quantity ahead and freeze in a container. Thaw overnight, heat at 350 degrees for 15-20 minutes, and serve to a large group or buffet. You can do the same with the cauliflower and serve to a large group.

Caramelized Onions (M: 2 cups packed)

My father used to travel a lot and knew a lot about cooking. He always said to use garlic, salt and pepper to cook onion, and if you want to make it healthy, add little turmeric and fresh crushed fennel seeds. I also, add 1 tbsp. balsamic vinegar almost at the end. You can carmelize them in a pan over the stove, stirring often, on low heat, or in the oven.

Ingredients: 1 tbsp. olive oil and 4 tbsp. melted butter; about 1-1/2 pounds (7-8 medium) yellow onions sliced about ¼-inch thick; ½ tsp. turmeric; salt and fresh-ground black pepper to taste; 1/4tsp. cayenne pepper (op); 1 tsp. fresh crushed fennel seeds.

Preheat the oven at 250 degrees. On a large baking tray with sides, place the oil and move around to grease the bottom and sides. Add onion, sprinkle with spices and butter, mix well; cover airtight with foil and bake 250 degrees for 90 minutes, turning the tray around every half hour. Open the cover after 45 minutes, stir well and cover again and roast, until soft, about another 45 minutes. If you prefer, add some lemon juice or balsamic vinegar to taste and serve on buns, sandwiches, or use in soups, fillings or garnishes.

Okra Vegetable (Bhindi Masala) (Serves: 6)

Okra (bhindi or lady fingers) is usually made dry. Buy okra soft and small, and wash them before you cut them; do not use any salt on cut okra, use only when they are done. If okra are tender, they take only 15 minutes to cook. Take the top off and slice them in about 1-inch pieces. Use a paper towel if they stick. The silky part (juice) is loaded with the nutrition. My father treated okra as the king of the vegetables. You always have to cook them with lemon to break down on the sticky juice.

Ingredients: 2 pounds, about 1 kg. fresh, soft okra, washed and cut; 3 tbsp. canola oil; ½ tsp. celery seeds; ½ tsp. turmeric; 3 tbsp. lemon juice; 2 medium onions cut in 1-inch cubes (cut in 8 slices lengthwise, then cut in half across); 2-3 medium plum tomatoes cut in thick slices, about 6 slices lengthwise; 1 tsp. granulated garlic powder; salt and pepper to taste

1. Heat a large, heavy-bottom pan on medium heat; when hot add 2 tbsp. oil and celery seeds, cook seeds for about 3 minutes until they start bubbling and light brown; move them aside and add the okra to the pan. Increase heat medium high, sprinkle ½ of garlic powder, turmeric and lemon juice all over, sauté for 2 minutes, add onion and stir well; add tomatoes on the top, do not stir, cover, lower the heat and simmer for 10 minutes; open, the okra should be done; if not, stir a little, cover again and cook another 5 minutes, until soft.

2. When okra are done, if there is any juice left underneath, let it dry out on medium heat, in open pan; do not cover. When all juices are gone, sprinkle garlic powder, salt and pepper to taste, and 1 tbsp. oil; stir a little and let it cook on low heat, open, for 5 minutes. Reheat and serve. You can sprinkle some parsley if desired.

3. If you want to make it spicy, brown the 2 tbsp. ginger-garlic and green chili paste in oil first, add ¼ cup water, cook 5 minutes covered and pour over the okra at the end.

Tips: When we have a party or company for dinner, we always add the all-purpose fresh-ground spices, about 1 cup, browned in the oil. This extra flavor makes okra a fancy vegetable.

Stuffed Okra (Stuffed Bhindi or Lady Fingers)

(Serves: 8)

These stuffed okra are very fancy. They take longer to stuff, but are very tasty. You can make a day ahead and freeze them in a container up to two months, then defrost overnight in refrigerator; just sauté in oil. Again, wash okra, cut the top off and make a slit on one side lengthwise to stuff.

Ingredients: 2 pounds fresh soft okra, washed, cut on one side lengthwise to stuff; 3 tbsp. lemon-pepper mix; 1 tbsp. granulated garlic powder; 2 tbsp. curry powder; 1 tsp. turmeric; salt and pepper to taste, 4 tbsp. canola oil (divided).

1. In a bowl combine: lemon-pepper mix, ½ of granulated garlic, curry powder, turmeric, salt and pepper, and 1 tbsp. oil; mix well. Take a small knife and take one okra at a time; open the slit with one hand and stuff the spices, picking with the knife and inserting in to the okra. Press down the spices into the okra, close the slit with the hand and put the stuffed okra in a platter.

2. When all okra are stuffed, heat a large sauté pan on medium-high heat, with 2 tbsp. of oil, add okra, sauté 1 minute, sprinkle 2 tbsp. of water all over, lower the heat, cover with the lid and cook okra for about 10 minutes. If okra are not cooked or soft yet, sprinkle another 1-2 tbsp. of water, cover and cook another 5 minutes. When okra are soft, sprinkle with rest of the garlic powder, a pinch of salt and pepper, and 1 tbsp. of oil, and sauté on high heat for 1 minute; serve or heat again later and serve with deep-fried bread, rice, bread and yogurt.

Tips: You can use frozen, whole okra. Just thaw overnight in the refrigerator, and roast them sprinkled with lemon juice in a 400-degree oven for about 15-20 minutes, then cook in the pan later.

Grilled Okra

You can grill stuffed okra very easily. Just thread them on two skewers, brush with the oil on both sides, and place the skewers on medium heat. Grill each until they are light brown and have brown specks on them. About 8 minutes on each side, depending the size of the okra. Serve on the skewers.

Stuffed Bittermelon (Stuffed Karela)
(Serves: 6-8)

I like to use Indian bittermelon for stuffing. They look good and the stuffing stays well inside each piece. If you use Chinese, you have to cut them in half, and they are less bitter. Just try to buy all bittermelon the same size. Here you stuff them with the spices, and also brown them outside with some spices. Just boil bittermelon, stuff them and brown in the oil and spices.

Ingredients: 2 pounds or about 1 kg. Indian bittermelon or 4 Chinese bittermelons; 4 tbsp. canola oil; 2 large onions thin-sliced; 2 tbsp. granulated garlic; 2 tbsp. fennel seed powder or fine crushed fennel seeds; about 2 tbsp. dry mango powder (amchoor) or lemon-pepper mix; 2 tsp. turmeric; 1 tbsp. sugar; salt to taste., ¼ cup fresh-chopped cilantro or parsley.

1. Wash the bittermelon, trim off the stem away from the body. Add them to a medium pot, cover halfway with cold water, add some salt, 1 tsp. turmeric; simmer until soft. When cool, make a slit on one side, lengthwise, scoop out the seeds and set them aside.
2. Heat a large sauté pan on medium heat, add 2 tbsp. oil and brown the onion. Sprinkle ¼ tsp. each salt and garlic, sauté well, cover and cook for 6-8 minutes until soft. Take out the onion in a small bowl and mix rest of the spices: gran garlic, fennel powder, mango powder or lemon-pepper mix, turmeric, sugar, cilantro, and about ½ tsp. salt, setting-aside: about ½ tbsp. of gran. garlic, 2 tbsp. oil, ½ tbsp. mango powder or lemon-pepper mix to coat outside.
3. Heat the same pan, on low heat, with spices set aside: 2 tbsp. oil, ½ tbsp. gran. Garlic; add stuffed bittermelon flattened and sideways; brown both sides on medium-high heat. At the end, sprinkle on one side of bittermelons: ¼ tsp. salt, ½ tbsp. mango powder, 2 tbsp. water, do not stir, cover, and cook on low 10 minutes. Serve as a side dish.

   Tip: Bittermelon are known to kill the germs and stomach virus. They are good for diabetic people. Some people take out the juice and drink it straight to get rid of diabetes.

Sliced Bittermelon Vegetable (Serves: 4-6)

Bittermelon not only cures cancer if eaten on daily basis, it also cures diabetes. My friend's mother, who had early signs of diabetes, drinks about ½ cup of juice every day. You also have to watch out for sugar and starch. This vegetable, you have to simmer for a long time; only then will the flavor of the spices and onion give it a good flavor.

Ingredients: 2 extra-large (about 10 inches long) chinese bittermelons, about 2 to 2-1/4 pounds; 2 tbsp. canola oil; ½ cup tomato sauce; 2 large onions peeled and sliced thick (about ½ inch thick); 1 tbsp. fennel seeds powder or 1 tbsp. fennel seeds, crushed fine; 1 tbsp. sugar; 1tsp. granulated garlic; salt to taste (no need for any pepper), 2 tbsp. fresh chopped cilantro.

1. Wash, and cut bittermelons lengthwise, scoop out all the seeds with a spoon and discard the seeds. Slice each piece across about ½-inch wide slices.
2. Heat a large non-reactive, heavy-bottom sauté pan on medium heat. When hot add oil and bittermelon. Sauté, stirring on and off for 5 minutes. Sprinkle lightly with salt, cover and cook on low heat for 5 minutes.
3. Open and stir the bittermelon well, top with sliced onion and sprinkle the onion with half of the gran. garlic, a little more salt and ½ of the fennel powder, about ½ cup water; bring to a boil and simmer on medium for about 45 minutes, stirring often, do not let it burn.
4. When melon is soft and onions almost disappear, pour the tomato sauce, sugar, rest of the gran. garlic and fennel powder and a little salt. Stir well and cook another 15 minutes on medium heat.
5. When ready to serve heat again, sprinkle cilantro and serve over rice or with Indian bread or garlic toasts.

Tip: My father liked spicy bittermelon with deep-fried bread (Poori). To make it spicier, add fresh-ground all-purpose spices, browned in the oil in the beginning. At the end, sprinkle with lemon juice, salt and pepper to taste.

Roasted Red Bell Peppers (Serves: 4-6)

These roasted peppers you can serve as vegetable, salad, over the cooked dishes or as garnish or in sandwiches. They are tasty as well as healthy. No need to add any salt.

Ingredients: 5 large, even shape, red bell peppers; 3-4 tbsps. Extra-virgin olive oil; 1-2 tbsp. pressed or grated fresh garlic.

1. You can roast the peppers over the stove until they are blackened all around, or roast them under a broiler in the oven. Wash and dry each pepper, then place them in a broiler tray, lined with aluminum foil. Sprinkle a few drops of oil on each and broil them, about 4-inches away from the heat source. When the peppers are charred, in about 4 minutes (first time), turn them over, and rotate them (top to bottom). Keep on rotating until they are charred all sides (the rest will take about 1-2 minutes on each side).
2. Take the tray out of the oven, fold the foil over the pepper and then cover them with a kitchen towel, completely. Let them rest on the counter until cool enough to handle, about 45 minutes.
3. Use a medium bowl for the pepper slices. Using a dinner plate, take one pepper at a time, cut off the skin from the stem, peel the skin off the pepper; take out the stem and seeds, then cut the pepper in the long slices; add to the bowl with the juice.
4. When all the peppers are done, sprinkle crushed garlic and 1-2 tbsp. e.v. olive oil. You can keep them in room temperature for one day, and in the refrigerator up to 4 days.

Tasty Greens (Bhajiya)

Bhajiya is a general term for all the tasty greens cooked without water in spices. Greens take only 20-30 minutes to cook and very little oil. The secret is not to use any salt on the leaves; it will turn into liquid and never dry out.

Wash big-leaf greens under running cold water stem side first (that's where all the dirt is) in a large bowl, with a few change of water. For the small leaves, you can cut off the hard stems, discard any bad leaf, thin-slice across and then wash in a large bowl with 1 or 2 changes of water. Pick the cut leaves in a bunch and place in a colander set over a platter to catch the water.

Cutting the leaves: Using a sharp, small knife, holding a few bunch of leaves, slice at the soft stem side (discard the tough stems) very thin, between ¼ or ½ inch across, while they are still wet.

If you want spicy greens, grind the fresh spices, like in chickpeas (chole), cook and brown the spices in oil first, and then stir them in the cooked greens. We serve these greens with hot corn, chickpeas or deep-fried breads with chutney and raita.

Beets Greens (Serves: 4-6)

Ingredients: 1-1/2 to 2 pounds fresh beets with green leaves on; 2 tbsp. canola or olive oil divided; 1 tsp. caraway seeds; 2 large garlic cloves sliced; 1 tbsp. instant chicken broth (op); ½ tsp. dry oregano; ¼ tsp. granulated garlic; about ½ cup cilantro or flat-leaf parsley soft stems and leaves, thin-sliced; 1 tbsp. lemon juice; salt and fresh ground pepper to taste.

1. Use 1 or 2 small beets together with the leaves. Peel the beets and cut them in half lengthwise. Take 1 half at a time and slice it paper-thin lengthwise. Slice stems and leaves across, about ¼ inch wide.
2. Heat a large heavy-bottom sauté pan on medium heat, add 1 tbsp. oil and caraway seeds. When seeds start bubbling in oil, add garlic, stir a little, and immediately add sliced beets; sprinkle a little salt and pepper, stir well, add parsley and cut leaves, reduce the heat to low, sprinkle 3-4 tbsp. water, cover and cook 15 minutes. Open add little more water if needed, cover and cook until soft, about 10-15 minutes.
3. Just before serving, heat the beets again, sprinkle, gran. garlic, oregano, chicken broth, 1 tbsp. oil; stir on high heat 1 minute, add lemon juice and serve.

Broccoli Rabe (Mustard Greens) (Serves: 4-6)

Ingredients: 1 large bunch of broccoli rabe (rapini) about 1-1/2 pounds; 2 tbsp. canola or olive oil, divided; 1 large onion thin sliced ; 2 large garlic cloves thin sliced; ¼ cup grated fresh ginger;1 large plum tomato chopped or ½ cup chopped sun dried tomatoes in oil; 1 tbsp. lemon juice or to taste; ½ tsp. gran. garlic; ¼ tsp. dry oregano;1/2 1tsp. onion salt or to taste; 1 tbsp. butter; ¼ cup grated parmesan cheese.

1. Cut off the hard stems, almost near the green leaves, holding the half or quarter of the bundle, pushing down with the tips of the fingers; carefully thin-slice the greens about ½-inch wide. Wash them in a large bowl and take out in a colander to drain.
2. Heat a large heavy-bottom pan with 1 tbsp. oil on medium heat and sauté onion 2 minutes; add garlic, ginger, fresh tomatoes, cover and cook on low heat until soft, about 5 minutes.
3. Take out the onion mixture and add the greens to the pan, sauté 2 minutes; cover and cook on low heat about 10-15 minutes until soft; if needed, sprinkle 1 tbsp. water, cover and cook until soft. When done, add back the onion mixture, gran. garlic, lemon juice and a little salt and pepper to taste; stir well, add butter and cheese and serve.

Collard Greens with Faro (Serves: 2)

Once the greens are cooked, sprinkle some lemon juice on them before serving. Greens have iron, and lemon helps digest the iron.

Ingredients: 1 bunch about 6-8 ounces fresh small collard green leaves or beets leaves; 3 tbsp. olive oil, 1 cup chopped onion, 2 large garlic cloves chopped; ½ tsp. turmeric powder; salt and pepper to taste; 1 tsp. lime or lemon zest; 2 tbsp. lemon or lime juice; 1 cup cooked faro or quinoa (use 1-1/4 cup of blanching water from greens, add faro or quinoa, bring to a boil, boil for 8 minutes for faro and 5 minutes for quinoa; stir in 1 tbsp. olive oil, and a little salt and pepper, cover and set aside to soften). To serve: 2 tbsp. extra-virgin olive oil, grated parmesan cheese, sliced tomatoes and garlic toasts.

Wash each leaf of collard green under running cold water, and take out the bottom hard stems. Blanch them for 3 minutes in boiling water, and take out. When cool enough, slit the stems in half lengthwise, and thin-slice them about ¼-inch wide across, together with the stems.

Heat a large pan with olive oil, and fry the onion for 2 minutes on medium heat; add garlic, turmeric, salt, pepper; cover and let them cook for 5 minutes until onion is soft. Add the sliced greens and cook open for 5 minutes on medium-high heat, stirring them constantly, until soft. Add the faro or quinoa, sprinkle salt, pepper, zest and lemon juice, stir well and serve sprinkled with some extra virgin olive oil, cheese, and sliced tomatoes and toast on the side.

Kale Greens (Serves: 4-6)

When buying kale, try to buy small and less curly leaves. You can wash each leaf under running cold water; strip them off the stems and blanche them if using in salad. Slice thin across.
Ingredients: 2 tbsp. canola or olive oil; 1 tsp. caraway seeds; 2 large garlic cloves sliced; 1 tbsp. instant chicken broth (op); 1 tbsp. lemon juice or to taste; ½ tsp. gran garlic; ¼ tsp. dry oregano; ¼ tsp. dry rosemary; ½ cup grated parmesan cheese.

1. Wash the Kale leaves and strip them off the stems, hold in small bundles and slice them about ½ inch wide.
2. In a large heavy-bottom pan, on medium heat, add 1 tbsp. oil and caraway seeds. When seeds sputter, add garlic, stir a little and add greens; sauté 2 minutes, sprinkle 2 tbsp. water, cover and cook on medium heat, about 10 minutes. Stir well and cook on low heat, covered until soft, about 10 minutes. Sprinkle gran. garlic, oregano, rosemary, 1 tbsp. oil; stir on high heat, add lemon juice to taste. Serve sprinkled with grated cheese, no salt needed.

Tip: Greens in general are loaded with vitamins and mineral. Make sure you use some lemon or tomato sauce with them to digest the iron. Kale has calcium and iron both.

Wine Mushrooms (Serves: 8)

Around Easter, Thanksgiving and Christmas, you can find a large basket of the button or Asian mushrooms at the supermarkets. I can't resist and always buy them, and we all love them.

Ingredients : 40 ounces (1.13Kg) button mushrooms; 2 tbsp. canola or olive oil; 4 tbsp. unsalted melted butter; 1 cup good red wine; 1 cup orange juice, ½ cup teriyaki marinade and sauce or 2 tbsp. lemon juice; 3 tbsp. light brown sugar; ¼ tsp. each cumin powder, fennel seed powder, salt and fresh-ground black pepper.

1. Heat a large heavy-bottom non-reactive pan on medium high heat, add 1 tbsp. oil, move around to coat the pan; off-heat, add wine and orange juice, cover halfway with the lid and reduce to ½ C. Add teriyaki sauce (or sugar, cumin and fennel powder, salt and pepper) and reduce to ¾ cup all together.
2. With a lightly damp paper towel, wipe the mushrooms and slice them about 1/3 inch thick. Heat a large, cast-iron pan, on medium-high heat. When pan is hot, add 1 tbsp. oil and move around to coat the pan. Add about half of the sliced mushrooms and pour over 1 tbsp. melted butter all over. Do not disturb and let the mushrooms cook for 7-8 minutes open, until they are golden underneath. Turn them over and cook another 6-7 minutes, or until golden and most of the moisture has evaporated. Take them out on a dinner plate and keep them open. Repeat and cook rest of the mushrooms in batches. When done, take them of the pan and add them to the reduced sauce in the non-reactive pan. Mix well and let them cook on medium heat until they are almost dry.
3. Turn off the heat. Taste for seasoning. Leave them partially covered. Serve immediately or reheat and serve later.
    Tips: Mushrooms should be cooked, uncovered, on high heat. When all the liquid has been evaporated add flavoring and add the salt only at the end, so that it doesn't get watery. Sugar and sweet liquid burns on the bottom, so stir constantly.

Stuffed Salad Tomatoes

These are small salad tomatoes (campari), about 2-3-inches in diameter. Buy them firm on the vine, and let them sit in room temperature for 2-3 days; they will be dark red and very sweet.

Ingredients: 1 pound about 24 salad tomatoes; about ½ cup shredded white cheddar, goat or your favorite cheese; ¼ cup grated parmesan cheese; 1 tbsp. Dijon mustard; 1 tbsp. ketchup, olive oil to drizzle, salt and pepper to taste.
1. Wash, dry tomatoes, put them stem side down in a platter, and cut them half way through, about ½ to ¾-inch deep, on the top, but leave them attached (do not take them apart).
2. In a small bowl, mix shredded and grated cheeses, mustard, ketchup, salt and pepper. With a small utility knife, stuff each tomato with about 1 tsp. of mixture. Put the tomatoes on an aluminum foil-lined baking tray. Drizzle some olive oil over the stuffing, then sprinkle with some grated cheese all over on the top.
3. Preheat the broiler and broil the tomatoes about 5 minutes, until light brown. Serve them with salad, sandwiches and even with dinner.

Stuffed Plum (Roma) Tomatoes

Follow the above broiling procedure. For 6 plum tomatoes, scoop out the pulp, use all juice and pulp, and some parsley; 1 cup each boiled mashed potato and shredded cheese, 1 tbsp. each Dijon and ketchup, ¼ tsp. each: salt, pepper and garlic powder. Cut off the top, stuff the tomatoes and put the top back on. Broil them, sprinkled with olive oil and grated or shredded cheese, for 5-6 minutes.

Collard Greens (Serves: 4-6)

Collard greens are so easy to cook that once you cook them, you will cook them over and over. They are loaded with nutrients and go well with almost any dish.

Ingredients : 1 large bundle of fresh green collard greens, about 1-1/2 pounds (about 6 cup packed leaves); 1 packet instant chicken broth (op); ½ cup orange juice, 2 tbsp. lemon juice; ½ tsp. each granulated garlic and dry oregano; 2 tbsp. butter, ¼ to ½ cup grated parmesan cheese.

1. Wash and pat dry the leaves and tear them off the stems. Take a few leaves, stack them on top of each other, roll them up in a bundle, and thin slice them with a sharp utility knife, on a diagonal, slicing them on the left, slicing them on the right, and then slicing them at the middle so that the slices are small, small, diagonal and will cook fast. You can thin-slice the soft stems as well.
2. Heat a large sauté pan on medium-high heat, add orange and lemon juices, add the sliced leaves and sauté on high heat until they are wilted halfway. Add more orange juice if needed. Cover, and simmer on low for about 10-15 minutes until soft. Sprinkle chicken broth, gran. garlic, oregano and butter and sauté on high heat 1 minute, or until all the liquid has been evaporated. Serve sprinkled with cheese and with any dish, especially with fried chicken and grilled meat.

Tips: You can blanche the greens in boiling salted water about 3 minutes, then cool them in ice water, to keep the green color. Or you can sauté with or without liquid in the butter if they have soft green leaves (almost like spinach).

Roasted Japanese Eggplants (Serves: 6-8)

This is our favorite dish. It is so easy, quick and very tasty, and goes well with almost any meal as a side dish. Japanese eggplants are loaded with compounds that helps lower the LDL bad cholesterol.

Ingredients: About 2-1/2 pounds or about 6 long Japanese eggplants (try to buy evenly slim and light-colored; dark colored are matured and can have tough seeds); about 2 tbsp. canola or vegetable oil and extra for greasing the baking trays; 4 tbsp. chili powder or 1 pkg. taco seasoning mix; 1 tsp. lemon-salt seasoning mix; 1 tsp. granulated garlic; salt and fresh ground black pepper to taste.

1. Preheat oven to 400 degrees. Line 2 large baking trays (12x18 inches and about 1-inch sides) with double parchment paper or aluminum foil, and grease it well.
2. Trim the eggplants and starting from the wider end, slice diagonally into long slices about 1-inch wide. Sprinkle the cut side with salt right away (before they turn brown). Place them in a large bowl. Sprinkle with half of the chili powder or taco seasoning, some more salt and pepper to taste, then with half of the oil. Toss with a wooden spoon and then sprinkle again with rest of the seasoning. Spread out in the trays in single layer.
3. Bake open at 400 degrees for 15 minutes and covered with aluminum foil for about 10-15 minutes until soft. If you wish, you can sprinkle with more seasoning while they are hot.
4. Serve warm almost with any meal.
5.

Spinach Balls (M:12)Error! Bookmark not defined.

You can prepare these ahead and bake just before serving.

Ingredients: 1Pg., 8oz. Herbal dry bread stuffing; 1/4 cup grated cheese; 2 packages frozen chopped spinach cooked and drain well; 1/2cup minced onion; 6 large eggs; 3/4cup butter melted; 1tsp. each onion and mustard powder; 1/2tsp. garlic powder; 1/2cup grated cheddar cheese; 1/2tsp. each thyme and fresh ground black pepper; 1/4cup grated (dry) cheese.

Mix all ingredients in a bowl and make about 12 firm balls. Place on a foil lined baking tray and refrigerate. About 45 minutes before baking take them out in the room temperature. Bake in a preheated 350 degree oven for about 15 minutes covered. Serve as a side dish or for appetizer with chutney.

Spinach and Watercress with Cheese
(Palak Paneer) (Serves: 8-10)

This is a famous Indian Palak Paneer means spinach with cheese, and is easy to make. You can use all spinach or add some watercress. You can make without cheese and it still tastes very good.

Ingredients: 4 tbsp. canola oil; 2 pkgs. each 10 ounces (284g) frozen chopped spinach; 1 bag 4 ounces (113g) washed and dried fresh watercress (or use just 3 pkgs. of frozen spinach); about 4 large onions sliced; about ¾ to 1 pound plum tomatoes, cored and chopped; 1 tbsp. sugar; 2 tbsp. lemon juice; 2 large bay leaves, vein taken out, crumbled very small and ground into powder in a grinder or coffee grinder together with 1 tbsp. grinded cardamom seeds; 1 tsp. turmeric powder; 1 tsp. fenugreek powder (op); ½ tsp. granulated garlic; ½ tsp. cinnamon powder; salt and pepper to taste; 1 can 13.5 ounces coconut milk; 1 pound browned, ready-to-use paneer cubes (you can make at home or buy at the Indian grocery stores. To serve: rice or poories.

Heat a medium stainless steel or non-reactive pot on low heat. Add oil, bay leaves, cardamom, turmeric, fenugreek, garlic, cinnamon, and sauté the spices 15 seconds. Add onion and little salt and pepper increase the heat to medium-high and sauté onion for 5-6 minutes, until they are transparent. Add the tomatoes and sauté another 5 minutes. Add the spinach and stir well. Reduce the heat to medium and cook spinach at constant simmer, for 15-20 minutes covered, until wilted and soft.

Puree the vegetables and raw watercress in a blender in two batches and pour back into the pot again. Add sugar, lemon juice, coconut milk, salt and pepper to taste; bring them back to simmer on medium-high heat. Stir well, add the paneer (cheese cubes); cover, reduce the heat to medium and simmer for 10-15 minutes until cheese is heated through. Serve with rice or poories.

Tips:

1. This vegetable freezes very well. Freeze in individual containers, defrost overnight; just simmer on low and serve. Do not add cheese if you are going to freeze. Add cheese cubes just before serving, heat through and serve.

2. Watercress contains about 18 vitamins and minerals.

Peas with Cheese (Matar Paneer)

Follow the recipe as above, up to Number 1. Puree the mixture and then add 3 pkgs. 10 ounces (284g) frozen peas to the mixture.

American frozen peas are soft and you can add them uncooked to the hot tomato mixture. But if you are using Indian frozen peas, they are hard and you have to brown them first in a little purified butter (2 tbsp. ghee); add a few tablespoon of water, cover and cook on low-heat until they are soft, and then add to the pureed mixture. Add the cheese (paneer) at very end.

Mashed Potatoes (Serves: 4)

Ingredients: About 1-1/4 pounds, or 4 large yukon gold or red potatoes; ¼ cup grated cheese; about ½ cup 2% or whole milk or half-and-half; ¼ cup fresh sliced scallion or chives; or ¼ tsp. each: granulated garlic and dry rosemary; at end stir in 2-4 tbsp. softened butter (op); salt and fresh ground black pepper to taste.

Peel the potatoes (or leave the peel on if using the red potatoes) and boil them in a medium pot with just enough water to cover them. Bring them to a boil on high heat, then simmer on low heat until soft, about 15 minutes. Stir them twice during the cooking. If potatoes still have some water left, then cook them open and dry out much of the liquid. Do not discard the cooking water, that's where all the flavor is. Add the milk and bring them to a boil again. Boil potatoes for another 5 minutes with the milk, then sprinkle the cheese, granulated garlic, rosemary and a pinch of salt and pepper; lower the heat and mash them right in the pot over the cutting board. Fold in the green onion and stir in the melted butter; salt and pepper to taste just before serving. Serve immediately or keep them warm over the simmering water.

If you want to make potatoes creamy: Boil the ½ cup heavy cream and 2 tbsp. of butter and whisk in the hot potatoes instead of milk. You can also add boiled potatoes in the food processor or blender, and pour in heated cream and butter, and cream all together. But here you will need 1 cup of heavy cream and 4 tbsp. of butter.

If you want to make with spinach or the kale, blanch the greens for 3 minutes, cool them in an ice-water bath, let them rinse out in a tilted platter, pat dry, slice into ½-inch wide, and then stir in the mashed potatoes.

I like to add 1 cup cooked and mashed peas together with ½ bulb of roasted garlic squeezed in, and then fold in the chopped roasted red bell peppers.

When you add some fresh herbs together with garlic, potatoes get tasty and you do not need to add too much of butter or cream.

Tip: Red potatoes are healthier and good for the brain. A substance 'choline' fund in red potato is very beneficial for the brain. So do not peel them, scrub clean and cook whole.

Sliced and Baked Acorn Squash (Serves: 2-4)

Acorn squash sliced and roasted is easy to make. Just prepare the glaze ahead, roast the squash and brush the glaze. Leave the skin on, you will have more fiber and nourishment. Buy the squash with some yellow on the skin.

Ingredients: For the Squash: 2 tbsp. olive oil; line a baking sheet with parchment paper, and grease it well; 1 whole acorn squash washed, cut across, scooped out and then sliced across in ½-inch wide semicircles and placed on the baking sheet; salt and pepper to taste.

Glaze: 1 tbsp. butter; ¼ cup marmalade or apricot jam; 2 tbsp. maple syrup;1 tsp. paprika; ½ tsp. cayenne pepper or to taste; salt to taste.

For the Glaze: Just before squash is done, melt all ingredients in a pot, bring to a boil and take off the heat. Keep warm until needed.

For the Squash: Preheat oven at 350 degrees. Drizzle the squash with salt and pepper, then with olive oil. Bake in a preheated oven for about 30 minutes, or until squash is tender. Brush with the glaze, turn over and glaze the other side. Bake another 5-6 minutes at 400 degrees. Serve warm.

Whole Baked Acorn Squash (Serves: 4)

This is the easiest and healthiest way to cook acorn squash.

Ingredients: 2 acorn squash, same size, about 1-1/4 pounds total; ¾ cup maple syrup; 2 tbsp. butter, plus extra to brush; ½ cup chopped nuts; ½ cup dry cranberries; fresh-grated nutmeg; salt and pepper to taste.

Preheat oven to 350 degrees. Line a rimmed baking sheet with foil. Make 4 aluminum foil rings to hold the squash halves. Cut the squash in half, scoop out the seeds and fibers. Brush the top with butter, then place the halved squash on the baking sheet in rings. Evenly divide the butter, maple syrup, nuts and fill in the squash. Grate a little nutmeg over each squash, then sprinkle a little salt and pepper. Pour about 1-2 tbsp. water into each squash halves to come up to ½-inch below the rim. Bake at 350 degrees, for about 45 minutes, or until the squash is soft. Serve warm holding with the rings.

Succotash with Avocado Dressing (Serves: 4-6)

This is a fresh bean salad with avocado. You can use black beans from the can or fermented beans from the can. Fermented beans are very salty, so use less.

Ingredients: 2 tbsp. butter; 2 fresh corns husk removed; 1 can 15 ounces (425g) black beans drained, washed and drained again, or about ½ cup (6 ounces) fermented beans (black), drained or 1cup frozen peas; 1 pkg. 12 ounces (340g) frozen shelled soybeans or lima beans cooked per package direction.

Avocado Dressing: 2 large garlic cloves crushed well; 5 tbsp. cider vinegar; 2 tbsp. Dijon mustard; 1 tbsp. sugar; ¼ tsp. salt and fresh-ground black pepper or to taste; 1/ 2c extra virgin olive oil; ½ cup sliced green onion; 1 ripe avocado.

1. Scrape the corn kernels in a bowl. Place the kernels in a large heavy-bottom pan, then scrape the corn milk off the cobs into the pan over the corn kernels. This is what it gives the best taste. Now add butter, peas, a little salt and pepper and sauté the corn on medium-high heat for 5 minutes, or until they are warmed through; cover and cook on very low heat for another 6-8 minutes. Take off the heat and place them in a large bowl. Add soybeans to warm up.

2. To make the dressing, whisk together garlic, vinegar, mustard, sugar, salt and pepper together, then whisk in the olive oil. Cut the avocado in half, take out the pit, and score the pulp inside the

skin into ½-inch cubes and fold the avocado cubes into the vinaigrette; cover airtight and set aside in refrigerator.

3. When ready to serve, place a portion of salad on serving plates, sprinkle fermented beans, and pour the avocado dressing on the top. Sprinkle with the green onions and serve.

Chutneys, Glazes, Sauces, Pickles etc.

Chutneys

We live on chutney and make fresh almost every day. Chutney makes everything tasty. You can mix in with the vegetables or pour over the toasts, use in sandwiches, roasted and baked food to give extra flavor. The best use, I think, of chutney is to fix burned food and make it tasty by adding more flavor and nutrients (discard the burnt part and use leftover with chutney). Chutneys are very versatile. They go well with meat, poultry, vegetables, bread, rice and for sure with the fried and grilled food. Leftover chutneys can be used for marinade, gravy, dipping sauce, rub and you can even cook rice and potatoes and other dishes with it. Chutneys are also loaded with vitamins and minerals when made mostly with fresh ingredients.

A simple meal can be perked up just serving with chutney and raita (yogurt relish). Store all fresh-made chutneys in a non-reactive bowl or a jar (glass or china) in the refrigerator and use them within one or two days of making. The secret of making chutney is to use as many fresh herbs and spices as possible and use as little water as possible; add salt at the end with a rubber or wooden spatula so it does not get watery. Chutney should not be runny, should have a little thicker consistency; it may be pureed or a little chunky. I prefer making it in the food processor, first pulse the ingredients and then grind them as per your taste.

The chutneys made with the fruits are better to make a little chunky; it looks better as well tastes better. When serving chutney, either pour or use a wooden or rubber spatula or spoon so you do not spoil. This goes with any sauce, chutney or paste. Store chutneys in a nonreactive bowl or a glass jar, covered in the refrigerator for about 3 days.

Amla Chutney- Indian Gooseberries (Y: about 1 Cup)

Amla is a light green vegetable, round, hard about 2-inch diameter, with a pit in the middle, a little sour tasting and loaded with vitamins, iron and mineral. It is good for eyes, hair, nails, etc. and is known to reduce cholesterol. We had this chutney almost every day with the meal. It is hard to find fresh, but you can find frozen, in the brine (pickled), and powder form in most Indian grocery stores.

Ingredients: 1 cup brined amla (in salt and vinegar water) chopped, 1 tab fresh-roasted caraway seeds, 1 medium onion chopped, ½ cup packed leaves and tender stems of cilantro (dhaniya) or parsley, 1 large garlic clove peeled and chopped, 1 or 2 serrano fresh green chili or 1 seeded and chopped jalepeno; salt to taste.

In a blender or food processor, grind the roasted caraway seeds, then grind the garlic and onion with a little water just until coarsely ground. Now add rest of the ingredients and puree with as little water as possible. Store in a small bowl in refrigerator up 4-5 days covered.

You do the same thing with the powdered amla. Add amla powder with cilantro and whisk in 4 tbsp. or to taste; lemon Juice at the end.

Frozen Amla Chutney (Y: 2-1/2 Cups)

This is very easy and tasty.

Ingredients: 1 bag, 1 pound (454Gm Frozen Amla, defrosted overnight in the refrigerator; 2 cups fresh chopped cilantro or parsley; 2 large fresh cloves of garlic chopped; 4 tbsp. or juice of 1 large lemon; salt and pepper to taste.

In a small pot with ½ cup of cold water, bring the Amla to a boil, reduce the heat and simmer on low for about 45 minutes. Cool and spilt each in half and take out the hard pit from the center and discard; chop the amla. In a blender add garlic, about ¾ C water, cilantro and puree first. Then add the amla and puree; add as little water as need to keep the chutney thick. Take out the pureed amla in a medium bowl and stir in lemon juice and salt and pepper to taste. You can freeze half of the chutney in an airtight container in a plastic bag up to a month.

Avocado Chutney (Y: about 1-1/2 Cups)

Avacado turns brown very fast, so cut it only just before using it. Avacado chutney is made in two parts. First, you grind all the ingredients and set them aside, covered in the refrigerator and when you are ready to serve you mash up the avocado in the lemon juice, add spices, garnish with cilantro and serve immediately.

Ingredients:1 tab roasted caraway seeds, ½ cup chopped onion, 2 serrano chilis or to taste, ½ cup fresh-squeezed lemon juice, 1-inch fresh ginger, ¼ cup tomatoes in oil, salt and fresh ground black pepper to taste, 2 ripe haas avocados, 1 tsp. chat masala (op), and about ½ cup chopped cilantro divided.

In a blender or food processor, grind all ingredients except half of the cilantro, avocado, chaat masala and lemon juice. Set them aside, covered, in the refrigerator until needed.

Just before serving, put the lemon juice in a glass bowl, then cut avocado in half; take out the pit (grab the pit with the sharp edge of the knife and discard), and scoop out the pulp into the lemon juice. Mash it well into the juice; then add rest of the ground ingredients. Garnish with remaining cilantro and serve immediately.

Coconut Chutney (Y: about 1 Cup)

In India, coconut is grown mostly in south India and that's where this chutney is widely used, and each family has its own version. You can make this chutney from fresh coconut but coconut powder is just as good. This is a chutney that is traditionally served with the dosa (a fresh-cooked jumbo wrap, made with rice and beans, and stuffed with spicy potatoes and some vegetables) and with other south Indian dishes.

Ingredients: 1 tab corn oil, 1 tsp. black mustard seeds, about 5 fresh curry leaves or 2 medium bay leaves, 1 slice of white bread toasted and cut into small pieces, or ½ cup cooked chick peas, ½ medium onion chopped, 1 or 2 serrano chilis, 1 cup packed fine ground coconut power, 1/3 cup fresh-squeezed lemon juice, salt and white pepper (op) to taste.

Heat a small sauté pan on medium heat; when hot add oil, increase heat to medium high and add mustard seeds; cover at once and cook, shaking pan just about 30 seconds. When seeds start popping add curry or bay leaves and stir and cook, just about 30 seconds or until light brown; take off the heat and set aside.

In a blender or food processor, grind chickpeas with a little water, add rest of the ingredients except the bread and puree well; then add the bread pieces at the end (if using) and puree just to combine. Add the salt and/or white pepper to taste, by hand using a wooden or rubber spatula so that it does not create any water. At the end, stir in the mustard seed mixture.

Cilantro Chutney (Coriander or Dhania) (Y: about 1 Cup)

This chutney is the main chutney, made almost every day for the meal. This chutney also has several versions and can be the base for several other fresh chutneys like mint, yogurt, tamarind and some fresh fruits. This recipe is very simple as well as tasty.

Ingredients: 2 cups chopped and packed cilantro leaves and soft stems; 1 large garlic clove peeled, ¼ cup chopped fresh onion, 1-inch fresh ginger, ¼ cup fresh-squeezed lemon juice, 1 tbsp. chat masala (homemade or bought from Indian grocery), ¼ cup toasted bread crumbs or 1 slice of bread toasted and torn into pieces; salt and pepper to taste.

In a food processor or blender, combine garlic, onion, cilantro, lemon juice and about ¼ C of water; pulse, then fine-grind all ingredients; add a little more water if needed and puree it again. Add bread or bread crumbs, grind again. Add chat masala, salt and pepper and mix well by hand. Store in refrigerator, in a non-reactive bowl, covered for about 3-4 days.

Healthy Cilantro Chutney (M: about 1 Cup)

Fresh chutney is made with fresh green serrano peppers (hot). If you like, add 1-2 or to taste. Cilantro has calcium; sesame seeds have magnesium, zinc, minerals and coconut has Omega-3 fatty acids, and mint is very refreshing, Lime juice and zest have healing power.

Ingredients: 2 large garlic cloves chopped; ¼ cup chopped onion; 2 cups packed cilantro leaves, chopped and thin sliced soft stems; 1cup fresh mint leaves or 1/4cup dry mint leaves; 2 tbsp. toasted sesame seeds; 2 tbsp. unsweetened coconut powder (op); ½ cup lime juice (about 3 large); 1 tsp. lime zest; salt and pepper to taste.

1. In a blender or food processor grind sesame seeds into powder and take out in a medium non-reactive bowl. Now grind garlic in 2 tbsp. water, then add the onion and puree well. Add lime juice and grind half of the cilantro well. Add a little more water, if needed, (1 tbsp. at a time) and grind rest of the cilantro and mint.
2. Take the chutney out in the same bowl and mix well with sesame seeds, salt and pepper to taste.
3. Store covered, in the refrigerator, for up to 3-4 days.
4. Note: First grind the fresh herbs in lime juice, if needed only then add little water at a time. Add salt, pepper and grinded sesame seeds by hand in the bowl, so you will not need too much liquid.

Cranberry, Apple and Pomegranate Chutney (Y: about 2-1/2 Cups)

This chutney is made with all healthy fruits and berries, and looks and tastes very good. This chutney lasts up to a month in the refrigerator and gets better with age. Just use a plastic spoon to get it out of the jar so you do not spoil it.

Ingredients: 1 tsp canola oil, 1 tsp. cumin seeds, ¼ tsp. red pepper flakes (op); 1cup pomegranate juice (about 2 medium pomegranates); 1 apple peeled, cut, cored and grated (if using dry cranberries then you need 2 grated apples); 1 10 oz. package of fresh cranberries or 1 cup dried cranberries, 3 tabs fresh-squeezed lemon juice, ¼ cup packed brown sugar; salt and fresh-ground black pepper to taste.

Heat a heavy bottom, nonreactive medium saucepan on medium. When heated add oil, increase heat to medium-high, add cumin seeds; when seeds start popping take the saucepan off the heat; add red pepper flakes, stir a little and put back on medium heat. Add pomegranate juice, sugar and bring to boil; lower the heat and reduce the juice by half on low heat. Add grated apple (or apples) bring to boil again and let it simmer, stirring occasionally for about 15 minutes; add cranberries, lemon juice and ¼ tsp. salt and stir well. Let it cook about 30 minutes until apple is soft and mixture is thick like paste. Taste and add seasoning as needed and cook 5 minutes longer. Take off the heat, cool and serve or store in refrigerator for later use.

Any cooked chutney can be made either juicy or thick in consistency just by cooking it longer and evaporating the liquid.

Hummus (Y: about 1-1/2 Cups)

This is also very versatile chutney or spread. Even though it can last longer, it is best to use within two or three days of making.

Ingredients: 3 tab. fresh roasted white sesame seeds; fresh roasted each: 1 tab caraway, 1 tsp. fennel seeds, 1 16-ounce can or fresh cooked chickpeas, drained; 2 garlic cloves peeled and chopped, 2-inch fresh chopped ginger, ½ cup chopped onion, 3 to 4 serrano chilis or to taste, 2 tabs apple-cider vinegar, 1 tsp. prepared mustard, salt and fresh ground black pepper to taste, 3 tabs extra virgin olive oil divided. For garnish: ¼ cup fresh chopped cilantro and ½ cup fine-chopped plum tomatoes.

In a blender or food processor first dry-grind caraway, fennel and sesame seeds. Then add fresh herbs and spices: onion, garlic, ginger, serrano chili, vinegar, mustard, about ½ tsp. salt and puree them together; then add the chickpeas and ¼ cup of water and puree them together; and if needed add a little more water (about 1 tbsp. of water at a time). Then slowly pour in 2 tablespoon of olive oil through the feed tube while machine is running. Taste and correct the seasoning. Take out the chutney in a bowl and garnish first with 1 tablespoon of olive oil, then with chopped tomatoes, and finally with chopped cilantro leaves. Serve or keep covered in the refrigerator airtight until needed.

Mango Chutney 1, Hot & Sour (Y: about 2 cups)

If you want real sour chutney, then buy green and very firm mangoes. Otherwise, buy green mangoes with a little yellow skin. You can make several different types of mango chutneys. This one is made with fresh green mangoes, without cooking.

Ingredients: 1 tab. roasted caraway seeds, 1 tsp. roasted fennel seeds, ½ tsp. salt, 2 medium green mangoes peeled and pulp taken out, and chopped, ½ cup chopped onion, 1 fresh garlic clove, 2 inches fresh chop ginger, 3 to 4 serrano chilis or to taste, 1 cup chop cilantro soft stems and leaves, 2 tabs honey, ¼ tsp. turmeric powder, salt and fresh-ground black pepper to taste.

In a food processor or blender, first dry-grind toasted caraway and fennel seeds with salt. Then add remaining ingredients and grind with a very small amount of water to a thick paste. Taste and correct the seasoning. Refrigerate in a nonreactive jar or a bowl, covered until needed.

Mango Chutney- 2, Hot & Sweet (Y: about 2 Cups)

This is my favorite one, easy, tasty and lasts long, for almost a month. In this chutney you can add your favorite nuts.

Ingredients: 1 tsp. canola oil, 1 tbsp. cumin seeds, ½ tsp. red pepper flakes, 1 tsp. black mustard seeds, ½ cup sugar, ½ tsp. salt, ½ tsp. crushed black peppercorn or to taste, ¼ cup dry cranberries, ¼ cup peeled and shredded almonds (op), 4 tbsp. apple cider vinegar, 2 large green mangoes a little ripe (with some yellow skin), firm-grated on the large holes of the grater.

Heat a heavy-bottom, non-reactive sauté pan on medium heat. When hot, add cumin seeds, raise heat to medium-high and add mustard seeds; when seeds start popping take off the heat, add almonds and toast for 15 seconds, shaking the pan. Put the pan back on the heat and add grated mango, and stir well for 1 minute, then add rest of the ingredients and keep on sautéing on medium high heat for 2 minutes, until mixture starts bubbling.

Reduce heat to low and keep mixture simmering, covered, for about 30 minutes until softened and all the liquid is evaporated, and chutney is thick in consistency, almost like a paste. Remove from heat, fill in the jar, cool, then refrigerate in an airtight jar until needed.

Mint Chutney-1 (M: about 2 Cups)

In India, we make mint chutney all summer long to keep cool from the hot weather. You need fresh mint and tamarind paste to make a tasty mint chutney.

Ingredients: 1-1/2 cups packed fresh mint leaves and soft stems; 2 cups packed fresh cilantro (dhania) leaves and soft stems chopped; 1 medium, about 1 cup, onion chopped; 2 tbsp. jaggery or light brown sugar; 3-4 or to taste serrano peppers chopped; 1 tbsp. tamarind concentrate; about ¼ tsp. or to taste salt.

In a blender, puree mint and serrano peppers with ½ cup water. Add cilantro and another ½ cup water and puree all; add onion and puree well. Add tamarind concentrate, jiggery or sugar and puree well. Pour in a non-reactive bowl and add salt to taste with a wooden spoon. Refrigerate covered with a lid, up to 5 days. Pour or use a wooden or a plastic spoon to serve.

Tips:

1. This chutney goes well with any roasted meat, potatoes, rice and bread. Mint goes well with cilantro. Use as little water as possible.
2. When making chutney, mix the salt at the end, by hand (not in the blender), otherwise it will get watery.

Peach Chutney (Y: about 2 Cups)

This fruit chutney can be made with almost any firm, juicy and flavorful fruit like apple, mango, plum, pear, etc. It is fresh-made so use it within a day or two. If you do not have green mango pickle (hot, sour and sweet-tasting), you can use one medium green mango with extra salt, cayenne pepper and sugar to taste.

Ingredients: 1 pound (about 3 large) fresh, firm and hard peaches, blanched in boiling water for 5 minutes, peeled, stoned and chopped, ½ cup green mango pickle, ½ cup chopped onion, 1 large clove of garlic, ½ cup packed cilantro leaves and soft stems, 1 tsp. sugar, salt and cayenne pepper to taste.

In a blender or food processor, grind all ingredients together. Taste, season with salt, pepper and sugar as needed, refrigerate covered until ready to serve.

Tomato Chutney (Y: ab. 2 Cups)

This chutney or relish tastes superb with a little work.

Ingredients: 6 large plum tomatoes (about 2 pounds), 1 large onion peeled and cut in ½ lengthwise, 1 red bell pepper, 2 large garlic cloves peeled, 2 tabs canola oil divided, ½ tsp. dry rosemary, salt and fresh ground black pepper, 1 tsp. cumin seeds, ½ tsp. red pepper flakes, 2 tbsp. cider vinegar, ¼ tsp. granulated garlic powder, ½ tsp. dry oregano, 2 tbsp. sugar.

Preheat oven to 400 degrees. Line up a large heavy-bottom baking tray (or broiler tray) with aluminum foil, spray or grease the foil with some oil. Core and cut tomatoes in half lengthwise and line them up near the edge on the tray, then onion and garlic and red bell pepper in the middle. Drizzle about 1 tbsp. of olive oil on the vegetables, and salt and fresh-ground black pepper all over, and bake open for about 25 minutes or until tomatoes are soft, turning the tray around once for even cooking. Take out of oven and let it cool.

When vegetables are cool enough to handle, chop them fine. Heat a heavy-bottomed, nonreactive sauté pan on medium heat; when pan is hot, add 1 table oil and brown the cumin seeds. Increase the heat to medium-high and add roasted chopped vegetables, red pepper flakes, vinegar, sugar, garlic powder, oregano, salt and coarse-ground black pepper to taste; bring it to a boil. Taste and correct the seasoning. Let it simmer, open for about 15 minutes until thick in consistency. Cool completely, then store in refrigerator, covered up to a week.

Tamarind Chutney (y: about 2 Cups)

This is a very famous chutney that my mother used to make. She always used raisins that taste good as well as look good when drizzled over the food.

Ingredients: ¾ cup water, ½ cup sugar, 1 tsp. cardamom seeds ground fine, ¾ cup apple sauce, ¼ cup tamarind concentrate, 1 to 2 serrano chili, ½ cup packed fresh cilantro, 2 tab chopped-fresh mint, ½ cup golden raisins, salt and cayenne pepper to taste.

In a saucepan, bring water to a boil, add sugar and cardamom powder and stir well to dissolve the sugar; lower the heat and add apple sauce, tamarind concentrate and raisins, let it simmer on very low heat covered about 15 minutes. Puree cilantro, mint and the serrano pepper in very little water in a blender and add to the mixture. Bring the mixture to a boil and simmer about 10 minutes until it is a slightly thick consistency. Taste and adjust the seasoning. Take off the heat, cool and keep in an airtight jar in the refrigerator for up to a week. Sprinkle over food or use as a dipping sauce.

Tamarind Concentrate: It is easy to buy tamarind paste in an Indian or Asian grocery store. But if you want to make your own, then buy 1 pound whole or broken dried tamarind pieces, peel them, then boil them in 4 cups of water in a nonreactive saucepan, and simmer, stirring often for about 2 hours. When all the extract is out, strain the juice and discard the seeds. Now heat a large heavy-bottom frying pan with 1 tsp. of oil, add the juice and ½ cup sugar, ½ tsp. salt and ¼ tsp. fresh-ground black pepper, and let it simmer; reduce to 1 cup. Store in refrigerator for about a month and use as a base to make the sauces and chutneys or use in cooking.

Yogurt-Cilantro Chutney (Y: about 2 Cups

)

This is a very tasty chutney that you can use almost every day, on almost any food. It is good to use with fried food to cut down on saturated fat. You can use 1 recipe of coriander chutney, just reduce the lemon juice in half, and add 2 pounds (about 4 C) of low-fat plain yogurt; stir well and add salt to taste and serve.

Ingredients: You can also make an easy version by grinding: 1 Tab toasted caraway seeds, ½ Tsp. curry powder, 2 large garlic cloves, 1-inch fresh ginger, 1 or 2 serrano chili, 1 cup packed cilantro soft stems and leaves, with ½ cup of water and then add to 1 pound (about 2 cups) low-fat plain yogurt; salt and pepper to taste, combine all and stir with a wooden spoon by hand. Store in a non-reactive bowl for almost up a week.

You can use regular or low-fat plain yogurt. Both have same results and by using low-fat yogurt, you will cut down on calories.

TIPS: To thicken the chutney: if you are cooking the ingredients then use a nonreactive pan and keep on simmering the mixture, about 10-15 minutes extra or until liquid is evaporated and chutney has a thick consistency; and if you are just pureeing the fresh ingredients, then use a slice of toasted bread, cooked chickpeas or toasted nuts like walnuts and almonds, etc. to thicken the chutney. You can also soak ¼ cup peeled and split mung beans in a little water for ½ hour and then cook them in ½ cup of water, and a pinch of salt, covered until soft; then grind or puree with rest of the ingredients. Mung beans are almost transparent and have a very mild flavor in the chutney.

Apple Relish (Serves: 4-6)

You can use this relish on almost anything: Pork chops, grilled food, ice cream, pudding, etc. It is tasty and easy as well as healthy.

Ingredients: 4 Granny Smith apples; 2 tbsp. apple cider vinegar; 2 tbsp. peeled and cubed ½-inch fresh ginger; ½ cup dry cranberries; 2 tbsp. sugar or to taste; ½ tsp. salt; ¼ tsp. fresh-grated black or white pepper; 1-2-inches long cinnamon stick; ½ cup water.

1. Peel, core and grate apples. Combine all of the ingredients in a non-reactive, medium pot. Bring to a boil, stir well, cover, lower the heat and simmer for about 45 minutes until soft and all the liquid is gone. Stir once during cooking and add a little more warm water if needed.
2. Use immediately or cool and refrigerate up to 4 days covered in a porcelain or a glass bowl.

Red Cabbage Relish (Serves: 8-10)

Do you know that red color fruits and vegetables are very healthy for you? So use as much as possible of red cabbage, beets, red onion, red lettuce, red or purple carrots, tomatoes, etc. Red cabbage is very common in Germany. In the 1970s, when I was in Berlin, I often bought food at the Berlin University cafeteria. They served Sauerbraten with Red Cabbage, and gave large purple grapes for the fruits, a healthy meal all the way.

Ingredients: 1 small red cabbage (discard the outer leaves if bruised), cut in quarters, cored, and thin sliced, about 5-6 cups; ½ cup apple cider vinegar; ¼ tsp. celery seeds; 1 cup water; ½ cup dry cranberries; ½ cup light brown sugar or to taste; 1 tsp. salt; ½ tsp. fresh-ground black pepper; 1 cup fresh or drained canned pineapple.

1. Combine all ingredients in a non-reactive pot, bring to a boil, stir well, cover, lower the heat and simmer for 45 to 50 minutes until cabbage is soft. Taste for the seasoning and add salt, pepper, sugar as needed.
2. Serve with grilled meat, German food, or almost with any food on the side. Store in a glass or porcelain bowl covered up to 3-4 days.

Tasty Pepper Relish (M: about 4-1/2 C)

This versatile relish is made with about eight different types of peppers to give a unique flavor. It goes very well with bread, vegetables, meat and the seafood.

Ingredients: Dry roast in a cast-iron pan for about 5 minutes on medium heat or until spices are fragrant; 1 tbsp. each: caraway seeds, fennel seeds, 2 medium bay leaves, black mustard, coriander seeds. Grind half of the seed mixture and broken bay leaves, and leave rest of the roasted seed as whole.

1 tsp. canola oil; 2 tbsp. butter; 1 c chopped onions; 1 tsp. granulated garlic; ½ tsp. turmeric; 1 Granny Smith apple peeled, cored and grated; all peppers seeded and chopped: 1 red bell pepper; 2 long anaheim, 2 poblano, 2 jalapeno, 2 Italian fryer; 1 tsp. cayenne pepper; 2 tbsp. paprika; 1 c sliced pickled hot cherry peppers, 1 c sugar; ¼ c chopped fresh mint leaf; ½ c cider vinegar; salt and fresh-ground black pepper to taste.

1. Heat a non-reactive pot on medium heat; when hot, add the oil and the butter and sauté onion with garlic and a little salt for 5 minutes. Add the grated apple and sauté 1 minute; cover with the lid and cook for 5 minutes. Add all peppers and stir a little, then cover and simmer on low for 10-15 minutes, stirring occasionally until the peppers are soft.
2. Move the peppers on one side, add the sugar, mint, vinegar, salt and pepper to taste. Stir until sugar is melted. Add half of the roasted and ground spices, simmer on low, uncovered for 10 minutes or until liquid is mostly gone and thickened. Stir in rest of the roasted whole spices. Take off the heat, cool and refrigerate covered until needed, up to one week.

Sauces and Condiments, Etc.

Whenever possible, use the zest and the juice of the lime. They both are very healthy. Take the zest out of the lime, lemon or the orange with a microplane zester, they zest very fine and you can use the zest over the salad and even over the desserts in preparing and in serving

.

Bechamel Sauce (M:1cup)

This sauce comes from France. It is a basic sauce you can use to make other sauces.

Ingredients: 2Tbsp. butter; 2Tbsp. all-purpose; 1cup heated whole milk; salt and white pepper to taste; pinch of fresh grated nutmeg.

Heat a large saucepan on medium heat and brown flour and butter until it is very light brown and cooked through. Take pan off the heat and slowly whisk in the milk. If you have any lumps, take out the mixture and strain back into the pan. Place the pan back on the heat, add salt and pepper, and whisk continuously until thick. Serve warm to your finished dishes garnished with a little nutmeg.

Variations:

Almond Sauce: Follow the recipe above. Use almond milk or 1/4cup lightly toasted slivered almond grinded into 3/4cup milk.

Coconut Sauce: Follow the recipe above. Warm coconut milk instead of whole milk, over simmering water or on low heat.

Creamy Mustard Sauce: Follow the recipe of béchamel sauce. When it is done, turn off heat and whisk in the Dijon type mustard to taste (about 1Tbsp.).

Barbecue Sauces

Mostly the barbecue sauces are vinegar- and tomato-based, but we also like the mango based. It's all up to you, which sauce you prefer. For the ribs we prefer vinegar-based and for the chicken we prefer the tomato-based. Mango-based sauce is more fruity and can be used on pulled pork, fish, etc.

Basic Barbecue Sauce (M: about 2 cups)

This is a thick barbecue sauce. Do not use too much oil so that it will stick better.

Ingredients: About 2 tbsp. canola oil; 1 cup chopped fine onion; 2 tbsp. chopped garlic cloves; ¼ cup fine grated fresh ginger; 1 jalapeno seeded and thin-sliced; 2 tbsp. cumin powder; 3 tbsp. tomato paste; ¼ cup Worcestershire sauce; ½ cup packed light brown sugar; 1/3 cup cider vinegar; 1 cup tomato ketchup; 1 tbsp. fine-ground cardamom seeds (op); 2 tbsp. fine-ground fennel seeds; 1 tsp. each granulated garlic and onion powder; 1 tsp. cayenne pepper; salt and fresh-ground black pepper to taste; 2tbsp. grated semi-sweet chocolate.

Heat a medium non-reactive pot on medium heat. Add oil and cook onion for 8 minutes stirring often. Add garlic, ginger and jalapeno and cook for 5 minutes. Add the tomato paste and cook stirring for 5 minutes. Now add rest of the ingredients except the chocolate, and bring it to a boil. Reduce the heat to a constant simmer, and cook the sauce covered on low heat for 15 minutes. Stir in the chocolate and take off the heat; keep covered for 10 minutes and use or transfer to a clean and dry glass jar; cool completely and refrigerate until needed. Store up to two weeks or freeze up to 2 months in a non-reactive container, wrapped with paper towels and placed in a plastic bag.

Vinegar Based Barbecue Sauce (M: 2-3/4 C)

This is a light and tasty BBQ sauce that goes well with almost with any meat, but the pork, fish, and vegetables taste best.

Ingredients: 1 tbsp. canola oil; ½ c each chopped: onion, celery and carrots; 2 large garlic cloves sliced; 1 large bay leaf; ¼ tsp. cayenne pepper; 1 tbsp. fennel seeds crushed lightly; ½ tsp. salt or to taste.

For the Syrup: 1 c granulated sugar; 1 c water; ¾ c maple syrup or any pancake syrup; ½ c plus 1 tbsp. cider vinegar; 2 fresh mint sprigs and 4 cilantro sprigs crushed lightly; 4 tbsp. prepared brown mustard; 1 tbsp. chili powder mix; 2 tbsp. ketchup; ¼ tsp. each salt and pepper or to taste.

Heat a large sauté pan on medium heat. Add the oil and sauté onion, celery, carrots, garlic for about 8 minutes or until translucent. Add 1 cup water, bay leaf, cayenne, fennel seeds, salt, and bring to a boil and simmer for 20 minutes. Strain the liquid, it should be about ½ cup.

In a pot, prepare the syrup. Heat water and sugar on medium heat, stirring until sugar is dissolved. Whisk in the mint, cilantro, cayenne, maple syrup, mustard, vinegar and bring it to a boil. Reduce the heat to low. In a cup, mix ketchup, chili powder, salt and pepper and vegetable liquid, and stir in the syrup in the pot. Simmer all on low heat for 15-20 minutes and turn off the heat. When ready to use just warm the syrup and brush on the meat.

Seafood Barbecue Sauce (M: about 1-1/2 C)

Even though this is for seafood, you can use it for almost anything. Just make sure you do not add too much of the fish sauce.

Ingredients: 1 tsp. canola or sesame oil (untoasted); 1 tbsp. onion powder; 1 tsp. granulated garlic; 1 tsp. ground cumin; ½ c concentrated frozen orange juice thawed; ¼ c ketchup; 2 tbsp. Worcestershire sauce; 1 tbsp. low-sodium soy sauce; 1 tsp. good fish sauce; ¼ c to 1/3 c sriracha sauce; 2 tsp. cider vinegar; ½ c cola; 1 tbsp. butter, salt if needed.

Heat a heavy-bottom pan, on medium heat. When hot, add the oil, onion, garlic, cumin powders and sauté for about 5 minutes. Add orange juice, ketchup, Worcestershire, soy, sriracha, cola and fish sauces and stir well. Add vinegar, butter and a little salt if needed. Bring to a boil, then lower the heat and simmer open for 15-20 minutes or until it is thickened slightly. Pour in a dry and clean jar, cool completely and use or refrigerate for up to a week.

Mango Barbecue Sauce (M: about 2-1/4 C)

This is a fruit-based sauce and very versatile. Make extra, freeze it in an airtight container for up to 3 months; thaw overnight in refrigerator and use more often.

Ingredients: 1-1/2 c mango puree; 1 c frozen concentrated orange juice thawed; 6 tbsp. ketchup; 1 tbsp. cumin powder; 1 tbsp. tandoori masala (Indian grilling spice) or chili powder; 1 tsp. granulated garlic powder; 1 tsp. cayenne pepper or to taste; ½ tsp. each salt and fresh-ground black pepper or to taste; ¼ tsp. turmeric powder (op).

In a medium pot, whisk in all the ingredients. Bring it to a boil on medium-high heat. Whisk for 2 minutes. Lower the heat and simmer covered for 30 minutes, until it is thickened slightly. Cool and refrigerate, covered for up to one week.

Chinese Black Vinegar (M: ½ C)

Chinese black vinegar is ready to use as it is, just like balsamic vinegar. If you prefer, you can dress it up with toasted sesame seeds and some grated ginger. You can also thin it with the fresh squeeze 2 tbsp. orange juice, and make it a little sweeter.

Foolproof Cocktail Sauce (M: 1 C)

Ingredients: 2/3 c hot and thick chili sauce; 1/3 c fresh-peeled and fine-grated horseradish or prepared horseradish sauce; 1 tbsp. fresh-squeezed lemon juice; a little salt and pepper or to taste.

Combine all ingredients, chill covered and serve with seafood. This is a sharp cocktail sauce; if you prefer, you can reduce the amount of the horseradish to taste.

Foolproof Hollandaise Sauce (M: about ¾ C)

This sauce is easy, thick and loaded with protein.

Ingredients: 3 large egg yolks; salt and white pepper to taste; 4 peeled and toasted almonds and 4 roasted cashews; 8 tbsp. (1 stick) melted and hot unsalted butter; 1-1/2 tsp. white vinegar.

Bring a small pot with about 4 cups of water to a boil and pour in the blender that you are going to use for the sauce. Heat another half pot of water and keep it warm.

Rinse out the blender with the hot water and add toasted chopped nuts, then yolks, salt and pepper. Cover and whisk all together for 1 minute until the nuts are ground. Open the top hole of the cover and pour in the hot butter, in a stream, while the motor is running. Take out the sauce from the blender into a medium non-reactive bowl and stir in the vinegar. Place the bowl over warm water, cover and keep it warm, stirring occasionally. You can turn the heat low, and on and off, but do not let the bowl touch the warm water. You can make the sauce one day ahead, cover and refrigerate, then reheat over the warm water and serve.

Mushroom Cream Sauce (M: about 3-1/2 C)

This is another versatile sauce that goes on steak, chicken, potatoes, eggs, rice and seafood, etc. This is a rich sauce and very tasty.

Ingredients: 1 tsp. canola oil and 4-5 tbsp. unsalted butter; 2 c thin-sliced leeks or yellow onions (use white part of leek, cut off the leaves and root, wash under running cold water, then submerge in a large bowl of water and wash between the leaves; take out and thin-slice across.); 1 pkg. 24 ounces (680g) baby bella mushrooms, cleaned and caps sliced ¼-inch thick; ½ c good white wine (op); 1 container, 1 qt. (946ml) heavy cream; ½ tsp. fresh-grated nutmeg; salt and fresh-ground black pepper to taste.

Heat a large heavy-bottom pan on medium heat. Add oil and 2 tbsp. of butter, sliced mushrooms and top with the leek. Increase heat on high and sauté the mushrooms until they release their liquid. Let the liquid evaporate by itself. Take the pan off the heat and pour over the wine. Put the pan back on the heat and let the wine dry out. Now take out the mushrooms and leave them tented with a foil in a platter.

Add rest of the butter and add the heavy cream; bring it to a boil on medium-high heat. Stir well and let it reduce in half, for about 45 minutes, stirring occasionally. Add the mushrooms back to the pan, and let it reduce again for 15 minutes until thick. Add salt, a lot of fresh-ground black pepper and fresh-grated nutmeg. Serve or Refrigerate up to 4 days in the refrigerator or freeze in a plastic container for up to 2 months. Thaw overnight, heat open in a pan on low and serve.

Orange Glaze or Sauce (M: about 1-1/2 C)

When I lived in Berlin, my brother used to buy all sorts or sauces, glazes and marmalades. This is one of the glazes that I still have taste for. Use a rubber spatula or a wooden spoon from start to finish. This glaze is versatile for use on fish, pancakes, oatmeal, fruits, cakes and pastries, etc.

Ingredients: About 1 tsp. melted butter; 3 c fresh-squeezed tangerine juice and ½ c pulp (buy 5 pounds of tangerines); 3 tsp. fine zest of tangerines (by microplane zester); 1 c sugar; 3 tbsp. lemon juice.

Heat a large, heavy-bottom, stainless steel or a non-reactive pan on low heat. With a damp paper towel, move the butter and coat the bottom of the pan. Add tangerine juice, zest, pulp, sugar and lemon juice; increase heat to medium-high and bring it to a boil. Stir well and let it reduce in half, stirring the bottom occasionally. It should take about 30 minutes to reduce and turn into a glaze. Turn off the heat, partially cover the pan with the lid and cool completely. Then fill the glaze in a clean and dry jar and refrigerate. Pour the glaze, do not dip any spoon. You can store it in the refrigerator for up to a month.

Tip: I add ½ c of Gran Marnier to the cooled glaze to give more volume, better taste and to last longer.

Pesto Sauce (M: about 2 cups)

I have a lot of fresh herbs growing in my garden in the large pots. I try to mix a little parsley to make it more nutritious.

Ingredients: 1 cup flat-leaf parsley; 2 cups fresh basil leaves; 1 tbsp. fresh garlic cloves chopped fine; 1 dry seeded serrano pepper or seeded and chopped jalapeno or to taste; 1 cup lightly toasted pine nuts or almonds; 4 tbsp. lemon juice or to taste; about ½ cup grated parmesan cheese; salt to taste; ½ cup extra virgin olive oil.

In a food processor pulse the pepper, garlic and the nuts first, then add the basil and parsley and pulse. Add lemon juice and cheese puree. Drizzle half of the oil and pulse just to mix. Take the mixture out of the food processor and whisk in the rest of the oil. Pour in a non-reactive bowl, cover the surface with the oily plastic wrap and then cover with a lid. Refrigerate until needed.

Steak Sauce (M: about 1-1/2 cups)

You can use this sauce on roast, eggs, toasts, or even on grilled vegetables and rice.

Ingredients: 2 tbsp. canola oil; 1 cup chopped fine onion; 2 tbsp. fine-grated fresh ginger; 1 tsp. each: cayenne pepper, paprika, onion powder, garlic powder; 1 tbsp. each: fennel seeds, and cumin seeds roasted and ground fine; ½ cup hoisin sauce; ¼ cup Worcestershire sauce; ¼ cup concentrated frozen orange juice, thawed; 2 tbsp. lemon juice; salt and pepper to taste.

Heat a medium pot on medium heat; add oil and cook onion for 5 minutes. Add ginger and cook another 5 minutes. Add rest of the ingredients, bring it to a boil. Boil the sauce for 1 minute, then lower the heat and simmer on low for 15 minutes. Cool and store in a non-reactive bowl, in the refrigerator for up to a week.

Tomato Salsa (M about 2/12 C)

This sauce goes almost with anything: pasta, seafood, grilled or baked food.

Ingredients: 3 anchovy fillets, rinse, pat dry and chopped fine; 2 tbsp. drained and chopped capers; ½ c chopped green or black pitted olives chopped fine; 1-1/2 c, about 4 large plum tomatoes, seeded and chopped fine; ¼ c yellow onion chopped fine; ¼ c fresh cilantro leaves chopped fine; ¼ to ½ tsp. dry oregano;1 tsp. fine lemon zest; 2 tbsp. lemon juice or to taste; salt and fresh-ground black pepper or red pepper flakes to taste; 1-2 tbsp. grated parmesan cheese (op).

Combine all ingredients and serve at room temperature, sprinkled with parmesan cheese if you prefer.

Foolproof Hoisin Type Sauce (M: about 2 C)

This sauce is easy to make, tasty and very thick, but is of pouring consistency and versatile. It goes well with chicken, turkey, grilled meat and vegetables, and you can even use in making brown gravy, etc. I sometimes make with sesame seeds: grind white sesame seeds first and then add a little water; puree well and make your own paste.

Ingredients: 1 tbsp. sesame oil or canola oil; 1 c sweet soybean paste (found in oriental stores); ½ c water; 1 tbsp. tomato ketchup; ¼ c apple cider vinegar; 2 tbsp. molasses; 2 tbsp. sugar; 1 tsp. salt or to taste; roasted and browned, on medium heat for 5-6 in a dry pan, 1 tbsp. each: caraway seeds, coriander seeds, half of medium star anise, black peppercorns, black cardamom seeds and then ground all roasted items in a spice mill or coffee grinder.

Dilute soybean paste with water. Heat a medium pot on low heat, add oil and diluted soybean paste, stir well and bring to a simmer on medium heat. Add vinegar, molasses, ketchup, sugar and salt and stir well. Simmer the sauce on very low heat, covered, for 15 minutes. If it is too thick, add little more water. If it is too thin, add a little more ketchup and ½ tsp. vinegar, and simmer 5 minutes. Taste for salt and pepper. Add all roasted and ground spices, stir well and take off the heat. Cool and store in a clean, dry, bottle air tight in the refrigerator for up to a month.

Horseradish Sour Cream (M: 1 C)

Ingredients: 1 c sour cream; ¼ c prepared horseradish; 1 tbsp. dijon mustard; 1 tbsp. lemon juice; salt and fresh-ground black pepper to taste.

Combine all ingredients in a bowl, cover and chill before serving.

Spinach Hummus (M: 2-1/2 C)

Ingredients: 1 cup baby spinach, blanched for 3 minutes, drained, and chopped fine;1 can, 16 oz., about 2 c chickpeas, drained and washed under cold water and drained well; 2 c cilantro leaves and soft stems, 1tsp. lime zest; ¼ c fresh lime juice (about 4 large limes) or lemon zest and juice; 1 jalapeno, seeded and chopped, or 2-3 serrano peppers, chopped; salt to taste; 2 tbsp. toasted white sesame seeds; 2 tbsp. chopped onion; ½ c seeded roasted red bell peppers from the jar; 4 large garlic cloves roasted; 4 tbsp. extra-virgin olive oil.

Grind and puree all the ingredients in a blender except the spinach and olive oil. Slowly pour the olive oil from the opening in the cover and blend all together into a paste. Take out the hummus in a glass bowl, stir in the spinach and serve, or cover and refrigerate for up to 4-5 days. Use a clean and dry spoon each time to take some out.

Kimchi Cream (M: about 1 C)

Ingredients: ½ c to ¾ c kimchi (Japanese fermented cabbage) with some juice; ½ c sour cream; ½ c mayonnaise; salt and fresh-ground white pepper to taste (op).

In a blender, coarsely chop the kimchi with the juice and the sour cream. Take out in a nonreactive bowl. Stir in mayo and season with salt and pepper to taste.

Pesto with Lemon and Lime (M: about 2 C)

Pesto is the famous Italian, healthy, thick sauce. Made with fresh herbs, nuts and cheese. This sauce requires a very good quality of olive oil.

Ingredients: ½ to ¾ c lightly roasted almonds; ¼ c Italian parsley leaves (flat-leaf); 1 c packed fresh basil leaves; 2 tbsp. chopped fresh garlic cloves; 1 tsp. each fresh oregano and tarragon leaves; ½ c fresh grated good quality parmesan cheese; 1 tbsp. lemon zest; 2 tbsp. each lemon and lime juice or to taste; ¼ c good dry white wine; about ¾ c high-quality olive oil; salt and fresh-ground black pepper to taste or 1 small and dry serrano pepper.

In a blender or food processor, pulse the almonds first to small pieces, then add rest of the ingredients except the olive oil and salt, and pulse until the herbs are coarsely chopped. Slowly pour the olive oil through the cover hole while machine is running and mix only just the sauce, thick and a little creamy. Salt to taste. Cover with a plastic wrap then with the lid until needed.

Pomegranate Molasses (M: about 1 C)

Pomegranate Juice: Buy a healthy and a large pomegranate. Trim off the ends and cut half only in the outer skin lengthwise. Insert the point of the knife on the crown side, halfway inside the pomegranate, and try to pull apart in two pieces. If it does not come apart, then make a cut on one side of the pomegranate and then pull it apart in two pieces. Now take one piece at a time and press it downward over a juicer placed on a cup (to catch the juice). Press down, lift up and press down again starting from the edges going toward the center. Any leftover seeds you can press in with your thumb inside the half piece, and then again press down on the juicer. This is a very fast process once you get used to it. You can also use a juicer after you have taken out all the seeds.

Ingredients: 2 c pomegranate juice, 1 c tangerine juice, ¼ c lemon juice, ½ tsp. salt, 1 c packed dark brown sugar, ¼ tsp. fresh-ground black pepper, ½ tsp. ground cinnamon, ½ tsp. fennel seed powder, ¼ tsp. cayenne pepper, 1 tsp. sesame or canola oil.

1. Heat a large heavy-bottom stainless steel sauté pan on medium heat, add oil and move around to coat the bottom. Add all ingredients, bring it to a boil on medium high heat.

2. Let it boil for 10 minutes, stirring constantly with a stainless steel spatula. Cover the pan with a lid halfway, reduce the heat to medium and let it simmer for about 1-1/2 hours, stirring every now and then until it is reduced to 1 C and has thickened. Take it off the heat and let it rest for about 5 minutes.
3. Pour in an airtight, clean and dry jar while it is still warm. Cool completely, then refrigerate up to three months. Use on baked, broiled vegetables and meat. I even use this for my breakfast.

Pomegranate Sauce (M: 1-1/2 C)

This sauce is so versatile that we use it almost on a daily basis and has substituted for ketchup. Pomegranate has antioxidant properties and this sauce does not have too much sugar or too much salt.

Ingredients: 2 c pomegranate juice, 1 c fresh squeezed orange juice, ½ c lemon juice, 1/3 c packed light brown sugar, ½ c salt or to taste, ½ tsp crushed each: anise and fennel seeds, 1 fresh jalapeño seeded and thin sliced, 1 tab fresh peeled and grated ginger, ¼ tsp. fresh-ground black pepper, 1/2 tsp. canola oil.

1. Heat a large heavy-bottom stainless steel sauté pan on medium heat, add the oil and move around to coat the bottom of the pan. Add all ingredients to the pan, bring it to a boil.
2. Boil for 5 minutes, stirring constantly with a stainless steel spatula. Cover the pan with a lid, reduce the heat to medium and let it cook for about until it is reduced to about one third or 1-1/2 C and thickened a little. Take it off the heat and cool about 5 minutes.
3. Pour in an airtight, clean and dry jar while it is still warm. Cool it completely then refrigerate up about one month. Use on almost everything.

Tip: When using the sauce, open the bottle and pour it into a spoon, or use a plastic spoon inside the jar so it will last longer. This goes for all sauces, molasses, pickles and preserved items.

Pomegranate Chipotle Sauce

Add about 2 tbsp. or to taste chopped chipotle from the can to the sauce. This sauce goes well with roasted meat and vegetables.

Tartar Sauce (M: 1-1/4 C)

This sauce is for fried food, especially the seafood, and also goes well on burgers.

Ingredients: ¼ c sour cream; ¾ c mayonnaise; 2 tbsp. lemon or lime juice; 1/3 c chopped fine sweet and sour pickles or India sweet relish; 2 tbsp. minced yellow or red onion; 1 tbsp. rinsed and chopped capers; ½ tsp. fresh chopped thyme or 2 pinches dry thyme; fresh-ground black pepper to taste.

In a small bowl, mix all ingredients, cover with the plastic and refrigerate until needed. Prepare at least 1 hour or overnight before serving so that the flavors can develop together with the pickles.

Stewed Tomatoes (M: about 3-1/2 C)

Ingredients: 2 pounds plum tomatoes, blanched in hot water for 2 minutes, peeled and seeded and chopped to 1-inch pieces; save all the juices; 2 tbsp. butter or canola oil; 1 tsp. fennel seeds crushed (op); 1 c each chopped onion, green bell peppers, 2 tbsp. sugar, 1 jalapeno seeded and chopped (op); 1 tbsp. tomato paste; ¼ tsp. granulated garlic; salt and fresh-ground black pepper to taste.

Heat a medium pot on medium heat. When hot, add oil and transparent the onion for 5 minutes; add the bell peppers and sauté a little. Add tomatoes with their juices, tomato paste, granulated garlic, fennel seeds and jalapeno, sugar, salt and pepper to taste. Bring to a boil, cover and lower the heat and simmer until all the vegetables are soft, about 20 minutes. Cool and serve as a side dish or puree, and serve as tomato chutney, or use as a gravy for meat or vegetable curries.

Basic Tomato Sauce

This is a basic tomato sauce you can use it on almost any pasta, pizza, chicken etc.

Ingredients: 3 tbsp. canola or olive oil, 1 large onion chopped fine;
½ cup each fine chopped: celery, carrots; 1 c thin-slice mushrooms; 3 tbsp. garlic chopped fine; 2 (28 oz.) cans plum tomatoes; 1 can 28 oz. plain tomato sauce; 2 tbsp. fresh-grated ginger; ½ c soft stems and leaves of parsley or cilantro; ¼ c chopped basil; 2 tbs. fresh thyme chopped (op); ½ tsp. dry oregano; 1 tsp. fine fennel seeds; 2 tbs. brown sugar (op); salt and fresh cracked black pepper to taste.

1.   Heat a large heavy-bottom pot on medium heat; when hot, add oil and sautéed onion to transparent about 5 minutes, add celery, carrots, mushrooms, garlic and ginger, fennel seeds, and sauté until vegetables are soft, about 10 minutes. Add tomato sauce, crush the plum tomatoes and add to the pot. Add sugar and half of the all herbs; salt and pepper to taste. Bring to a boil and simmer covered for 20 minutes.
2.   Add remaining herbs, taste for seasoning and add a little salt and pepper as needed, stir well, cook open 5 minutes and turn off the sauce.

Tips: Ginger and fennel seeds give very good flavor with the tomato and are very healthy. For extra flavor, you can add chopped jalapeno, extra basil, roasted nuts, lemon juice and granulated or roasted garlic. Make the sauce and keep in a dry, clean, glass jar, airtight in the refrigerator for at least up to a week. When using the sauce, pour from the jar in a cup on spoon. Never pour into a cooking pot (steam will get into the jar) and never put a spoon in the jar (it will get watery) and will spoil fast.

Red Wine Sauce (M: 1 C)

This sauce goes well over almost anything, especially on fish, chicken, roasted and grilled meats and vegetables.

Ingredients: 2 c good red wine; 4 tbsp. brown sugar; 1 tbsp. lemon juice; ¼ c fresh squeezed tangerine or orange juice; salt and fresh-ground black pepper to taste; 6 tbsp. cold butter cut into cubes.

1. Heat a large heavy-bottom pan on medium on medium and move around 1 tsp. butter to coat the pan. Off heat pour the wine, lemon and orange juice, sugar, and a little of salt and pepper, in the pan and bring to a boil on medium heat, stir well, reduce the heat and stir for 2 minutes. Cover the pan ¾ with a lid and let it simmer, stirring on and off for about 1 hour, until the wine mixture is reduced to almost 1 cup.
2. Take the mixture off the heat and stir in the butter in 2-3 batches, whisking constantly. Taste for the seasoning. Pour in a gravy boat or serving bowl. Keep covered. Serve right away or just reheat in the microwave on high for 1 minute.

Pickles

We grew up with balsamic vinegar pickles. My mother used to make her own balsamic vinegar and will pickle whole green mango, red and white watermelon pickles, cauliflower, thin-sliced turnip. She also made preserved lemons, bittermelon pickles, cucumber and garlic pickles etc.

Bittermelon Pickles (M: about 3 cups)

Bittermelon is very common in Indian and Asian cooking. If you eat a few slices of the raw bittermelon every day, it will cure your stomach illnesses. It is also good for diabetic people. The key of this pickle is using a cast-iron pan that somehow soaks up the bitter taste. Wash out all the equipment after using to get rid of the lingering bitter taste.

Ingredients: 1 pound (about 4 large) Indian bittermelon, sliced whole about ½-inch thick slices; 4-5 tbsp. canola oil; spice mixture: 1 tbsp. each of crushed fennel seeds, turmeric powder (or more), garlic powder, fenugreek powder (op); ½-tsp. or to taste salt; 2 tbsp. brown sugar; 4 tbsp. cider vinegar.

Heat a cast-iron pan on medium-high heat. When hot, add 1 tbsp. oil and spread out the bittermelon slices in a single layer; cover and lower the heat slightly. Cook until they are golden brown underneath, about 7-8 minutes. Sprinkle 1 tsp. of oil all over the slices and turn them over, and cook the other side for another 6-7 minutes until soft. Take them out in a bowl and cook rest of the slices in batches same way.

Heat a stainless steel non-reactive pan on medium heat. Add 1 tbsp. oil, spice mixture, salt, sugar and vinegar; bring to a boil, lower the heat and add the cooked bittermelon slices. Stir to coat the slices with spice mixture for about 10 minutes, until heated through. Cool and fill the jar. Refrigerate for up to one week in the refrigerator; serve with almost any meal.

Red and White Watermelon Pickles (M: about 3 cups)

Watermelon is loaded with folic acid. The red pulp and white rind both are very nutritious. Just cut the watermelon into 1x3-inch strips, leaving at least 1-inch of the red pulp intact, and peel off the green skin; take out all the seeds.

The Basic Pickle Mixture: 4 cups boiling water; 1-1/2 cups white vinegar; 1 tbsp. each crushed spices: mustard seeds, black peppercorns, coriander seeds, red pepper flakes (op), sea salt to taste; 1-2 bay leaves; 1 tsp. turmeric powder (op); 1/3 cup sugar; 4 garlic cloves peeled and pierced all over with a wooden toothpick; about 3 cups, 1x3 inches long, peeled watermelon strips.

In a non-reactive medium pot, bring water to a boil, add all spices, simmer for 5 minutes, add the watermelon pieces and cook on constant simmer for 5 minutes. Pour the mixture in a cleaned, dry, pickling jar, leaving about 1-inch space on the top. Cover the jar loosely with the lid. Then put the jar in simmering water, submerge halfway through, for 10 minutes. Take out the jar with tongs, cool completely and refrigerate for 2 weeks. They are ready to eat immediately. Take out the pickles with a wooden dry fork; do not use wet spoon.

Variations

Use the same basic pickling mixture from above, and make all sorts of pickles, such as: pieces of cauliflower, sliced cucumber, whole okra, sliced turnips, thick sliced onion, sliced celery, whole garlic cloves (pierce them with the wooden toothpick all around) and sliced carrots.

Desserts

Cookies, Cup Cakes, Muffins, Pies, Cakes, Desserts, Frosting etc.

I think cookies are second favorite treats after the cakes. They are loved by everyone, child, adult, young and old. They are a bundle of sweet treats that can be eaten any time of the day. In 1982 when I went to Berlin to visit my brother on Christmas, one of his friends who was a doctor had invited us for coffee. His mother, who was born in Italy but had lived in Berlin, had her own newspaper business and was very fond of cookies. She had baked at least 25 different types of cookies, filled in porcelain jars, and had stocked the shelves of a large glass cabinet. When she start taking out the porcelain jars after jars, we all were amazed to see that how quickly she had filled a large dining room table with the fancy cookies. Almost every cookie was very decorative, tasty, and had a history behind it. Some of these recipes were carried in the family for almost 4 generations. Well, I always like German and Italian food and to my surprise, this was a taste of the life time.

Make sure you use Double acting Baking powder in all your baking.

General tips for Baking Cookies

1. Line a large baking sheet with double parchment paper. This way, cookies will not burn on the bottom.
2. Bake cookies on the middle self, in a preheated oven. I first heat the broiler for 2-3 minutes, shut it off and then heat oven at 350 degrees for about 2 minutes, before placing the cookies in the oven.
3. Leave enough room, at least 1 to 2-inches between each cookie. They will spread while they are baking.
4. . Butter cookies tastes better. Use softened butter to the dough so that cookies do not spread out too much.
5. Chill the dough or the cookies about half of an hour in the refrigerator or about 8-10 minutes in the freezer before baking.
6. Use an ice cream scoop or a tablespoon to drop the copies on the tray, then smooth out or shape them, with lightly wet fingers.
7. Bake cookies on an ungreased tray; they won't spread too much.
8. After cookies are baked, take them out of the oven and immediately shape them in round by pushing the edges in with a metal spatula.
9. Take the baked cookies out of the oven, let them stand in the baking tray for about 5 minutes. Then loosen with a metal spatula carefully, and transfer them to a wire rack, upside down, to cool completely.
10. Store them in an airtight container lined and covered with paper towels.

Cheese Filled Cookies(M: about 120)

These cookies are somewhat Indian gujhiya, but they are not fried, they are baked.

Ingredients:
For the Crust: 1 box 16.5 ounces white cake mix; 1 pkg. 8 ounces cream cheese mixed together by hand into a smooth dough.

For the Filling: 1 pound part-skim ricotta cheese; 2 tsp. vanilla extract; 2 tbsp. butter; 1 pkg. about 1cup non-fat dry milk; 1 cup sugar; about ½ cup powdered sugar to garnish. Some melted butter to roll the dough into balls.

To make the Filling: In a large sauté pan heat butter on medium heat, add the cheese, increase the heat to medium-high and sauté the cheese to reduce the liquid for about 10 minutes. Lower the heat to medium, sprinkle the cheese with the dry milk and then with the sugar and mix well. Add the vanilla extract and sauté for another 5-10 minutes, do not let the cheese burn. Cool the mixture completely.

On a cutting board, spread out the plastic wrap. Using a tablespoon, drop the dough over the plastic about 10 places. Roll each dough into the balls. If hands are sticky wash and grease them with melted butter. Now using a dinner knife, press down the balls into about 2-inch rounds. Top each round with 2 tsp. of cheese filling. Pick up one round at a time, fold in half and pinch the edges together to make the semi-circle. Do not worry if the cheese is spilling out, just pinch the dough together.

Make the cookies, place them on a parchment-lined tray about ½-inch apart, and refrigerate them covered. When all are done, bake them in batches in a preheated 325 degree oven for about 12 minutes. Take the tray out of the oven, wait for 1 minute and with a spatula move the cookies into a platter. When cooled, sprinkle with the powder sugar. Store them in the refrigerator between the paper towels in a container.

Chocolate Chips Chocolate Cookies (M: about 26, 2-1/2")

Do you know that cocoa powder is very healthy for the intestines? I use Hershey's Special Dark Cocoa Powder, and that is even better.

Ingredients: 1 pkg. 4oz. (113.5g) 60% cacao bittersweet chocolate chopped; 2 ounces semi-sweet chocolate grated; 1 cup semi-sweet chocolate chips; ½ cup packed light brown sugar; 1 cup granulated sugar; 16 tbsp. (2 sticks) softened unsalted butter; 2 extra large eggs; 2 tsp. vanilla extract; a mixture of: 3 cups un-sifted all-purpose flour; ½ tsp. salt; 2 tsp. baking soda; 2 tbsp. unsweetened natural cocoa powder or special dark cocoa powder.

In a microwave for 30-second intervals, stirring or over the warm water, melt the bittersweet chocolate. Take off, cover and let it cool. When cooled, whisk in the sugars. In a large bowl, whisk the eggs well, then add the chocolate chips, vanilla extract and the grated chocolate, melted chocolate mixture, and then soften butter. Now with a wooden spoon or a fork, whisk the flour mixture. Combine all well until no traces of the flour are left.

Drop about 2 heaping tablespoonful of batter on 4 to 5 dinner plates. With wet hands, shape and make the neat rounds, and refrigerate for 15-20 minutes until firm. Preheat the oven at 375 degrees. Line two large baking sheets with parchment paper. Take out 6 rounds and place them about 2 inches apart on each baking sheet. Wet your hands and flatten the rounds to ¾ inches high. Bake in a preheated oven for about 8 minutes, turning the tray around halfway during baking. Take out the baking sheet and let cookies cool for 5 minutes. Then with the spatula, turn them over on a cutting board and cool completely. Repeat with rest of the dough. When cookies are cooled serve, or store them in a cookie jar, between the paper towels and/or parchment paper, for up to 3-4 weeks.

Cookie Bouquet (M: 40 pieces of cookies and truffles)

I had made this bouquet for the Woman's Club in Nov. 2015. We baked and packed over 130 cookie containers to distribute to the Food Bank, Senior Citizen Center and several other organizations. You can use your favorite: macaroons, chocolates, and truffles. But make sure you can insert them with the skewers. Just make sure you do not make the container too heavy, so it does not turn over with the weight.

Ingredients: One medium, about 6 to 8-inches tall cookie container and a vase of same height, just big enough to fit inside the cookie container with a smaller opening; 1 bag 20 pieces assorted (colorful) Lindor truffles or any other truffles; 10 pieces coconut macaroons; 1 pkg. mega stuff golden Oreo cookies; 4 oz. (113g) Baker's white chocolate, melted in 4 tbsp. heavy cream; red and green sprinkles or sugar crystals; 20 10-inch-long bamboo skewers; 20 11.75-inch lollipop sticks (can be purchased at a craft store); wax or parchment paper to line the baking sheet.

1. **To prepare the Oreo Skewers**: Line a large baking tray with wax or parchment paper. Pile up the sprinklers or sugar crystals, each in a separate plate. Take 1 Oreo cookie at a time, insert the lollipop stick in the middle, separating one cookie from the sugar (or the cookie will fall apart). Brush some melted chocolate on and around the inserted part of the lollipop stick, paste the loose cookie back together the way it was (make it double again), and hold a few seconds. Now brush outer side of one cookie, then dip in the sugar crystals or in the

sprinklers. Place the skewer facing up, on the wax/parchment paper. So you will have red or green Oreo cookies. Wait for about 2 hours for chocolate to dry.

2. Now insert the skewers in the macaroons and in the truffles; make sure they do not come outside of the pieces on the top.
3. **To arrange the Bouquet:** Tie a fancy ribbon on the neck of the vase. Hold the macaroons and Oreo sticks together and insert into the vase. Now push in the truffles sticks all around, on the outside. Secure the vase into the cookie container with mushed foil or the paper.
4. Place the bouquet in the center of the buffet or dessert table.

Fancy Fruit Cookies (M: 25)

These fruit cookies with cherries in the center not only taste good, but look very pretty. They are best suited for the holidays.

Ingredients: 2 sticks, 1 cup unsalted butter melted and cooled; 1-3/4 cup sugar; 2 jumbo eggs; 1 tsp. tangerine fine zest; 1 container, 16 ounces 453.6g fancy fruit cake mix candied fruits; 1 cup chopped candied pineapple; 1 cup chopped walnuts; 1 cup slivered almonds; 3 cups unsweetened coconut powder or 1 bag unsweetened angel flakes coconut (if using sweetened, reduce the sugar by ¼ cup); 3 cups unsifted all-purpose flour; ½ tsp. salt, 3 tsp. baking soda; to garnish: 1 container, 8 ounces (226.8g) candied cherries.

1. Line a large baking tray (12x18x1-inch) with double parchment paper and very lightly grease the paper with butter. Melt the butter in a large bowl and cool completely; whisk in sugar, eggs, zest well. Add candied fruits, pineapple, walnut, almonds mix well. Sift the flour, baking soda and salt and mix in the hand into the fruit mixture.
2. Using an ice cream scoop drop ¾ scoopful mixture about two inches apart over the parchment paper. With lightly wet hands, flatten the cookies to 1 inch and push in one cherry in the center. Chill the tray in the refrigerator for 20 minutes.
3. Bake in a preheated oven for 12 minutes or until the edges are light brown. Turn the tray around half way during the baking.
4. Take the tray out of the oven, shape the cookies in a round immediately. Cool the cookies in the tray for 5 minutes, then take out with a metal spatula and turn over and cool over a kitchen towel or over the cutting board.
5. Store the cookies in large trays between aluminum foil in one or two layers. Because of the weight of the fruits they are soft and may break, so store in a wide container or tray in room temperature for 4-5 days, and then place in the refrigerator covered with the foil.

Oats, Fruit and Nut Cookies (M: 30)

Follow the recipe of Fancy Fruit cookies and make following adjustments:

Use all-purpose flour only, 1 cup, add 3-1/2 to 4 cups of quick-cooking oatmeal as needed.
Take out the tangerine zest and add 2 tsp. of vanilla extract
Use only 2 tsp. of baking soda.

Peanut Butter Cookies (M: about 55 cookies)

I make several different types of peanut butter cookies. These are the most common ones. My husband loves all of them as long as they are loaded with peanut butter.

Ingredients: 2 cups all-purpose un-sifted flour; 1 tsp. baking soda; 1/3 tsp. salt; 1 stick (8 tabs) unsalted softened butter; ¾ cup creamy peanut butter; 1-1/2 cup sugar; 1 large egg; 1 tsp. pure vanilla extract; for garnish: ¼ cup sugar and ¼ cup roasted and halved peanuts.

Line a large (1/2 sheet) baking sheet with double parchment paper.

Sift the dry ingredients: flour, baking soda and salt in a small bowl.

In a large mixing bowl, cream butter and sugar with an electric mixer. Grease a measuring cup with oil or melted butter and take out ¾ cup of peanut butter and add to the bowl. Add one beaten egg and vanilla extract to the bowl, cream all liquid ingredients together. Slowly in two batches add the dry ingredients to wet mixture by hand with a wooden spoon.

Preheat oven to 400F. Use a small ice cream scoop, scoop out an overflowing scoop with cookie dough, then press the dough in the scoop with a thumb and drop out the extra dough from the scoop; turn over and release the dough ball over a clean and dry dinner plate. Make about 15 dough balls; pick one ball at a time, dip the round top in the sugar, place on the parchment paper about two-inches apart. When all are dipped in the sugar, top and press in each ball with a piece of roasted peanut.

Chill the tray in refrigerator for 5 minutes. Bake in the preheated oven, on the middle rack, for about 12 minutes, turning around the tray 2-3 times in each direction. The cookies should be lightly browned on the edges. Take the tray out of the oven, leave it outside the oven for 5 minutes, then with a metal spatula gently pick up each cookies and cool on a wire rack to cool. Repeat with the rest of the cookies dough.

I cool my cookies on a counter lined with aluminum foil. Once they are cooled in about 10 minutes, I pile them up on top of each other in a neat row so I have room for more to cool in single layer. After cookies are cooled, I slide the aluminum foil, holding both ends in, to a large baking tray and leave them in a cooled oven for 3-4 days, or pack in an airtight container lined and covered with a fancy paper napkin to give them as a gift.

Tip: Make sure you chill cookies before baking. Chilled cookies can take higher temperature, therefore they bake longer and are crispy.

As with any other baking, if you want you can also decorate the top with colorful sprinkles or other nuts before baking.

Jumbo Peanut Butter Cookies with Morsels (M: 25)

These cookies are very attractive, tasty and easy to make. You can also use peanut butter or chocolate kisses, instead of morsels.

Ingredients: 2 large jumbo eggs; 3 cups sugar; 2 sticks 8 tbsp. unsalted butter melted but cooled; 2 cups super chunky peanut butter; 2 tsp. vanilla extract; 1 pkg. 1 cup instant non-fat dry milk; 3 cups unsifted all-purpose flour; 2-1/4 tsp. baking soda; ¼ tsp. salt; to garnish: ½ cup sugar and 1pkg. 1 1ounce (311.8g) butterscotch morsels (or peanut butter chips).

1. In a large bowl, add melted butter and sugar whisk well; add the eggs and whisk; grease a cup with a little oil or butter and measure the peanut butter and whisk in the egg mixture; add the vanilla extract, dry milk and whisk well. Add flour, baking soda, salt and using a fork, mix all together by hand.

2. Line a large baking tray with sides (12x18x1-inch) with double parchment paper. Spread out the ½ cup sugar and butterscotch morsels separately on two different dinner plates.
3. To make cookies, fill the mixture in an ice cream scoop, pat it down with a dinner knife and drop over the sugar, pick up the cookie with a metal spatula, turn over and drop it over the morsels, press down to adhere some morsels and also to make cookie about one-inch thick. Pick up the cookie and line up in the prepared tray about 2 inches apart. These cookies are coated one side with sugar and the other side with peanut butter morsels. Chill the cookies in the refrigerator for 20 minutes or in the freezer for 8 minutes.
4. Bake in a preheated oven about 12 minutes, or until light brown on the bottom. Turn the tray around halfway during the baking.
5. Take the cookies out of the oven, shape them in round with a metal spatula immediately. Cool in the tray for 5 minutes, then turn them over on a wire rack or on a kitchen towel lined over a flat space.

Coconut Macaroons (M: 25 Jumbo)

Everyone loves my Macaroons, so I bake a lot and give out a lot. These macaroons are baked first at a lower temperature, then with higher temperature to puff and brown them lightly. To make Chocolate covered, just dip them in melted chocolate and let them dry.

Ingredients: 2 bags 14 oz. (396G) each, angel flake sweetened coconut; ½ cup white cake mix (or ½ cup all-purpose flour, ¼ tsp. baking powder and ¼ cup sugar); 2 extra large egg whites or 3 large egg whites; 1 can 14 oz. (396g) sweetened condensed milk.

1. In a large bowl beat the egg whites, add the condensed milk, whisk well, add the cake mix and whisk well. Add 1 bag of coconut at a time and mix well, by hand, with a fork.
2. Prepare two large trays with at least 1-inch sides (12x18x1 inches); first line the trays with aluminum foil, then with parchment paper or two layers of parchment papers, and lightly grease the paper with oil or butter.
3. Fill a regular size ice cream scoop with the mixture and neatly press in the mixture all around the edges, then pack the mixture neatly and drop on to the tray about 1-1/2 inch apart. When done, shape the macaroons with lightly wet fingers. Chill the macaroon trays for 20-30 minutes.
4. Preheat oven at 350 degrees. Bake one tray at a time on the middle self. Bake macaroons for 10 minutes at 350 degrees and about 8-10 minutes at 450 degrees or until light brown.
5. Take the trays out of the oven, wait 5 minutes and then take the macaroons out with a spatula, turn them over and cool on a wire rack or over the counter on the kitchen towel. Serve them with the tea or coffee.
6. When cooled completely (after a few hours), store them in a large glass jar, cover with paper towels or in a plastic bag lined with the paper towels. They freeze well, so freeze the plastic bag inside a plastic container up to 3 months. Defrost overnight in the refrigerator and serve.

Cupcakes

Cupcakes are a lot of fun to make and eat. You can take a basic recipe and put in different flavors, fillings and toppings, and it's a whole lot of different game. Just make a list and do all your shopping ahead so you have everything on hand. If you have to make a lot of cupcakes, then bake them a day ahead and ice them only the day you are going to serve them. They stay well overnight in a turned-off, cool oven, in the baking trays, except in the hot weather.

I make them large, fill with chocolate covered caramel, lemon, lime or pineapple curds or with chocolate kisses and then top with icing and decorate them with the candied fruits, chocolate or sprinklers etc. and people love them. Just use your wild imagination, lot of flavors, colors, fancy paper cups and you are a pro.

Fancy Chocolate Cupcakes (M: 24 Large)

The secret to these cupcakes is the filling and the chocolate liqueur. These cupcakes take only 3 to 4 tablespoons of batter, so try to under bake them, about 15 minutes. Do not insert the toothpick to test them, because of the filling; just make sure the top is firm. You can use any white or dark chocolate frosting. You can also freeze them covered in a plastic bag, in a plastic container, before you frost them. We prefer Hershey's Special Dark 100% Cacao, a mixture of natural and Dutch process cocoa powder.

Ingredients: For the cocoa melt – ½ cup whole milk; ½ cup heavy cream, 6 tbsp. special dark 100% cacao cocoa powder, ¼ cup granulated sugar. Heat all on low heat just to warm for about 5 minutes; stir well, take off the heat and cool.

For the Cookies:1/2 cup heavy cream; 1pkg. 4 ounces (113g) semi-sweet chocolate chopped; 2-1/2 cups bleached all-purpose flour; ½ tsp. salt; 2 tsp. baking powder; ½ tsp. baking soda; 3 large eggs; 1-1/2 cup granulated sugar; ½ cup canola oil; ¼ cup chocolate liqueur; for filling 1pkg. 4oz. (113g) semi-sweet chocolate grated on the large holes of a box grater; for the topping: chocolate frosting.

1. Grease the top of a 12-muffin large tin, then line the tin with the paper cups, spray the cups lightly with cooking oil spray. Place an oven shelf in the middle and heat the oven at 350 degrees. In a small pot heat the ½ cup heavy cream and take off the heat; add the chopped chocolate, cover for 5 minutes. Then stir well to melt the chocolate; set aside to cool.
2. In a medium bowl, sift all the dry ingredients together: flour, salt, baking powder and the baking soda.
3. With an electric mixer, whisk the eggs and the sugar until pale and smooth, for about 5 minutes. Add the oil and whisk in well. Add the chocolate liqueur and the melted, cooled chocolate and whisk well. Now alternate with cocoa melt and the dry ingredients. Add half of the cocoa melt and whisk well, then half of the dry ingredients and whisk just to mix; then add remaining cocoa melt and finally remaining flour mixture, whisk just to mix. Scrape the bottom well.
4. Pour in about 3 tbsp. batter into each paper cup then place about 1 tsp. of the grated chocolate on the top; press down the chocolate with the back of a spoon or a finger, then drizzle another tablespoon of the batter on the top to cover the chocolate. Bake in preheated oven about 15 minutes. Turn the tin around halfway during the baking. When the top is firm, take out the cupcakes and cool in the tin for 5 minutes, then cool completely on the wire rack.
5. Bake and cool all the cupcakes, then either pipe the frosting or spread out on the top with a wooden spoon.

Chocolate, Cheese Cupcakes (M: 30)

These cupcakes are better than cheesecake and are everyone's favorite. Buy or make your own toppings one day ahead and chill in the refrigerator before using.

Ingredients:

For the crust: 4 tbsp. melted unsalted butter; 4 tbsp. sugar; 2 cups graham cracker or sugar cookies crumbs.

For the Filling: All the dairy ingredients should be at room temperature. 4 packages 8 ounces each cream cheese; 2 cups sugar; 4 large eggs; 4 tbsp. all-purpose flour; 1 envelope 7 grams about 1 tbsp. unflavored gelatin; 2 tbsp. melted butter; 2 tbsp. lemon juice; ½ cups heavy cream; 1 package 3.4 ounces (966 grams) instant vanilla pudding mix; 1 dark chocolate bar, 6.8 ounces (192g), broken across into 4 pieces together at the score, then cut them in half across, to make 1-inch square pieces.

Crust: In a bowl, mix together crumbs, sugar and butter with hand. Line the muffin tin with 12 paper cups, spray with cooking spray. Then drop about 2 tbsp. crumb mixture in each paper cup. Press down well the crumbs with a small glass or a flat-bottom bottle and set aside.

Filling:

1. Soak the unflavored gelatin in 4 tbsp. water and set aside for 5 minutes to bloom. In a large bowl whisk together cream cheese, sugar, flour and eggs until cheese is incorporated well with the other ingredients. Whisk in gelatin, lemon juice and half of the vanilla pudding mixture and half of the heavy cream.

2. In a small bowl whip together ½ C prepared cheese batter, remaining vanilla pudding mix and rest of the heavy cream for the topping.

3. Fill about 1 regular ice cream scoop of cheese batter in each paper cup, filling almost up to the top. Push in 1 piece of the chocolate, standing up inside each cup and cover the chocolate with 1 tsp. each the set-aside cheese and pudding batter. Even out the top with wet fingers.

4. Bake in a preheated 325-degree oven. Place a large tray in the oven, then place the muffin tin inside the large tray and pour in from the side about 1-1/2 cups to 2 cups of boiling water, just enough for baking or to come almost half way to the muffin tin. Bake about 30 minutes, until cupcakes are puffed up and firm to touch on the top. Carefully turn around the tray halfway during the baking for even baking. Turn off the oven and let the cupcakes rest in the warm oven for 15 minutes. Then cool completely on a wire rack.

5. Chill the cupcakes from 2 hours to overnight before placing the topping. Place about 1 tbsp. topping on each cupcake and then top with fresh berries, glazed pineapple chunks or sliced, dried apricot on the top. Serve immediately or refrigerate for later.

Chocolate-Orange Icing

Chocolate and orange go together very well. You can use orange liqueur or orange-flavor drink powder. This icing is enough for 24 cupcakes or for a 4 layer, 9-inch cake.

Ingredients: ½ cups heavy cream, plus 2 tbsp. for finishing at the end; 1 tbsp. chocolate cake mix (mixture of flour, baking powder and sugar); ½ cup light brown sugar; ¼ cup unsweetened cocoa powder; ½ cup orange drink mix powder; 1 stick (8 tbsp.) unsalted butter softened and cut into slices; 2 cups about 1 pound powdered sugar.

1. In a measuring cup heat ½ cup heavy cream, brown sugar, cake mix, cocoa powder, for 1 minute; stir, cover and let it melt for 5 minutes. Pour in a large bowl and cool completely.
2. Whisk in orange drink mix powder. Using an electric mixer add half of the butter and the powder sugar. Then slowly whisking, add the rest of the butter one tablespoon at a time. Whisk in 2 tbsp. heavy cream. Use icing right away or let it chill covered and use it later. Whisk well before using.
   Chocolate-Mocha Icing: Use ½ C Suisse mocha powder (hot chocolate mix) instead of orange drink mix.

Fruit Toppings

Pineapple:

Ingredients: 1 can, 20 ounces about 2 cups, crushed pineapple; ½ cup sugar; 2-3 drops of butter or oil to grease the pan.

Heat a large nonreactive pan on medium heat. When hot add butter or oil and move around to coat the bottom. Add the pineapple and increase the heat to medium-high. Cook pineapple until all the liquid has evaporated, stirring occasionally, for about 15 minutes. Add the sugar, mix well and reduce the heat to medium or low as necessary and dry out all the liquid again, stirring occasionally for about 10 minutes. Take the pan off the stove, cool and refrigerate the topping in a bowl, to chill overnight.

Blueberry:

Ingredients: About 2-3 drops canola oil or butter; 2 pints, about 4 cups fresh blueberries; 1 cup sugar; 2 tbsp. lemon juice; 1 peeled, cored and grated apple; 2 tbsp. corn starch.

Heat a large and deep sauté pan with oil or butter. When hot, add the grated apple, fresh blueberries and lemon juice and cook on medium-high heat for 5 minutes. Add sugar and stir well. As soon as you see some liquid, take out about ½ cup in a small bowl, cool it, and add corn starch, whisk well and set aside for later. Bring the apple and blueberries mixture to a boil for about 8-10 minutes. Add cornstarch mixture and stir well, still on medium-high heat until mixture is thicken for about 6-8 minutes. Take off the heat and cool completely then chill in a bowl, in the refrigerator overnight.

Apricot:

Ingredients: About 2 cups apricot jam; 1 tbsp. lemon juice; ¼ cup orange juice; 3 tbsp. corn starch.

Heat the apricot jam in a large nonreactive sauté pan on medium heat and bring to a simmer. Mix corn starch, lemon juice and orange juice; whisk well and add to the pan. Increase the heat to medium-high, stir well and bring to a boil. Cook for 5-6 minutes until mixture is thickened. Cook completely, then chill in the refrigerator at least 2 hours before using as a topping.

Banana, Raisin & Nut Muffins

Follow the recipe of Banana, Raisin & Nut Bread, under Breads. Just line a muffin pan with paper cups, spray the cups with cooking spray, pour the batter in to 15 cups, bake in a preheated 350 degrees oven for 12 to 15 minutes and serve warm or cooled.

Blueberry Muffins or Cupcakes (M: 18 large)

My husband loves these muffins fresh and hot, right out of the oven with plain butter. In Jersey we get an abundance of blueberries around Fourth of the July, so I freeze the whole pint or even whole box of six pints, as it is, in the plastic bag and take them out as needed for pancakes, muffins, pies and even just for ice cream and fruit salads.

Ingredients: 1-1/2 cups bleached all-purpose flour, 1-1/2 tsp. baking powder, ¼ tsp. salt, 3 large eggs room temp., 1 cup and 2 tbsp. fine sugar, 4 tbsp. unsalted butter softened, 2 tbsp. canola oil, 1 cup sour cream, ¼ cup water, 1 tbsp. vanilla extract, 2 cup fresh blueberries, 2 tbsp. of flour mixed with a pinch of baking powder, ½ cup chocolate chips.

Topping: 2 cups mocha filling or any other topping, 1 cup sweetened whipped cream, ice cream or ice cream sandwiches and some fresh blueberries to serve on side.

1. Preheat oven at 350 degrees. Line a muffin tin with paper cups and grease or spray them with cooking spray.
2. On a large platter or wax paper, shift together flour, baking powder and salt and set aside.
3. In a large bowl, with a hand electric mixer or stand mixer with whip attachment, beat the butter and sugar well. Add eggs and beat well again until yellow ribbon forms about 5 minutes. Whisk in ¼ cup water, 2 tabs of oil and vanilla extract. Now whisk in half of the flour mixture and beat only just to incorporate. Add sour cream and whisk well to mix the ingredients. Add rest of the flour and whisk just to combine.
4. Wash and pat dry the blueberries, spread them out on a dry platter, then sprinkle over the 2 tabs of flour mixed with a pinch of baking powder, shake a little to coat blueberries well with the flour. Using a rubber spatula, fold in by hand, the blueberries and chocolate chips into the batter. Use an ice cream scoop and fill the batter in paper cups neatly up to about half-inch below the rim. Try to distribute the blueberries evenly if possible.
5. Bake one tray at a time, on the middle shelf, in a preheated 350 degrees oven for about 20 to 25 minutes until light brown.
6. Take blueberries out of the oven, let them rest for 10 minutes then with the help of a spoon and a fork, pick them up and cool on the wire rack completely for icing, or serve warm just with butter.
7. Use a large piping bag and pipe about 2 tabs of icing on each cooled muffin, then top each with the sweetened whipped cream and a fresh blueberry.
8. Serve each decorated muffin with ice cream or ice cream sandwich and some fresh blueberries on the side.

Fancy Red Velvet Cupcakes (M: 18 Large, 24 Regular)

You can make red velvet cupcakes either fancy or low-calorie; they both are tasty.

Ingredients:
For the Cake: dry ingredients: 2 cups bleached all-purpose flour or cake flour; ¼ tsp. baking powder; ½ tsp. baking soda; ¼ tsp. salt; 2 tbsp. unsweetened cocoa powder; wet ingredients: 1-1/3 cups sugar; ¾ cup (1-1/2 stick) unsalted butter softened; 2 extra large or jumbo eggs room temperature; 1 bottle,1 ounce (28.3g) red food color gel (red icing color); 1 tsp. pure vanilla extract; 1 cup low fat buttermilk, room temperature, mixed with 2 tbsp. canola oil and 2 tbsp. lemon juice; berries to serve.

For the Filling: About 1cup thick strawberry jelly or apricot jam.

For the Frosting: One package, 8-ounces softened cream cheese; 2 sticks (1 cup) softened unsalted butter; 2 cup sifted powder sugar; 2 tbsp. orange juice; 1 tsp. pure vanilla extract.

1.   Grease a 12 cups muffin tin inside the cups and on the surface well. Line the tin with paper cups. Spray the cups with cooking spray. If you are greasing the paper cups, keep them in the stack; dip a lightly moistened piece of paper towel, hold the stack in one hand and grease the cups with the other hand, then line the muffin tin.
2.   Sift the dry ingredients together in a medium bowl. In another large bowl, cream butter and the sugar together with an electric mixer; add the eggs, break the yolk and cream together for 1 minute. Add the food coloring and the vanilla extract and cream together, scraping the bottom well. Now alternating with flour mixture in three times, and the buttermilk mixture in two times, starting and ending with the flour mixture, add the dry and the wet mixtures. Beat after each addition just to mix the ingredients; do not over mix. Using an ice cream scoop about ¾ full, fill the paper cups with the batter about half-inch below the rim.
3.   Bake in a preheated oven on a cookie sheet or a baking sheet for about 20-25 minutes; they are done when the top is puffed and springy, and a toothpick inserted in the center comes out clean. Cool in the pan for 5 minutes, move a knife around the edges of the tin cups and invert the cupcakes on a platter. Cool right side up on a wire rack completely. Bake the second batch the same way.

To Fill the Cupcakes: Using an apple corer, take out the center of the muffin; using a knife, pull out the crumbs, then drop about 1 tsp. of thick jelly/jam in the hole.

To Frost the Cupcakes: Whisk the cream cheese in a medium bowl with an electric mixer, then beat in the butter well. Add the powdered sugar and beat well. At the end fold, in the orange juice and the vanilla extract. Refrigerate then pipe the frosting on the top of the cupcakes, covering the jelly hole and dot the edges with the frosting. Serve with berries.

Low-Calorie Red Velvet Cupcakes

Follow the recipe above for the Red Velvet Cupcakes, just reduce the butter in the cake to ½ cup (1 stick) and fold in ½ cup of the apple sauce at the end, in the batter. Do not fill and do not frost the cupcakes. If you wish, press in one shelled almond or the pistachio on each muffin just before baking.

White Fudge Cupcakes (M: 24)

These cupcakes are filled with white fudge and topped with white chocolate frosting. What could be better than that? These are a fun to make and fun to eat.

Ingredients:

For the Cake: 2 cups bleached all-purpose flour; 3 tbsp. softened butter; ¾ tsp. baking soda; ½ tsp. baking powder; ¼ tsp. salt; 1 tsp. vanilla extract; 2 cups sugar; 2 extra large eggs room temperature; ¾ cup sour cream, ¾ cup whole milk.

For the Filling: ½ cups heavy cream; 1 pkg. 4oz. (113g) premium white chocolate baking bar, chopped; ½ c marmalade or apricot jam.

For the Frosting: 2 sticks (½ pound) unsalted butter softened; 2 cups confectioners' sugar; 1 pkg. 4oz. (113g) premium white chocolate baking bar, chopped.

For the Cake: Grease the top of a 12-cup muffin tin, then line with paper cups; spray the cups with cooking spray or grease them lightly with a piece of oily paper towel. Move an oven rack in the center and preheat the oven at 350 degrees.

In a large bowl, mix together the flour and the butter by hand, then whisk in the baking soda, baking powder and the salt. Take out the mixture on a platter.

In the same bowl with an electric mixer, whisk eggs and the sugar on high speed for 1-2 minutes, then add the sour cream and vanilla extract and whisk in well. Now on medium speed, alternate with half of the milk, whisk in well, then half of the flour mixture, whisk in just to combine, then whisk rest of the milk and the rest of the flour mixture just to combine. Pour the batter in the prepared cups with an ice cream scoop, about ¾ inch below the rim.

Bake the muffins for 17 to 18 minutes until the top is firm to touch. While the cupcakes are baking, turn the tin around halfway during the baking. Take them out of the oven and cool them in the pan for 5 minutes, then take them out of the tin with a teaspoon onto a wire rack. Bake the second batch same way, and cool completely.

For the Filling: Heat the marmalade or jam in a pot on medium heat for 5 minutes or until it is liquid, then strain through a sieve into a small bowl, scraping the bottom of the sieve to get all the mixture out in the bowl. You can save the grated orange from the sieve and top the cupcakes later.

Heat the heavy cream in the same pot, take the pot off the heat and add the chopped chocolate; cover and set the pot aside for 5 minutes. Stir the mixture with a whisk and when the chocolate is melted, add the strained marmalade or the jam and whisk just to mix. Using an apple corer, take out about 1 inch of center of the cupcakes (do not go all the way to the bottom) and fill with 2 tsp. of the white chocolate fudge.

For the Frosting: Melt the chocolate in the microwave oven, stirring every 20 seconds for about 1-1/2 minutes, or over the warm water and set aside. Whisk the softened butter with an electric mixer (use a knife to get the butter out of the mixer) then add the powdered sugar and whisk in well. Now add the cooled chocolate and whisk just to mix in.

Top the cupcake with about 2 tbsp. of frosting or pipe over them with a piping bag. I use a mini whisk, dipping the whisk in the frosting, and go in a circle to top the frosting. Now garnish the frosting with a little jam or shredded drained orange from the sieve.

Store the cupcake in a tray for 1 day in the room temperature (I keep the platter in the turned-off cooled oven), then refrigerate them in the cake-saver container. Bring the cupcakes out of the refrigerator 2-3 hours before serving; serve them now or heat them in the microwave oven for 15 seconds to melt the fudge inside.

Tip: Greasing the top of the muffin tin helps the cupcake or the muffin get out of the pan easily.

If you do not have cooking spray, dip a small piece of paper towel (3x3 inches) in water, squeeze out the water and then dip in about ½ tsp. of oil or melted butter at a time; hold the stack of the paper cup (do not separate the cups) and go around the sides and grease the cups then grease the bottom. The paper cups will stay in shape while you are greasing them.

Cupcakes Variations

Lemon Cupcakes

Follow the cup cake recipe above for the White Fudge Cupcakes and bake the cupcakes. For the filling prepare: 1 box 2.75 ounces (77g) lemon pudding and pie filling and pipe about 2 tsp. in the center of the cupcakes, Add remaining prepared pudding mix to the frosting.

Orange Cupcakes

You can do the same as for the Lemon Cupcakes, using the orange flavor of the pudding mix, or add about ¼ cup orange drink mix powder in the batter, and another ¼ cup orange drink mix powder in the frosting.

Pistachio Cupcakes

Follow the recipe above for White Fudge Cupcakes but mix in the batter: 1 box 1 ounce (28G) of pistachio Jello pudding and pie filling, and bake the cupcakes with the same fudge filling as above. For the Frosting: also mix 1 box 1 oz. (28g) pistachio Jello pudding & pie filling to the prepared frosting.

You can also whisk in 3-4 tbsp. green tea powder to both the cupcake batter and the frosting, to give green color, and/or add about ¼ cup of Irish cream to the frosting to give Irish flavor.

Pineapple Cupcakes

Follow the recipe above for the White Fudge Cupcakes, just mix in the batter: 1 box, 1 oz. (28g) pineapple Jello pudding and pie filling and then bake the cupcakes. Also, mix in the prepared frosting: 1 box 1 oz. (28g) of the pineapple Jello pudding and pie filling. Garnish with pineapple topping: bought in an 8-ounce bottle, or use the crushed and well drained pineapple (op).

Coconut Cupcakes

Follow the whole recipe above for the White Fudge Cupcakes, just increase the amount of the milk from ¾ cup to 1cup and add 1cup of coconut flour or coconut powder in the better. Coconut powder/flour gives a very good taste to the cupcakes. If you wish, garnish the top with a little grated coconut. (Coconut flour or the powder is very inexpensive at the Indian grocery stores. It comes in the clear plastic bags.)

Fudge & Fruit Cupcakes (M:12)

Some of my friends asked me to whip up something fantastic and something fast. Here is a recipe that almost anyone can do it. This is what I had baked for our local police department on Valentine's Day. Sgt. Griffin and Patrol Officer D'Alessandro welcomed me with open arms.

Ingredients: 1 Box 15.25oz (432G) Super-moist Triple Chocolate Fudge Cake Mix; 3 large eggs; 1-1/4cup water; 1 cup unsweetened apple sauce; 1/2cup vegetable oil; 1box 1.4oz (39G) instant chocolate pudding mix; 1 cup semi-sweet chocolate chips.

Topping: ½ Cup milk; 8oz. semi-sweet chocolate chopped; 1/4cup heated and strained orange marmalade (save zest for garnish etc.); 1 container, 8oz. glazed cherries; sprinklers (op).

Preheat oven at 350 degrees. Grease or spray with cooking spray the top of the muffin tin. Take the stack of the paper cup liners, lightly damp a paper towel, and then dip lightly in the oil and move around inside each paper cup liner and place them inside the muffin tin.

In a large bowl whisk eggs and water first for 2 minutes, add the apple sauce and oil; whisk for 2 minutes. Whisk in the cake mix and the pudding mix. With an ice cream scoop fill the cup cake liners about half inch below the rim. Now plant about 5-6 chocolate chips in the center of the batter. Bake in a preheated oven in the center for about 25 minutes turning the muffin tin around halfway once during the baking. Take them out of the oven and let them cool in the muffin tin for 10 minutes. Loosen the edges and turn them over in a platter. Place them right side up and cool completely.

Topping: This topping is a ganache (Chocolate sauce). Place the chopped chocolate in a medium bowl. Bring the milk almost to a boiling point and pour over the chocolate, cover, and let it seep for 5 minutes. Then whisk in the strained marmalade, cool a little. Using a tablespoon spread out the sauce over the cooled cup cakes. Top with a cherry and some sprinklers. Serve immediately or store overnight in a cooled oven.

Tip: You can make your own Super-moist Triple Chocolate Fudge Cake Mix: take one chocolate cake recipe, add 1cup grated semi-sweet chocolate, and 2Tbsp. each corn starch and dark brown sugar whisk well to combine.

Corn Muffins (M:12)

These muffins are so tasty and so easy to make that even a 12-year-old child can make them. Serve them warm for full flavor.

Ingredients:

Dry: 1 cup medium texture yellow corn meal; 1/2cup dry milk powder; 3/4 cup all-purpose flour; 1 c sugar; 1 tsp. baking soda; ¼ tsp. salt;

Wet: ¾ cup, plus 2Tbsp. orange juice; 1 large egg; 4 tbsp. vegetable oil.

Preheat the oven at 400 degrees. Line a 12-cup muffin pan with the paper cups and light grease or spray them with cooking oil.

In a large bowl whisk together the dry ingredients. In a small bowl, whisk together the orange juice and the egg. Then whisk in the oil and pour over the dry ingredients. Mix just to combine. Fill in the paper cups evenly and bake them about 15-20 until golden and the tooth pick inserted in the center comes out clean.

Serve warm with coffee, milk or tea. Do not refrigerate, just leave them on the counter, tented with the foil, and they all will be gone.

Quinoa (Keen-wah)

How to Buy: Buy whole grain organic premium natural quinoa. Do not buy ground or colored. It is a gluten-free, high-protein, high-fiber and contains 9 essential amino acids, vitamins, enzymes and phytonutrients.

How to Cook: In a medium pot add 1 cup quinoa, 1-1/4 cup water and 2 pinches salt. Bring to a rolling boil, stir for 5 minutes, cover, turn off the stove and let it sit on the stove for 20 minutes. It's ready to use. You can keep in room temperature and it will stay fresh for about 2 hours

Quinoa-oatmeal Muffins (makes: 18)

Ingredients: 3 large eggs, 1 cup apple sauce, ½ tsp. cinnamon, 4 tbsp. canola oil, 2 cups cooked quinoa, 1 cup old-fashioned quick oats pulsed in the blender to crumbs, ½ cup all-purpose flour, 1-1/2 tsp. baking powder, ½ tsp. baking soda, ½ tsp. salt, 1 tbsp. pure vanilla extract,1 cup semi-sweet chocolate chips or ¾ cup dry cranberries, 3 bananas cut in quarter-lengthwise, then cut across in ½ inch cubes, about ¼ cup chopped walnuts.

Preheat oven at 350 degrees, Line a 12-cup muffin tin with paper cups and spray with the cooking spray.

1. In a large bowl, whisk together eggs, add apple sauce and cinnamon, whisk well. Add oil, quinoa, oatmeal, flour, baking powder, baking soda and salt and whisk well. Add chocolate chips or cranberries and mix well. Fold in the vanilla extract and banana cubes.
2. Using an ice cream scoop, fill in the paper cups with the mixture about halfway; heat in oven at 350 degrees for about 20-25 minutes until golden on top. Leave the muffins in the turned-off oven until cooled, about 35 minutes. Serve warm. No sugar added; natural sugar is sufficient.

Oat, Coconut & Pineapple Muffins (M: 15)

Every ingredient in these muffins is a healthy ingredient. So these are healthy as well as very tasty muffins.

Dry ingredients: 1 cup all-purpose un-sifted flour; ½ cup wheat germ; 1 cup old-fashioned rolled oats; 1 cup dry unsweetened coconut powder or peeled and very fine-grated fresh coconut; 2 tsp. baking powder, ½ tsp. baking soda; ¼ tsp. salt.

Wet ingredients: 2 large eggs; ½ cup light brown sugar; 1 cup low-fat plain yogurt; ¼ cup water; ¼ cup canola oil; 1 large ripe banana mashed; ½ cup glazed pineapple cut into ½-inch pieces; 1 cup chopped almonds; ½ cup dry cranberries or chocolate chips.
For garnish: ¼ cup coconut powder or fresh sliced or grated coconut mixed with ¼ cup concentrated pineapple juice.

Line the muffin tin with paper cup liners and grease lightly or spray with the cooking spray.
In a medium bowl, stir together the dry ingredients and set them aside. In a large bowl whip together eggs and sugar well. Add yogurt, water, mashed banana, oil and whip all together just to mix. Add pineapple, almonds and cranberries on one side, using only half of the liquid. Add and whip in the dry ingredients on the other half side, in the liquid. Then combine all together. Chill in the refrigerator for 30 minutes.
Preheat the oven at 400 degrees. Place about 2 cups water in an aluminum pan on one side of the middle rack. Fill the muffin cups up to half-inch below the rim. Spread out 1 tsp. garnish on the top. Bake in a preheated oven for about 20 minutes or until puffed and light brown. Take the muffins out of the tin with a spoon and a fork and cool a little on the wire rack. Serve warm with coffee, milk or tea.

Tips:

1.   Unsweetened, dry coconut powder and glazed pineapple are available at Indian grocery stores.

2.   To add extra flavor, replace garnish with ½ cup of pineapple topping. Also, add 1 cup chopped pineapple and use only ½ cup chopped almonds.

3.   Oat muffins tend to dry slightly. Baking with a pan half full of water will keep the muffins moist.

Lattice Top Apple Pie (M:One 9-inch Pie)

From August to November we make a lot of Apple pies and Apple Crumbles. This coconut Lattice Top is so tasty, it just crumbles in your mouth. You can cook Apples two days ahead and make the dough one day ahead, if you prefer. Just bring the cooked Apples, in room temperature, one hour before making pie. Practice makes perfect, so after making one pie you will master the tricks. This dough is for 2 crusts: top and bottom.

Ingredients:

For the Dough: 1 Stick, 8Tbsp. unsalted cold Butter; 2cups All-purpose Flour, plus extra for dusting; 1/2cup fine grated or powdered Coconut; 1/2Tsp. Baking Soda, 1/2Tsp. Salt; 1/2cup Sugar; 1/4cup cold Sour Cream; 3-4Tbsp. Ice Water.

For the Filling: 2Tbsp. Butter; 4 Granny Smith Apples and 4 Golden Delicious Apples; a mixture of:1cup Sugar mixed with 1Tbsp. Corn Starch, 1/2Tsp. Salt, and 1/2Tsp. Cinnamon; 2Tbsp. Cookie Crumbs; 2Tbsp.Butter for dotting the Apples, and extra melted butter to brush the top.

Make the Filling: Peel, cut and core the apples, then slice them about 1/3-inches slices, so you will have 12 slices from each apple. Heat a large saute pan on medium heat. Add butter and saute the apples on medium-high heat for 3-4 minutes. Lower the heat and cook covered for another 10-15 minutes, until they are soft. When they are cooled toss them with the sugar & Cinnamon mixture. If you do not want to cook the apples, then use only Golden or Red Delicious apples, and slice them very thin.

Make the Dough: In a large bowl place 2cups flour, coconut, baking soda and salt and whisk. Grate the cold butter or slice it very thin over the flour mixture. Mix and separate each slice of butter into the flour. Spread out the sour cream and mix and then ice water and mix by hand or in the food processor. As soon as dough comes together, knead it a little dusting with the flour. Divide the dough into two parts, one slightly larger than the other. Wrap the smaller portion in plastic wrap and refrigerate.

For the Lattice Top: Using a large plastic wrap, make a square disk between two layers of the wrap then roll out in a 9X9-inch square. If the dough is sticky place it in the freezer for 3-4 minutes or proceed. Cut out the square into 1/2 to 3/4-inch strips. Place a piece of parchment paper in a cookie tray and make the lattice top over it.

First lay down half of the strips vertically, spacing about 3/4-inch apart from each other, on the parchment paper. Then starting from the left fold back every other strip (fold back to the left 2,4,6, and 8th strips). Now lay down one strip vertically, starting from the left. Unfold the strips over the vertical strip. Now alternating the strips, fold the 1,3,5,7th strips to the left. Lay down another strip vertically and then unfold the folded strips over it. Proceed with the same procedure. You need a 9X9 lattice top. When all are done turn over a 9-inch pie plate over the lattice top and trim out the excess. Freeze the lattice top, until you are done making the bottom crust. Make or save about 3 extra long (9-inches) strips to cover and crimp the lattice top edges, set the strips aside until needed.

Roll out the smaller portion of the dough from the refrigerator, between two layers of the plastic wrap, into 10-inch diameter. Lift off the top plastic, and place the pie plate upside down over the dough, invert the pie plate together with the dough and the plastic wrap, and line the pie plate with the dough. Now press down the dough into the pie plate, pressing over the plastic wrap all around the corners. Shape the edges, to come up to the rim, redistributing the dough with the plastic wrap. Then peel off the plastic wrap.

Preheat the oven 350 degrees. Brush the lined dough with melted butter. Sprinkle the cookie crumbs in the center of the pie plate, then fill in with the apples, and press down the applies to shape in a round. Dot with 2Tbsp. butter. Now bring the lattice top from the freezer, scrap it off the bottom and slide over the apples. Using 3 set aside strips of the dough cover the edges, then crimp them by placing the index finger on the edge and pressing the dough around the finger. Brush the lattice strips generously with butter.

Bake the pie in a heavy bottom baking tray, in a preheated 350 degrees oven for 50 to 55 minutes until golden. Turn around the pie halfway during the baking and then tent the top with a foil. Turn off the oven but leave the pie in the off oven for another 10 minutes to crisp. Serve immediately or wait until it comes to a room temperature.

Blueberry Pie

This Pie is very tasty and well settled when refrigerated. I use 2 tabs of ginger snaps crumbs (or your favorite cookie crumbs with a pinch of ginger) to soak up the liquid in the bottom and give a good flavor.

Ingredients: One 9-inch Pie shell; 2Tabs unsalted Butter plus extra to brush; 1 apple peeled, cut, cored and grated; 1-1/4cups sugar, 2 pints (551 ml each) fresh blueberries; pinch Salt; 2Tbsp. lemon juice;

2Tbsp. (2) ginger snaps; 1Tbsp. (about .50 Ounce, 14G) unflavored gelatin; 1/2cup toasted almond or walnuts (or a mixture of both) chopped fine for the topping.

1. Soak gelatin in 4Tbsp. of water and set aside to bloom.
2. Preheat oven at 350 degrees. Take out the frozen pie shell and bake loosely covered in a preheated oven for about 10-minutes on a baking tray.
3. In a heavy bottom and a nonreactive sauté pan heat the butter on medium - heat, add grated apples and cook stirring constantly for 2 minutes until bubbly. Increase the heat to medium-high add sugar, save about 1/2-C large blueberries and add rest of the blueberries to pan, lemon juice, salt, gelatin, stir well and cook blueberries for about 10 minutes just until sugar is dissolved and blueberries start getting thick. Take off the stove and cool a little.
4. Take the pie shell out of oven brush all over with butter then sprinkle the ginger snap crumbs in the bottom and pour in the blueberry. Now drop the large blueberry (set aside) in the center, In a single layer and gently push them down in the mixture. Cover the edges with the aluminum foil completely, place the pie shell on the tray and bake for about 30-35 minutes until center is set and crust is light brown. During the baking turn the pie shell half-way around for even cooking. Take the pie out of the oven, open the edges and sprinkle the almond and walnut crumbs in a circle all around the edges, leaving the center open. Put the pie back in the oven, bake for 5-minutes and turn off the oven. Leave the pie in the oven to cool for 15 minutes. Cool pie on a wire rack in the room temperature. Serve the pie or chill in refrigerator to set further.

Cherry Pie (S:6-8)

You have to make this pie when cherries are in the season, around summer time. Once you make this pie you will love to make it over and over again. This is so tasty and original, and nothing like home baked. I use this yogurt curst and coconut topping in lot of my pies.

Ingredients:

For the Crust: 1-1/2 Cups All-purpose Flour, plus extra for dusting; 1/2Tsp. Baking Soda; 1/4Tsp. Salt; 1/3cups Plain Yogurt; 4Tbsp. lightly soften Butter, plus extra for baking.

Make the Crust: In a bowl whisk in flour, baking soda, and salt, then rub in the butter, add the yogurt and mix all together with the hands, and make a disc. Use a large piece of the plastic wrap, dust it with some flour and roll out the dough into about 10-inch round circle. Grease or spray a 9-inch pie plate, fold the dough in half, then line the pie plate. Push the dough all around the corners, and fold the extra dough underneath the edges. Now crimp the edges by using the forefinger and pushing the dough around it with the other hand. Make some holes in the bottom with the tines of a fork, cover loosely with the foil and bake halfway, at 350 degrees preheated oven for 15 minutes. Take out the crust and brush the edges with the butter.

For the Filling: 1 Pound stemmed, halved and pitted fresh Cherries, 1/4cup dry Cherries or Cranberries; a mixture of 4Tbsp. Corn Starch with 1cup of Sugar, and 1/2Tsp. of Cinnamon; 2Tbsp. Cookies or Cracker Crumbs.

For the Topping: 1 Cup All-purpose Flour, 1stick, 8Tbsp. lightly softened Butter; 1cup fine grated unsweetened Coconut; 1cup Sugar.

Assemble the Pie: In a bowl place the fresh and dry cherries or dry cranberries, sprinkle over the sugar mixture, and stir well with a wooden spoon. Now sprinkle the cookie crumbs in the bottom of the partially baked crust and pour over the cherry mixture. Now turn over the top cherries facing the cut side down and skin side up.

Place the Topping: In a bowl mix together all topping ingredients by hand. Take out about 1/2cup of the topping in your hand, make a fist, and firmly press the topping in your hand to make a roll. Then break the roll over the filling into about 1-inch pieces (balls), and starting from the rim of the pie line up the topping balls in a circle. Keep on making the topping balls and keep on covering the cherries.

Place the prepared pie on a large baking sheet and bake it loosely covered with the aluminum foil, in a preheated 350 degrees oven for about 30 minutes. Take off the foil, rotate the tray half way, and bake another 20-25 minutes open, until golden brown and bubbly. Take out the tray and let it rest for 30 minutes till all the juices are gone back to filling. Serve as it is or with the 1/2cup sour cream whipped together with ½ cup whipped cream, or with ice cream.

Pecan Pie (1-9-inch Pie)

Ingredients: 1 Pie crust lined in a 9-inch pie pan (see apple or cherry pie) partially baked for 10 minutes at 350 degrees; 2 extra-large yolks and 1 whole egg; ¼ cup light brown sugar; ¾ cup maple syrup; 1Tsp. vanilla extract; 1/4Tsp. salt; 1oz. semi-sweet chocolate grated; 1/2cup chopped pecans; 1cup halved pecans; butter to brush on the edges.

In a medium bowl beat together egg, yolks, salt, vanilla extract, sugar and syrup well. Pour the mixture into the pie shell. Sprinkle the grated chocolate all over. Now line the halved pecans on the edges of the mixture going in a circle, holding carefully and working with a fork and knife to hold pecans in its place. Sprinkle half of the chopped pecans in the center. Brush the edges with the butter then cover with the strips of foil. Place the pie on a baking sheet and bake in a preheated 300 degree oven for about an hour or until center is settled. Sprinkle the rest of the chopped pecans in the center, cool and serve with or without whipped cream.

Pumpkin Pie (S:6-8)

This doesn't have to be Thanksgiving tradition. You can bake this pie all year round. It is healthy as well as tasty. Bake a day before so it settles well. It is so tasty that you will bake it over and over again.

Ingredients: Crust: 1-1/2Cups All Purpose Flour; 1Tsp. Baking Powder; 1/2Tsp. Baking Soda; 1/4Tsp. Salt; 4Tbsp. cold unsalted Butter; 1/4cup cold low fat Plain Yogurt.
Filling: 2Cups Pumpkin Puree from the can (or make your own puree by roasting the fresh pumpkin, cored, cut in large wedges and drizzled with some oil, in a baking tray, at 400 degrees for about 25 minutes or until it is soft); 1 large Egg; 1can, 14 ounces sweetened Condensed Milk; 1/4Tsp. Salt; each1/2Tsp.: Ginger Powder, Cinnamon; 1/4Tsp. ground Cloves; 3Tbsp. Dark Chocolate Liqueur, such as Godiva.

Crust: In a medium bowl whisk together flour, baking powder, baking soda, salt then grate the cold butter over the flour mixture and mix well. Add the yogurt and mix well to make a ball. If needed you can add 1-2 tbsp. cold ice water. Roll out the dough between 2 plastic wraps, into about 10-1/4-inch circle for an 9-inch deep dish pie plate.

Line the pie plate with the crust pressing the curst against the plate then fold the extra handing edges underneath the edge. Now put the index finger on the folding edge and push in the crust all around the finger to make a scallop edge. You can also press the edges with the tines of a fork, if you prefer. Poke the fork in the bottom of the crust about 1-inch apart. Cover the curst with a piece of the aluminum foil and chill in the freezer for 15-20 minutes. Then place pie plate in a baking tray and bake at 350 degrees for 20 minutes.

Filling: While pie is chilling, whisk together the filling ingredients in a bowl. Slowly pour in the filling in the baked pie crust and place on a baking tray again, cover the edges with strips of aluminum foil and bake pie at 350 degrees for about 1 hour. Let pie cool in the room temperature and then chill overnight in the refrigerator before serving. Serve with or without whipped cream.

Cakes

Chocolate, Cocoa Powder and How to Melt Chocolate

Chocolate and cake go together very well. Dark chocolate is a "super food." It has polyphenols (especially the flavonols) the super nutrients that act as the dietary antioxidants, anti-inflammatories, antimicrobials and antifungals. They help lower the bad cholesterol (LDL), and raise good cholesterol (HDL), reduce blood pressure and risk of heart disease.

Chocolate is made from the cocoa beans. It has very little caffeine, about 11 mg in a bar of chocolate.

The cocoa powder has half of the fat because the fat content is taken out during the process. Use Dutch-processed cocoa powder; it is refined and has less acid. When using the natural cocoa powder, try to use with some baking soda to reduce the effect of the acid.

Cocoa power is readily available for baking around my house. To get the effect of the chocolate, use cocoa powder with warm liquid. I call it cocoa melt. Use cocoa with warm water or warm milk, or for a smooth and silky flavor use light or heavy cream, and a little light brown sugar. If you add some dark chocolate with it, it will be smoother and more flavorful.

I also like to use chocolate liqueur occasionally, both with cocoa powder and chocolate to give a real chocolaty flavor. The white chocolate liqueur goes almost with any cooking to give an intense flavor of chocolate. My low-fat cheese cake and eggnog are made with the chocolate liqueur. People go crazy with the eggnog.

Buy a good dark chocolate with high contents of cocoa solids, somewhere around 60% to 70%. This way you will have more flavor and more polyphenols. Also, use unsweetened and semi-sweet chocolate so can control the sugar. Try to avoid buying the milk chocolate to avoid using extra calories and less polyphenols. White chocolate is not a real chocolate, but it gives the taste of cocoa butter.

Cocoa Melt: I melt cocoa powder in warm liquid, with some sugar and butter; it tastes better and becomes almost like chocolate.

How to Melt the Chocolate

Direct Heat: Heat about ¼ cup to ½ cup of milk, half-and-half or heavy cream, on low heat in a pot (do not boil); add the fine-chopped chocolate, stir once, cover and set aside for 5 minutes. Open and stir well. The chocolate should be melted. If not, heat the mixture over low heat again just for a few seconds. You can also add butter, instant coffee, cocoa powder, vanilla extract, etc.

Microwave: Use a microwavable medium bowl, add chopped chocolate or any other ingredients such as: a little heavy cream, or a few slices of butter, instant coffee, etc. Heat on high for 1 to 2 minutes, stirring the chocolate every 25-30 seconds.

Double Boiler: Use the top part of double boiler or make your own double boiler by heating a half-full medium pot of water and placing the chopped chocolate in a large glass or stainless steel bowl on the top. Stir the chocolate until it is melted. Do not let the pot touch the water.

Chocolates and Chocolate Liqueur

You not only want to bake a delicious cake, but a cake that is out of this world. When the chocolate-lovers eat one piece of my luscious chocolate cake or chocolate cheesecake, they go like "aah," and some ask "did you bake this or buy it?" The secret is fine chocolate together with the chocolate liqueur to boost the flavor. I buy 1 bottle, 375 ML, of the chocolate liqueur, and it last me for over a year. I even use this in my eggnog, and in the beet red velvet cake. It gives good aroma as well as a good taste.

When it comes to white chocolate, in most of my white frosting I use white chocolate. It settles well and it gives a unique flavor. When I have an Irish meal with my Irish family, I also add some Irish cream to my frosting. You can also use green tea powder to give green color to the frosting.

Cakes

Baking the Cakes: When baking cakes, be careful of the moisture in the atmosphere. If it is raining, it will take less liquid and may have different baking results. To bake a cake, have the cake pan ready. First grease the pan in the bottom with butter or cooking spray, line with the round parchment paper, grease the parchment well, sprinkle about 1 tsp. of flour, shake the pan to spread out the flour and then tap out the excess flour. Greasing the pan first makes it easy to invert the cake, and greasing and flouring the parchment paper makes it easy to peel off the paper.

When baking cakes, have all the ingredients ready and count the ingredients against the recipe. I like to count the items, comparing with the recipe before making the cake. Any dairy product that is to be mixed in the batter should be at room temperature.

Cakes are baked better with cake flour or pastry flour. You can also use sifted all-purpose flour. Most of the cakes are baked with all-purpose flour. Use both butter for flavor and oil for texture. Most of the cakes are baked at 350-degree temperature. Bake on the middle shelf and rotate halfway through baking, and rotate the pans if you are baking two pans at the same time. Some cakes like pound cakes are baked in the cold oven, so follow the instructions. To test the cake, insert a toothpick in the center and only few crumbs (3-4) should come out attached on the toothpick. Cool the cake in the pan for about 5 to 8 minutes; move a dinner knife around the edges to loosen the cake, then invert on a greased wire rack, peel of the paper and let it cool completely (at least 1 hour), slice, fill and/or frost the cake.

Baking and Storing the Cake

Always bake a cake on the middle shelf, in a preheated oven. If you have three cake pans, put two pans on the middle shelf and one in the center on the lower third shelf and rotate them top to bottom, and turning half way around during the baking.

To store the cake: Place some toothpicks over the cake and cover loosely with plastic wrap and/or use a cake saver (cake container with a lid) and refrigerate for up to a week. If you are baking cakes ahead or freezing them, wrap them in plastic wrap, place in a container and store in the refrigerator or freeze them. Thaw overnight and frost them before serving.

Basic Layer Cake

Layer cakes are tastier than just plain cakes. You can bake 1 cake or bake 3 separate cakes in three cake pans. If you are baking 3 cakes, make sure you slice off the top to even out the tops, brush off the crumbs and then assemble them. I also like to invert the top layer (bottom side up) for a smooth finish.

Ingredients for the Cake: 2 cups granulated sugar; 2 sticks (1 cup) softened (room temperature) unsalted butter, plus extra for greasing the pan; sift together the dry ingredients: 3-1/2 cups all-purpose bleached or cake flour, 2 tsp. baking powder, ½ tsp. baking soda, ½ tsp. salt; 3 extra-large eggs, and 1 extra-large egg white; 2 tsp. pure vanilla extract; ½ tsp. almond or 1 tsp. coconut extract; 1 cup light buttermilk whisked with ¾ cup sour cream.

For the Frosting: 4 stick (1 pound) softened unsalted butter; 6 cups, 1-1/2 pound sifted confectioner's (powder) sugar; 2 tsp. pure vanilla extract; ½ tsp. almond or 1tsp. coconut extract; to decorate: glazed fruits, grated chocolate, or sprinkles, etc.

Preheat the oven at 350 degrees. Grease or spray with cooking butter spray, 3 round, 8- or 9-inch cake pans, line with the parchment paper, and grease again.

In the clean and dry bowl of a stand mixer with the whip attachment, cream the sugar and the butter on low speed, until it is creamy, about 5 minutes. Increase the speed of the mixer to medium and cream the mixture for another 10 minutes, until it is fluffy and double or triple in volume, scraping the sides with a rubber spatula as needed. Beat the eggs and the egg white in a small bowl, and add them in 3 times, whisking the mixture well after each addition until they are incorporated well, and before adding the next batch. Add the vanilla and the almond or coconut extract, and beat well. Now, ending with the dry ingredients, and adding in two batches, add half of the buttermilk mixture and incorporate well for about 3-4 minutes, then add the dry ingredient mixture and incorporate well for about 3-4 minutes; repeat in the same order one more time.

Pour the batter evenly in prepared pans, even out the top, and bake in a preheated oven for about 18-20 minutes, depending on the size of the pan and the oven, or until a toothpick inserted in the center comes out with only a few crumbs on. Do not over-bake. Rotate the pans during the baking, from top to middle shelf, for even baking. Take the pans out of the oven, cool the cakes in the pan for 5 minutes. Move around a dinner knife on the edge, shake the pan a little, and invert the cake over a wire rack; cool for 15 minutes, take off the parchment paper and cool completely before frosting.

Frosting: In a large bowl on medium speed, or in a stand mixer, whisk together the softened butter until it is creamy, for about 5 minutes. Slowly add the powdered sugar in 4 batches, whisking each batch for about 2-3 minutes until it is incorporated well, before adding the next batch. Beat in the vanilla and almond or coconut extracts well. Now beat in 2 tbsp. of milk to make a spreadable consistency of frosting. If needed, add more milk 1 tsp. at a time. If the frosting is too thin, whisk in some more sugar. Decorate the cake after frosting it.

Assembling the Layer Cake

1. Bake cakes in two or three 9-inch cake pans or as per recipe. When cakes are cooled completely, slice them horizontally in to two slices or as desired. Put cake on a large cutting board or rotating stand. First, slice off the top with a serrated knife and make the top even. Using a small bread knife, score and cut edges about one inch deep, slicing the cake in two. Then, using a large serrated knife and rotating the platter, slice cake in to two horizontal slices, following your one-inch-deep cut as a guide. Brush off all the loose crumbs from the cut surface and slide the slices onto cardboard or aluminum foil or parchment paper, and place them on a cutting board. Slice the whole cake the same way.

2. Prepare a large cake-serving platter; cover the edges of the platter with wide strips of parchment or wax papers, drop about 2 tsp. of the frosting in the center to hold the cake. Place one flat-bottom slice of the cake on the platter (save the other flat bottom for the top.) Now, brush the bottom slice with the syrup. Then, using a metal spatula, take out about 1 cup of filling and spread on the bottom slice evenly. Take out and slide another cake slice onto the bottom slice; press it down firmly so that the cake is solid. Repeat with syrup and the filling until the whole cake is assembled.

3. When all cake slices are assembled, frost the side of the cake. Place about 3 tbsp. of frosting on the top of the cakes near the edge, and carefully slide down some of the frosting, on an angle, on the side of the cake. When side is frosted, use the rest of the frosting to cover the top. Again divide the frosting and drop it on the edges, and even out frosting covering the top of the cake. Note: If you are not using the same frosting on the top, then frost the side of the cake with icing on the metal spatula from the bottom and moving to the top, on the side. Then with a clean spatula, just smooth out the side of the cake. This way top of the cake will remain untouched.

4. To decorate the cake on the side, use some coconut flakes, chocolate crumbs, and roasted chopped nuts. Tilt the platter and sprinkle, or press in the crumbs on the side. If you have any crumbs left, use them on the top near the edges in a circle. At the center, put something different: nuts, dry/fresh fruits and berries. You can also pipe some of the frosting on the top and bottom edges of the cake, or just decorate the top with cinnamon sugar, cocoa powder or write with a contrast-color icing, etc. Carefully, take out the wax/parchment papers from all around, pushing the frosting back into the cake with the edge of a small sharp knife.

5. Store the cake in the cake saver or covered container, inside or outside of the refrigerator per recipe. If you want to refrigerate the cake, place some toothpicks on the top in a circle and loosely tent the cake with aluminum foil or plastic wrap. Do that so the decoration on the top of the cake is not disturbed.

Almond and Pistachio Cake (Serves: 12)

This is an easy, healthy and very tasty cake. I have made something like my mother used to make - the almond square cake.

Ingredients: About 2 cups 10 oz. (283 g) bag slivered almonds, divided; 1 cup, 6 oz. (170g) bag shelled pistachios; about 2 cup, 1 bag 12 oz. (340g) white chocolate morsels; 8 tbsp. softened, unsalted butter, divided plus extra for greasing the tray; 1-1/2 cups sugar; 1 tsp. almond extract or 1 tsp. ground cardamom seeds, divided; 4 extra-large eggs; 1-1/2 cups unbleached all-purpose flour; 1-1/2 tsp. baking powder; ½ tsp. salt; 1-3/4 cup low-fat 2% milk, heavy/light cream or whole milk.

1. Preheat over 350 degrees. Line a half sheet (12x18 inches) with parchment paper and grease the paper well with butter.
2. Grind about 1-1/2 cups almonds in food processor or blender and take out in a baking tray, mix ½ cup sugar, 2 tbsp. softened butter and ½ tsp. ground cardamom seeds by hand; set aside. Grind 1 cup pistachios, mix 1 tbsp. softened butter, ½ tsp. ground cardamom seeds and 1 tbsp. sugar mix well with hand in a separate baking tray. Bake both ground nuts in a preheated 350 degrees oven, for about 8 minutes, light brown. At the same time toast ½ cup leftover slivered almonds in one corner of the baking tray until light brown.
3. Melt the rest, 5 tbsp. butter, and let it cool. In the bowl of stand mixer or in a large bowl by hand electric mixer, cream eggs and 1 cup sugar, on low speed for 5 minutes. Increase the speed to medium and whisk for 10-12 minutes, until mixture is doubled in volume. Add ½ cup milk and almond extract, (if using, whisk well). Slowly add the melted butter and cream for 1 minute. Mix flour, baking powder and salt and mix with the wet ingredients just to combine.
4. Pour the batter evenly in the prepared pan, even out with the spatula. Now carefully and evenly sprinkle the ground and toasted almonds on the top. Bake in a 350-degree oven for about 15-18 minutes, until toothpick comes out clean when tested in the center. Cool the cake on a wire rack completely.
5. In a medium pot, bring almost to a boil, 1-1/4 cup milk or cream, add chocolate morsels, take off the heat, cover, set aside for 5 minutes. Stir and melt the chocolate, take out 3 tbsp. of melted chocolate to brush the sides of the cake; in the rest of the melted chocolate, add ground pistachios and stir well. It should be of a spreading consistency (if needed, add more warm milk or cream). Cut cake in half across, together with the parchment paper. Keep on piece in the bottom, spread less than half of the pistachio icing evenly over the bottom piece of the cake, on the almond side; turn over the second piece of cake over the icing, (almond side down, keeping the smooth side up). Spread rest of the pistachio icing on the top evenly. Brush the side with the reserve melted chocolate and press in the toasted slivered almonds. You can serve the cake right away.
6. To serve, cut cake in strips, about 2x4 inches. Store in room temperature for up to two days, loosely covered, then in the refrigerator, covered well.
7.

Tips: According to experts, 1 cup of Almonds have 30 grams of protein and 18 grams of fiber. Almonds should be eaten after they are soaked in water, with skin on for at least 3 hours. Chocolate-covered Almonds have vitamin E; and help you live longer.

Pistachios are high in protein, have fiber, vitamin B6, vitamin E, thiamin, zinc, copper, and manganese. The nut and the purple skin both have antioxidants. Pistachios have lutein and phenolic acid. Lutein is good for the eyes.

Basic Cheese Cake

This is the basic cheesecake batter. You can make plain cheesecake in a 9-inch round spring-form pan, or pour the batter over the thick layer of any cookie crumbs in a 8x12 platter; baking time will be a little less. I bake batter in the platter, let it settle overnight in the refrigerator, then cut into 2x2 squares, and just before serving, put in paper cups and serve topped with melted apricot jelly and fresh colorful fruits like grapes and berries. Do not put cut squares in paper cups overnight, they may get soggy.

Ingredients: Crust: 2 cups ginger cookie crumbs; 2 tbsp. melted butter; 2 tbsp. sugar; ¼ cup walnut crumbs; ½ tsp. ground cinnamon.
cake: 1-1/2 cups sugar; 4 large eggs; 3 pkgs. 8 ounces each cream cheese; 1 cup sour cream; ½ cup heavy cream both in room temperature; ½ cup crumbled tofu or ¼ cup pancake flour; 1 tbsp. pure vanilla extract, 1 tbsp. fine grated lemon zest; 2 tbsp. lemon juice; ¼ cup chocolate liquor or orange liquor (op); 2 tbsp. (.5 ounces) clear gelatin; ½ cup orange juice; 2 tbsp. melted butter; fruit and berries for garnish; chocolate pieces and/or chocolate syrup to serve.

Crust: Heat the oven at 325 F. In a small bowl combine together cookie crumbs, melted butter, sugar, walnut crumbs, cinnamon. Line a 9-inch spring-form cake pan with round cut of parchment paper; grease the paper with the non-stick cooking spray and spread out the crumbs over the parchment paper. With a flat-bottom glass, press down the crumbs in the bottom of the pan evenly. Bake the crumbs in a preheated oven for about 10-15 minutes, until light brown. Take the pan out of the oven and let it cool.

1. In a small bowl add ½ cup of orange juice, sprinkle the gelatin and stir a little and set aside for 5 minutes. Then add ¼ cup hot water, stir well and set aside covered.
2. In a large bowl add 1-1/2 cups sugar, 4 beaten eggs, cream cheese, sour cream, heavy cream, tofu, zest and vanilla extract. Beat all together with an electric hand mixer, scraping the mixer with a knife, until well combined, about 10 minutes. Add lemon juice and bloomed gelatin to the batter and mix in well; add chocolate or orange liquor and melted butter and mix in well.
3. Pour half of the batter in the prepared pan and bake in a baking tray in a preheated 325 F oven for 25-30 minutes. Take out the cake and pour the rest of the cheese batter, and bake again for about 25-30 minutes.

4. Cool cake in the oven for 15 minutes, then on a wire rack, tented with the aluminum foil until cooled about 3-4 hours in room temperature.
5. Garnish cake with fruits and berries or leave it plain. Cut cake with a heated knife and serve with fruits, chocolate and chocolate syrup.

Chocolate Cheese Cake (Serves: 12-14)

This chocolate cheesecake is out of this world, and easy to make.

Ingredients:

Crust: 1-1/2 cups graham cracker or ginger cookies crumbs with 1 tsp. cocoa powder, or thin chocolate-wafer crumbs; 2 tbsp. melted butter (plus extra for the pan); 1 tbsp. sugar.
Cake: 1 pkg., ¼ ounce clear gelatin bloomed in ¼ cup cold water; ½ cup heavy cream; 1 pg. 4oz. (113g) each bitter-sweet and semi-sweet chocolates chopped; all in room temperature: 4 pkgs. each 8oz. (227g) cream cheese, 1 cup sour cream, and 4 extra-large or 5 large eggs; 2-1/4 cup sugar; 2 tbsp. lemon juice; 4 tbsp. chocolate liqueur; 4 tbsp. pancake mix (I Prefer Aunt Jemima brand); 2 tbsp. melted butter.
Topping: 1 pkg. 4oz. (113g) semi-sweet chocolate chopped and melted with ½ cup your favorite, jam or jelly. Or, melted and cooled semi-sweet chocolate whipped with ½ cup sour cream. To serve: fresh berries and/or 1 can, (16 oz.), about 2 cups cherry or blueberry pie filling.

For the Crust: Move the oven rack to middle and preheat oven to 350 degrees. Butter a 10-inch spring-form cake pan bottom (only) with butter; line it with a cut out round circle of the parchment paper and butter the paper well. In a bowl, mix together the crumbs, melted butter and the sugar, and spread the crumbs in the bottom, then press them down with a flat-bottom glass. Bake the crumbs for 8-10 minutes, then let it cool. Now, wrap the pan bottom half-way up with aluminum foil. Prepare a large roasting pan with a large piece (put 2 pieces together) of foil to cover airtight. Boil about 6 cups of water for the roasting pan.

For the Cake: Heat the heavy cream in a small pot, add the chopped chocolates, cover and set aside 5 minutes to melt, then stir well. In a large bowl, with electric mixer, whip half of the sugar with the eggs well, then add the softened cream cheese, sour cream, rest of the sugar, lemon juice and chocolate liqueur, and whisk all well in to a smooth cream. Add melted cooled chocolate, and mix well, scraping the edges and the bottom well. Sprinkle the melted butter on the top then the pancake flour, and using a rubber spatula, fold them in the batter by hand.
This is very important: pour the batter in the prepared pan in a steady stream, in the center, then tap the pan edges on all 4 sides against the counter to settle it well and break any bubbles. Pour hot water in the roasting pan, place the pan over the grades, cover airtight with aluminum foil and bake covered at 350 degrees for 45 minutes; turn around the pan halfway and loosen the cover first, staying away from the steam; carefully take out the foil and bake uncovered at 325 degrees for another 45, until the center of the cake is almost settled. Cool cake in the oven for 1 hour and then place on a wire rack on the counter and cool completely.

Topping: Melt chocolate and the jam together, and spread on the cooled cake. Or, melt and cool the chocolate, and whip in the sour cream, and spread on the top.
Serve, topped with pie filling, and fresh berries all around. Slice and cut the cake with a heated knife. Heat the knife under the running hot tap water and wipe it well, or heat over the stove and wipe the knife after each slicing.

Chickpeas Balls or Squares - Besan Laddu or Burfi (M:25-30)

Chickpeas balls (Laddu) or squares (Burfi) are very famous old fashion dessert.

Ingredients: 3 cups chickpeas flour (Besan); 1-1/2 cups fine sugar; 1pound unsalted butter; 1Tbsp. fresh grinded cardamom seeds; 1/2cup slivered almonds.

Grease a 9 X 14-inch glass platter or baking sheet with rim. Heat a large heavy bottom skillet on medium heat and melt half of the butter, add chickpea flour and start stirring to brown it. Add the cardamom after 5 minutes. Keep the heat at medium-high and stir constantly for 10 minutes. If it starts burning in the bottom then lower the heat for a short time and raise the heat again. When it starts giving nice aroma and the color is darker, it is done. Turn off the heat and stir in the sugar then rest of the butter sliced and mix well. Now pour the mixture in the prepared pan even out and sprinkle the almonds on the top. Then press down from the back of the metal spatula and make the mixture solid firm by pressing all over. You can also make the balls using about ½ cup of the mixture at a time. Cool it first, then refrigerate for 2-3 hrs. until it is firm, cut with a knife into 2-inch squares and serve.

Basic Chocolate Cake (Serves: 12)

This is the perfect recipe for chocolate cake. You can serve as it is, serve with berries and whipped cream, or make a 2- or 4-layer cake and decorate with icing or frosting.

Ingredients:

Cocoa Melt: ½ cup heavy cream; 6 tbsp. unsweetened cocoa powder (substitute 3 tbsp. dark cocoa powder if you want to make a dark-color chocolate cake), ½ tsp. instant coffee powder, ¼ cup sugar, 3 tbsp. canola oil; heat all on low heat, in a pot, whisking together, until combined (about 5 minutes) and set aside to cool.
Dry ingredients: 2 cups all-purpose flour, 1 tsp. baking powder, ¾ tsp. baking soda, ¼ tsp. salt; whisk all together in a bowl and set aside.
wet ingredients: 1stick (8 tbsp.) softened unsalted butter, 1-3/4 cup sugar, 3 extra-large eggs at room temperature, 1 tsp. vanilla extract, 1 cup milk at room temperature.

1. Grease the bottom of a 10-inch spring-form cake pan with softened butter or cooking butter spray, sprinkle 1 tsp. of flour, shake to coat the bottom with the flour, then tap out the excess flour. Preheat the oven at 350 degrees.
2. In a large bowl, with an electric mixer, cream the butter, then add 1-3/4 cup sugar and whisk well on low speed for 5 minutes, then medium speed for another 6-8 minutes until the mixture is doubled. Add one egg at a time and beat in well, break the yolk first then beat in the eggs well, scrape the sides and beat all for 30 seconds on high speed. Whisk in the cocoa mixture and vanilla extract on high speed until well combined. Now on medium speed, add ½ cup milk and whisk well, alternating with half of the dry ingredients, then milk and last the rest of flour mixture. At the end whisk all for 30 seconds at high speed.
3. Pour the batter in the prepared pan, in the center. Then pick up the pan at the top, on the rim, and tap against the counter, going all around, about 4-5 times to break any bubbles and to settle the batter.

4. Bake the cake on a light baking sheet for 45 to 50 minutes until a wooden toothpick inserted in the center comes out almost clean. Cool the cake in the pan on a wire rack completely.
5. Serve as it is or slice in two layer and frost the cake.

Variations

With the Frosting: Melt 4 oz. of semi-sweet chocolate over water or in the microwave and cool. Whisk 3 sticks unsalted softened butter, add 3 cups sifted powdered sugar; whisk in the melted chocolate, then whisk in 1 tbsp. of cold milk or orange juice.

Cut cake in to two layers, slide on the cardboard piece and brush out the crumbs. Divide the frosting in to 3 parts. Use one part between the layer, another on the side: place the frosting on the top of the cake and with a dinner knife, slide down a little at a time and frost the side, going all around. Then use rest on the top.

Bake with the Chocolate Chips: Buy 1 bag, 12 oz. (340G) semi-sweet chocolate chips. Use 1 cup in the batter, fold in at the end. Use the rest of the chips in the frosting by melting.

Serve with fresh Berries and Whip Cream or a Scoop of Ice Cream: Berries and the chocolate go together very well. Cut a slice of the cake, and serve with fresh berries and the whip cream or the ice cream. To go all the way, drizzle some chocolate syrup on the top of berries and ice cream.

Store the Cake: Place the cake in the cake-saver container, place some toothpicks on the top to protect the frosting, cover loosely with plastic wrap, place the cover on, and refrigerate. If cake has no icing or frosting, you can leave the cake container in room temperature overnight.

Light and Dark Chocolate Cake
or
Double Chocolate Cake (Serves: about 10)

This is an easy and the tastiest of all the cakes. It has white chocolate layer and the dark chocolate layer. No skills involved; just bake and frost.

Ingredients: 1 box super-moist chocolate fudge cake mix (or any chocolate cake mix; just add: 3 tbsp. brown sugar and ½ cup semisweet grated chocolate in the batter); 3 large eggs; ½ cup canola oil; 1pkg. 4oz. (113.5g) white chocolate premium baking bar chopped; 1 can 14 oz. (397g) sweetened condensed milk; 1 cup coconut powder or fine-grated coconut; 1 box, 4 oz. (113.5g) semi-sweet premium baking bar chopped; 1 tsp. instant coffee; ¼ cup heavy cream or milk; 3 tbsp. butter.

For the Cake: Preheat the oven at 350 degrees. Prepare two 9-inch round cake pans, grease the pans then line with the parchment paper circles and grease the paper. In a bowl of stand mixer, or in a large bowl with an electric mixer, whisk together 1 cup and 2 tbsp. water and eggs well. Add ½ cup oil and whisk all together for 8-10 minutes. Now fold in the cake mix, just until combined. Pour evenly in two prepared pans, even out the top, then hit the edges all around over the counter to spread the batter and break any air bubbles. Bake on the middle shelf for about 20 to 25 minutes, until a toothpick inserted in the center comes out only with a few crumbs on.

Cool the cake in the pan for 5 minutes, then line a wire rack with the parchment paper and invert the cake to cool completely.

White Chocolate Frosting: In a medium pan, on medium heat, lightly brown the coconut for 5 minutes. Take out the coconut and add the condensed milk. When the milk starts bubbling on the edge, add the coconut back to the pan. Stir well for 5 minutes. Take the pan off the heat and cool until the frosting is thick, or refrigerate for 10 minutes.

Dark Chocolate Frosting: Heat the butter, heavy cream and the instant coffee in a small pot, add the semi-sweet chocolate; on low heat, stir to melt the chocolate for about 1-2 minutes. Take the pot off the heat and cool completely.

When ready to frost the cake, slice the top off each cake to make it even, brush off the crumbs and place one cake bottom side down on the serving platter. Pour the white chocolate frosting on the top and let it drip all around. Place the second piece of the cake flat side up, and frost the top with only half of the melted chocolate. Refrigerate the cake for 30 minutes or longer. Then frost the top second time with rest of the dark chocolate. Serve. This cake freezes well. Freeze unfrosted cake up to 3 months, well wrapped, in a plastic container.

<h3 align="center">Triple Chocolate Layer Cake (Serves: 16)</h3>

This yummy chocolate cake loaded with chocolate and is a chocolate lover's paradise. You can melt the chocolate in the microwave, stirring every 20 seconds, or over the warm water in a bowl, making sure bowl does not touch the water.

For the Cake: 2 cups self-rising cake flour; 5 tbsp. Dutch-process cocoa powder; 1box 3.9 oz. (110g) chocolate fudge pudding mix (or 2 tbsp. corn starch, 2 tbsp. dry nonfat milk powder and 1 tbsp. cocoa powder); 1 cup water; 4 large eggs; 1 cup sugar; ½ cup vegetable/canola oil; ¾ cup low-fat sour cream.

For the Mocha Filling (M: 5-1/2 cups): 1 pkg. 4oz. (113g) Ghirardelli chocolate, premium baking bar, semi-sweet chocolate, melted and cooled; 1-1/2 cups chilled heavy cream whipped; 3 cups confectioner's sugar; 6 tbsp. Hills Bros. cappuccino-double mocha powder or mocha café mix, or just 1 tbsp. instant coffee diluted in 2 tbsp. of hot milk.

For the Chocolate-Orange Icing: 1 box, 4oz. (113g) Baker's unsweetened baking chocolate bar 100% cocoa, chopped; ½ cup orange marmalade; ½ pound, 2 sticks (16 tbsp.) unsalted butter softened; 2 cups confectioner's sugar.

For the Decoration on the Side: 1 giant 6.8oz., (192g) Hershey's special dark, mildly sweet chocolate bar, shaved with a potato peeler.

For the Decoration on the Top: 1 pkg. 8oz. (226g) Hershey's milk chocolate drops (op).

<h3 align="center">Prepare the cake</h3>

Prepare 3 round 9-inch cake pans. Grease or spray the pans with cooking spray, line them with round circles of parchment paper, spray the paper, sprinkle a little flour, shake around to coat the bottom, then tap out the excess flour. Preheat the oven at 350 degrees.

Shift together cake flour, cocoa powder and the pudding mix in a medium bowl. In a large mixing bowl with electric mixer on medium speed, beat the eggs, water and sugar together until foamy, about 5 minutes. Add oil and beat again to mix well for 2 minutes. Add half of the sour cream and half of the flour mix and beat 1 minute at low speed; scrape the side of the bowl with a rubber spatula, then beat about 2 minutes on high speed. Add rest of the sour cream and rest of the flour mixture, and beat on low 1 minute and on high 2 minutes. Scrape the sides and mix the batter well by hand.

Pour batter in three prepared pans evenly (about 1-2/4 cup in each pan). Even out the top and place 2 pans on the middle shelf and one on the bottom third, in a preheated oven. Halfway during the baking, rotate 1 pan from top to bottom and then turn halfway around. Bake 20 minutes and check the cake - it should spring back when pressed with the fingers; turn off the oven and leave the pans in the oven for another 5 minutes. Cool the cake in the pan for 15 minutes, then invert them on wire racks over 2-3 strips of the parchment paper. Peel off the bottom round of parchment paper. Cool cake completely. Slice each piece into two slices and take off some crumbs from the center of each slice to make a little depression, then slide each cake slice onto the cardboard carefully without breaking.

Prepare the Mocha Filling

Prepare the Filling: Chill the electric beaters and a large bowl in the refrigerator for 1 to 2 hours Pour the heavy cream into the chilled bowl and beat on high speed for 1 minute, until thick; add melted cooled chocolate, 3C powder sugar and mocha powder, or diluted instant coffee, and whip all just to mix first, then whip on high speed until thick. Refrigerate the filling for about 1 hour until thick and spreading consistency.

Follow the Assembling the Layer Cake procedure (under The Basic Layer cake), or place one flat slice of cake on the serving platter, flat side down, spread out about 1 cup of filling on the slice, then repeat the icing, placing rest of the cake slices cut side down and flat side up; chill the cake in refrigerate to harden the filling for ½ hour. Ice the cake on the side, then on the top. Press in the shaved chocolate on the side and decorate the top with chocolate drops. Place the cake in the cake server. Serve the cake. You can leave in room temperature for 1 day, then refrigerate up to 4-5 days. After refrigerating cut the slices or take out the cake at least one hour before serving.

I spoke to a person in a local bakery and they mentioned that during the day, they take out the cakes and place in the glass-covered display shelves, and at night, they refrigerate all cakes.

Prepare the Chocolate-Orange Icing: Place the chopped chocolate in a large bowl. Heat the marmalade in a small pot or in the microwave until it is melted; strain the marmalade over the chopped chocolate. Whisk both together until the chocolate is melted and combined. Let it cool completely. Now in a large bowl, beat the butter with the electric mixer well; add the powder sugar and beat together. Then add the marmalade mixture and beat all together. Spread the icing on the side of the cake, then on the top. Press in the shaved chocolate on the side of the cake all around.

Decorate the Cake

Decorate the top with a few chocolate drops if desired, or serve on the plate all around the chocolate slice.

This cake tastes best when served in room temperature or with each serving piece heated in the microwave for 20 seconds. All senses will hit your palate and you will be in the heaven.

Tofu-Chocolate Cheese Cake (Serves: 12-16)

This luscious cheese cake is made with firm tofu for lighter texture. Cheese gives tasty flavor, and a top chocolate layer creates a heavenly taste in your mouth. This is an easy cake that has chocolate on the top and bottom and cheese in the middle. You will need a 9-inch spring-form pan.

Ingredients: Crust: 1 cup chocolate or plain graham cracker crumbs; 2 tbsp. butter softened; 2 tbsp. sugar; ½ tsp. ground cinnamon.

Chocolate: 24 ounces 680g semi-sweet chocolate chips (divided); 4 tbsp. butter; ½ cup light brown sugar, ½ tsp. tangerine or orange zest; ½ tsp. instant coffee powder.

Cake Batter: At room temperature: 4 large eggs, 3 pkgs. 8 ounces each light cream cheese, 1 container 16 oz. light sour cream; about 1-1/2 cups 8 ounces (268g) firm tofu crumbled; 1-1/2 cups sugar; 2 tbsp. pure vanilla extract; 2 tbsp. lemon juice; 2 tbsp. .50 ounces (56g) clear gelatin; ½ cup orange juice; 4 tbsp. butter and 1 cup powder sugar; 2 tbsp. milk; fresh berries and/or chocolate syrup for garnish.

Make Crumbs: Line 9-inch round spring pan with a round parchment paper and grease it well. In a small bowl, mix all crust ingredients together, cover the bottom of the cake pan, then press it down firmly with the flat bottom of a glass. Bake crust in a preheated 300F oven for about 10 minutes until light brown. Take out of the oven and let it cool.

For the Cake:

1. To melt the chocolate, heat water in the bottom of the double boiler or in a medium pot about three inches deep, and simmer on low. In a large metal or glass bowl, add 4 tbsp. butter, save ½ cup of chocolate chips (for garnish) and add rest of the chocolate chips, brown sugar, coffee powder, zest to the bowl and melt the chocolate, whisking over the simmering water. Do not let the bowl touch the water. When chocolate is melted, set the bowl aside, covered, and prepare the batter.

2. In a small non-reactive bowl, add orange juice, sprinkle the gelatin over the top and let it sit aside for 10 minutes. Then heat ¼ cup water to boiling point and stir in the gelatin with a wire whisk; set aside until needed.

3. In a large bowl, whip the eggs together, then add cream cheese, sour cream, sugar, crumbled tofu and vanilla extract, and beat with an electric hand mixer until all combined well, about 5 minutes. Add lemon juice and bloomed gelatin, and whip well to incorporate the gelatin. Take out ½ cup of the cheese batter in a cup, cover it well with a piece of aluminum foil and refrigerate for the topping.

4. Preheat the oven at 325F.

5. Take out 1/3 of the melted chocolate in glass bowl; keep it covered and set aside for the topping. Take out a little less than half of the cheese batter and add to the melted (two-thirds) chocolate; stir well and pour over the crumbs in the prepared cake pan. Place the cake pan in a baking tray. Bake chocolate-cheese layer in a preheated oven at 325F, on the middle shelf, for about 25-30 minutes, turning once during the baking.

6. Take out the cake from the oven let it rest 5 minutes, then pour rest of the cheese batter slowly, in a circle, starting from the edges going to the center and over the chocolate layer. Even out the cheese layer on the top with a wet wooden spatula or wet fingers. Bake the cake in the oven for about 30 minutes, turning once during the baking. Turn the oven off, cool the cake in the

oven for about 10 minutes. Then cool on a wire rack, tented with an aluminum foil. When cake is cooled in about 3 hours, chill the cake in the refrigerator, on a platter, tented with the foil.

7. Just before serving, make the chocolate topping. Heat the melted chocolate again over the boiling water, add ½ cup set aside cheese batter, add 4 tbsp. softened butter, whisk well until warmed about 10 minutes, set aside, covered, to cool. When topping is cooled, add 1 cup of powder sugar and whip well. Slowly pour in half of the melted chocolate over the cooled cake and spread out evenly on the top. Now whisk well the remaining half of the chocolate mixture and pour over the cake in a thin stream, covering the top of the cake. Shake the cake platter from all sides to spread the melted chocolate. At this point you can either serve the cake or let the chocolate settle in the refrigerator until it hardens. Cut the cake with a heated warm knife, wiping the blade often with a paper towel. Serve cake with fresh berries and/or chocolate syrup and with some of the set-aside chocolate chips.

Pumpkin or Sweet Potato Cake: Follow the direction for chocolate cheese cake. Just add pumpkin or sweet potato puree or any other fruit filling together with a 3 ounces of vanilla pie filling to make puree a little thicker.

Luscious Jumbo Chocolate Layer Cake (Serves: 12-16)

This is my party chocolate cake. I make a big cake and double the ingredients. To cut down on work and time, I buy chocolate mixes and bake the cake a day before, then just assemble and decorate next day. This cake is very light, fluffy and delicious. The secret is the chocolate liqueur that transforms the whole cake.

For the Cake: 2 boxes, each 6.5 ounces 468g dark chocolate fudge, moist cake mix. Save 2-3 tbsp. cake batter for the topping.

Make your own cakes: Follow the recipe for the basic chocolate cake. Bake 2 cakes separately.

For the Syrup: 1 cup orange marmalade or apricot jam; 4 tbsp. water, heat together, melt, strain in a small bowl and let it cool. This syrup is for the cake layers and for the topping.

Topping: 4 oz. (113g) semisweet baking chocolate chopped; 4 tbsp. unsalted butter; ¼ cup heavy cream; 1 cup powder sugar sifted; 2 tbsp. chocolate liqueur; leftover orange syrup. To decorate: ¼ cup each chopped chocolate or chocolate drops and some glazed cherries.

For the Filling and Frosting: 2 pkgs. each 4 oz. (113g) semi-sweet chocolate chopped; ½ cup heavy cream; ½ cup dark chocolate liqueur; 8 tbsp. unsalted butter, sliced, melted over warm water or in microwave oven;

2 Containers each 16 oz. (453g) whipped topping; or 2 containers each 1 quart (846ml) heavy cream (divided: save for the melting the chocolate) whipped with 1 cup powder sugar. Whip the cream in batches, using about 2 tbsp. of powdered sugar per cup of heavy cream.

For the Side the Chocolate Curls or Crumbs: 1 6.8oz. (192G) giant Special Dark Hershey's chocolate bar; heat the bar in the microwave or in the oven over parchment paper for 15 seconds, and shave with potato peeler or grate on the large holes of the grater.

To Bake the Cake: Bake 2 separate cakes per instruction on the package of cake mix in to a 10-inch spring-form cake pan and cool completely.

To make the Topping: Heat a medium pot half-full of water and bring to a simmer on low heat. In a large bowl, place heavy cream, sugar, butter, chocolate liqueur, and stir well to cook over warm water, for 5 minutes or until thickened; add the chocolate, stir well, and take off the heat. Cover the pot with the lid and set aside for 5 minutes. Stir well when chocolate is melted; save 1 tbsp. of syrup for the shine over the topping), and whisk in rest of the syrup (almost ½ cup) into the chocolate mixture; set aside covered in room temperature.

To make the Filling and Frosting: Use half of the cream and half of the melted and cooled chocolate at a time, and mix cream and chocolate together.

Now, slice each cake: Take off the uneven top of the cake to make the top even. Then slice the cake with a large serrated knife into 3 equal and horizontal slices, and slide each slice on cardboard, aluminum foil or parchment paper. Brush off the crumbs.

To assemble the cake: Turn the cakes upside-down. Use one flat bottom of the cake in the bottom and the other one on the top. Then place one flat bottom on the serving platter, covering the open edge of the platter with the parchment paper wide strips all around to catch any frosting. Use about 2 tbsp. of syrup and pour in a circle over the cake piece, or use a pastry brush to brush the syrup on the cake slice. Take a large metal spatula and pick up about 1-1/2 cups of filling and spread out over the syrup evenly. Top with another cake slice and press it down all over with your palm to make an even cake and repeat with syrup and filling.

When all six layers are assembled, frost the side of the cake with the filling, starting from the bottom and going to the top with the spatula, on the side of the cake. After frosting the side, just smooth the side with the clean and warm spatula. Now press in the crumbs or the curls on the side. Take a handful of crumbs, spread out on your hand and press into the cake, starting from bottom and going to the top.

For the topping: Spread out half of the melted and liquid chocolate topping on the top of the cake (or heat the chocolate mixture again; if it has thickened, over the warm water or in the microwave oven, stirring constantly). Then use 1 tbsp. of syrup on the top of the topping, mostly in the center, (about 1-1/2 inches away from the edges) to shine the topping. Carefully remove the parchment paper.

Decorations: Whisk in all the leftover topping and the filling, and pipe over on the edges on the top and the bottom of the cake all around. Decorate the top with chocolate and cherries. When serving, cut each slice with one hand and hold the cake slice, on the side, with the other hand. Serve immediately or leave in the cake-server container, or poke a few toothpicks in a circle, on the topping, and tent it loosely with aluminum foil, and refrigerate until serving.

Chocolate Torte (Filled Chocolate Cake)

(Serves: 16-20)

According to my husband, "Chocolate torte is better than chocolate." I had baked this for him on his 86th birthday, with cannolis and cheese cookies. He loved them all. Chocolate torte is a filled-chocolate cake that tastes almost like chocolate bars.

Ingredients:

For the Crust: Each ½ c: all-purpose flour, grated or crumbled semi-sweet chocolate, sugar and graham cracker crumbs; 3 tbsp. unsweetened coco powder; ¼ tsp. salt; 4 tbsp. unsalted butter plus extra for greasing; 1 large egg beaten with 1 tsp. vanilla extract.

For the Filling: 1 cup dark chocolate cookies crumbs; 1 cup roasted pecans ground into fine crumbs; 2 large egg whites; ½ cup sugar; 1 pound dark chocolate: ½ cup grated and rest chopped; ½ cup heavy cream, 2 tbsp. butter, ½ cup strawberry jam, and 2 tsp. vanilla extract and 1 tsp. almond extract; to garnish: ¼ cup each glazed pineapple, sliced thin and roasted pecans; ½ cup white chocolate melted to make design (op).

For the Crust: Grease the bottom and sides of a 10-inch spring-form pan with butter. Preheat the oven at 300 degrees. In a bowl, mix together all-purpose flour, grated or crumbled semi-sweet chocolate, sugar, graham cracker crumbs, coco powder, salt, butter, egg and vanilla extract, and sprinkle all over on the bottom of the pan. Grease a large piece of the plastic wrap, cover the crumbs and press down on the crumbs evenly over the bottom of the pan. Discard the plastic wrap and sprinkle 2 tbsp. grated dark chocolate on the top of the crumbs, and bake in a 300-degree oven for 12 minutes. Take the pan out of the oven.

For the filling: In a bowl, mix together cookie crumbs, pecan crumbs, ½ cup sugar and egg whites and sprinkle over the crust. Then sprinkle rest of the grated dark chocolate on the top. Bake at 350 degrees for 10 minutes until all settled. Take the pan out of the oven.

In a medium pot heat the heavy cream and butter first; when heated through, add the jam and both extracts. Stir well to combine. Take off the heat and add the chopped dark chocolate; cover and set aside for 5 minutes to melt. Stir the chocolate with a whisk and it should be melted completely. Pour the melted chocolate over the filling. Tent the pan with aluminum foil and leave in room temperature to cool. After 30 minutes, or when chocolate settled, garnish with the pineapple and pecans. If you prefer, you can make designs with the melted white chocolate. Serve when settled or refrigerate overnight and serve thinly sliced.

Coffee Crumb Cake with Apples (Serves: about 12)

This is an easy cake to make. It is tasty and serves a lot of people. After it is baked, you can leave it in room temperature for up to one day, then cover with plastic wrap and refrigerate.

Ingredients:

For the Cake: 3 large eggs; ¾ cup 2% milk; a mixture of: 1 cup sugar, 1 tsp. lemon or tangerine fine zest, and 8 tbsp. melted butter whisked together for 5 minutes; the flour mixture: 2-1/2 cups bleached all-purpose flour; 2-1/2 tsp. baking powder; ¼ tsp. salt; the fruit topping: 1 can, 20 oz. (567g) sliced apple or blueberry pie filling, or make your own filling (see below).

For the Crumb Topping: 1 cup all-purpose flour; 1 tsp. ground cinnamon; ½ tsp. salt; 1 cup quick cooking oats; 1 stick (8 tbsp.) unsalted butter melted; 1 cup packed light brown sugar; 1/2cup dry cranberries; ½ cup slivered almonds or chopped walnuts (op).

1. Line a 12x14-inch lasagna pan with double parchment paper and grease well with the oil or butter and set aside. Place the oven rack in the middle and preheat oven at 350 degrees.
2. **For the Topping**: Combine flour, cinnamon, salt, oats, butter, brown sugar and cinnamon in a medium bowl and mix together by hand. Then add the cranberries and nuts. Mix well with the hand, and set it aside.
3. **For the cake**: In a large bowl with an electric mixer, whisk together eggs well and then whisk in the milk. Add the sugar and butter mixture, and whisk to combine all. Now sift on the top the flour mixture and, using a whisk, incorporate the flour just to mix. Do not over-mix.
4. Pour the batter in the prepared pan, tap the pan all around gently against the counter to break any bubbles. Using a fork and a knife, top the batter with the apple slices flat on the surface, or spread out the blueberry filling evenly. Now sprinkle the topping mixture evenly on the top, covering the entire surface.

5. Bake the cake in a preheated oven for about 30-35 minutes. Cool the pan on a wire rack for 30 minutes; cut into 2-inch squares and serve warm with coffee, milk or hot chocolate, or cool it completely and serve later.

Apple Pie Filling (M: 2 cups)

Ingredients: 2 Granny Smith apples or other firm apples, peeled, cut in to 8 slices, cored; 2 tbsp. unsalted butter; 1 tbsp. lemon juice; 2 tbsp. sugar; 1 tbsp. cornstarch diluted in ½ cup of cold water.

Heat a large heavy bottom, non-reactive pan over medium heat. Add butter and when butter is melted, move around the pan to coat the bottom. Add the apples and increase the heat to medium-high. Stir the apples continuously for about 5 minutes, until they are coated with the butter and have changed color slightly.

Reduce the heat to low, sprinkle the sugar, and pour the cornstarch mixture on the top; cover and let them cook for 15-20 minutes, or until the apples are soft.

Fruit Cake (S: 14 to 16)

Fruit cakes are mostly for Christmas, but they are so festive and tasty that you can use for other holidays in cold winter. Bake the cake first and save some fruits and nuts to decorate it right after baking. There are a lot of ingredients but this cake is easy to make. You will need non-stick an angel food cake pan 9-1/2x3-3/4 inches.

Ingredients: 2 sticks unsalted softened butter, 1 cup granulated sugar, 1 cup packed light brown sugar, 5 large eggs, 2 tsp. pomegranate molasses, 2 tbsp. orange drink mix (like Tang) or ¼ cup juice and 1 tbsp. tangerine fine zest. 2 cups all-purpose unbleached flour, ½ tsp baking soda, ½ tsp. salt.

1 container, 16 oz., 1lb (453.6g) holiday fruit and peel mix, 8 oz. each: green and red candied cherries, 1 cup chop walnuts, 1 cup chop pitted dates,1 cup slivered almonds, ½ cup chopped crystallized ginger, 1 cup chop crystallized pineapple, ½ cup shelled pistachio, 1 cup golden or dark raisins.

1 cup good brandy or dark rum (divided), 4 tbsp. sweet orange marmalade.

1. Cut out a circle of parchment paper, measuring the base of the pan, then fold the circle in 4 folds, then in 8 folds, and cut the corner off about 1 inch to make a hole in center, to fit in the bottom. Grease and flour the pan and paper. Preheat the oven at 350 degrees.
2. In a large bowl, or in the bowl of the stand mixer, whisk the butter and sugars with an electric mixer for 10 minutes at medium speed; add the orange drink mix, lightly beaten eggs, molasses, whip all about 1 minute. Sift dry ingredients: flour, salt and baking soda, and pour in the bowl and whip together, do not over-mix. Now pour in all the nuts and fruits (set aside about ¼ cup each for decoration) and only ½ cup of brandy. Now, mix all up and down with a rubber spatula to mix well. Pour into the prepared pan, tap pan on the counter, then even out the top.
3. Bake cake on a baking tray in a preheated oven 10 minutes at 350 degrees, 90 minutes hour at 300 degree and about 15 minutes at 250 degrees, until a toothpick inserted in center of cake comes out with only a few crumbs on. Turn the cake around together with the tray 3 times during the baking.
4. While cake is baking, heat the marmalade in a small saucepan and cool it. Now take the cake out of the oven and pour ½ cup of brandy all over the cake; brandy will go down in a few minutes on the warm cake. Then brush half of the marmalade over the top of the cake, decorate the cake with fruits and nut, then pour rest of the marmalade over the decoration and put the cake back in the oven. Turn off the oven and let the cake cool down completely. Cover the cake with plastic wrap, then cover the pan with aluminum foil, put on a plate and refrigerate up to two weeks, letting it marinate in the brandy until it matures. Cake is ready to serve after 10 days.
5. Serve with coffee/tea with or without cream.

Tip: When decorating the cake, try to use colorful crystallized fruits and nuts. If you prefer after decorating, you can cover the cake with a double cheese cloth and pour brandy/rum in 2 or 3 times while the alcohol is soaking in the cake in a two week period. (use ½ cup brandy/rum before baking and other ½ cup or so later on).

Black Forest Cake

(Bake at 350 F for 30-35 minutes)

This German cake is my husband's favorite. It has lot of flavors. Just bake the cake and use filling of: cherry brandy, jelly and cherry filling top with whipped topping; then cover the sides with whipped topping and top with chocolate crumbs. Finally, decorate top with whipped topping, cherries and chocolate curls.

Cocoa Melt: 1/3 cups Dutch processed, unsweetened cocoa powder (good quality), 1/3 cups brown sugar, 2 tbsp. canola oil, 1 tbsp. vanilla extract, ½ cup hot water.

Ingredients: 2-1/4 cup sifted all-purpose flour, 2 tsp. baking soda, ½ tsp. salt, ½ tsp. baking powder, 1 stick unsalted butter softened, 1-1/4 cup sugar, 3 large eggs, ½ cup low-fat buttermilk, ½ cup sour cream.

For Topping: ½ cup strawberry or cherry jelly, 2 Tab corn starch, 1 Bottle 16 oz. (454G) maraschino cherries with stems (divided), 1- 4 ounces dark chocolate bar for shaving, about 8 ounces whipped sweet cream or whipped topping chilled; 3 to 4 tbsp. cherry brandy (Kirschwasser).

Line two 9-inch round cake pans with parchment paper and grease them well with butter. Combine cocoa ingredients in a measuring cup, stir well and set aside covered; cool completely. Preheat oven to 350F. Sift together flour, baking soda, salt and baking powder, and set aside.

In a large bowl, or the bowl of the stand mixer, cream butter with an electric hand mixer until fluffy; add sugar and combine together well about 6-8 minutes. Slowly add one egg at a time, whisking well after each addition. Now add half of the flour mixture and buttermilk and mix on medium speed just to combine, then add the other half of the flour mixture, sour cream and coco melt and mix just to combine. Do not over-mix.

Pour batter evenly in two prepared pans, tap the pans on the counter to take out any air bubbles. Place pans on the middle shelf on aluminum foil, side by side. Bake in a preheated oven for about 30 to 35 minutes until a toothpick inserted in the center comes out almost clean. During the baking, rotate the pans from left to right, turning them halfway around to bake from all sides. Cool cake in the pan for 5 minutes, then loosen the edges with a dinner knife and reverse over a wire rack; peel off the parchment paper, and cool completely.

While cake is baking, melt the strawberry jelly in a small saucepan on low heat. Mix 2 tabs cornstarch with 4 tbsp. of water and stir in to the melted jelly. Raise the heat medium-high and continue whisking the jelly until it is bubbly and thick, for about 5 minutes; set aside to cool completely. Drain about 15 stem cherries (save another 10 stem cherries for the topping) on a paper towel; take off the stems and slice them in half and set aside. Using a vegetable peeler, shave the chocolate bar on the side to make curls. If bar is too hard, melt it slightly in the microwave for about 20 seconds.

Assemble the cake: When the cake is completely cooled, put it on a cutting board and using a large bread knife, slice each cake in to two slices, then take off the top crust, slicing very thinly on the top. Brush off all the crumbs from the cake slices. Keep slices in the same order on parchment paper strips on platters or cutting board, to slide them easily. Brush all cake slices with about 1 tbsp. of cherry brandy on each, starting from the edge and going towards middle of the slice.

Use a cake stand or a large platter to assemble the cake. First drop 1 tbsp. of whipped topping in the center of the platter to hold the first slice of the cake; place one bottom slice (flat side) on it. Spread out one-third of the jelly mixture on it, stay away about ½ inch from the border. Spread out about one-third of the halved cherries over jelly.

On the second slice of the cake spread about 3 tbsp. whipped topping in a thin layer and turn it over, touching the jelly surface. Repeat the filling with other two layers. Make sure you save flat-bottom slice for the top for your decoration.

Cover the sides and top of the cake with cream. Put some of the cream on the edge and, using a large icing knife or offset spatula, slide the cream on the side and cover the sides while moving the cake platter with the other hand. If you have a Lazy Susan, put your platter on it. Pipe the whipped cream 8 places on the top or use eight white sugar roses. Pile up the saved chocolate in the center and decorate the side of the cake with chocolate crumbs. Decorate the top with the stem cherries. Refrigerate the cake for an hour to firm the cream. Cut and serve each piece of the cake with some chocolate crumbs all around.

Pistachio Pound Cake (Serves: 8-10)

This healthy cake is one of our favorite cakes.

Ingredients: 1 stick lightly softened unsalted butter; ¾ cup light sour cream; ¼ cup canola oil; 2-1/2 cups sugar; 4 extra-large eggs at room temperature; ¾ cup 2% milk mixed with 2 tbsp. pure vanilla extract; the dry ingredients mixture: 2 cups all-purpose unbleached flour, 1 cup toasted shelled pistachios ground into flour, 1 tsp. baking powder, 1 box, 3oz. pistachio pudding mix; topping: 2 cups sifted powder sugar whisked in with 2-3 tbsp. lemon juice in a thick pouring consistency; ½ cup each dry cranberries and toasted and shelled whole walnuts to garnish.

Preheat oven at 350 degrees. Grease well, then sprinkle with flour a non-stick tube pan; tap out the excess flour.

In a food-processor bowl or in a large bowl with electric mixer, cream the butter, oil and sour cream for 2 minutes, adding the sugar slowly. In a small bowl, beat the eggs well, then whisk in the butter mixture for 1 minute. Now in 2 portions, whisk in half of the milk, half of the flour mixture, then the rest of the milk and ending with the flour mixture. Pour the batter in the prepared pan. Tap all around on the counter to break any bubbles. Bake in a preheated oven for about 75 to 90 minutes, until a toothpick inserted in the thickest part comes out only with a few crumbs on. Cool completely on a wire rack.

Drizzle the sugar-lemon topping, and sprinkle with cranberries and pistachios; slice and serve.

Sweet Potato and Chocolate Cheese Cake (Serves: 10-12)

This is a healthy, tasty, light and colorful cake. Make a cream cheese mixture and divide it into chocolate, sweet potato and sour cream layers; garnish and bake. You need to bake it a day before to chill overnight.

Ingredients: 2 cups chocolate graham crackers crumbs; 3 tbsp. butter softened; 3 tbsp. sugar; 2 pkgs. each 8 ounces light cream cheese, softened; 1 cup heavy cream; 1 container, 16 ounces (453g) sour cream, divided; 1 cup sugar; ½ cup cold 2% milk; 2 pkgs. each 1.4 ounces (396g) instant Jello chocolate fudge pudding; about 1-1/4 pounds or 2 medium sweet potatoes baked (wrapped in foil, baked 350F for about 1 hour), peeled and mashed with a fork; 1pkg. 3.4 ounces (96g) instant Jello vanilla pudding, divided; ¼ cup pumpkin seeds; ¼ cup slivered almonds; 1 tsp. ground cinnamon for garnish; fresh blueberries and/or chocolate syrup for serving.

Line a 9-inch round spring-form pan with parchment paper. In a bowl, mix together graham cracker crumbs, 3 tbsp. sugar and 3 tbsp. butter, and press it down in the cake pan over the parchment paper with the bottom of a glass, bringing the crumbs about 1 inch high on the side. Bake the crumbs in a 350F oven for about 10 minutes to firm.

In a large bowl with an electric mixer, beat cream cheese, half (1 cups) of the sour cream, heavy cream, and 1 cup sugar on medium speed for 5 minutes.

In the remaining 1 cup sour cream, add ½ cup cream cheese mixture and 2 tbsp. vanilla pudding; mix well and set aside for the topping.

Divide into two bowls the rest of the cream cheese mixture. In one bowl of cheese mixture, add ½ cup of milk, and both chocolate pudding mixes; whip with a wire whisk just to combine and pour it immediately into the cake pan; smooth it out with wet hands.

In the remaining cheese mixture add sweet potato puree and remaining vanilla pudding; whip with the electric mixer and immediately pour over the chocolate pudding in the cake pan.

Top sweet potato layer with the sour cream topping (set aside); smooth the surface with a knife or a metal spatula. Garnish with pumpkin seeds all over, top with almonds and sprinkle cinnamon all over. Chill in the refrigerator for about 1 hour.

Preheat oven 350F. Bake cake for about 1 hour, until set. Turn off the oven and cool the cake in the oven for about 3 hours Chill in the refrigerator overnight.

Serve cake with fresh blueberries and/or chocolate syrup.

Tips: If you need to serve this cake right away, just use 1 pkg. of softened light cream cheese in the mixture instead of two packages. Fold into chocolate pudding 2 cups of whipped cream or Cool Whip.

No need to use any heavy cream in the mixture. Keep the sweet potato and topping same (whisk in the cheese mixture). Roast the almonds and pumpkin seeds in a dry skillet, over medium heat, shaking for about 8 minutes. Assemble the cake; garnish with nuts and cinnamon and chill in the refrigerator at least 1 hour and serve with berries and chocolate syrup. This will be a no-bake cake.

Pound Cake (Serves: 12-16)

This cake is based on the Indian Wedding Cake, which people ship all over after weddings. It is not too rich, and is easy to make.

Ingredients: 4 leveled tbsp. semolina soaked in 4 tbsp. milk for at least 2 hours then mixed with 2 tbsp. softened butter; 4 large eggs; ½ cup sugar; ½ can sweetened condensed milk; 2 tsp. rose water or vanilla extract; ½ cup canola oil; 2 cups self-rising flour; ½ cup 2% or whole milk; about ½ cup powdered sugar to sprinkle on the top.

1. Preheat oven at 325 degrees. Use cooking spray or 1 tbsp. softened butter to grease a nonstick tube pan well, then sprinkle with 1 tbsp. flour all over and tap out the excess.
2. In a large bowl or in the bowl of the stand mixer, whisk the eggs and rose water or vanilla extract, then add the sugar and whisk both well for 5 minutes on medium speed. Add the soaked semolina and whisk well. Whisk in the oil. Whisk in half of the flour, then ½ cup milk. Now whisk in rest of the flour to combine. Do not over-mix. Pour the batter in the prepared tube pan and tap the pan on the counter on all 4 sides to break any air pockets.
3. Place the cake pan on a piece of aluminum foil and bake for 55 to 60 minutes, until golden brown on the top and a toothpick inserted in the center comes out almost clean. During the baking, turn the cake pan around halfway after 30 minutes. When the cake is done, turn off the oven, take out the cake pan and let it sit for 5 minutes. Using a dinner knife, loosen the cake all round, shake the pan, then cover with a dinner plate and invert the cake. Garnish the warm cake with powder sugar. Cool the cake completely on a wire rack. Serve thin sliced warm or cold.

Pumpkin Cake (Serves: about 16)

This is my mother's recipe. She used to make eggless squash cake and squares. You sauté the ingredients in a pan, and layer in a cake pan. It takes only about 30 minutes, plus to cool. This is a very tasty layer cake, which we make a day ahead of Thanksgiving.

Ingredients:

For the Crumbs: 1 cup graham cracker or cookie crumbs, mixed with 2 tbsp. each butter and sugar.

For the Filling: 1 tbsp. butter; 1 can, 29 ounces pumpkin puree; 1 box, 3 ounces (85g) butterscotch, or orange pudding; 1 box 4 ounces (113g) lemon pudding, divided; 2 pkgs., 8 ounces (227g) each cream cheese, room temperature; 1-1/2 cups sugar; ½ cup Post Grape Nuts or any cold cereal; 1 bag, 11 ounces (311g) butterscotch or white chocolate morsels, divided.

To decorate the top: 1 container, 8 ounces (226g) whipped topping or Cool Whip; ½ cup each roasted pumpkin seeds and fresh pomegranate seeds (op). To serve: orange-lemon glaze.

1. Line a 10-inch spring-form cake pan with parchment paper and grease it well. Preheat the oven at 350 degrees. Press down the crumbs on the bottom of the cake pan with a flat-bottom glass, then bake in the oven for 10 minutes.

2. Heat a heavy bottom sauté pan on medium heat. Add the butter and coat the pan. Add the pumpkin puree, increase the heat to medium-high and sauté the pumpkin for 10 minutes, until it is very hot. Sprinkle the whole box of butterscotch pudding, only half of the box of lemon pudding (lemon flavor should be less) on the top and sauté for 1 minute; combine well. Now reduce the heat to medium, cut the cream cheese in the wrappers to 1-inch cubes and add to pan; add the sugar. Increase the heat to medium-high and sauté again until the cream cheese and sugar is diluted, about 8-10 minutes. Pour half of the mixture over the crumbs, even out the top and sprinkle the cereal, then about a half cup of chocolate morsels. Now pour rest of the mixture over the cake and even out the top. Leave in room temperature for 30 minutes or until it is cooled.

3. Spread the whipped topping evenly over the cake, then sprinkle the remaining chocolate morsels, pomegranate seeds and pumpkin seeds. Serve drizzled with caramel sauce.

Tip: Instead of making the cake, you can make two 9-inch pies same way. Just double the amount of the crumbs and whipped topping, to cover two pies.

Orange-Lemon Glaze (M: 1 cups)

I mostly prepare this glaze for pumpkin cake, but you can use this on pies, cakes, glazed carrots, Brussels sprouts, even on roasted chicken and turkey.

Ingredients: 2 tbsp. unsalted butter; 1 cup apricot jam or marmalade; ¼ cup caramel sauce; ½ cup sugar; 1 tsp. paprika; 2 ounces lemon pie and pudding filling (left over from pumpkin cake); ¼ tsp. salt.

Melt all ingredients in a pot, bring to a boil; take off the heat, strain or use as it is when cooled.

Pistachio Ice Cream Cake (Serves: 12-15)

This is our famous ice cream cake that we make on St. Patrick's Day.

Ingredients: ½ gallon pistachio ice cream; ½ gallon French vanilla ice cream; 1 cup half and half or heavy cream; 1 tsp. fine-ground cardamom seeds; ¼ cup sugar; 1 cup slivered almonds lightly toasted, then ground; ½ cup honeydew melon liqueur; ¼-½ cup torn fresh mint leaves; 1 cup sliced pistachios; 1 cup chopped semi-sweet chocolate or chocolate chips; garnish each piece before serving with more melon liqueur or chocolate syrup.

1. Line a 9- or 10-inch spring-form cake pan with parchment paper and grease the paper. Take out both ice cream containers and leave in room temperature on a platter. Heat the cream, almonds and cardamom seeds in a pot on medium-high heat. Bring it to a boil and take off the heat. Pour the cream in a small bowl and cool it, either over ice water or in the freezer.

413

2. In a large bowl, whip together both ice creams; add the cream and whisk well. Spread out half of the ice cream mixture in the prepared cake pan and top with the ½ of mint leaves, liquor and pistachios. Now, spread out rest of the ice cream, even it out and garnish with rest of the liquor, mint leaves and pistachios, and then sprinkle with the chocolate chips. Freeze immediately until firm, from 4 hours to overnight.
3. Slice cake with a heated knife and after cutting each slice of the cake wash the knife under running water and wipe out with kitchen towel. Garnish with more melon liquor or chocolate syrup.

Red Velvet Cake (Serves: 12)

This is the traditional Red Velvet Cake. I make it with chocolate flavor.

Ingredients: 2 cups all-purpose flour; 1 tsp. baking powder; ¾ tsp. baking soda; ¼ tsp. salt; 1 tbsp. unsweetened Dutch process cocoa powder; 2 cups sugar; 2 extra-large eggs; 2 tbsp. lemon juice; 2-ounce bottle of liquid red food color; 4 tbsp. chocolate liqueur; 4 tbsp. melted and cooled unsalted butter; 1 cup canola oil; 1c buttermilk.

Frosting: 1.5 lbs. 1-1/2 cups softened unsalted butter; 1 lb. sifted powder sugar; ½ cup heavy cream; 2 bars 4 ounces(113g) white chocolate, one bar chopped and melted in warm heavy cream and cooled.

1. Grease the bottom of a 10-inch spring-form cake pan with 1 tbsp. softened butter. Sprinkle 1 tsp. of flour, shake to coat the bottom, then tap out the excess flour. Preheat the oven to 350 degrees.
2. In a medium bowl combine all dry ingredients: flour, baking powder, baking soda, salt and cocoa powder.
3. In a large bowl or in the bowl of the stand mixer, with the electric mixer or whisk attachment, combine sugar and the eggs together. Add the lemon juice, chocolate liqueur and the food color and combine well. Add the butter and combine well for 5 minutes. Alternate with half of the buttermilk and mix well, then half of the flour mixture and mix just to combine, then add other half buttermilk, combine, and finally the rest of the flour mixture and combine well. Now scrape down the sides and the bottom, and mix well.
4. Pour the batter in the prepared pan. Tap the pan all around against the counter to dissolve any bubbles and to make the cake even. Bake in the preheated oven, on a light baking sheet or a cookie sheet, for about 55 minutes or until the toothpick inserted in the center comes out clean. Cool the cake ½ hour in the pan over the wire rack, then take out the cake from the pan, turn over onto the rack and cool completely.
5. **Assemble the Cake:** Make the frosting: in a large bowl, whip the softened butter well, slowly add the sugar and whisk well. Then whisk in the cooled melted white chocolate.
6. Using a large corrugated knife, slice the cake on the top to make it even, then slice it into two even horizontal slices. Slide the top slice on cardboard. Brush off any crumbs.
7. Place the top slice of the cake upside-down on the cake platter. Then cover the open part of the platter with wide strips of parchment or wax paper. Place ¼ of the frosting over the cake slice and even out with a metal or icing spatula. Place the second slice on the top and press it down to firm the cake. Apply another ¼ of the frosting on the side of the cake. Place a little frosting on the top edge of the cake and slide it down onto the side, and spread it out with a icing spatula or a dinner knife neatly. Then use ¼ of the frosting on the top.
8. To decorate the cake: Fill in the rest of the frosting in a piping bag using a small Star Tip (#18 Wilton) to pipe the frosting on the top edge. Take out the parchment paper carefully and pipe the rest of the frosting at the bottom edge.

9. Heat lightly the other white chocolate bar, in a microwave or in a heated oven, over parchment paper; just to make it a little soft, and shave the chocolate bar, with a potato peeler, over the cake. Keep the cake in the cake-saver container covered for a few hours, then refrigerate until serving.

Red Velvet Cake with Beet Juice (Serves: 12)

This nutrient-loaded cake is baked with low-fat yogurt and raw beet juice, and no one can tell a difference.

Ingredients: For the juice: place 1 tbsp. lemon juice and 1 tbsp. sugar in a large mug. Peel 1 large carrot and 2 large beets (about 1 pound) and take out about 1-1/2 cups juice in the mug and set aside.

For the Cake: 2 cups bleached all-purpose flour; 1 tsp. baking powder; 2 tbsp. semolina; ¼ tsp. salt; 2 cups sugar; 3 extra-large eggs plus 1 large egg yolk; 1 cup canola oil; 4 tbsp. chocolate liqueur; 1 cup low-fat yogurt.

1. Grease with soft butter one 10-inch spring-form cake pan, then line it with a cut-out round circle of parchment paper; butter the paper and sprinkle 1 tsp. flour, shake to coat the bottom of the pan and tap out the excess flour. Preheat oven at 350 degrees.
2. In a medium bowl whisk together the dry ingredients: flour, baking powder, semolina, salt, and set aside.
3. In a large bowl with electric mixer, whisk together sugar and the eggs and yolk on medium speed for 5 minutes, until creamy. Add the oil and whisk together until all are combined. Add beat juice and chocolate liqueur, whisk in and combine. Now alternating with yogurt and flour, add half of the yogurt, combine well, then add half of the flour mixture and mix well just to combine, then yogurt and the flour mixture. The mixture will be thin.
4. Pour the batter in the prepared pan. Bake in a preheated oven on a light baking tray or a cookie sheet, for about 1 hour or until the toothpick inserted in the center comes out clean. Cool the pan on a wire rack for half hour. Then loosen the rim, and loosen the cake with a dinner knife; cover the pan with a dinner plate and turn over the cake on to the dinner plate; cover the wire rack with strips of the parchment paper and slide the cake over the parchment strips; cool on the wire rack completely.
5. For the frosting, follow the Red Velvet cake recipe above

.Baking, Pans & Temperature

There are a few basic things to follow with any type of baking. Make sure the oven is preheated, unless the recipe is called for a cold oven (like in pound cake). **Position the oven rack in the center, before preheating the oven,** unless you are baking two trays at the same time. Turn the trays half way around at the middle of baking for even baking. Switch the trays from top to bottom.

Keep an eye on what you are baking. Don't let it burn. Test it with a toothpick in the center. It should come out clean, with only a few crumbs attached. Cool the baked goods for about 5 minutes in the baking pan, then on a wire rack.

Glass baking pans retain the heat fast and longer, so bake with a little lower temperature with the glass pans and dishes.

I use club soda instead of water in most of my baking because it makes the cakes and muffins soft.

Baking Temperatures

2 Round Cake Pans: Line with round parchment paper, spray with cooking oil or butter spray or grease well with soft butter; sprinkle about 1 tsp. of dry cake flour, shake well to coat the bottom, then tap out excess flour. Pour in the batter, then tap two-three times on the counter to release any air bubbles. Bake about 30 minutes on the middle rack. Check with a toothpick for doneness. Cool in the pan for 5 minutes, then invert on a wire rack, peel off the parchment paper and cool completely.

12x10 Baking Pan: Baking time will be approximately 35 minutes following the above procedure.

24 cupcakes: Baking time will be about 20 minutes with baking tin ¾ full. Make sure you line the tin with paper cup liners and spray with cooking spray or grease the bottom well with soft butter. Cool in the tin for 5 minutes, then invert on a wire rack and cool completely before icing.

Bundt Pan: Baking time will be about 40 minutes. I always line my bundt pan. Cut out a round parchment for the bottom, then fold the round 4-5 times and snip off the pointed center of the parchment, about 1-1/2 inch, making a hole in the center. Grease the center pole very well with soft butter, sprinkle with flour and line the pan with parchment paper.

Almond-Coconut Balls (M: about 30 large)

This is an old recipe that my mother used to make for us in the winter. We ate these energy balls all day long. Ingredients used here can be found at the Indian grocery stores. Just like other nuts, keep the almond flour in the refrigerator once it's open.

Ingredients: 1-1/2 cup semolina (sooji); 1 tsp. cardamom seeds fresh-ground; 1 cup almond flour; 1 stick unsalted butter, divided; 1 bag 1pound, (454g) about 4 cups fresh-grated frozen coconut thawed; 1 can 14 oz. (396g) sweetened condensed milk or 1 cup mava (reduced milk), ¼ tsp. salt; 1 cup coconut flour to roll in.

Heat a large wok or a large heavy-bottom frying pan on medium heat. Add the semolina, 4 tbsp. butter, and the cardamom. Stir constantly until light brown about 8 minutes. Add the almond flour, salt and half of the grated coconut (about 2 cups) and stir for another 5 minutes; do not let it burn.

Now sprinkle the sugar on the top, then add 1-1/2 cup water, increase the heat to medium-high and stir fast for 2-3 minutes, to absorb the water. Lower the heat to medium again, add another 4 tbsp. butter and condensed milk. Stir again, scraping the bottom for about 5 minutes or until it is bubbly and turns to a thick paste. Now reduce the heat to low, sprinkle remaining grated coconut on the top and push it in the mixture; stir and combine the ingredients well for about 5 minutes. At this point the mixture should be all puffed up. Take the mixture off the heat. Sprinkle 2 tbsp. coconut flour on a large baking tray (12x18 inches); using an ice cream scoop, drop about 1/3 cup of the mixture over the coconut. When all are done, place the remaining coconut flour in a small bowl, pick up one piece of the mixture in your hand, roll into a ball, and then roll in the coconut flour and place in a large platter.

You can serve them any time with coffee, milk or tea. Leave them out tented with a plastic wrap in room temperature for a few hours then refrigerate covered up to a week. I place half of them in a zip-lock bag, place the bag in a plastic container, and freeze them for up to 2 months. Thaw overnight and serve.

Almond Christmas Biscotti (M: 1x3-inch, about 40 pieces)

On Nov. 28, 2016 at my Woman's Club, we were packing cookies for seniors, food bank, and for nursing homes when I came across these green and red, thin and small cake cookies. So, next day I baked these almond Christmas biscotti. My husband loved them. I don't bake them twice. If you want them crispier, cut them, turn over, and bake them at 325 degrees for 25 minutes. We like them soft, they are more tasty.

Ingredients: Sift the dry ingredients together: 4 cups unbleached all-purpose flour, 1 cup almond flour, 3 tsp. baking powder, ½ tsp. baking soda, ½ tsp. salt; 4 extra-large eggs at room temperature; 2-1/2 cup sugar; 1 tsp. each almond and vanilla extracts; 1 pkg. 8 ounce, light cream cheese in room temperature; ½ ounce (141g) each red and green food color; 8 tbsp. (1 stick) melted and cooled unsalted butter.

Preheat the oven at 350 degrees. Grease a 13x9x2-inch baking pan with butter or spray, line the pan with parchment paper extending the parchment on two sides extra to make handles. Grease the parchment paper. In a medium bowl sift all the dry ingredients and divide them into two portions.

In a large bowl, whisk eggs first, then add the sugar and whisk well for about 2 minutes. Add the almond and vanilla extracts. Cut the cream cheese into about 1-inch pieces and add to the mixture and whisk well. Now divide the egg mixture into two equal bowls. Whisk in the green color in one bowl, and the red color in the other bowl. Using a wooden spatula fold in and mix the dry ingredients half and half in each bowl. Now mix in half of the melted butter in each. Drop the green batter in the pan first, spread out evenly with a knife or cake spatula. Then do the same with the red batter. Take some melted butter in your hands, and press down the red dough evenly.

Bake in a preheated oven for about 35 minutes, until the edges are brown, and a toothpick inserted in the center comes out clean. Turn off the oven, and leave the pan in the off oven for 10 more minutes. Take the pan out of oven and cool on the wire rack for 2-3 hours. Loosen the edges with a knife and take out the biscotti on a cutting board. Cut 5 strips across (about 2-1/2-inches wide), then cut each strip into 1-inch wide slices. Serve fresh or leave overnight in the off oven. Then take out the pieces, or wrap the tray airtight, place in a large plastic bag, and refrigerate for up to two weeks.

Tip: If you prefer, you can sprinkle more sliced almonds on the top, press them down just before baking the biscotti.

Black Sesame Seeds Squares (M: about 40 2x2-inch)

Black Sesame Seeds are loaded with nutrients including: protein, magnesium and zinc. These are my father's favorite squares. You can make extra, wrap and freeze in a plastic container up to four months.

Ingredients: 3 bags, 7 ounces (200G) each (total about 4 cups) black sesame seeds, picked over and cleaned; 1 cup sugar; 3 tbsp. water; 1 pkg., 1 cup instant non-fat dry milk powder; ½ cup pistachios slices; ½ cup slivered almonds, 1 tbsp. butter to grease the parchment paper.

1. Preheat oven to 350 degrees. Line a large baking tray with aluminum foil, spread out the sesame seeds and bake for about 15 minutes, stirring once. Turn off the oven and let them cool in the

oven. When cooled, grind only half of them in batches in the blender or the food processor, into coarse crumbs; do not grind in to powder. They grind very fast. Mix up the ground and the whole sesame seeds together. Pour them in to a large bowl.

2. Position an oven rack in the middle. Preheat the oven at 350 degrees. Line a 9x13-inch baking tray with parchment paper and grease the paper well with butter.

3. Heat a large sauté pan with 4 tbsp. water on medium heat, add the sugar, stir a little to melt the sugar and pour over the sesame seeds. Stir well with the metal spatula. Sprinkle ½ cup to 1 cup of dry milk powder as needed to make a thick mixture; stir well and pour over the prepared tray. Spread out the mixture on the parchment paper about 1-1/2-inch thick, using a knife to spread out evenly and top with nuts. Grease a 12-inch-long parchment paper with butter, put butter side down and pat the mixture well on the baking tray. Bake the mixture in a preheated oven for 15 minutes, a little puffed. Take out, cool a little, then transfer the parchment on the cutting board and score into 2x2-inch squares. Cool completely and serve.

Tip: You can use beige or white sesame seeds and with buttered hands make balls instead of squares. Also, if you prefer you can add some nuts and raisins.

Sticky Buns (M: 12 large)

Make the dough about 1 hour before you are ready to roll out the dough. This is my basic pizza dough recipe, just added eggs, milk, and extra sugar. I partially raise the dough, so it is easy to handle, roll, cut, and pick up each slice and place in the syrup. Then I let them rise again in the syrup until almost doubled. You will need about ½ pound of pecans.

Ingredients:

For the Dough: 1 Recipe of naan bread, with the dough raised almost double.

For the Syrup: 1 cup light brown sugar; ¼ cup orange juice; 2 pinches salt; 4 tbsp. unsalted butter; 1 cup toasted and chopped pecans or walnuts.

For the Filling: 2 tbsp. melted butter; 2 tbsp. ground cinnamon mixed with 1 cup packed light brown sugar; ½ cup toasted and chopped pecans or walnuts; 2 tbsp. melted butter to brush the buns before baking.

For the Glaze: 1 cup sifted confectioners' (powder) sugar mixed with 2-3 tbsp. lemon juice mixed to a pourable but thick consistency.

To make the Syrup: While the dough is rising, make the syrup. In a medium pan, on medium heat, place the sugar, add the orange juice, salt and stir to dilute the sugar, and bring it to a boil. Add the butter, lower the heat and simmer 6-8 minutes, until it is slightly thick. Take the syrup off the heat cool, and mix in the pecans. Then pour the syrup in a 10x14-1/2x2-inch greased glass platter.

Assemble and Bake the Buns: Punch down the dough. Place a large plastic wrap on the counter, dust it well with the flour, and make an oblong disk of the dough. Dusting with flour, roll out the dough into 16x10-inches.

Butter the dough on the top with the melted butter, then spread out the sugar and cinnamon mixture leaving a ½-inch border all around. Then sprinkle the pecans, and press down slightly with a spatula. Now starting at the longer border nearest you, start rolling the dough, holding the filling in its place and pressing down with the plastic wrap. Make a long and tight roll, taking the plastic off the dough as you go. Pinch the ends to hold the filling in. Using a bread knife, cut the roll into 12 equal slices, and carefully place the slices in the syrup, cut side up. Give a quarter turn to the dough before cutting the next slice, and make 12 slices in total. Let the buns rise again in the syrup, until almost doubled, for an hour. Buns will expand more while baking.

Brush the buns with the melted 2 tbsp. butter. Bake the buns in a preheated 350 degree oven for about 25 minutes, or until golden. Cool the buns completely. Then scrape the buns together with the syrup and place on a serving platter upside down. Drizzle the glaze all over the cooled buns in a circular motion with a tablespoon and serve.

Mini Cannolies (M: 24)

You don't have to be an Italian, just taste these treats and you will love them. They are so easy to make. Just buy the mini cannoli shells from the supermarkets or order them any time from the Italian bakery. To make your own shells, you need the molds.

Ingredients: 2 boxes (12 shells each) mini cannoli shells; 2 tbsp. butter; 2 pounds part-skim ricotta cheese; ½ cup heavy cream; 6 ounces white chocolate chopped; 3 tbsp. dark chocolate liqueur; ½ cup each pistachios and glazed pineapple chopped (op).

Preheat oven at 300 degrees. Bring out the ricotta cheese about 45 minutes ahead in the room temperature. Line a broiler tray or a heavy-bottom baking tray with double parchment paper and grease it with the butter. Move a sharp knife around the edge inside the cheese container to loosen the cheese, and dump the cheese onto the parchment paper. Slice the cheese into 4 slices. Place the tray in the oven and reduce the liquid by baking for 30 minutes. Turn off the oven, move the tray around halfway and let it dry out for 1 hour.

In a medium pot, heat the heavy cream and the chocolate liqueur; when bubbly, take off the heat and add the chopped chocolate, cover for 5 minutes and whisk to melt the chocolate. Now whisk in the reduced ricotta cheese. When it is cooled completely, fill a piping bag with the cheese and pipe into the shells halfway; push in a slice of pineapple and then fill the shell at both ends. Push in some pistachios. Serve or refrigerate in a container, between the parchment paper and topped with a paper towel and cover. Paper towel will absorb the moisture and will keep it fresh.

Tip: Brush the melted, dark, and cooled chocolate on cannoli shells to make the chocolate cannolis.

Caramel Apples (M: 4)

These apples are not only for the kids. We all love them as well, especially when they are dipped in Chocolate caramel and coated with the large pieces of chocolate. Raw apples can be stored on the counter or in the refrigerator for up to 5-6 weeks.

Ingredients : 4 unbruised Granny Smith or your favorite medium-size apples, wax removed by dipping them in boiling water and turning around for 5 minutes, then pat dry with paper towel; 1-2 tsp. soft butter; 1 bag, 7oz, (198.5g) hard caramel candies (i prefer Werther's Original), you can also use chewy caramels; 2 bars, 4.25 oz., (120g) dark chocolate bars (I prefer Hershey's) both chopped into ¼-inch pieces (divided); ¼ cup sugar; 1/3 cup evaporated milk; 4 lollipop sticks; 1 cup colorful (assorted) sprinklers and ½ cup grated sweetened coconut (op).

1.   Line a baking sheet with parchment paper and grease well with the butter. Spread out the chopped chocolate in a platter and the sprinklers and grated coconut each in another platter. Push in the lollipop sticks at the stems, in each apple.
2.   Grease a medium, deep, microwave safe bowl, lightly with butter. Place milk, sugar, and unwrapped hard caramel candies in the bowl and heat on high 1 minute at a time and stir well with a spoon after each heating. Heat a total of 2-1/2 to 3 minutes until caramel is melted and bubbly. (You can do this in a greased medium pot as well.) Stir in and melt half of the chopped chocolate. Immediately dip the apples in chocolate caramel, rotating all around and then pour over the some caramel with a spoon to cover the top, and dip in to the sprinkler mixture or in chocolate mixture. Place the apples on the greased parchment paper. Repeat with rest of the apples.
3.   Place the baking sheet in a cold oven overnight or until apples are hard and dried. I dip two apples in sprinklers and two in the chocolate pieces. You can dip apples halfway in the caramel or all the way if you have enough left over. If the apples are large, I cut them in to wedges before serving.

Chocolate Fruits and Nuts Balls

These are very easy. My friends love them so much that they keep on asking me to bake some. You can use all fruits or all nuts, as you prefer. Just make sure you make the mixture tight by adding enough fruits and nuts.

Ingredients: 2 tbsps. coconut butter; half can 7 ounces (save the other half for the pudding) sweetened condensed milk; 1 bar, 4 oz. (113g) unsweetened chocolate premium baking bar with 100% cacao (I prefer Ghirardelli) chopped fine; 1 bag, 12 oz. (340g), semi-sweet chocolate chips; about 3 cups glazed pineapple chunks; 1 cup lightly toasted pistachios or cashews.

In a medium pot, on medium heat, heat coconut butter and condensed milk. When it starts bubbling on the edges, add the chocolate and the chips, cover, and take off the heat. Leave it covered for 5 minutes.

After about 5 minutes whisk the chocolate well; it should be melted, if not, then heat again on the low heat whisking constantly. Leave the pot open, away from the heat, and cool the chocolate mixture for about 10 minutes. Then pour over the fruits and nuts. Mix well with a spoon. Using a medium ice cream scoop, drop the mixture on a parchment paper-lined tray, about one inch apart. Let it cool completely, peel off and serve. Refrigerate in a paper towel-lined plastic container, for up to a month.

Chocolate Mousse (Serves: 2)

These are white and dark chocolate mousse, made with avocado and apple sauce instead of traditional whip cream. They are reduced half in calories and are healthy and very tasty.
Ingredients:
For the Dark Chocolate: 1 pkg. 4 ounces chopped semi-sweet chocolate; ½ tsp. instant coffee; 1 ripe haas avocado; 2 tbsp. light brown sugar mixed with 2 tbsp. unsweetened cocoa powder; ¼ cup milk; 2 tsp. vanilla extract; to garnish: chopped walnuts, glazed pineapple pieces and chocolate syrup to drizzle.

For the White Chocolate: 1 pkg., 4 ounces chopped white chocolate; 2 tbsp. chocolate liqueur; 2 tbsp. roasted and ground almonds; about 3 tbsp. apple sauce.
For the Dark Chocolate Mousse: In a bowl melt chopped chocolate, vanilla extract and instant coffee, either for 1 minute in the microwave, stirring every 20 seconds, or over the warm water. In a blender puree together milk, chopped pulp of the avocado, cocoa powder and sugar mixture, and melted and cooled chocolate. If needed add little more milk by the tablespoon, and make a soft mousse. Take out the mixture and fill in a zip-lock sandwich bag.

For the White Chocolate Mousse: Melt the chocolate and liqueur as above, and whisk in the almonds and then the apple sauce as needed. Fill in a sandwich zip-lock bag.
Cut one of the corners of the plastic bag and pipe out the dark chocolate mousse, first in serving fancy glasses on one side. Then pipe the white chocolate on the other side in the glasses; make sure they both are touching each other. Garnish and serve. You can prepare these just before you serve dinner, and leave in a cooled oven or in the refrigerator, tented with a foil, in a serving tray.

Chocolate Tartlettes(M:24)

These chocolate cups are filled with chocolate and nuts. You can also fill them with cream or fruit preserve etc.

Ingredients: Flour mixture: 1-1/2 cups all-purpose flour mixed with 1Tsp. baking powder, 1/2Tsp. baking soda, 1/2Tsp. salt, 1/4cup sugar, 2Tbsp. cocoa powder, 4Tbsp. grated chocolate; 8Tbsp. softened butter, 8oz softened cream cheese; for the filling: 8 oz. melted and cooled semi-sweet chocolate, whisked with about ½ cup sweetened whipped cream and 2Tbsp. orange marmalade; to garnish: 1/2cup toasted and chopped pistachios or almonds.

In a large bowl whisk together butter and cream cheese then mix in the flour mixture. Drop about 1Tbsp. of dough into the mini muffin cups (about 1-3/4-inch muffin cups) and press onto the bottom and sides of the cups to form tartlettes. Place the muffin tin in the refrigerator for 10 minutes. Preheat the oven at 325 degrees and bake about 25-30 minutes until golden. Take out and cool.

Fill in the cups with the mixture of melted chocolate, whipped cream and marmalade, and sprinkle the nuts on the top. You can freeze them after baking, without filling, wrapped in a foil and placed in a plastic container for up to 2 months. Thaw overnight, fill with cream and serve.

Crème Brulee (Serves: 8)

This creamy custard, in French it is "burned cream," is very easy to make. The secret is to bring all the dairy products to room temperature. You can use eight 5 ounce crème brulee molds or four to six large oven-proof bowls, depending on the number of the people you are going to serve.

Ingredients: 1 tsp. melted butter; 3 cups heavy cream; 1 cup whole milk; 3tbsp. chocolate liqueur (or 2 tsp. vanilla extract); 8 large egg yolks; about ¾ cup sugar, divided; ¼ tsp. salt; to garnish: 1/3 cup light brown sugar; to serve: fresh berries.

Boil a large kettle full of water. Lightly grease eight, 5 ounces molds or crème brulee dishes with butter and place them in a large roasting pan. Preheat oven to 300 degrees.
In a large bowl, whisk heavy cream, milk, half of the sugar and the chocolate liqueur. Leave about ¼ cup of the mixture in the bowl behind, and heat rest of the mixture, on low heat, in a medium pot with a good handle.

Now in same bowl whisk the leftover ¼ cup cream mixture, egg yolks, ½ of the sugar, and salt. Increase the heat to medium and heat the cream mixture to almost boiling point, but do not let it boil. Slowly pour about ¼ cup of the hot cream mixture into the egg mixture in a thin stream, whisking constantly. Repeat the process until all the hot cream mixture has been incorporated into the egg mixture. Now pour the mixture straining into the prepared molds. Carefully, pour the hot water into the roasting pan with the kettle, half way up to the molds.

Carefully, place the roasting pan into the heated oven and bake at 300 degree for about 35 minutes, until the cream mixture almost start foaming. Turn off the oven; leave the roasting pan in the off oven for 5 minutes. Then take the roasting pan out of oven and with the help of tongs and a plate, take out the molds and place on the wire rack to cool completely, for about an hour. When they are cooled, place them in a baking tray, cover with the plastic and refrigerate for at least 2 hours, until they are settled, or up to 2 days.

A half hour before serving, take them out of the refrigerator, sprinkle about 1 tbsp. brown sugar, and move a kitchen torch flame over them, or place under the broiler for 3 minutes, to melt and caramelize the sugar on the top. Serve with berries.

Cream Puffs (M: 15)

Cream puffs are made with French pastry dough pate a choux. They are baked on high temperature so that the steam is trapped inside and after they are fully baked, they are hollowed out. We like them filled with icing or pastry cream. A few years back, I took my husband to Berlin, Germany. When we visited a local bakery we saw that they have baked cream puffs about 6-7-inches high and with two tiers. Each of them was filled with tasty whipping cream. We bought some and at home we had to use knife and fork to eat them.

Ingredients: ½ cup water; ½ cup 2% milk; 2 tsp. sugar; 1/3 tsp. salt; ½ cup (1stick) sliced unsalted butter; 1 cup sifted all-purpose flour; 4 extra large eggs; 1-1/2 cup cream or icing for filling; 2 oz. chopped semi-sweet chocolate to drizzle on the top.

1.   In a large pot bring water, milk, sugar, salt and butter to a rolling boil. Boil them for 1 minute and take off the heat. Immediately add all the flour and using a hand-held electric mixer, mix together to form a thick dough. Now break in one egg at a time, break the yolk first, then on medium speed whisk in the eggs completely. Whisk the dough 1 minute at medium speed, scraping the edges, then whisk for 2 minutes at high speed. The mixture will be soft, shiny, smooth, and still a little warm. Let the dough stand for 5 minutes.

2.   Line 2 large baking sheets with parchment paper. Preheat oven 400 degrees. You can drop the dough in a mound, one tablespoon at a time, on ungreased parchment paper; or use a plastic bag, snipping off about ¼ of the corner and dropping about 2 tablespoons, or use a piping bag fitted with a plain ¾-inch tip, and pipe them on the parchment paper about 1-1/2-inch apart. With lightly wet fingers, shape them in mounds. Place the baking sheet to chill for 3-4 minutes in the refrigerator. Bake them in a preheated oven, 400 degrees for 20 minutes, then reduce the temperature to 350 degrees and bake for 10-15 minutes until golden brown. Take them out of oven and place them over the warm stove on a wire rack. Bake the second sheet the same way. Place all the puffs in the turned-off warm oven for another 15 minutes. Check one to make sure they are hollow inside.

3.   You can pipe the filling with a piping bag or cut each puff horizontally halfway (leave both pieces attached), open the puff with one hand and with the other hand fill in a teaspoonful filling in the puff, wiping the spoon off against the top slice. When filled with the cream, place them on a platter and drizzle the melted chocolate on the top, or dip the top of each puff into melted chocolate. Serve immediately or leave in the room temperature for one day, then cover and refrigerate.

Fresh Fruit Custard (Serves: 4)

This fresh fruit custard we are making is from childhood. We mostly make it in the summer when all kinds of fresh fruits are in season, and you can get a good bargain.

Ingredients: 4 to 6 cups chopped fresh fruits, such as: sliced banana, strawberries, and kiwi, or chopped apple, pineapple, mango, melon, etc.; 2 boxes each: 3.4oz. (96g) pudding and pie filling with flavors such as mango, pineapple, lemon, etc.; about 3-1/2 cup milk; ¼ cup dry cranberries and/or ½ cup roasted and chopped pistachios or walnuts.

Place the chopped fruits in four serving bowls. In a medium pot, whisk together the pudding mix and the milk on medium-high heat. Whisking constantly, bring the mixture to a boil. Lower the heat and whisk on a constant simmer for another 5 minutes or until it is thickened. Pour the warm custard over the fresh fruits and serve garnished with cranberries and nuts, or let it cool and serve in a room temperature. Do not refrigerate.

Doughnuts (M: 15 with holes and 12 long jelly doughnuts)

These doughnuts are made with butter (not shortening); milk powder keeps them fresh.

Ingredients: 3 cups unbleached bread flour plus extra for dusting; 1/2Tsp. salt; 4Tbsp. sugar; 1 stick (8Tbsp.) cold butter; 1pkg. 1/4oz. quick-rise yeast; 1/4cup dry milk powder; 3/4cup warm water (110 degree, that doesn't burn back of your hand); 2 large eggs; canola oil to deep fry. Icing: 2cups powdered sugar sifted; 2Tbsp. lemon juice. If prefer jelly filled then about 1-1/2cup your favorite jelly such as: grape, strawberry, apricot or pineapple.

1. In a large bowl whisk together flour, salt and sugar. Thin slice the butter and mix with the flour mixture with both hands until it resembles bread crumbs. Whisk in the yeast then the milk powder. Pour in the warm water mix with wooden spoon and mix in the beaten eggs. Wash your hands and kneed the dough for five minutes until it is pliable. Make a dough ball. Wash and dry the bowl; place about 1Tsp. oil in it and move around the dough ball to coat it on all sides. Cover the bowl with a damp cotton cloth and place in a turn off lightly warm oven (Heat the oven at 200 degrees for 5 minutes and turn it off.) Leave the bowl in the warm oven for about 1 hour until dough is doubled.

2. Take the dough out of the oven, punch down and kneed for 5 minutes. Now divide the dough into 15 equal pieces. Roll each piece into a smooth ball. Using 2 pieces of plastic wrap and dusting with the flour, roll out each portion into 3-inch diameter. Use a 1-inch cookie cutter or a soda bottle cap; stamp out the center and make holes (op). Gather all the centers and reroll by hand into a doughnut. Use a large baking tray about 12 X 18-inch, grease it lightly with the oil, and spread out the doughnuts in single layer. Place the tray back in the warm oven and let the doughnuts rise for another 45 minutes.

3. When doughnuts have puffed up, heat about 2-inch deep oil in a fryer or in a wide medium pot. Heat oil to 325 degrees. Carefully lower 3 or 4 doughnuts in the hot oil; wait for 30 seconds, and start turning them over. Cook them about 4 minutes total, turning each side over about 4-5 times. When they are golden-brown take them out on a paper towel lined platter and repeat with the rest of the doughnuts. Cool them slightly and dip in the icing and coat them all over. Serve immediately.

4. To make long jelly doughnuts, after the dough has risen (step 1), kneed and divide it into 10 pieces. Take each piece in the hand, roll it into 3 X 2-inch rolls and place them in the greased tray to rise 2nd time. Let them rise 45 minutes then fry them as above. When they are cooled, with a utility knife make a pocket and slit them inside, leaving about 1/2inch border alone all around. Fill them with about 2Tbsp. jelly with a pipping bag. Serve them immediately. You can also freeze them without filling with the jelly.

Baked Almond-Blueberries Doughnuts (M: about 18)

My husband and I both love doughnuts. So, I invented these healthy ones, and now we do not feel guilty to have these treats once in a while. To bake these doughnuts you will need a non-stick doughnut baking pan.

Ingredients: 4 tbsp. softened unsalted butter, plus 1 tbsp. for the baking pan; 1 cup sugar; flour mixture: 1-1/2 cup almond flour, 1-1/2 cup all-purpose bleached flour or cake flour plus 2 tbsp. for the pan and the blueberries; 1 tsp. rapid-rise active dry yeast, ½ tsp. baking soda, 2 tsp. baking powder, ½ tsp. kosher salt; egg mixture: 3 large eggs whisked well first then add ¾ cup low-fat yogurt, 2 tsp. vanilla extract, and 2 tbsp. water whisked together; 2 cups frozen blueberries (do not thaw).

For the Glaze: 2 to 2-1/2 cup sifted confectioners' (powder) sugar whisked with 2 tbsp. lemon juice and 2 tbsp. orange juice; 1/3 cup roasted and sliced pistachios.

Preheat oven at 350 degrees. Grease the doughnut pan with soft butter inside and on the cavity edges first, then sprinkle with 1 tsp. flour, especially around the middle knob; tap out extra flour.

In a large bowl with the electric hand mixer, cream the butter and sugar. Add half of the flour mixture and whisk on low speed to combine well. Add the egg mixture and combine. Add rest of the flour mixture and combine, scraping the sides. Now take out the frozen blueberries, sprinkle with 1 tbsp. flour, and mix in by hand. Add the blueberries to the batter and fold in with the hand, just to combine.

Using a piping bag or a teaspoon, fill in the doughnut cavity with about 4 tbsp. batter. Wipe clean all drippings and bake in a preheated oven for 12 to 15 minutes light brown. Wait and cool for 5 minutes If the batter has covered the top, make a cross on the top with a spoon, and push in the spoon all around the knob, making a hole in the doughnut. Cool completely. Repeat with rest of the batter.

To glaze the Doughnuts: Place a wire rack on the baking tray. Dip one cooled doughnut at a time in the glaze, and place on the wire rack. Push in and garnish with the roasted pistachios on the top, and serve.

Tip: To secure the partially used and the opened packet of rapid-rise yeast, get the air out, fold it, and place in an aluminum foil; fold and seal well, and keep in the refrigerator for a short period of time.

Peanut Butter-Almond Doughnuts

Follow the Blueberry Doughnuts recipe: just take blueberries and add: 1/2cup Milk powder, 1/2cup Almond flour and 3/4cup peanut butter. Bake 12-15 minutes golden. Serve as is or dip doughnuts in 4oz. White or dark Chocolate melted in 1/2cup heated Heavy Cream.

Eclairs (M: about 10)

Follow the recipe for the Cream Puffs above, but use 4 large eggs (instead of using 4 extra large eggs). Just pipe the eclairs in a tube-like fashion, about 4-1/2- inches long on the ungreased parchment paper and shape them with a wet knife, then with the wet finger to make them in even shape. Baking time is a little longer. Bake in a preheated 400 degree oven for 30 minutes, then reduce the temperature to 350 degrees and bake another 20-25 minutes golden brown. Turn the oven off and place them in a warm oven for another 25-30 minutes or until hollowed out inside.

Make a long slit on the top of each éclair, hold it open with one hand and pipe the pastry cream inside, filling the whole length. Dip or drizzle the melted chocolate on the top.

Pastry Cream (M: about 1-1/2 C)

Ingredients: 2 cups whole milk; 4 tbsp. corn starch; pinch of salt; ½ cup plus 1 tbsp. sugar; 3 tbsp. unsalted butter; 3 large egg yolks; ½ tsp. vanilla extract; ½ tsp. almond or coconut extract.

Bring milk and half of the sugar to a simmer in a saucepan, on medium heat. In a medium bowl whisk in cornstarch, salt, rest of the sugar, vanilla and almond or coconut extracts and yolks. Slowly whisk in warm milk ½ cup and using a hand-held electric mixer, whisk all. Then slowly add half of the milk into the egg mixture, whisking constantly. Now whisking slowly, pour in the egg mixture into the warm milk and whisk well. Place the saucepan over the low heat and bring to a simmer while whisking constantly. Increase the heat to medium-high heat, whisk in the butter and whisk until thickened. Take off the heat, pour into a bowl and place a plastic wrap on the surface of the cream to keep from forming a skin on the top. Let it cool in the room temperature for an hour, then chill for 1 hour in the refrigerator before using.

Energy Bars (Serves: 15-20)

These chocolate, nut, oat and coconut bars are out of this world. You can serve them any time of the day. They are very easy to bake; bake the layers 3 times, about 6 to 8 minutes each.

Ingredients: 2 cups plain or chocolate graham cracker crumbs, mixed with 4 tbsp. butter, and 4 tbsp. sugar; 1 bar, 4 ounces semi-sweet chocolate; 2 bags each: 11 oz. (311.8g) butterscotch morsels (peanut butter chocolate chips); 1 bag, 12 oz. (340g) white chocolate morsels; 1 container, 16 oz., 454g shelled walnuts quartered or chopped; 2 cups each whole: pistachios and pumpkin seeds (about ½ pound each); ¾ lb. (2 c) slivered almonds; 1 can, 14 oz. (396) sweetened condensed milk; a mixture of ½ cup quick cooking oatmeal, and 1 cup fresh-grated or fresh-frozen and thawed coconut.

1. Preheat the oven at 350 degrees. Line a 12x18x1-inch baking sheet with a large and double parchment paper, 2 short sides with a little overhanging, to grab the paper as handles. Then fold the paper, other two long sides underneath, to fit the tray. Grease the paper well, with cooking spray or butter. Spread out the crumb mixture and bake for 10 minutes. Wait for 15 minutes, to cool a little, then grate the semi-sweet chocolate bar all over on the top.
2. Now spread the walnuts evenly over the crumbs, then one bag of butterscotch morsels evenly, then spread the pistachios evenly. Bake in the preheated oven for 6-8 minutes, just until morsels are soft. Take the tray out of the oven, place on the cutting board. Grease a metal spatula with cooking spray or butter. Press down the nuts firmly with a metal spatula, pressing down the flat part with one hand and holding the handle with the other hand, moving the spatula all over (to break the morsels so that they adhere to the nuts).
3. Now spread the white chocolate morsels, then make a layer with the pumpkin seeds, another layer with the butter scotch morsels, then spread out the slivered almonds. Bake again for another 6 to 8 minutes. Take the tray out of the oven and again press down firmly with the metal spatula to break the morsels.
4. Now in a very thin stream, pour the condensed milk, starting from the edges and going towards the center. Then sprinkle with the mixture of coconut over the milk, and press down with the metal spatula all over to flatten and firm the layers. Bake again for 6 to 8 minutes, or until the oatmeal is light brown. After the baking press down again with spatula to flatten the top.
5. Take the tray out of the oven. Let it cool for 1 hour over a wire rack. Then cut about 3-inches wide strips across, going over the cut 2-3 times and separating the bars slightly. Cool on the counter 1 hour. Then chill in the refrigerator overnight, until the chocolate has hardened. Loosen the edges all around, with a small knife, holding the paper handles, slide the parchment paper over the cutting board and cut into desired bars or squares. These freeze well in a parchment paper-lined plastic container for up to 3 months, or leave in the refrigerator covered airtight in a plastic container, for up to two weeks.

Stuffed Figs (Serves: 4 -6)

This is a tasty, healthy and quick-fix dessert in the summer.

Ingredients: 1 box 18 ounces, (456g) fresh black mission ripe figs; ¼ cup peanut butter or ½ cup cottage cheese or both; 2 tbsp. honey; whip cream or ice cream to serve (op).

Wash, pat dry the figs and take out the stems. Heat for 1 minutes in the microwave or in the oven until they are just warm, then cool the figs.

Cut the figs in half lengthwise; spread about ½ tsp. of peanut butter on one side and ½ tsp.of cottage cheese on the other side. Put both pieces together again and drizzle with the honey. Serve immediately 4 to 5 pieces each as it is or with whip cream or a scoop of ice cream.

Fruit Crumble (Serves: 8-10)

You can bake Apples alone or bake apples with the mixed fruits. If the fruits are not in the season, use some in cans.

Ingredients: 1 tbsp. butter to grease the bottom of the pan; 6 golden Delicious apples peeled, cut into 8 wedges, cored and sprinkled with a mixture of: 2 tbsp. sugar, 2 tbsp. corn starch and ½ tsp. cinnamon; all canned fruits drained: 1 can, 20 oz. (567g) pineapple chunks, 2 cans each 15.25 oz. (432g) halved apricots in syrup, 1 bottle, 25 oz. (709g) ready to eat whole prunes (make a slit and take out the pits), 1 can (397g) whole berry cranberry sauce; for topping a mixture of: 1 stick soft unsalted butter mixed with 1 cup of unsifted all-purpose flour and 1 cup packed light brown sugar, then mix with ½ tsp. cinnamon and 2 cups fine grated sweetened coconut.

Grease a 15x10x2-inch glass pan with butter and layer the drained fruits in the order they are listed. Mix all the topping ingredients and sprinkle on the top. Bake in a 350 degree preheated oven for 35-40 minutes until they are bubbling. Turn off the oven and leave the platter in the oven for another 10 minutes for apples to soft. Serve any time of the day.
Tip: Fruits are healthy for you. Try to use less sugar and less butter. Prunes are loaded with fiber, have vitamin A, and are good for the eyes.

Quinoa Oat Halwa - Dry Pudding (Serves: 4)

Halwa is almost like a dry pudding. It is soft, tasty and very nutritious. I make Halwa for the temple and people love it. Traditionally, it is made with semolina (cream of wheat), and loaded with butter, cream, coconut and nuts. You can serve this any time of the day.

Ingredients: 1 cup whole grain quinoa round in the food processor or blender for 5 seconds, and then add 1 cup old-fashioned oatmeal and grind together in to fine crumbs; soak 30 minutes or up to overnight, covered in ½ cup heavy cream and ½ cup milk; 4 tbsp. butter; about 3 tbsp. light brown sugar or jaggery (Indian brown cane sugar); 2 cups warm water; ½ cup dry cranberries; ½ tsp. ground cinnamon; ½ cup shredded coconut; 1 cup fresh berries to serve.

Heat a large heavy-bottom pan with butter on medium heat, when hot add the soaked quinoa mixture and sauté for 8-10 minutes until it is light brown. Take the pan off the heat, add 2 cups warm water, whisking slowly. Place the pan back on the heat. Increase the heat to medium-high, add cranberries, cinnamon and sugar, and stir constantly to dry out the water, scraping the bottom. If the mixture is burring, reduce the heat to medium, adjusting back and forth from medium to medium-high heat. When the mixture stops sticking to the bottom and the butter starts coming all around, and the mixture is light brown and dry, after about 10 minutes, sprinkle the coconut and turn off the heat and mix the coconut well. Serve warm, garnished with fresh berries, and warm milk or tea.

Tip: This is a traditional breakfast and offering at the temples in India. I am using quinoa and oatmeal that are loaded with protein and fiber. I have reduced the heavy cream and butter in half. Instead of nuts, I am using dry and fresh berries that are good for the heart and have fiber and vitamin C.

Ice Cream in Chocolate Cups (Serves: 6)

In 2014 we gave a farewell luncheon to our gym teacher in a café in New Jersey. For dessert we had these ice cream cups that we all loved very much. You need 1 to 2 days ahead to make the cups.

Ingredients: 1 container, 1.5 qts. (1.42 l) strawberry ice cream (or your favorite ice cream) 3 boxes, each 4 ounce (113g) chopped semisweet chocolate; ½ cup heavy cream mixed with 3 tbsp. dark chocolate liqueur and 2 tbsp. sugar; 6 very small balloons filled with air and blown in about 3-inches in diameter, spray the round part of the balloons with cooking spray and lightly wipe out with the tissue paper; topping: 6 tbsp. pineapple topping or strawberry jam; ¼ cup chopped pistachios and chocolate syrup to drizzle over the top.

1. Line a large baking tray with the parchment. Then pick up the parchment paper and draw 6 circles, about 1-1/2 inches in diameter, and then encircle those with the larger circles, about 3 inches in diameter, close to each other in two rows, or use two trays.
2. Melt the chocolate: Heat the sugar, heavy cream and chocolate liqueur on low heat; take off the heat, add the chopped chocolate, cover for 5 minutes, then stir well, Keep the chocolate bowl over the warm water so it is melted. When cooled a little, drop about 2 tbsp. of melted chocolate in the smaller circles and let the chocolate dry for 1/2 minute. Now dip the balloons halfway around the bottom round part, rotating into the chocolate to coat completely; make sure it is not dripping, then carefully place the balloon on the smaller circle, hold the balloon for a minute, making sure it is straight and can stand on its own. Then just let it go, and balloon will stand on its own when chocolate gets hard. When all are done poke a match to the balloons and break the balloons and discard them. You will have nice chocolate cups now.
3. Take out the ice cream and leave in the room temperature for 3-4 minutes to let it get a little soft. Scoop out the ice cream and make a ball over a large piece of plastic wrap, press from all around and fill in the chocolate cups; you can squeeze the ice cream ball to fit into the cups. Shape the top with the slightly wet hands, cover and freeze the balls overnight.
4. Take out the cups just before serving. Serve ice cream cups in small glass bowls with topping and drizzle the chocolate syrup on the top.

Hand Made Ice Cream (M: about 1 Qt.)

You do not need any ice cream maker with this recipe. You just need to stir with a wooden or plastic spoon 2-3 times during freezing process.

Ingredients: 1 tsp. butter; 1 can, 14oz. sweetened condensed milk; ½ cup lightly toasted and ground almonds or pistachios (op); 1 tsp. vanilla extract; about 1-1/2 cup whipped cream; ½ tsp.table salt.

Heat a medium pot on medium heat, add the butter and coat the bottom. Add the almonds and the condensed milk and mix well with a fork. Let the mixture come to a simmer (you will see some bubbles on the edge). Add the vanilla extract and the salt. Take off the mixture and pour in a lightly greased 9x12-inch glass or a porcelain platter. Cool completely. Then fold in the whipped cream, just enough to combine the mixture. Freeze covered for 3-4 hours. When the ice cream start to freeze, stir in with the plastic or wooden spoon. Let it freeze for about 7-8 hours, stirring 2-3 times during the process. Scoop out and serve over the fresh fruits, topped with the chocolate syrup.

Fudge Brownies (36 2x2 inch pieces)

These soft, chocolaty brownies are loaded with flavor. Eat, cover and refrigerate, or freeze them for the future, wrapped with the plastic wrap, in a plastic container, for up to three months.

Ingredients:
For the Brownies: 2 cups bleached all-purpose flour or cake flour; 1-1/2 tsp. baking powder; 2 pinches (about 1/8 tsp.) baking soda; ½ tsp. salt; ¼ cup shredded sweetened coconut; 1 cup granulated sugar; 3/4 cup packed light brown sugar; 1/2cup grated semi-sweet chocolate; 1-1/2 stick (12 tbsp.) unsalted butter; 2 tbsp. canola oil; 1 cup heavy cream or half-and-half, 1/3 cup (about 6tbsp.) unsweetened cocoa powder; 1 tsp. instant coffee powder; 3 whole large eggs and 2 large egg yolks; ½ tsp. fine grated orange zest; 1/2cup chopped walnuts (op).

Topping: 1 bag, 10 ounces, 283.4g (about 2 cups) semisweet chocolate or dark chocolate chips with about 55% cacao, divided; ½ cup heavy cream or half-and-half; 1 tbsp. unsalted butter; ¼ tsp. finely grated orange zest; 1 tbsp. packed light brown sugar; one pinch of salt; 1 cup chopped walnuts or lightly roasted slivered almonds.

1. Grease a 9x12-inch metal baking pan with butter or cooking spray, line it with the parchment paper and spray the paper well, sprinkle ½ tsp. of cake flour, shake around the pan and tap it out.
2. Sift the dry ingredients together in a large bowl: flour, baking powder, baking soda and salt; set aside. In a small pot melt 1 stick of butter and pour over the dry ingredients. Whisk the butter well in to the dry ingredients well or use your hand to incorporate it well. Add the coconut mix well and set aside. Make the cocoa melt: Cocoa melt is almost like melted chocolate. Heat 1 cup of heavy cream and 4 tbsp. butter in the same small pot, bring it almost to a boil. Take off the heat and add cocoa powder, brown sugar, instant coffee; whisk it well, cover with the lid and set aside to cool. After 5-6 minutes whisk it well and add the ½ tsp. orange zest.
3. Beat the eggs and egg yolks and whisk in 1-1/4 cup granulated sugar together well and set aside.

430

4. Take the dry flour mixture and whisk in the cocoa melt and oil, incorporating all the flour. Now whisk in the egg mixture well into the batter. Fold in the grated chocolate and walnuts (if using). Pour the batter into the prepared pan and even it out with a dinner knife; tap on the counter a little to take out all the air bubbles.
5. Bake in a preheated 325 degrees oven for a total of 20 minutes. Turn around the cake halfway after 10 minutes. After the 20 minutes turn off the oven and let the brownies rest in the oven for 1-2 minutes, no more. Take the brownies out of the oven and cool completely on a wire rack for about 1-1/2 to 2 hours before applying the topping.

    Topping: Heat over the stove (or in the microwave oven) 1/2 cup heavy cream or half-and-half. Take off the heat and add 1 cup chocolate chips, 1 tbsp. brown sugar, and 1 tbsp. unsalted butter, ¼ tsp. fine orange zest and a pinch of salt. Whisk well, cover and cool.

After 5 minutes when brownies are cooled, pour only about half of the melted chocolate over the brownies, spreading it out up to the edges with a knife and covering the entire surface with the chocolate; sprinkle the nuts and about 1 cup (remaining) chocolate chips evenly over the brownies. Refrigerate the brownie pan for chocolate to settle about 15 minutes, then pour rest of the melted chocolate across or on the edges (wherever it is needed) or just decorate on the top. Refrigerate the pan until ready to serve. Cover with the aluminum foil. Cut and serve the brownies as needed.

Variations

With Apple Sauce: To make cocoa melt use 1 cup hot water instead of heavy cream. Add 1 cup apple sauce together with the cocoa melt in the batter.

To make brownies more chocolaty: Add 4 ounces of fine chopped semisweet chocolate in the heated heavy cream in making the cocoa melt.

You can substitute the 10 ounces of chocolate chips with 10 ounces of semi-sweet, fine-chopped chocolate. Melt half of the chocolate to spread on the top and use other half chopped chocolate with the nuts to garnish.

Jalebi - Fermented Rings in Syrup (Serves: 6-8)

Jalebi are known to help relieve headaches. Also, the fermented batter is good for you. Jalebi are somewhat like the funnel cake. They are rings of fermented batter, dipped in lemon syrup and sprinkled with almonds. It takes about 2 days to have the batter ready. You will need a 2-pound clean ketchup bottle or a 12x12-inch cotton cloth with a 1/10-inch hole in the center, with button stitches sowed all around to hold its shape, to drop the batter in the hot oil.

Ingredients

For the Batter: 2 cups sifted all-purpose flour; ½ cup chickpea flour (besan); 1 tbsp. sugar; ½ cup thick plain yogurt, room temperature; 2 tbsp. warm vegetable oil; about 1/3 to ½ cup warm water as needed; ¼ cup corn starch; vegetable oil to deep-fry.

For the Syrup: 3-1/4 cup sugar, 2-3/4 cup water; 1 tsp. cardamom seeds ground into powder; 2 tbsp. lemon juice, to garnish: ½ cup sliced almonds.

To prepare the Batter: In a large bowl, whisk in both flours and the sugar, add hot oil and whisk in the oil. Add the hot water 1/3 cup only (or as needed) to make a thick batter, the yogurt, and whisk all well. Cover with a cotton cloth, tie the cloth with the kitchen twine, and place in a warm place for 24 hours in the summer; on hot days, you need only about 12 hours

For the Syrup: Just before deep-frying the batter, prepare the syrup. In a medium and wide pot, heat sugar, cardamom powder, and the water; bring to a boil, let it boil for 5 minutes, skim out the foam, add the lemon juice, then simmer for another 20 minutes on low heat, skimming out the foam.

To make the Jalebi: Heat a medium wok or a frying pan, on medium heat, add about 2-inch deep oil. Whisk the corn starch into the batter well, then fill the batter in a clean, fresh-washed and dried-out bottle, or freshly washed and rinsed out cotton cloth with a hole. Use half of the batter at a time. When the oil is hot, about 375 degrees, squeeze out the batter in a double circle, at the 4 corners, ending the batter by making a line in the center of the circle. (This line will hold the circle well). Cook for 4-5 minutes on each side, until it is light golden and crisp. Using a fork and spatula, pick up the circles and drop them in the syrup. Immediately, take out the circles (rings) and place them in a platter. Repeat with the rest of the batter. Sprinkle the almonds on the top and serve warm.

Tip: Do not leave the rings in the syrup too long, they will get soggy.

French Apple Tart I (Red Heart)(Serves 8-10)

Just like my mother, I like desserts with fruits. This apple tart is pretty, easy to make and very tasty.

For the Crust: 1-1/4 cup all-purpose flour; 1 cup almond flour; 1 tsp. each: baking soda and baking powder; 1 stick (8 tbsp.) unsalted butter cut up into bits; ½ cup sour cream; ½ tsp. salt; 2 tbsp. sugar; 1 tbsp. lemon juice; 3 tbsp. melted butter to brush on the tart.

For the Filling: 5 large Gala apples; ½ cut lemon to rub on the cut apples; 3 tbsp. sugar; 1 tbsp. cinnamon powder; for the topping: 3 tbsp. sugar; ¼ cup orange marmalade.

1. To prepare the crust: In a large mixing bowl combine 1 cup flour, 1 cup almond flour, baking soda, baking powder, salt; add butter and rub well between two hands to incorporate butter and flour into small crumbs.
   You can use a food processor and pulse until mixture resembles small crumbs (small pea size). Add sour cream, sugar, lemon juice and mix well with a wooden spoon and shape into a disk; wrap loosely in plastic wrap and refrigerate at least 1 hour until chilled and hard.
2. To prepare the filling: Wash, and core apples with corer and cut each into 2 pieces lengthwise; rub the cut side with lemon and turn them over to pile them in a large bowl.

3. Now take out the crust and roll it out between two plastic wrap dusting with flour into 10x14-inch rectangle plus ½ inch larger than the size of the tray. At the end you can also stretch it by pressing with both hands on a parchment paper-lined baking tray. Brush the tray with melted butter, especially the edges, and sprinkle the whole crust with 1 tab mixture of sugar and cinnamon; save rest of the mixture for later. Place the tray in the refrigerator and chill for 6-8 minutes.

4. Preheat the oven to 350F. Take one apple at a time, cut in half lengthwise; core it with a small spoon or a knife, rub the cut side with the lemon juice. Take one piece of apple at a time and turn it over, cut side down, on the cutting board and slice paper-thin across; keeping the slices in place, move the cut piece with a spatula or knife, together in a platter. When almost all the pieces are sliced then bring out the crust tray and start laying them down, cascading them in the tray. Start from the shorter side of the tray leaving at least ¼ to ½ inch of crust all around. When you lay down the second row, overlap a little to cover the cut part of the apples. Use all the large pieces first and save the tiny ones for later if needed. When the crust is covered with the apple slices, then fold the crust edge inward to hold the slices; brush pieces carefully by dabbing the brush on apples.

Red Heart Tart: To make a red heart of apples: slice two red delicious apples, and 4 yellow delicious apples. Spread out the crust, then draw a heart in the crust with a knife (outline it), fill the heart with the red apple slices first. Then take the yellow delicious apple slices and fill in the space all around the heart going to the edges. Follow the recipe.

Place the tray in the center of oven and bake 350F for 20 minutes. Then take out the tray out of oven sprinkle rest of the sugar and cinnamon mixture; increase the oven temperature and bake another 10 minutes at 450F until apples are soft.
Brush the apples with marmalade, cool on the wire rack.
Serve warm or cooled with whip cream or a scoop of Ice cream and or drizzled with caramel sauce.

French Apple Tart II (Serves: 6)

In this tart, apples are quartered and baked in the cast-iron skillet or 9-inch tart pan topped with the Crust. You can use one type of mixed variety of apples as long as they are not mushy.

Ingredients for the Crust: 2 large eggs; 1 stick butter softened, divided; 2 tbsp. lemon juice; 1-1/2 cup all-purpose flour; ½ cup sugar; 1 tsp. baking powder; 2 tbsp. peanut butter (op); ½ tsp. baking soda; ½ tsp. salt; 1 tbsp. milk if needed.

For the Filling: ½ cup quartered pecans or walnuts; ½ cup orange juice; 1-1/2 cup sugar; 2 tbsp. hot water; 4 tbsp. unsalted butter; 5 granny smith apples, peeled, quartered, cored; ½ cup dry cranberries.

For the Topping: 4 tbsp. butter cut into ½-inch bits; ¼ tbsp. marmalade; to serve: ice cream or whipped cream.

For the Crust:

1. In a large bowl whisk eggs and peanut butter with sugar until foamy. Add and rub the butter to the dry ingredients: flour, baking powder, baking soda, salt. Add the flour mixture to the egg mixture, and make a dough. Kneed a little and make a disk. Use 1 tab milk, if needed, to make a pliable dough.

2. Place disk between two plastic wraps and roll out, moving plastic and peeling off the dough every now and then, into 10-inch crust. Then peel off the plastics and put back again and refrigerate the crust in a tray, still between the plastic wrap.

For the Filling:

1. Greece a 9-inch pie plate or a tart pan with soft butter, then line up pecans or the walnuts on edges in a circle.

2. Heat a large cast-iron pan on medium heat, and add 4 tbsp. butter and quartered apples and sauté on medium for 8-10 minutes until soft. Add orange juice, sugar, stirring constantly bring it to a boil, and boil for 5 minutes until the juice is thickened. Take out the apple pieces and line them up in a circle in the pie plate, hollow side up, and then cover the open spaces with rest of the Apple pieces, cranberries, and juices.

3. Move oven shelf to middle and preheat oven to 350F.

4. Now drop rest of the half-stick of butter bits on top of apples and cover with crust. Fold the extra crust underneath the crust on the edges, Push the edges in slightly making a scallop edges. Make 2-3 cuts in the crust. Put pan on a sheet pan and bake in a preheated oven.

5. Bake in at 350F for 25 to 30 minutes until golden brown. Take tart out of oven and place on a wire rack to cool. Within 5 minutes, loosen the edges with a dinner knife; put a large platter on the top and turn over the tart into a serving plate while it is still warm. Brush marmalade over the tart all over.

Serve tart wedges with the ice cream or whipped cream.

Baked Whole Apples (Save Ka Murabba)

When my mother's middle sister Kaushilya came to stay with us, she was sick and having migraine headaches. The doctor gave her some pills and asked her to eat one preserved apple every morning to get rid of the headache. Since then my mother started cooking these apples very often for our family.

Ingredients: 12 Granny Smith apples unbruised; juice of ½ lemon about 2 tabs plus ½ tsp. salt; 2 cups water and 2 cups sugar; 1 tbsp. cardamom seeds freshly crushed into powder

1. In a medium pot heat 2 cups water and add sugar stir to dissolve, add half of the cardamom powder and simmer on low heat for 15 minutes covered. Turn off the heat and keep it warm.
2. Wash, peel, and core apples with a corer then rub lemon all over inside and out on apples. With a sharp knife make about ½ an inch cut all over (3-4 places) on the apples in the center.
3. Preheat oven to 425F.
4. Grease a 10x14 platter with butter and spread out apples in platter, then pour over the warm syrup, sprinkle the rest ½ tab of cardamom power and salt; cover tightly with aluminum foil.
5. Bake 400F for 30 minutes, then turn over the apples with two large spoons cover and bake again about 30 minutes more until apples are soft. Turn off the oven and let the apples sit in over uncovered for 2 hours, then cool them on a rack.
6. You can fill cooled apples in a jar or large bowl and keep in the refrigerator up to 3 weeks.

7. Serve with or without ice cream or whipped cream. You can also chop the apples and use as garnish on any pudding or pastry, even on pancakes and French toasts.

Dark Chocolate Fudge (M: about 20 pieces)

This fudge is not only tasty, but is a pure fudge. You can also melt the chocolate over warm water in a bowl, making sure the bowl does not touch the water.

Ingredients: 2 pkgs., each 8 ounces (226G), Bakers' unsweetened baking chocolate squares 100% cacao, chopped fine; 3 tbsp. unsalted butter plus for greasing the dish; ¼ tsp. salt; ½ cup superfine sugar or to taste; ½ tsp. instant coffee (op); 1 tsp. vanilla extract; 1 tsp. fine grated tangerine or lemon zest; ½ cup heavy cream; 1 cup chopped walnuts (op).

1. Grease an 8x8 baking dish, line with the parchment paper and grease well with butter or cooking spray and set aside. In a heavy-bottom pot, on medium-low heat, add 1 tbsp. butter. Move the butter around to coat the bottom, just 5 seconds, and immediately add the cream and bring it to almost to a boil.
2. Take the cream off the heat add chopped chocolate, zest, vanilla extract, salt and the sugar; cover with the lid and set aside for 5 minutes; do not stir at this point.
3. After 5 minutes, stir the chocolate with a wooden spoon until the chocolate is melted completely and the mixture is thickened. Add the remaining 2 tbsp. of butter and dissolve it completely. If the chocolate is too thicken or not melted, put the pot back on the low heat, covered for 1-2 minutes, open the cover and stir the chocolate. Add the chopped walnuts and stir fast before chocolate hardens and immediately pour into the prepared baking dish. Leave the chocolate in room temperature, away from heat and draft for a few hours or overnight.
4. Take the fudge out together with the parchment paper on a cutting board and cut into about 1-1/2-inch squares. Store in a container in a dark and cool place, in a room, away from the spices or other smells. Never store chocolate in the refrigerator.

White Chocolate Fudge (M: about 20 pieces)

You can use all white chocolate just like the dark chocolate fudge, or use milk and chocolate both. I like the combination, it is healthy as well as tasty.
Ingredients: ½ cup whole or 2% milk boiled with 1 tsp. fine crushed cardamom seeds and cooled; 4 tbsp. unsalted butter plus for greasing the dish; 1 can, 14 oz. (396g) sweetened condensed milk; 1 cup low-fat dry milk powder; 1 tsp. vanilla extract; 1 pound chopped white chocolate or 1pkg. 10oz, about 1-3/4 cup white chocolate chips; ½ cup dry cranberries; ½ cup sliced pistachios.

1. Grease an 8x8 baking dish with butter, line with the parchment paper and grease well again with the butter or cooking spray and set aside. In a large and heavy-bottom pan, on medium heat, add 1 tbsp. butter, coat the bottom and add the condensed milk. Bring milk to a simmer, stir with a spatula, and let it simmer on low heat for 4-5 minutes.
2. Mix the dry milk powder and remaining 3 tbsp. of butter by hand in a bowl, then add to the simmering milk; add the vanilla extract and mix well. Take off the heat and add the white chocolate or chips, cover immediately with the lid and let stand for 4-5 minutes. Open the cover and stir the chocolate well. If chocolate is hardened, put the pan back on the low heat

and stir the chocolate until it is melted. Take off the heat and strain over the cardamom infused milk. Stir the chocolate until all the milk is absorbed. Pour the mixture over the prepared dish and sprinkle first the dry cranberries, then the sliced pistachios. Press down with a clean spatula and cool in the room temperature a few hours or overnight. Take the chocolate out together with the parchment paper on a cutting board and cut into 1-1/2-inch squares. Store in room temperature, away from heat and smell in a cool and a dark place.

Chocolate fudge with nuts and seeds: In a dry skillet on medium toast 1/2 cup each pumpkin seeds and peeled and sliced almonds for 2 minutes, add 2tbsp. each black sesame seeds and quinoa and toast for 3 minutes. Cool and spread nuts and seeds on the parchment paper first and pour over the fudge, follow the recipe above.

Apricot and Cheese Danish (Serves: 10-15)

This exotic Danish is loaded with flavors and nutrients. You need all dairy products at room temperature. For the crust you can also use the puff pastry if you like. This pasty is very easy. First you make nut layer and bake for 15 minutes, then pour the preserve and bake 5 minutes, and finally pour the cheese mixture and bake about 30 minutes; chill, cut into the bars and serve. We freeze half of the pastry in a container and rest we use slowly with milk or serve to company. Everyone loves it.

Ingredients :

For the Crust: 1 cup each ground pistachio, almond and walnut; ½ cup plain all-purpose flour; 4 tbsp. (1/4 c) corn starch, 4 tbsp. unsalted butter soft and ½ cup sugar; 2 egg whites at room temperature, ¼ cup superfine sugar, 2 tbsp. lemon juice; 1 cup apple sauce; ¼ tsp. salt.

 For the Filling: 1 jar 12 oz. (340g) about 1 cup apricot preserve or 1 cup orange marmalade melted in a small saucepan; 3 large eggs; ½ 2% or whole milk; 1 cup sugar; 1 container, 16 oz. 453g sour cream; 1 pkg., 8oz. (227g) cream cheese; 1 tbsp. lemon zest; 2 tbsp. lemon juice; 1 tsp. corn starch; 2 pinches salt; 4 tbsp.(1/4 c) plain flour; 2 tbsp. soft unsalted butter; to decorate: 4 tbsp. (1/4 c) pumpkin seeds; ½ cup (8 tbsp.) dry cranberries.

1. Line a baking sheet 12x14x2 inches with parchment (baking) paper, grease with butter or spray the paper. Preheat the oven at 350 degrees.
2. In large bowl combine flour, salt, 4 tbsp. soft butter, and corn starch together. Add the 3 cupss of ground nuts and 1/2 cup of sugar and ¼ tsp. salt, combine all together well. In a medium clean and dry porcelain or metal bowl, whisk the egg whites with an electric mixture on low speed until foamy, about 30 seconds. Slowly add the 2 tbsp. lemon juice and some superfine sugar and whisk, increasing the speed; keep on adding the sugar slowly while increasing the speed until the soft peaks form, about 2-3 minutes. Add apple sauce and combine it well.
3. Now make the crust layers. First sprinkle ½ of the nut mixture over the parchment, press it down to make even with a metal spatula. Slowly pour all over the apple sauce mixture and cover the nut layer (spread out the apple sauce mixture with a butter knife). Now sprinkle other half of the nut mixture over the apple sauce. With the tines of a fork, make holes all over the crust, about 1-inch apart, then even out the crust again with the spatula. Bake in a preheated oven for about 15 minutes until it is firm.
4. While the crust is baking, make the filling. In a large mixing bowl with an electric mixer, beat the eggs and ½ cup of milk together well, add 1 cup sugar, soft cream cheese cut up in cubes, the sour cream, lemon zest, lemon juice, 1 tsp. corn starch, salt, ¼ cup plain flour; beat on low speed to combine, then beat on high speed to incorporate all well. Add the soft butter and mix it well.

5. After the crust is baked for 15 minutes, take the tray out and pour the melted apricot preserve or orange marmalade all over, and bake for 5 minutes to let it settle down a little.

6. Take out the tray and pour the cheese mixture evenly all over the preserve; top with pumpkin seeds and dry cranberries and bake at 350 for about 30 minutes, until edges are lightly brown and pastry is settled. Cool in the oven for ½ hour, then on the counter for about 2 hours. Cut into to 2x4-inch bars. You can also cut into 2x2-inch squares and serve in paper cups. Serve right away or cover and refrigerate for later.

Coconut Flan (Serves: 4-6)

This flan is very flavorful. I did not use coconut milk and whole milk, so it is lot less in calories as well as in fat.

Ingredients: 1pkg. 7ounces (198g) about 1-1/2 cup sweetened coconut flakes (divided), ½ cup sugar, 2 tap water, 1 tab lemon juice, ¼ tsp. ground cinnamon, 3-1/2 cup 2% (or whole) milk, 1 can 14 ounces (396g) about 1-1/2 cup sweetened condensed milk, 5 large eggs, ¼ cup sugar, 2 tabs coconut extract, chocolate syrup to drizzle on each serving.

1. Grease an oven-proof medium glass bowl or large glass pie platter with butter spray and set aside. Boil about 10 cup water in a kettle or a pot and keep warm until needed. Preheat oven at 350 degrees. Have a baking tray with sides or a roasting pan ready to bake the flan in hot water.

2. Line a baking or cookie tray with aluminum foil and spread out the coconut and bake, stirring often, for about 8-10 minutes until light brown. Take coconut out of the oven and set aside.

3. In a small heavy-bottom saucepan, melt sugar while shaking the pan (do not stir) until brown color. Add the mixture of 2 Tab water and 1 Tab lemon juice. Shake the pan until it is thick. Then pour the melted sugar in the prepared bowl or pie plate and set aside to cool.

4. Whisk the eggs in a medium bowl then whisk in 1 cup of cold milk and ¼ cup of sugar and set aside, In a medium heavy-bottom pot, heat the rest of 1-1/2 cup of milk with 1 cup of toasted coconut flakes. Bring milk to a boil, then slowly, in a steady stream and stirring constantly, add the condensed milk to the milk mixture. Bring the mixture to a boil and lower the heat. Now temper the eggs: Pour about ½ cup of the hot milk in a stream while whisking into the egg mixture and repeat one more time, adding another ½ cup of the milk. Take the milk mixture off the heat and add the egg mixture slowly into the hot milk and coconut mixture while whisking constantly. Put the combined mixture back on the stove and, while stirring constantly on medium to medium-high heat, bring the mixture to a boil. Immediately take the mixture off the heat and strain it through a strainer into the prepared glass bowl or pie dish, over the melted brown sugar. Sprinkle over the coconut extract and place the bowl carefully in the roasting pan in the oven. Then pour the boiling water into the roasting pan or tray, up to halfway up to the bowl; cover loosely with aluminum foil and bake at 350 degree for 30 minutes. Turn the bowl halfway around and take out the foil, and bake open about 30 minutes more until top is set. The flan will set as it cools. Cool the flan bowl in room temperature on a wire rack completely, then refrigerate overnight.

5. Take out the bowl or pie plate from refrigerator, loosen the edges with a knife, move around in a circle, cover with a serving platter and invert onto the platter. Serve flan garnished with rest of the toasted coconut mixed with ¼ tsp. of cinnamon and/or chocolate syrup.

Foolproof Gulab Jamun- Milk Balls in Syrup (M: 40 large)

This is one of the best and greatly admired desserts of all. Gulab means rose, and jamun means berries. They are soft, round, fluffy, tasty and the look is like large berries. Traditionally, they are made by reducing whole milk (khoya or mava). But we have developed an easier version with the same results.

Ingredients: 2 cups 2 packages nonfat milk powder; 1 cup unbleached all-purpose flour; 1 cup plus 2 tbsp. pancake flour (I prefer Aunt Jemima); 2 cups cold heavy cream; about 3 tbsp. melted ghee (clarified butter) or canola oil plus more for deep-frying.

Syrup: 6-1/2 cup sugar; 5-1/2C water; 1 tbsp. fine crushed cardamom seeds.

1. To make the syrup: mix sugar, water and cardamom seeds in a large and wide pot and bring to a boil, stirring constantly, to melt the sugar. When sugar is melted, in about 8-9 minutes, lower the heat to medium and cook the syrup, skimming the foam on the top, for about 20-25 minutes, until syrup is a little thick.
2. To make the balls: whisk together milk powder, both flours well. Make a well and pour in 1 tbsp. oil and then the heavy cream. Using a wooden spoon or a rubber spatula, incorporate dry and wet ingredients well. Sprinkle 1 tbsp. of oil at a time, work with the dough, bring it together, then divide in to two portions. Using a few drops of melted ghee or oil at a time, knead each dough portions about 8-9 times or until dough is pliable.
3. Make the long rolls of the dough and cut out 20 portions from each roll. Now take 1 piece of the dough at a time, dipping your hands in little ghee or oil, pressing hard; make a 2-3-inch firm log first, then roll into a soft ball. Make all 40 balls first. While you are making the balls, heat about 2-inch-deep oil in a large and wide pot or in a large wok, on medium heat.
4. Frying the balls is the trickiest part. Increase heat to medium-high and when the oil is hot, immediately and carefully drop about 8-10 balls, from the side, rolling into the hot oil and immediately scraping the bottom with the metal spatula; turn the balls over in a group or keep on moving the handle of the wok in a circular motion to turn the balls around themselves. Be careful not to splash the oil.
First you have to brown lightly all sides of the balls on medium-high heat for about 3 minutes, then lower the heat to medium; cook, stirring (in a group, digging from the bottom and moving to the right, away from you) for about 6 minutes. When all the balls are browned, increase the heat to medium-high again and cook all around for 1 minute, to firm the outside.
If any time you see a ball is cracking, just increase the heat high and start turning the balls over fast, turning the cracks towards the bottom.
When the balls are done, take them out with the spatula or perforated metal spoon, on a paper towel-lined platter. Let the balls sit on the platter for 5 minutes, then drop them in the syrup. Keep in the syrup for 5 minutes; stir and dip them well all around to coat with the syrup; take them out on a glass or porcelain platter and keep in a single layer. After all the balls are soaked in the syrup, any leftover syrup just pour over the balls. Keep them in room temperature for 3-4 days, or refrigerate covered. These balls are served at room temperature.
5. The gulabjamun freezes well in an airtight plastic container placed in a plastic bag, up to three months. Thaw overnight in the refrigerator and serve as it is or lightly heat in the microwave to freshen up the flavor.
6. Serve them with colorful nuts, fresh berries and/or coffee or tea, even with milk.

Halwa: Suji (Semolina Pudding) (Serves: 4)

This traditional halwa is mostly used for offerings to God at home and in the temples. Also it is served for breakfast and as a dessert after a meal. The body of the halwa looks like scrambled eggs and the taste is like a pudding. It is very easy to make.

Ingredients: 1 cup suji rawa (semolina), 1 cup heavy cream, ½ cup chopped walnuts, ½ cup slivered almonds, ½ cup golden raisins, 5 tab unsalted butter or ghee, ½ cup sugar or to taste,1/4 tsp. salt (op), ½ tsp. crushed cardamom seeds.

1. Soak suji in the heavy cream, in a bowl, covered, in room temperature for about one hour.
2. In a heavy-bottom pan or wok, dry-roast nuts and raisins on medium heat for about 6-8 minutes until light brown. Take the nuts out and spread them on a plate and set aside until needed.
3. Wash the same pan under running water, dry it with towel and heat it again on the medium heat. When pan is heated, add 3 Tab butter and suji and stir on medium heat for 5 minutes. Increase the heat to medium and brown the suji, stirring constantly, patting down, turning over for about 10 minutes or until light brown. Take out suji in a clean bowl, cover and keep it warm.
4. Put the same pan back on the stove, add 2-1/2 cup water, cardamom seeds and bring the water to a boil; add sugar, stir well to dissolve, then bring to a boil again. Now lower the heat and add suji, half of the nuts and stir to combine well for 5 minutes; add last 2 Tabs of butter. Now increase the heat to medium; at this point the mixture will start bubbling and splattering, so be careful and hold the lid of the pan with one hand with a long gloves on, covering the pan about one-third. Start stirring the halwa until it is thick. Take the lid off and stir the halwa only until it is thick and dry and stops sticking in the bottom, about 10 minutes. Halwa is done when it is almost dry and some butter will start showing in the bottom.
5. Serve halwa warm, garnished with toasted nuts and hot coffee or tea on the side.

Pecan Praline (M:12-14)

When we visited New Orleans we saw several stores making these pralines at their windows. People go inside and buy them fresh made. You just can't resist.

Ingredients: 1-1/2 Cups light brown sugar packed; 1-1/2 cups granulated sugar;1/4cup maple syrup; 2 pinches salt; 1-1/4 cup and whole milk; 2tsp. vanilla extract; 1oz. semi-sweet chocolate grated; 2Tbsp. grated coconut (op); 1-1/2cups halved pecans.

Line 3 large trays with wax paper or cover two large cutting boards with foil and then with wax paper and set aside.

In a medium pot combine both sugars, maple syrup, salt, milk, vanilla extract and heat on medium heat stirring constantly. Brush the edges of the pot with a lightly wet brush (if bubbling out). Do not let the syrup burn. Bring the mixture to a soft ball stage 236 degrees. When a drop of the syrup dropped in a glass of cold water it forms a soft ball. Take the pot off the heat, and let it cool to about 110 degrees, stirring often. Now whisk in the coconut and the chocolate and bring it to a lukewarm stage. Immediately using a wooden spoon drop the mixture about 3-inch round patties and about 1-inch apart, distributing the pecans evenly (mostly towards the center). Let them cool completely. When they are firm, peel them off the paper and wrap them in the parchment paper, place in a plastic container or a jar until serving. Keep the pralines away from heat, store in a cool place for up to 2-3 weeks. Serve them as they are or use them as garnish on almost any dessert.

Pfeffernusse (M:20 large)

These are German nut cookies that you see around Christmas time. They are easy to make.

Ingredients: Flour mixture - 3/4 cup all-purpose flour; 1/4tsp. each baking powder, nutmeg and salt, 1/2tsp. each cinnamon, cloves and cardamom; 1 large egg and one egg yolk; 1/2cup sugar; 1 cup grinded pecans (flour); to coat: 1cup sifted powder sugar.

Preheat oven at 350 degrees. Line a large baking sheet with parchment paper. Whisk the egg and yolk well add sugar and flour mixture and combine all ingredients together with a fork. Fold in the pecans. Using a 1-1/2 ice cream scoop drop about 1 tablespoonful mixture on the prepared sheet, about 1-inch apart and shape them with wet fingers. Bake for 10-12 minutes until they are puffed up and bottom is light brown. Take the sheet out of oven, cool 5 minutes, scrape the bottom with a metal spatula and dip each pfeffernusse in the powder sugar, coating them twice and serve.

Banana Pudding (Serves: 4 to 6)

This is a very tasty pudding. You cut the bananas, pour over cheese sauce and serve. If prefer top with a dollop of whipped cream. We serve this cheese sauce on mixed fruits, cakes and brownies, pancakes, etc. This sauce is versatile.

Cheese Sauce (M: about 2-1/2 cup)

Ingredients: 2 extra large eggs; 1 cup milk; 1 pkg., 8 oz. cream cheese softened to room temperature; ½ cup sugar; 3 tbsp. corn starch; 2 tbsp. chocolate liqueur; pinch of salt.

In a bowl whisk together eggs with 1 cup water. In another bowl whisk cream cheese and sugar well, then whisk in chocolate liqueur and corn starch well. Now whisk in milk. Slowly pour in the egg mixture in a thin stream, whisking constantly.

Heat the mixture in a medium pot on medium-high heat, whisking constantly, and bring it to a boil. Lower the heat and simmer for 5 minutes, whisking occasionally. Take off the heat and let it cool.

To serve: Slice 4 large bananas about ½-inch thick in an 8x8 dish and pour over the cheese sauce; shake the pan to even out the pudding. Serve immediately sprinkled with some toasted nuts if you wish or refrigerate covered and serve later.

Pistachio Pudding (Serves: 4)

This famous pudding I make on St. Patrick's Day. Make sure you have at least ½ cup lightly roasted shelled pistachios. You can make it gluten-free by using rice or tapioca flour instead of semolina.

Ingredients: 1 box 1 ounce (28g) instant pistachio pudding; 2 cups almond milk; 2 cups 2% or whole milk; 1 tbsp. sugar; 1 tsp. vanilla extract; 5 tbsp. semolina; to garnish: ½ cup shelled and lightly roasted pistachios and some fresh green or purple grapes.

1. Make pistachio pudding first per package direction. Whisk in pudding mix into the almond milk and set aside.
2. Heat 2% or whole milk in a medium pot just to warm. Take off the heat and whisk in the sugar, vanilla extract and semolina well. Put it back on the medium-high heat and bring it to a boil. Lower the heat and simmer for 8-10 minutes, until it is thick. Take off the heat and whisk in the prepared pistachio pudding. Serve warm or cold garnished with pistachios and grapes.

Tips:

1. If you want to make **Irish Pistachio Pudding**: whisk in about 3 tbsp. Irish whisky or ¼ cup Irish cream halfway during the cooking.

2. If you want to make it without pudding mix, then in a medium bowl whisk in 2 large egg yolks, 2 tbsp. sugar and a few drops of green food color. Whisk all well first, then whisk in 1 cup almond milk. When semolina is done, take the pot off the heat and whisk in the egg yolk mixture. Put the pot back on medium-high heat and whisk for another 8-10 minutes until it is bubbly.

Easy Rice Pudding (Serves: 4)

One thing you have to remember with rice pudding is that the rice takes a lot of liquid. In the beginning, use some water or milk and save about ½ cup of good liquid for the end.

Ingredients: 1 cup fresh-made or leftover plain rice; 1 cup milk; 1-1/2 cup coconut, or almond milk; 2 tsp. vanilla extract; pinch of salt; ¼ cup granulated sugar and ¼ cup light brown sugar or to taste; ½ cup lightly toasted pistachios; 1/3 cup raisins; ½ cup mini chocolate chips (op).

In a medium pot heat 1 cup milk and 1 cup coconut or almond milk; bring it to a boil. Add the sugar and vanilla extract and stir well. Add the rice and bring it to a boil again; lower the heat and simmer on low. After 10 minutes add the raisins and stir well. Simmer for another 10 minutes. Check the liquid, if you need more add some milk.

Just before serving, add the rest ½ cup heated coconut milk and serve garnished with pistachios and chocolate chips, or chill in separate bowls and serve it chilled later.

Rasogullah - Cheese Balls in Syrup(M: about 12 large)

This is a special sweet that is made around the holidays. They look like (and are) large ricotta balls. These balls come out perfectly round in a pressure cooker. Because of the steam, they puff-up better.

After they are cooked, we cut them in half, top with coconut topping, and they are called Chum-Chum. I like these better.

Ingredients for the Balls: 1 tbsp. butter; 1 gallon (3.78l) whole milk ¼ to 1/3 cup as needed; white vinegar.

For the Syrup: 2 cups of water; 3-1/2 cup sugar; ½ tsp. rose extract.

For the Syrup: Bring all the ingredients to a boil, stirring constantly, on medium-high heat until the sugar is dissolved. Simmer on low for 5 minutes, then turn it off.

For the Cheese Balls: Heat a large and a heavy-bottom pot on medium heat. Add the butter, coat the bottom. Add the milk and bring it to a boil on medium-high heat. Stir in the ¼ cup vinegar and keep on stirring for 5-6 minutes, until milk separates and you can see the curd and the whey clearly (if needed, add a little more vinegar). Now place a large strainer over a large bowl and pour in the mixture carefully. Take out the curd in a large platter. Keep the platter tilted to rinse out all the water.

Heat the syrup on low heat. Now using the heel of the hand, knead the curd for about 5 minutes. Make long strokes with the heel of the hand, pressing into the curd so that the curd turns into the cream and all the cheese pieces are gone, for about 4-5 minutes. Take small portion of the curd, make a log, then make the ball. You should have about 12 balls.

Increase the heat to medium and when the syrup is simmering, place the cheese balls into the syrup carefully. Simmer for 4 minutes on low heat; turn them over with a spoon, simmer another 3-4 minutes. Now increase the heat high and boil for 1 minute on each side. Turn off the heat, let them sit in syrup for 5 minutes, then take them out on a platter with rim, together with the syrup. Serve each piece with some syrup.

Chum-Chum- Cheese Rolls with Topping (M: about 24)

Follow the recipe above for the rasogullah. Instead of making the balls, just roll slightly into an egg shape. When the balls are cooked in syrup, slice them in half horizontally.

The Coconut Topping (M: about 1-1/2 cup)

Ingredients: 1 tbsp. butter; 1 can, 14 oz. (397g) sweetened condensed milk; 1 tsp. fine crushed cardamom seeds; 2 cups coconut flour or fine grated coconut.

Heat a heavy-bottom pan on medium heat. Add the butter, coat the bottom, then toast the coconut and the cardamom seeds, stirring constantly for 2 minutes, until light brown. Add the condensed milk, increase the heat to medium-high and stir for 1 minute, then lower the heat and stir for 2-3 minutes until it is thickened. Take off the heat.

Immediately, take the topping mixture with a tablespoon and top the cut balls, on the cut side, with the topping. Cool and serve without any syrup.

Chocolate Covered Strawberries (M: 12-15 pieces)

You need fresh, unblemished and if possible large or same-size strawberries. If you want to make all the same size, buy an extra pint and pick the ones with the same size. Carefully clean them with a lightly damped cloth, then dry them in room temperature. Do this in nice, sunny and dry weather. Damp weather may spoil them.

Ingredients: 2 pints (about 25-30) fresh and unblemished strawberries; each ½ cup toasted walnut and almonds or pistachios ground in to coarse crumbs; ½ cup dark chocolate bar grated; ½ c, about 3 squares, white chocolate chopped fine; ½ cup semisweet chocolate, about 3 squares chopped fine; 2 tsp. unsalted butter and 4 tbsp. heavy cream or whole milk.

1. In a tea cup, place the 1 tsp. butter, semisweet sweet chocolate add 2 tbsp. heavy cream and microwave on high for 20 seconds. Stir well with a fork and heat again for another 20 seconds; stir well. The chocolate should be melted by now. You can also melt the chocolate over warm water and then pour back in a tea cup for dipping. Melt and cool the white chocolate the same way.
2. Have a large cookie sheet lined with wax or parchment paper ready. Holding the strawberries' green leaves backward, on the top, dip 1 strawberry at a time in the melted chocolate, about ¾ up, leaving the top exposed about ¼ inch. (The more chocolate they have, the better they taste). Then roll them into any one of the three: chocolate, walnut, almond or pistachio crumbs, all around and place them in a row on the prepared cookie sheet. You can dip in dark chocolate, let it dry out and then make white chocolate linings over the dark chocolate with a small parchment paper funnel.
3. Let the strawberries dry out overnight, loosely tented with aluminum foil, in the refrigerator or in room temperature away from the draft. Serve them soon while they look fresh.

Chocolate Dipped Dry Fruits and Nuts (Serves: 10-12)

We dip dry fruits partially and leave the top exposed. This way they are very colorful and easy to identify. When working with chocolate, try to pick a dry and a sunny day so that chocolate can dry easily.

Ingredients: 8 ounces, about 1 cup each dry or glazed fruits such as: apricots, papaya, pineapples, prunes, mangoes, dry and sliced coconut, and 1 cup of each toasted nuts like whole peeled almonds, cashews, walnuts etc. One day before dipping, rub each dry fruit and nut with paper towels to take off any powdery stuff or sugar, and spread them in large trays to dry completely; 1 can, 14 oz. (396g) sweetened condensed milk; 2 tbsp. canola oil; 1 pkg. 8oz. (226g) 8 squares unsweetened 100% cocoa, chopped; ½ tsp. unsweetened cocoa powder; 1 cup 2% warm milk together with 2 tbsp. unsalted butter softened or 1 cup heavy cream.

1. Line 4 large baking trays (half sheets) with aluminum foil or parchment paper and lightly grease or spray them and set aside.
2. Grease a 3-quart medium pot with 1 tsp. butter on low heat and add the condensed milk, oil, and simmer for 6-7 minutes until bubbly. Take the pot off the heat and add cocoa powder and chopped chocolate; cover the pot with the lid, swirl the pot around a little then set aside for 3-5 minutes. After 3-5 minutes, whisk the chocolate mixture well, put the pot back on low heat and

whisk in slowly 1 cup milk, then rest of the butter. When chocolate is creamy, in about 2 minutes (about 85 degrees), take the pot off the heat .

3. Place the chocolate pot on the cutting board and start dipping the dry fruits about halfway in the melted chocolate; wipe out extra chocolate from each piece on the edge of the pot and place on the prepared sheets in a row. At the end, dip nuts individually or place the nuts in a small bowl and pour over some melted chocolate, then drop the nuts in small mounds, separating with a knife, over the baking tray. You may have to heat chocolate on very low heat when it starts getting thick; whisk the chocolate well and proceed. Set the trays of dipped fruits and nuts on the counter, away from the heat, or in the cooled oven, and let them dry overnight. Then turn them over with a knife and let them dry completely. To store, fill the dry fruits and nuts in plastic containers lined with parchment paper, place the chocolate-dipped fruits and cover with paper towels to absorb the moisture. Store in the refrigerator until needed or up to 3-4 weeks.

Strawberry Topping or Sauce (M: 1-1/2 C)

This sauce goes well on almost any dissert, like pudding, cake, pastry and ice creams. During the season I make a lot and freeze in separate containers, each for one time serving.

Ingredients : 1 Pound (454g) fresh strawberries, cored and chopped; 1 apple peeled, cored and grated; 2 tbsp. lemon juice; 1 cup sugar; pinch of salt; 1 tbsp. clear gelatin (op), bloomed in ½ cup water for 5-10 minutes.

1.   In a heavy-bottom medium pot, on medium to medium-high heat, place the grated apple, sugar and lemon juice, sauté a few minutes; when bubbly add the strawberries, salt, bring to a boil for 5 minutes. Stir well, cover and simmer on low heat for 15 minutes. When most of the water is gone, and sauce is reduced and thick, stir the gelatin well and add to the pot; increase the heat to medium-high, stir well, and dilute the gelatin. Cook for 5 minutes, turn off the stove and pour the sauce in a serving bowl or boat. Cool completely, use or refrigerate covered.
2. Store in the refrigerator up to a week.

Variations

Instead of using clear gelatin, you can use ½ cup strawberry preserve and reduce the amount of sugar to ½ cup in the sauce.

Tiramisu (Serves: 8)

Traditionally this stack of pastry filled with cream and dipped in the espresso or in coffee is made with ladyfingers. I have noticed that sometimes they are too sweet. So I use sponge cake; you can also use the thin layers of pound cake.

Ingredients: 3 layers, each 8x8-inch square ladyfingers or thin (about 1/3 inch) layer of sponge cake; 2 cups, 16 oz. sweetened whipped cream or whipped topping or traditional mascarpone cheese, folded into 4 tbsp. chocolate liqueur; 1 cup orange marmalade or apricot jam, divided; 1 tbsp. lemon juice; 2 tbsp. Grand Marnier (op); 1 cup fresh made espresso or coffee whisked in with 1 tbsp. sugar, 1 tbsp. cocoa powder and 1 tbsp. chocolate liqueur. To garnish: ½ cup sliced pistachios and 2 tbsp. unsweetened cocoa powder; 1 recipe of the cashew cream.

In a small pan heat all marmalade or apricot jam with Grand Marnier and mix well; simmer for 2 minutes. Take out half of the marmalade and set aside. With the remaining marmalade whisk in 2 tbsp. water and lemon juice, and simmer on medium heat for 2 minutes, then strain in a cup. Brush this syrup on one side of all cake layers.

Place one layer of the cake in an 8x8 square pan, marmalade side up; top with half of the whipped cream spread out evenly. Now place another layer of the cake marmalade side down, and brush the coffee mixture on the top evenly. Then take a half cup of remaining marmalade that was set aside and spread all over the cake evenly. Now place the final layer of the cake on the top, the marmalade side down. Brush the top with the coffee mixture, then spread about 2 tbsp. of the whipped cream. Sprinkle the pistachios, then place the remaining (2 tbsp.) cocoa powder in a fine strainer and sprinkle all over the tiramisu. Cut into 8 pieces and serve with a small dollop of whipped cream on the side over the cashew Cream. Store, loosely covered, with foil in the refrigerator.

White Chocolate Squares (M: 96 2x2-1/2-inches)

These white chocolate squares are very easy, fast and tasty. In 2014, I had made these for the temple. You can make even a week ahead or freeze in the container for a party up to 2 months.

Ingredients: ½ cup heavy cream; 2 tbsp. unsalted butter plus for greasing the tray; 4 cans each: 14 oz. (396g) sweetened condensed milk; 4 envelopes each: 1 cup (to make 1 qt. milk) instant nonfat dry milk; 1 bag, 12 oz. (340g) premier white chocolate morsels (chips); 3 packages, each 4 ounces (113g) all-natural white chocolate chopped fine.

For Toppings: 1 cup each slivered almonds, shelled pistachios and dry cranberries.

1. About 1/2 hour ahead of making the squares: use a large baking tray 12x18x2, line it with parchment paper, grease the paper well. Heat the heavy cream in a medium pot, bring the cream almost to boil, take off the heat; add 1 bag of white chocolate chips (about 2 c), cover the pot with the lid, let it stand for 5 minutes. Open the cover, stir the chips and when they are melted, pour all over the parchment paper to make the base of the squares. Let it cool.
2. Heat a large, heavy-bottom, sauté pan (5.5 qt., 5.2 l) on low heat, when hot add the 2 tbsp. butter, move around to coat the bottom and add all the condensed milk. Increase the heat to medium. Stir the milk with a metal spatula in the bottom for about 5 minutes. When the condensed milk starts bubbling on the edges, add all the dry milk. Reduce the heat again to low and, using a potato masher, press down the dry milk into the condensed milk for 6-7 minutes. Take the pan off the heat, add chopped white chocolate. Stir a little, cover and leave it off the heat for 5 minutes. Open the cover and stir the chocolate well with the metal spatula. If the chocolate does not melt, put the pan back on the very low heat, stir well to melt the chocolate a couple of minutes.
3. Pour the contents all over the prepared chocolate base and then even out the mixture with a metal spatula. Top it with the almonds, cranberries, pistachios. Press down the topping with a clean and wide spatula, and leave on the counter to dry overnight. Slide the parchment paper with the contents over to a cutting board. Cut into 12 bars across then each bars into 8 pieces.

Serve in paper cups. Store in a container on the shelf for up to 2-3 days, then refrigerate. These freeze very well wrapped in a container; thaw overnight and serve with coffee, tea, milk at any time of the day.

Frozen Yogurt Snacks (M: 34)

These are frozen yogurt drops. To make them attractive and precise, use a piping bag and pipe them on a parchment paper-lined baking tray, and sprinkle with the toasted and ground nuts of your choice.

Ingredients: 1 container, 6 oz. (170g), Greek yogurt, black cherry flavor, and one container peach or pineapple flavor; 24 pieces of pistachios or any other nuts; 24 pieces of dry cherries or any other dry fruits; 1 bottle 12 oz. (340g) pineapple topping or ½ cup chocolate chips, melted or unmelted.

1. Line a mini muffin tray (of 24 cups) with 2 pieces of plastic wrap, covering the ½ tray with each piece of wrap. Covering with one piece will pull all over; covering with 2 different pieces holds down better.
2. Drop a piece of fruit and a piece of nut in each muffin slot, top with 1-2 tsp. of yogurt, then top with pineapple topping or melted or whole chocolate chips. Freeze for about 3 hours or overnight.
3. Take the tray out of the freezer, pull the plastic wrap and the snacks will fill right in your hands. Serve immediately or keep frozen in a plastic bag.

Vermicelli Pudding or Semanyan (Serves: 8)

Vermicelli (very thin wheat noodles) pudding can be made alone or mixed with tapioca. It is a traditional pudding that is made with milk, with condensed milk and even by adding reduced milk (mava or khoya). The thicker the milk you add, the better it tastes. It is served a little warm, and each time you reheat, it takes a little more liquid, so use either warm milk alone or half-water and half-milk heated together.

Ingredients : About 2 cups (225g) roasted and broken into small pieces vermicelli; 1 tbsp. butter; 4-5 c, 2% or whole milk; 1 extra large egg whipped well with ½ cup water(op); 1can, 1 c, 14 ounces (396g) sweetened condensed milk or 6 cups whole milk reduced to 2 c; 1 tbsp. cardamom seed crushed fine; 1 cup toasted slivered almond or pistachios or a mixture of both; ½ cup raisins; ½ cup dry cranberries; ½ cup shredded coconut (op).

Topping : 4 peeled, cored and chopped apples cooked in ¼ cup sugar and 2 tbsp. corn starch until soft, or store-bought pie-filling apples.

1. Heat a large, heavy-bottom pot or Dutch oven on medium heat. When hot, add butter and 2 cups vermicelli, stir around for 5 minutes until vermicelli are heated through. Take out the vermicelli in a bowl.
2. In the same pot over medium-high heat, bring 4 cup milk and 2 cups of water to a boil; slowly stir in the toasted vermicelli, stirring constantly; bring it to a boil, lower the heat and add the egg mixture; cook for 1 minute and add ¾ can or ¾ cup of condensed milk, in a thin stream (save rest of the milk for some other use). Add ½ of the: roasted nuts, raisins, cranberries, crushed cardamom seeds, and all of the coconut; cook and simmer the pudding on low heat for 10 minutes. When vermicelli are floating on the top, turn off the stove and cover the pudding halfway with the lid.

3. Serve warm garnished with cooked apples, remaining nuts, cranberries and raisins.

Xmas Wreath

This wreath is made of pretzels. It takes only 30-40 minutes to make but you have to let it dry out for 3-4 days on each side, before placing in a large and clear plastic bag and hanging on the front door. These pretzels will make two wreaths.

Ingredients: On a platter, about 18-inches in diameter; 1 tsp. canola oil to grease the plastic wrap; about ½ cup heavy cream plus extra if needed; 1 bag 10 ounces (283g) miniature marshmallows;1 cup white chocolate chips; 1 bag tiny twists, original pretzels; 1 bag, sourdough, extra dark "the pounder" large pretzel; red and green candy melts (each bag: 12 ounces (340g), found at Michael's craft store; you will need less than half of the bag); red ribbon to make a bow.

Line the platter with a double layer of the plastic wrap and grease the plastic in the bottom and the sides. Pour about 1/3 of the pretzels (of same size) in two separate platters. Heat a medium pot half full of water. Save about ½ cup of marshmallows, and place rest in a large Pyrex or stainless steel bowl; add the chocolate chips on the top. Heat the heavy cream in a small pot and pour over the chocolate and marshmallows. Place the bowl on the simmering water and whisk until they are melted well.

Take one pretzel, dip in the chocolate mixture, wipe out extra against the rim and place over the plastic wrap at the edge, in the platter. Keep on placing the pretzels next to each other. Now make the second row of the same pretzels, starting between two pretzels. Now make the third row. This time, dip the large pretzels (the pounder) and make a row again between two pretzels. At the end, break up the last pretzel to fit in between.

To decorate the Wreath: Take out red chocolate drop (candy melts), place ¼ tsp. of melted chocolate on the back and paste on the large pretzel. Paste 3 red drops, then one green, after that surround them with some white marshmallows. Or make your own design. Leave the wreath to dry for 3-4 days. To turn it over, loosen the bottom plastic wrap with a metal spatula, cover the wreath with large pieces of double plastic wraps, pick up the bottom plastic and turn it over carefully over the new plastic wrap. Let it dry 3-4 days, make a bow, then tie the ribbon to hang; place in a large clear plastic bag and hang it carefully, or place it in a glass cabinet.

Tip: I always place the wreath in a clear plastic bag and hang it inside the house, just before the party. It becomes a conversation piece and a tempting dessert.

Frosting, Glazes, Creams & Sweet Sauces

Cashew Cream (M: about 2 cups)

To make your desserts tasty and attractive use sauces, creams either in the bottom or on top. Also whipped cream together with some shaved chocolate or glazed fruits makes desserts mouth-watering.

Ingredients: 1 cup lightly toasted and fine-ground cashews; 2 cups heavy or light cream (or coconut milk; just heat, do not boil); ¼ cup sugar; 2 tbsp. white chocolate liqueur.

This luscious sauce is my favorite one. Bring all ingredients to a boil and simmer, stirring on low heat for 10 minutes. Serve on fruits or almost over any dessert.

Coconut Glaze (M: About 2 cups)

This glaze is versatile and goes almost with any baking.

Ingredients: ¼ cup orange juice; 1 tsp. fine grated lemon zest (on microplane zester) ½ cup lemon juice; 1 cup sugar; about 1 tbsp. cornstarch; ¼ tsp. salt; ½ of the package (8 ounces) unsweetened frozen coconut thawed, or about 1 cup fresh coconut, peeled and grated.

In a medium pot whisk together: orange juice, lemon zest and juice, cornstarch, sugar, ¼ cup water, and salt. Heat on medium-high heat and bring it to a boil, stirring constantly. Lower the heat to a simmer, stir occasionally for 10 minutes until the sugar is melted. Add the coconut and stir another 5 minutes. Take off the heat. Cool a little and pour over the warm cake and pastry, or cool completely and dip or glaze almost anything.

Hot Fudge Sauce (M: about 2 cups)

This sauce is very addictive. You can use it on cakes, brownies, fruits, fruit pancakes, muffins and even on puddings and pies.

Ingredients: 1 bar 4 ounces bittersweet chocolate, chopped; 1/3 cup strawberry jelly (or ½ cup orange marmalade, heated and strained); 4 tbsp. unsalted butter, cold but sliced thin; 1 tsp. vanilla extract; 1 cup packed light brown sugar; ½ cup water; 1 tsp. lemon juice; 2 pinches of salt.

In a medium pot, heat the water, sugar, salt, lemon juice and the jelly together, and bring it to a boil on medium-high heat. Reduce the heat to low and simmer about 8 minutes until well combined. Add chocolate, vanilla, stir a little and take off the heat. Let it sit for 5 minutes, then whisk in to melt the chocolate well. If chocolate is not melted, put it back on low heat and whisk to melt the chocolate.) Off-heat whisk again and slowly whisk in the butter slices; cool and serve, or refrigerate covered and reheat stirring over the warm water.

Orange Pastry Cream (M: about 1-1/2 cups)

Ingredients: ½ cup frozen concentrated orange juice thawed overnight; 1/3 cup sugar; ¼ cup corn starch; 1 cup water; 2 tbsp. unsalted butter.

In a bowl whisk in water, corn starch, and sugar, and whisk in the orange juice. Heat a non-reactive large saucepan on medium heat, and add the mixture. Whisk the mixture constantly until it is bubbly and thickened for about 10 minutes. Add the butter and whisk well to incorporate the butter. Pour into a non-reactive bowl, top with a plastic wrap on the surface so that it does not form a skin on the top of the cream. Chill in room temperature first, then refrigerate and chill a little before using.

Lemon Pastry Cream

Follow the instructions above for the Orange Pastry Cream, just substitute the orange juice with ½ cup frozen concentrated lemonade, thawed overnight. You can also use the lemonade powder; just add extra ½ cup water.

Foolproof Whipped Cream (M: 16 oz., 3 cups)

Whipped cream is very tricky. You need to chill the cream in the refrigerator. Place the bowl and the beaters in the freezer first for one hour. The cream should be made a few minutes before using. I mostly buy the whipped topping that can stay in the refrigerator for about a week. But once you open the container, you should use it within 2 days. This whipped topping also freezes well. We use cornstarch to stop it from turning into water, and gelatin to hold the whipped foamy shape.

Ingredients: 2 cups well-chilled heavy cream; 1 tbsp. cornstarch; 1Tsp.clear gelatin; 2Tbsp. powder sugar sifted; chilled large bowl, and chilled electric balloon wire whisk.

Place the chilled cream in a large chilled bowl, tilt the bowl slightly to make oval and long stokes. Holding the bowl with one hand and scraping the bottom, and making long oval strokes, whip the cream on medium speed, with the chilled electric whisk, for about 1 minutes. When it is foamy, sprinkle the cornstarch and whisk on medium speed for 1 minute. Then whisk on high speed for 1 minutes until it is thickened. The cream should be very thick. Do not over whisk or it will turn into butter. You can serve it right away. If you want to serve later then sprinkle the powder gelatin and whisk on high speed for 30 seconds. Then sprinkle the powder sugar and just fold it in the cream.

Use or refrigerate the cream. Keep the whipped cream in a covered container up to 4 days. You can also freeze, thaw about 4 hours in the refrigerator, whisk a little, and serve

Use or refrigerate the cream. Keep the whipped cream in a covered container up to 4 days. You can also freeze, thaw about 4 hours in the refrigerator, whisk a little, and serve.

Beverages

Drinks can be healthy, delicious, keep you hydrated and replenish the electrolytes in the body. Try to make them fresh just before serving if possible. There is no need to use salt and sugar. You can use all sorts of fruits, nuts and vegetables together with lemons, limes, oranges, pineapple, yogurt, coconut water, soda water, seltzer, sparkling water, cucumber, dates, berries and water, or a drizzle of maple syrup or honey. Garnish drinks with the wedges or slices of fresh or frozen fruit. You can add crushed ice in the blender and puree, chill in the refrigerator or serve fresh right away. My favorite drink is half and half sparking water and any fruit juice or crushed berries.

Avocado Drink - The Green Drink (Serves: 2)

Ingredients: 1 cup orange juice, 1 cup coconut juice; ¼ cup lemon juice; 1 haas avocado cut in half, pitted and scooped out of pulp; ¼ cup fresh cilantro or flat-leaf parsley; ½ cup kale leaves off the stems. To garnish: avocado slices or any fruit of your choice.

In a blender, puree all, adding more coconut water as needed. Use within a day.

The Berry Drink - The Red and Purple Drink (Serves: 6)

Ingredients: 1 pint each strawberries, blueberries and ripe and pitted cherries; 1 tsp. lime zest and 4 tbsp. lime juice (about 2 large limes); soda water or seltzer as needed or to taste.

Puree the berries in the blender with zest and lime juice. Add 3-4 cups of seltzer water and serve on ice. Keep refrigerated, airtight, and use within 1-2 days.

Tip: Berries are good for the heart and help reduce cancer.

Coconut Drink (Serves: 4-6)

Ingredients: 1 fresh coconut (or 1 bag 16 ounces, frozen grated coconut) or use coconut water (from the supermarket); warm water as needed; 1 pint strawberries and about 2 cups pineapple chunks.

When buying fresh coconut, shake it and listen the sound of the water inside the coconut to make sure it is fresh. Make a hole in the 3 eyes of the coconut (one of the eye will be soft) and pour out the water in a glass and save. Heat the coconut in a preheated 400-degree oven for 15-20 minutes or until coconut is cracked. Wrap the coconut in a thick layer of newspaper. Place outside on the ground and hit it all around to break the shell. Then using a thick knife, peel off the shell, peel off the brown skin with a potato peeler and grate the coconut.

Puree the grated coconut with warm water in the blender, in batches, and place on a double layer of cheese cloth; squeeze and take out the milk. Then puree the coconut milk, coconut water and pineapple chunks. Serve on ice. Store airtight in the refrigerator. Use within a week. If preferred, garnish with fresh strawberries and pineapple chunks.

Cranberry Drink - The Red Drink (Serves: 2)

Ingredients: ½ cup fresh beet juice (about 1 large beet chopped, take out juice from the juicer); 2 c watermelon chunks or ½ c dry cranberries; sparkling cranberry water or seltzer, or coconut water, or water to taste.

Puree all together in the blender and serve within 1-2 days.

Tip: Beet Juice helps reduce the blood pressure.

Grapefruit Drink (Serves: 2-4)

Ingredients: 2 large pink grapefruits, one juiced and the other ¼ sliced for garnish and other ¾ grapefruit sectioned (peel the skin deep, into flesh, then take out the slices with a knife, leaving behind the hard dividing membrane); 2 cups fresh-squeezed watermelon juice.

Pour some crushed ice in the glasses, top with grapefruit and watermelon juice, then drop the grapefruit segments on the top. Garnish the glasses with grapefruit slices cut into ¼ pieces. Serve with straws.

Note: You can also garnish with mint sprigs and crush a few leaves in the glasses with the ice before pouring the juice.

Nut Drink - The White Drink(Serves: 2)

Ingredients: ¼ cup slivered almonds and ½ cup cashews lightly toasted in a dry pan, on low heat for 8-10 minutes until light brown; 2 cups coconut water or 2% milk.

Puree all together in a blender and serve on ice. Use within 2-3 days.

Orange Drink - The Yellow Drink (Serves: 2)

Ingredients: 2-3 cups orange juice (or fresh-squeezed orange juice); ½c ripe mango pulp; 2 tbsp. lemon juice; ½ ripe banana (op).

Puree all together in a blender and serve on ice within a day.

Frozen Fruit Slush (Serves: 4-6)

Ingredients: 1 can coconut milk 13.5 oz. (480ml), frozen in ice-cube trays a night before; 2 large ripe peaches or mango peeled, pulp cubed and frozen in zip-lock bags; 1 pint each strawberries hulled, and blueberries frozen in bags; 2 tbsp. lemon juice; about ¾ cup strawberry or blueberry jam; 1 cup coconut water or as needed. To garnish: fresh mint leaves and/or 1 cup ripe diced mango or any other fruit of your choice.

Pulse all ingredients together in a blender, serve in chilled stem glasses and garnish with mint and fresh fruits. Sip or eat with dessert spoons.

Fruit Shake (Serves: 4-6)

Follow the recipe above, just add 1 pint of strawberry ice cream and 1 cup low-fat milk in the blender, and puree all together. Serve with straws, in tall glasses, garnished with mint sprigs.

Christmas Eggnog (Serves: 4-6)

This eggnog is cooked, and if you prefer you, can use all organic egg whites.

Ingredients: 2 large or jumbo eggs separated; 2-3 tbsp. sugar or agave nectar; 1 qt. whole or 2% hot milk, heated in a pot with ¼ cup chocolate liqueur. To garnish: a sprinkle of fresh-grated nutmeg or cinnamon.

In a large bowl, whisk the egg white over hot but turned-off water, until foamy.

In a double broiler or in a bowl, or over the boiled but turned-off water, whisk the egg yolks with sugar until foamy. Slowly whisk in a ladle at a time the hot milk. Now pour the hot milk mixture slowly, whisking into the beaten egg whites, and let it cool slightly. Then fill in the clean bottles or pitcher; cover and refrigerate. Serve sprinkled with nutmeg or cinnamon.

Tip: This eggnog tastes better when you use whole milk, and chill overnight in the refrigerator.

Whey Protein with Chocolate (Serves: 4-6)

Ingredients: 1 quart whole milk; ¼ cup fresh squeezed lemon juice; 4 ounces semi-sweet chocolate chopped.

In a non-reactive pot, bring the milk to a boil. Stir in the lemon juice. Keep boiling the liquid for another 5 minutes until the whey is separated from the curd. Strain through a cheese cloth into a large non-reactive bowl. Save the cheese for the salad or cheese (paneer) dishes. Whisk the chopped chocolate into the whey. Pour the drink in the clean airtight glass bottles, chill in the refrigerator and serve. Store in the refrigerator for up to two weeks.

Watermelon Punch (Serves: 12-15)

This is our famous punch for the summer. I buy the biggest watermelon that I can find, and make punch to give out to our neighbors. Kids and adults both love it very much.

Ingredients: 1 large watermelon, sliced (remove the rind) into about 2-inch chunks; save some thin pieces for garnish; 2 cups orange juice; 1 container 12 oz. (355 ml) concentrated frozen lemonade, thawed; 2 bottles each 24 oz. (750 ml) sparkling cider or sparkling water.

Puree the watermelon pieces in a blender, in batches, and pour back in a large punch bowl. Add orange juice, lemonade and mix well. Add the sparkling cider or water, stir and serve; garnish with a piece of watermelon, either in the punch or on the rim of the cup.

Nutritional Milks

Drinking a glass of juice, smoothie, milk, tea or coffee made at home is more nutritious, fresh and tasty than bought at the store. These are good alternatives for the people who have dairy allergies.

Almond Milk (M about 2 cups)

Almond milk is more nutritious when made with whole unpeeled almonds soaked overnight, and mixed with raisins. In India, we always add some flavor such as rosewater, honey, cardamom seeds, fresh or dry fruits, etc.

Ingredients: 1 c whole almonds with skin on; 2 drops rosewater; 1 tsp. honey (op); 2 cups water; 1 tbsp. dark raisins

1. Wash and soak Almonds and Raisins, cover with the cold water in two separate bowls, and soak overnight.
2. Wash the soaked Almonds, peel the skin off and discard, then puree them in a blender with 1 cup of water.
3. Strain the mixture through a fine strainer in a bowl and puree the ground mixture again in the blender with the raisins, then strain it again. You will have about 2 cups of milk. Serve immediately or store in refrigerator in an airtight glass jar, and use it within a day.
4. You can also make this milk with regular dairy milk: add 1 cup of pureed almonds to 1 cup of 2% milk, heat in a microwave and serve immediately with or without honey. Use microwave on high one minute at a time and be careful not to let it boil out.

Coconut Milk (M:about 2 cups)

Coconut is good saturated fat. Coconut milk or coconut water both are good for you.

Ingredients: 1 coconut; 3-4 cups of water (as needed depending on the size of the coconut and the consistency of the milk)

1. Heat the oven at 400 degree. Peel off the outer fibrous covering from the coconut. Puncture one of the three eyes (the softest one) and take out the coconut water in a large cup. Then roast the coconut in a preheated oven for about 15 minutes or until the coconut is cracked.
2. Immediately wrap the coconut in paper towels; then in a thick layer of newspaper and with a hammer, start hitting the coconut from all around until it is cracked and broken into pieces (you will hear the cracking sound). Now use a dinner knife and from edges push the coconut out of the hard shell. Wash, peel off the brown skin with a vegetable peeler, chop by hand into small pieces or grate the coconut in the food processor.
3. Puree the grated coconut in a blender with one cup of water at a time. Strain the milk and puree the crushed coconut two more times to get all the juice out.
4. Serve the milk immediately or keep in room temperature, covered in a glass jar, or refrigerate and use within 2 to 3 days. The refrigerated coconut milk will get thicker and even get solid, or will separate, with the cream on the top and the liquid on the bottom. I use this milk mostly for cooking.

Sesame Milk (M: about 1-1/2 cups)

This is another healthy milk. According to my father, this milk gives you a healthy skin. When used with fruits and nuts, it is more nutritious.

Ingredients: ½ c raw sesame seeds; 1 tbsp. raw cashews; 1 tbsp. raw pistachio; about 1-1/2 c water.

1. In a blender, grind sesame seeds, cashews and the pistachios together. Add water in two parts and grind to a fine puree.
2. There is no need to strain the milk. You can serve the milk immediately as it is or with 1 tsp. of honey.
3. You can lightly toast and then cool the sesame seeds to give the milk a nutty flavor

454

Soy Milk (M: about 2 cups)

Soy milk is loaded with cancer-fighting properties and rich in iron.

Wash and soak the 2 cups raw soy beans, covered with water overnight. Grind and puree fine in a blender with about 2-1/2cups of water. Strain the milk in a fine sieve. Serve the milk immediately with or without honey, or store in the refrigerator in an airtight glass jar up to 2 to 3 days.

Just like any other fresh food, fresh-made milks should be served soon after they are made. If you store in the refrigerator, the freshness is gone to some degree and because of the refrigeration, the taste will be gone to some degree as well. So make only what you are going to consume that day.

Hot Toddy (Serves: 1)

Ingredients: 1 shot of brandy (about ¼ cup); 8 oz. hot water; 2 drops of lemon juice; ½-inch-by 2-inch lemon rind; 1 tbsp. honey; sprinkle of cinnamon.

Pour brandy in a clear glass with handle. Add lemon juice, rind, and hot water. Stir in honey and just sip slowly and enjoy on cold days, or if you have cold or flu.

You can also buy prepared at the liquor stores. Some liquor stores carry it around the Christmas holiday.

Mango Drink (Serves: 10-15)

Ingredients: 2 bottles each 2 liters orange soda; 1 bottle 1 liter, 33.8 oz. lemon-lime flavor sparkling seltzer; 1 can 30 ounces (850g) mango pulp; 2 pinches turmeric; ½ cup (about 4-5 lemons) fresh-squeezed lemon juice.

Chill all ingredients in the refrigerator the night before and mix together in the order they are listed; stir and serve. You can also mix together all ingredients a night before in two large bottles. I use two Tropicana orange juice bottles with handle, each 86 oz. 2.63L; make the punch a few days before, chill well and take them to the party. These bottles are easy to chill, easy to pour, and keep all the flavor fresh.

Pumpkin and Apple Smoothie (S:2)

Ingredients: 1 apple peeled, cored and chopped, 1 cup baby spinach or watercress; 1-1/2cup orange juice; 4 almonds soaked and peeled; 1/2Tsp. each cinnamon and ginger; ¼ cup lightly toasted pumpkin seeds; 1/4Tsp. turmeric.

Whisk all together in a blender and serve.

Spanish Coffee (Serves: 1)

We used to work in Newark, New Jersey within walking distance of some famous Spanish restaurants. Spanish coffee was our favorite drink.

Ingredients: 1 to 1-1/2 cups fresh-brewed hot coffee; 1 shot each of kahlua and liquor 43; whipped cream for topping; sprinkle of cinnamon.

In a large round (globe) wine glass, fill about 1 to 1-1/2 cups fresh-brewed coffee and stir in Kahlua and liquor 43. Top with some whipped cream and sprinkle with cinnamon. Serve with straw to sip.

Yogurt Drink or Lassi (Serves: 4)

To make the sweet yogurt drink: In a blender whisk together 1 pint of whole or low-fat yogurt, 1 cup water, ¼ cup sugar or to taste, ½ cup toasted almonds or pistachios and ½ cup crushed ice. Serve sprinkled with cardamom seed powder, or garnish the glasses with a slice of fresh mango, orange or pineapple.

To make a salty drink: follow the procedure as above, just use a little salt and fresh-ground black pepper, do not use any sugar and garnish with dry or fresh mint.

Recipes from Family and Friends

When I hear people are talking about food, my ears perk up, and I start listening what people are co

oking or what they have enjoyed in the restaurant. To show the interest in cooking was a big pleasure of my father, and I too like to learn the new family recipes that people brought them over from all around the world.

Hamantashen

These are the famous jam or preserve triangle cookies. You see them in the markets around Jewish holidays. I like anything that has fruit filling.

Ingredients:

For the Crust: 2 large eggs; ½ cup sugar; ½ cup canola oil; 1 tsp. vanilla extract; juice and zest of ½ orange; 2-1/2 to 3 cups of all-purpose flour as needed; 2 tsp. baking powder; ¼ tsp. salt.

For the Filling: ½ pound prunes; ½ cup dark raisins soaked overnight; ½ cup nuts; juice and zest of 1 lemon; ½ cup sugar; 1 beaten egg for egg wash.

For the Filling: Chop the soaked prunes and the raisins, and add nuts, juice and the zest of the lemon and sugar, and mix well.

For the Crust: Mix the ingredients in the order they are listed. In a bowl, whisk eggs and the sugar well, then whisk in oil, vanilla extract, zest and the juice of the orange. Sift the flour, baking powder and salt together, then whisk into the egg mixture. Roll out the dough into ¼-inch thickness. Dusting the rim of a glass, cut out the rounds and place spoonful of filling in the center. Draw up the three sides to form a triangle and pinch edges firmly. Brush the tops of hamantashen with the egg wash to give a glossy look. Bake in a preheated 350-degree oven for about 30 minutes. Filling may also be marmalade or the apricot preserve.

- Sheila Basem

Stuffed Eggplant (Bharali Wangi)

(S:4-6)

This recipe comes from my friend and neighbor, Supriya. Her husband, Sachin, is the president for several years of our townhouse association. They are originally from Bombay, India. You can make your own goda powder or buy at the Indian grocery stores. If you wish you can add some cubed potatoes in the pan with the eggplant.

Ingredients: 12-14 baby eggplant (seedless, if possible); ½ cup peanuts; ¼ cup sesame seeds; 1 cup fresh or fresh frozen grated coconut; 2 medium onions finely chopped; ¼ cup tamarind paste; ¼ cup or to taste, jaggery or light brown sugar; 1 tbsp. red chili powder or to taste; 4-5 garlic cloves chopped; ½ tsp. turmeric powder; ¼ cup goda masala (see recipe below); ¼ cup oil; ½ tsp. mustard seeds; ½ tsp. cumin seeds; a pinch of asafoetida or hing (op); 2 cups water; salt to taste; cilantro leaves to garnish.

Wash the eggplant and quarter them from the top but leave them attached at the stems, and soak them in the salted water.

Dry roast the peanuts in a dry skillet on medium heat, when they turn very light brown add sesame seeds, and then coconut. Roast until they are fragrant and light brown.

When coconut, sesame seeds, and peanuts are cooled add them to the blender/grinder with half of the chopped onions, and the garlic. Grind to a smooth paste with a little water. Do not make it too thin. Add to the ground peanut mixture the goda masala, red chili and turmeric powder.

Pat dry the eggplant in and out well, and stuff them with the ground spice mixture. Heat a large frying pan on medium heat, add the oil and the stuffed eggplant; stir and fry them on medium-high heat for 5-6 minutes, just to brown all around. Add tamarind pulp, jiggery, water, salt, and cover; lower the heat and cook on constant simmer for about 30 to 35 minutes, or until eggplant are soft. Garnish with coriander leaves and serve hot with rice, chapatti or poories.

Goda Masala (Maharashtrian Spice Mixture) (M: about 3 cups)

Ingredients: 1 cup each: coriander seeds and grated dry coconut; ¼ cup caraway (cumin) seeds; 1/3 cup white sesame seeds (teel); 2 tbsp. cloves (lavang); 2 tbsp. whole black cardamom (big cardamom); 2 tbsp. cinnamon sticks broken (dalchini); 1 tbsp. black peppercorns); 1 dry serrano pepper; 2 tbsp. dagadphool (lichen) optional; 10-12 medium bay leaves (tamalpatra); 1-2 tsp. oil to roast;

Roast all ingredients one by one, take out in a bowl, cool, and grind. Store in a clean and dry jar, in the refrigerator. You can make this mixture a few days ahead.

- Sachin and Supriya Brahme

Bread Ring with Pecans

My friend Nicki and her son are very good cooks. The family owns three Pizzerias. This is a traditional Italian savory recipe but it is made with cream cheese and sugar.

Ingredients: 4 ounces softened cream cheese and 1 large egg whisked together; 1 envelope (about 1Tbsp) active dry yeast; 1 cup warm water (110 degrees); 2Tbsp. sugar; 1/2Tsp. salt; 3-1/2 cups all-purpose unbleached flour plus extra for dusting; 1Tbsp. canola oil; 1 egg whisked for egg wash; 1cup halved pecans; 1cup powder sugar mixed with 1Tbsp. lemon juice.

Use a food processor with metal blade or a stand mixer with dough hook to whisk the yeast, warm water and 2Tbsp. sugar. Then add the flour, salt and combine. Add softened cream cheese mixture and mix well. Take out the dough and knead on the counter dusting lightly with the flour until it is pliable, about 6-8 minutes. Place the oil in a large clean bowl roll the dough ball in the oil to grease all around then cover with a lightly damp cotton towel. Let it rise until almost doubled takes about an hour.

Punch down the dough and divide into 2 equal pieces. Roll each piece into a 20-inch long roll. Hold both ropes together and give them a little twist. Now place them on a greased baking sheet lined with parchment paper in a circle. Pinch the ends together to form a circle. Roll and flatten lightly with the rolling pin to 1-inch thickness. Brush the ring all over with the egg wash and sprinkle the pecans on the top. Let the ring rise again for 30 minutes. Preheat oven at 350 degrees and bake for about 50 minutes until golden brown. Turn off the oven and let it cool in the off oven for 5 minutes. Take out of the oven, place on the serving platter. Cool and drizzle with powder sugar and lemon glaze, serve.

- Nicolina and Mike Cappola

.

-

Seared Pork Chops with Vegetable Gratin (Serves: 2)

This recipe is from Jennifer Cox, a dear friend who works for a wine company, and is travelling all the time. She emailed this recipe saying, "This is a fantastic recipe, and amazingly quick!"

Ingredients: About 2 tbsp. olive oil; 6 ounces cremini mushrooms cleaned with a damp paper towel and quartered; 1 tbsp. fresh tarragon leaves chopped; 1 medium shallot peeled and chopped; 1 medium zucchini rinsed, sliced in half lengthwise, then sliced ¼-inch thick into half-moons; about 6 to 8 oz. 2 pork chops bone or boneless; ½ cup fresh shelled peas; ½ cup heavy cream; 1 oz., about ½ cup shredded gruyere cheese; 3 tbsp. panko (Japanese) bread crumbs; 2 tbsp. grated pecorino cheese; ¼ cup white wine; 2 tsp. butter; salt and fresh ground black pepper to taste.

Preheat oven at 425 degrees. Heat 1 tbsp. olive oil in a heavy-bottom pan, on medium-high heat. When oil starts simmering add mushrooms and zucchini. Sauté until softened, about 5 minutes. Add peas, season with a little salt and pepper, and sauté until peas are bright green, about 1 minute.

Transfer the vegetables to an 8x8-inch baking pan. Add heavy cream, gruyere cheese, scatter the bread crumbs and pecorino cheese over the top. Put pan in the oven and bake until bubbling and golden, about 12 minutes.

While the gratin bakes, season the pork chops all over with salt and pepper. Add 1 tbsp. olive oil to the pan for the vegetables and heat over medium heat. When the oil is simmering, add the pork chops and sear until browned and cooked through, about 3 to 5 minutes, depending on the thickness. Remove the pork chops from the pan and set aside in a platter.

Reduce heat under the pan to medium, add shallots, sauté until translucent. Stir in white wine, and cook scraping up the brown bits until liquid is reduced in half, about 1 minute. Add the tarragon and cook stirring until combined. Remove the pan from heat, and stir in chilled butter. Return the pork chops to the pan to coat with the wine sauce.

Divide pork chops and vegetables between 2 plates, and serve shallot and wine sauce drizzled over the pork chops.

- Jennifer Cox

Bean Stew (Sambar) (Serves: 4)

Sambar is the main meal that is used in South India with rice, fritters and bread, and is served with almost all the meals. It is a mixture of beans, vegetables and spices, and served in combination of coconut chutney (see recipe in Sauce and Chutney section). All these ingredients are available at the Indian grocery store.

Ingredients: Garnish (Baghar) Spices: 3 tbsp. vegetable oil; 1 tsp. each of mustard seeds, urad dal, chana dal; 1 pinch of hing, 8-10 fresh curry leaves; 1cup peeled and split tur dal (tur beans); about 3cupmixed and cut vegetables such as: onion, tomatoes, long Chinese beans and okra; 3 serrano peppers; 2 tbsp. sambar powder bought or made; 1 tsp. sugar; 2 tbsp. tamarind paste diluted in ½cupwarm water; salt to taste; cilantro to garnish.

Cook tur dal with 2 cups of water in a pressure cooker until soft; mash and set aside. In a medium pot bring 1 cup of water to a boil, add the vegetables, cover and cook for 5-8 minutes, until par-boiled. Add tamarind water and cook 5 minutes. Next, add cooked dal, and a little water to a pouring consistency. Add sambar powder, serrano peppers, salt and sugar, and bring to a boil. Simmer all ingredients for 5 minutes or until vegetables are soft; turn off the heat and keep covered.

For the hot Garnish (baghar): In a small pan, heat the oil on medium heat; add garnish spices: first add mustard and wait until it splits (starts popping), then urad and chana dals; cook stirring 1-2 minutes until light brown; add curry leaves and wait 1 minute until they are transparent; add hing, stir well and immediately pour into the sambar pot, stir well once, and cover immediately. Serve garnished with cilantro with side dishes.

- Shreenivas and Sunitha Durbha

Peanut Chutney (M: about 1-1/2 cups)

This recipe is from my friend's teenage daughters who love to cook and love to eat good food.

Ingredients: 1 cup roasted or unroasted peanuts; ½ cup grated coconut; 2-3 serrano peppers or to taste; handful of cilantro leaves; salt to taste.

Roast the unroasted peanuts in a dry skillet on medium heat without any oil, until they are light brown. Cool, rub off and remove the pink skin. Blend the roasted peanuts, coconut, peppers, cilantro and salt with a little water to form a fine paste of sauce like consistency.

- Shreya and Amoolya Durbha

Cheese Squares (Kalakand) (Serves: 8-10)

These are ricotta cheese squares that are made all different ways, but all taste very good.

Ingredients: 4 tbsp. butter; 3-pound container ricotta cheese; 3 cups non-fat dry milk; 1 cup sugar or to taste; seeds from 5 cardamom pods, crushed; to garnish: ½ cup slivered almonds.

In a large and a heavy-bottom pan, on medium heat, heat the 3 tbsp. butter, add the cheese and stir well. Increase the heat from time to time to reduce the cheese and dry out some water. Stir for about 30 minutes, then slowly add the dry-milk power and stir well. Add the sugar and the cardamom seeds, and turn off the heat.

Preheat the oven at 300 degrees. Grease a 9x12-inch glass baking pan or a non-stick baking sheet with some butter and pour in the cheese mixture. Spread out evenly. Bake the mixture loosely covered with a foil, for about 30 minutes at 300 degrees. Turn off the oven and leave the cheese mixture in the off oven until it is cooled completely, about 2 hours. Take out and score into 2-inch squares. Serve in paper cups.

- Suresh, Prem, Saaket & Alka Gupta

Rich Chocolate Cake with Buttercream Frosting

My niece, Melissa, sent me this recipe from Joanne Hancharick. Melissa also sent a recipe from her mother Lorraine Krisanda. Her mom Lorraine is a very good cook. For her grandson's baptism, Lorraine and friends had cooked meals for over 100 people. There were several tables filled with over 50 desserts, and they were delicious.

Ingredients: 2 cups sifted flour; 2 cups sugar, ¾ cup cocoa; ½ tsp. salt; 2 tsp. baking powder; 2 tsp. baking soda; ½ cup Crisco vegetable oil; 1 cup hot coffee; 1 cup milk; 1 tsp. vanilla extract; 2 large eggs.

Preheat oven to 350 degrees. Grease and flour a tube or bundt cake pan. Place the first 6 ingredients in a large mixing bowl and mix well with a spoon. Add the remaining ingredients and mix at medium speed for about 2 minutes. Fill the pan with the batter, and bake at 350 degrees for 45 minutes. Cake is done when a toothpick inserted at the thickest part comes out clean. Cool and frost with buttercream.

Buttercream Frosting – Cooked

Ingredients: ¾ cup sugar; 5 tbsp. flour; ¾ cup milk; 1 tsp. vanilla ext.; 12 tbsp. softened butter; ¼ cup confectioners' sugar.

Mix the flour and the milk together until well-combined. Place the mixture into a small saucepan and cook over medium-high heat until mixture thickens, stirring constantly. Let the mixture cool, then refrigerate. Mixture must be cold before making rest of the frosting.

Cream the butter and sugar together until fluffy, and sugar granules are blended. Add vanilla and mix well. Take cold flour mixture and mix well with a whisk. Add it to the butter mixture and beat well until mixture is light and fluffy. Add the confectioner's sugar and mix well. Frost on a cooled chocolate cake.

- Joanne Hancharick, and Melissa & Thomas Hennessy

Beef Bourguignon

Ingredients: 2 pounds cubed beef; 3-4 medium carrots diced; 4-6 medium potatoes cut small; 1 cup chopped celery; 2 onions sliced; 2 cups canned tomatoes; 1 cup tomato sauce; 1 large garlic clove crushed; 3 tbsp. minute tapioca; 1 tbsp. sugar; ½ cup burgundy red wine; 2 cups mushrooms.

Preheat the oven to 250 degrees. In a 4-quart casserole dish, combine all ingredients, except the mushrooms. Cook for 4 hours, then add the mushrooms. Cook for one more hour. Let it set aside for 5 minutes before serving.

- Lorraine Krisanda and Melissa Hennessy

Bean Fritters (Vada) (M: about 15, 3-inch rings)

Bara are fritters that look almost like doughnuts with holes. They are made of beans and are very famous in South India. My friend, Krishna, and her husband own a couple of restaurants called Dosa House, where they sell these as side dishes.

Ingredients: 2 pounds, skinless urad beans (gotta), picked over and soaked in water for at least 3 hours; about ¼ tsp. heing; 5-6 small fresh curry leaves; ½ cup chopped each fresh: ginger cilantro, and the serrano peppers; 1 tsp. each salt and black pepper; vegetable oil to deep fry; to serve chutney, and sambar. All spices are found at the indian grocery stores.

Drain the soaked beans and grind them without or with very little water in the food processor. Mix all the spices, and set aside in the room temperature covered for about 4 hours to rise. When ready to cook, heat about 2-inch-deep oil in a wok, on medium heat (360 degrees). Take about ½ cup, or one ladle mixture in lightly wet hands, roll it like a ball, press down to 1-inch thickness, make a hole in the center with a wet finger, and carefully drop in the hot oil near the edge. Cook underneath until golden brown, about 6-7 minutes; turn over and cook the other side, golden brown, maintaining the temperature between medium and medium-high. Serve warm with chutney and the sambar or raita.

- Krishna and Giri Karuru

Plum Cake (Pflaume Kuchen)

Bake: at 350 degrees for 20 minutes.

This famous recipe came from Germany.

Ingredients: ½ cup soft but cold butter; ½ cup sugar; 2 large eggs; 2 cups all-purpose flour; 2 tsp. baking powder; ½ tsp. salt; 1 tsp. pure vanilla extract; 1-2 tbsp. milk or water; fruit mixture: about 2 cups thin-sliced fresh (or canned and well-drained) plums or peaches; the topping mixture: in a bowl blend together by hand 1 cup all-purpose flour, ½ cup sugar, a pinch of salt, ½ stick (4tbsps.) softened butter, ½ tsp. cinnamon. Filling: about 4 fresh pitted and sliced plums or apricots, mixed with a mixture of 1 tbsp. each flour, sugar and about ½ tsp. cinnamon.

Preheat the oven at 350 degrees. Grease 8- or 9-inch spring-form pan well, then sprinkle with the flour.

In a bowl cream the butter, sugar and the eggs. Sift over and fold in: the flour, baking powder, salt, vanilla extract, and 1 to 2 tbsp. milk or water as needed. Press in the mixture into the bottom of the prepared pan. Sprinkle the plum or apricot mixture on the top evenly. Then sprinkle the topping mixture over the fruits evenly. Bake in a 350 degree preheated oven for about 20 minutes or until topping is browned.

- Frances Bremer

- Hildegard Heinz and her mother from Germany.

Cucumber and Tomato Relish (M: about 2-1/2 quarts)

This recipe is from my Jewish friend. She is a very good cook and any time you talk about food, she will tell you how to cook.

Ingredients: 2 garlic cloves peeled and sliced thin; 1 medium green and 1 medium red bell pepper, seeded and chopped fine; 4-5 medium Kirby cucumbers, peeled or unpeeled, chopped; 1 cup minced onion; 1 cup shredded green cabbage; 1-1/4 cup sugar mixed and diluted with 1 tbsp. salt and 1-1/4 cup cider vinegar ; 1 tsp. celery seeds; 1 tsp. red pepper flakes (op); 2 tbsp. mustard seeds.

Have one large (about 3 quarts) or two jars, clean and dry. Mix all ingredients in a large non-reactive bowl. Then fill in the jar/jars with a plastic or a wooden spoon. Chill in the refrigerator for two days, shaking it well several times. Serve on the side or over the burgers and sandwiches.

- Ellen Dash

-

Korean Beef (Bul Gozi) (Serves: 4)

These three recipes are from my Korean friend, Yunie Driscoll. She is also the author of "My Garden of Life." She makes smoothies every day for breakfast.

Ingredients: 1-1/2 pounds boneless rib-eye steak or sirloin steak, partially frozen and sliced paper thin; 4 tbsp. sugar; ¼cupsoy sauce; 3 garlic cloves crushed and then chopped fine; ¼ tsp. black pepper; 1 tsp.

462

sesame oil; 2 tsps. white or rice wine. To garnish: 3 scallions cut into 1-inch pieces. To serve: plain rice or of your choice.

In a large bowl, mix meat and sugar and let it rest for 2 minutes. In a small bowl, mix together rest of the ingredients: soy sauce, garlic, black pepper, sesame oil and wine, and pour over the beef. Let it marinate in room temperature for about an hour, or overnight in the refrigerator.

Preheat a large, heavy-bottom pan over moderate heat for 2 minutes. Add a few meat slices, spread them out straight, and sear them without any oil until they are browned on both sides, or use outdoor grill. Serve with rice garnished with scallions.

Tofu Hot Pot (Soon Dubu)

(Serves: 4)

Ingredients: 4 tsps. chili powder (or less depending, on how hot you prefer); 2 garlic cloves, minced; 2 tsps. salt or 1 tsp. salt and 1 tsp. soy sauce; 2 tsps. sesame oil; 9 ounces soft tofu; 8 clams; 8 large shrimps peeled and deveined; 4 oz. cleaned squid sliced 1-inch length; 3 cups chicken stock or broth; 3 cups water; 4 large eggs. Rice to serve.

In a small bowl, combine the chili powder, garlic, salt and sesame oil and set aside.

In a large pot, heat chicken broth, water, tofu, clams and bring them to a boil; add squid, shrimp and seasoning that is set aside. Let simmer on low heat (about 6-7 minutes) until seafood is cooked through. Add the green onions before serving.

Serve hot over a raw egg added to each soup bowl, and serve immediately with rice.

Breakfast Smoothie (Serves: 2)

Ingredients: One of each peeled, cored and chopped: medium carrot, apple, orange or clementine; 1-inch fresh ginger; about 2 tbsp. onion; 1 cup fresh berries; ½ cup mixed nuts and seeds (such as almond or pistachio, sunflower or pumpkin seeds); and 2 cups milk.

In a smoothie maker or in a blender puree all ingredients, and serve immediately.

-   Rusty & Yunie Driscoll
-
-

Lemon Punch (Serves: about 24)

These three recipes come from my dear friend. They made these punches for the open house that they had before Christmas.

Ingredients: 3 cups water; 2 cups cranberry juice; 1 can 6 ounces frozen orange juice concentrate, thawed; 1 can 6 ounces frozen lemonade concentrate, thawed; ½ cup sugar; 1-1/2 liter frozen lemon/lime soda, chilled.

Mix first 5 ingredients in a bowl with sugar, chill for 1 to 2 hours, add soda just before serving.

Cran-Apple Punch

Ingredients: 1 quart cranberry juice; 1 quart apple juice; some ginger ale or soda water; lemon and orange slices, and cinnamon sticks or cloves to float.

Combine juices, add ginger ale or soda for sparkle. Float fruits on the top. Serve on plenty of ice.

Apple Coffee Cake

Ingredients: 1 box yellow cake mix; 1 stick cold butter but lightly soften; 1 can Comstock apple slices; 1 cup sour cream, whisked with 1 large egg.

In a bowl, mix together cake mix and the butter until crumbly, reserving 2/3 cup aside, pat rest of the cake mixture in a greased 9x13 baking pan. Top with apple slices evenly. Pour over the sour cream mixture evenly. Bake in a preheated 350 degrees oven for about 30 minutes until golden. Serve warm with cream or ice cream.

- Caral Harrison, Ex-President, Woman's Club

Deep-Fried Beans Bread (Pithi Poori)

(M: about 15)

In India, breads are made with white whole wheat flour that is called atta, or bread or chapatti flour. You need to soak the beans for 2 hours and then grind with the spices. This is a protein bread to serve with vegetables and/or raita (yogurt salad) and chutney. This is my sister's son and daughter-in-law's recipe.

Ingredients: ½ cup thick yogurt; 2 cup bread flour (atta) plus more for dusting; ¾ cup semolina (sooji); ¼ tsp. baking soda; 3 tbsps. softened butter; 1 cup urad or moong skinless and split beans soaked for 2 hours in water, drained and then grinded coarsely in food processor, with very little water, 2 tbsp. chopped ginger, 2 tbsp. fine fennel seeds, 1 or 2 chopped serrano peppers or to taste; salt and pepper to taste; oil to deep-fry. To serve: vegetable, raita and chutney.

In a large bowl, rub the butter with the 2cupflour, baking soda, and semolina by hand. Add the yogurt, and mix well. Add the bean mixture and mix well; add about ¾ cup to 1 cup of water as needed and make a stiff dough. Knead the dough for 2 minutes, and set aside for 40 minutes, covered with a lightly damp kitchen towel. Then knead the dough again, using a few drops of water; if it is still tough, sprinkle about 1 tsp. salt to make it a pliable dough.

Now heat about 2-inch-deep oil in a wok on low heat. Divide the dough into 15 equal portions. Take one portion at a time, make a ball, then a disk, and dusting with the flour, roll out to about 2-inch-diameter round poori; dust with the flour, turn over and then roll on the other side, into 3-4-inch diameter. Make sure you roll out evenly, and the edges are not thin, or the center is not broken. Roll out about half of the poories and spread them out on the plates, in a single layer. Increase the oil to medium-high heat. When oil is hot, about 360 degrees, drop one poori at a time, wait for 30 seconds, then carefully turn it over. It will puff right away. Keep on cooking and turning over until both sides are golden brown. Make sure you turn each poori about 3-4 times on each side to cook well. Take out the cooked poories from the wok onto a paper towel-lined platter. Make rest of the poories same way. Serve with vegetable, raita and chutney while they are still hot.

- Abhishek and Anjana Katiyar, Delhi, India

Grilled Eggplant (Serves: 4)

These young cooks, the teenagers, are my sister's grandson and granddaughter. They love to cook and love to eat.

Ingredients: 6 to 8 medium size, about 3-inch diameter fresh and soft eggplant; 2tbsps. Fresh-ground garlic cloves; 1 tbsp. cumin powder; ½ tsp. turmeric; salt and cayenne pepper to taste; about 3 tbsps. vegetable oil; 3 tbsps. lemon juice. To serve: cilantro and mint chutney and soft buns.

In a bowl, slice the eggplant across about ½-inch-wide slices, then sprinkle them with cumin powder, turmeric, garlic, salt, pepper, and sprinkle with lemon juice and oil. Toss well with a spoon, coating each piece well. Prepare a medium-hot grill and grease it well. Spread out the eggplant slices in a single layer, cover and let them cook light brown. Turn over and cook the other side until soft. Take out on a platter, and serve sprinkled with chutney and the bun on the side.

-   Ayush and Anushri Katiyar, Lucknow, India

Fermented Beans and Carrots Dumpling (Gajar Kanji Bara)

(Serves: 8-10)

My middle sister is an expert in this. This is a fermented bean stew, made with bean fritters and carrots, which takes 3-4 days to ferment; refrigerate and use for another 5-6 days. This is a unique dish from my family. My mother will prepare a large batch in a clay pot with a small neck, and tie with a cheese cloth and place in the hot sun for 2-3 days. Around the Dewali festival, friends and family will enjoy this for over a week. It is nourishing, tasty, digestive and unique.

Ingredients: 1 cup urad beans, skinned and split, soaked in the water for 3 hours, then ground with 1 tsp. fenugreek powder, ½ tsp. each salt and cayenne pepper, 1 tbsp. fresh ginger and very little water; oil to deep-fry; about ½ pound carrots peeled, cored and cut into large match sticks (3 inches long, about ½-inch wide and ¼-inch thick).

For the Liquid: about 8 cups water, 2 tbsps. tamarind paste, 3 tbsps. lemon juice, 2 tsp. black salt (found in Indian grocery stores), 1 tsp. or to taste table salt, 4 tbsp. crushed black mustard seeds, 2 tbsp. roasted and crushed caraway seeds, ½ tsp. heeing powder (Asafoetida) or ginger powder,

Heat oil in a wok about 2-inch deep on medium heat. Now, whisk the bean mixture well until it is soft and little thicker to drop in the hot oil. Heat the oil to 350 degrees or until a bread piece dropped in the oil, floats and browns immediately. Using two tablespoons or a medium (about 1-1/2-inch diameter) ice cream scoop, scoop out the bean mixture and drop the balls in the hot oil, in a single layer. Wait for about 2 minutes or until they are browned underneath, then turn over with a metal spatula and cook the other side. After they are browned all over, turn them over two more times on each side for even cooking. Take them out and place on a paper towel-lined platter. Cook rest the same way.

Place the carrots sticks and the bean balls in one or two clean, dry, glass or cooking clay jars. Heat the liquid ingredients in a pot, bring it to a boil, then simmer for 5 minutes and pour over the bean balls and the carrots. Cover the top with double cheese cloth and leave in room temperature for 24 hours, then cover with a lid or a bowl and refrigerate for 2 full days. You can also place in the hot sun for 1 or 2 full days, then cover with the lid and refrigerate for 2 days. Serve 2 balls and 2 pieces of carrots with about ½cup liquid per person. Store in the refrigerator for up to 4 days.

-   Shail Katiyar, Lucknow, India

Idli (Semolina Cakes) (Serves: 2-4)

Idlies are semolina cakes, about 2-1/2 to 3-inch diameter, and about 1-inch high. These are mostly made of rice flour, and are used in place of rice. Since these are steamed, they are healthy and taste good. You can use the traditional mold and just steam in the roasting pan as I do all the time.

Ingredients: 1 cup semolina (aka: sooji or rava); 1 cup thick yogurt, the more sour the better; about ½ cup water; ½ tsp. salt; to serve sambar and chutney.

Mix all ingredients together in a non-reactive bowl and set aside in room temperature, covered with a kitchen towel, for two hours.

Boil 6 to 8 cups of water. Grease or spray a 9x12 glass platter, pour in the mixture in the platter. Place a large roasting pan in a 350-degree heated oven, pour in boiling water up to the wire rack; place the platter over the wire rack, Using aluminum foil (put 2 pieces together), seal the roasting pan on the edges airtight. Steam the mixture for about 15 minutes. Turn off the oven and leave the roasting pan in the oven for 5 minutes. Be careful and open the foil away from you. Take out the platter and cut the idli into 2-inch squares or large diamond shapes. Serve with sambar and chutney.

- Madhu Mistry

Pasta E. Fagioli (Serves: 4)

Below listed recipe is from my friend Maddy. She is a teacher and does a lot of good cooking. She has written to me: "Sue, I got this Italian recipe from Morristown Memorial Hospital. It is a healthier version of the traditional Pasta E Fagioli. I make it for our church's soup kitchen every year and get great reviews. I think it is delicious. I quadruple the amounts."

Pasta E Fagioli

Ingredients: 1 13-14 oz. can lower sodium chicken broth; 5-6 chopped sun-dried tomatoes; 1 cup chopped celery, including leaves; 1-2 cloves garlic, crushed
1 15-19 oz. can un-drained cannellini beans; ¾ cup canned crushed tomatoes; 1 1/2 cup cooked macaroni (I used Ditallini and reserve 1 cup of cooking liquid); 1/8 tsp. red pepper flakes (or to taste; I use half of that because we are not spicy people, but like the flavor); 2 tbsp. chopped parsley

In a medium saucepan, bring broth, sun-dried tomatoes, celery and garlic to a simmer and cook until celery is crisp yet tender (about 7 minutes). While the broth is simmering, remove about ¼ of beans from the can and smash/crush them (to thicken the sauce.) Add all the beans, tomatoes, pasta and red pepper flakes, bring to a simmer and cook for 5 minutes. If dish is too thick, add small amounts of the cooking liquid, water or tomatoes. Add parsley just before serving.

Dietary information (per serving); calories 193; fat 1g; saturated fat 0g; protein 12g; carbohydrates 34g; fiber 6g

- Maddy and Frank Onofrio

Favorite Pound Cake

My friend and her husband are both professors. He is still a professor for over 30 years in a university in New Jersey. This is their favorite family pound cake.

466

Ingredients: 2 sticks (1/2 pound) unsalted butter lightly softened; ½ cup sour cream or vegetable shortening; 3 cups sugar, 5 large eggs; 3 cups all-purpose flour; ½ tsp. salt; ½ tsp. baking powder; 1 cup milk; 1 tsp. vanilla or lemon extract.

Preheat oven at 350 degrees. Grease a non-stick tube pan with butter, then sprinkle with flour and tap out the excess flour.

In a bowl, cream butter and sour cream, adding a little sugar at a time. Whisk in eggs. Combine flour, baking powder and salt, and starting with the flour mixture, alternate flour and milk into the butter mixture. Whisk in the vanilla or lemon extract. Pour into the prepared pan, tap the pan on the counter to break any air bubbles. Bake cake for 1 to 1-1/2 hours until a toothpick inserted in the thickest part comes out almost clean. Cool and serve with fruits, berries or ice cream, coffee and/or tea.

- Rev. Dr. Forrest and Barbara J. Pritchett

Mixed Vegetables with Coconut (Aviyal) (Serves: 4)

This recipe is from my friend, from Kerala, India. South India is famous for growing coconut, so they use it almost every day.

Ingredients: Chopped vegetables (you can use any vegetable of your choice): 2-3 drumsticks (long beans grown on trees); 2 medium carrots; about 1 cup string beans; 1 large yam (elephant); 2 medium Kirby cucumbers; 2 medium potatoes peeled; 2 cups chopped snake gourd or zucchini; 2 medium plantains, peeled, 2-3 serrano chili, slit lengthwise and stems removed; salt to taste; 5-6 medium curry leaves or cilantro to garnish.
Fresh-ground spices: about 1-1/2 cup fresh or frozen grated coconut, ½ tsp. cumin seeds, 1 tbsp. garlic cloves, 3-4 serrano peppers, 1-2 tsps. chili powder or to taste,1/4 tsp. turmeric powder.

For the Sauce: ¼ cup to ½ cup yogurt or to taste for tanginess or 2-3 slices of green mango or ¼ cup tamarind juice, 1 tbsp. coconut oil.

Place all the vegetables in a large pot and add enough water just to cook them soft; add salt, turmeric, and chili powder. Bring them to a boil, lower the heat and simmer until they are halfway done.

In a food processor, coarsely grind the coconut, cumin seeds, garlic and green chilies. When the vegetables are half-cooked, add these ground spices, and yogurt or mango slices or tamarind water, and salt and pepper to taste, stir well. Simmer until they are soft, then remove from the fire. Drizzle a tbsp. of coconut oil and add the curry leaves or the cilantro. Serve warm with rice or breads.

- Jayashri Ramesh and Ramesh Nair

Lamb with Okra (Serves: 4-6)

My friend Ray is a retired cook. His parents came from Syria long time ago. This is his family recipe.

Ingredients: 3-4 tbsp. butter or oil; about 1-1/2 pound lamb shoulder meat, cut into 1-inch cubes and all fat taken out; ¼ cup all-purpose flour; 4 tbsp. tomato paste; 3 cups chicken stock; 1 pound fresh okra, cut 1-inch, slightly on bias, or frozen okra: scattered on a baking tray, sprinkled with 1-2 tsp. oil and little lemon juice and roasted at 400 degrees for about 20 minutes, until they are partially cooked and all liquid evaporated; 1 cup each chopped fine: onion and celery stocks or seeded green bell pepper; 1 tsp.each: cumin powder, garlic powder, sugar, cayenne and allspice; cilantro to garnish. To serve: naan, pita or any other kind of bread; yogurt, and/or rice.

In a 5 qt. pot, heat 2 tbsp. oil or butter on medium heat. When hot, cook onion for 5 minutes, add the celery and the bell pepper and cook for 5 minutes, and take out. Now sprinkle the flour all over the meat, add rest of the oil to the pot, add the meat cubes to the oil in single layer, cover the pot with the lid and let them brown underneath on medium heat, for about 6-7 minutes. Turn over the meat and brown on the other side. Add the tomato paste and stir on high heat for 5 minutes, until tomato paste dries out. Add chicken stock and bring it to a boil. Lower the heat and simmer for 15 minutes, until meat is tender. Add the spices, lemon juice, and the okra and simmer covered for another 15 minutes, until okra are tender. Serve hot with bread, yogurt, and/or rice.

- Raymond Asbaty

Tasty Stuffed Squash (Stuffed Lauki) (Serves: 4-6)

This is the way to eat a squash. My niece and her family are expert in this. You can boil, stuff and refrigerate covered. Just deep-fry or shallow-fry just before serving.

Ingredients: About 2 pounds long, slim lauki or medium soft zucchini, cored, peeled (if skin is hard), cut into 4-inch pieces, scooped out of all pulp, then boiled or steamed with the pulp, just until soft.

Filling: Boiled pulp hard with seeds removed, 1 cup boiled potatoes peeled and mashed, 1 tbsp. cumin powder, salt and black pepper to taste, ½ cup grated onion, 1 tbsp. diced garlic cloves, 1 tbsp. fresh grated ginger, 1 tbsp. lemon-pepper mix or dry mango powder (amchoor); mix all and press into the squash pieces.

Batter: You can dip in the pancake batter or mix 1cupall-purpose flour and ½cupcorn starch, salt and pepper to taste with about 1-1/2cupwater or as needed to make the batter of pancake consistency; oil to deep-fry.

Boil the squash pieces with the pulp, stuff with the filling. Heat the oil for deep-frying at 350 degrees in a wok or a frying pan at medium-high heat. Carefully slice the stuffed pieces into 2-inch wide pieces. Then dip in the batter, and deep-fry golden in hot oil in batches. Or shallow fry in 2 tbsp. oil in the pan; when they are browned underneath, drop 2 drops of oil on the top, turn over and brown the other side. Serve as snacks or side dish with the meal.

- Amit, Anupam, & Anshul Schan, Haiderabad, India

Lamb Keema or Lamb Chile (Serves: 8-10)

This recipe is from my brother, who cooks a lot of Indian food for parties. Keema is like chili, it looks like chilie, but is not so hot. If you prefer, you can add hot peppers or hot sauce.

Ingredients: About 4 pounds ground lamb shoulder or leg meat; 4 tbsp. canola oil; 4 large onions very thin sliced whole, across, into thin rings or just sliced thin; 2 large bay leaves; ¼ cup grated fresh ginger; ¼ cup fine chopped fresh garlic cloves; 3 tbsp. tomato paste; 2 Tsp. turmeric powder; 2Tbsp. chili powder or mustard powder; 4 tbsp. curry powder; ½ cup thin sliced soft cilantro stems; 1 pound plain yogurt; 1 pound thick tomato or pasta sauce; 1 pkg. 10 ounces frozen peas; 1 tsp. each granulated garlic and cayenne pepper. To garnish: 1 cup each grated fresh radishes and thin sliced green onion. To serve: naan, rice, raita, and mint chutney.

1. In a large heavy-bottom pot, with tight-fitting lid, heat the oil on medium heat. When hot, add bay leaves and stir a little for 5 seconds. Add sliced onion, increase heat to medium-

high and sauté onions for 8-10 minutes, until they are transparent. Lower the heat to medium, add garlic, ginger, turmeric and sauté 5 minutes. Move the ingredients on the side, add the tomato paste, chili powder, curry powder and sauté well 1 minutes. Add the meat and stir well with the tomato paste. Now add the cilantro stems and tomato sauce and stir well. Increase heat medium-high and stir for 5 minutes until sauce is heated through.

2. Add yogurt, stir well, bring to a boil. Now reduce the heat and cook on constant simmer, covered for about 1 hour or until meat and spices are mixed well and cooked through. Add frozen peas and garlic powder, salt and pepper to taste; cook another 10 minutes until peas are done.

3. Serve garnished with radishes and green onions with rice, bread, raita and chutney.

- Yadvendra N. Singh, Berlin, Germany
-

Red Kidney Beans (Rajma)

(Serves: about 6)

This family recipe comes from 4 generations. My mother, Bhagvati Devi, my older sister, Saroj, her daughter, Kanchana, and her daughter, Vasvi, all are expert in cooking these beans. Red kidney beans are good for your eyes.

Ingredients: 1 Bag, 16 ounces red kidney beans, picked over, washed, and soaked overnight covered with water; ¼ cup vegetable oil; fresh spice mixture: 1 large onion thin sliced, ¼ cup garlic cloves chopped, ¼ cup fresh unpeeled ginger chopped, 2 tbsp. each caraway, fennel and coriander seeds, 1 tbsp. cardamom seeds, 1 large bay leaf with veins taken out and broken into small pieces and then all ground fine with very little water; 1 tsp. each fenugreek and turmeric powder, 1 cup thick tomato sauce or 1 can 14oz. stewed tomatoes; 1Tbsp. mustard powder; salt and pepper to taste; ½ cup cilantro to garnish; deep-fried bread (poori) or rice to serve.

Rinse out all the soaking water, and then wash the soaked beans with cold water. Put the beans in a heavy-bottom medium pot, covering with water 1-inch higher than the beans. Bring to a boil for 10 minutes, skimming the foam from the surface. Cover the beans with the lid; lower the heat to a constant simmer, and cook until fork tender, about 1 to 1-1/2 hour Do not use any salt.

While beans are cooking, heat a large wok or frying pan on medium heat, add the oil, and cook the fresh-ground spices and fenugreek powder; stir for 5 minutes, add a little salt and pepper, cover and simmer on the low heat for 15 minutes. Turn off the heat. When the beans are done, strain out the water, save about 1 cup of water, and add the beans to the spice mixture. Increase the heat to medium-high, sprinkle turmeric powder, tomato sauce or stewed tomato, mustard powder, salt and pepper to taste and bring them to a boil; simmer for 10-15 minutes. Add some cooking water if needed. Serve sprinkled with cilantro, and rice or bread on the side. You can also use this recipe for chickpeas (Cholay).

- Late Bhagvati Devi Singh, Late Saroj Chaudhary
- Kanchana, and Vasvi Singh

Sweet, Sour & Cruncy Snacks (Bhel Puri) (Serves: 4)

This is a famous Mumbai street food. We make layers of crunchy, sweet, sour, boiled and deep-fried food. Once it is assembled, you just have to dig in before it gets soggy. You can eat this with crackers, hot dog buns or just as it is with a fork. All ingredients can be found at the Indian grocery stores. This recipe comes from my older sister Saroj's son. He was in the military.

Ingredients: 1 cup each spicy cilantro-mint chutney and sweet tamarind chutney; 20 papdis or 4 cups tortilla chips broken into 1-inch pieces, or 2 cups Indian puffed rice; about ½ pound potatoes boiled, peeled and mashed roughly or cut into ½-inch cubes; about 1cupcooked chickpeas; 1 cup raw or ripe but firm mango, peeled and diced; 1 cup diced onion; 1 pound ripe tomatoes cut into 1-inch cubes; to garnish: 1 cup fine chickpeas noodles (nylon sev); 3-4 tbsp. chat masala; ½ cup cilantro leaves. To serve: crackers or hot dog buns.

Spicy Cilantro-mint Chutney (M: 1 cup)

Ingredients: 1 tsp. caraway/cumin seeds and ½ cup peeled almonds both toasted in a dry pan a shade darker (about 6 minutes on medium heat); 2 cups firmly packed cilantro leaves and soft stems; 1 cup packed mint leaves and soft stems; 1 tbsp. amchoor (green mango powder) or 1 tbsp. lemon-pepper mix or to taste; about 5 serrano or fresh thai chilis to taste; 1 tbsp. chopped garlic cloves; 2Tbsp. brown sugar; 1/3 cup fresh lemon juice; ½ tsp. Salt or to taste.

Grind all in a blender or food processor to a fine paste or thick sauce, and set aside in a non-reactive bowl, cover and refrigerate for up to 2 days.

Sweet Tamarind Chutney (M: 1 cup)

Ingredients: ¼ cup tamarind paste; ½ cup pitted, dated, chopped; 1 tbsp. each toasted coriander, cumin seeds; 1 tsp. cardamom seeds; ½ cup jaggery or ¼ cup packed light brown sugar; ¼ cup each cilantro and mint leaves; 1 tsp. cayenne pepper or to taste; ½ tsp. salt or to taste.

Grind all ingredients in a blender or a food processor with about 1cupwater or as needed. Place the ingredients in a pot, bring to a boil, lower the heat and simmer 5 minutes. Transfer to a non-reactive bowl, cover, cool and use or refrigerate up to 2 days.

Assemble the Plates:

First spread papdis, tortilla chips or puffed rice in 4 dinner plates equally. Top with potatoes, onion, sprinkled with little salt and pepper then with 2 tbsps. each cilantro and tamarind chutney, then chickpeas, mango, tomatoes, little salt, 1 tsp. chat masala, again with tamarind and cilantro chutney, and some cilantro and chickpea noodles. Serve with crackers and buns, and extra chutney on side, if preferred.

- Vishvadeepak and Ila Singh, Bombay, India

Golden Egg Float (Boiled Eggs in Thick Nut Gravy)

(Serves: 2 to 4)

This recipe is from my older sister Saroj's son and daughter-in law. He was a Naval officer, and lived coast to coast.

Ingredients: 3-4 tbsp. Olive Oil; 4 to 6 hard-boiled eggs peeled; 1 tbsp. lemon juice; ½ tsp. turmeric powder; 2 medium onions chopped; 1 tbsp. each ginger , garlic and chili pastes; 2 ripe tomatoes diced (about 1 cup); ¼ cup cashews or almonds, lightly toasted and ground into powder; about 2 cups almond or coconut milk; cilantro to garnish.

Heat about 1 tbsp. olive oil, in a large frying pan, on medium. Add eggs and brown all around lightly about 2 minutes. Then sprinkle with turmeric and lemon juice; stir well and take out of the pan.

Add 2 tbsp. of oil and brown onion for 5 minutes. Add garlic, ginger, chili paste and salt and pepper to taste; stir well, top with tomatoes, cover and cook on medium heat until they are soft, about 5 minutes. Add the almond or cashew powder and stir well; add almond or coconut milk and bring it to a boil; add the eggs and cover for 5 minutes, until the eggs are heated through. Serve sprinkled with cilantro, in a shallow dish, with sides.

- Ex. Navy Commador, Rajkeerti Singh and Sarla Singh, Delhi, India

Baked Kale and Spinach Fritters (Serves: 4)

This recipe is from my nephew and his wife. These fritters are easy to make. Just use extra bread crumbs and eggs to hold them together. You can drop them as a 1-1/2-inch balls or flat 1-inch high pieces on a baking sheet, and bake until golden.

Ingredients: 2 tbsp. Butter; 2 cups packed each baby spinach and kale leaves, stems taken out, washed, pat dried; 1 cup sliced onion; 2 tbsp. chopped garlic cloves; ¼ cup grated ginger; 2 extra large eggs; 1 cup ricotta cheese; ½ cup grated parmesan cheese; ½ cup chickpea flour; 1 to 1-1/2 cups dry bread crumbs either panko or seasoned; salt and pepper to taste; 2 tbsp. olive or canola oil; your favorite chutney or sauce to serve.

Blanch the kale in boiling water for 3-4 minutes, take out and drain and chop. Heat a large frying pan, add 1 tbsp. butter and cook onion on medium heat for 5 minutes. Add kale, torn spinach leaves, 1 tbsp. butter and cook kale and spinach for about 8 minutes on medium heat until it is wilted. Take off the heat and cool. Then add garlic, ginger, bread crumbs, ricotta, parmesan cheese, flour, salt and pepper to taste, and bread crumbs.

Preheat the oven at 400 degrees. Prepare a baking sheet, line with parchment paper, and spread out 1 tbsp. oil. Using a cookie scoop, or two tablespoons, pack the mixture, roll like a ball, and drop over the oil, about 1-inch apart. Drizzle one or two drops of oil on each ball. Bake in the preheated oven for 15-20 minutes until golden. Turn them over once during the baking. Serve with your favorite sauce or chutney.

- Dr. Pradumn Singh and Dr. Laxami Singh, Scotland

Breakfast Souffle (Serves: 8)

These recipes are from our friend Richard and Betty. Richard is a fire fighter for over 30 years, just like my brother-in-law, Tom Hennessy, in Breezy Point, N.Y. They both have a good heart, always asking how my husband is doing. They both do a lot of charity work.

Ingredients: 6-8 slices of bread, torn into pieces; 9 large eggs beaten with ½ tsp. dry mustard, 2 tbsp. flour, 2 tbsp. fresh parsley chopped, 1-1/2cupgrated cubed cheese, such as jack or cheddar, and mix well; then whisk in 3 cups of milk; 1 to 2 cups sausage, ham or bacon, cooked.

Preheat oven at 350 degrees. Grease a 9x13-inch pan and place the bread pieces. Top with meat, and pour over the egg mixture. Refrigerate overnight, or about an hour. Bake in a preheated 350-degree oven for about 1 hour, until it is settled. Serve warm with extra cheese or extra herbs.

Sweet and Sour Pork (Serves: 8-10)

This recipe comes handy when you have to feed a large group of people.

Ingredients: 3-4 tbsp. corn oil; 3 pounds boneless pork cut up into bite-size pieces; 18.5 ounces can pineapple chunks; 6 cloves garlic chopped; ½ green bell pepper chopped; 1/3 cup cider vinegar; 1-1/2 cups corn syrup or 1 cup maple syrup mixed with ½ cup sugar; 6 tbsp. ketchup; 6 tbsp. corn starch.

Heat a large pan on medium heat, add oil, and brown the pork in single layer, in batches. When it is browned underneath, turn over once and brown the other side. Add pepper and garlic and stir well; add corn starch and stir well. Now add ketchup, vinegar, syrup, sugar (if using) and pineapple; stir well and bring it to a boil. Lower the heat and simmer for about 20 minutes until thickened. Serve over rice.

- Richard and Betty Tuers

Osso Buco

This recipe is from my friend, Mark Vogel. He has his own website and occasionally prints recipes in the local newspaper.

Ingredients: 4 veal shanks, salt and pepper to taste; 3 tbsps. olive oil; 1-1/2 cup each: roughly chopped parsnips and turnips; 4 cloves of garlic chopped; 2 tbsps. tomato paste; 1 cup red wine; 1 cup beef or veal stock; 2 tbsp. parsley, chopped; 1 tbsp. rosemary, chopped; 1 tbsp. thyme, chopped.

1. Season the shanks with salt and pepper and brown them in a large skillet with the olive oil for about 5 minutes on each side.

2. Place the shanks in a large oven-proof casserole dish or Dutch oven with a tight-fitting lid.

3. In the same skillet you browned the shanks, sauté the vegetables for about 3-4 minutes, adding more olive oil if necessary. Add garlic and tomato paste and sauté for a few minutes more, being careful not to burn the paste or the garlic.

4. Add the stock, wine, and herbs and bring to a boil.

5. Pour everything over the shanks and place the casserole dish in a preheated 350 degree oven for 1 hour and 45 minutes.

6. Add salt and pepper to taste at the end.

- Mark Vogel, Author & website: Foodforthoughtonline.net

Spanakopitankia (Pastry with Spinach Filling)

This pastry is baked in filo sheets. Each filo sheet should be brushed with the melted butter well before stacking them on top of the other. This is a Greek recipe.

Ingredients: 2 pkgs. 10 ounces each frozen spinach thawed; 1 small onion grated; 3 tbsp. butter; 2 whole eggs plus 4 yolks, slightly beaten; ½ pound feta cheese; ½ tsp. each salt and fresh grated nutmeg; 1 tbsp. chopped parsley; 1 tbsp. grated toast; ½ pound filo pastry; ½ pound butter or margarine melted for brushing.

Defrost spinach completely and drain well. Sauté onion in 2 tbsp. butter, add spinach and cook until dry. Remove from heat and add eggs, cheese, salt, nutmeg, parsley, and grated toast, mix well. Cool completely.

Grease and line an 8x8x1-1/2-inch baking pan with half filo sheets, brushing each sheet generously with melted butter. Spread the filling over the filo. Cover with remaining ½ filo sheets, brushing each layer with butter. Pour any remaining butter on the top. Bake at 350 degrees for 1 hour. Cut into 12 large pieces.

- Elaine Xenitelis

Know How to do Things

How to Set the Table

You do not need expensive items to set up a table. Make sure whatever you present is neat, polished and attractive. If using a tablecloth, make sure it is ironed. Use napkins all the time, either cloth one or paper.

To Set the Table:

Place the dinner plate in the center. On the right side of the dinner plate, place the dinner knife facing the edge of the knife towards the dinner plate or service knife, then a fish knife (if you have), and then the soup spoon.

On the left of the dinner plate, place the salad fork next to the plate, then dinner fork, and then the fish fork. If you do not have a fish fork, you can use a salad fork. Place the napkin next to the fish fork.

Above the dinner plate, place the dessert spoon and the cake fork.

On the top right corner (close to dessert spoon and fork), place the water glass, white wine glass and then the red wine glass.

On the top left corner, close to the dessert spoon and the cake fork, place the bread and butter plate and the butter knife.

The Charger Plates: The charger plates make the serving more attractive. They are not required. They are used under soup plates or a soup bowl. You can take them away before the dinner is served.

To Serve the Food:

1. If you are serving food buffet-style: arrange the food in order. Keep the salads together, hot food together and cold food together, etc. Keep napkins and silverware at the end or at a separate table. Keep desserts and coffee at a separate table.
2. If you are serving at the table, the platters are passed from right to left. Most of the people are right-handed, therefore it is easier for them to handle the food.

To make the Dinner more pleasant:

1. One rule we had in our family: before entering the kitchen, whether in the morning or any other time of the day, comb your hair, wash your face and put a smile on for a pleasant attitude. This goes for the cook, and the host, to make the guests comfortable and welcomed.
2. The other rule we had: Go to bathroom, wash your hands. You don't want to ask to be excused during dinner, to go to the bathroom.
3. The centerpiece should be low so that people can see each other's face during conversation. I mostly use fresh flowers with some herbs during the summer and attractive fruits during the winter for my centerpiece.
4. As a courtesy, do not talk about religion, political affiliation and personal matters. Have more general conversation such as a movie you saw, a restaurant you went to, your kid's basketball game, etc. I always talk about my latest cooking and gym experience, and the charity work I am involved in.
5. Understand the importance of being polite in talking to others, in representing yourself and in respecting others. Try to leave a pleasant dinner experience so that people will remember you for years to come.

Food Safety

Food safety and cooking go hand-in-hand. We were not allowed to enter in the kitchen even to eat breakfast until we brushed our hair, washed our face and hands, and had a pleasant attitude. Whether you are cooking, serving or preparing, you need to pay attention to sanitation.

Wash hands, vegetables and cutting boards; wipe the meat juices. Cross-contamination is another big problem. Avoid using a dirty knife or the cutting board after slicing the meat and then using same utensils for the fruits and vegetables. Wash after each use and after each ingredient. If possible, use the dishwasher to sterilize the utensils.

Baking at the High Altitude

The high altitude, areas surrounded by the mountains or situated above 3,000 feet and above, the texture of the baking goods changes due to the low pressure. They rise above the normal baking and texture may change considerably.

Reducing the amount of the leavening agents, baking powder, eggs, sugar, and increasing the amount of liquid, will help keep the texture in its place. Also, reducing slightly the amount of fat and increasing the oven temperature slightly to bake fast will help as well. You may have to work with trial and error to determine the altitude with baking.

Taking Care of Whole Fish

You can ask your fish monger to clean the fish for you unless you want to do it yourself. Fish are two types: round like salmon, and flat or oval body like flounder. They both can be cooked, baked, grilled or broiled, and can be filleted or cut into pieces, etc.

Scaling the Fish

1. Place the fish in a large, clear plastic bag.
2. Place both hands inside the plastic bag, hold the fish by the tail and using a blunt knife like a butter knife or a fish scaler, scrape the skin gently, using a long strokes, toward the head. Do not scale the head, it will come out and can be used in stock. Use gentle strokes all around so that the scales stay inside the bag. Wash the fish, knife and work surface to avoid the scales from sticking.
3. After you have scaled the fish, take out the head. Place the fish on the cutting board, head near you and belly away from you. Using a sharp chef knife in one hand, and holding the fin behind the head with the other hand, cut behind the pectoral fin, through the flesh on both sides, and pull out the head.

Gutting the Fish

1. You can do this before or after scaling. Place the fish on the cutting board with head to the right and tail to the left. Using a sharp knife, split the belly lengthwise from behind the pelvic fin to the anal vent, just to cut into the flesh; do not go deep. Then with your hands pull out the entrails (guts) from the cavity. Cut it off the near the head and discard.
2. With a sharp heavy scissors, cut off the gills underneath on both sides.

Filleting the Fish

1. After scaling, place the fish on a cutting board, with the body away from you and head towards the right. Using a filleting knife, start filleting from the right; insert and cut the flesh above the backbone, using and resting on the backbone, keeping the knife edge lightly downward; gently cut flesh in a sawing motion, lengthwise toward the tail. Stay on the back bone base (parallel to the body) and do not go in the rib cage. Take out the long sliced piece.
2. Position, cut and repeat exactly the same procedure (from the beginning to end), and take out the fillet on the other side.
3. Now use the back of the knife or, gently using your finger, find any bone left in the fillet. Pull out the bones from the fillet with a plier or a tweezer. Usually these bones are in a row, so it is easy to find them by pressing the back of the knife or the tip of the index figure into the flesh.

Skinning the Fish Fillet

1. Place the fillet on the cutting board, skin side down and tail side to the left.
2. Using a thin-blade, flexible, sharp knife, hold the tail with left hand (if you are right-handed), hold the knife with the right hand and carefully insert the knife between the skin and flesh, at an angle; cut and separate the skin, then grab the skin end, and move the knife slightly pointed downward; cut and move to the right, separating the skin from the flesh.
3. I never separate the skin unless I am deep-frying the fillet because skin has a lot of good fat (polyunsaturated fat) near the flesh that helps cook the fish, and keeps it from drying out. After the fillet is cooked, the skin will come out by itself.
    I heat the heavy-bottom pan on high heat; off the fire add a little oil; when oil starts almost smoking, I add the fish (sprinkled with salt and pepper) and cook on high heat on flesh side, until it is golden brown, about 1-1/2 minutes. Turn it over, reduce the heat to low, cover half

way and cook skin side for about 4-6 minutes. The fish is moist and cooked, the skin comes off.

Cleaning and Shucking the Oysters

To clean: Soak the oysters and clams in about ½ cup of cornmeal, covered with cold water for about 15 minutes. Then wash each, rubbing with a brush, under running cold tap water. The dirt will come right off and they will be shiny and clean.

To Shuck the Oysters
Fold a clean cotton towel in few folds; hold the oyster with round side down, place the oyster the hinge side away from you, fold over and cover the oyster with the towel; pressing the oyster on the cutting board or holding in the hand (wrapped in the towel) insert the oyster knife into the hinge, then twist a little and try to loosen the top shell by twisting the knife and wiggling it a little to open the top shell. Now run the knife all around the top shell and disconnect the muscle, holding the meat. Hold the bottom shell still, remove the top shell and save the oyster liquor (juice) from spilling.

Shucking the Clams
1. Clean the clams as mentioned above.
2. Place the clam in a folded, clean cotton towel, facing the hinge inward the towel.
3. Place the sharp edge of the clam knife between the crack (groove) of two shells. Carefully press in, twist and push the point into the crack, and pry open the shells. You can also try the other side, the hinge side and push open the knife into the crack. Be careful and save the liquor.
4. The easiest way to open clams and oysters is to steams them in a little chicken broth or white wine, or the combination of both. Heat and bring the liquid to a boil, add the clams, cover, let the liquid simmer on low heat for 1-2 minutes, take out the clams, hold in the towel and pry open them.

Cut Up a Chicken in Standard Eight Pieces

Buy a whole chicken according to the use of the chicken pieces. If making a juicy chicken, the best one will be the roasting one, about 5 to 6 pounds. If you are going to fry the pieces, then buy the fryer one, about 4 pounds. In any way, cutting up a chicken into pieces depends upon practice. The first few times it will take longer, then you will be able to cut into 8 pieces within 3-4 minutes. I take my time and do slowly and carefully, making sure the knife doesn't slip. You can use a sharp chef's knife, a sharp utility knife or a sharp and small paring knife. The backbone is easier to cut with a pair of poultry shears. The secret of cutting a chicken into pieces is to cut the skin around the joint and snap it backward; you will hear the crack; then separate the pieces between two bones, cutting through the cartilage and mussels.

1. Use a kitchen counter and a glass cutting board and place the cutting board over paper towels to catch any running juices. Make sure the chicken is completely defrosted. Place the whole chicken on a cutting board and take out the neck and liver package from inside.
   To take off the leg, put the chicken on its back and cut the inside leg skin at the joint where it is attached to the body of the chicken. Then take off the clear thin membrane.

Turn the leg backward and pop the leg out of the socket (you will hear the cracking sound). Now cut between the two bones at the joint, separating the leg bones from the body.

2. To separate the drumstick from the leg, cut through the fat separating the thigh and the drumstick, right on the top of the drumstick. Then turn the drumstick backward to snap it from the thigh and cut between two bones to separate the thigh and the drumstick.

3. To separate the wings, put the chicken breast side down and cut the skin all around the wing joint at the body. Then snap the wing backward, pop the joint and cut through the cartilage to separate the wing from the body.
    Working with one wing at a time, separate the wings into pieces. Cut the skin at the middle joint between two parts of the wing, snap it backward and cut through the cartilage and mussels to separate the two large parts of the wings.
    You can cut off the tip and save for the soup or broth.

4. To take off the backbone, place the chicken breast side down. Starting from the tail end, using the poultry shears (the best and safest), cut the backbone along the ribs, from both sides, and take out the backbone. Then trim off the ribs from the breast and save for the soup or the broth.

5. To take out breasts, spread out the chicken in butterfly fashion, with the breast side up; using a paring knife, cut both sides of the breast bone to separate it from the flesh. Then bend the breast towards the back and separate it from the breastbone. Pull out the breastbone with the fingers of one hand, while separating and scraping off the meat with the knife from the other hand. Now you can separate and halve the breasts.
    Wash your hands and wash and pat dry the chicken pieces and place them in a clean platter for cooking, or refrigerate at once.
    Now, using paper towels, wipe clean the cutting board, knives, shears and any other dish that you may have used. Then using soap and running hot water, scrub clean everything including the kitchen counter and dry with paper towels.
    To avoid salmonella poisoning, do not touch anything while working with the chicken.

Lobster: How to boil and take out the meat

The key to buy a good lobster is the freshness and the size. A 1 to 1-1/2 pound lobster is the best. The bigger and heavier ones can be tougher. Also, it is believed that the hardest shell outside will have soft meat. The spring is the month when the shells are generally hardest. In summer, you will find a big supply of the lobster in the market and they are fresh as well. Try not to buy the frozen lobster and the one sitting in the tank for a long time. You can boil, steam, or grill the lobster. In any case, you have to prepare the lobster before you cook on heat.

Bring a large pot of water with some white vinegar (about 3 to 4 tbsp. of vinegar per lobster) to a boil.

Hit the lobster over the head with a hard object (like the handle of a chef's knife) to knock out the lobster and immediately plunge it in the water, head first; cover with the lid and hold down the lid for a few minutes and boil the lobster for about 6 to 7 minutes for a 1-pound lobster. If you are going to cook or reheat the lobster later on, then do the minimum cooking; just as the lobster changes the color, plunge it in an ice-water bath to stop the cooking right away. Reheat later on just before serving.

To take out the lobster meat before boiling, put a large glass or plastic cutting board on a thick layer of the newspapers, lined on the top with paper towels to absorb the liquid spilling out of the lobster. Use a large (about 10-inch) sharpened chef's knife to cut open the lobster in half. Insert the knife in the back of the head, at the indentation, and split the head in half between the two eyes, then turn around for easy handling and cut the lower part of the body in half. Remove the waste (the dark or green stomach and intestinal waste) the roe or coral, feathery lungs, the head sac from the head, etc.

Once the lobster is boiled, split it in half lengthwise. Put the lobster on the cutting board right side up. Cut the lobster in half between the two eyes, through the front body, the turn around for easy handling and cut through the rest of the body and the tail in half.

Now, turn over the lobster on the stomach side and crack open the underneath side lengthwise and take out the long and thin intestinal track near the tail; take out the roe or coral, the feathery lungs, head sac and any liquid found there.

For the tail, twist off the tail and separate from the body, cut open the tail shell with a pair of kitchen shears or just push the tail meat upward where it was attached to the body. Take out the tail meat in one piece. Remove the tough vein running through at the top of the tail. Refrigerate meat covered with plastic until needed, or serve as it is, or thick sliced like scallops.

For the claws, twist the knuckles and break off (or cut with the chef's knife) and remove the claws. Then put claws and all small pieces in a freezer plastic bag and crack open the meat with a hammer. Hit and crack the shells, but do not damage the meat. If needed, wiggle a sharp utility knife and loosen the meat. If the meat does not come out of the claws, then make a little cut at the top of the shell, push through or blow through the hole to release the meat and make it come out easily.

For the knuckles, the best way is to cut off the top joint that was attached to the body, then cut the shell along at the outside edge of the knuckle with kitchen shears; using the fingers of your both hands, open the shell and take out the meat.

Take out all the shells, discard, or save for the lobster or seafood broth to be made later on, and freeze them in plastic freezer bags.

Tip: If you are boiling lobster for a large crowed, you can do the same what some of the restaurants do: Boil the lobsters, cut them in half lengthwise, and serve warm on a large platter. If lobsters to be served buffet-style, then serve them on ice, in an attractive large bowl or platter.

How to Peel and Devein Shrimp

I try to buy the large (30-32 count) or jumbo shrimp (24-26 count). Most of the time, the jumbo shrimp have veins on the top and bottom, so take out both of them.

1. Keep shrimp refrigerated, in a bowl, over ice. Try to use them within a day or two of buying.
2. Hold one shrimp at a time. Take a small sharp knife (utility) and cut open the whole shell lengthwise, at the bottom by the feet. The shell near the tail is hard, so break it, with your fingers, all around the tail and leave the tail on. Take out the shell.
3. Now look for the black veins. It will look like a black thread going through the length of the shrimp near the legs, and also over the head. Leave about ½-inch near the head, on the top, and make a cut about 1-inch long, right over the black thread, push in the point of the knife, and lift up the thread like soft vein, then pull out the vein at the head and at the tail, from both sides. Press down the vein on a paper towel to discard. Do the same on the bottom. Sometimes you do not see the vein, but make a cut, push the point of the knife, and pull out

the vein if there is one. Some of the veins are clear (not black). Wash the shrimp under running cold water. Pat them dry before using.

4. To keep the shrimp from curling, make ¼-inch deep cuts in to the shrimp, at the 1/3 and 1/2 of the length across on the underside, near the head.

How to Carve a Turkey

After baking the turkey, let it rest on a cutting board, tented with aluminum foil for at least 15 to 20 minutes, so that the juices will go back to the meat .

The easier way to carve the turkey at the table is to take off left leg and the left wing from the body (if you are right-handed) and slice the left breast with an angle as thin as possible, and serve right at the table on serving platters.

If you want to carve the turkey in the kitchen and bring out the platter to the table, then take off both legs and wings. Then cut the breast lengthwise in half and then slice each portion across, and place in the platter in one piece. Follow this procedure:

To separate the Legs: Push down the thigh away from the body and cut off the skin between the leg and the breast. Put the tip of the knife at the thigh joint and, holding the leg away from the body with a large meat fork, cut down and separate the leg at the joint. You can turn backward and crack the joint to separate the leg, then carefully use the knife to separate it completely.
Now you can separate the drumstick from the thigh at the joint. First, cut the skin at the joint, turn backward and crack the joint, and then separate it into two pieces.
To separate the Wings: Use a large meat fork and pull away the wing from the breast, then make the cut at the joint where the wing is attached to the body, turn wing backward, make a crack and separate the wing with the knife from the body. Now separate the wing in to two parts but cutting down at the joint and cracking it backward.
To cut the Breast in to two pieces: Make a cut in the middle of the breast, right along the breast bone, lengthwise, separating the breast in to two. Holding one breast at a time with a large fork, use the knife with an angle and separate the breast from the rib cage. Now put the halved brCst on the cutting board and slice thin across first, then slide the knife at the length of the breast and, holding the meat with the other hand, carefully pick up the sliced breast and place it neatly on the serving platter. Do the same with the other breast.

How to cut Artichokes

How to Buy: Buy an artichoke that is fresh, has pretty green color, firm, heavy, leaves are compact and the stem is still thick and green. My favorite ones are the heavy, green globe artichokes. You can also buy baby artichokes that are fresh, heavy and have compact leaves. It depends which recipe you are going to use. For pickling or marinating, small ones are the best. For stuffing, the larger ones are the best.

How to Clean:

1. Have a large glass or porcelain bowl ready with half full with water. Add 2-3 tbsp. of lemon juice.

2. Take off the one or two outer layers of the hard leaves.

3. Cut the top off about 1/3 and take out the hard ends of the leaves. Peel the stem with potato peeler.

4. Cut the artichoke in half lengthwise and take out all the fuzzy fibers from the heart of the artichoke. Immediately rub the empty cavity of the heart with lemon all around and drop it in lemon water.

5. Now you can boil the artichokes in lemon water, just enough to cover, and turn the cut side down into the water. Bring to a boil, cover and simmer on low until they are soft.

6. You can pat dry with paper towels and drizzle with light vinaigrette (1 part vinegar and 3 parts olive oil); sprinkle with little salt and pepper and granulated garlic. Cover and let it marinate for couple of hours in the room temperature.

How to eat artichokes: If you don't want to marinate the artichokes, you can just boil, steam and grill the whole artichoke without peeling and cutting in half. After cooking the artichoke, just peel off the leaves of the outer layer and discard them. Then pull out one leaf at a time and dip the bottom, the soft part in a dipping sauce and suck the soft part. To get to the heart, just cut the artichoke in half and using a spoon, take out all the fuzzy parts and discard it, and eat the soft meat all around dipping in the sauce.

How to Chop Onion

Wearing glasses helps the eyes. Also, I rub 3-4 drops of vegetable oil into my hands and after cutting the onions, I rub the hands on the paper towel, and wash with soap. First find a place near the stove, and put the kitchen fan on. Dampen a kitchen towel, squeeze out all the water, place the cutting board over it. Place the onion on a clean cutting board and using a chef knife, cut it in half vertically. Take one piece of the onion at a time, and peel the onion skin, pushing the skin backward gathering the peel towards the root, for an easy grip. Place the onion cut side down on the cutting board.

Slice the Onion: Either thin-slice the onion in half circles or holding the onion root end, with the point of the knife, slice the onion lengthwise, then just cut it off the root end.

To Chop the Onion: Holding the onion at the root end, make about ½-inch wide long slices into the onion. Then just slice across ½-inch wide. To chop fine, just make cut ¼-inch-wide and make the pieces smaller.

To Mince the Onion: Holding the onion at the root end, make 2-3 horizontal slices (about ¼-inch wide) with the center part of the blade first. Then make ¼-inch-wide long slices with the point of the knife into the onion. Now starting at the tail part, thin-slice the onion across, and you will have minced onion pieces.

How to Cut the Hard and Tough Items

The hard squash such as winter squash (acorn), take off the stem completely. Then place it on the cutting board stem side down, and make a light cut on the top. Then using the heel of the knife, and inserting the knife into the cut, place one hand to hold the handle of the knife, and the palm of the other hand on the top of the knife (the dull side); slowly cut down, and split the squash into two vertically. Now scoop out the seeds with a teaspoon.

If you are going to stuff the acorn squash and bake it on an aluminum foil ring, then split it horizontally.

How to Measure Flour

For the Baking: If you are big on baking, then place the cup on a large piece of wax paper, place the strainer over it, scoop out the flour with the measuring cup, and sift the flour into the cup. You can also sift the flour onto the wax paper and just slide the flour into the cup, level it out with a knife, and pour it into a bowl. Do not shake the cup, it will settle in the bottom. Keep it fluffy.

If you just want to measure the flour, place the cup over a dinner plate, take out the flour from the bag with a large spoon and drop into the cup, then level it out with a knife, and carefully pour it in a work bowl, before it gets dense.

Do not dip a cup into the bag of flour, it will push in and will measure incorrectly.

How to Knead the Dough

Take the rings from your fingers, wash your hands with soap and dry them well. Have some extra flour to dust the surface and the hands as needed. Place the prepared dough ball on the work surface over the sprinkled flour.

Now using the heel of the hand, knead the dough by pressing the heel into the dough in the same direction, until the dough is stretched out a lot thinner than it was before. Fold the length of the dough, rotate the dough to a 90- degree angle, dusting the hands and the dough; again knead the dough and stretch it out again thinner than before. Do this a few times until the dough is smooth, pliable, and a little springy.

How to Prepare an Ice Water Bath

Use a large glass or porcelain bowl, fill halfway with tap water, then about 2 cups crunched ice or ice cubes. This bowl is now ready to cool off vegetables, lobster, etc. after partial cooking.

How to Blanche the Vegetables

Bring a large or a medium pot, half full of water, to a boil. Add a little salt (op) and plunge about 1 to 2 pounds of vegetables like green beans, asparagus, mustard greens, Brussels sprouts, broccoli, etc. into the boiling water. Using a spider or a slotted spoon, turn them around in the boiling water, boil 2-3 minutes, take them out and plunge in an ice-water bath to stop cooking.
These vegetables are partially cooked to retain their color and also to soften them a little. You can then sauté them in a pan with a little oil and fresh crushed garlic. Also, you can chop and add them in soup etc.

How to Roast Bell Peppers

2 red, yellow, orange or green bell peppers with stems attached; 1 tsp. canola oil.

In the Oven:

1. Preheat the broiler. Rub the peppers with the oil all over and place them in the broiler tray. Char-broil all sides, turning them over with tongs.
2. When the peppers are charred all over take them out, place them in a large bowl, cover with plastic wrap and then with the lid. Cool the peppers for about 30 minutes and peel off the charred skin; cut in half, take out the seeds. Then refrigerate and save with the juices until needed. If using same day, leave covered on the counter top. Add raw crushed clove of garlic and some olive oil and serve.

On the Stove top:

1. Rub peppers with the oil and place on stove, over medium heat. When the peppers are charred underneath, turn them around holding the stem, and keep on turning around until the pepper is completely charred. Then follow the step 2 above.

How to Peel Tomatoes

Prepare an ice-water bath. Bring a medium pot with half full of water, place on the medium-high heat and bring it to a boil. Using about 4 plum tomatoes, make an X on the skin on the bottom of each tomato. Plunge them in the water, boil for about 2 minutes. Take the tomatoes out of the water and plunge them in the ice-water bath to stop cooking, for 5 minutes. Take out, peel and use them in cooking.

How to Segment an Orange or Lemon

Wash and dry the orange, If you need the zest of the orange, take out the zest using the microplane zester first.

Use a sharp utility knife to trim off top and bottom of the orange, mostly taking off the zest and the white pith. Now let the orange stand on the cutting board (flat surface) and slice off the zest and the white pith together, following the shape of the orange or lemon, and expose the segments (do not cut into the segments).

Place a medium bowl underneath (to catch any juices and segments) and holding the orange above the bowl, cut off the each segment, between the membranes, and let it fall into the bowl. When the orange is segmented, squeeze out the mass of the membrane to get all the juices out. Now with a spoon, discard the seeds. Use segments whole or cut into small pieces as required in the recipe, and use the juice for the recipe or set aside for other use.

How to Clean Dinnerware, Pots and Pans

I think buying the right pan and cleaning them as you finish using them is the key, and is part of cooking. To clean the pots and pans, you need to know following:

Buy the right type of pan. Spend a little more money and it will pay off in the long run. Buy heavy-bottom pots and pans. Light pans burn fast, and food also is not tasty. Heavy pots and pans give even heat, and the food cooks slowly and tastes better.

The key to cleaning the metal is wash them right away after the use. If your pots and pan are burned, take out the burned food, scrape the pan with a metal spatula and then clean out the pan. But if it is stuck badly, then boil some water in it and keep on scraping with the metal spatula.

If the pot is still badly burned, then heat some water, add some lemon juice and then scrape out with the metal spatula. You can also heat the pan with a little water, throw out the water, sprinkle some scarring powder and scrape with a copper or aluminum-mesh scrubber.

Also, you can soak the pot in hot water and with some vinegar, cover and set aside for a few hours; scrub with metal scrubber and clean it out with the dish soap.

How to Clean Wood and Rubber Utensils

As mentioned before, wash them as you go. Don't let them pile up for later. If you are using a spoon, cutting board or spatula, etc., wash with plain water right after using. If the food is stuck, just scrape off with a knife and wash right away. Don't let it dry up. You can also drizzle some lemon juice and scrub clean, or use equal parts of baking soda, salt, a little water, and scrub clean, then wash well with the warm tap water.

How to Clean Dinnerware and Silverware

To hand-wash the dishes, first clean the sharp knives first, carefully, then crystal, glassware, smaller dishes, flatware, the large dishes, then pots and pans. Dry the dishes with a kitchen towel. Heat the pots and pans on low heat, dry them out with a towel, and put them away.

If you have fine china, right after the dinner, wipe clean all the food off the china with napkins, and discard the food right away. Wear rubber gloves, fill the sink halfway with the warm water, add 2-3 squirts of dish soap and using a soft sponge, clean the dishes and rinse under running warm water. If you have two sinks, fill one with soap and the other one with clean warm water. Then either rinse the plates under running water and set them aside to clean later. Or just go ahead and clean them by hand right away. We do not put fine china in the dishwasher. Many of our friends do the same because if anything is broken it is hard to replace. The same goes with the fine silverware. Dry with a kitchen towel and put them away. If you prefer, you can drip dry them on a large kitchen towel or dish dryer, and then dry them well with a kitchen towel, and put them away. If you are loading the dishwasher follow the manufacture instructions, and don't over-load. Use a good quality soap.

Utensils, Cooking Techniques & Oven Temperatures

I have to tell you that we were told not to use plastic containers, bowls etc., aluminum pots and pans, and copper pots and pans in cooking. They all discharge some bad chemicals that gets in the food. The best ones are stainless steel pots and pans, cast iron pans for bread, steak and hamburgers etc. Use glass and porcelain instead of plastic. Even some studies suggest not to use non-stick pans. If the non-stick pan is scratched throw it out right away.

You need various types of Kitchen utensils for various cooking. It all depends what type of cooking you are doing. For everyday's cooking you may need the basic items. But if you are baking, entertaining, giving parties, or catering you need more equipments to meet different types of need.

Knives

You can have a large collection of knives or a small one with a few important one. I mostly use three main ones: a large Chef's knife, Paring knife for most of my cutting, and a Serrated knife for bread and cakes etc. Keep your knives sharp so it does the job well as well as it does not slip and cause a mishap. No knife will keep a razor-edge for a long time. So keep your knives sharpened on a good electric knife sharpener, whetstone or sharpening steel. Use plain, carbon steel knives that are easy to sharpen. Wash them by hand (not in the dishwasher) right after you have finished using them and done with your work.

Paring knife: This is a small knife about 2-1/2 to 3- inches long and used for all small jobs like peeling, slicing etc.

Boning knife: This is a thin flexible, about 6-inches long knife that does the trimming of fat and removing the bones goes all around the bone easily.

Carving knife: This knife is good for slicing the roast meat. With the flexible blade you can thin slice the meat.

Chef's knife: You can buy 6, 8 or 10-inches long knife. I prefer the 10-inches one that does the job alright. It is a strong knife and does almost all the chopping, cutting, mincing etc. In other words you can get by only with one chef's knife.

Icing knife: This is a old fashioned knife to spread the icing on the cake. Now a days an offset spatula is used for the icing. To me this long and flexible blade knife is all purpose knife for the baking needs. I use for icing, folding and rolling the dough for cinnamon buns, and for spreading the nuts. When rolling out the pizza or pie dough I just side the knife underneath and loosen the dough if it is stuck on the surface.

Serrated knife: The serrated edge is good for slicing the bread. I use this knife for slicing the cake layers and then making the design over the icing of the cake.

Using the knife: Using the chef's knife you can: slice, julienne, chop, cube, dice or mince. When you cut onion lengthwise into thin slices it is slicing, in to matchstick cut is julienne, coarsely chopped (without any specific size) is chopped, and cutting into about one inch squares is cube. When you fine chop into smaller and same size pieces is dice and chop into very fine pieces is minced (like minced garlic). For soup or stews I chop the vegetables. For rice pilaf I thin slice the onion that gives more flavor then chopping.

A Citrus Reamer: This wooden tool to juice the citrus is handy in everyday cooking. If you juice a lot, you can also have a electric juicer, where you press down the half cut piece of the orange or lemon and the juice will collect in a cup or a glass.

Pots and Pans & Dutch Oven: I like to have heavy duty, All-Clad stainless steel or Hard-anodized pots and pans, one 12X2-inches, one medium size sauté pans, one large and one medium saucepan. Also a good quality, heavy bottom, unlined, and solid copper medium or large pan is good to have for melting sugar on a high temperature. I prefer, a large, an All-Clad, Stainless Steel, 8-Qt. Stockpot. This is where I make the meatball and transport them to the parties without spilling.

One 12-inches skillet Calphalon or All-Clad pan with one or two inches of sides. Also, you need one 12-inch Cast Iron skillet (keep well seasoned all the time). Indian bread – chapatti, roti or paratha require a cast iron skillet or Tawa. I prefer at least an inch of sloping sides that catches any dry flour from the rolled out dough.

Dutch Oven are good for making stews, braising and meat curries etc. We like Le Creuset , 7-1/4-Qt., Round French Oven with a tight-fitting lid.

You will also need a Wire-mesh Skimmer with wooden handle to scoop out the food from the hot liquid or oil.

If you can afford , it's good to have various sizes pots and pans. Heavy bottom skillet conduct heat evenly and stay hot longer. First heat the pan on medium heat till hot and then before cooking add the oil, move around to coat the bottom when pan is hot enough, proceed with cooking or turn off the heat and let it rest a few minutes and heat it again whenever you are ready to do the cooking. Remember, the pan has to be heated first before you add the oil or butter for cooking.

Omelet Pan: You need a nonstick, either 8-inches or 12-inches pan for eggs. The best one is Calphalon or All-Clad. Omelet need to cook in a nonstick pan so they slide out easily without burning.

Roasting Pan: A roasting pan should be large enough to accommodate the large piece of meat like Turkey and also heavy enough to use on the top of the stove to make gravy. I have a large stainless steel one with a V shape roasting rack and I also use another roasting rack that fits perfect in the pan. It is not necessary to buy a roasting pan with a lid. I do have a lid but hardly use it. Just wrap the pan with a heavy duty aluminum foil and cover the meat well. Also, I line the bottom of the pan with foil for easy cleaning.

Saucepan: You can use several saucepans with all different sizes. In the small one you can whip up the sauces quickly, medium one are all purpose and the large ones are good for braising and stocks. I prefer All-clad and good stainless steel one. Try to buy with curved bottoms so that the food will not deposit on the edges. Some new mixed metal pans called Alloy are available.

Wok: In Indian and Chinese cooking a wok is a very important pan. It serves the purpose of a pan and a pot. Due to its shape it is easy to stir the food, deep fry and cook the food. You just have to get used to it. Buy a heavy bottom wok, made of good Iron which helps to cook the food evenly without burning in the bottom. I cook Gulab-Jamun (Indian Dessert-milk balls) in it as by moving the handle in a circular motion the balls roll over in all direction by themselves, no need to turn them over. But cooking with the citrus you need to use a stainless-steel pan.

For the Baking

Baking Sheets: Heavy duty non-stick or stainless steel are the best. More you have better you are and have various sizes. Remember to use parchment paper all the time and double parchment paper for cookies. For baking vegetable use aluminum foil and then parchment on top to conduct the heat well and also protect it from burning.

Cake and Pie pans: I prefer non-stick 9-inch cake pan. To make a layer cake buy two or three separate pans of even size or just buy one pan with at least 3-inches sides and removable bottom and after baking just slice the cake in desired layers. This way each layer will be soft and even sizes. You will need to reduce the baking temp. from 350 F to 325 F. The dark color pan makes cake a little darker and light color the stainless steel one make a lighter cake. In any case grease the pan, line with parchment, grease the paper and then sprinkle with the flour, shake the pan and tap out the excess flour. The best ones are non-stick cake pans of different sizes according to your baking needs. I prefer three different sizes of cake pans to make a tier cake. These cake pans also come handy in making tiered rice pilaf with different flavors for a large gathering. If you use various metal moulds try to buy them in stainless steel or non-stick metal. Parchment paper for baking is very important.

Marble Slab: These are a must for making sugar candies and rolling out the chilled dough for pastries etc.

Springform Pan: You need these pans to make cheese cake, Ice cream cake and even for strawberry short cake. The nonstick one are the best.

Cake Rack: I prefer separate racks for each cake. Take the cake out of the oven and let it rest in the pan for about five minutes. Spray the rack with nonstick spray, turn over the cake onto a dinner plate, peel off the parchment paper and turn over the cake onto the cake rack right side up, cool cake completely before icing.

Casseroles Dishes: For all your left over or to make from scratch casseroles, you need one medium and one large casserole dishes. The Indian recipe for baked Keema (the baked spicy beef) needs a good size of casserole pan either with a lid or a heavy duty aluminum foil.

Loaf Pan: A nonstick large loaf pan about 9-1/2X5-1/2X2-1/2-inch pan, can be an all purpose for bread, meatloaf, making layered salmon spread, pound cake and even making an stuffed omelet. Even though it is nonstick but line it with the parchment paper overhanging on two side to use as handles.

Muffin Tin: The nonstick one are the best for muffins and cup cakes, line them with the paper cups, spray with nonstick spray before baking cup cakes for easy removal.

Pie Plate: I prefer the deep-dish pie plate and the glass one. You can always use the Tart pan for easy removal of the crust.

Souffle Dish: I use this dish for soufflé, gelatin mold, and doing small baking like custard for the fruit. You need one 1-1/2-quart size dish for most of the baking. The individual ramekin cups can be used for individual servings.

For the Grilling

Buy an indoor or a large outdoor grill, according to your grilling needs. Unless you have a gas grill, you will need a Chimney to start the fire. You will also need a wire brush to clean the grill, a long handle tong, and a long handle spatula and a pan to place the wet wooden chips for smoking.

Essential Kitchen Tools

Cutting Board: You can use a fiberglass, about 12-inch for daily use or a large wooden one about 20X 15-inches. For rolling out the dough you need to use a large and a clean and dry surface wooden board. Wash you cutting board each time you use for meat, fish or poultry with the soap and hot running water and keep your board clean all the time after you finish chopping and cutting. Use a one part vinegar and three part water solution to scrub clean the board and then rinse out well under running hot water.

Colander, Sieve and Strainer: I prefer a large colander for pasta, straining the stock, washing the fresh vegetables etc. For salad I wash the green in two or three changes of water in a large bowls filled with water and then let it dry in the colander and later one I just spread out on the cotton kitchen towels (unless you have a salad spinner) This is way I clean my herbs, if I am going to make Chutney and stuff the Paratha (bread). You need two different sieves or strainers one fine mesh and the other one with large mesh wire of holes to do various jobs.

Kitchen Scale: For more accurate and precise measurements you need a scale. Try to use same measurements cups, grams or ounces, so you get used to it. I just prefer Tablespoons and cups, the easiest way we all are taught.

Mandolin or Vegetable Slicer, Box graters, & Microplane zesters: You can never beat a old fashion mandolin or a V-slicer. I use mine very often to make paper thin chips with potato, sweet potatoes, parsinips etc. The vegetable peeler should be sharp, fast and smooth to get the job done easily without clogging up the peels. The box graters are good to grate onion, soaked nuts and cheeses. The Microplane zesters do wonderful job with zests. I prefer the tangerine zest with cheese so as soon as I see tangerins in the market I buy them and zest along as I serve or eat them. The citrus rinds zested, wrapped in plastic wrap then frozen in a container lasts almost four months.   So, my microplane zester works for me all year round even for garnishing with the chocolate & ginger as well.

Peeler: Whether you use a fixed blade or swivel peeler depends on your choice. The swivel blade does the job better and quicker. But for garnish and decorations you peel the vegetable first and use a fixed blade peeler to thin slice the cucumber, and fruits etc.

Shellfish Suchkers: You need heavy duty work gloves and an Oyster or clam knife to open the shell. Some people just use the squat screwdriver, the stubby end of the screwdriver does the job well. It all takes practice, once you get used to opening the shells you get expert in opening.

Spatulas: I prefer a large stainless-steel spatula for all sorts of cooking. A heat resistant rubber spatula for baking etc. and a wooden one for nonstick pots and pan and also mixing the batter etc. The wooden spoon and spatula both should be very sturdy for baking and cooking both.

Steamer: You necessarily need not to buy a commercial steamer. You can stem the vegetable etc. in a wok or a large pot using a rack and cover the lid. Just make sure the water does not touch the food. I prefer the collapsible stainless basket that you can use in a large pot or use a stackable steamer.

Thermometer: There are a few thermometers you can use in cooking. An instant-read digital thermometer is the best to check doneness of roast, baked etc. A deep –frying thermometer is good for deep frying. It can be clipped on the pot to give you constant oil temperature while you are frying. A sugar thermometer which is marked with different stages of syrup making is also important to have on hand if you like making candies.

Timer: Timer is important if you do a lot of baking and cooking. Buy a good one a three-way timer, like West Bend that shows three different timings. I prefer my big kitchen clock with large numbers, facing the living room, that I can see without getting up right from the living room.

Tong: This is multi-purpose tool. I use for serving salad, turning over the meat on the grill, and a flexible Indian Tong (Chimta) with two long blades for the bread when working with the open fire.

Wire Whisk: This is something you need to buy the right one: a flexible, medium size. Most of the work is done by electric mixers, you just need to whip up few things.

Miscellaneous Items: I prefer cotton kitchen towels and one clean white one to use over the dough and pastries and making Paneer (cheese). If you are going to use a cheese cloth make sure you use atleast double layer to do the job right. Mortar and Pestle for crushing the herbs and spices. Kitchen scissors, rolling pins, wooden ruler for measuring rolled out dough for pasties and cinnamon buns, cotton string for trussing chicken, roast beef etc., a ladle for stews and soups, aluminum foil, wax paper, parchment paper, tooth pick, wooden and metal skewers, a food mill is good for mash potato etc, a double boiler if you really need one, otherwise you can melt chocolate etc. in a bowl over a hot water in a pot , just make sure bowl does not touch the water, an ice cream maker if you like to make your own ice cream, a pasta machine, pizza cutter and pizza stone, squeeze bottles for sauces, candy and meat thermometers etc. Baking sheet with rims and Wire Racks are very important for baking, broiling, and roasting. I prefer a heavy duty sheet pan : Wear-Ever Half Size Sheet Pan by Vollrath. You also need a Wire Rack or a Cooling Rack, we prefer CIA Bakeware 12 X 17 wire rack.

Electric Appliances

Electric Deep Fryer: You can always use a wok or large wide pot for deep frying. You can also buy an electric deep fryer they have built- in temperature that comes very handy to keep an even temperature while frying.

Coffee Grinder: This is very essential with Indian cooking. We grind fresh spices almost every day. Keep a coffee grinder for grinding coffee separate and keep one for grinding the spices. This way you do not have to taste spices in the coffee.

Electric Griddle: This is like indoor grill. I use this for making large Dosa and a large amount of Pan cakes when we have company. Dosa (Indian large pancakes, bean crusted and stuffed) are very healthy and very easy to make once you have prepared the batter. I prefer Vitantonio model with even cooking that covers the whole Dosa.

Blender: A good blender does all the work for you. I like blenders to make smoothies and other drinks.

Food Processor: A heavy duty food processor does the good job. It is good for chopping, pureeing, and mixing the dough etc. I prefer Cuisinart Custom, with 14 cups capacity.

Standing Mixer: If you do a lot of baking you should have one good stand mixer. A six-quart bowl serves all purpose. The KitchenAid also comes with grinding attachment. A mixer should have a whisk, paddle and a dough hook. Dough hook is very important if you make breads.

Waffle Iron: Any Waffle Iron will do the job. If you use on a regular basis buy a good one and read the instruction well before using it.

In short, more equipment you have better you are if you do a lot of cooking, baking on a regular basis. I remember when I came from India, I had only one suitcase, when I moved in to an apartment I had only one set of pot and pan, when I bought the first house I still had one or two knives and 3or 4 pot and pan, and now when I started cooking and baking a lot I have a large cabinet full of utensils but I still think I need a lot more and can use a lot more if only I can afford them and find a large space to store them.

Panini or Sandwich Maker: These electrical appliances can be luxury unless you are making a lot of Panini or sandwiches everyday and on regular basis. I just use my cast iron griddle pan to make sandwiches.

To Transport the Food

You will need coolers and boxes to keep the cold food cold and the hot food hot. A small cooler is handy in the car when shopping for the seafood. A large cooler with ice comes handy for the drinks.

Cooking Techniques

Cooking is all about using heat in one way or the other. You can cook on gas, charcoal, wood or electric. All are slightly different. Gas, you can have more control of the temperature. Electric it takes a little longer to heat and a little longer to bring the temperature down. To grill food on charcoal, first you have to prepare fire and then grill the food directly or indirectly. You get some kind of sense about using the stove or grill after using them a few times.

Following are the cooking techniques. You can use more than one technique for one dish at one time depending on the recipe.

Baking:

Baking is done mostly in the oven with a controlled temperature, mostly low, for items like bread, cake, pastry, etc. You can also use a handmade oven (old-fashioned) where ladies used to burn wood inside, make coal, and bake breads. Tandoor ovens (clay) for cooking naan (bread) are still in use. Now-a-days with the control of the knob, everything is easy and neat. Baking is done mostly with the items that have moisture or liquid, so when it is baked, the steam helps cook, raise and brown the item.

Boiling:

This basic method is very easy. You either heat or use cold water to start cooking. It is used mostly for dried items like beans, rice, etc. and to make stocks and broths with bones and vegetables. From a health point of view, just plain boiled food (mostly vegetables) can lose some important vitamins and minerals. If you have to use this method, use a little water as possible and open the pot and let the water evaporate (like for mashed potatoes), or after boiling, sauté the food in a little butter and then season it.

You can also par-boil food like french fries, then cook them in the oven or deep-fry in the oil to finish the cooking.

You can also poach the food, which is also cooking slow in liquid. You can poach the food in flavored juices and liquid, and then serve both food and poaching liquid. Fish are the great example of poaching. If you do not have a poaching pa,n use a regular large sauté pan.

Broiling:

This is almost inside grilling. I love this method because with a turn of the knob, you have your grill ready. The only thing you have to do cook food in the broiler tray, about 5 to 6 inches away from the heat source, cooking under the fire instead over the fire. Just turn over the food and cook both sides. I broil my bread, like Naan and Chapati, as well as broil meat like London Broil, Tandoor Chicken, fish and jerk meat.

Braising:

This is mostly cooking on low heat in liquid. You can sauté the food first, or just braise directly in the seasoned liquid. Braising the vegetables, mostly leafy ones, gives a moist result. Braising is also good for the tough piece of meat or, for that matter, you can braise or simmer a lot of things. I make chicken tikka in curry sauce and cook meat first either by roasting or braising it in a small amount of apple juice. The meat cooks perfect and is ready to add to the heated curry sauce.

Frying:

Frying can be deep-frying in oil, stir-frying in a pan with a little amount of oil, or butter and turning over the vegetables constantly with the spatula. You can shallow-fry the food in a small amount of oil. If possible, serve all fried food either with yogurt raita (salad), or with yogurt chutney - it is healthy, tasty and cuts down on oily effect.

Deep-frying is cooking in the large amount of oil, usually 2-3 inches deep, in an electric fryer or a deep and heavy-bottom saucepan, or in a wok, which cooks and browns fast. To deep-fry, heat oil to around 350F, 180C, or Gas Mark 4; drop a piece of the bread. If the bread starts sizzling and gets brown, the oil is read to deep-fry. Do not crowd the pan; cook in batches for perfect cooking and browning.

The fried food may be tastier, but it has extra oil, which you do not want to do too often. Although certain foods like fried chicken, fries, fish and chips and doughnuts are traditionally cooked this way. You can help better the process to a certain extent by using good cooking oil that is not too heavy, like canola or grape seed. Cook on high temperature around 375F; use clean oil and after cooking, take out fried food on a paper towel and immediately press down and soak up extra oil on the top with another paper towel. The fast-food restaurant are famous for fried foods. Indian fried food like samosa and pakoras are very addictive with tasty chutneys. After deep-frying, cool the oil a little, and line a large strainer with a double layer of the paper towels, and strain the oil in to a large bowl or large glass bottle. Place the bottle in a large bowl, leave it open until cools completely, then put away the oil for the next use.

Grilling:

Grilling is very common in the outdoor in the summer, although you can grill indoors all year-round in indoor grills. But there is nothing better than cooking outdoors in the open air, in good weather, with family and friends. Grilling is done on open flame, whether on gas, electric, charcoal or wood. When buying the grill, buy the one that is convenient for your cooking. Buy one with a lid on so that you can smoke as well as cook slow and long. You can cook on hot grill directly on the fire, or on indirect heat away from the flames, covered or uncovered. Thin pieces of meat can cook on direct heat, like fish, chicken breast, etc., but thick pieces of meat should be cooked on indirect heat to cook it all the way through. You can butterfly meat like chicken and, after marinating the meat, cook in the pan or directly on the fire with a weight on the top; when meat browns underneath turn it over and cook on the other side. For grilling you should marinate the meat first for a couple of hours or overnight; bring to room temperature, grill and then at the end pour some sauce or marinade; let it wait about 5 minutes cut and serve.

You can grill almost anything: meat, vegetable, fruits, even desserts.

Roasting:

Roasting is done in the oven in a roasting pan. Temperatures are mostly high, but vary depending on the meat. You start high to seal the juices, and then you lower the temperature to cook even and cook through. At the end, you can lower the temperature if the meat is cooking too fast. I usually start with around 400F for about 15 minutes in a preheated oven, then lower the temperature to either 350 or 375F It usually 15 minutes per pound to roast meat, but follow the recipes for the exact temperatures.

Sauteing:

This is like stir fry. Sauteing is a main technique in Indian cooking. We always sauté in hot oil, clarified butter and spices (almost all vegetables and meat) that develop a special flavor, seals the juices and gives a special taste. For this type of cooking also, I prefer the wok, because of its sloping sides, the vegetables cook evenly. First, you heat a wok or a pan with sloping sides well, then add the oil and heat to smoking. Either add the vegetables right away or add the whole spices; first when they are light brown and start giving aroma, then add the vegetables and start turning them over quickly on medium to medium-high heat, and cook briefly a few minutes (about 5 to 10); add spices or pastes and sauté first until fragrant and then sprinkle 2 to 3 tbsp. of water or broth; cover and simmer on low heat until done. This method does not take too much water because first you stir-fry the vegetables so they are almost half-cooked; then by sprinkling the water and covering it, the vegetables will cook in the steam. All nutrients and flavor will stay in the vegetables.

Searing: Searing is browning the surface of the meat (mostly before roasting or simmering) until it is caramelized. This way, meat cooks fast and stays intact.

Stir-fry:

This method will retain the nutrients as well as cook vegetables quickly. You first cut the vegetables medium to fine. Heat a wok or a heavy-bottom skillet or a cast iron pan; when hot add some oil (1 or 2 tbsp.) and quickly start stirring the vegetables until they are soft, but still crunchy. I prefer to use a wok. Its round shape helps vegetables cook faster. If cooking roots vegetables then cover with the lid for 5 minutes more, lower the temperature and they should be done.

Steaming:

Steaming is the healthiest way of cooking food. You can use a commercial steamer. I prefer the pressure cooker. But you can use a collapsible metal steaming rack or insert and steam almost in any pot or pan you like. Pressure cooking is the fastest way to steam and cook items. Steaming is a moist but dry-cooking method. You fill a pot with about 2-3 inches of water, depending on the amount and type of food, then put food on a steaming rack and cook covered until food is done. You can steam fish, vegetables, custard, etc. Most of the time, I steam my chicken with bones, and steam cauliflower before deep-frying with batter in oil, to cut down on frying time and fat absorption. If you prefer, you can first steam and then sauté vegetables briefly in butter for more flavor.

Whatever method you choose, make sure you are comfortable with it and try to handle the food carefully around fire. If in doubt, use two burners, one for low cooking and one for high-heat cooking and alternate to low and high cooking as needed.

Blanching and Shocking: Most of the greens and some soft vegetables like carrots, zucchini, asparagus, broccoli, Brussels sprouts are blanched and shocked to keep their bright colors and crispness. Boil enough water with some salt to submerge the vegetables, add the cleaned vegetables, turn over to cook well for about 2-3 minutes, soft but still crunchy. Then with a tong, take out the vegetables and shock them in an ice bath (a bowl filled with water and a lot of ice) to cool and stop the cooking right away. Turn them over, cool, and take out on a platter, pat dry and sauté fast (about 1-2 minutes, just to dry the water and give some flavor) in a little oil; add salt and pepper and little granulated garlic, and serve right away.

Tandoor (cooking on open fire or under the flames)

Tandoori cooking: A special Tandoor oven is used. Also, the meat is soaked overnight or for a few hours, in special spices called Tandoor Masala. You can go all the way with the Tandoori cooking, or just use Tandoor spices and grill, braise, sauté, or roast the meat.

You can also make breads (Roti) in the Tandoor oven. Use yogurt in the dough or on outside of the rolled-out bread with some spices. Place the bread on a cushioned pad and slap the bread inside the moderately-heated oven. It will stick on the side of the oven, on the wall. The bread will puff up, cook on both sides, and as soon as it has some brown specks and is done, you take it out by poking a long metal bar or with a long Tong (Chimta). Serve hot bread with juicy meat or vegetables.

Oven Temperatures

There are different types of ovens that use different temperatures.

275F, 140C, Gas Mark 1

300F, 150C, Gas Mark 2

350F, 180C, Gas Mark 4

400F, 200C, Gas Mark 6

425F, 220C, Gas Mark 7

Safe minimum internal temperatures recommended by the USDA

Chicken Breasts: 165 F

Cooking with Eggs: 160 F

Ground Beef: 160 F

Fish: 145 F

Roasts and Steaks: 145 F

Whole Poultry: 165 F

The Restaurant Chef's internal cooking temperatures

Chicken: Light meat: 160 F, Dark Meat: 165 F

Beef: Rare, between 120 to 125 F

 Medium-Rare, between 125 to 130 F

 Medium, between 130 to 135 F

Lamb: Rare, between 128 to 130 F

 Medium-Rare, between 130 to 135 F

 Medium, between 135 to 140 F

Pork: Medium-Rare, between 145 to 150 F

 Medium, between 150 to 155 F

Various Food Measurements

Some of these measurements are approximate. Actual measurements depend on the types and varieties of food used.

Food	Volume	Weight: US	Metric Weight
All P. Flour:	1 c	5 ounces	142 grams
Whole-Wheat Flour:	1c	51/2 oz	156 g
Apple: 1Medium,	1Cup sliced,	4.2 oz	119 g
Apple Sauce:	1Bottle,5C,	3lb,2oz,	1.42kg.
Asparagus:	1 Bunch,2C,	9.5oz,	269g
Baking Powder:	1Tsp.,	.15oz,	4g
Baking Soda:	1Tsp.,	.18oz,	5g
Beans:	1c DRY,	6.5oz,	184g
(Pinto,Lima,Chickpeas)			
Brown Sugar:	1 c	7 oz	198 g
Chickpeas:	1Can,4c,	1lb,13oz,	822g
Bell Pepper,Med.	1c chop,	5.2oz,	147g
Bread crumbs,fresh: 1c,		3.5oz,	100g
Broccoli florets:	1c,	2.5oz,	71g
Broth fat free:	1-3/4c,	14-1/2oz,	411g
Butter:	1stick,8Tbsp.(1/2c),	4oz,	113g
Carrot:	1c chopped,	5oz,	142g
Celery:	1/2c chop,	2oz,	57g
Cheese hard:	1c grated,	3.75oz,	106g
Chocolate chips:	1c,	5.5oz,	156g

Food	Volume	Weight: US	Metric Weight
Cocoa Powder:	1 c	3 oz	85 g
Coconut fresh:	1c,	2.75-3 oz,	78-85 g
Confectioners' Sugar:	1 c	4 oz	130 g
Corn kernels:	1c,	5.75oz,	163g
Cornstarch:	1Tbsp.,	.3oz,	8.5g
Garlic:	1Tsp.diced	.125oz,	3g
Granulated Sugar:	1 c	7 oz	198 g
Giardiniera (Pickle Veg)2C		32 Fl.Oz.	946ML
Ham:	1c diced,	4oz,	113g
Herbs fresh:	1Tbsp.minced	.115oz,	3g
Honey:	1Tbsp.,	.75oz,	21g
Jalapeno:	1Tbsp.diced,	.30oz,	9g
Kale:	1c chopped,	2.5oz,	71g
Lemon juice:	3Tbsp.,	1.5oz,	43g
Lentils green:	1c dry,	6oz,	170g
Milk condensed sweetened:1c,		14oz,	396g
Mushroom (Button):	3-1/2c chop,	8oz,	227g
Mustard prepared: 1Tbsp.,		.5oz,	15g
Nuts:	1c chop,	4oz,	113g
Onion:	1c minced,	4oz,	113g
Orange 1medium:	1/2c juiced,	4oz,	113g
Pepper, ground:	1Tsp.,	.07oz,	2g
Potato, Red,1 medium: 1/2c chop fine,		2oz,	57g
Raisins, Cranberries dry: 1c,		6oz,	170g

Food	Volume	Weight: US	Metric Weight
Rice Pancakes	1Pkg.	4.7oz.	134G
Salad greens:	1c chop,	2.5oz,	71g
Salt, table:	1Tsp.,	.25oz,	7g
Spices, ground:	1Tsp.,	.07oz,	2g
Sugar (white):	1c	7 oz	198 g
Sugar (brown):	1c	7 oz	198 g
Sugar (confectioners):	1c	4 oz	113 g
Tomato:	1c chop,	5.75oz,	163g
Water Chestnuts:	3/4C sliced	8oz.	227G
Yeast, dry:	2-1/4Tsp.,	1/4oz,	7g
Zucchini:	1c minced,	4oz,	113g

Conversion Charts

For Oven Temperatures

Fahrenheit	Celsius	Gas Mark	Description
250	120	½	very slow oven
275	140	1	very slow oven
300	150	2	slow oven
325	160	3	slow oven
350	180	4	moderate oven
375	190	5	moderate hot oven
400	200	6	hot oven
425	220	7	hot oven
450	230	8	very hot oven
475	240	9	very hot oven
500	250	10	extremely hot oven

To convert temperature from Fahrenheit to Celsius:

Subtract 32, then divide by 9 and finally multiply by 5, and get the Celsius.

From Celsius to Fahrenheit:

Reverse: divide by 9, multiply by 5 and add 32, to get the Fahrenheit.

Liquid Measures

1cup = 240ml =8 fl. Oz. 1 fl. Oz. = exactly 29.57 milliliters.

US Standard	UK Imperial	Fluid Oz.	Metric Rounded
1 Tsp.	1 Tsp.	5 ml	
1 Tbsp.	1 Tbsp.	½ fl oz 15 ml	
¼ cup	4 Tbsp	2 fl oz 60 ml	
½ cup	8 Tbsp	4 fl oz 120 ml	
¾ cup	12 Tbsp	6 fl oz 180 ml	
1 cup	½ pint	8 fl oz 240 ml	
1-1/2 cup	¾ pint	12 fl oz 360 ml	

2 cups	1 pint	16 fl oz 480 ml
1 Qt	2 pints	32 fl oz 950 ml (1Liter)
1 Gallon	4 Qts.	128 fl oz	3.75 Liter

Weight Conversions

US Standard	Imperial Pounds	Metric Rounded
½ oz		15 grams
1 oz		30 grams
2 oz		55 grams
4 oz	¼	115 grams
8 oz	½	225 grams
1 lb (16 oz)	1	450 grams
2 lb (32 oz)	2	1 kg
5 lb (80 oz)	5	2.25 kg
10 lb	10	4.5 kg.

Glossary

Al dente: To cook mostly pasta (or some vegetables) until it is cooked tender and is still firm. It should not get mushy at all.

Amchoor: One of the Indian spices. Mango Powder that is made with green, dried mango. It has very powerful sour taste. You can use fresh green mangoes whole or sliced instead of grinding into powder.

Anchovies: These tiny fish fillets can be used on pizza, in sauce, in paste etc. They store well in refrigerator. .

Annatto Seeds: These are mostly used in Latin cooking for color. In India we used turmeric, a powerful antioxidant that gives yellow color in food. You can make annatto oil just before cooking by using 2 tabsp. of seeds and ½ cup of canola oil on medium high heat to start for 1 minute, then on low heat for about 10 to 15 minutes, until it is deep orange color. Use this on rice and other dishes.

Arrowroot: Is a white color root powder like corn starch and is used in thickening the liquid. It helps to digest the food. Store is in an airtight container.

Atta (White Whole Wheat Flour): In India Bread, or Roti, or Chapati is made daily (mostly in Northern part) and the flour is used is called Atta. It is made with white wheat berries, using the whole wheat so it is healthier as it contains inside and outside of the whole wheat berry; nothing is taken out. It looks good and the bread comes out tasty when the Roti is cooked in the pan first then on the open flames over the stove. This is the same flour used for Poori – deep-fried bread and Paratha – shallow-fried bread. Available at Indian grocery stores or you can order on line.

Barbecue: This is one of the cooking methods; usually you rub the food with spices, and grill the food over charcoal, wood or gas, and then brush with the sauce at the end.

Baste: When you pour liquid, fat, butter or juices over the food while it is cooking, to moisten the food.

Batter: This is a thin mixture of liquid and flour. It is poured and made into dishes such as pancakes, cakes, fritters, etc.

Bisque: This is a thick or creamy soup made with vegetables, crustaceans and finished with the butter.

Blanche: You first bring the water to a boil and plunge the vegetables into the boiling water to soften or to wilt them lightly, about 1 to 3 minutes, and then take them out of the boiling water and submerge them in an ice-water bath, or just simply run the cold water over them. Ice water bath: fill a large bowl with halfway with cold tap water, add some ice cubes. The ice water stops the vegetable from cooking further by bring down their temperature. This is also used to keep the vegetable in dark-green color and in some cases to remove the too-strong taste such as for cabbage, etc.

Bouquet Garini: A bundle of herbs and spices used in cooking. Usually they are tied together in a cheese cloth, such as parsley, cilantro, thyme, bay leaves and ginger. I also include the chopped leaves of celery for digestive purpose. You can use your own flavoring spices and herbs according to the dish.

Braise: First you brown the food in fat/butter and then you cook in a covered pot in liquid. The food gets soft and stays juicy.

Brine: This is a seasoned salt-water curing or marinating of the food. Usually turkey and the chicken are brined first, and then roasted or deep-fried.

Broth: This is liquid made with vegetables, meat, spices and herbs, and simmered for long time, so that turns into an aromatic liquid or gel. Then it is used in soups, stews, and even braising and boiling the food. Now-a-days, you can buy low-sodium broth that is more suitable for various cooking, and is healthy as well.

Bulgur: This is the cracked wheat can be found dried, cracked and steamed. I buy medium or fine. Usually you can use equal amount, i.e. 1 cup bulghur add to 1 cup boiled water, add seasoning, cover, let it soak about 25 minutes, then fluff with fork and serve warm.

Butterfly: Just like a butterfly, you cut open usually seafood or meat, almost like a book. Then you rub the spices or marinades and cook. If the item is large and thick, such as the leg of lamb or the whole chicken, you press it down with a weight for even cooking.

Caramel: Caramel is made with sugar and heavy cream mostly. Try to make it in sunny and dry weather. Sugar will absorb water in rainy and humid weather, and will get sticky.

Caviar: These are fish eggs used for garnish and gourmet cooking, often served cold. They come from female sturgeon, mostly from Beluga, Ossetra and Sevruga, and in black and brown colors. The tuna caviar are a pretty orange color. Use a plastic knife to take them out of the cans or jars; store in refrigerator and use them within 10 days.

Ceviche: Marinating uncooked seafood into citrus juice, mostly limes and lemon juices. This depends on the type of seafood; it may take from a few minutes to several hours. The seafood is then mixed with fresh or dry herbs and spices. Some of the seafood can be precooked until tender and then added to the mix.

Chapati (Bread) Flour: Chapati is Roti and flour is Atta (in India) Chapati is a fresh-made daily bread. Chapati flour is hard wheat and can be made in white or brown depending on the color of wheat used. Since bread is in the daily diet in most of India, a majority of people buy their own wheat berries, clean and wash them, and then take them to flour mills to be grinded. This way you get fresh and pure wheat flour as well as you save a lot of money.

Chorizo: Spanish and Mexican, spicy, cured pork sausages; can be sweet or hot. Whether chopped, sliced, sautéed or browned, they give good flavor to the food they are used in. Their shelf life is longer than regular pork sausages.

Chutney: Chutney are the mixture of mostly fresh spices, herbs, lemon, lime, yogurt, vinegar and vegetables, served mostly with fritters, pakoras, curries, rice and breads. It can be cooked or uncooked depending on the ingredients used. You can also buy at the Indian grocery stores and supermarkets.

Cocoa powder: This dry dark-brown powder is made from chocolate liquor. You do not need chocolate in recipes, the powder works just as well when mixed with hot water or coffee; and for a more chocolaty flavor; whisk in some butter and a little powdered sugar. Mostly Dutch-processed cocoa powder gives a smooth and complex flavor. I prefer to use part cocoa powder and part semi-sweet chocolate, the combination comes out better. If you want a strong flavor of chocolate, then just add a teaspoon of instant coffee or espresso powder.

Consommé: A purified and aromatic broth strained of all impurities.

Cornstarch: This is the starch extracted from dry corn, and is used mostly as a thickener.

Cream of Tartar: This white powdery substance is an acid. Mostly used in whipping egg whites and baked goods. You should store in airtight bottle, in a cool place for a long time. You can also use 1 tablespoon vinegar for ½ teaspoon of cream of tartar.

Crostini: Toasts made with olive oil and Italian bread or topped with herbs, greens and beans etc. can be used with dips and open sandwiches, with soup and stews, etc.

Cruciferous Vegetables: These vegetable are in the cabbage family and include broccoli, cabbage, cauliflower and Brussels sprouts. They are antioxidant-rich and keep cancer away. They have calcium and are loaded with vitamin C.

Curry Powder: Curry powder is the blend of spices: Turmeric, Coriander, Cumin, Cayenne and/or Black peppercorns, Cardamom, Cinnamon, Cloves, Fennel seeds, Fegugreek seeds, and sometimes some of the ingredient of garam masala are added. You can make raw powder, or roast the spices first and then grind them. The word Curry is mostly known mainly in other countries. In India, Curry Powder or Curry are not very common. It is mostly called Masala, which is a blend of spices. The blend of spices can be dried or the fresh-ground. The wet ones always have fresh Onion, Garlic, Ginger and/or Cilantro stems.

Daikon: This is large white Radish used mostly in Asian cooking. It can be used raw sliced or shredded, cooked and stuffed or pickled.

Dhana Dal: These little seeds look like split Moong Beans. They are split baby Coriander seeds, roasted in oil and seasoned. These are very fragrant, nutritious and help in digesting food. You can also grind them into powder and garnish any savory dish. You can find them in the Indian grocery stores.

Dredge: Coat food with the flour, spices or other dry ingredients, then shake off the excess and then cook ingredients per recipes.

Falafel: These are dry chickpeas fritters, sometimes made with beans like fava beans. These are Middle Eastern, where they are used on sandwiches or served separately with various sauces. I like to make them with dry green chickpeas; not only they are appealing but tasty as well.

Fillet: These are meat slices, mostly poultry and the fish, without any bones.

Filleting Knife: This is a boning knife that has a flexible blade, for easy access to the meat.

Gold leaves and Gold Powder: Traditionally Indian sweets are decorated with edible gold leaves or silver leaves. Silver is told to be better for the health. You can find about 20 to 22 karat gold to decorate either leaves or powder form.

Garam Masala: Spice mixture. See Spices & Spice Mixtures.

Gelatin: Gelatin in powder form can be proofed in room temperature water or milk for a few minutes before adding to the recipes. It is made from animal products like bones etc. Recipes made with gelatin will thicken when refrigerated for a few hours.

Ghee: This is clarified butter made at home by simmering unsalted butter and taking out all impurities. One pound of butter usually takes only 30 minutes, to melt and cook on constant simmer. This butter or ghee is used on bread, rice and in many recipes.

Gluten-free: Wheat, barley and rye mostly have gluten. Gluten-free is the flour or the ingredients that does not contain the gluten, or the elastic protein that is produced when the wheat is moistened at the time of milling, and making the flour.

Gujhiya: This is a Indian dish similar to Empanada, mostly famous for sweet filling, but we also make with bean crust like stuffed Bara that are filled with nuts, ginger, raisins and herbs.

Herbs: See Herbs in Food and Health Section.

Hoisin Sauce: This is Chinese sauce can be used as a glaze or sauce has a sweet, little sour and spicy taste and brown in color. It can be diluted with fruit juices or water or used as it is.

Horseradish: Horseradish can be used in small amounts as fresh-grated or prepared with seafood, eggs and other dipping sauces and dressings. It has a sharp and a pungent flavor.

Kalaunji: These black onion seeds are also called Nigella seeds. They have a sharp flavor between pepper and onion. It is used mostly crushed in cooking and in pickles.

Kewra Extract: This extract is used mostly in desserts and drinks and sometimes in fancy savory dishes like Nut Pulao. This is the essence taken from the Screwpine flower and smells very close to Jasmine flowers. You can substitute it with crushed Cardamom seeds in the cooking.

Kuttu: This is a small grain filled with nutrients, just like Quinoa. It is about ¼-inch long, in black shell, in triangular shape. After it is peeled it looks almost like Pearl Barley. We use it crushed with oatmeal, and ground into flour for bread. This is almost considered as fruit, and used on the fasting days. It has iron and other minerals.

Maca: This is a vegetable root that is ground into powder and used by the teaspoonful in food such as yogurt, drinks, oatmeal, pancakes and bread dough. It is an old medicine from Peru to give energy and boost libido. Should be used in small quantities.

Maple syrup: This is extracted from the sugar maple tree and then processed into pure maple syrup. Maple syrup can be graded A and B. Grade B has much richer flavor, but both can be used for baking and serving, depending on your taste.

Matzo Meal: Made from unleavened cooked bread, used in various cooking including in meatballs.

Miso: Made from fermented soybean, used in Japanese and other cooking, in soup, dips, dressing, spreads and sauces. This is a fermented bean paste usually made with soybeans, barley or rice. It comes in jars, tubes or in bags. It can be purchased as a sweet, mild or salty.

Molasses: This thick, syrupy liquid is made from sugarcane juice that is refined, browned and reduced. There are three types of molasses: light or mild molasses, dark molasses and blackstrap, which is from a third and final boiling and has strong and bitter flavor. In baking try to use light or dark molasses so they do not overpower the recipe. I make my own Pomegranate molasses, which I started using in almost all the recipes.

Monounsaturated Fat: This is plant-based fat, a healthy fat found in foods such as nuts, olives and avocados.

Munakka: These are large, dark raisins with seeds. They are about 1 to 1-1/2-inches long; dried ones are flat, but have about ¼-inch long 3 to 4 seeds in each. We soak 4 to 5 of them overnight and eat them before breakfast with soaked almonds.

Oats: These can be Silver cut, Quick oats or Old-fashioned oats used in hot cereals, baking, garnishing and topping, etc. Made from oat seeds, hulled and then processed into oats. Rolled oats are steamed and rolled flat, so they cook fast. Sliver cut are healthy.

Orzo: This is small pasta shaped into rice, used as a rice or in soups and salad etc.

Palm Sugar: Used in sauces and making desserts. In India it is used as Jaggery that comes in small to large molds. It can be refined into grains.

Paneer: This is Indian cheese. Where milk is boiled and with lemon juice, the curd and whey is separated. The squeezed-out curd cut in cubes is called paneer and is used in cooking and in desserts and salad.

Parboil: Cook food partially, usually halfway or even less. Like boiling the fries halfway before frying them in the oil.

Peanut oil: Made from peanuts and has a high smoking point. Sometime it is used to fry chicken pieces because it does not burn fast.

Phyllo Pastry: These are paper-thin flaky pastry sheets used in baking in various cooking. While working with this pastry, keep it wrapped under a clean kitchen towel as it dries very fast.

Pilaf: The rice or the grain-fluffed dish. First onion and some spices are sautéed in oil or butter, then rice or the grains are added and sautéed for a few minutes, and then cooked in water, broth etc. and garnished with aromatics herbs, spices, vegetables and/or nuts. Also called: Pullao or Pilau.

Polenta: This is cornmeal cooked in various forms and served with dishes.

Polyunsaturated Fat: This is also plant-driven fat, with more than one bonding site that are not filled with a hydrogen atom, such as safflower, soy, corn, sunflower oils, etc.

Protein: This is the life line. Essential for building and maintaining the hormones, tissues and enzymes. It is found both in animals and in plant-based food such as beans, nuts and grains.

Quinoa: Use whole grain Organic Premium Quinoa. It is a gluten-free superfood. Quinoa is the little seeds of a plant from Peru. It is complete protein, has all 9 essential Amino Acids that the body needs. It contains minerals, fiber, antioxidants and phytonutrients. A good source of phosphorous, calcium, iron, magnesium, and vitamins A, E & B. It is a meal in itself. I use it as rice, with oatmeal, in burger patties, in baking, bread, pudding, salad and halwa, etc. It takes 5 minutes to cook in boiling water (just like rice), then leave it covered for 10 minutes to fluff.

Rose Water: This an essence made from roses and used in savory, sweet dishes and drinks. You can buy rose water or rose syrup at the Indian grocery stores. To make your own rose water: Use about 6 cups of water in a large saucepan (about 5-6 quart pan) and drop the petals of 12 large unsprayed, fragrant, pink or red roses, cover with a lightly-hollowed metal lid, and pile the ice cubes over the lid in a single layer, up to the edges of the pan. Heat the pot and bring the water to a boil, then lower the heat and simmer until all the ice cubes are evaporated and about ½ cup of water is left over the lid. This is the precious rose water. Collect the water with a dropper or plastic spoon and fill in a clean and dry bottle. Cool the rose water and store in the refrigerator up to three months.

Saffron: The most expensive spice of the world. It gives yellow color in cooking and has a special flavor. It is the fine reddish-brown threads of the flower of crocus plant. It takes close to 80,000 flowers to make one pound of saffron. It is used both in sweet and savory dishes. You can soak in milk or water or fold in aluminum foil and heat over the stove just to warm, and then use it or simply just add to the cooking liquid to give flavor and color. It also has a medicinal value. Buy saffron in thread form; the ground saffron may not be pure and will lose its flavor fast.

Sake: Light rice wine good for drinking and cooking.

Sauerkraut: This is fermented cabbage from Germany. When I lived in Berlin for a few months, my brother used to buy it in a bottle made with white wine. We used it with sandwiches almost every day. It is good for the colon health and digestive tract, and gives good bacteria. Just remember to use it as it is; do not heat it and do not wash it.

Sauté: Sauté is actually stirring the food in the hot oil. When you sauté the food it browns as well as it softens. Most of the Indian spices and vegetables are sautéed in the hot oil to bring out their flavor. Just make sure you pat dry the vegetables before you add them in the hot oil. Also, make sure you do not crowd the pan. By sautéing the meat ,you can also seal the meat juices so it stays moist.

Score: Make a cut in the food to indicate the separation. First you score the food, then later on you can cut and separate them at the score, using the score as a guide line.

Sesame Seeds and Oil: Sesame seeds come in white, beige, and in black. The most beneficial ones are the black sesame seeds. They are loaded with nutrients like potassium, magnesium, calcium, iron, copper, etc. You can dry-roast them covered by shaking the pan for 8 to 10 minutes, until they start sputtering, and use them as garnish, make chutney or add to sweets. They help in constipation and digestion, so use moderately. The roasted and unroasted white sesame seeds are also used to make oil, and used in cooking and to flavor the dishes or garnishes. They are good for the complexion, and purifying the blood. Eaten in a large quantity, they can give diarrhea.

Seeds: Flax, poppy and sunflower seeds are loaded with healthy fiber and minerals. Flax seed oil is a healthy one. Sunflower seeds can be used on salad. Poppy seeds and be used ground as spices in cooking Indian food. All these seeds can be used in baking breads and rolls.

Semonlina: Also called Sooji or Rava in India, Semolina is made from durum wheat in granules. Semolina is used in both sweet and savory dishes as a base for the meat and vegetarian dishes instead of rice; as desserts, for breakfast like cream of wheat, as a crust to make fried food crispy, in dosa, idle and in fritters, etc.

Shaoxing Wine: This wine has distinctive flavor and is usually used in sauces and other cooking.

Slurry: This is the mixture of water and starch, made as thickener in cold water and added to the food. Then cook on high heat to make the liquid thick. Do not make slurry in hot water; it will form lumps.

Sorghum: This small grain is is almost like quinoa. It is full of protein, has iron and potassium, and is gluten-free.

Sour Cream: Has a cream and yogurt flavor. It can be used both in cooking and prepared food or as a topping. Its sour flavor comes from adding lactic acid and gives very good results in baking. For prepared foods, try to use low-fat sour cream to avoid extra calories without losing any flavor.

Soy Beans: A legume widely used in Asia and now around the world. It is rich in oil, iron, protein and other minerals. Bean curd Tofu is made from these beans and is used globally.

Soy Sauce: Made from fermented soy beans, water, salt, wheat, etc. Use low-sodium soy sauce to avoid extra salt.

Tahini: This protein-rich fermented soybean product can be used in dishes sautéed with spices as it absorbs the flavors very well. This is the sesame paste mostly used in Hummus to flavor the dish. In India roasted sesame seeds are ground and used in Chutney, and in sweets as a paste or powder.

Tamarind: The pulp from the beans that grow on a huge evergreen tree. Even the leaves are sour. This tree grows in warm climates. There are green Tamarind and Red Tamarind beans, and they both have almost same taste. You can buy it in the concentrated pulp form, or as actual dried beans and make your own pulp by cooking in the water and straining them.

Tapioca: Made from the root of the cassava plant into flour and pearl, etc. Tapioca is used as a thickener, as a flour to be used as crumbs to deep-fry seafood, poultry or fritters, and used in desserts and puddings, etc.

Tawa: This is a cast-iron pan with handle, used to make chapatti (bread), dosa, paratha and even to roast spices, etc.

Tenderloin: This is a cut of a very tasty, soft and expensive meat. It cooks fast, and comes from usually from beef and pork.

Tofu: This is a bean curd made from soy beans. It is full of nutrients like protein and iron. It can be used raw in salad, fried, sautéed, squeezed-dry and crumbled, and also in shakes and desserts like cheese cake.

Tortillas: Corn or flour tortillas ae as used as enchiladas, burritos; seasoned, cut and baked as chips, and deep-fried as crispy with fillings. Today they are not only Mexican and Latin, but are used universally.

Tomalley: This is the Lobster liver that is light green in color. Some people add this to the stuffing for the lobster, and some just discard it.

Truffle oil: Made from the truffles and is very flavorful; used mostly for garnishes.

Truss: Trussing is the tying of meat with kitchen twine. It could be a roast or poultry, for even cooking and a compact shape.

Turmeric: See Food and Health.

Unsaturated Fat: This is either monounsaturated or polyunsaturated fat, which has at least one bonding site that is not filled with hydrogen atom. They source from vegetables and stay liquid in room temperature (do not thicken like shortening).

Utility Knife: This is a small and a light knife, easy to handle, and has a sharp 5-to-7 inch blade for multiple uses. It is a handy knife, a smaller version of the chef knife.

Vanilla Beans: These are the beans from a climbing orchid plant. The vanilla flavor is used in mostly sweet dishes, chocolate, shakes and in milk dishes. You can use beans or extract to flavor the dishes.

Vegan Cooking: This is vegetarian cooking where no animal products are used.

Vegetable oil: The best for cooking as well as light is canola oil. You can also use corn oil or vegetable oil. Vegetable oils are made from seeds, plants or nuts, or a combination.

Wasabi: Wasabi is a root like horseradish that comes from southeast Asia, mostly from Japan. It can be hotter than chili powder. Make the wasabi paste with water just before using, otherwise it will lose flavor. Store wasabi powder just like any other ground spice, in an airtight container.

Waterchestnut (Singhara): This is a fruit grown under water in ponds. It is triangular with green and red color, with two small thorns sticking out just like animal horns. It is considered a fruit, but dried and crushed it is used in oatmeal, and halwa etc. The flour is used in the bread. It has minerals such as potassium, and iron and turns a little darker in cooking.

Zest: Zest is the outer part or skin of the citrus fruit, such as lemon, limes, grapefruit, orange and tangerine. Try to use tangerine zest when they are in season; it is much more flavorful than any other zest in cooking. Also, lime zest is very good for the body. Use a microplane zester that gives you a very fine zest.

Inspirational Books

I love to read a good book, just to get ideas how to shop, how to use shortcuts, how to cook certain food , and the various health benefits.

BAKHRU, H.K., Herbs That Heal, 1992. Published by, Orient Paperbacks, a Div. of Vision Books Pvt. Ltd., Madarsa Road, Kashmere Gate, Delhi 1100. There is no end of learning in the life. Almost every day you come across something that will help you, along the way in the life.

BALCH, M.D., James and BALCH, C.N.C., Phyllis, Prescription for Nutritional Healing, Avery Publishing Group, Inc., 1990.

BERNARD, Francoise, La Cuisine, Rizzoli, New York, 2010.

BHARADWAJ, Monisha, India's Vegetarian Cooking, Kyle Book, an imprint of Kyle Cathie Limited, 2006.

CASTLEMAN, Michael, The Healing Herbs, Emmaus, PA, Rodale 1991.

CLEVELY, A. and RICHMOND, K., The Complete Book of Herbs, Smithmark Publishers, A Division of U.S. Media Holdings, Inc, N.Y., 1994.

CUNNINGHAM, Scott, Cunninghams's Encyclopedia of Magical Herbs, St. Paul, MN, Llewellyn 1994.

Dr. DiNICOLANTONIO, James, The Salt Fix, Harmony Books, N.Y., 2017.

DORIT. Celebrating Our Raw Nature, Summertown Book Publishing Co., 2007

DUYFF, Roberta Larson, Complete Food and Nutrition Guide, American Dietetic Assn., John Wiley & Sons, Inc., 2006.

FERGUSON, MS, CN, Robert, Diet-Free for Life, Penguin Group (USA), Inc., 2011.

FLECKENSTEIN, M.D., Alexa with Weisman, Roanne, Health 2 O, McGraw- Hill, 2007.

GUPTA, MD, Sanjay, Cheating Death, Wellness Central Hachette Book Group, 2009.

HEINERMAN, John, Heinerman's Encyclopedia of Healing Herbs and Spices, Englewood Cliffs, NJ, Parker, 1996.

HUFFINGTON, Arianna, The Sleep Revolution: Transforming Your Life, One Night at a Time, Harmony, New York, 2016.

KHALSA, Gurucharan, and Yogi Bhajan, Breathwalk: Breathing Your Way to a Revitalized Body, Mind, and Spirit, Broadway Books, New York, 2000.

MALHI, Manju, India with Passion, Interlink Books, 2005.

MARS, A.H.G., Brigitte, The Desktop Guide to Herbal Medicine, Basic Health Publications, Inc., 2007.

McGEE, Harold, On Food and Cooking, New York: Charles Scribner's Sons, 1984.

PARENT, Joseph and Nancy, and Ken Zeiger, The Best Diet Book Ever, The Zen of Losing Weight, Zen Arts Press, CA, 2015.

PARKES, Simon & Sarkhel, Udit, The Calcutta Kitchen, Interlink Books, 2007.

PRATT, M.D., Steven G and MATTHEWS, Kathy, Super Foods Health Style, Willliam Morrow, an Imprint of HarperCollins Publishers, 2006.

PURSER, Jan & Joshi, Ajoy, Indian Cooking Made Easy, Periplus Editions, 2007.

SARAN, Suvir & Iyness, Stephanie, Indian Home Cooking, Clarkson Potter Publishers, N.Y. 2004.

SCHREIBER, Martin J. and Cathy Breitenbucher, My Two Elaines, Learning, Coping, and Surviving as an Alzheimer's Caregiver, Book Publishers Network, 2017.

SIEGEL, Marc, Inner Pulse, John Wiley & Sons, Inc., 2011.

STEVENSON, Violet, A Modern Herbal, How to Grow, Cook and Use Herbs, Crescent Books, A Division of Crown Publishers, Inc., N.Y.,1974.

STEWART, Martha. Pies & Tarts. New York: Clarkson N. Potter, Inc., 1985.

Dr. VERNI, Ken, Psy.D., Happiness The Mindful Way, DK Publishing, N.Y., 2015.

Dr. VRANICH, Belisa, Breathe, St. Martin's Griffin, New York, 2016.

WARREN, Rick, The Purpose Driven Life, Zondervan, 2002.

Dr,WEIL,MD, Andrew, Spontaneous Happiness, Little, Brown And Company, 2011.

YOGI RAMACHARAKA (William Walker Atkinson), The Hindu-yogi Science of Breath, Yogi Publication Society, Chicago, 1905.

Resources

The key to good cooking is shopping for the right food in the right places with affordable prices. Each place and each season, depending on where you live, can give a large selection.

There are certain common places where you can do most of shopping.

Supermarkets, Warehouses and Large Discount Stores: I do a lot of shopping at supermarkets for whatever I can't find in the Indian grocery stores like meat, cheeses, skin care, baking goods and some specialty items. It is important to look out for the special sale items in supermarket circulars, or go on the line and check out their websites. Now-a-days, most of the supermarkets have a large selection of cheeses, nutritional grains, milks and other good products. When we go to Las Vegas, we buy most of our grocery in bulk together with my sister-in-law at the warehouses and large discount stores.

Indian Grocery Stores: Most of the vegetables that I cook, either for Indian cooking or American cooking, are found in Indian grocery stores. Coconut powder, and almost all bean flours, are found in Indian grocery stores. Basmati rice both white and brown are found here. So every week I get all my fresh vegetables, fruits, spices, milk, juices, coconut water, nutritional beans, brown rice and flours from there. The prices are very good on spices, beans and flours and vegetables. You can also find some Middle East stores where you will find pomegranate molasses, and some of the Indian spices as well.

Oriental Grocery Stores: Chinese and Japanese stores carry special items like tofu, soy sauces, marinades, Chinese five-spices mix powder, sushi ingredients, wasabi, sprouts and vegetables. I like Japanese eggplant: it is nice, long and very soft, and Chinese bittermelon, which is long and less bitter than other bittermelons; dry mushroom caps and fermented beans, bamboo shoots, fresh noodles and soybean products are all available here as well.

Farmers Markets: They are seasonal, but you cannot beat them for freshness of the fruits and vegetables. I prefer to get my fresh corn and tomatoes in the bulk from there. You can buy organic produce at a great price. In India, my mother went for shopping at a farmers market in the evening, just before closing, and came back loaded with fruits and vegetables at half price.

Natural Food Stores: They are a big source for the specialty items. You can buy in bulk and save a lot of money rather than buying pre-packaged food. Certain food we buy in bulk in our neighborhood and chip in the price for that item.

Online shopping: For people who do not have time or do not want to go all around looking for certain item, online shopping is very convenient. You can buy almost anything online.

Acknowledgements

I am so very fortunate to get the unique, valuable advices, recipes and the articles from the following peoples. Starting from the childhood through my adult life I have been always impressed by many people, in many ways and have learnt many things for which I will always be obligated, and can never pay back for their contributions in my life and for the book.

Sincere thanks to Dr. Mehmet Oz, who gave me advice and guidance just like my father did all his life. He gave me inspiration to write this cookbook and tell others all about my family tradition and the healthy food. His books, his show, his staff, and all the doctors and authors who contributed to his show have helped us in all different ways to have a healthy lifestyle. I have asked my friends all around me to watch and learn something from his show.

I like to hear from a higher authority. Thanks to Pastor Rick Warren for the life teaching moments he gave us in his book, "The Purpose Driven Life." I quote this book every now and then.

One of the best book I ever read on memory is: "Intelligent Memory." Dr. Barry Gordon, coauthor explains in detail how your memory works and how you can improve it. Thanks to Dr. Barry Gordon your book is a big help. Also, the book, "Magnificent Mind At Any Age." By Dr. Daniel G. Amen, New York Times Bestseller, Harmony Books, N.Y., 2008, is a great book. It tells you how to take care of a balanced mind and succeed in your life.

I want to thank Dr. Gary Small and Gigi Vorgan for their book, "2 Weeks To A Younger Brain." This is also one of the best book that I came across. I have suggested to my friends and family to read this book. It is an eye opener.

I was inspired and supported to write this book by my nephew Edward Wolf who asked me to write a book, every time he ate my Cheesecake and other mouth watering desserts.

My heartfelt thanks to my friends in the neighborhood who are always having parties and serving good food, reminding us that we are a big family and we are still fond of good Indian food. I want to give my sincere thanks to my friend and her husband: Sunitha and Shrinivas Garbha, for helping me with my computer whenever I needed their help.

I am very humble to all my friends at the Gym who have taken the time and have written their messages and have given their family recipes. I am sure we all will benefit from them. Special thanks to Michael Papera who spent months, and helped me get the Tax-exempt status.

There is no end of learning. You learn from cradle to grave. I have learnt a lot and am still learning every day at Fox New and Fox Cable. We used to gather together faithfully to watch our favorite program, "The House Call." Dr. Marc Siegel and Dr. David Samadi are very experienced and qualified doctors who gave us tons of advice on food and health. Our sincere thanks to Dr. Marc Siegel and Dr. David Samadi, Dr. Manny Alvarez, Dr. Devi Nampiaparampil, Dr. Sejal Shah, Dr. Keri Peterson, Dr. Mendez and other who have contributed their expertise to our lives. We have learned a lot from all of them.

Thanks to Dr. James DiNicolantonio for writing the book," The Salt Fix." We have learnt a lot from the book. My sister-in-law's sister (a Nun) passed away with salt-deficiency.

Thanks to my father's favorite Indian writer: H.K.Bakhru, for his book on Herbs, that my father loved it, read it, learnt from it and left behind for us to learn more. In 2013, when I visited India, I brought back some of my father's books with me, and this one is my favorite one. I am sure my father is smiling and looking down on us from heaven.

I want to give my sincere thank to The Star- Ledger newspaper for their Health section. Since they have added the Health section on Thursdays, I have learnt a lot. It is a wealth of information right on your fingertips. You just need a will to follow a healthy life style.

I have to admire Mr. Martin J. Schreiber with Cathy Breitenbucher for writing his book, "My Two Elaines, Learning, Coping, and Surviving as an Alzheimer's Caregiver, Book Publishers Network, 2017. The courage, the suffering, the surviving as a spouse and as a caregiver, and telling us what difference he could have done to get better results and make life better. The resources that are available on your fingertips etc. are remarkable. Only a strong willed person, an adventurous, and avid lover for his and his spouse's life could have survived. I am glad he is making this place better for all of us. Also I want to thank a million to Book Publishers Network for giving permission to quote from the book.

Thanks to the Parsippany Library for all those books and courteous service that I have received over the years. In the month of June 2017: The Alzheimer's Disease Awareness and Brain Month, I donated the book, "My Two Elaines." Although I will never be able to pay back for their services, I will try to support them and appreciate them in the future as well.

Angels do exist. I call all the volunteers at the Woman's Club, "The Little Angels". They will have a special place in the Heaven. They work hard, have several projects going on at the same time, go out do the shopping, do not hesitate to spend their own money, do the fund raising and help out poor, needy, and destitute. They make this world a better place to live. I do collect the Angels, and have a small collection of the Angels. I am glad I believe in Angels.

When I started writing this book, I wanted to make it very special. Teach people about food and health, they both are related and very important in the life. We all can use guidance and direction when it comes to health. I want to thank Dr. Gilbert Mandal, M.D. for contributing article on Food and Health. Also, thanks to Anil, Michael and Offer Cohen, Dr. Jyotsna and Sudhir Mehta, Vasvi Singh, M.D, and Saurav Luthera M.D., for their health messages. I also want to thank Xceed Fitness, Michael Cohen and Offer Cohen for advising on Physical Fitness. Thanks to Anil & Veena for their health message.

I will never be able to thank enough Tony Dearing, Director, Advance Media, Star Ledger News Paper, for the article, "Six Steps to Brain-healthy Life," and his unwaivering support. Tony lost his mother with dementia. He was publishing a series of articles on Dementia in the Star Ledger, I read about three articles, the 4th one was on Brain-health, and I wanted to print that in my book. He gave me permission. Then I noticed that most of the articles he is publishing in the newspaper are also mentioned in my book. So I kept on reading, giving my opinion and getting ideas, and to this date I still enjoy reading his articles, he is doing a great service to mankind.

I want to thank Dr. Howard Fillit, a Geriatrician and Neuroscientist of Alzheimer's Discovery Foundation and Executive Director, who gave us insight and a promising future for Alzheimer's. Also, many thanks to Alzheimer's Association for sending me news letter and keeping me up to date. I love the brain tour that explains in detail the progression of the disease.

Special thanks to everyone at The Star Ledger newspaper. I can't wait to read Thursdays Health Section. Also, I love the Book page on Sundays. This was the reason I came across the book, "My Two Elaines," and donated to four families who were affected with Alzheimer's and Dementia. My book has a chapter on it, and I try to find ways to help these families.

Special thanks to my friend, Millie Ringer, who sold me his autographed copy of the book (May 23, 2017), " The Best Diet Book Ever, The Zen of Losing Weight," by Dr. Joseph and Nancy Parent with Ken Zeiger, 2015. She also consulted her nephew Dr. Joseph Parent and gave me permission to quote from his book (pages 102 & 103).

I also want to thank my family, and friends for their wonderful and unique recipes from all around the world: Sheila Basem, Sachin and Supriya Brahme, Nikki and Mike Capola, Jennifer Cox, Shrinivas,

Sunitha, Shreya and Amoolya Durbha, Suresh and Prem Gupta, Joanne Handcharick and Melissa and Thomas Hennessy; Lorraine Krisanda; Krishna and Giri Karuru, Frances Bremer, Hildegard Heinz, Ellen Dash, Rusty and Yunie Driscoll, Caral Harrison, Abhishek and Anjana Katiyar, Ayush and Anushri Katiyar, Shail Katiyar, Madhu Mistry, Maddy and Frank Onofrio, Dr. Forrest and Barbara Pritchett, Jayashri Ramesh and Ramesh Nair, Raymond, Amit, Anupan and Anshul Schan, Yadvendra Singh, Bhagvati Devi Singh, Saroj Chaudhari, Kanchana and Vasvi Singh, Vishvadeepak and Ila Singh, Rarkeerti and Sarla Singh, Richard and Betty Tuers, Mark Vogel, Elaine Xenitelis.   It saved me a lot of time searching the books and recipes in the Libraries.

A good night's sleep is just as important as food and air for the body. In her book, The Sleep Revolution" Harmony Books, N.Y., 2016, Arianna Huffington proved that very well by presenting the facts. Everyone should know the consequences of sleep deprivation.

No matter how good you are in Yoga and breathing exercises, I think every one should read the book, "Breathe" by Dr. Vranich, St. Martin Press, 2016. She has explained breathing exercises going back to ancient Indian practices. I feel like I am in India again. My sincere thanks to her and her associates for helping us making this book more interesting for all of us.

My sincere thanks to Dr. Ken A. Verni, Psy,D. for giving advice on Happiness. He left no stone unturned when it comes to happiness.

You know that god works in a mysterious way. I went to attend a seminar about how to publish your own book, and the instructor giving the seminar, who is also an author of six books decided to help me out. Mr. and Mrs. Westhoven are always helping others. My husband was an English Teacher, and an Editor of a Religious magazine and now he is sick and can not proof read my book. I want to give million thanks to Mr. & Mrs. Westhoven for helping me out while they are extremely busy.

I want to thank Mike and Joan Meeh for helping me with the computer and putting my book together. It's good to have friends who help you in need.

A million thanks to all those people who were involved in publishing and promoting this book. This was my first book and I thought I will never get it published. You all made my dream come true.

Finally, I want to thank to all, anyone and everyone whose knowledge and experience is contributed to this book. You just don't know that you all are doing a great charity work, by helping others. This book is for charity, and all of you are part of this charitable work. You all will be rewarded in your life for the God's work.

Index

A

C

D

F

G

H

I

K

L

M

P

R

S

X

About the author:

Sushil Katiyar Hennessy was born and raised in India. She got her Masters of Social Work degree from University of Lucknow, India. She received her Accounting Diploma from Essex College of Business, Newark, New Jersey. She has taken several courses at the American Institute of Banking, which led her to work for over 25 yrs. for Wells Fargo Bank as a Secretary, Supervisor and Loan Analyst where she received three Quality Idea Awards for her work (donated all to charity). She also worked for Weichert Financial Services, a mortgage company as an Underwriter for over 6 yrs. She cooks for the local temple and other charitable organizations as a volunteer. Her recipes are a big hit in the community. When a neighbor moves in she welcomes them with a famous Indian or American dinner. She also sends out a monthly message to over 90 people about Random Acts of Kindness/health. In family tradition they used natural remedies and traditional Indian food all their life. Coming to the United States was a privilege. She gave parties and prepared all the food at home for a large crowd. She is married to her husband Richard for over forty years and lives in New Jersey.

Sushil, grew up in a vegetarian family this food and culture gave her life, kept disease free and to this date shaped many lives around her. This book will successfully guide you to a healthy diet and mouth-watering recipes. Remember you can't buy your health no matter how much money you have. You just have to take care of it. Following is the water color painting by the author.